CHAPTER 28: Tarukus and the Dark Knight Blueford PART 3

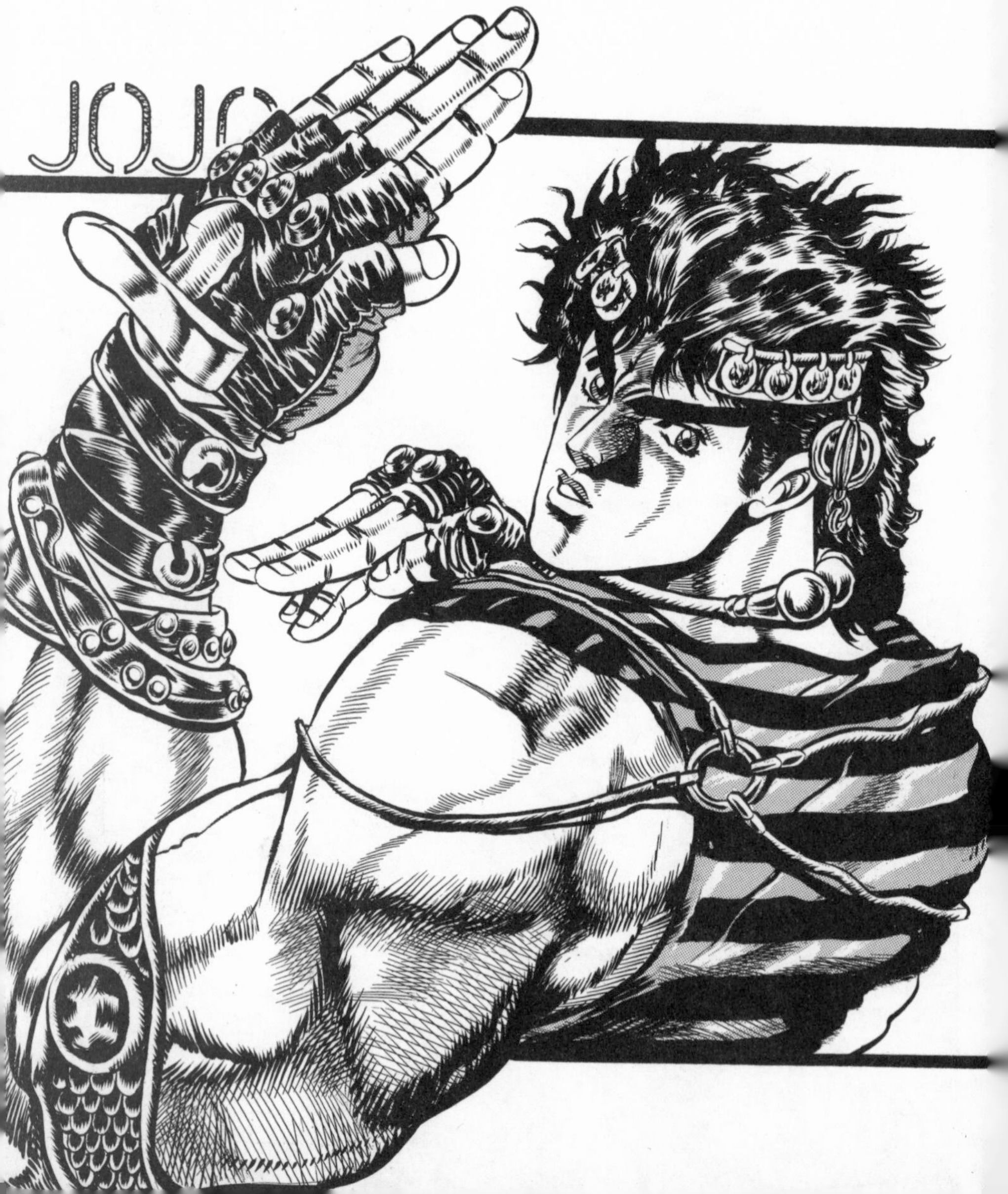
JOJO

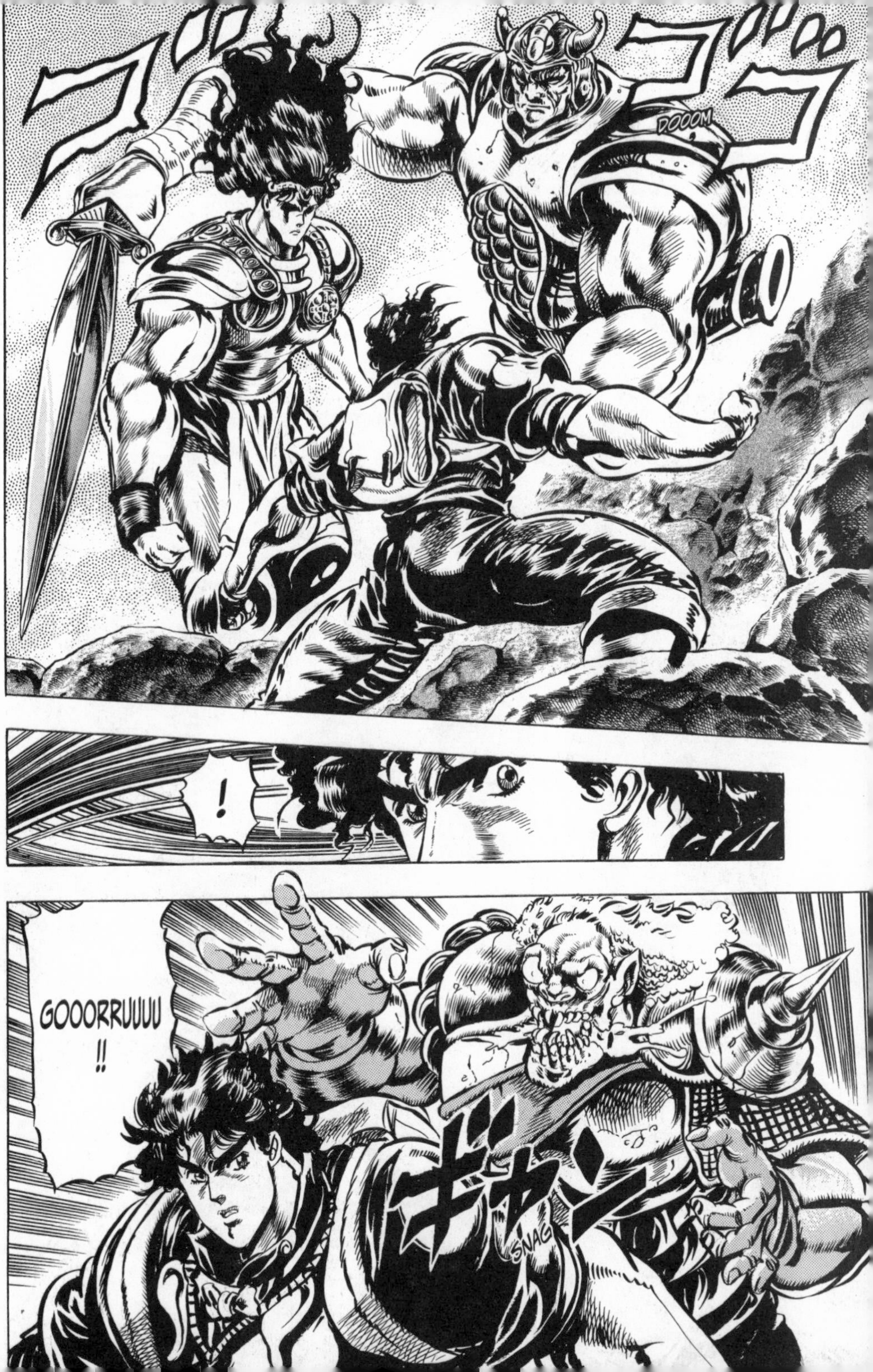
DOOOM
!
GOOORRUUUU !!
SNAG

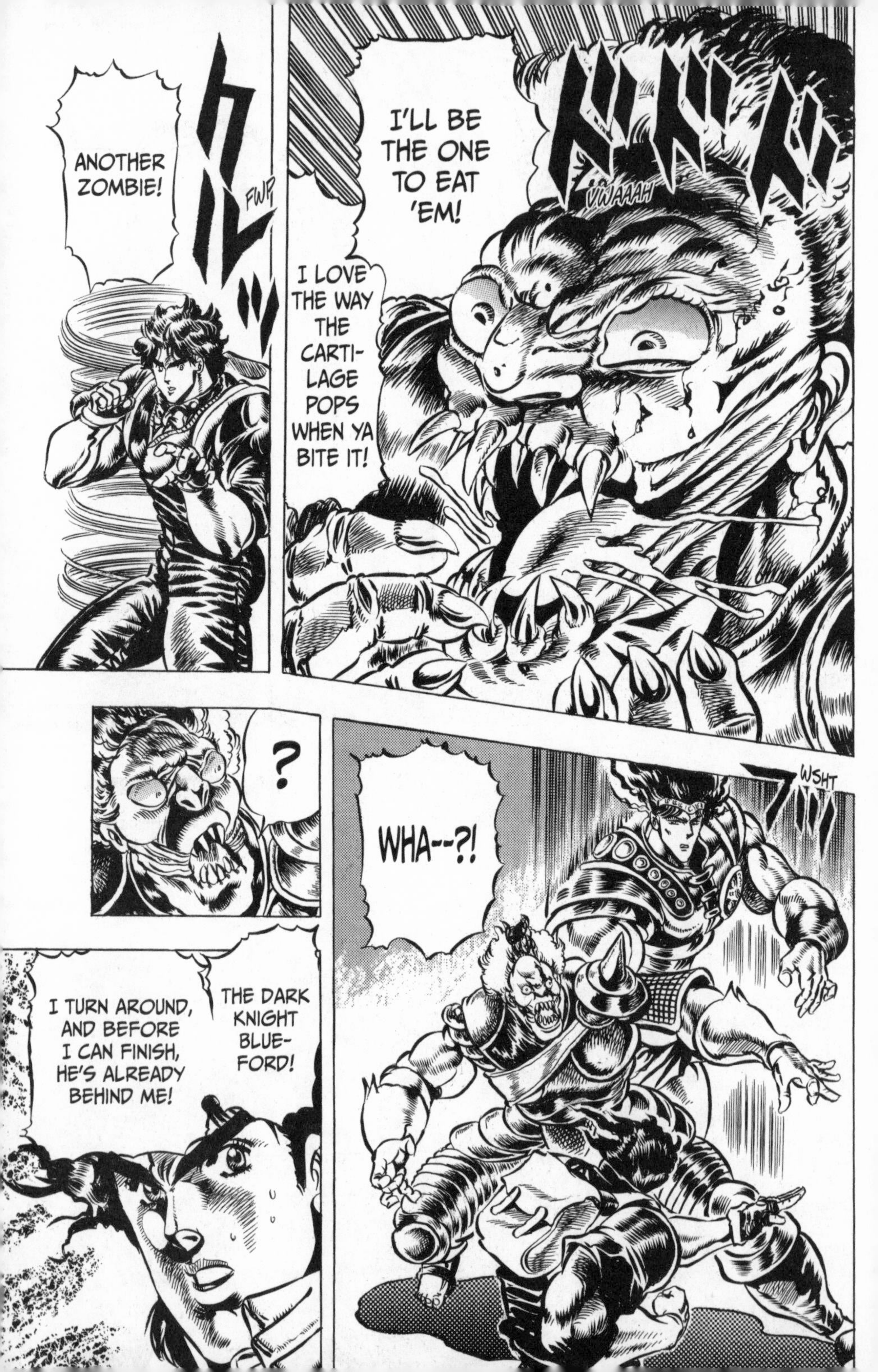
I'LL BE THE ONE TO EAT 'EM!
VWAAAH
I LOVE THE WAY THE CARTI-LAGE POPS WHEN YA BITE IT!
ANOTHER ZOMBIE!
FWP
WSHT
WHA--?!
?
THE DARK KNIGHT BLUE-FORD!
I TURN AROUND, AND BEFORE I CAN FINISH, HE'S ALREADY BEHIND ME!

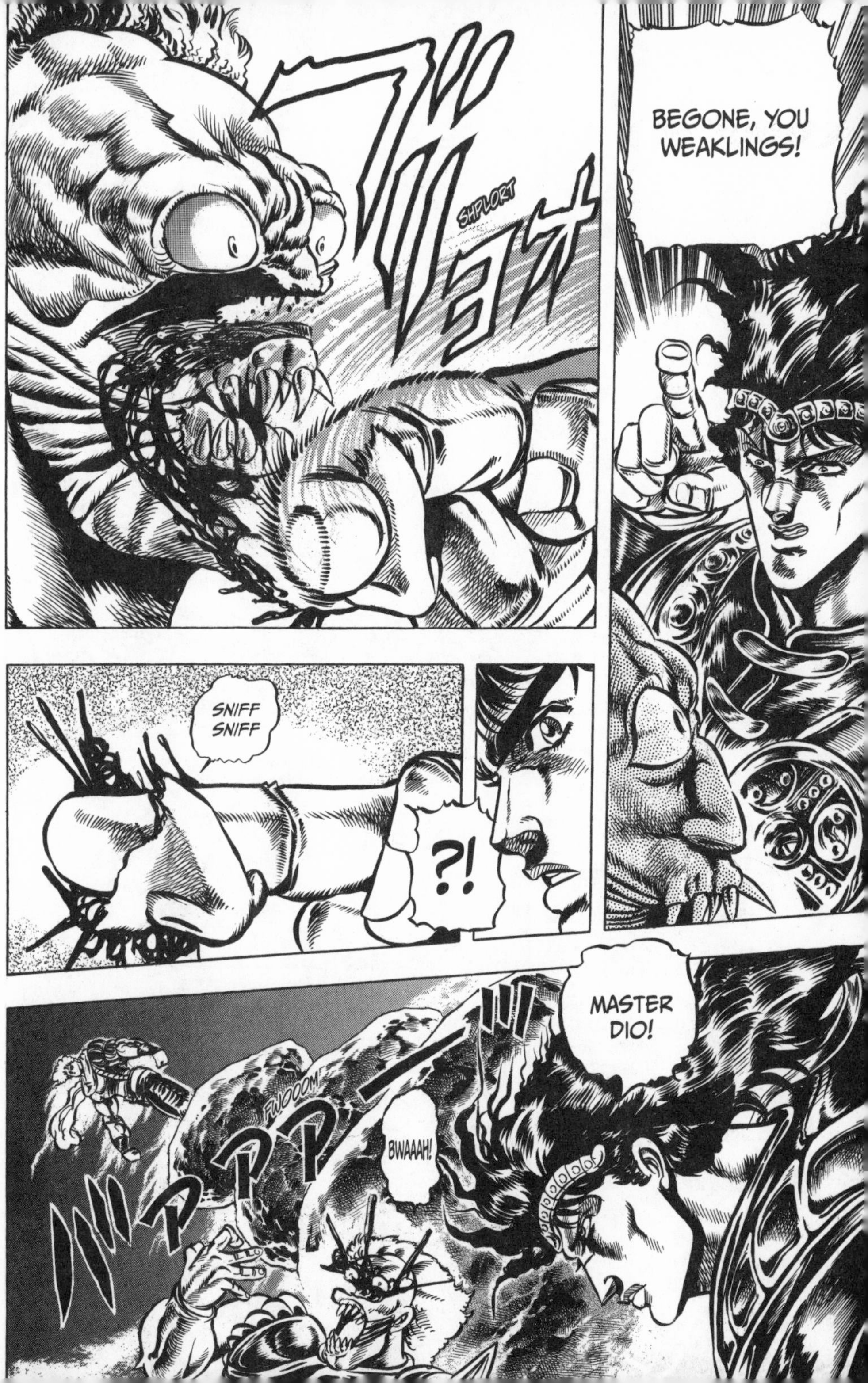
BEGONE, YOU WEAKLINGS!
SHPLORT
?!
SNIFF SNIFF
MASTER DIO!
FWOOOM
BWAAAH!

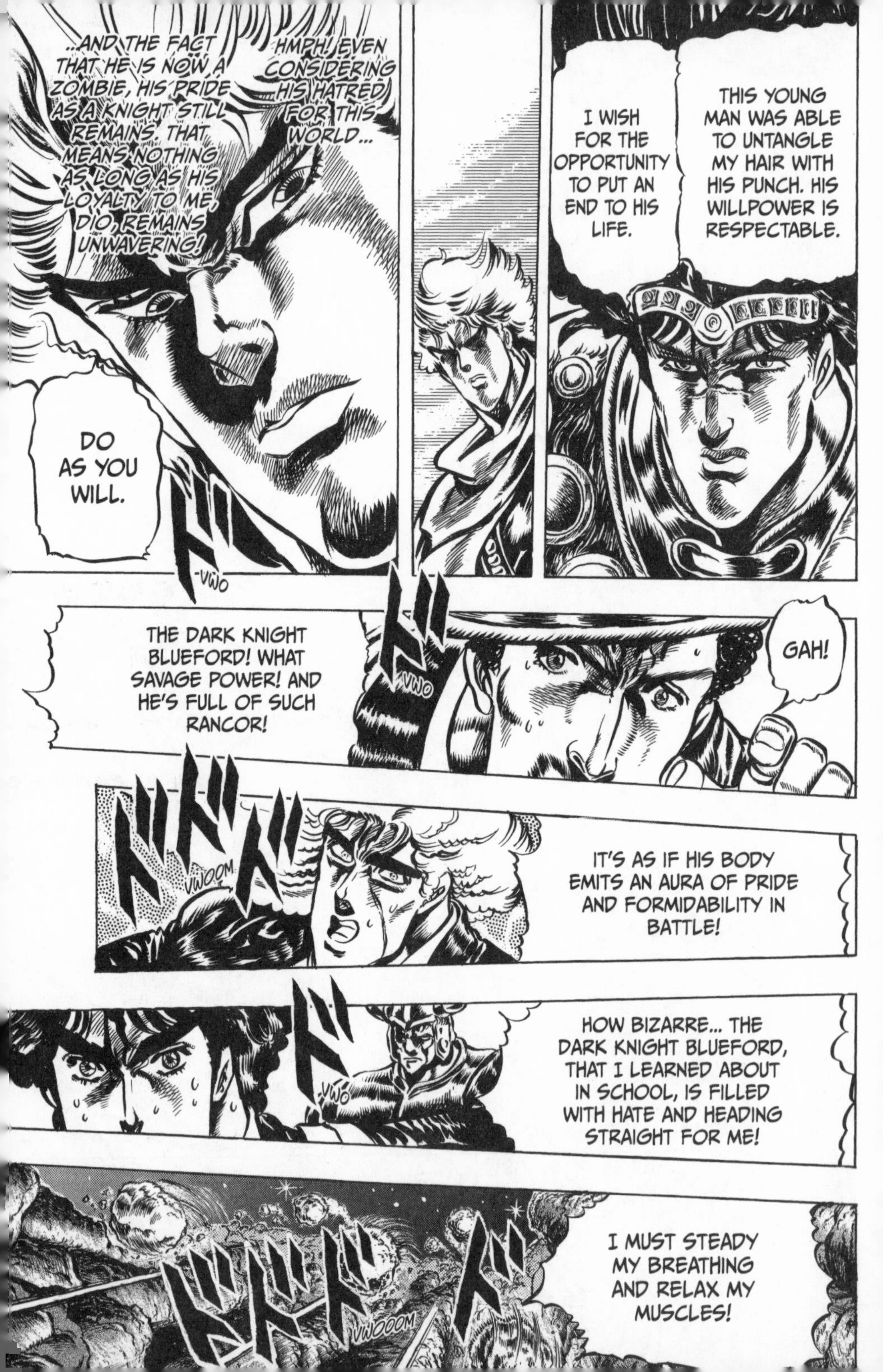
THIS YOUNG MAN WAS ABLE TO UNTANGLE MY HAIR WITH HIS PUNCH. HIS WILLPOWER IS RESPECTABLE.
I WISH FOR THE OPPORTUNITY TO PUT AN END TO HIS LIFE.
HMPH! EVEN CONSIDERING HIS HATRED FOR THIS WORLD...
...AND THE FACT THAT HE IS NOW A ZOMBIE, HIS PRIDE AS A KNIGHT STILL REMAINS. THAT MEANS NOTHING AS LONG AS HIS LOYALTY TO ME, DIO, REMAINS UNWAVERING!
DO AS YOU WILL.
VWO
GAH!
VWO
THE DARK KNIGHT BLUEFORD! WHAT SAVAGE POWER! AND HE'S FULL OF SUCH RANCOR!
IT'S AS IF HIS BODY EMITS AN AURA OF PRIDE AND FORMIDABILITY IN BATTLE!
VWOOM
HOW BIZARRE... THE DARK KNIGHT BLUEFORD, THAT I LEARNED ABOUT IN SCHOOL, IS FILLED WITH HATE AND HEADING STRAIGHT FOR ME!
VWO
I MUST STEADY MY BREATHING AND RELAX MY MUSCLES!
VWOOOM

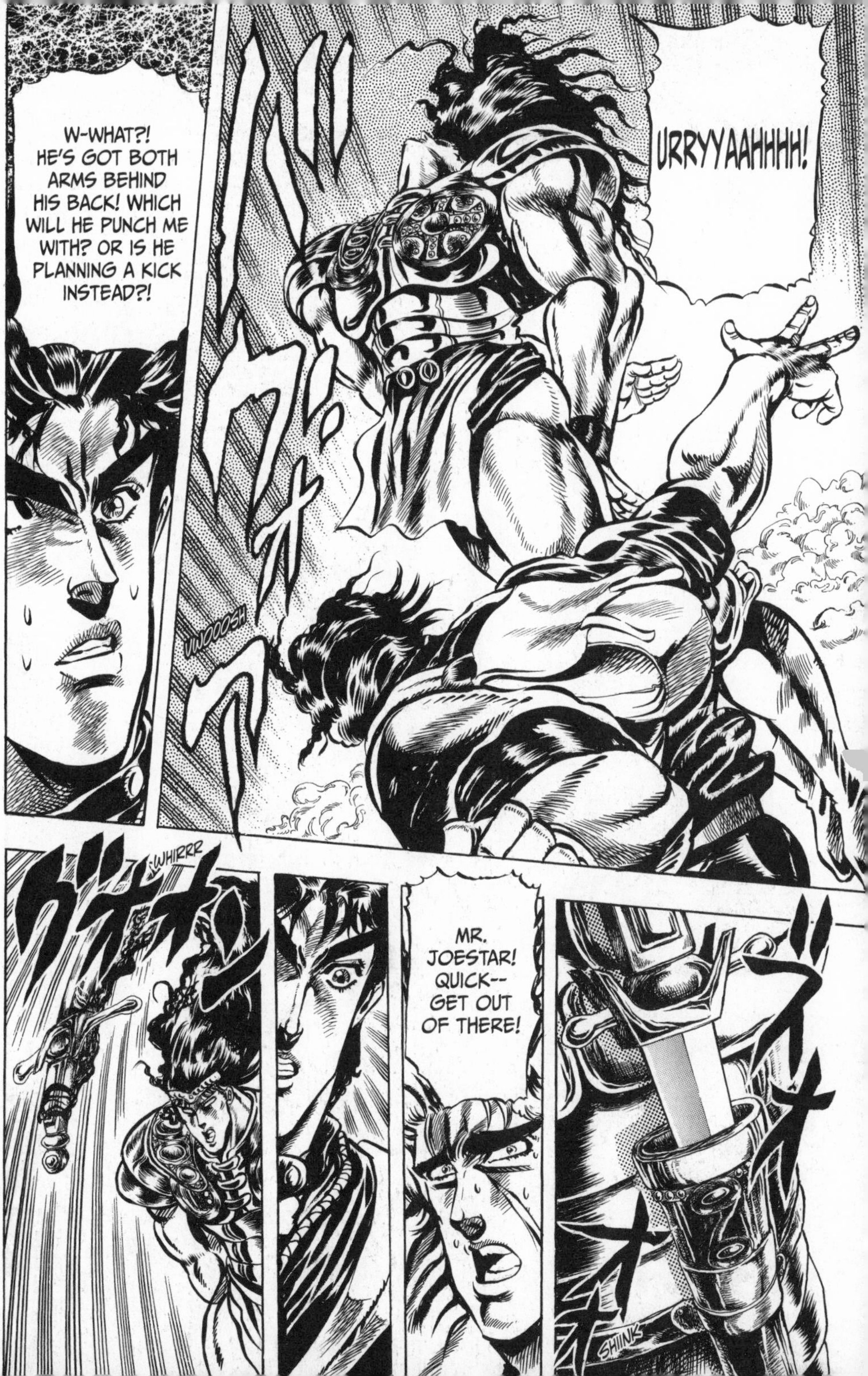
URRYYAAHHHH!
WHOOOSH
W-WHAT?! HE'S GOT BOTH ARMS BEHIND HIS BACK! WHICH WILL HE PUNCH ME WITH? OR IS HE PLANNING A KICK INSTEAD?!
SHIINK
MR. JOESTAR! QUICK-- GET OUT OF THERE!
WHIRRR

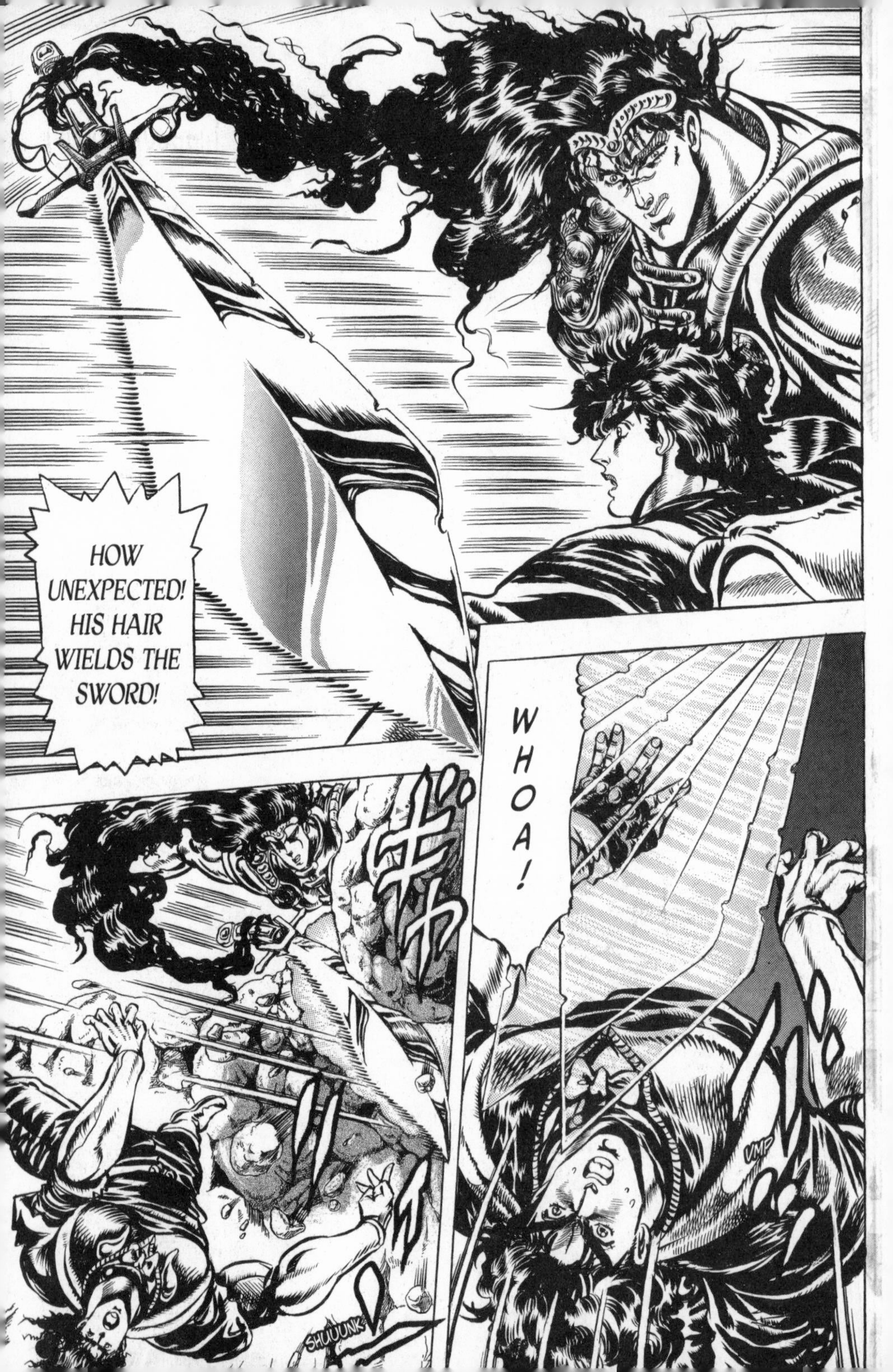
HOW UNEXPECTED! HIS HAIR WIELDS THE SWORD!
WHOA!
UMP
SHUUUNK

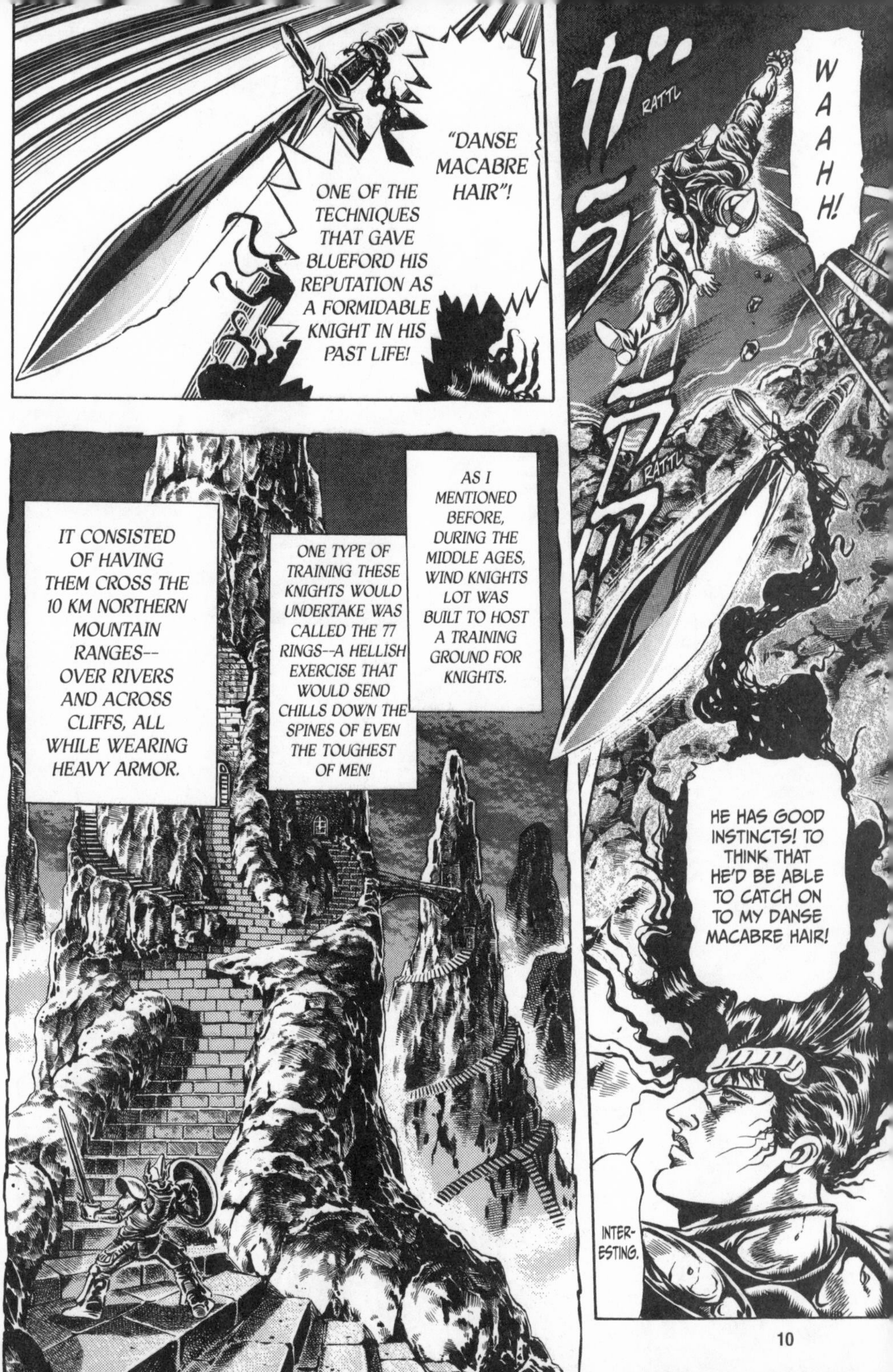
RATTL
WAAAHH!
RATTL
HE HAS GOOD INSTINCTS! TO THINK THAT HE'D BE ABLE TO CATCH ON TO MY DANSE MACABRE HAIR!
INTER-ESTING.
"DANSE MACABRE HAIR"!
ONE OF THE TECHNIQUES THAT GAVE BLUEFORD HIS REPUTATION AS A FORMIDABLE KNIGHT IN HIS PAST LIFE!
AS I MENTIONED BEFORE, DURING THE MIDDLE AGES, WIND KNIGHTS LOT WAS BUILT TO HOST A TRAINING GROUND FOR KNIGHTS.
ONE TYPE OF TRAINING THESE KNIGHTS WOULD UNDERTAKE WAS CALLED THE 77 RINGS--A HELLISH EXERCISE THAT WOULD SEND CHILLS DOWN THE SPINES OF EVEN THE TOUGHEST OF MEN!
IT CONSISTED OF HAVING THEM CROSS THE 10 KM NORTHERN MOUNTAIN RANGES-- OVER RIVERS AND ACROSS CLIFFS, ALL WHILE WEARING HEAVY ARMOR.

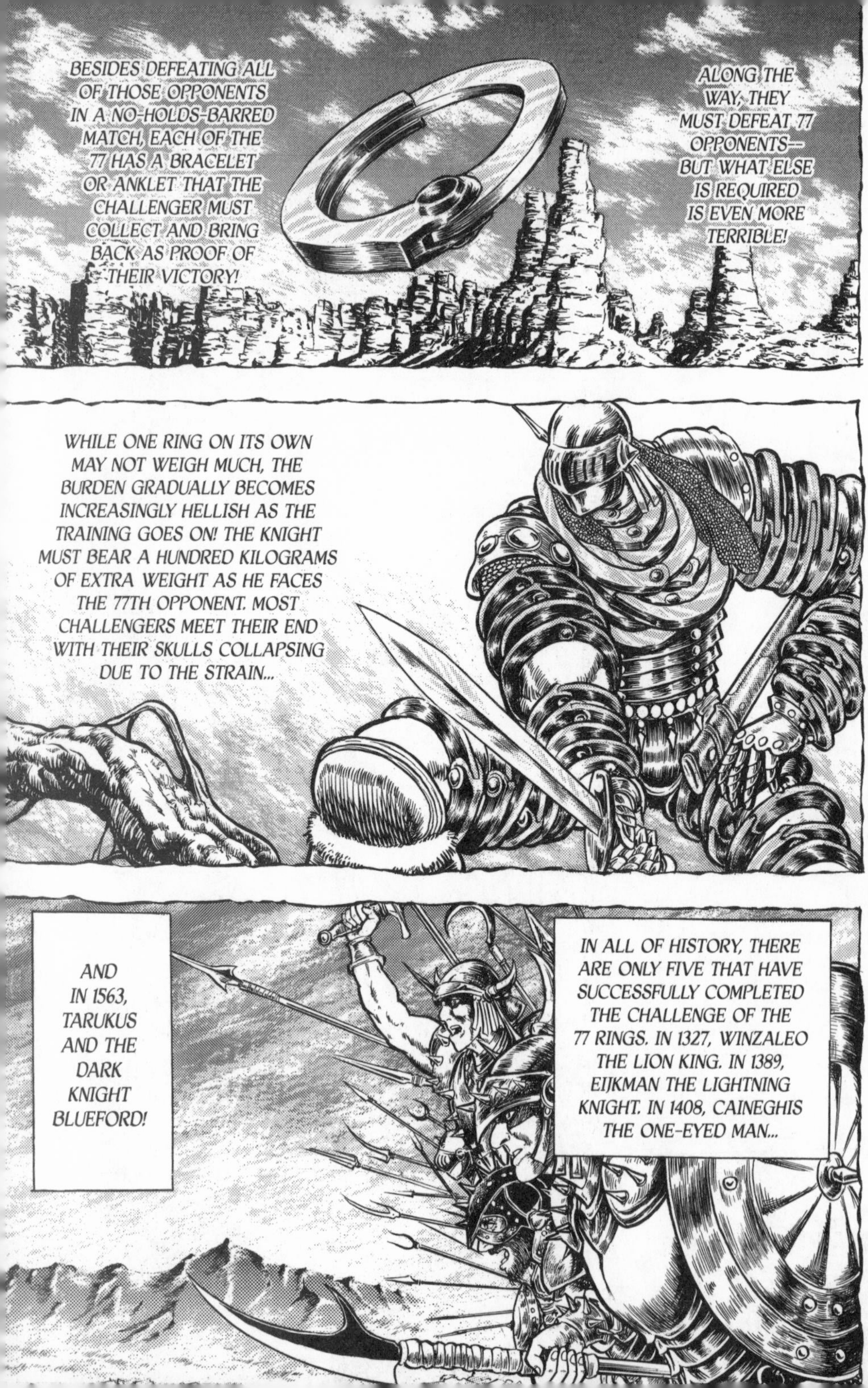
ALONG THE WAY, THEY MUST DEFEAT 77 OPPONENTS-- BUT WHAT ELSE IS REQUIRED IS EVEN MORE TERRIBLE!
BESIDES DEFEATING ALL OF THOSE OPPONENTS IN A NO-HOLDS-BARRED MATCH, EACH OF THE 77 HAS A BRACELET OR ANKLET THAT THE CHALLENGER MUST COLLECT AND BRING BACK AS PROOF OF THEIR VICTORY!
WHILE ONE RING ON ITS OWN MAY NOT WEIGH MUCH, THE BURDEN GRADUALLY BECOMES INCREASINGLY HELLISH AS THE TRAINING GOES ON! THE KNIGHT MUST BEAR A HUNDRED KILOGRAMS OF EXTRA WEIGHT AS HE FACES THE 77TH OPPONENT. MOST CHALLENGERS MEET THEIR END WITH THEIR SKULLS COLLAPSING DUE TO THE STRAIN...
IN ALL OF HISTORY, THERE ARE ONLY FIVE THAT HAVE SUCCESSFULLY COMPLETED THE CHALLENGE OF THE 77 RINGS. IN 1327, WINZALEO THE LION KING. IN 1389, EIJKMAN THE LIGHTNING KNIGHT. IN 1408, CAINEGHIS THE ONE-EYED MAN...
AND IN 1563, TARUKUS AND THE DARK KNIGHT BLUEFORD!

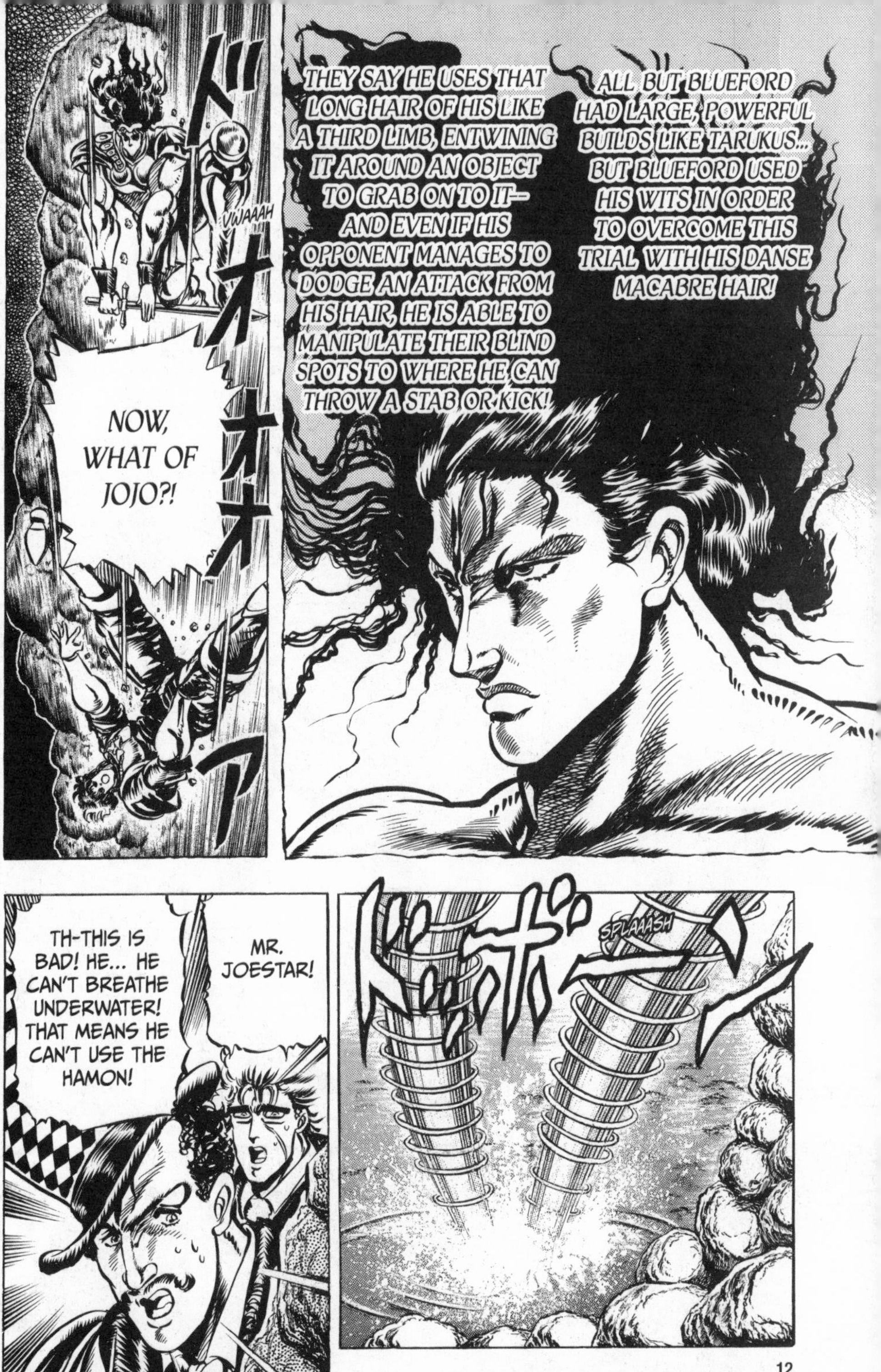
ALL BUT BLUEFORD HAD LARGE, POWERFUL BUILDS LIKE TARUKUS... BUT BLUEFORD USED HIS WITS IN ORDER TO OVERCOME THIS TRIAL WITH HIS DANSE MACABRE HAIR!
THEY SAY HE USES THAT LONG HAIR OF HIS LIKE A THIRD LIMB, ENTWINING IT AROUND AN OBJECT TO GRAB ON TO IT— AND EVEN IF HIS OPPONENT MANAGES TO DODGE AN ATTACK FROM HIS HAIR, HE IS ABLE TO MANIPULATE THEIR BLIND SPOTS TO WHERE HE CAN THROW A STAB OR KICK!
VWAAAH
NOW, WHAT OF JOJO?!
SPLAAASH
MR. JOESTAR!
TH-THIS IS BAD! HE... HE CAN'T BREATHE UNDERWATER! THAT MEANS HE CAN'T USE THE HAMON!

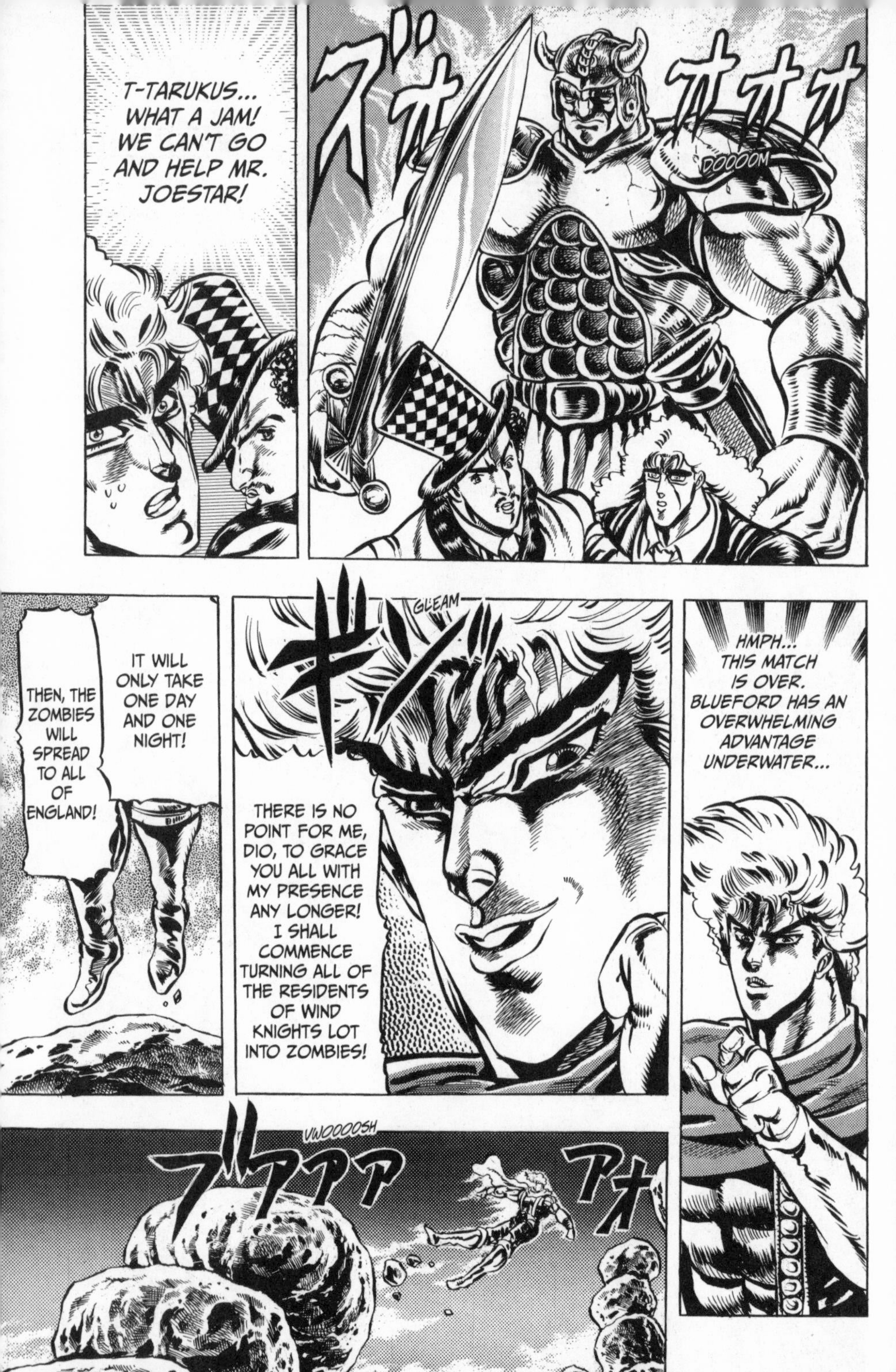
DOOOOM
T-TARUKUS... WHAT A JAM! WE CAN'T GO AND HELP MR. JOESTAR!
HMPH... THIS MATCH IS OVER. BLUEFORD HAS AN OVERWHELMING ADVANTAGE UNDERWATER...
GLEAM
THERE IS NO POINT FOR ME, DIO, TO GRACE YOU ALL WITH MY PRESENCE ANY LONGER! I SHALL COMMENCE TURNING ALL OF THE RESIDENTS OF WIND KNIGHTS LOT INTO ZOMBIES!
IT WILL ONLY TAKE ONE DAY AND ONE NIGHT!
THEN, THE ZOMBIES WILL SPREAD TO ALL OF ENGLAND!
VWOOOOSH

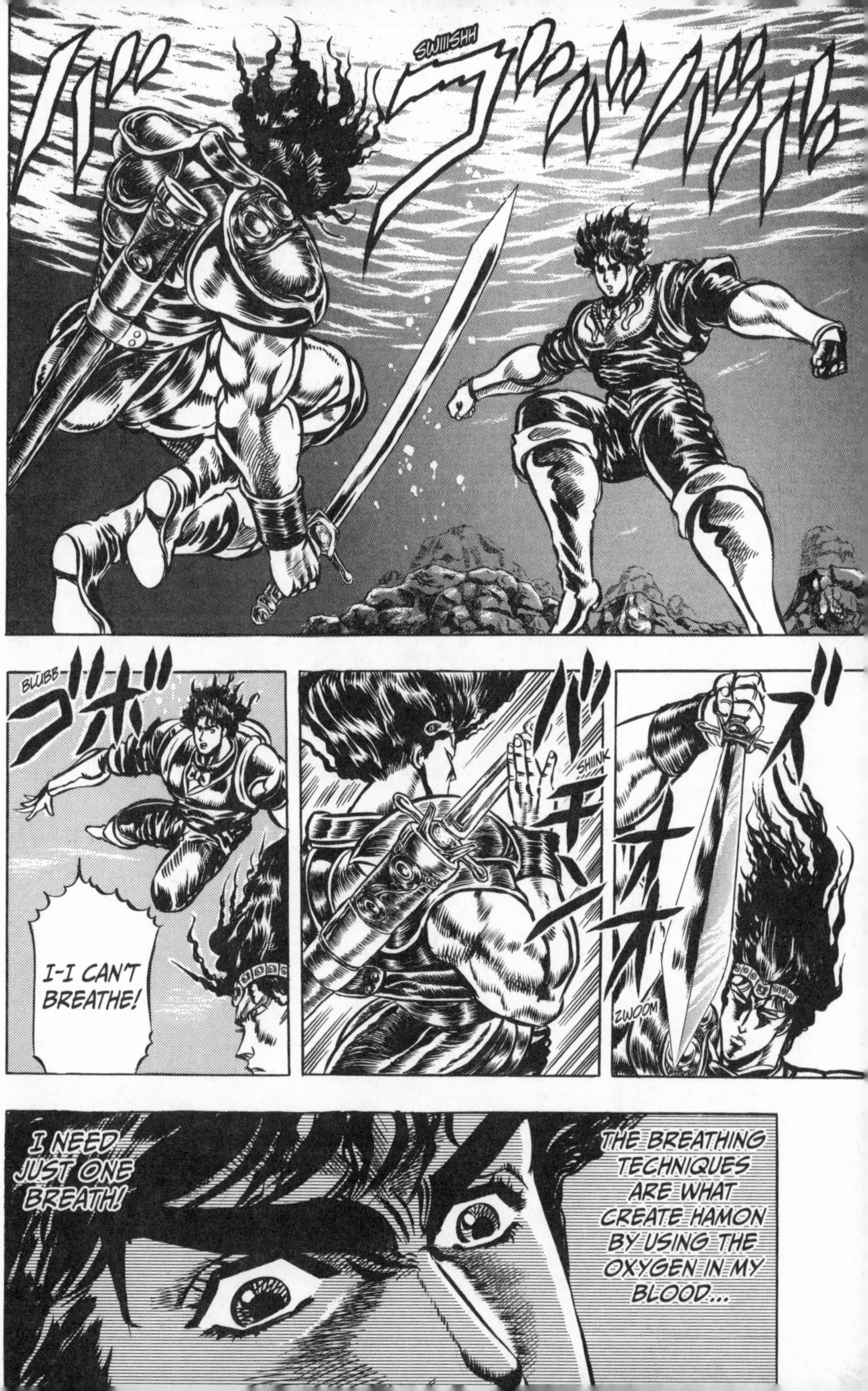
SWIIISHH
ZWOOM
SHIINK
BLUBB
I-I CAN'T BREATHE!
THE BREATHING TECHNIQUES ARE WHAT CREATE HAMON BY USING THE OXYGEN IN MY BLOOD...
I NEED JUST ONE BREATH!

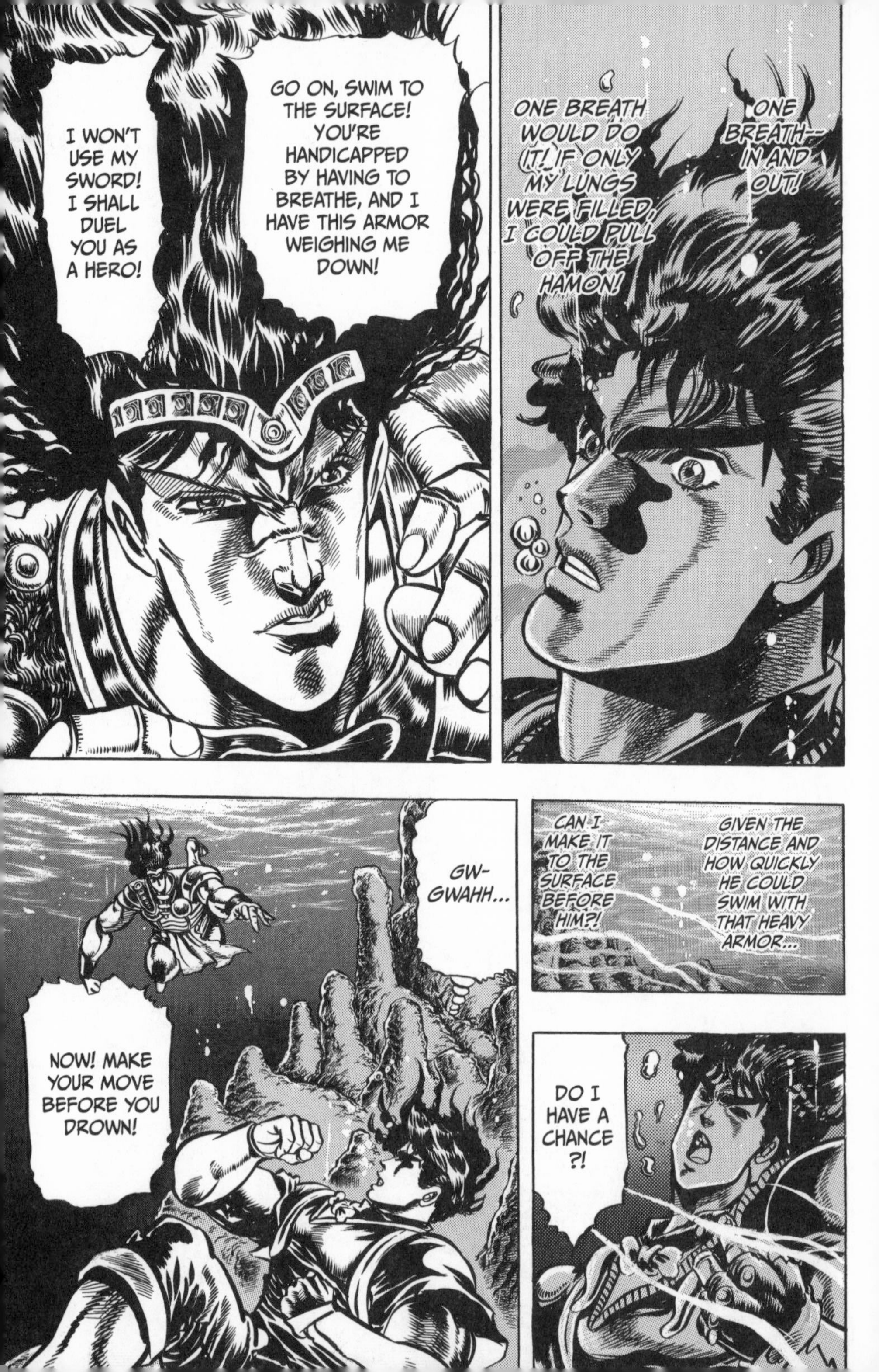
ONE BREATH— IN AND OUT!
ONE BREATH WOULD DO IT! IF ONLY MY LUNGS WERE FILLED, I COULD PULL OFF THE HAMON!
GO ON, SWIM TO THE SURFACE! YOU'RE HANDICAPPED BY HAVING TO BREATHE, AND I HAVE THIS ARMOR WEIGHING ME DOWN!
I WON'T USE MY SWORD! I SHALL DUEL YOU AS A HERO!
GIVEN THE DISTANCE AND HOW QUICKLY HE COULD SWIM WITH THAT HEAVY ARMOR...
CAN I MAKE IT TO THE SURFACE BEFORE HIM?!
DO I HAVE A CHANCE ?!
GW- GWAHH...
NOW! MAKE YOUR MOVE BEFORE YOU DROWN!

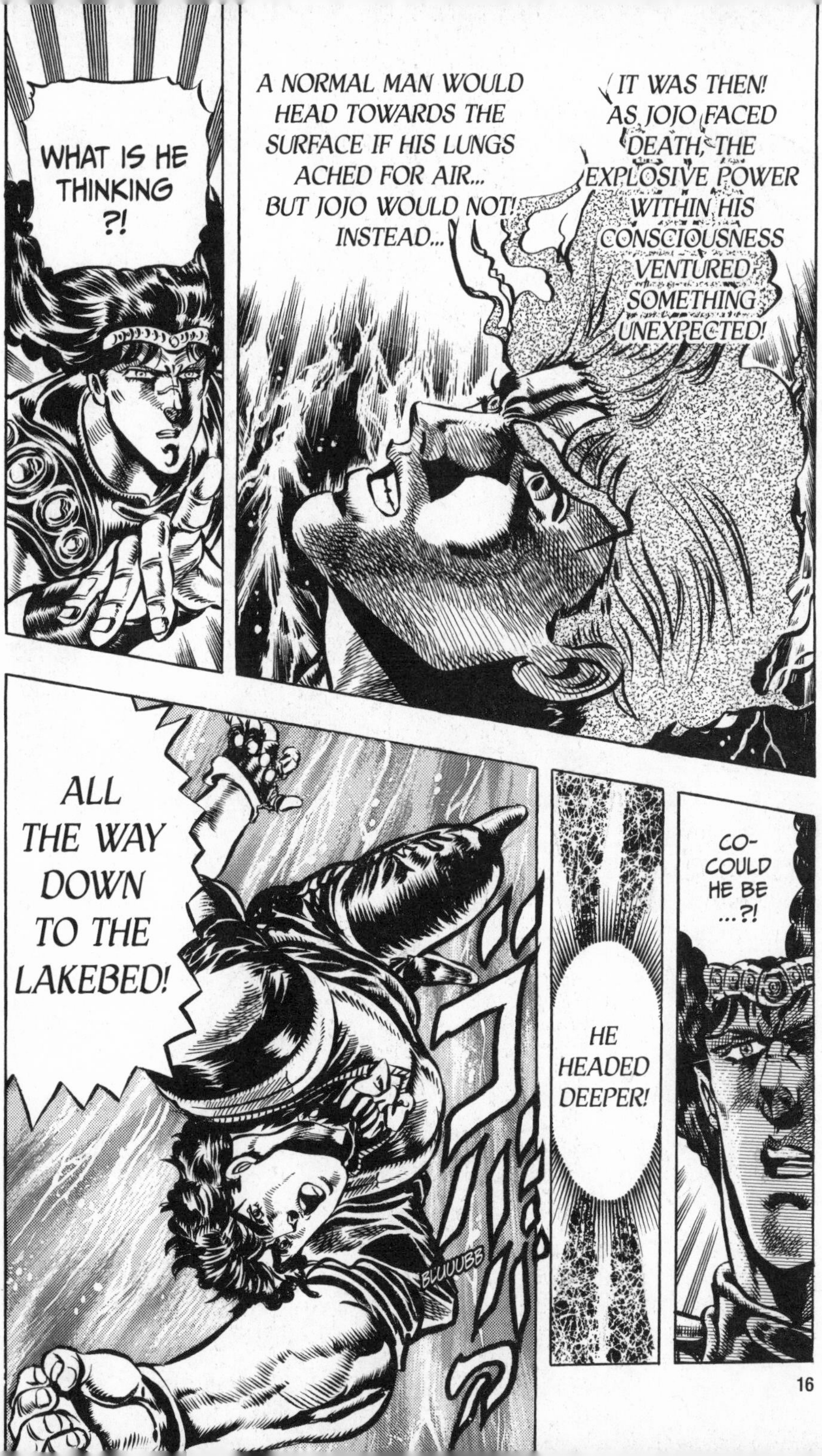
IT WAS THEN! AS JOJO FACED DEATH, THE EXPLOSIVE POWER WITHIN HIS CONSCIOUSNESS VENTURED SOMETHING UNEXPECTED!
A NORMAL MAN WOULD HEAD TOWARDS THE SURFACE IF HIS LUNGS ACHED FOR AIR... BUT JOJO WOULD NOT! INSTEAD...
WHAT IS HE THINKING ?!
CO- COULD HE BE ...?!
HE HEADED DEEPER!
ALL THE WAY DOWN TO THE LAKEBED!
BLUUUBB

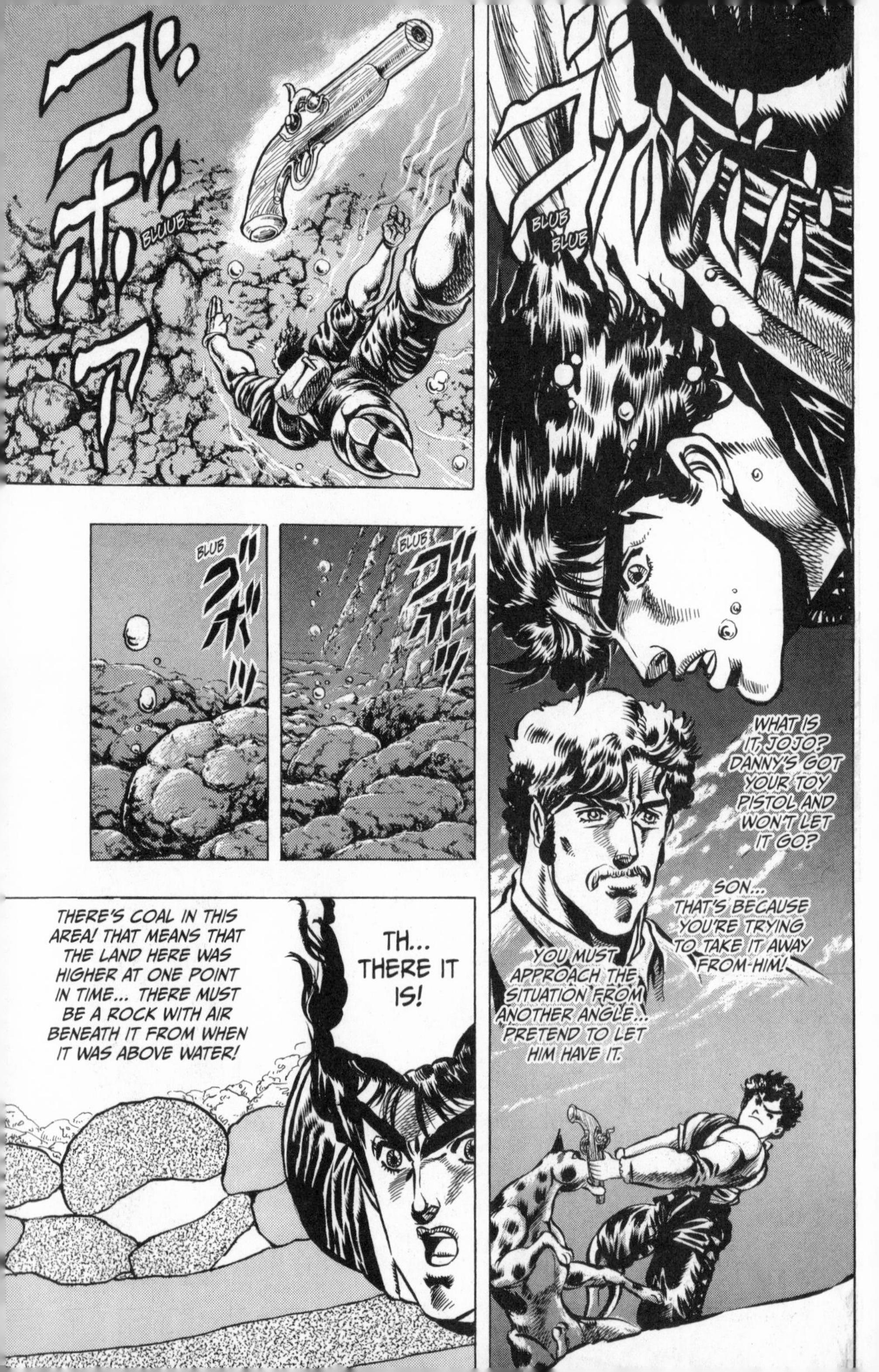
BLUB
BLUB
WHAT IS IT, JOJO? DANNY'S GOT YOUR TOY PISTOL AND WON'T LET IT GO?
SON... THAT'S BECAUSE YOU'RE TRYING TO TAKE IT AWAY FROM HIM!
YOU MUST APPROACH THE SITUATION FROM ANOTHER ANGLE... PRETEND TO LET HIM HAVE IT.
BLUUB
BLUB
BLUB
TH... THERE IT IS!
THERE'S COAL IN THIS AREA! THAT MEANS THAT THE LAND HERE WAS HIGHER AT ONE POINT IN TIME... THERE MUST BE A ROCK WITH AIR BENEATH IT FROM WHEN IT WAS ABOVE WATER!

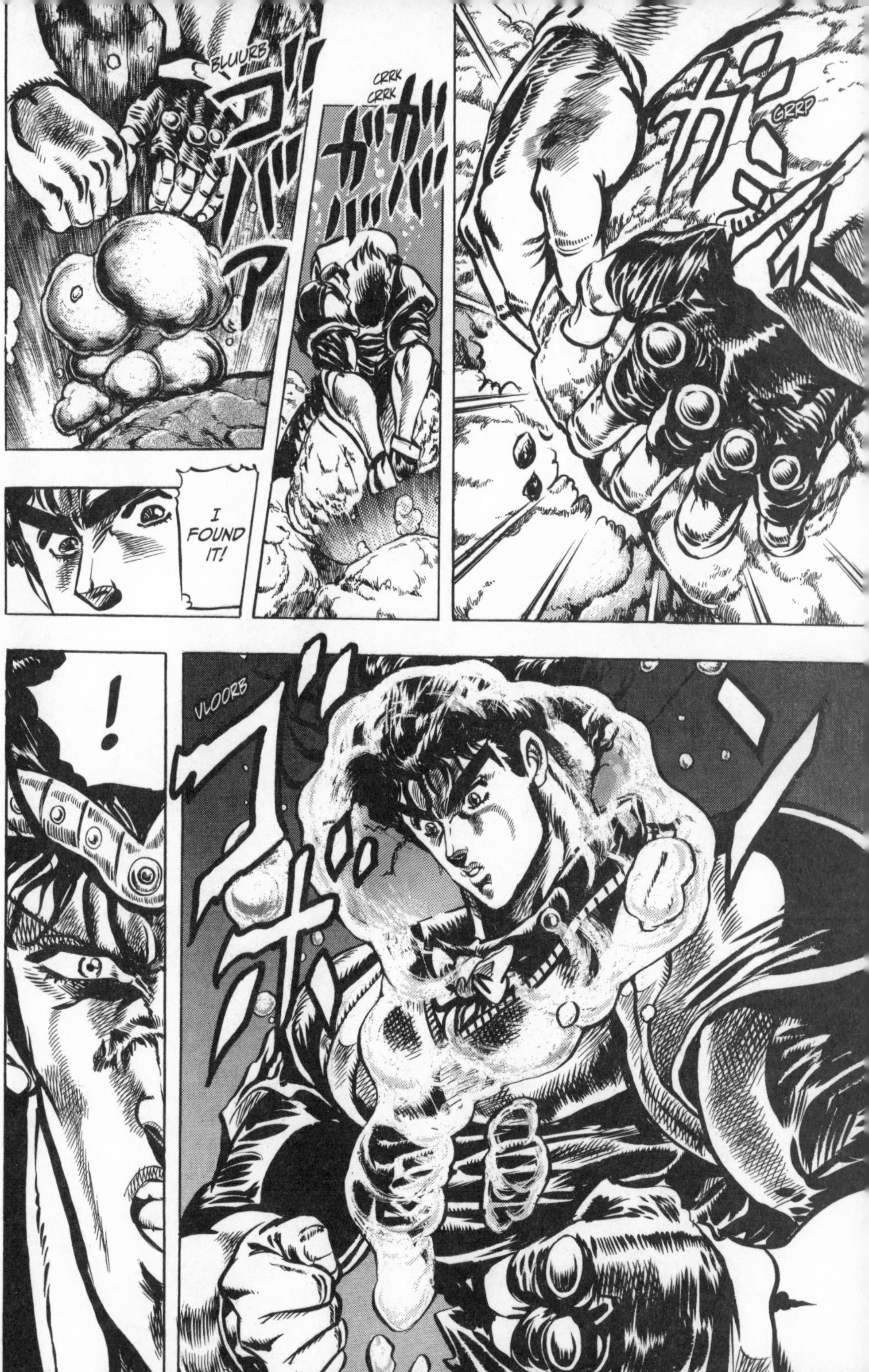
GRRP
CRRK
CRRK
BLUURB
I FOUND IT!
VLOORB
!

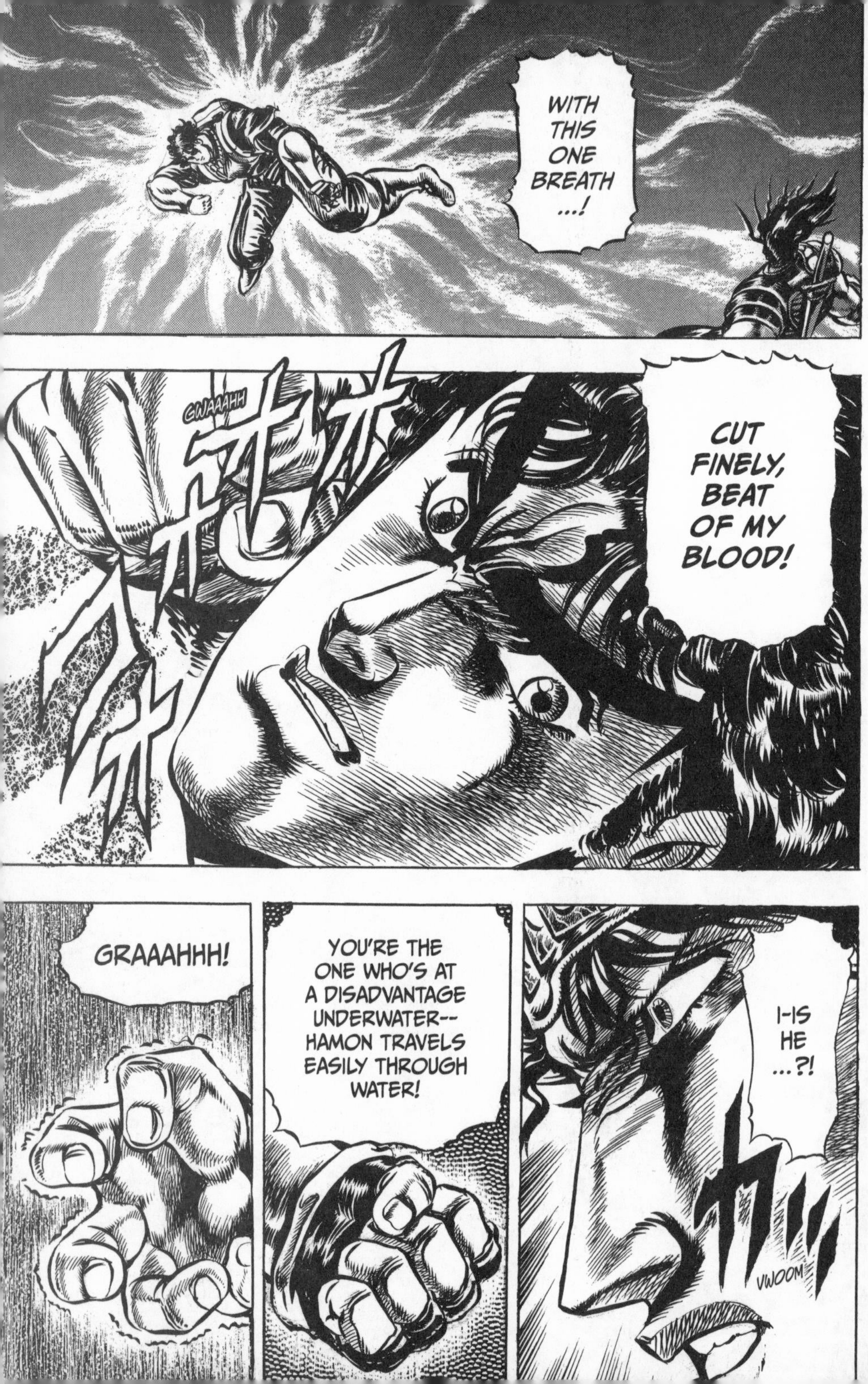
WITH THIS ONE BREATH ...!
CUT FINELY, BEAT OF MY BLOOD!
GWAAAHH
I-IS HE ...?!
VWOOM
YOU'RE THE ONE WHO'S AT A DISADVANTAGE UNDERWATER-- HAMON TRAVELS EASILY THROUGH WATER!
GRAAAHHH!

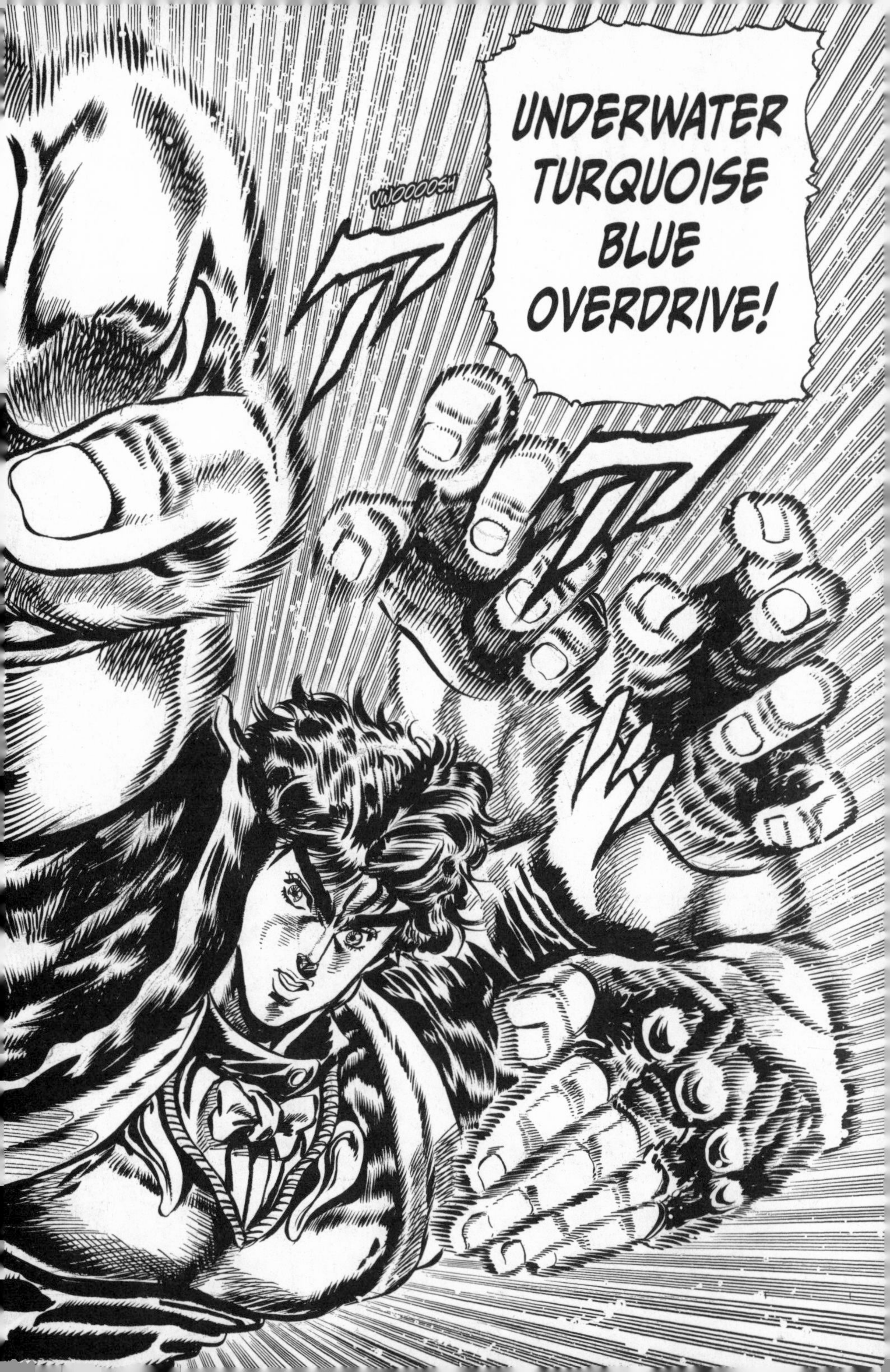
UNDERWATER TURQUOISE BLUE OVERDRIVE!
VWOOOOOSH

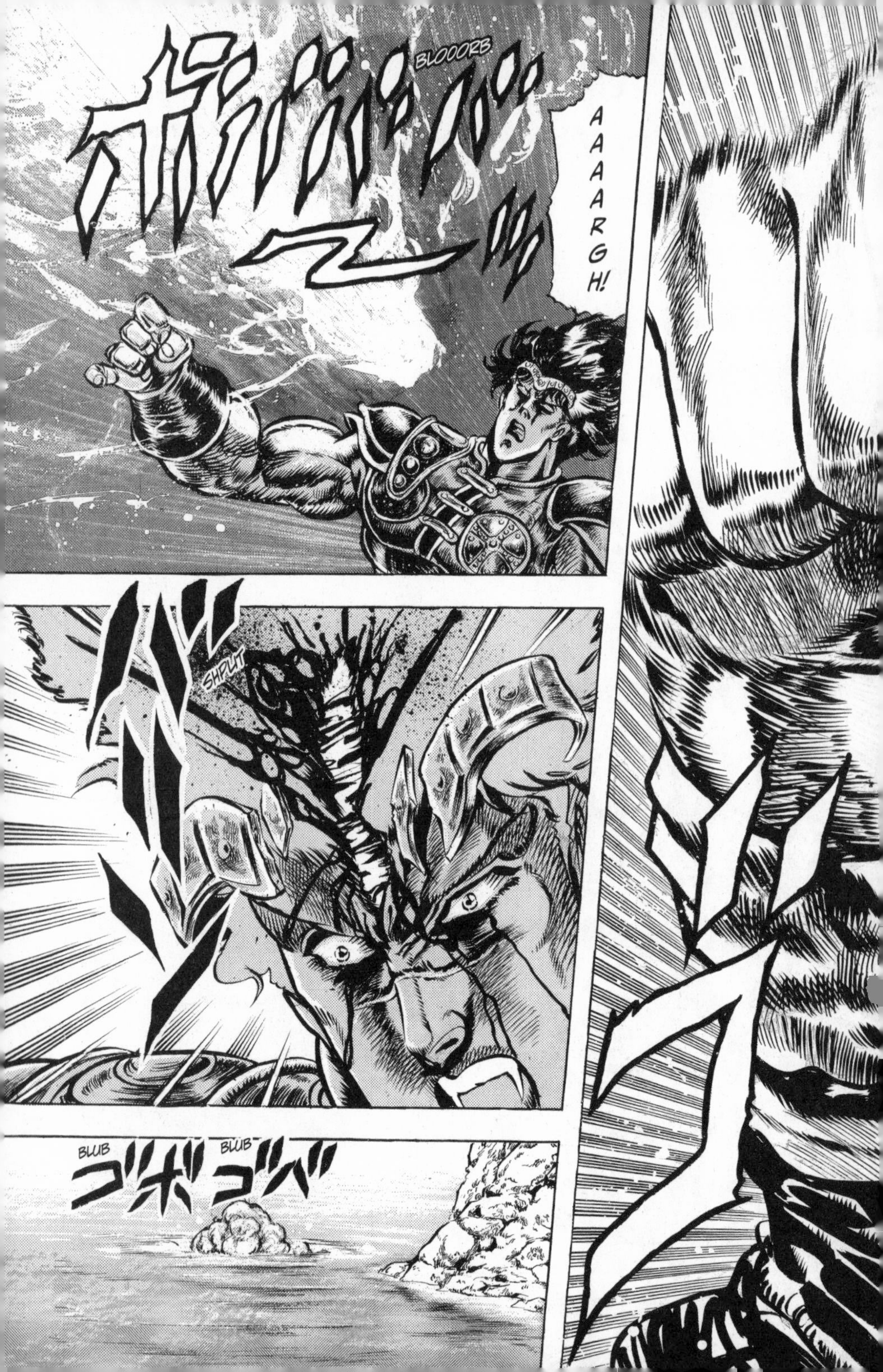
BLOOORB
AAAAARGH!
SHPLIT
BLUB
BLUB

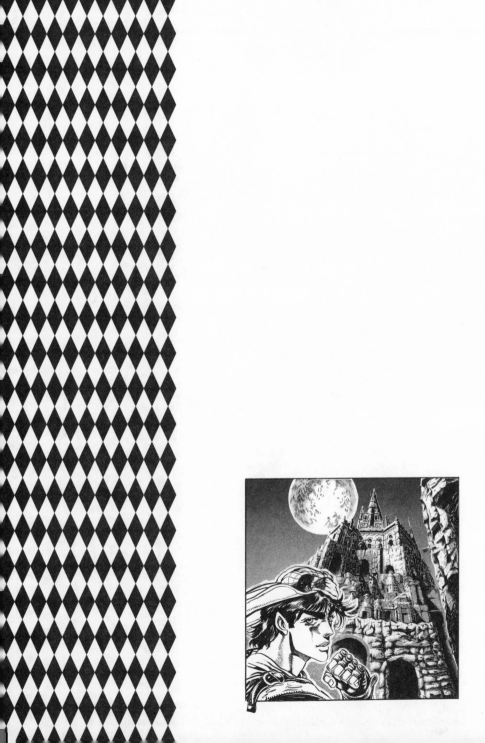

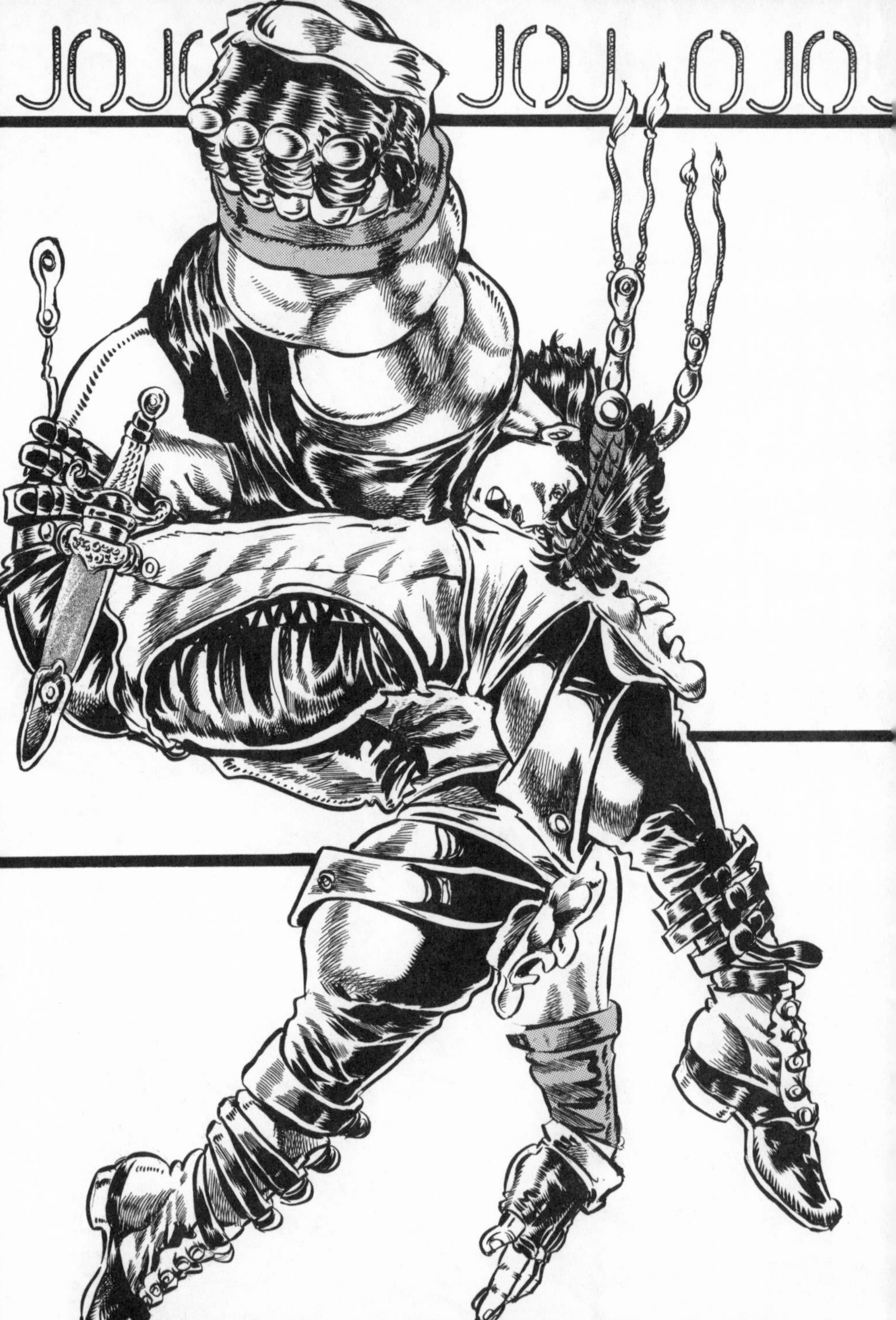

CHAPTER 29: Tarukus and the Dark Knight Blueford PART 4

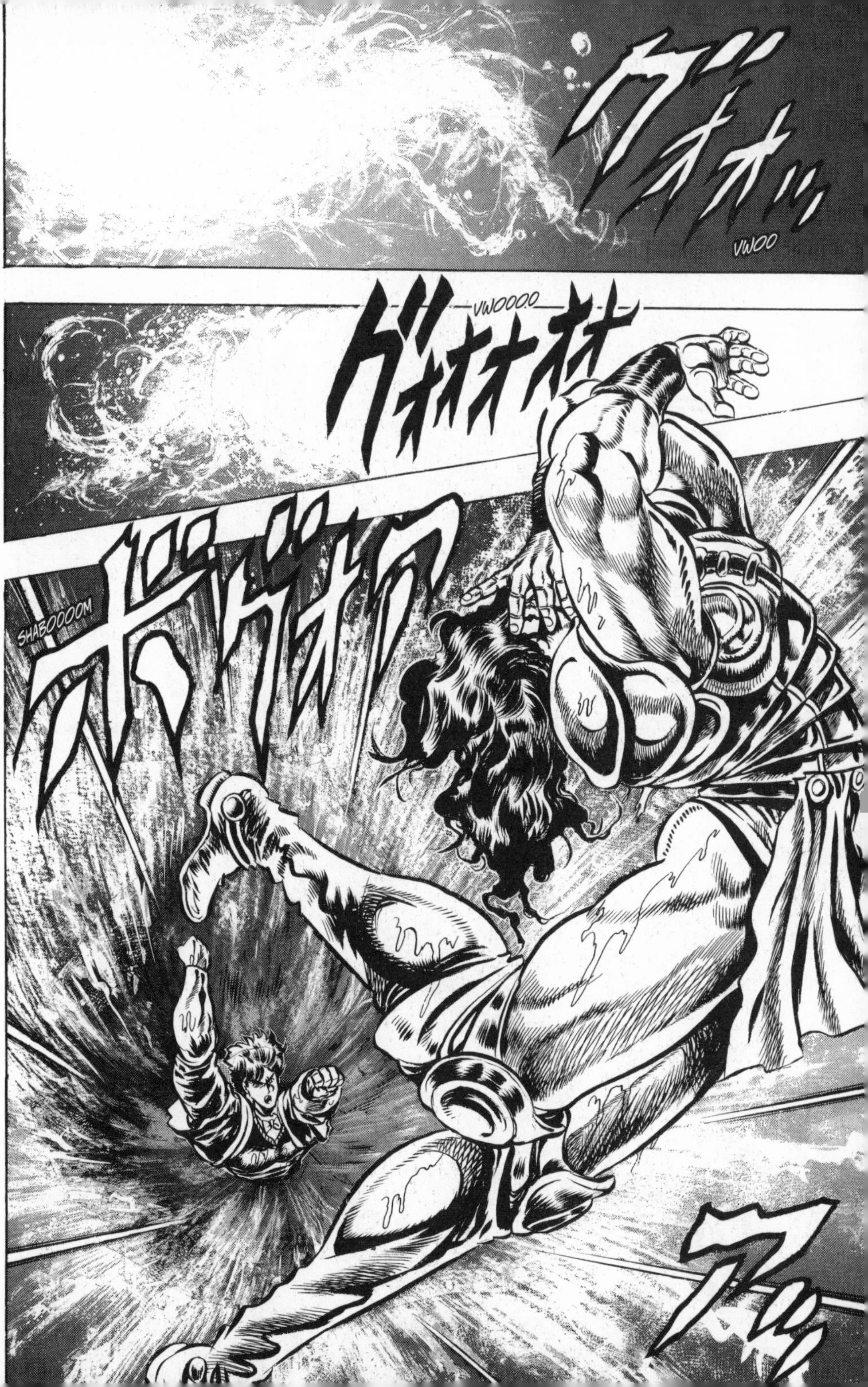
VWOO
VWOOOO
SHABOOOOM

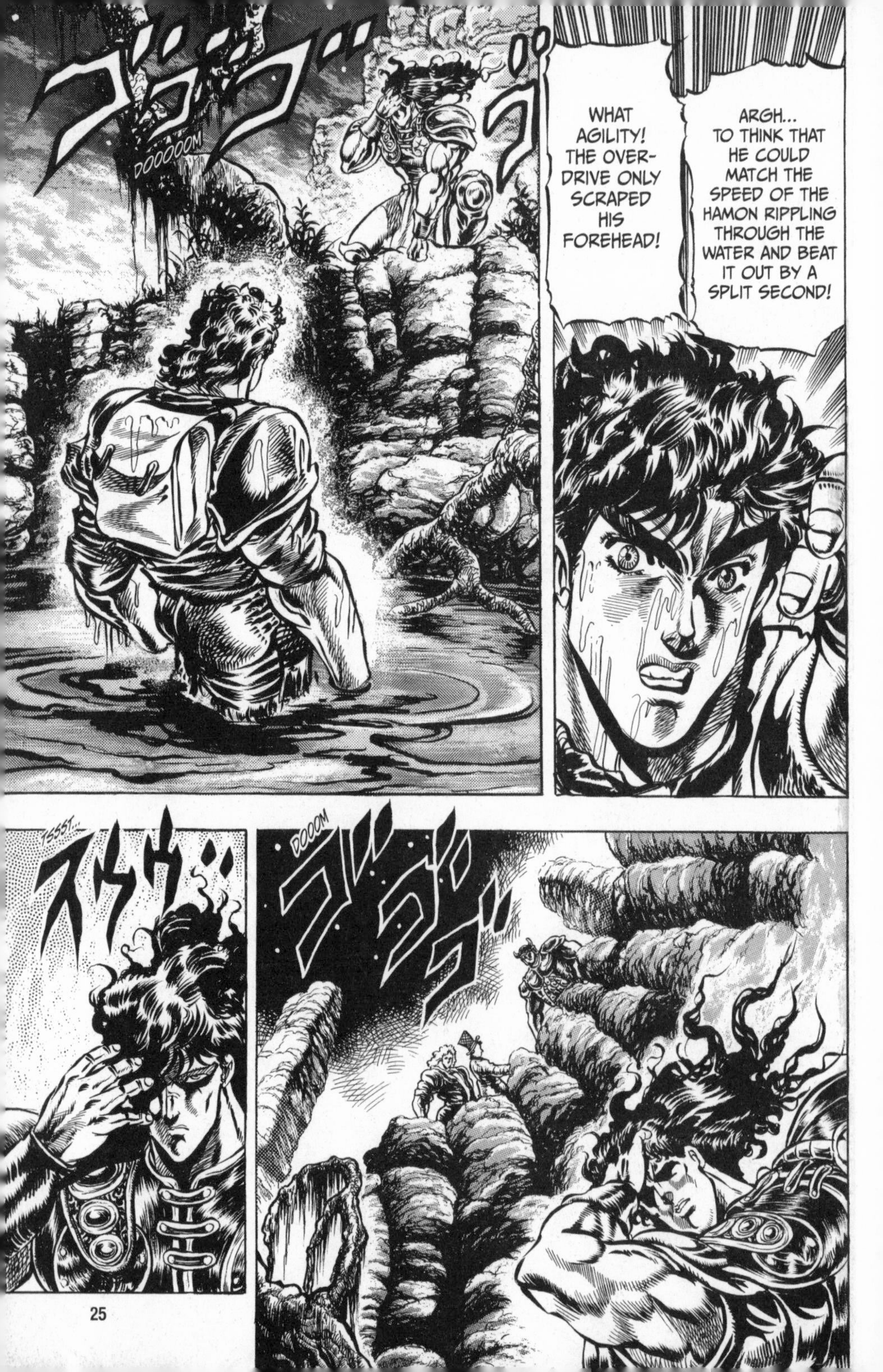
ARGH... TO THINK THAT HE COULD MATCH THE SPEED OF THE HAMON RIPPLING THROUGH THE WATER AND BEAT IT OUT BY A SPLIT SECOND!
WHAT AGILITY! THE OVER-DRIVE ONLY SCRAPED HIS FOREHEAD!
DOOOOOOM
DOOOM
TSSSST...

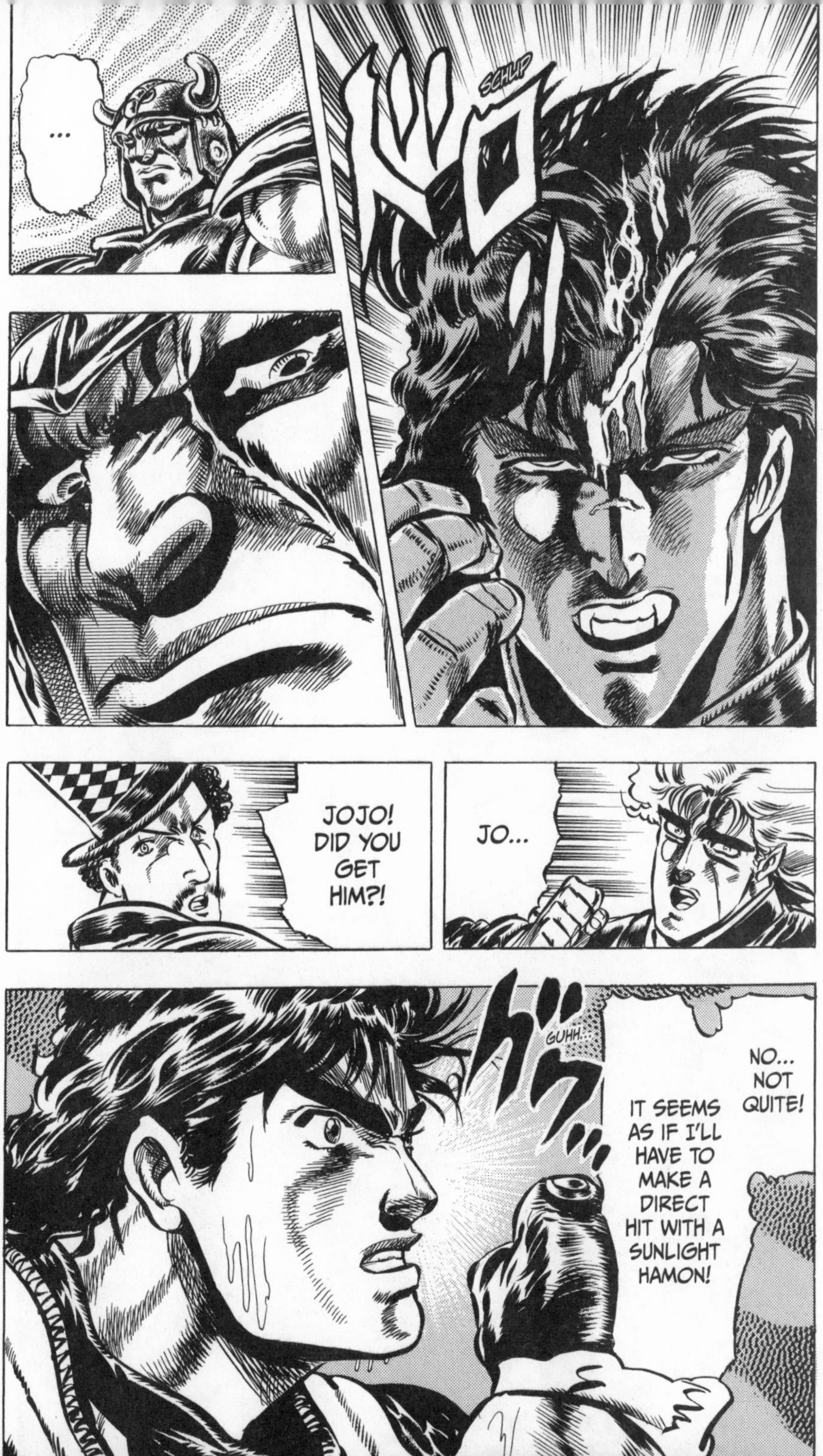
SCHUP
...
JO...
JOJO! DID YOU GET HIM?!
GUHH...
NO... NOT QUITE!
IT SEEMS AS IF I'LL HAVE TO MAKE A DIRECT HIT WITH A SUNLIGHT HAMON!

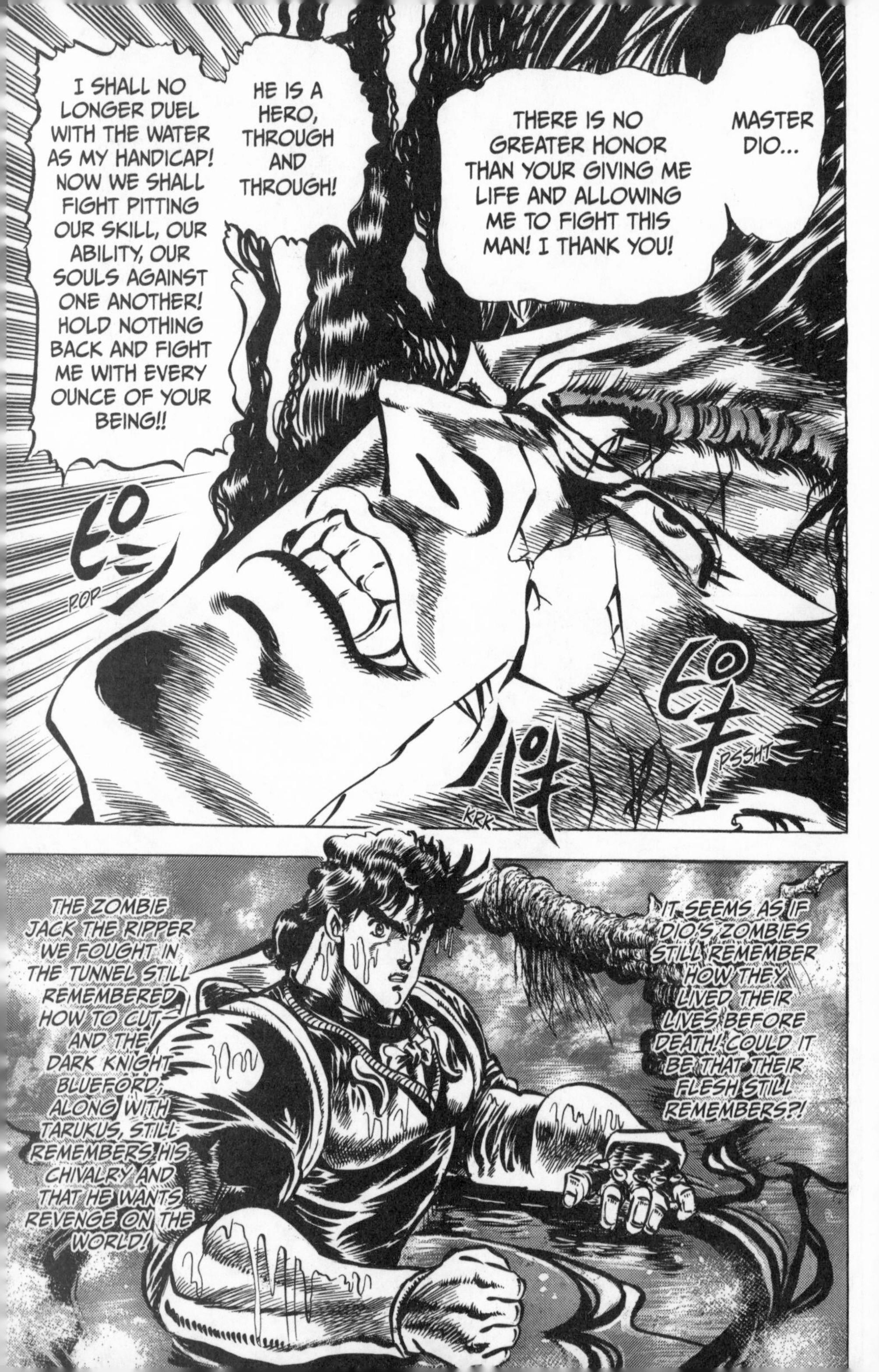
MASTER DIO...
THERE IS NO GREATER HONOR THAN YOUR GIVING ME LIFE AND ALLOWING ME TO FIGHT THIS MAN! I THANK YOU!
HE IS A HERO, THROUGH AND THROUGH!
I SHALL NO LONGER DUEL WITH THE WATER AS MY HANDICAP! NOW WE SHALL FIGHT PITTING OUR SKILL, OUR ABILITY, OUR SOULS AGAINST ONE ANOTHER! HOLD NOTHING BACK AND FIGHT ME WITH EVERY OUNCE OF YOUR BEING!!
PSSHT
KRK
POP
IT SEEMS AS IF DIO'S ZOMBIES STILL REMEMBER HOW THEY LIVED THEIR LIVES BEFORE DEATH! COULD IT BE THAT THEIR FLESH STILL REMEMBERS?!
THE ZOMBIE JACK THE RIPPER WE FOUGHT IN THE TUNNEL STILL REMEMBERED HOW TO CUT-- AND THE DARK KNIGHT BLUEFORD, ALONG WITH TARUKUS, STILL REMEMBERS HIS CHIVALRY AND THAT HE WANTS REVENGE ON THE WORLD!

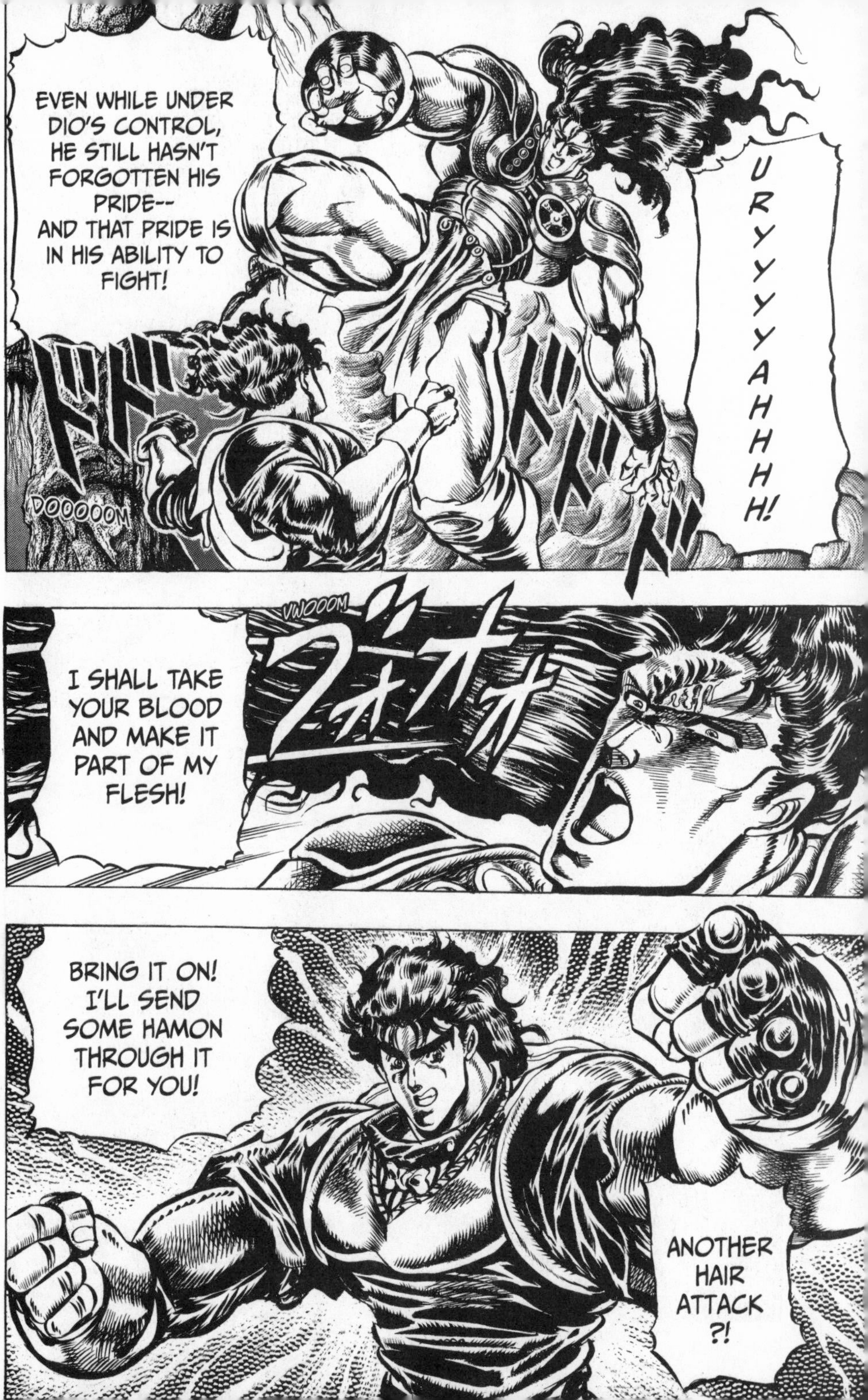
URYYYYAHHHH!
EVEN WHILE UNDER DIO'S CONTROL, HE STILL HASN'T FORGOTTEN HIS PRIDE-- AND THAT PRIDE IS IN HIS ABILITY TO FIGHT!
DOOOOOM
VWOOOM
I SHALL TAKE YOUR BLOOD AND MAKE IT PART OF MY FLESH!
BRING IT ON! I'LL SEND SOME HAMON THROUGH IT FOR YOU!
ANOTHER HAIR ATTACK ?!

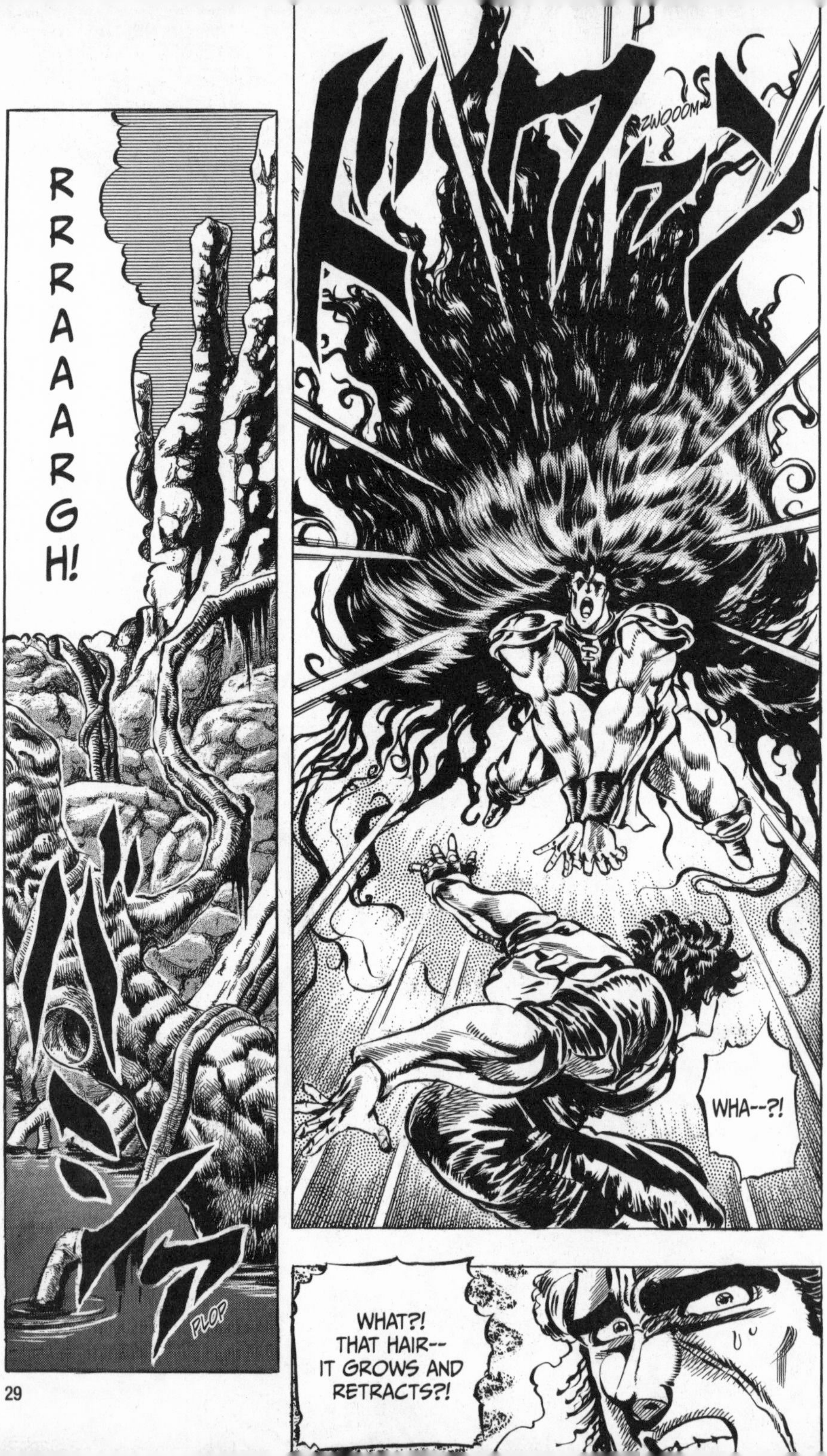
ZWOOOM
WHA--?!
WHAT?! THAT HAIR-- IT GROWS AND RETRACTS?!
RRRAAAARGH!
PLOP

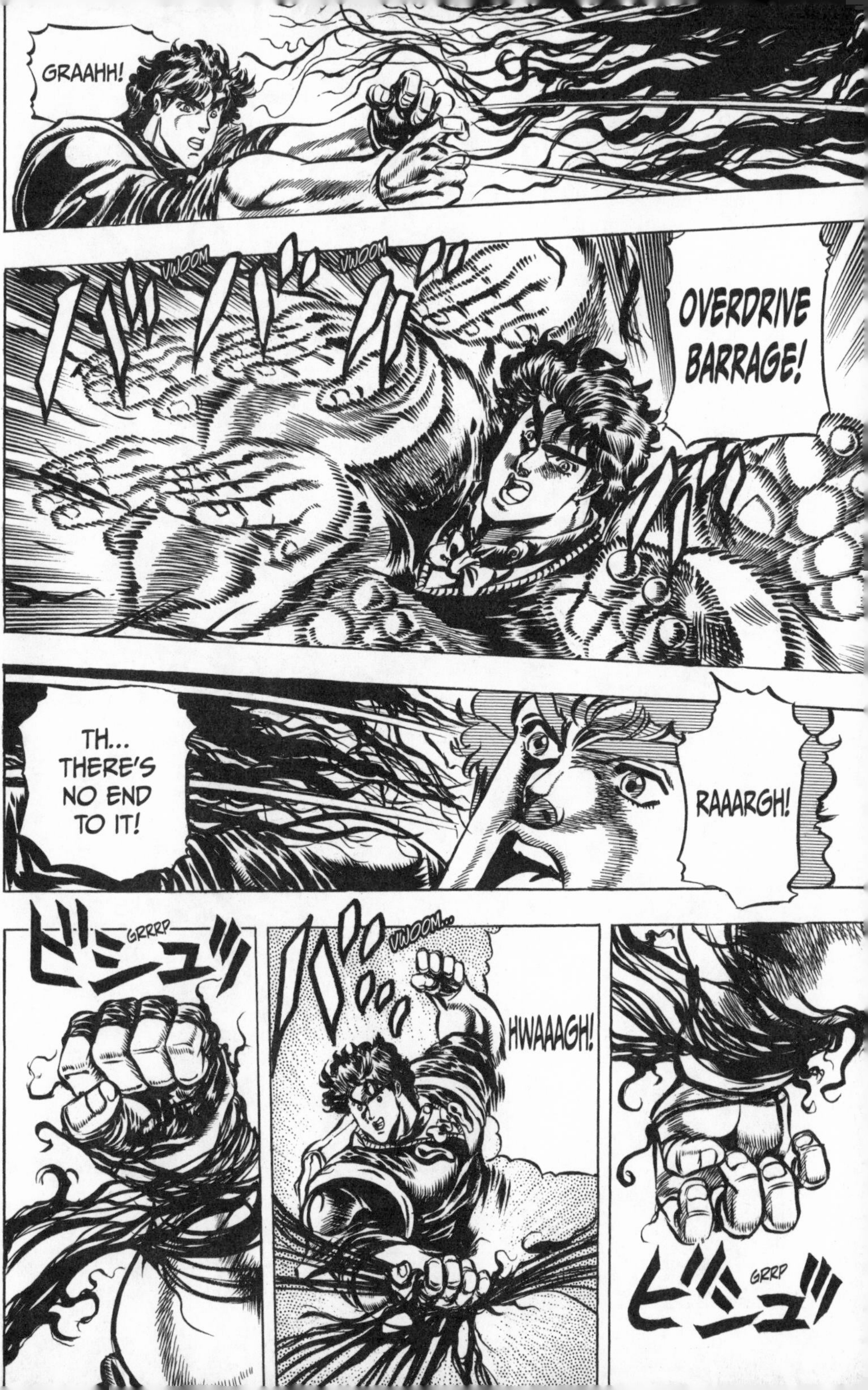
GRAAHH!
OVERDRIVE BARRAGE!
VWOOM
VWOOM
RAAARGH!
TH... THERE'S NO END TO IT!
GRRP
VWOOM...
HWAAAGH!
GRRRP

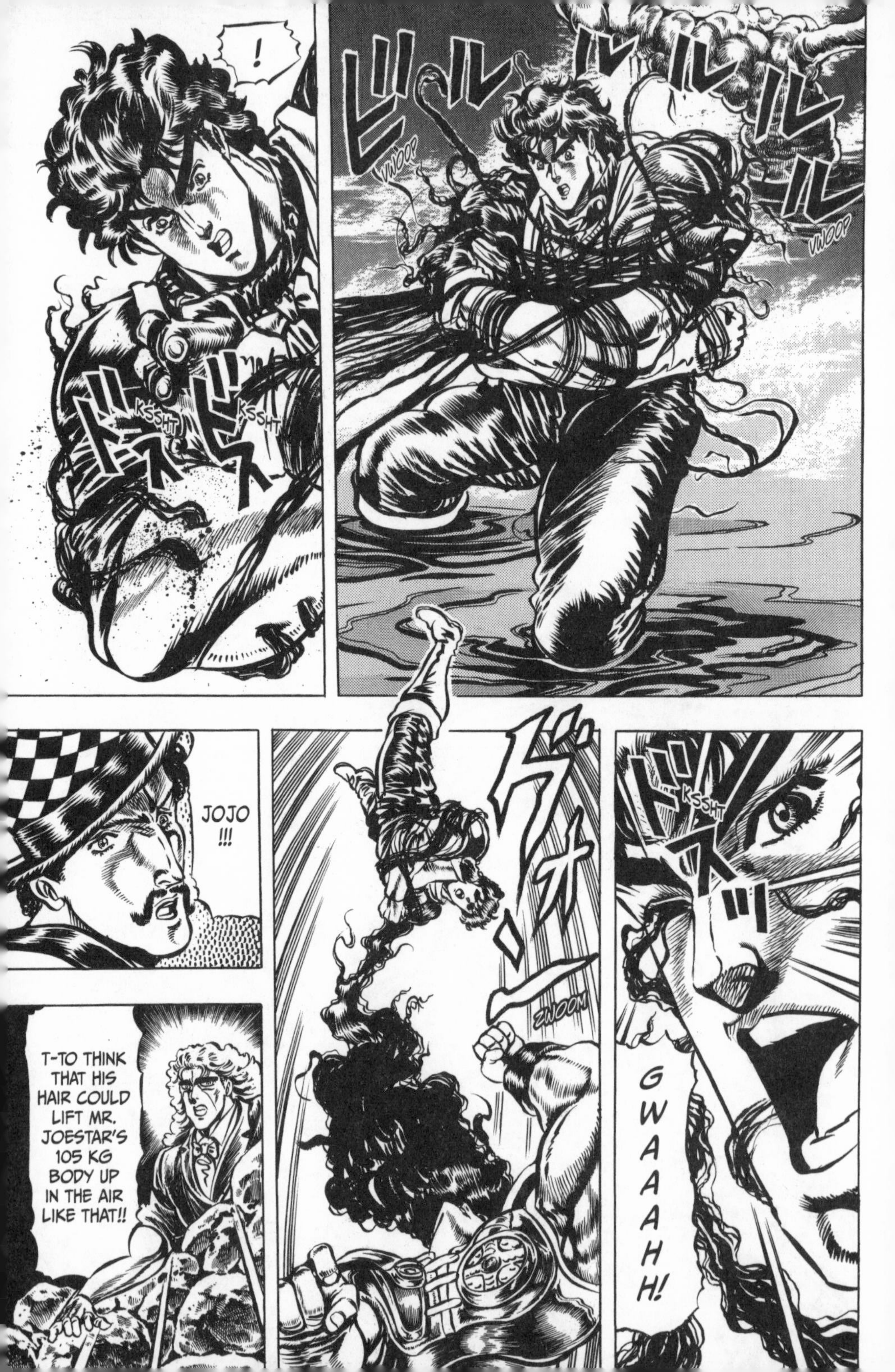

VWOOP
VWOOP
!
KSSHT
KSSHT
KSSHT
GWAAAAHH!
ZWOOM
JOJO !!!
T-TO THINK THAT HIS HAIR COULD LIFT MR. JOESTAR'S 105 KG BODY UP IN THE AIR LIKE THAT!!

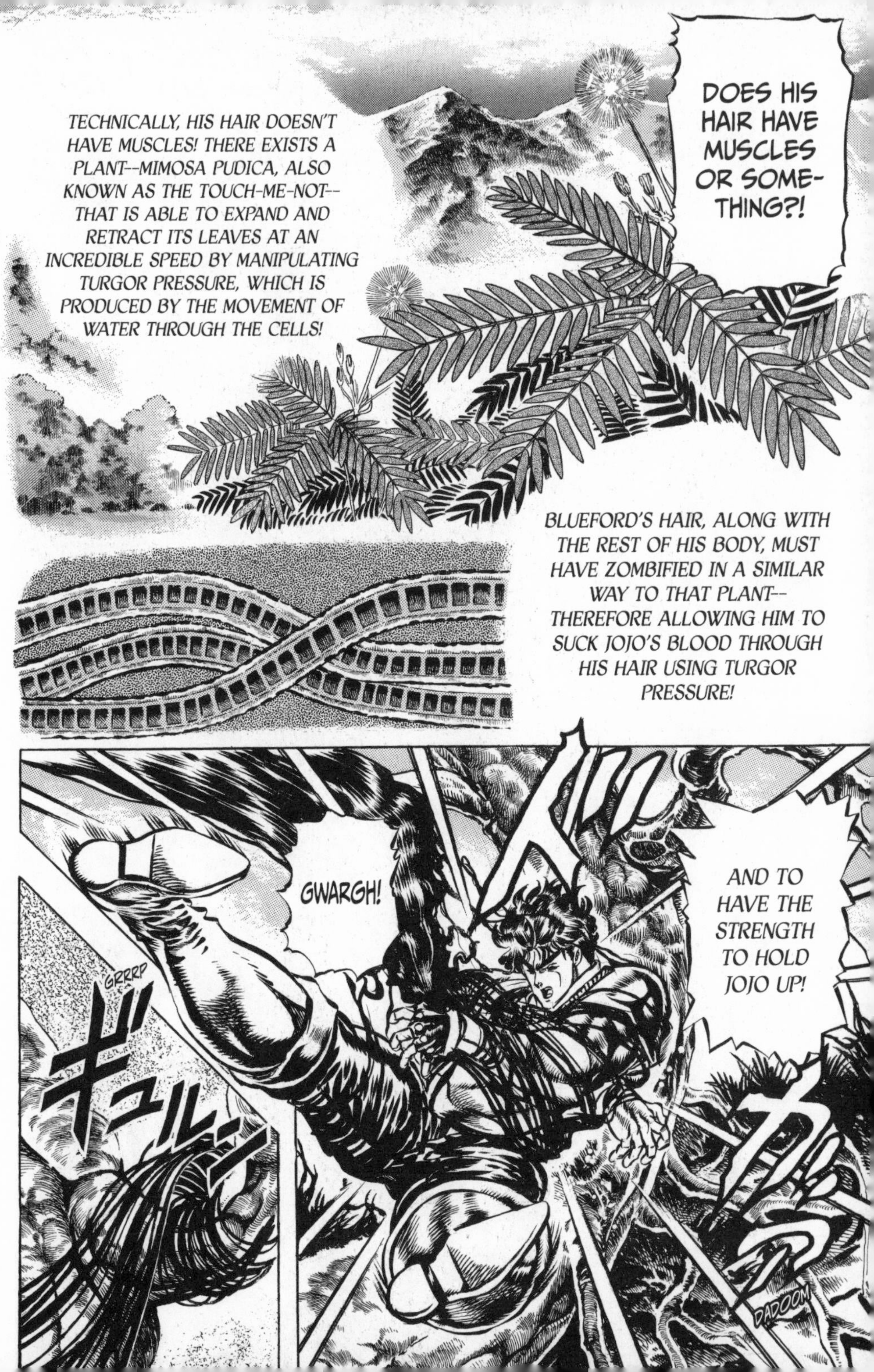
DOES HIS HAIR HAVE MUSCLES OR SOME-THING?!
TECHNICALLY, HIS HAIR DOESN'T HAVE MUSCLES! THERE EXISTS A PLANT--MIMOSA PUDICA, ALSO KNOWN AS THE TOUCH-ME-NOT--THAT IS ABLE TO EXPAND AND RETRACT ITS LEAVES AT AN INCREDIBLE SPEED BY MANIPULATING TURGOR PRESSURE, WHICH IS PRODUCED BY THE MOVEMENT OF WATER THROUGH THE CELLS!
BLUEFORD'S HAIR, ALONG WITH THE REST OF HIS BODY, MUST HAVE ZOMBIFIED IN A SIMILAR WAY TO THAT PLANT--THEREFORE ALLOWING HIM TO SUCK JOJO'S BLOOD THROUGH HIS HAIR USING TURGOR PRESSURE!
AND TO HAVE THE STRENGTH TO HOLD JOJO UP!
DADOOM
GWARGH!
GRRRP

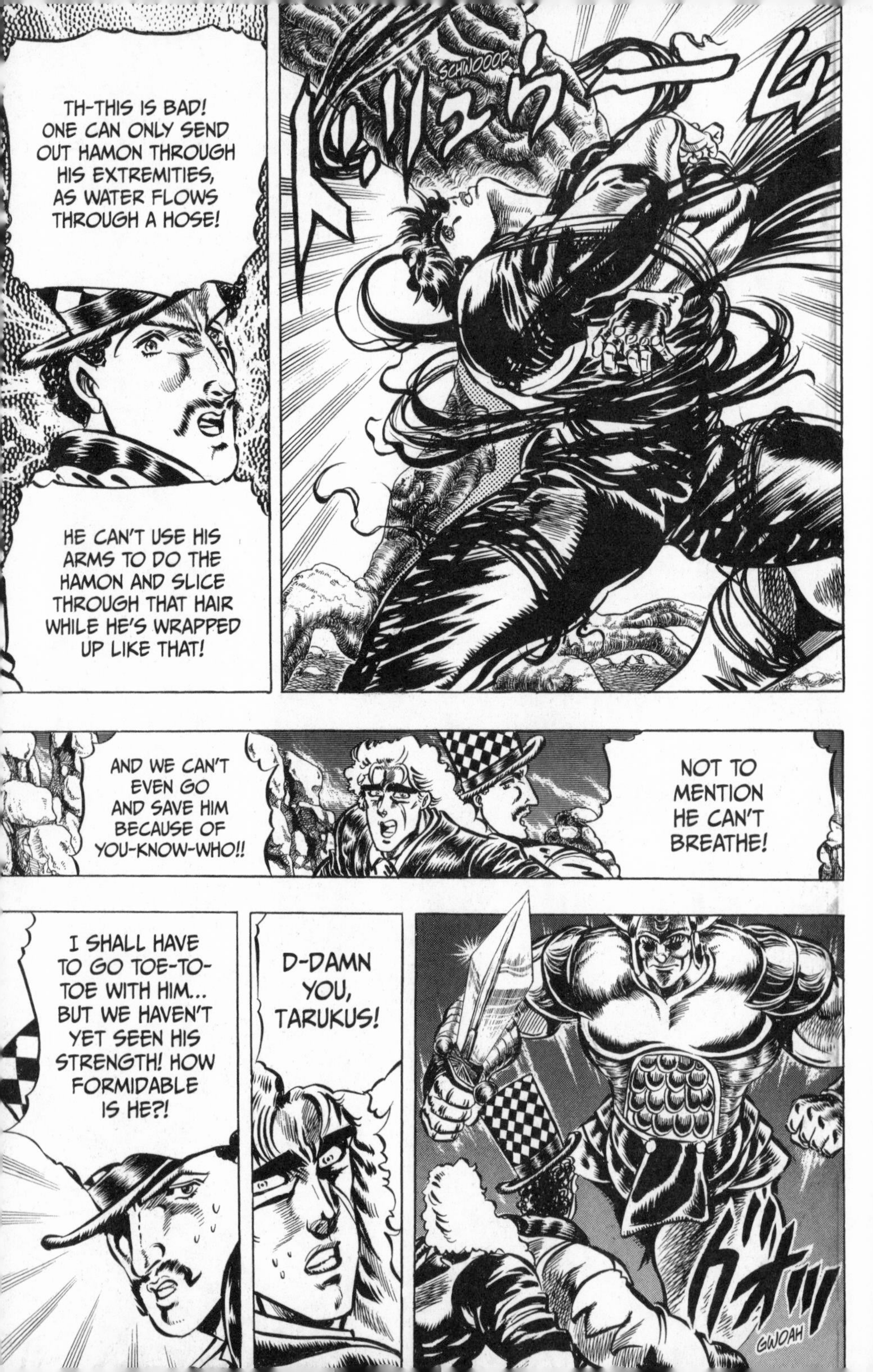
SCHWOOOP
TH-THIS IS BAD! ONE CAN ONLY SEND OUT HAMON THROUGH HIS EXTREMITIES, AS WATER FLOWS THROUGH A HOSE!
HE CAN'T USE HIS ARMS TO DO THE HAMON AND SLICE THROUGH THAT HAIR WHILE HE'S WRAPPED UP LIKE THAT!
NOT TO MENTION HE CAN'T BREATHE!
AND WE CAN'T EVEN GO AND SAVE HIM BECAUSE OF YOU-KNOW-WHO!!
GWOAH
D-DAMN YOU, TARUKUS!
I SHALL HAVE TO GO TOE-TO-TOE WITH HIM... BUT WE HAVEN'T YET SEEN HIS STRENGTH! HOW FORMIDABLE IS HE?!

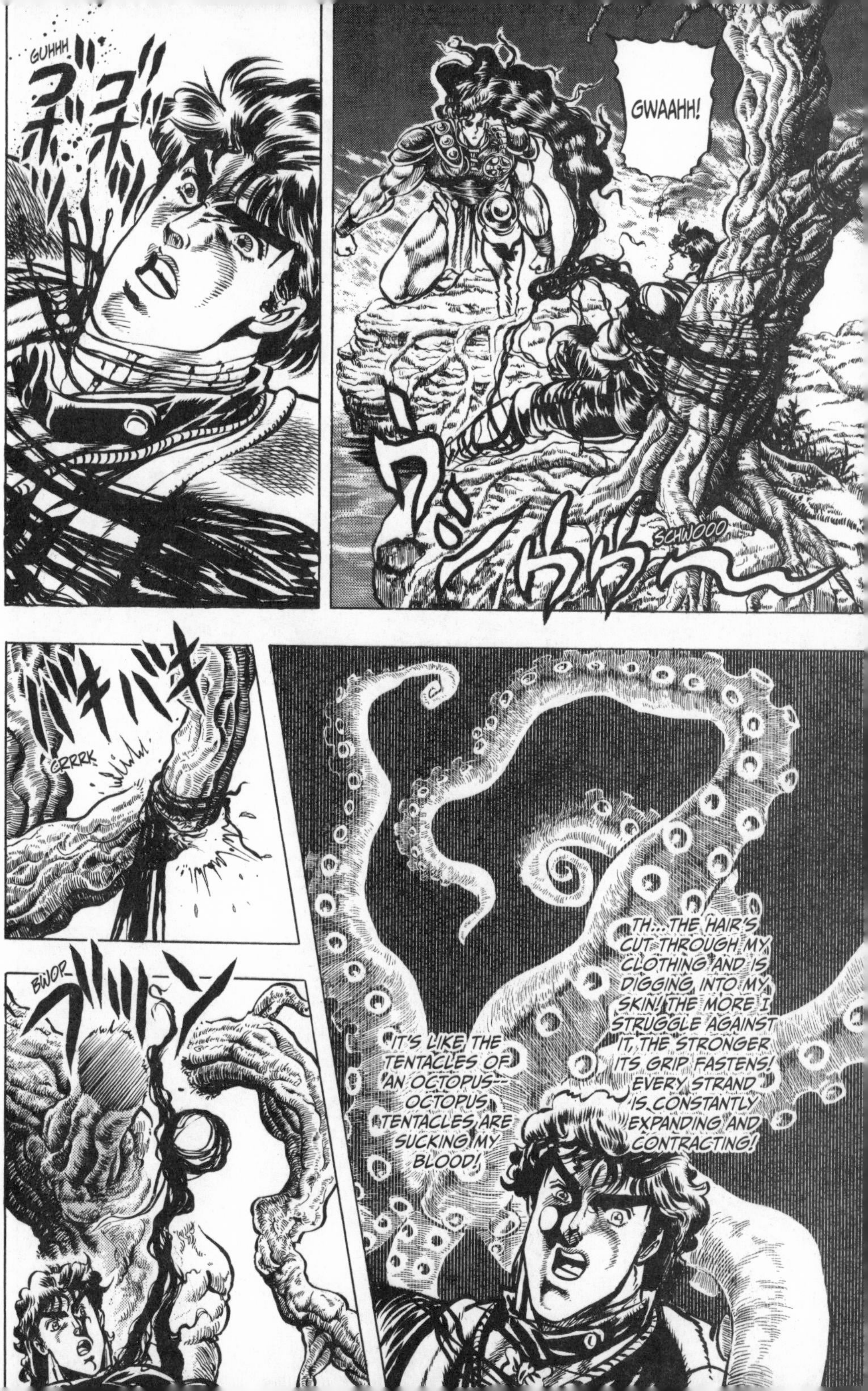
GWAAHH!
SCHWOOO
GUHHH
TH... THE HAIR'S CUT THROUGH MY CLOTHING AND IS DIGGING INTO MY SKIN! THE MORE I STRUGGLE AGAINST IT, THE STRONGER ITS GRIP FASTENS! EVERY STRAND IS CONSTANTLY EXPANDING AND CONTRACTING!
IT'S LIKE THE TENTACLES OF AN OCTOPUS-- OCTOPUS TENTACLES ARE SUCKING MY BLOOD!
GRRRK
BWOR

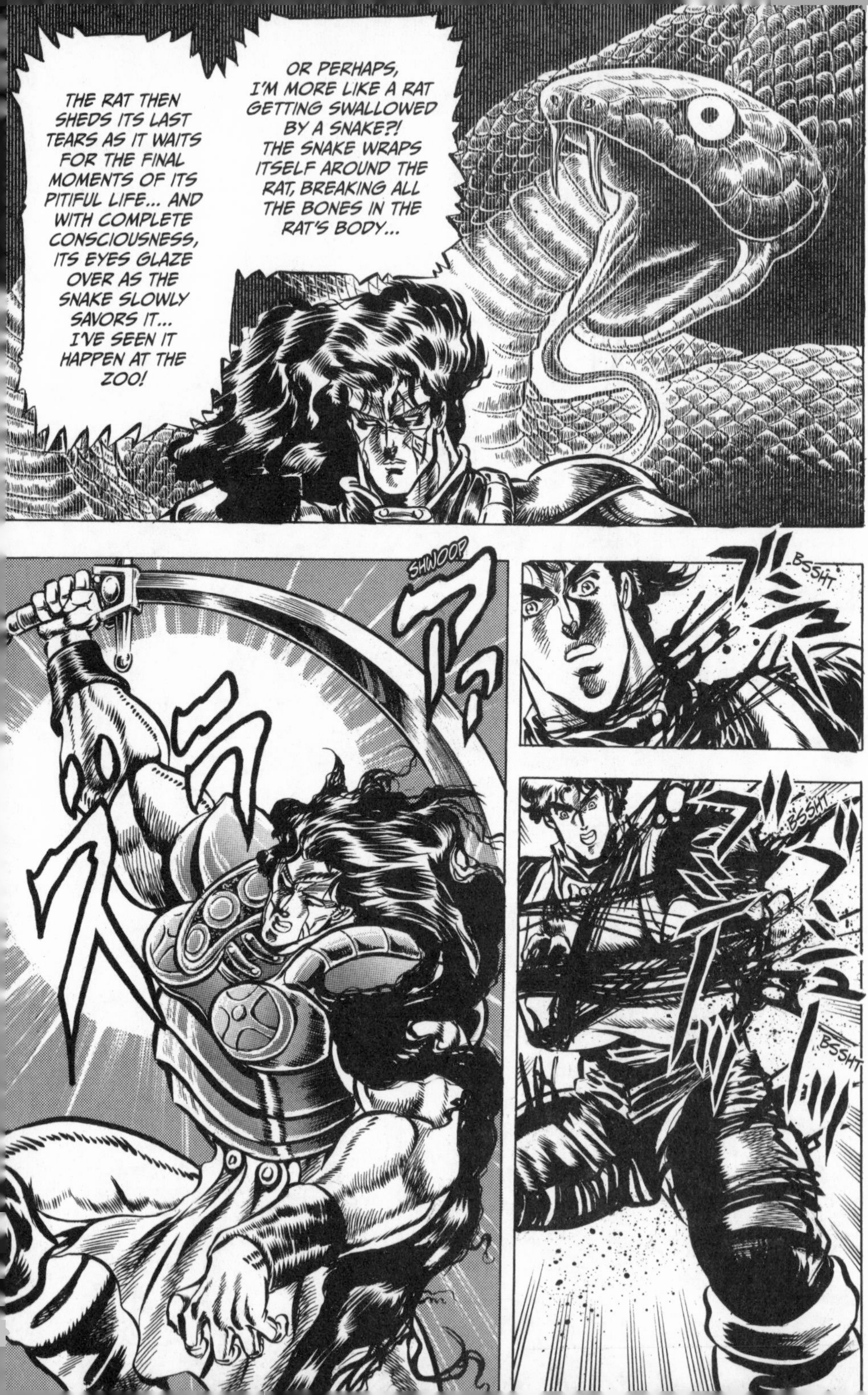
OR PERHAPS, I'M MORE LIKE A RAT GETTING SWALLOWED BY A SNAKE?! THE SNAKE WRAPS ITSELF AROUND THE RAT, BREAKING ALL THE BONES IN THE RAT'S BODY...
THE RAT THEN SHEDS ITS LAST TEARS AS IT WAITS FOR THE FINAL MOMENTS OF ITS PITIFUL LIFE... AND WITH COMPLETE CONSCIOUSNESS, ITS EYES GLAZE OVER AS THE SNAKE SLOWLY SAVORS IT... I'VE SEEN IT HAPPEN AT THE ZOO!
BSSHT
BSSHT
BSSHT
SHWOOP

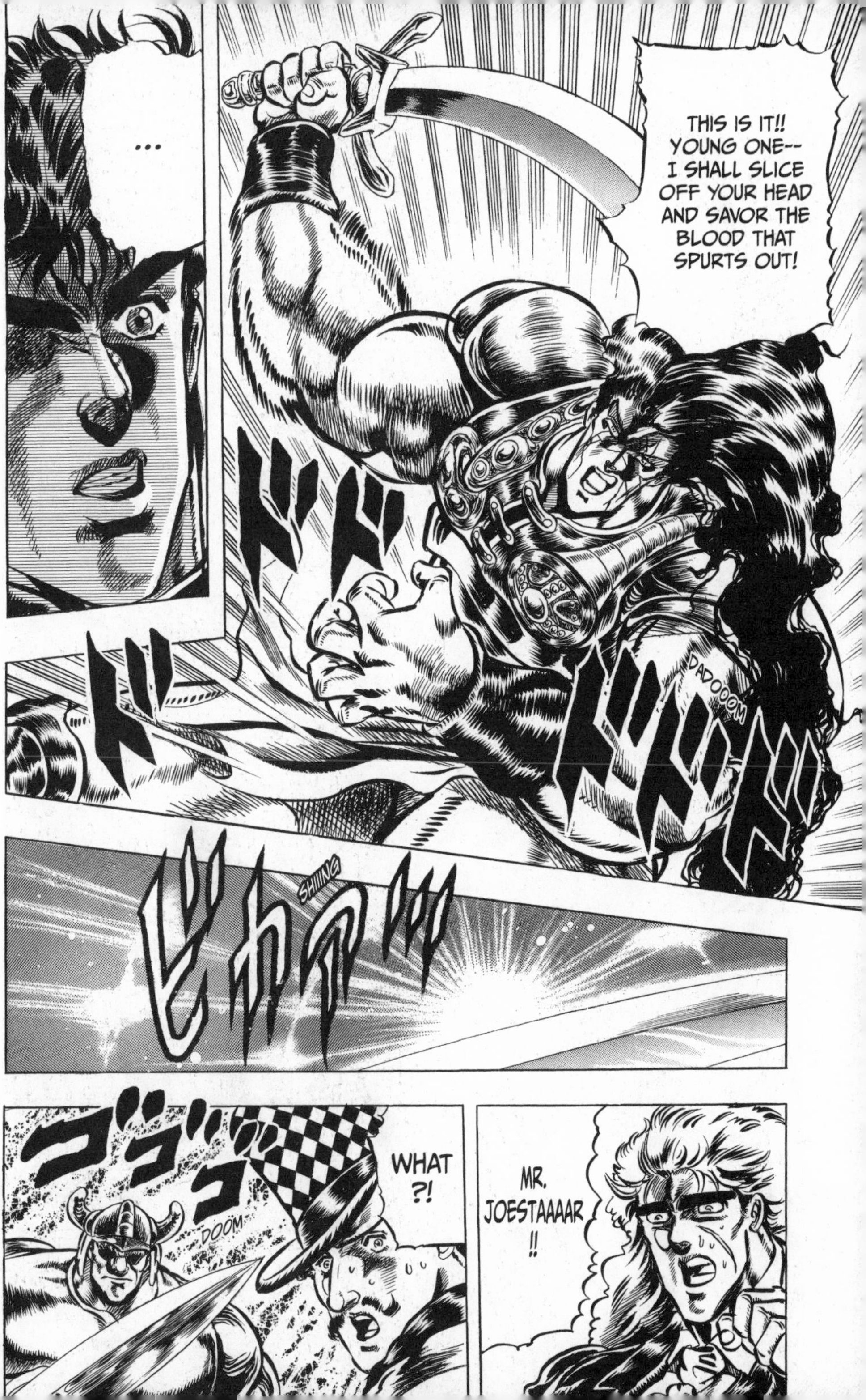
THIS IS IT!! YOUNG ONE-- I SHALL SLICE OFF YOUR HEAD AND SAVOR THE BLOOD THAT SPURTS OUT!
...
DADOOOM
SHIIING
MR. JOESTAAAAR !!
WHAT ?!
DOOM

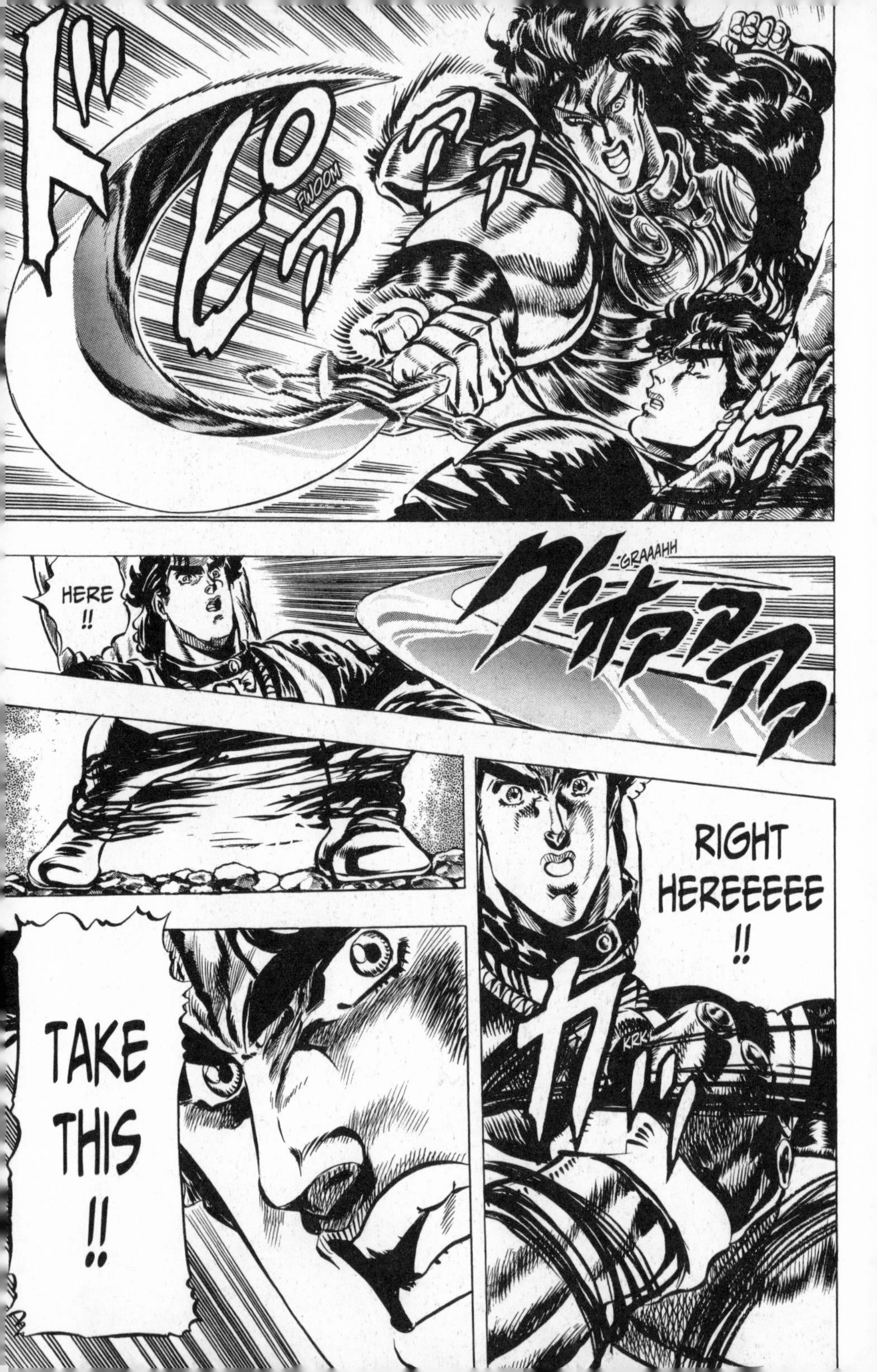
FWOOM
GRAAAHH
HERE!!
RIGHT HEREEEEEE!!
KRK
TAKE THIS!!

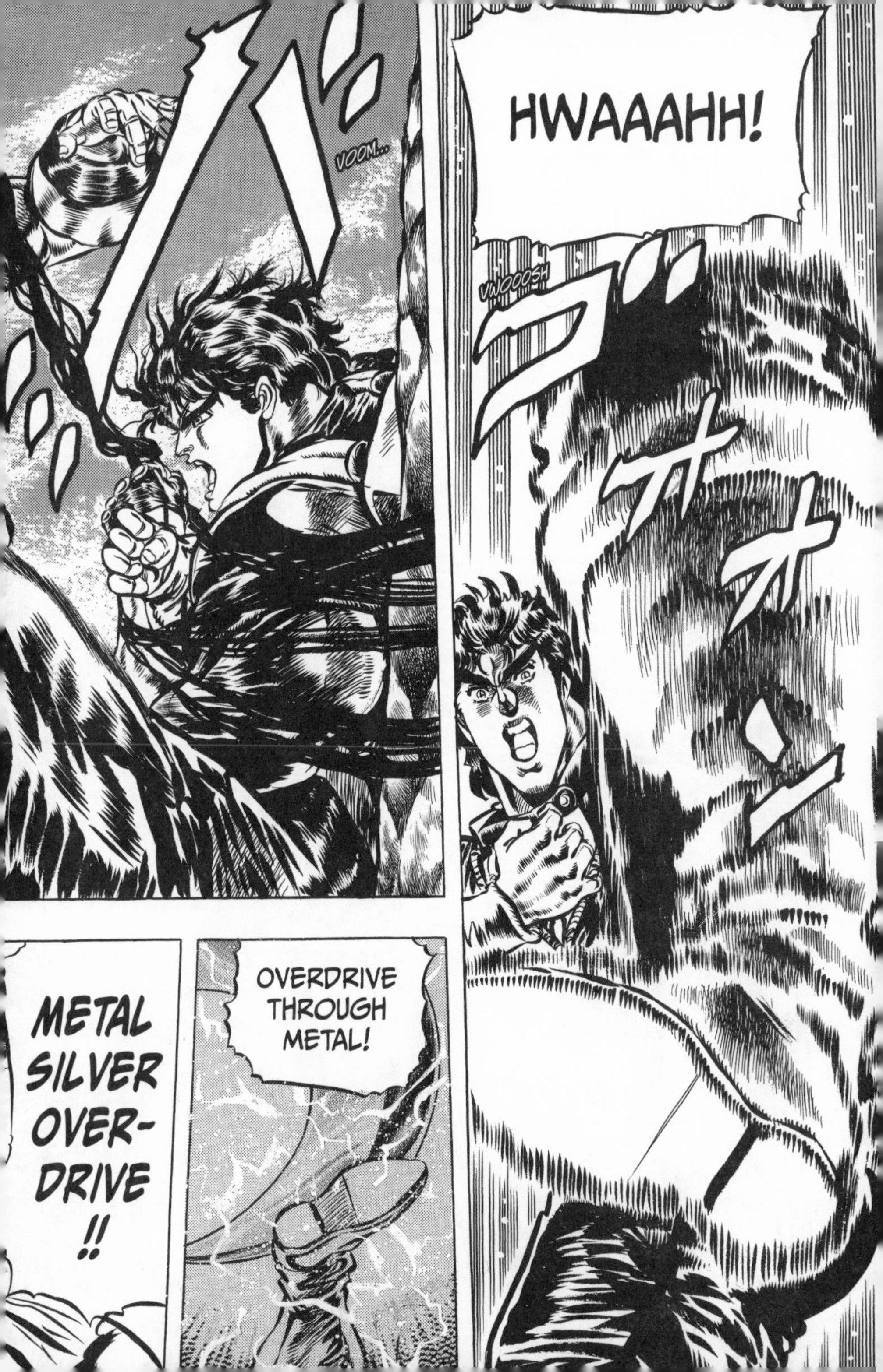
HWAAAHH!
VWOOOSH
VOOM...
OVERDRIVE THROUGH METAL!
METAL SILVER OVER-DRIVE !!

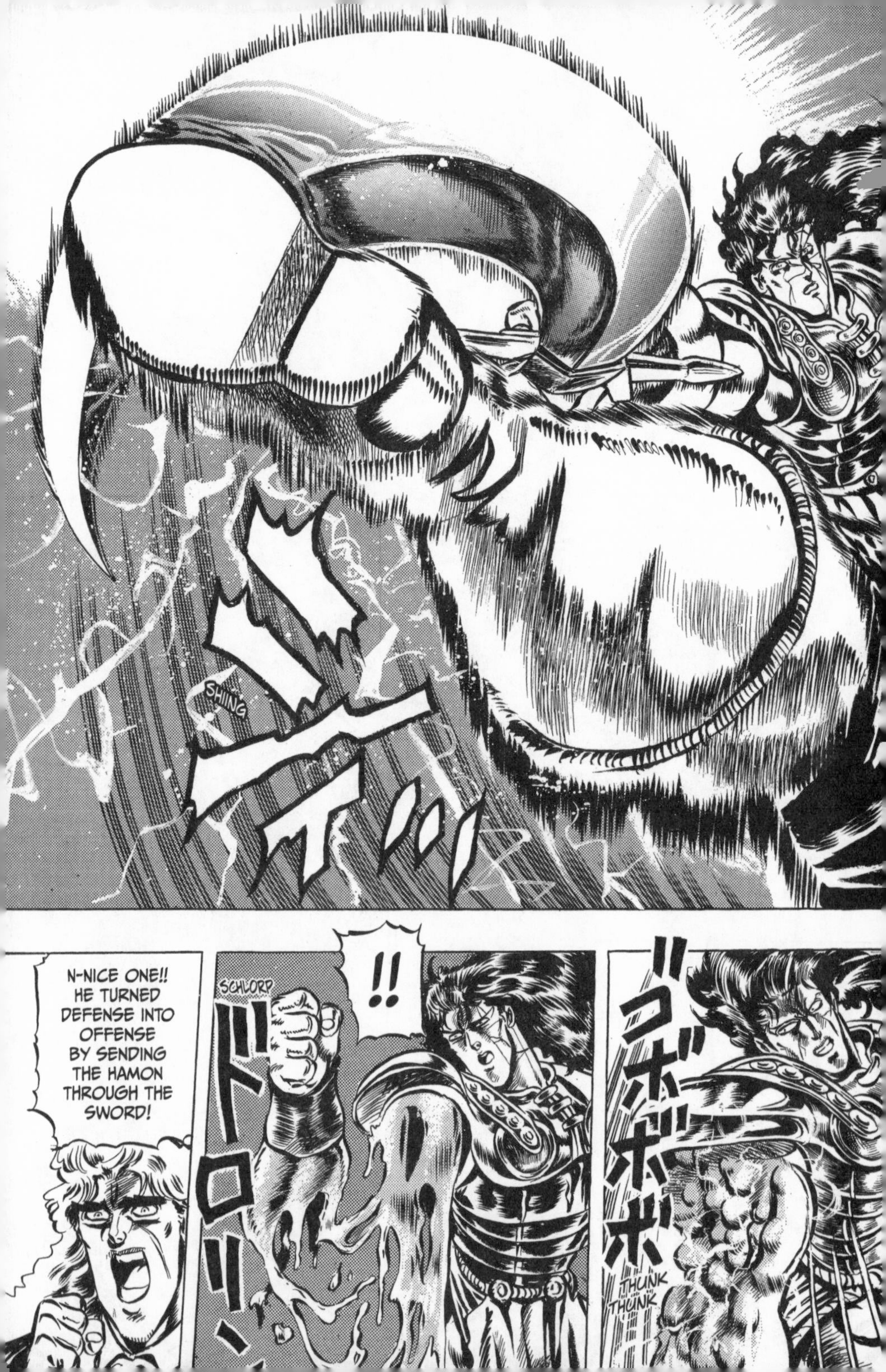
SHING
THUNK THUNK
!!
SCHLORP
N-NICE ONE!! HE TURNED DEFENSE INTO OFFENSE BY SENDING THE HAMON THROUGH THE SWORD!

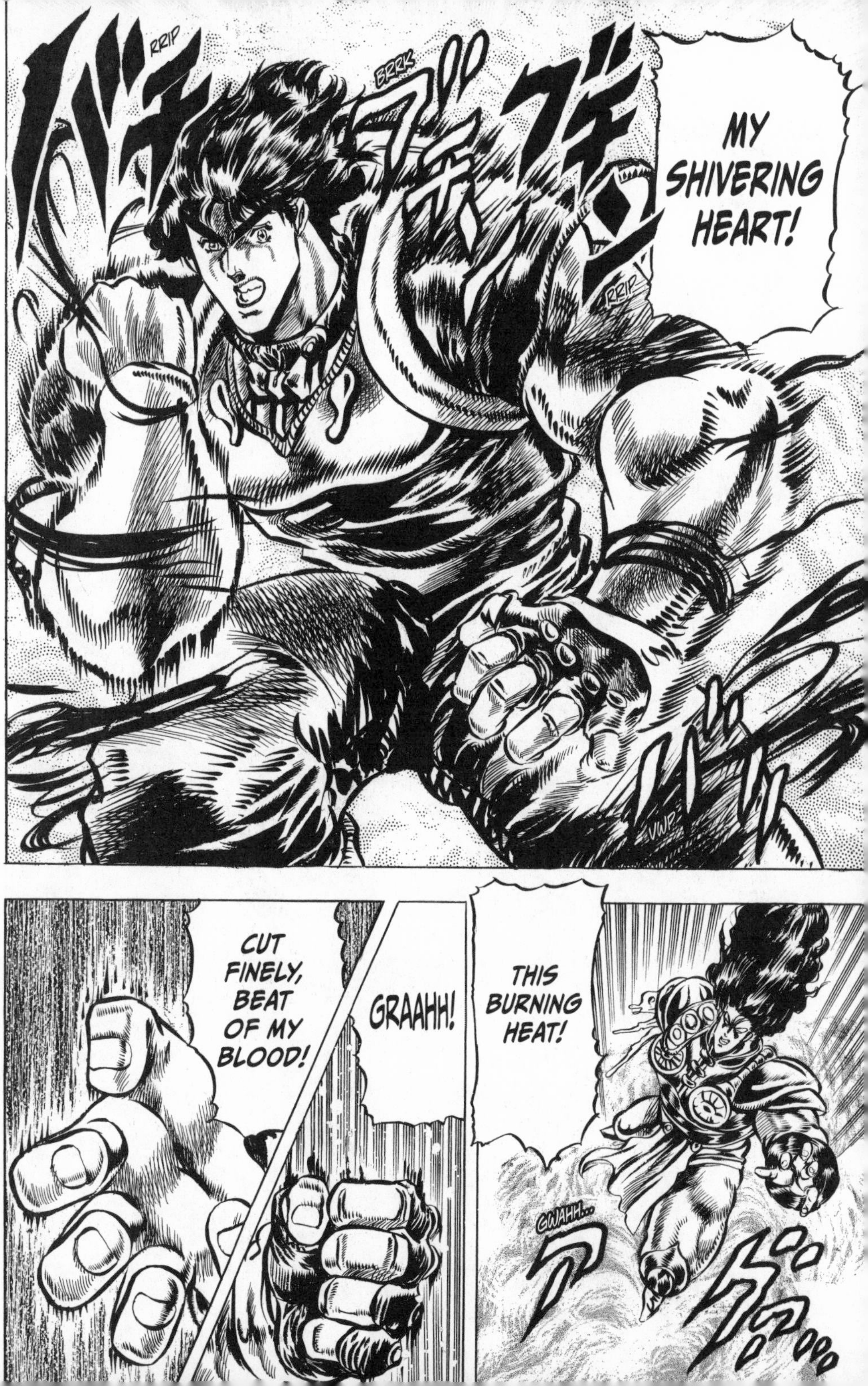
MY SHIVERING HEART!
RRIP
BRRK
RRIP
VWP
THIS BURNING HEAT!
GWAHH...
GRAAHH!
CUT FINELY, BEAT OF MY BLOOD!

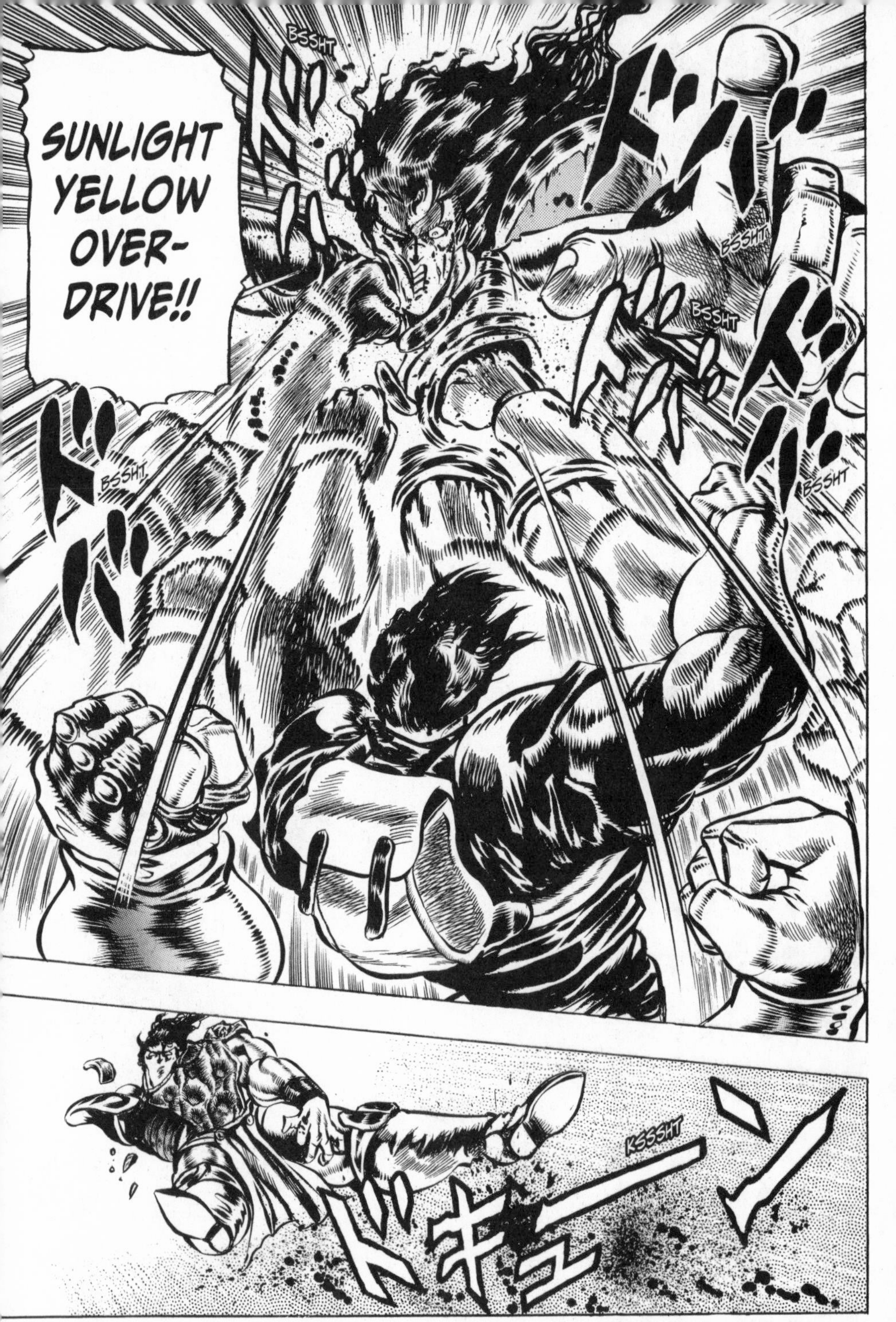
SUNLIGHT YELLOW OVER-DRIVE!!
BSSHT
BSSHT
BSSHT
BSSHT
BSSHT
KSSSHT

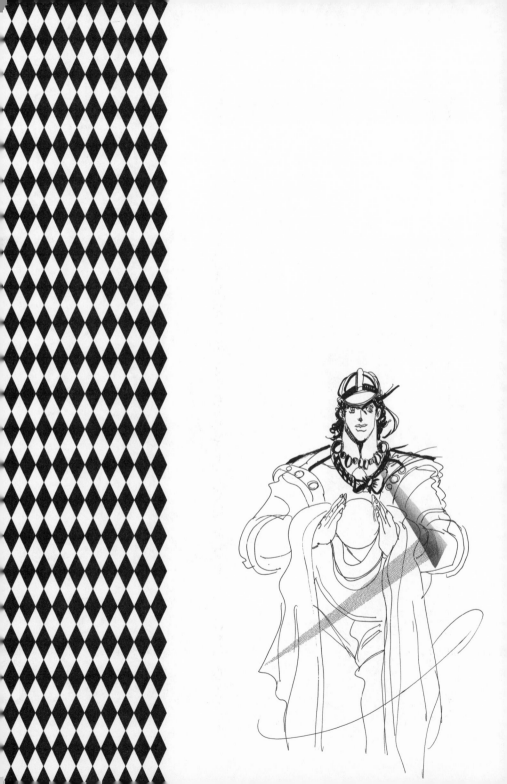

CHAPTER 30: Sleep as a Hero

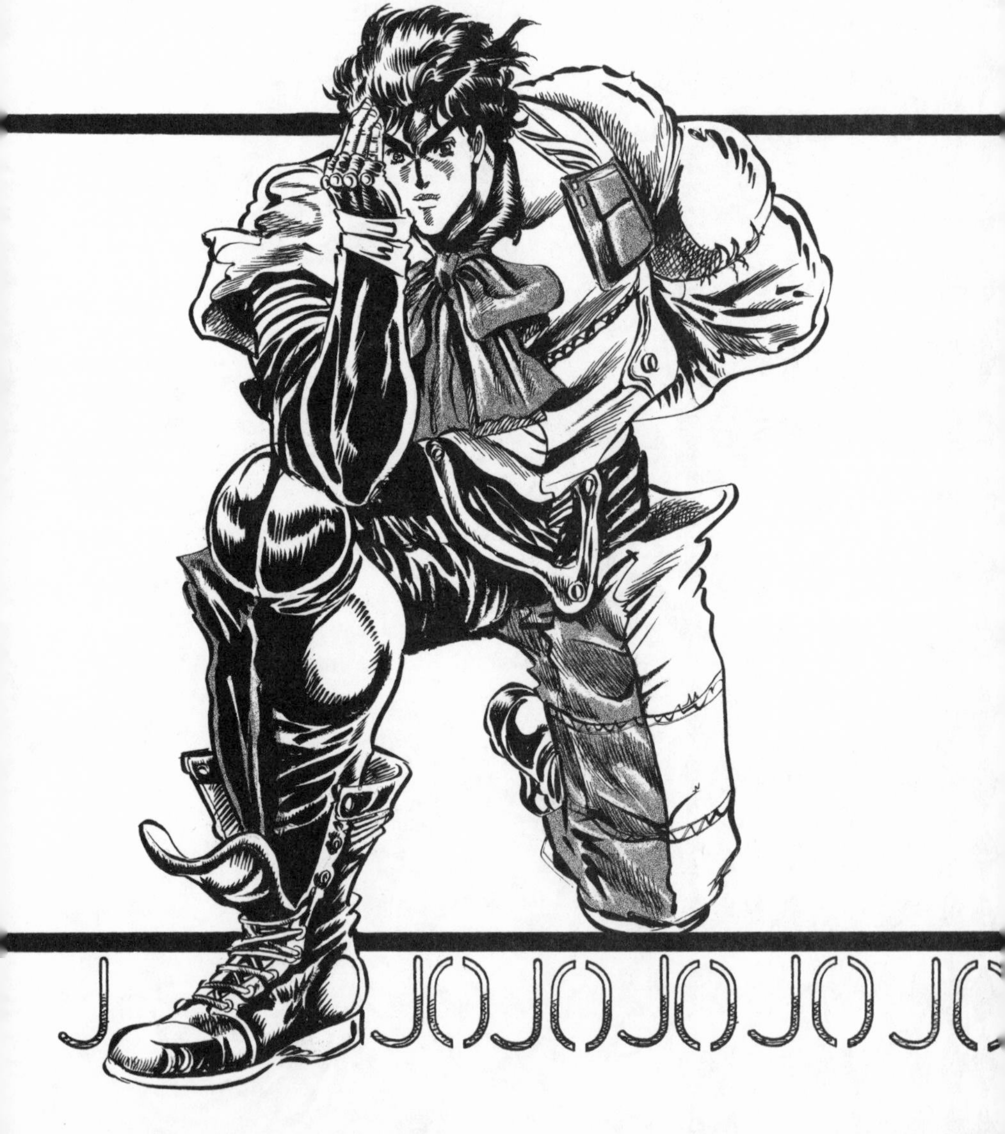

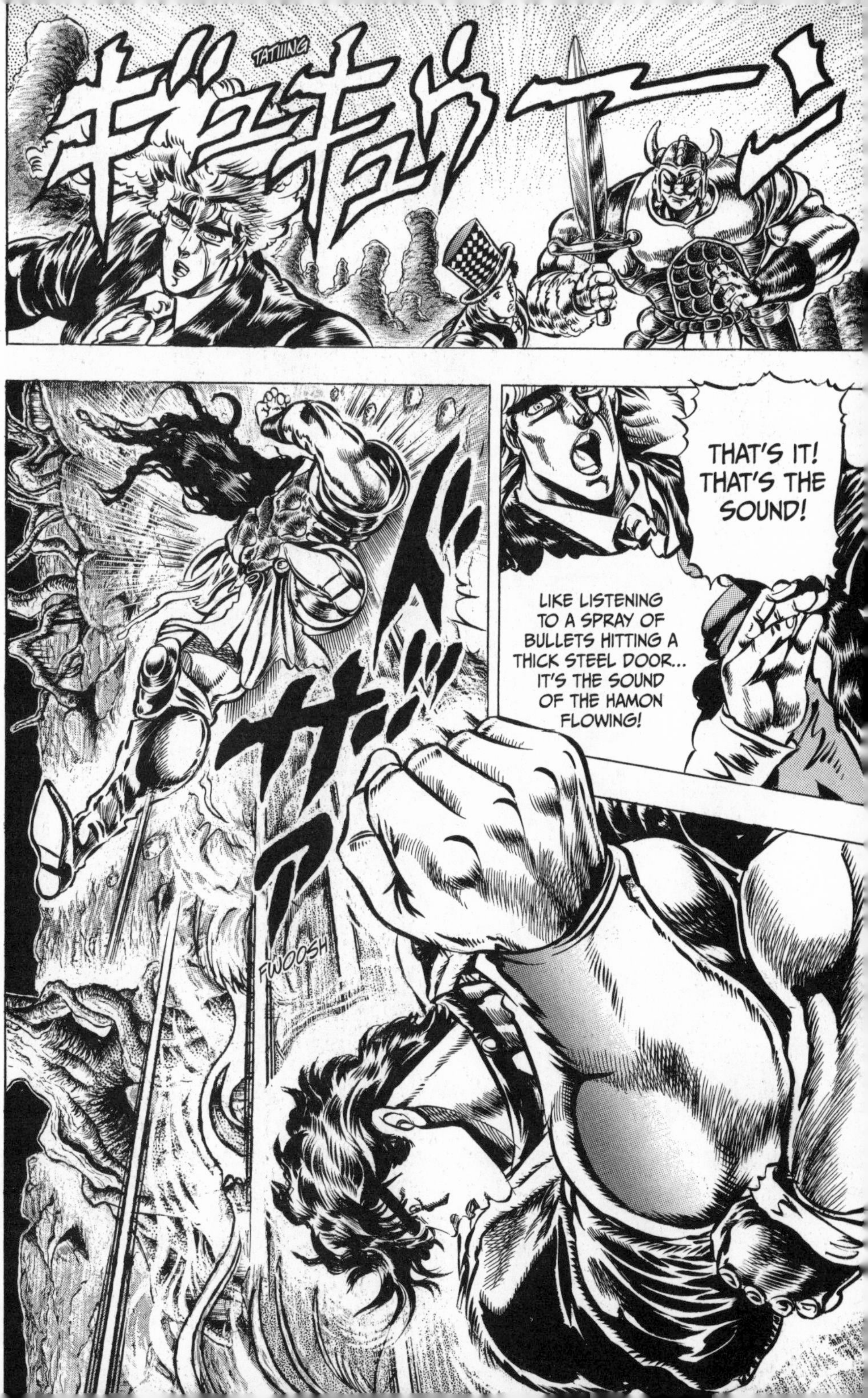
TATIIING
THAT'S IT! THAT'S THE SOUND!
LIKE LISTENING TO A SPRAY OF BULLETS HITTING A THICK STEEL DOOR... IT'S THE SOUND OF THE HAMON FLOWING!
FWOOSH

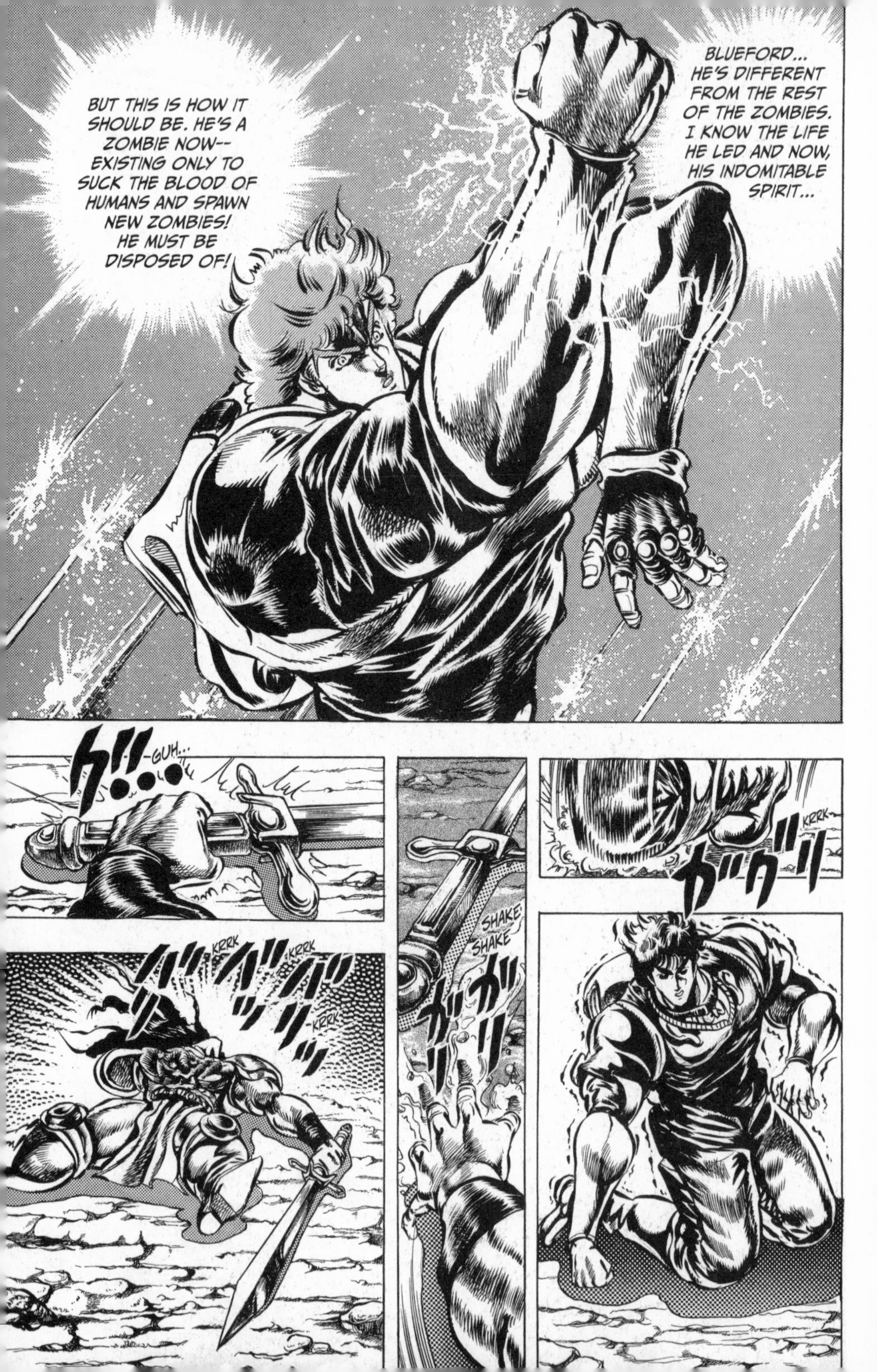
BLUEFORD... HE'S DIFFERENT FROM THE REST OF THE ZOMBIES. I KNOW THE LIFE HE LED AND NOW, HIS INDOMITABLE SPIRIT...
BUT THIS IS HOW IT SHOULD BE. HE'S A ZOMBIE NOW-- EXISTING ONLY TO SUCK THE BLOOD OF HUMANS AND SPAWN NEW ZOMBIES! HE MUST BE DISPOSED OF!
KRRK
SHAKE SHAKE
-GUH...
KRRK
KRRK
KRRK

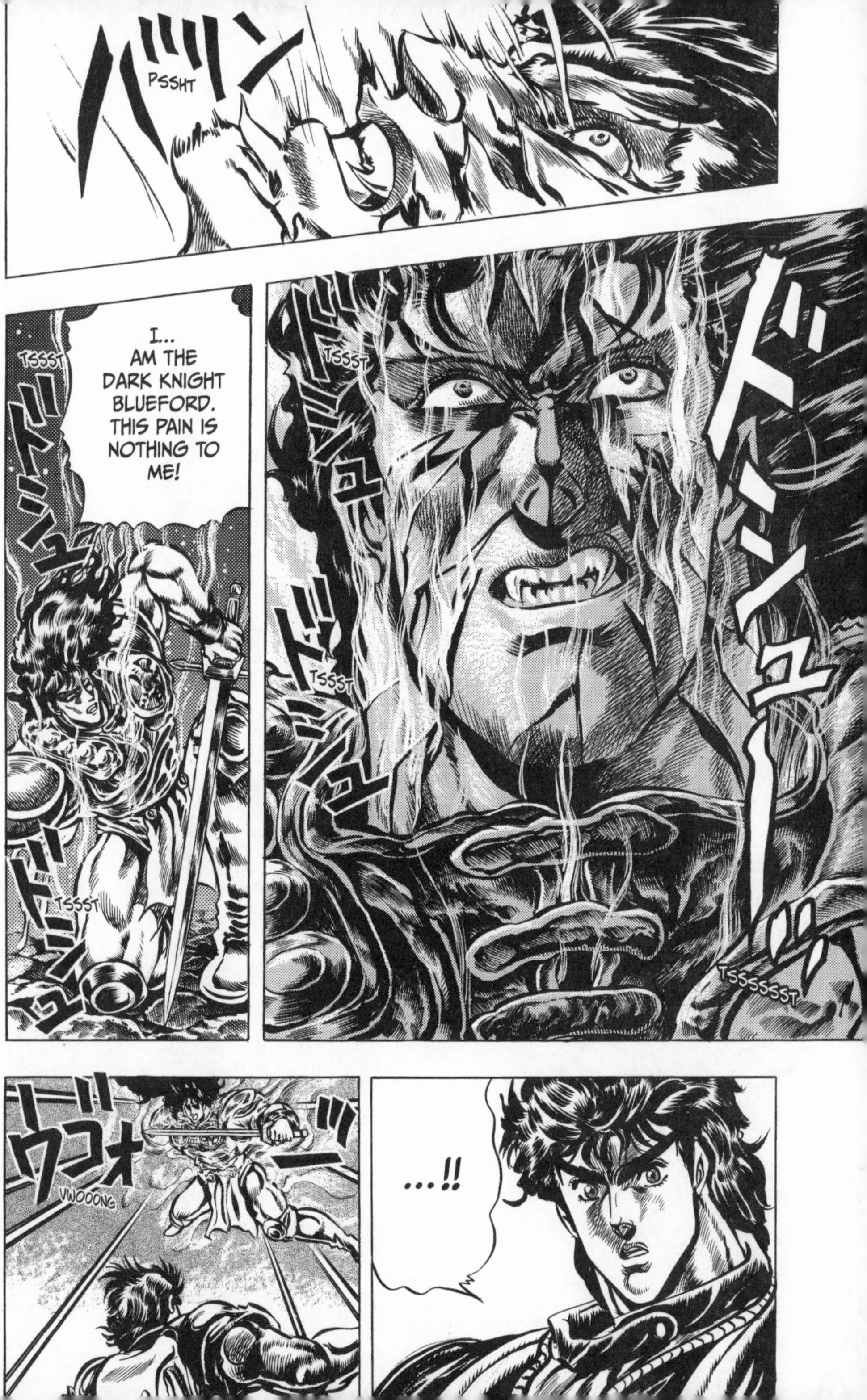
PSSHT
TSSST
TSSST
TSSSSSST
I... AM THE DARK KNIGHT BLUEFORD. THIS PAIN IS NOTHING TO ME!
TSSST
TSSST
...!!
VWOOONG

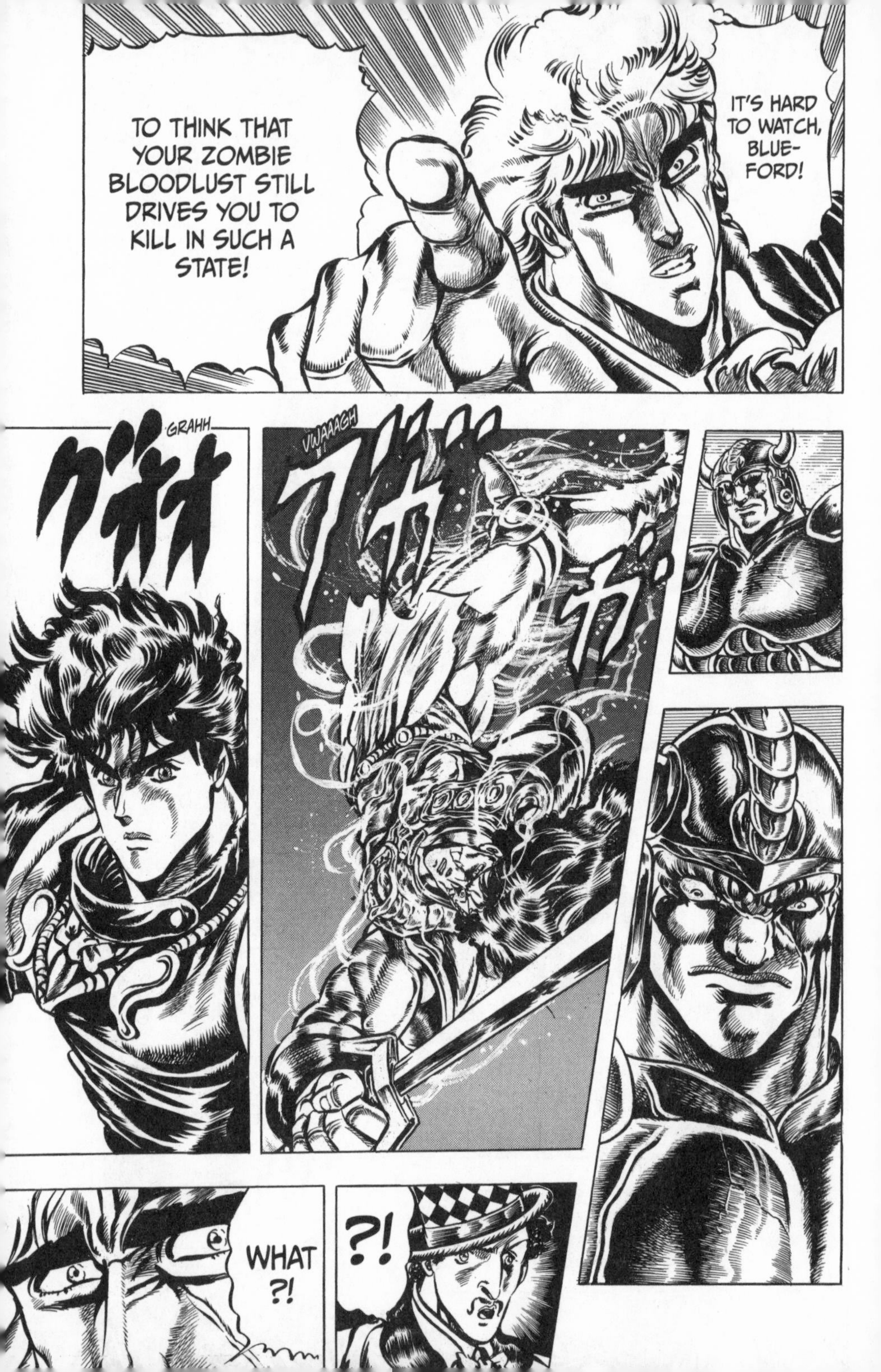
IT'S HARD TO WATCH, BLUE-FORD!
TO THINK THAT YOUR ZOMBIE BLOODLUST STILL DRIVES YOU TO KILL IN SUCH A STATE!
VWAAAGH
GRAHH
?!
WHAT ?!

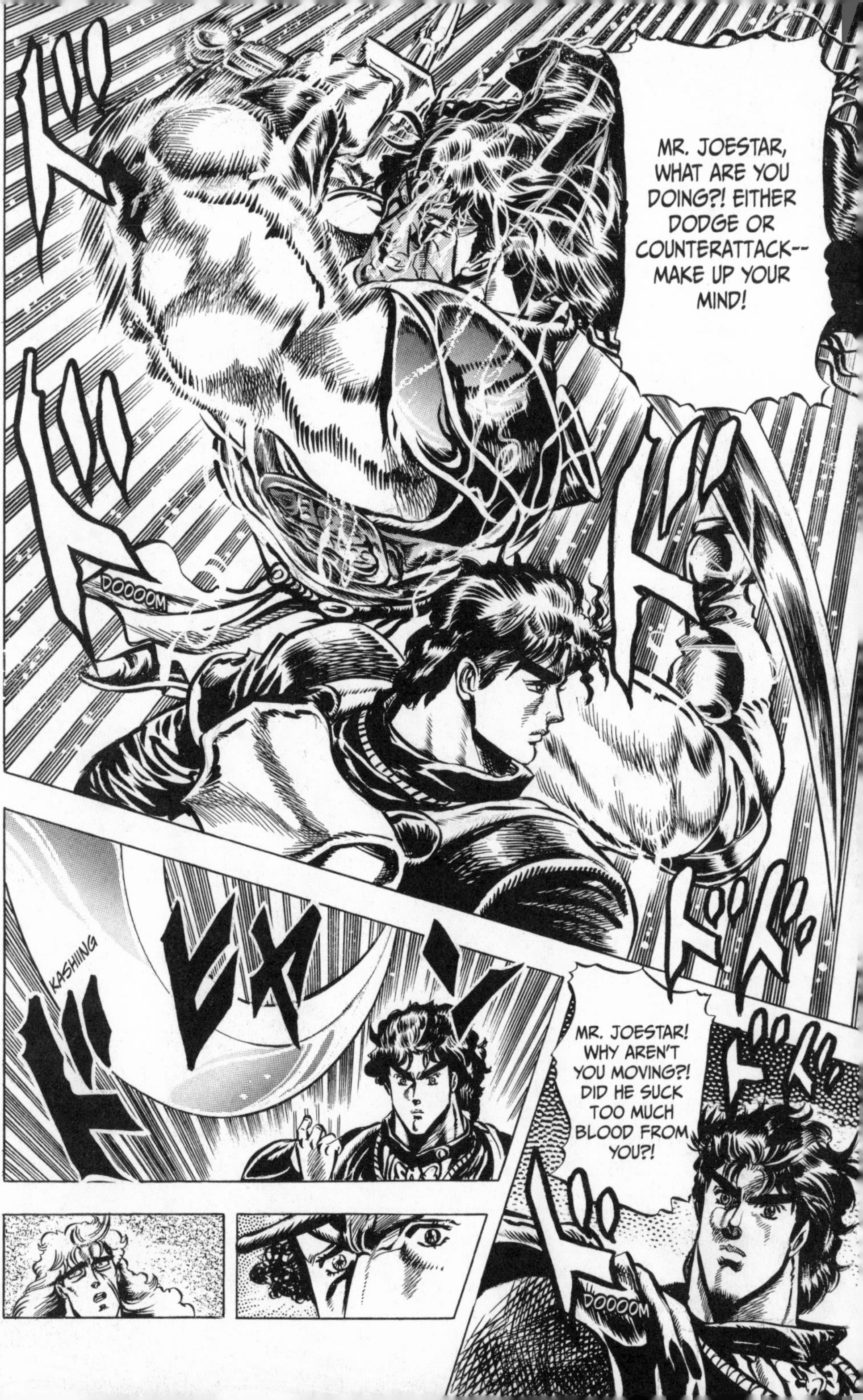
MR. JOESTAR, WHAT ARE YOU DOING?! EITHER DODGE OR COUNTERATTACK-- MAKE UP YOUR MIND!
DOOOOM
MR. JOESTAR! WHY AREN'T YOU MOVING?! DID HE SUCK TOO MUCH BLOOD FROM YOU?!
DOOOOM
KASHIING

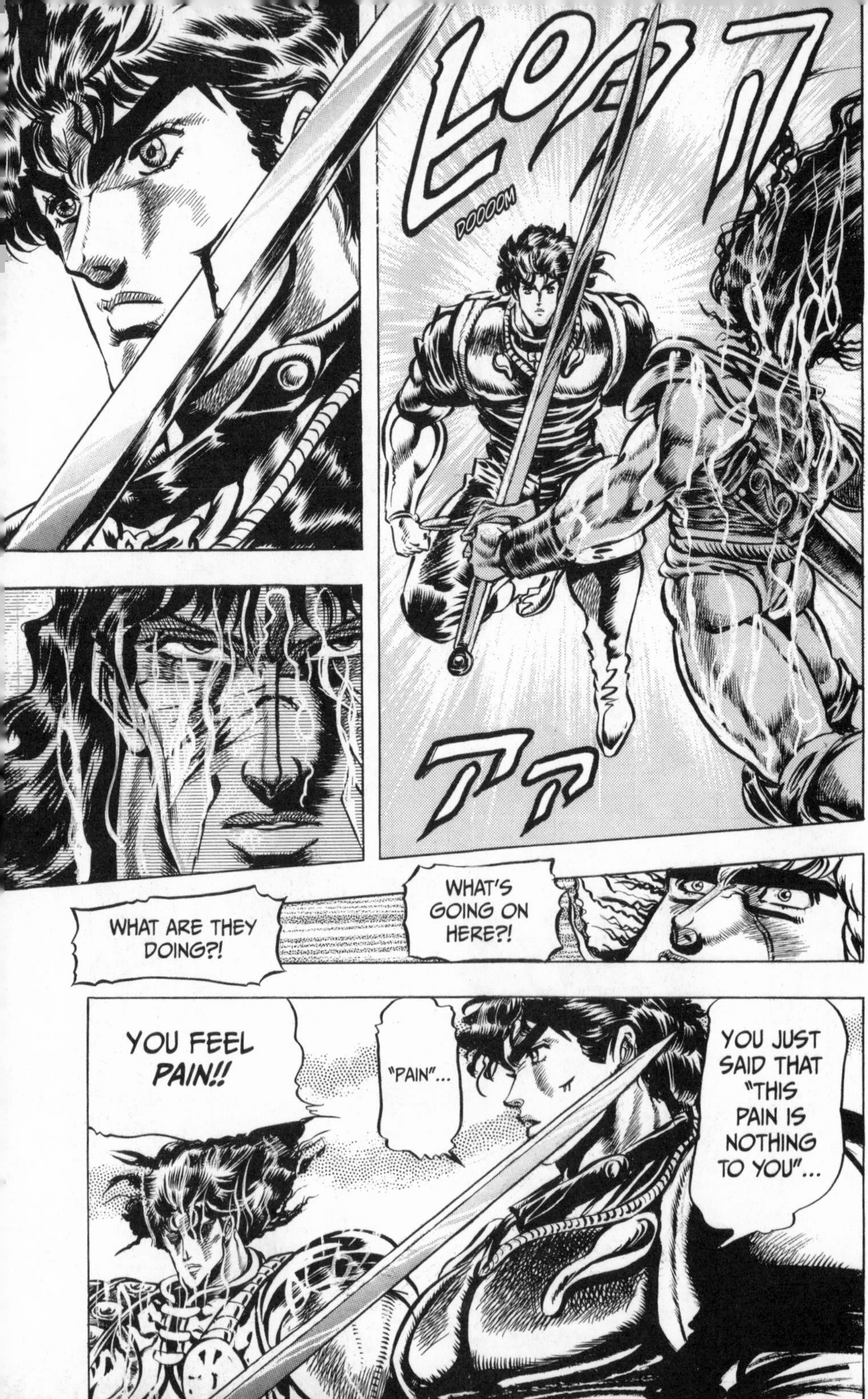
DOOOOM
WHAT'S GOING ON HERE?!
WHAT ARE THEY DOING?!
YOU JUST SAID THAT "THIS PAIN IS NOTHING TO YOU"...
"PAIN"...
YOU FEEL PAIN!!

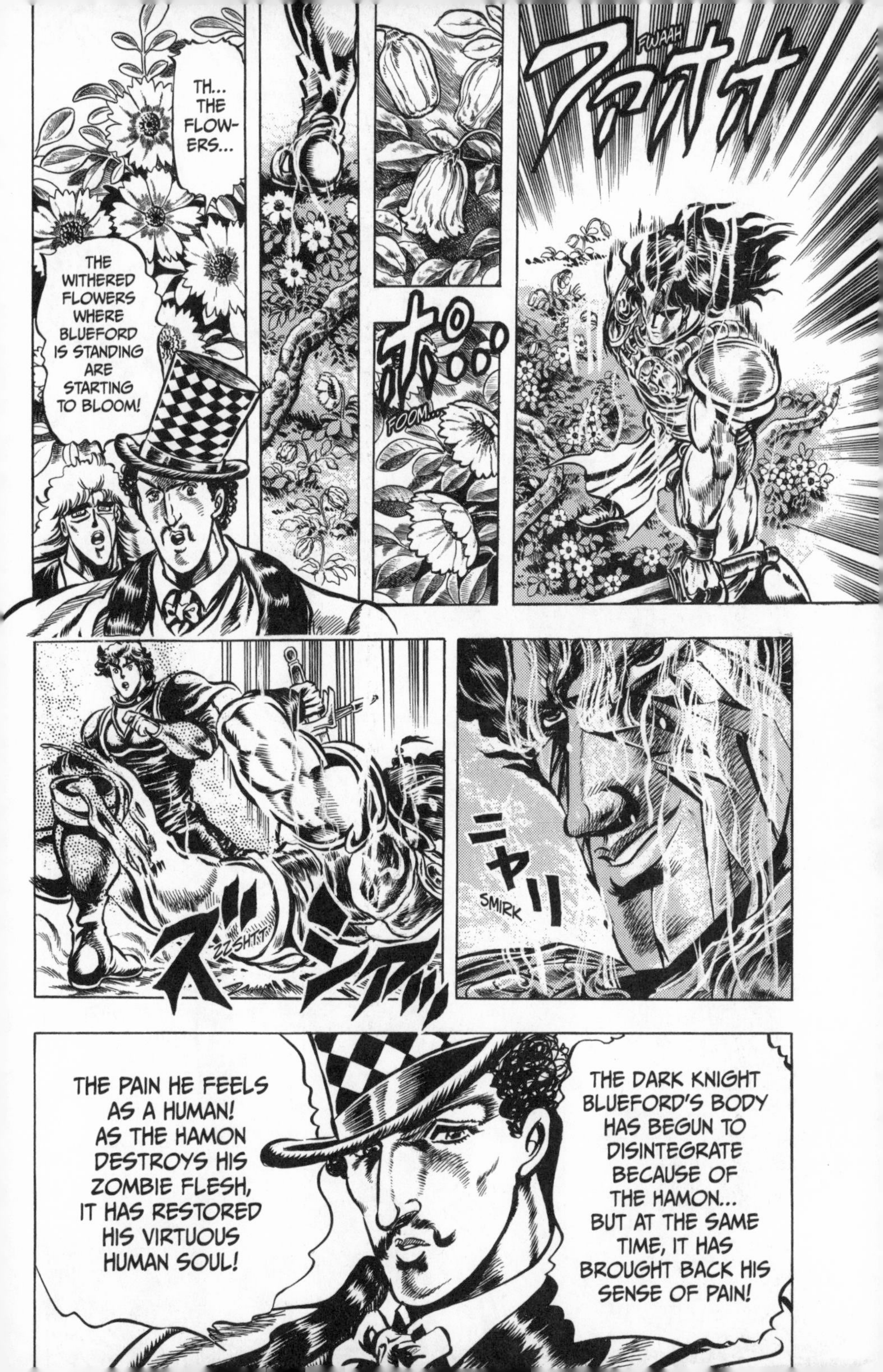
FWAAH
FOOM...
TH... THE FLOWERS...
THE WITHERED FLOWERS WHERE BLUEFORD IS STANDING ARE STARTING TO BLOOM!
ニヤリ
SMIRK
ZZSHT
THE DARK KNIGHT BLUEFORD'S BODY HAS BEGUN TO DISINTEGRATE BECAUSE OF THE HAMON... BUT AT THE SAME TIME, IT HAS BROUGHT BACK HIS SENSE OF PAIN!
THE PAIN HE FEELS AS A HUMAN! AS THE HAMON DESTROYS HIS ZOMBIE FLESH, IT HAS RESTORED HIS VIRTUOUS HUMAN SOUL!

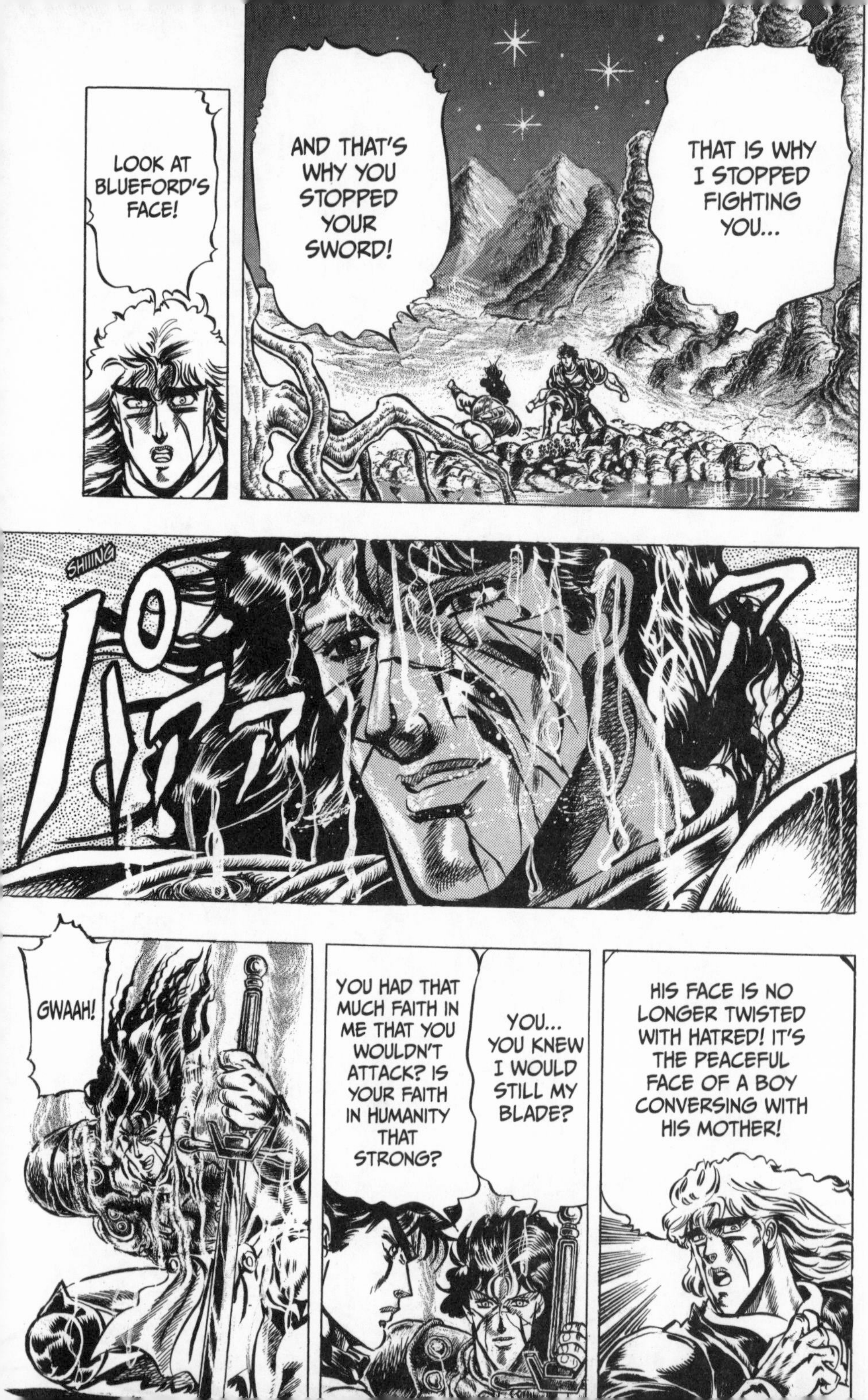
THAT IS WHY I STOPPED FIGHTING YOU...
AND THAT'S WHY YOU STOPPED YOUR SWORD!
LOOK AT BLUEFORD'S FACE!
SHIIING
HIS FACE IS NO LONGER TWISTED WITH HATRED! IT'S THE PEACEFUL FACE OF A BOY CONVERSING WITH HIS MOTHER!
YOU... YOU KNEW I WOULD STILL MY BLADE?
YOU HAD THAT MUCH FAITH IN ME THAT YOU WOULDN'T ATTACK? IS YOUR FAITH IN HUMANITY THAT STRONG?
GWAAH!

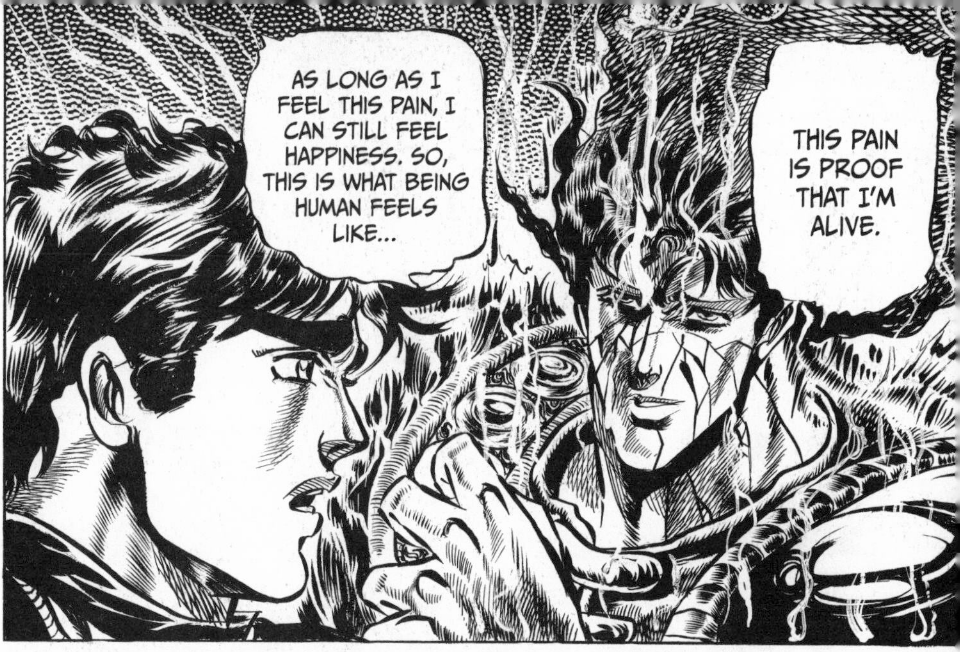
THIS PAIN IS PROOF THAT I'M ALIVE.
AS LONG AS I FEEL THIS PAIN, I CAN STILL FEEL HAPPINESS. SO, THIS IS WHAT BEING HUMAN FEELS LIKE...

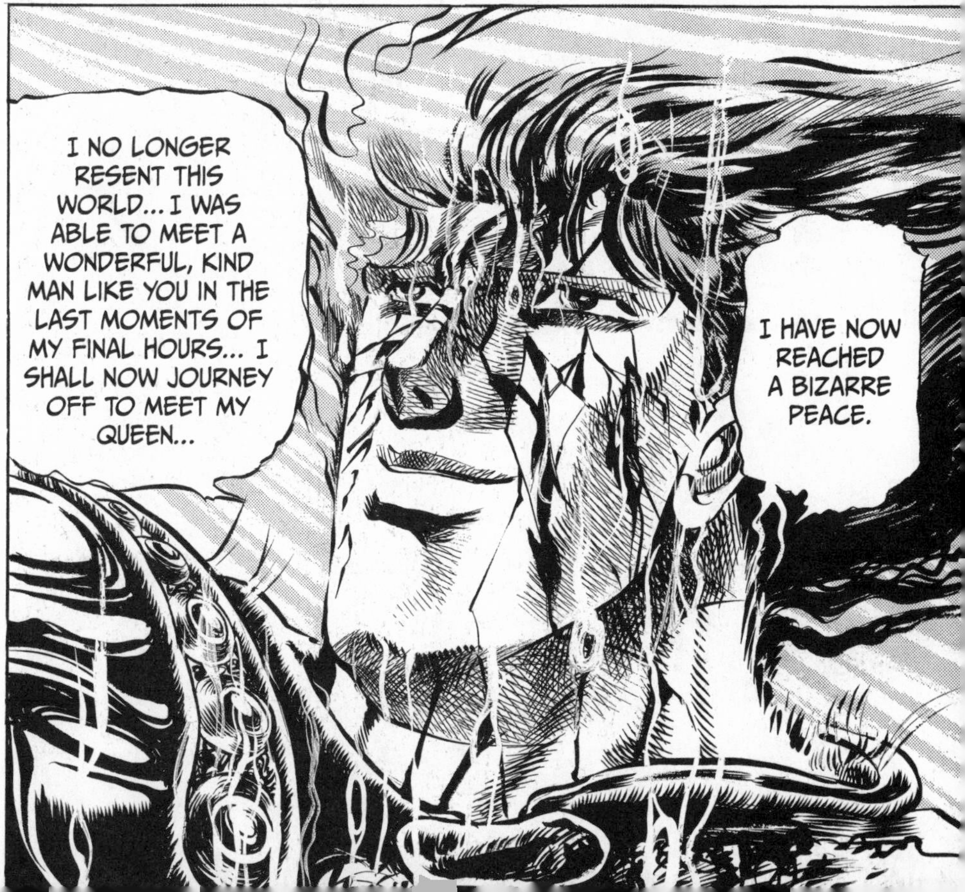
I HAVE NOW REACHED A BIZARRE PEACE.
I NO LONGER RESENT THIS WORLD... I WAS ABLE TO MEET A WONDERFUL, KIND MAN LIKE YOU IN THE LAST MOMENTS OF MY FINAL HOURS... I SHALL NOW JOURNEY OFF TO MEET MY QUEEN...

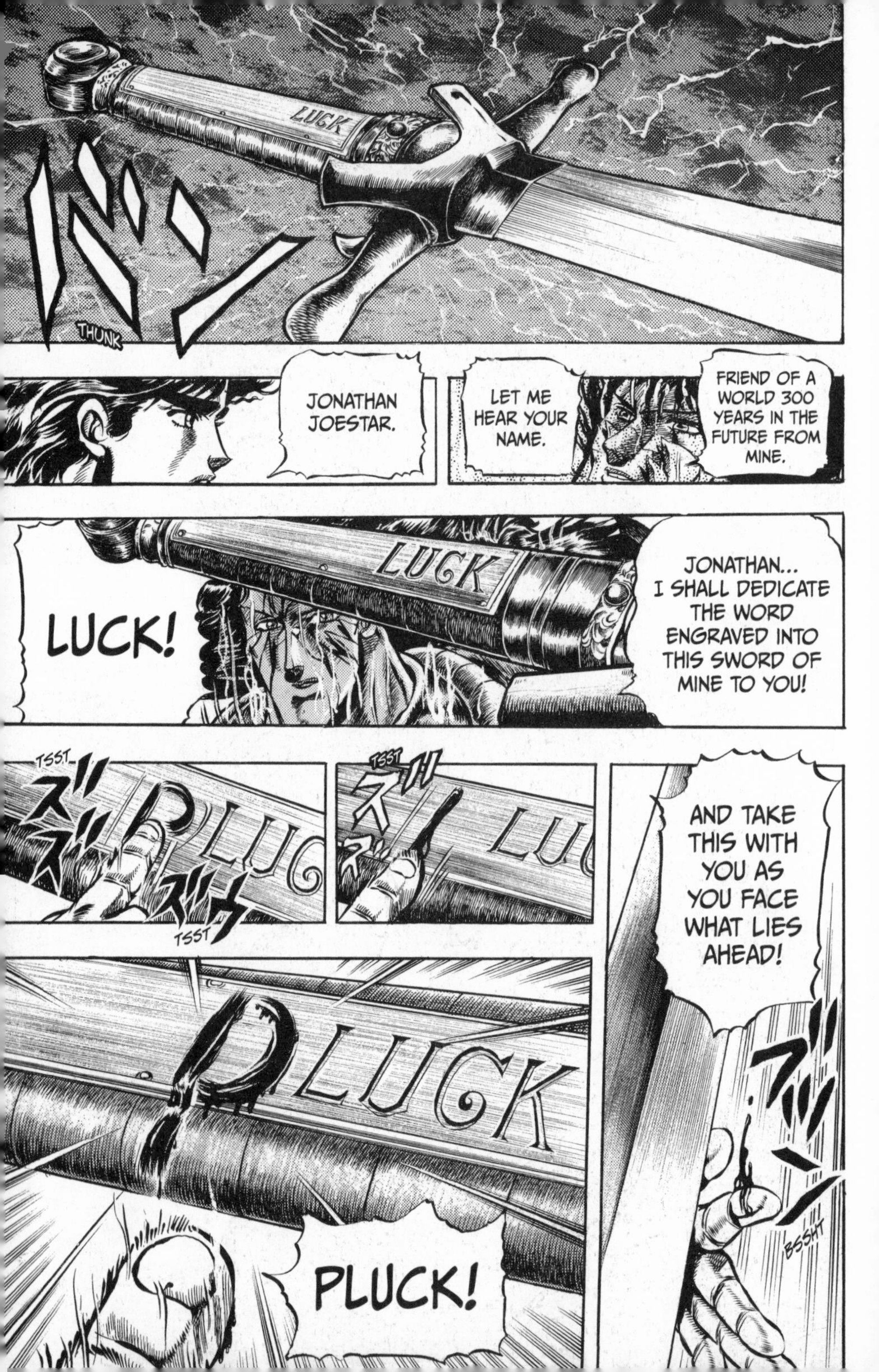
LUCK
THUNK
FRIEND OF A WORLD 300 YEARS IN THE FUTURE FROM MINE.
LET ME HEAR YOUR NAME.
JONATHAN JOESTAR.
JONATHAN... I SHALL DEDICATE THE WORD ENGRAVED INTO THIS SWORD OF MINE TO YOU!
LUCK!
AND TAKE THIS WITH YOU AS YOU FACE WHAT LIES AHEAD!
BSSHT
TSST
TSST
TSST
PLUCK!

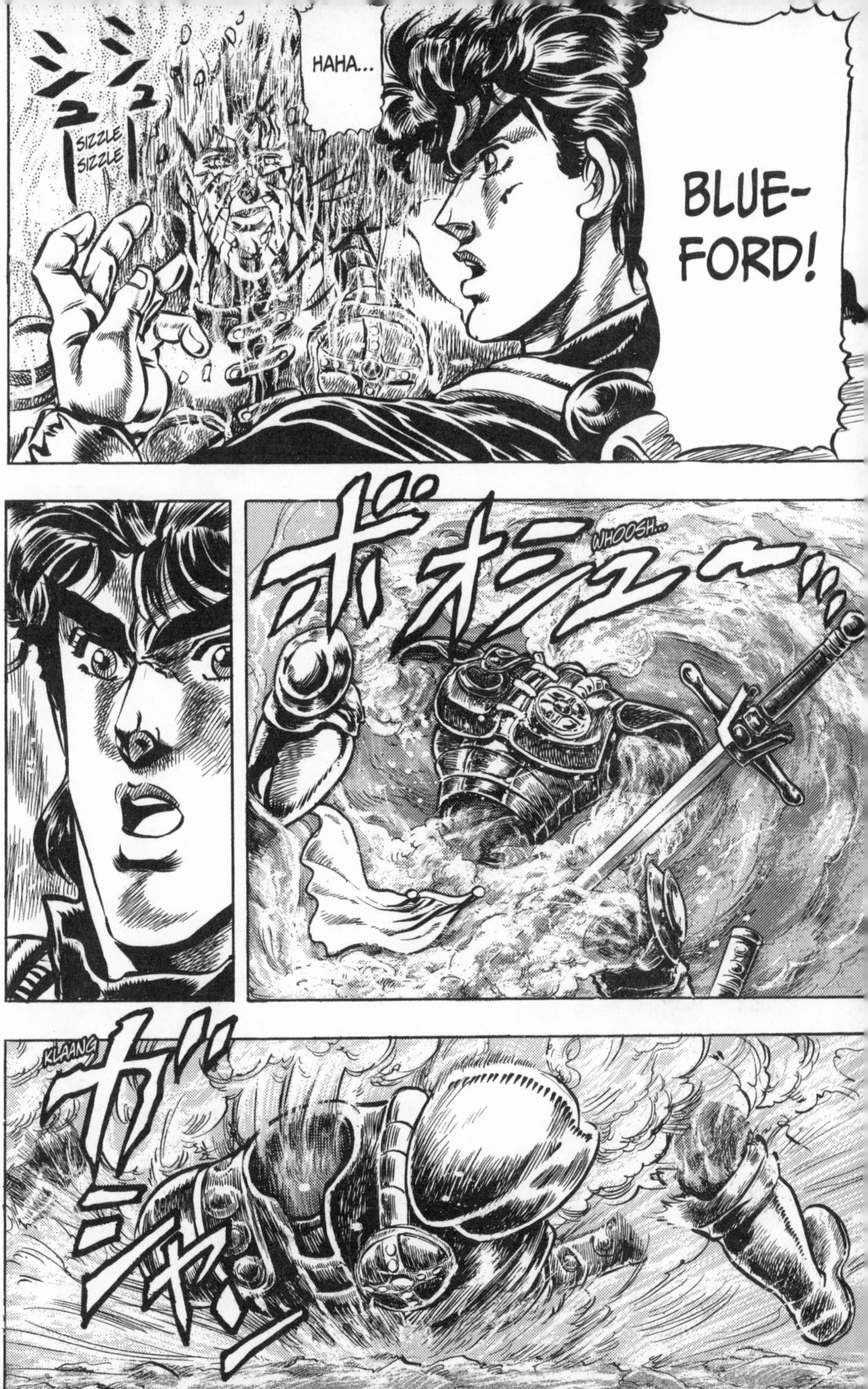
BLUE-FORD!
HAHA...
SIZZLE SIZZLE
WHOOSH...
KLAANG

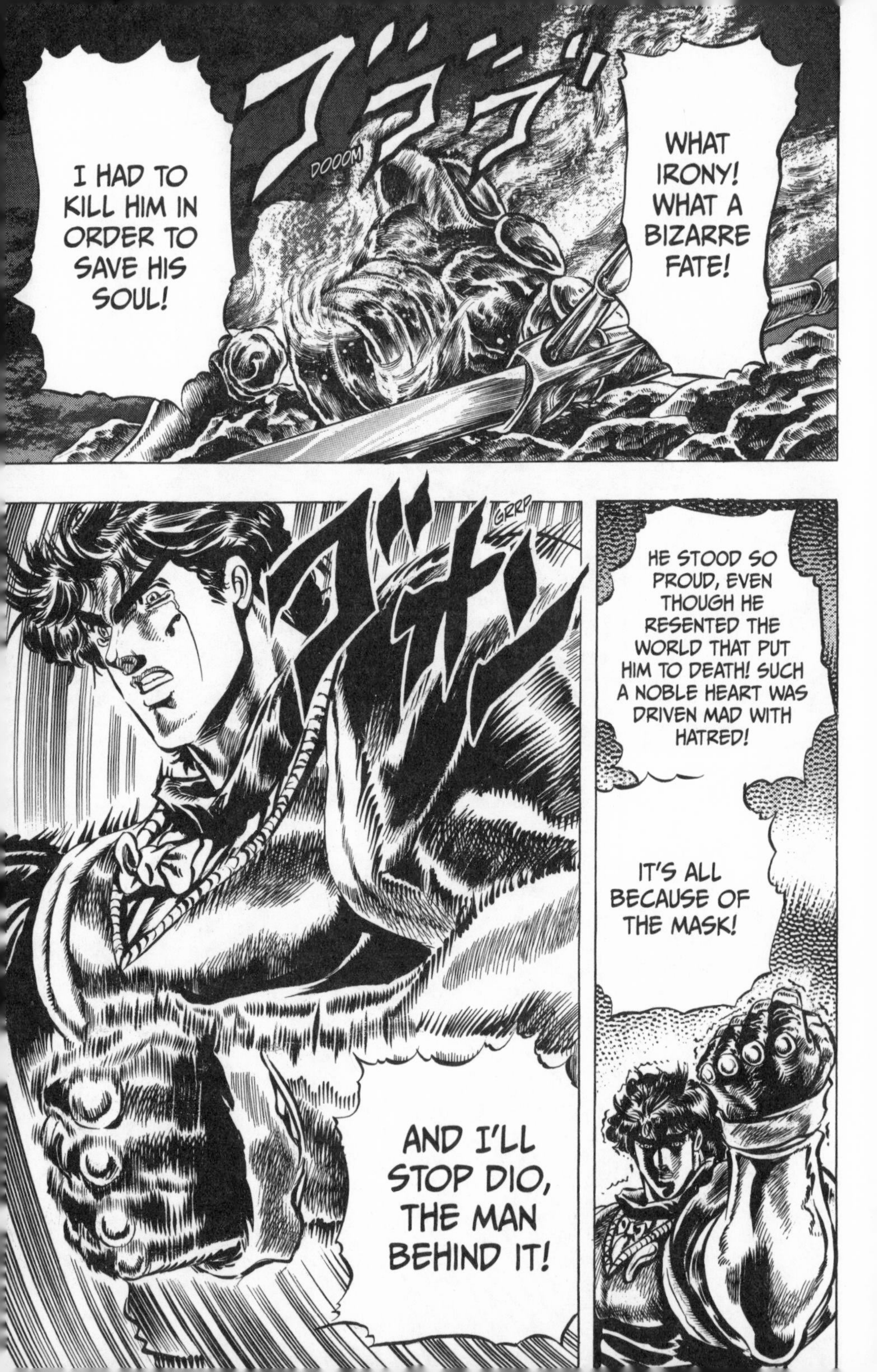
WHAT IRONY! WHAT A BIZARRE FATE!
DOOOM
I HAD TO KILL HIM IN ORDER TO SAVE HIS SOUL!
HE STOOD SO PROUD, EVEN THOUGH HE RESENTED THE WORLD THAT PUT HIM TO DEATH! SUCH A NOBLE HEART WAS DRIVEN MAD WITH HATRED!
IT'S ALL BECAUSE OF THE MASK!
GRRP
AND I'LL STOP DIO, THE MAN BEHIND IT!

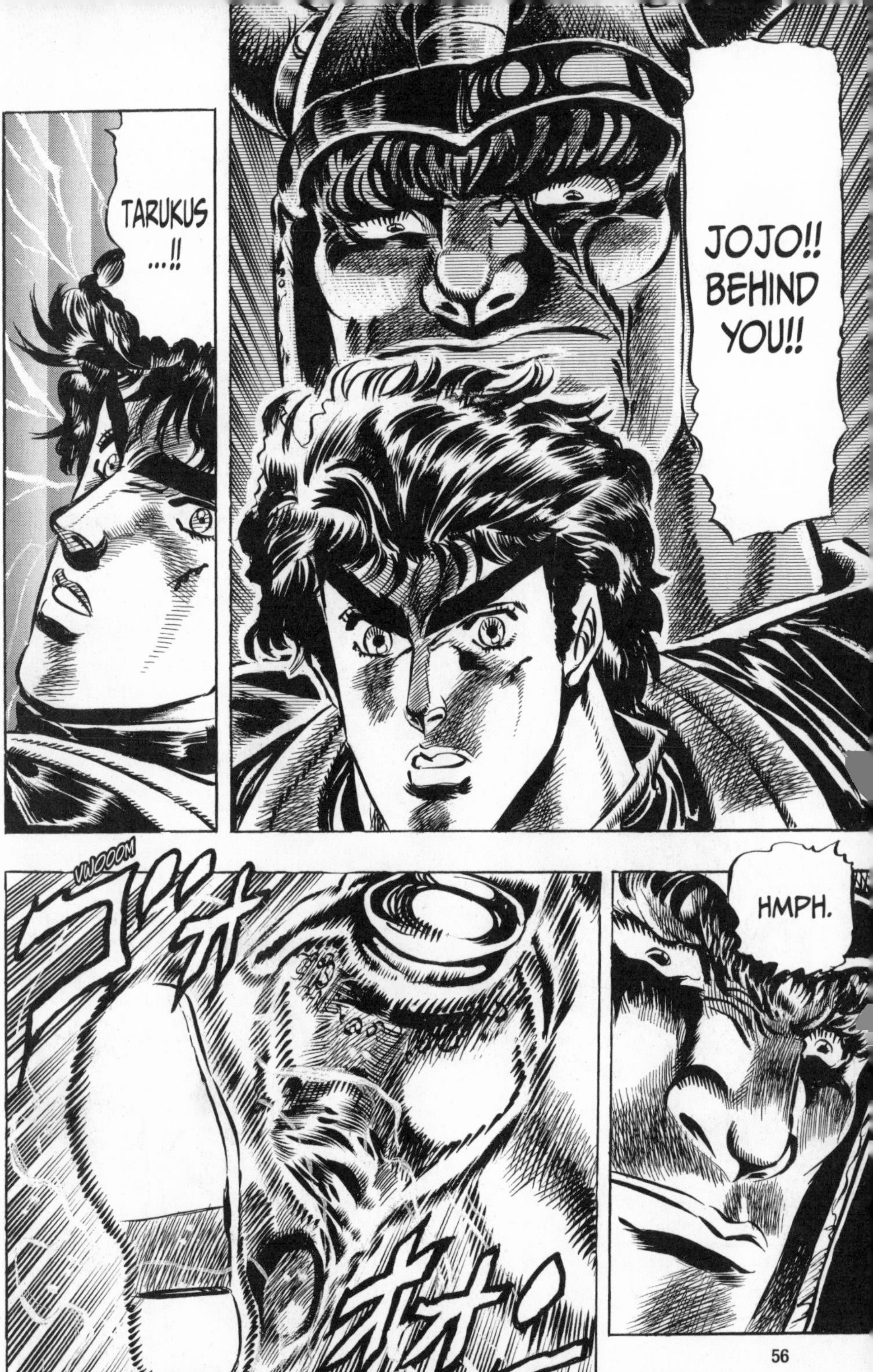
JOJO!! BEHIND YOU!!
TARUKUS ...!!
HMPH.
VWOOOM

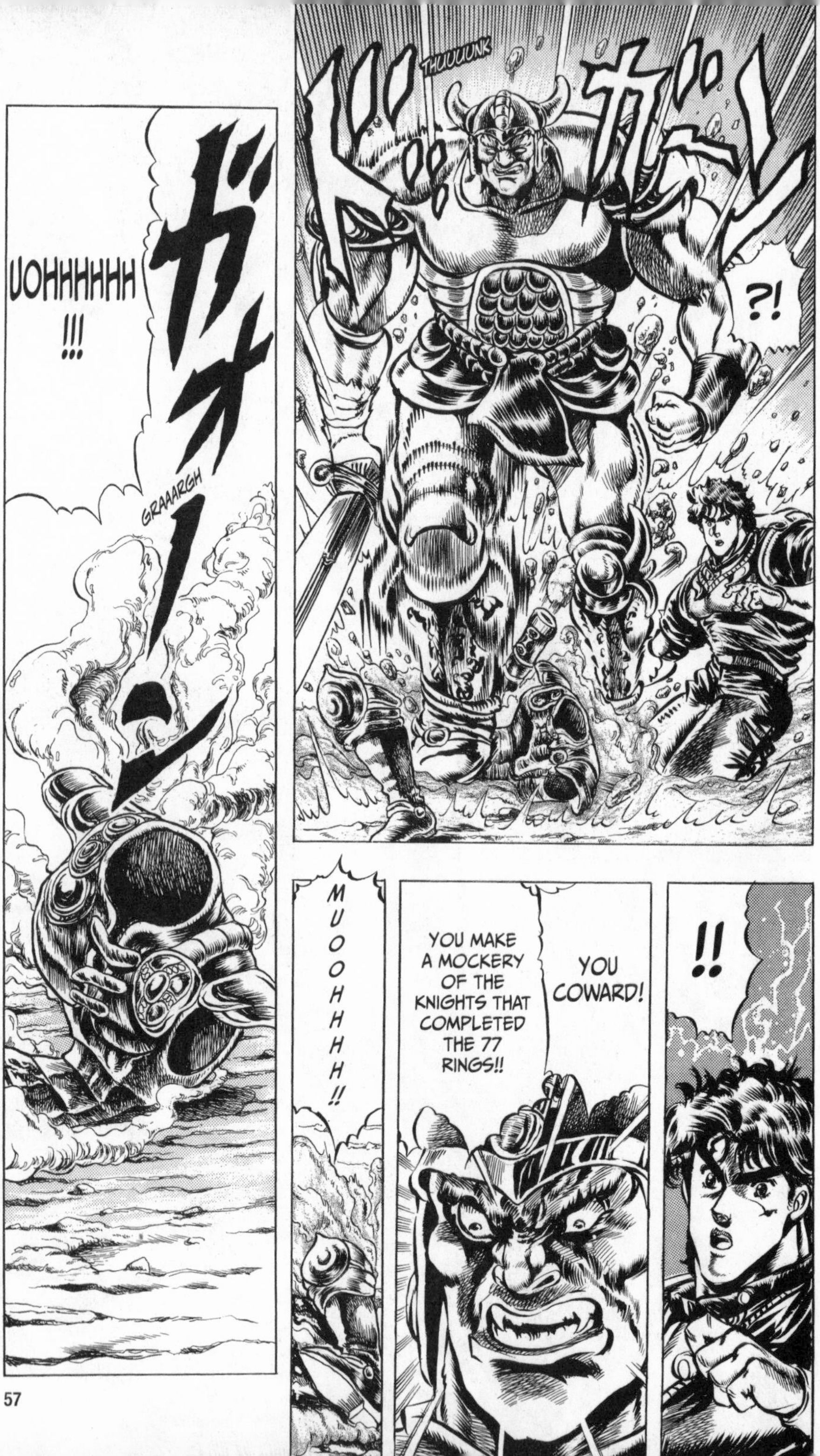
THUUUUNK
?!
!!
YOU COWARD!
YOU MAKE A MOCKERY OF THE KNIGHTS THAT COMPLETED THE 77 RINGS!!
MUOOHHHHH!!
GRAAARGH
UOHHHHHH!!!

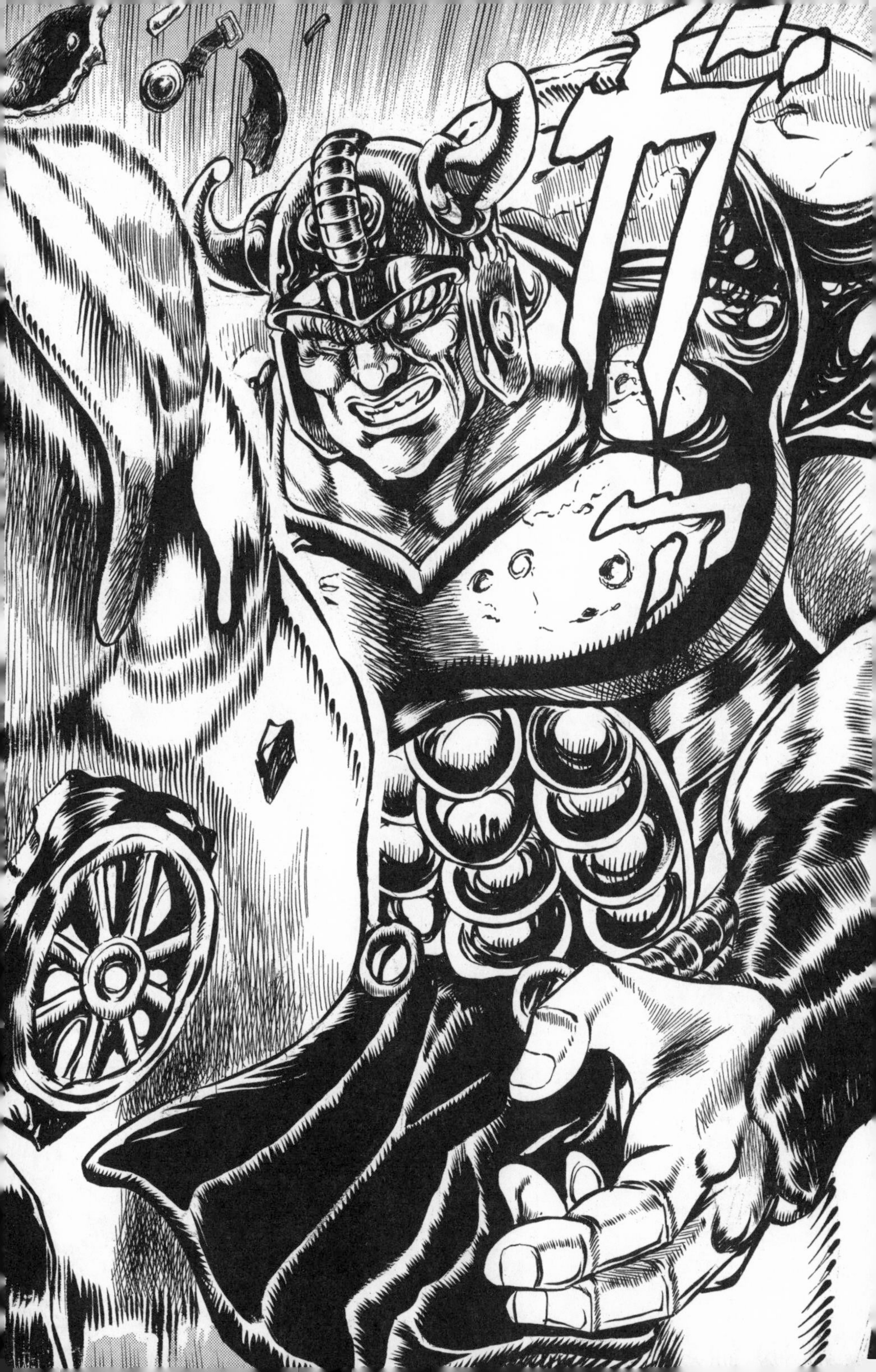

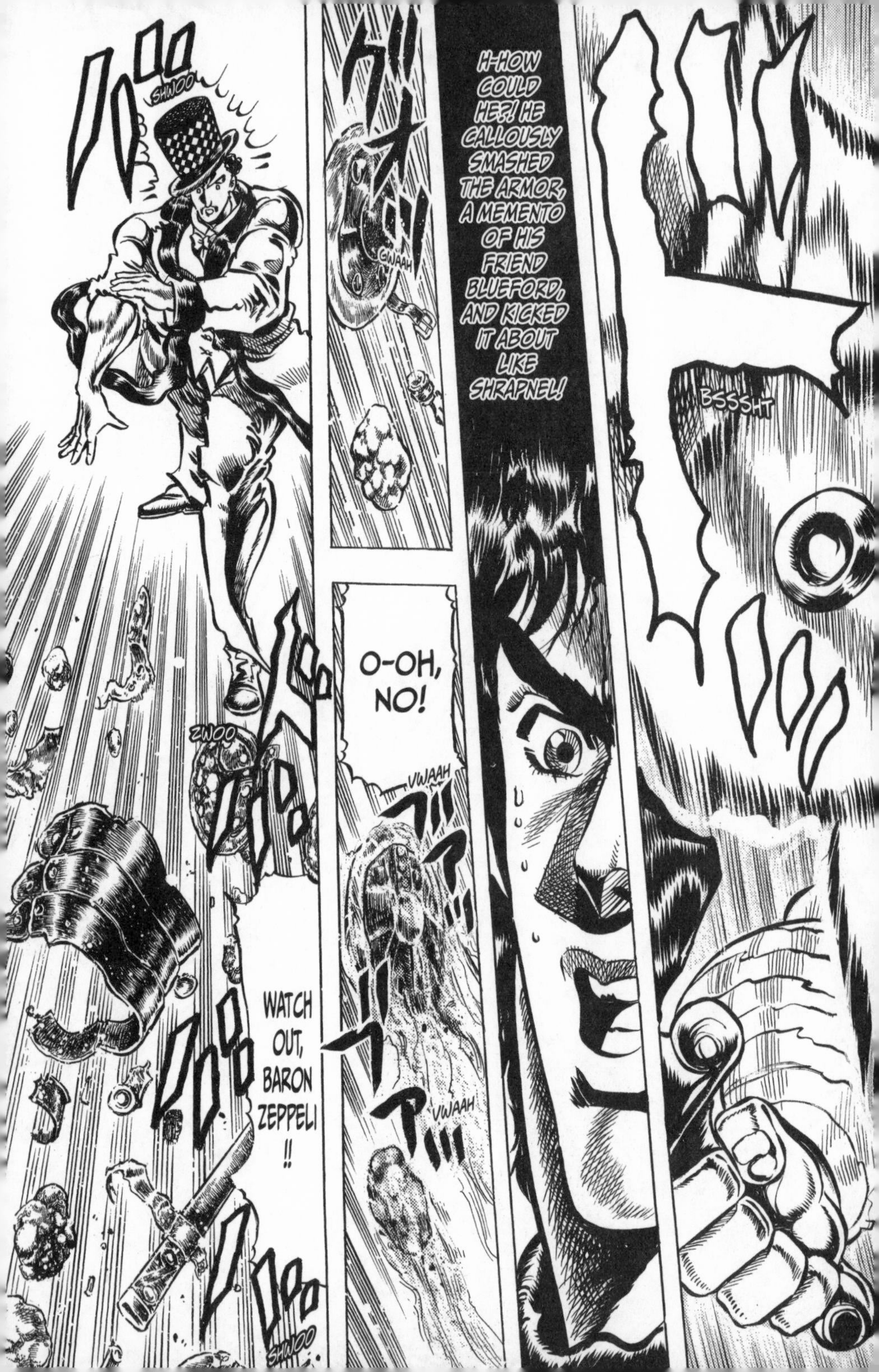
BSSSHT
H-HOW COULD HE?! HE CALLOUSLY SMASHED THE ARMOR, A MEMENTO OF HIS FRIEND BLUEFORD, AND KICKED IT ABOUT LIKE SHRAPNEL!
GWAAH
O-OH, NO!
VWAAH
VWAAH
SHWOO
ZWOO
WATCH OUT, BARON ZEPPELI !!
SHWOO

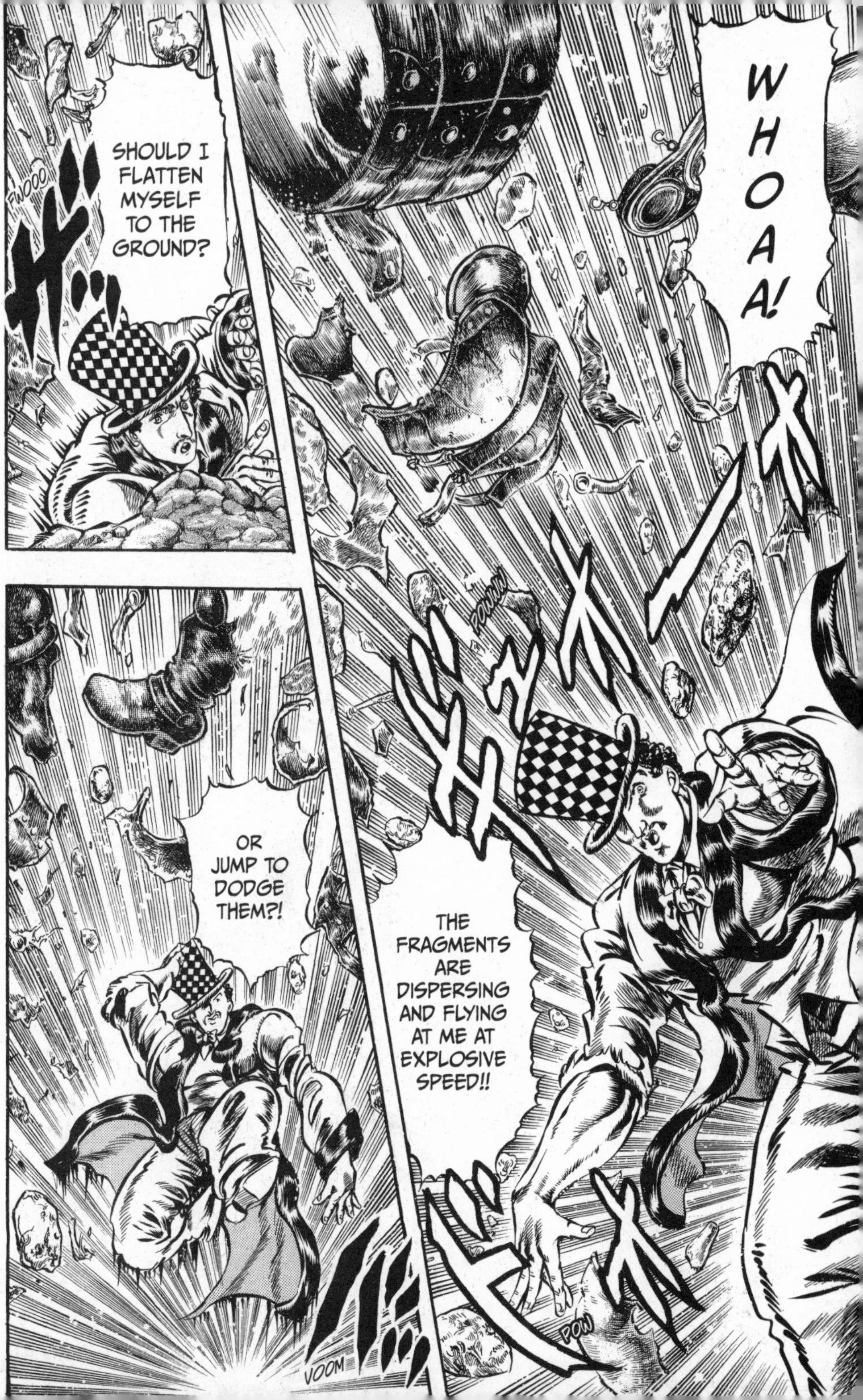
WHOAA!
POWW
THE FRAGMENTS ARE DISPERSING AND FLYING AT ME AT EXPLOSIVE SPEED!!
POW
FWOOO
SHOULD I FLATTEN MYSELF TO THE GROUND?
OR JUMP TO DODGE THEM?!
VOOM

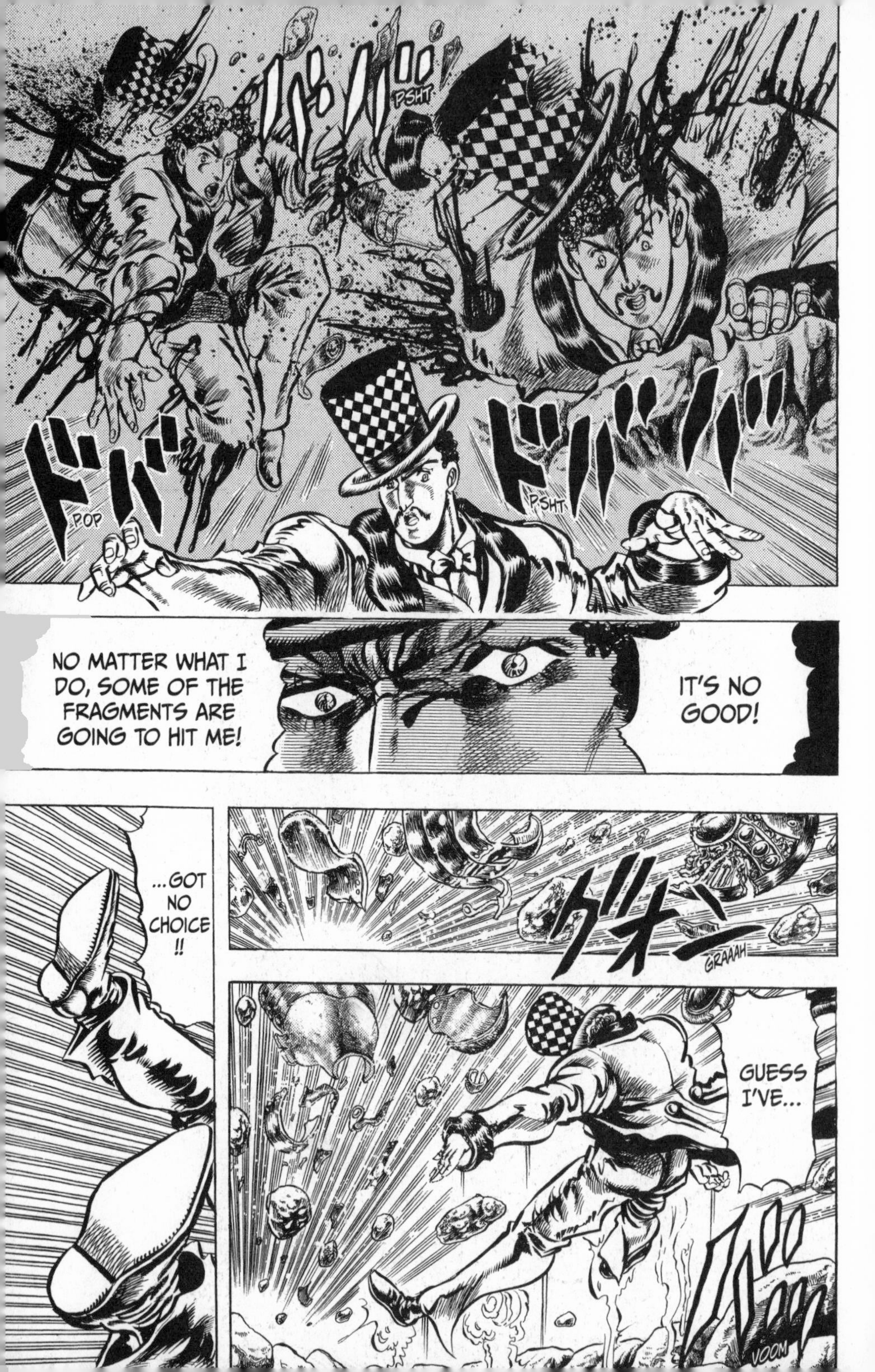
PSHT
PSHT
POP
IT'S NO GOOD!
NO MATTER WHAT I DO, SOME OF THE FRAGMENTS ARE GOING TO HIT ME!
GRAAAH
GUESS I'VE...
VOON
...GOT NO CHOICE !!

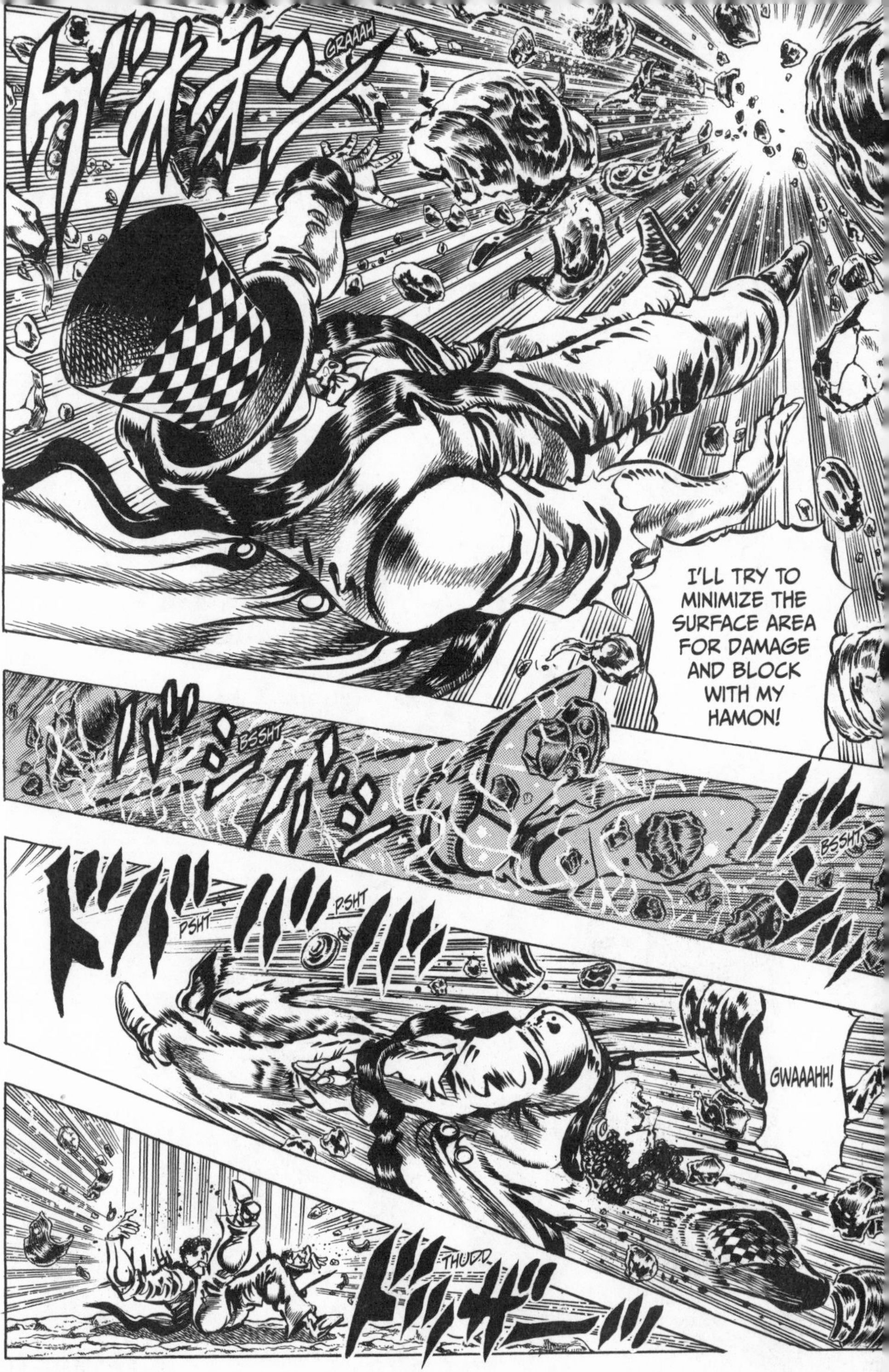

I'LL TRY TO MINIMIZE THE SURFACE AREA FOR DAMAGE AND BLOCK WITH MY HAMON!
GRAAAH
BSSHT
BSSHT
GWAAAHH!
P-SHT
PSHT
THUDD

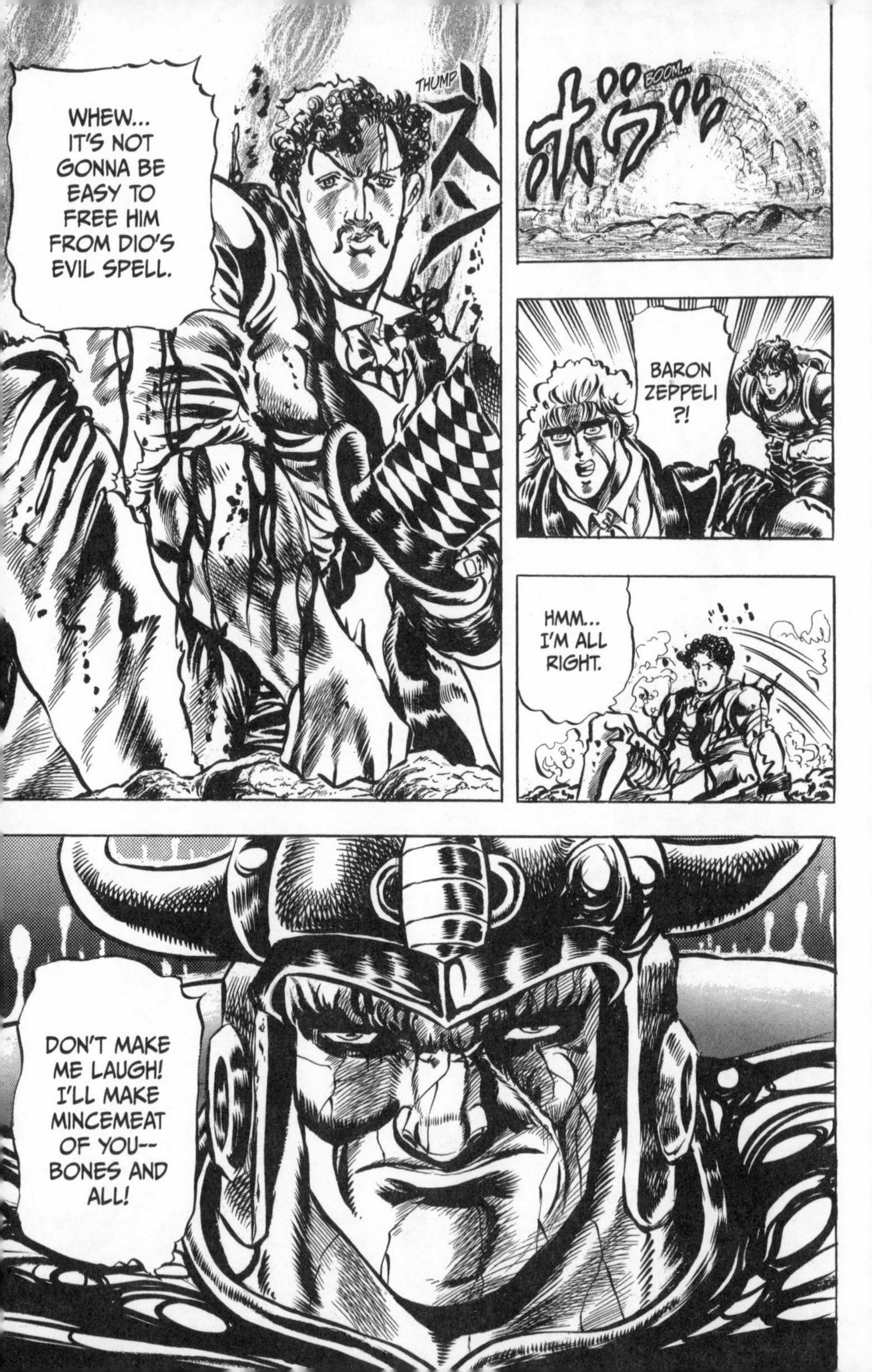
BOOM...
BARON ZEPPELI ?!
HMM... I'M ALL RIGHT.
THUMP
WHEW... IT'S NOT GONNA BE EASY TO FREE HIM FROM DIO'S EVIL SPELL.
DON'T MAKE ME LAUGH! I'LL MAKE MINCEMEAT OF YOU-- BONES AND ALL!

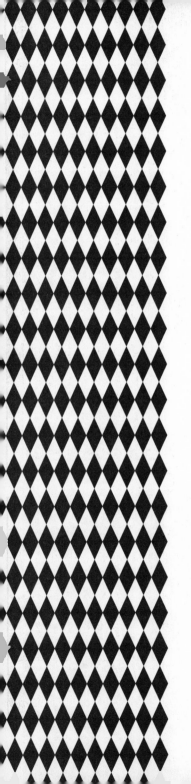

JoJo's
BIZARRE ADVENTURE

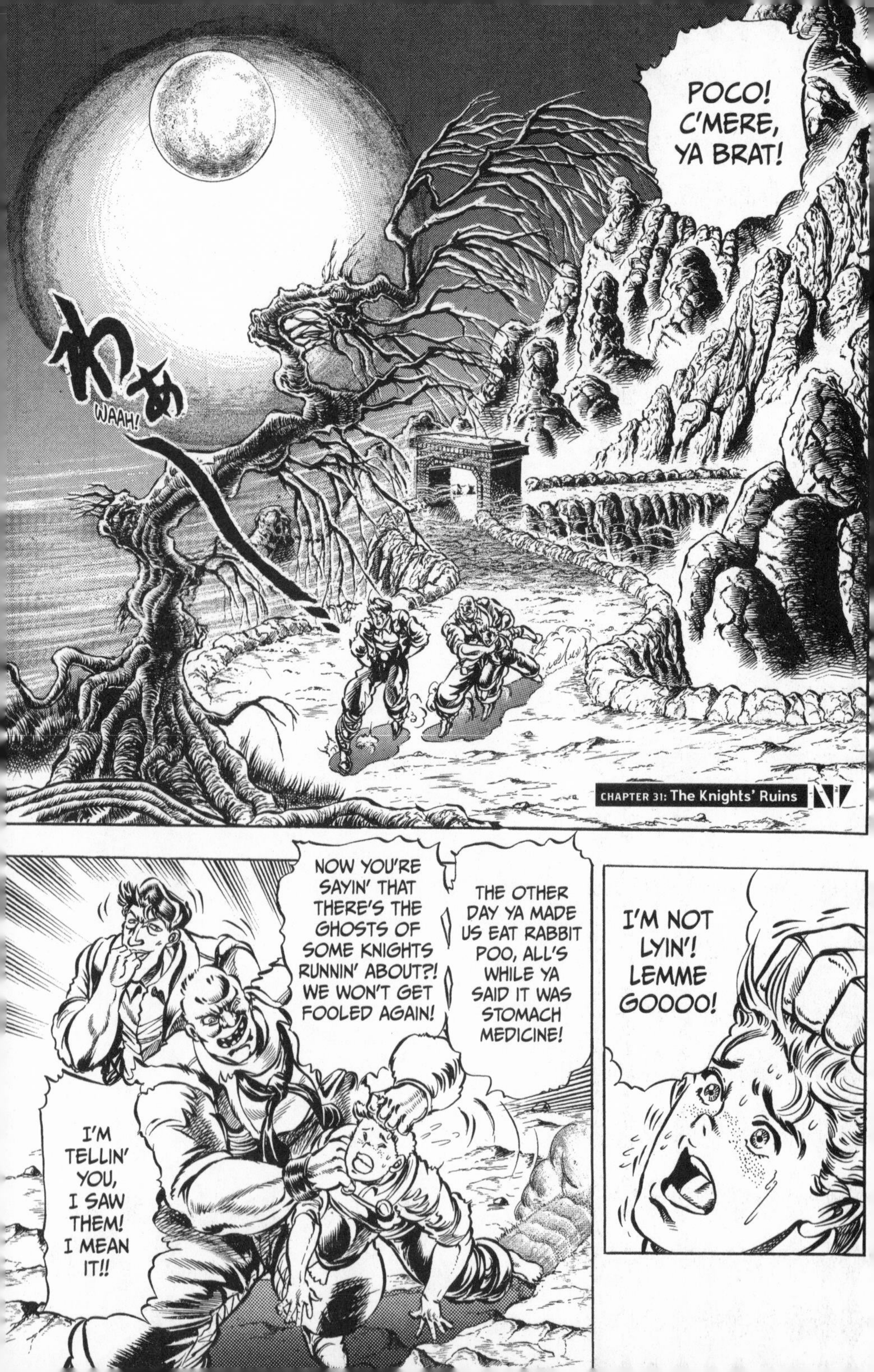
POCO! C'MERE, YA BRAT!
わあ
WAAH!
CHAPTER 31: The Knights' Ruins
I'M NOT LYIN'! LEMME GOOOO!
THE OTHER DAY YA MADE US EAT RABBIT POO, ALL'S WHILE YA SAID IT WAS STOMACH MEDICINE!
NOW YOU'RE SAYIN' THAT THERE'S THE GHOSTS OF SOME KNIGHTS RUNNIN' ABOUT?! WE WON'T GET FOOLED AGAIN!
I'M TELLIN' YOU, I SAW THEM! I MEAN IT!!

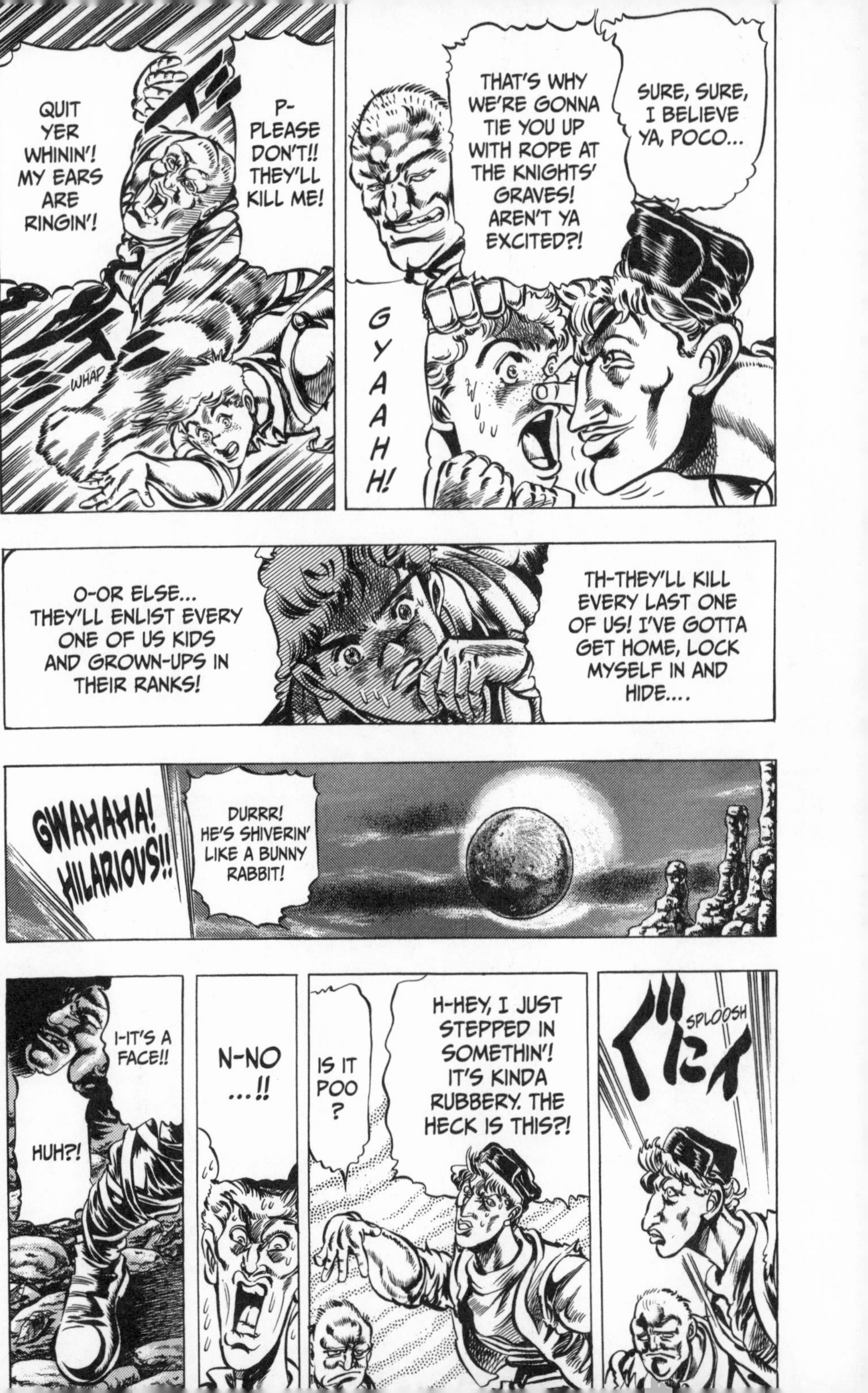
SURE, SURE, I BELIEVE YA, POCO...
THAT'S WHY WE'RE GONNA TIE YOU UP WITH ROPE AT THE KNIGHTS' GRAVES! AREN'T YA EXCITED?!
GYAAAHH!
P-PLEASE DON'T!! THEY'LL KILL ME!
QUIT YER WHININ'! MY EARS ARE RINGIN'!
WHAP
TH-THEY'LL KILL EVERY LAST ONE OF US! I'VE GOTTA GET HOME, LOCK MYSELF IN AND HIDE....
O-OR ELSE... THEY'LL ENLIST EVERY ONE OF US KIDS AND GROWN-UPS IN THEIR RANKS!
DURRR! HE'S SHIVERIN' LIKE A BUNNY RABBIT!
GWAHAHA! HILARIOUS!!
SPLOOSH
H-HEY, I JUST STEPPED IN SOMETHIN'! IT'S KINDA RUBBERY. THE HECK IS THIS?!
IS IT POO?
N-NO ...!!
I-IT'S A FACE!!
HUH?!

CHAPTER 31: The Knights' Ruins

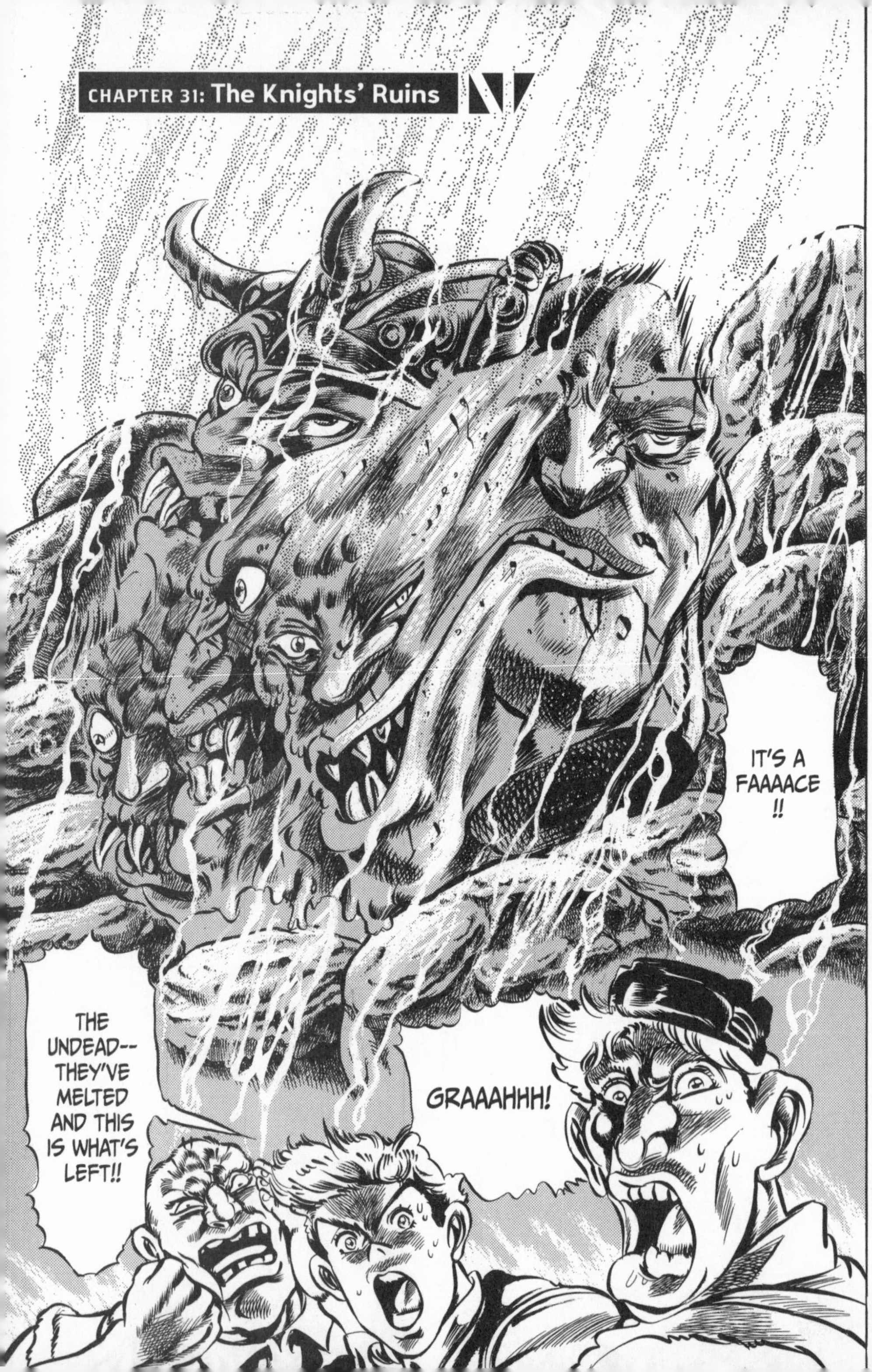
IT'S A FAAAACE !!
GRAAAHHH!
THE UNDEAD-- THEY'VE MELTED AND THIS IS WHAT'S LEFT!!

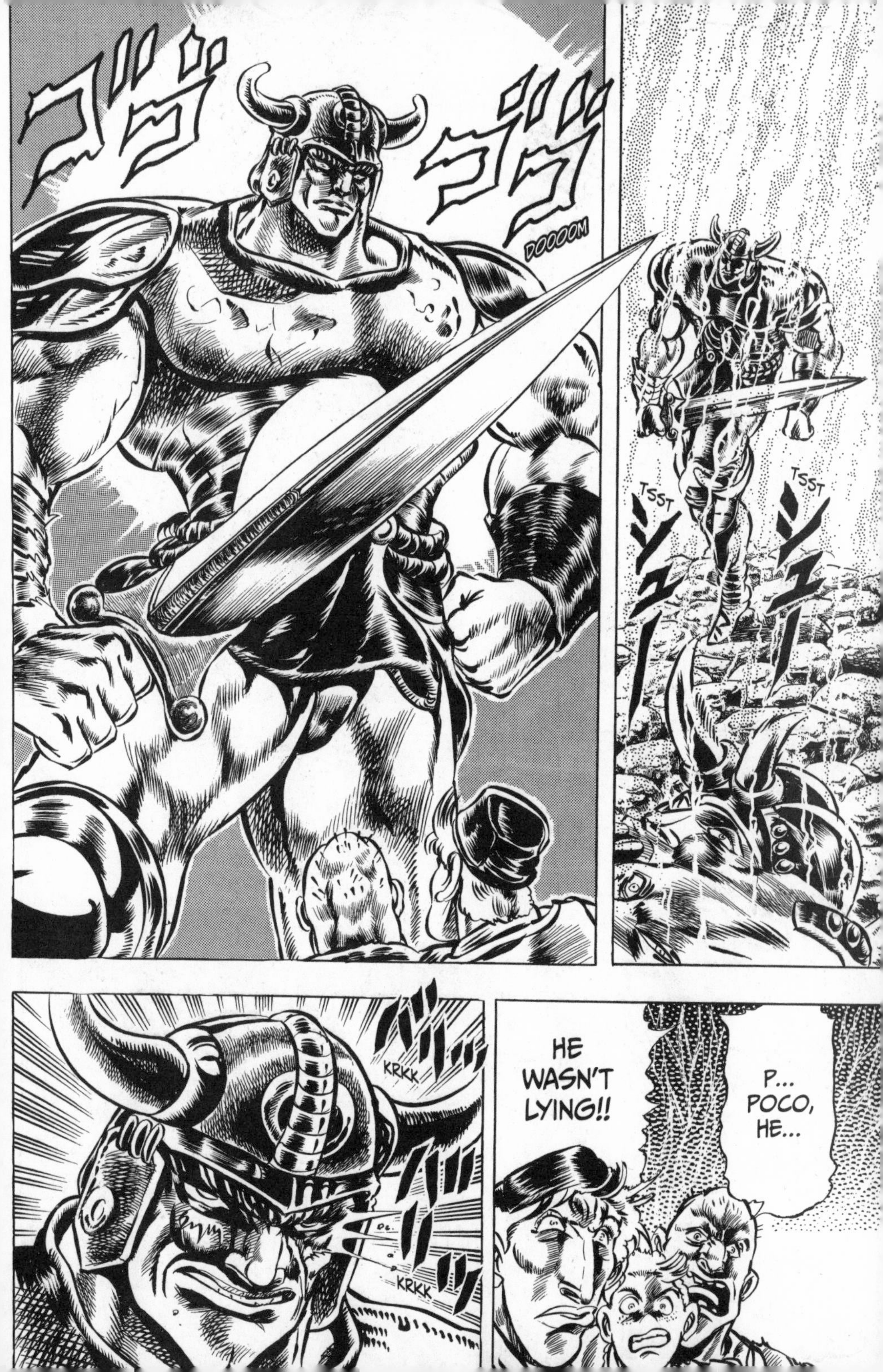
TSST
TSST
DOOOOM
P... POCO, HE...
HE WASN'T LYING!!
KRKK
KRKK

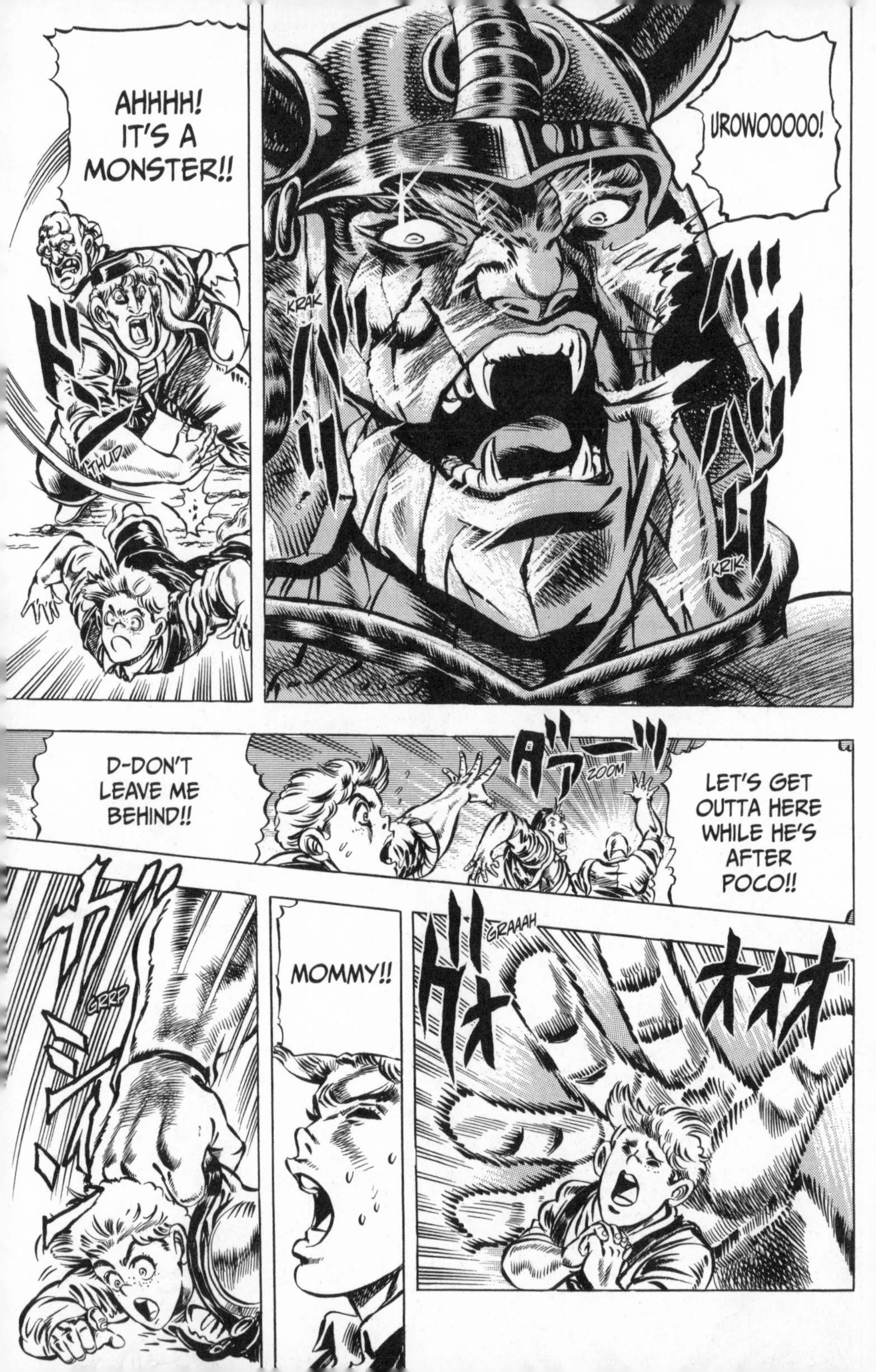
UROWOOOOO!
KRAK
KRIK
AHHHH! IT'S A MONSTER!!
THUD
LET'S GET OUTTA HERE WHILE HE'S AFTER POCO!!
ZOOM
D-DON'T LEAVE ME BEHIND!!
GRAAAH
MOMMY!!
GRRP

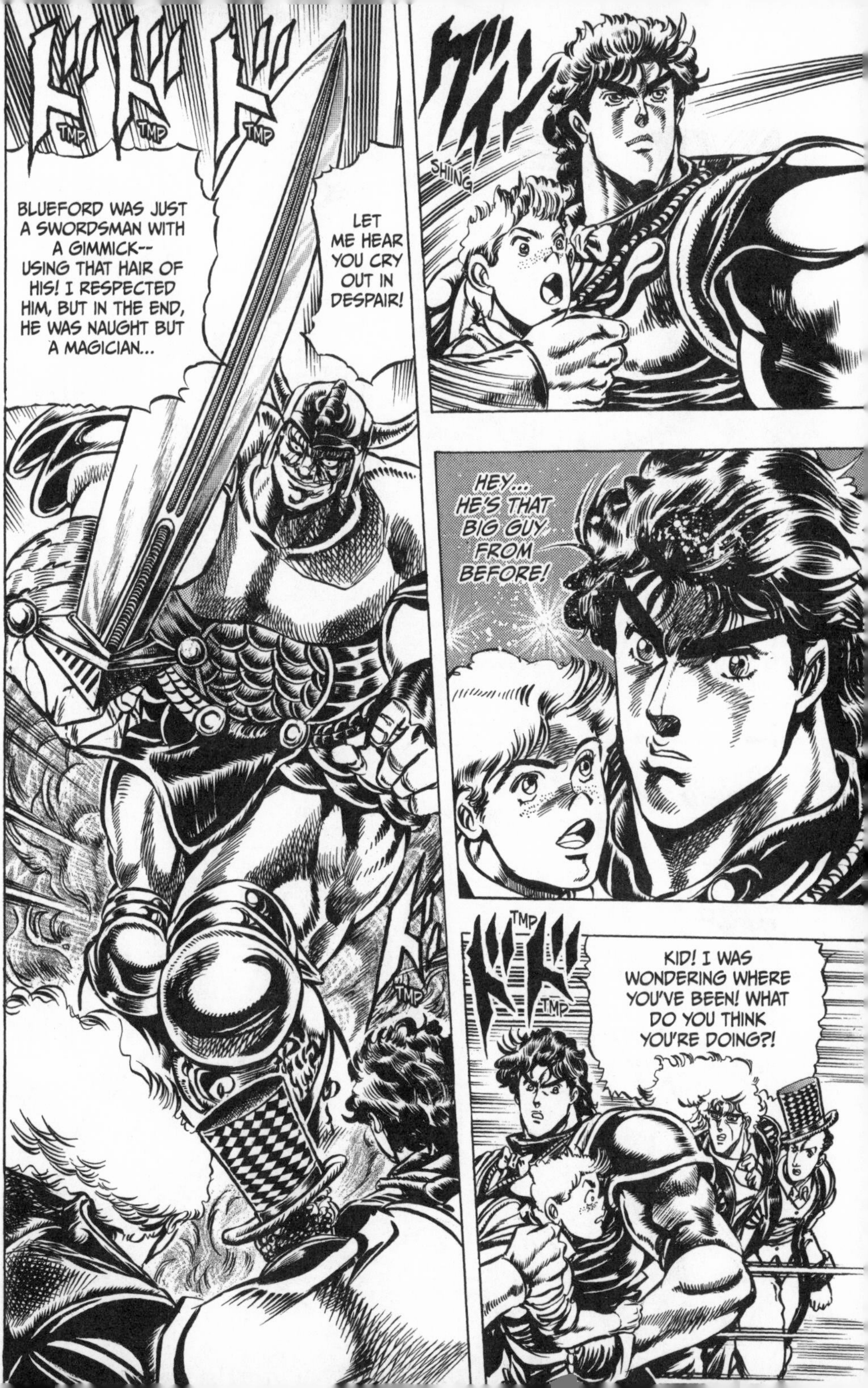
SHING
HEY... HE'S THAT BIG GUY FROM BEFORE!
TMP
TMP
KID! I WAS WONDERING WHERE YOU'VE BEEN! WHAT DO YOU THINK YOU'RE DOING?!
TMP
TMP
TMP
LET ME HEAR YOU CRY OUT IN DESPAIR!
BLUEFORD WAS JUST A SWORDSMAN WITH A GIMMICK-- USING THAT HAIR OF HIS! I RESPECTED HIM, BUT IN THE END, HE WAS NAUGHT BUT A MAGICIAN...
TMP

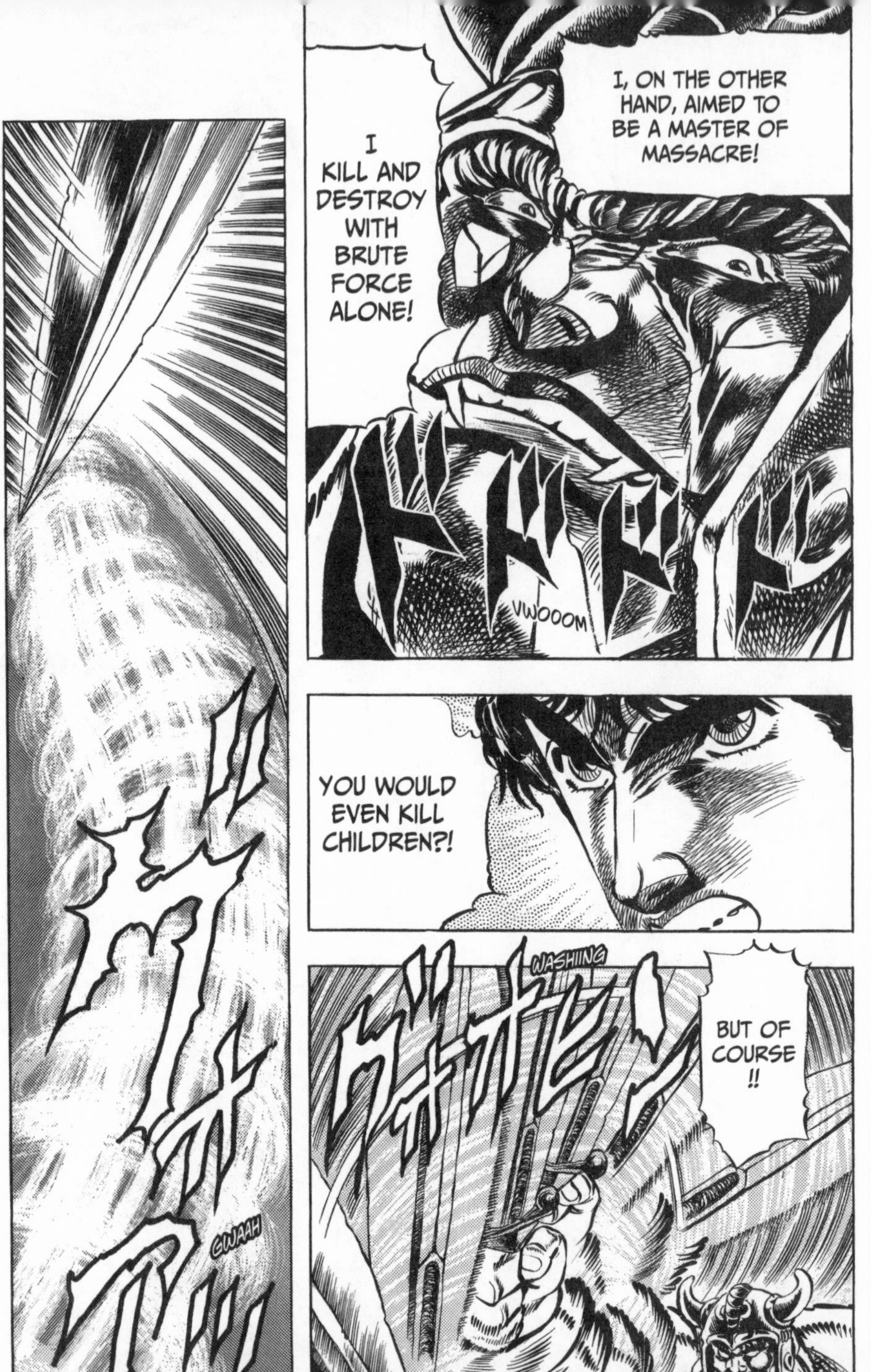
I, ON THE OTHER HAND, AIMED TO BE A MASTER OF MASSACRE!
I KILL AND DESTROY WITH BRUTE FORCE ALONE!
VWOOOM
YOU WOULD EVEN KILL CHILDREN?!
BUT OF COURSE !!
WASHIING
GWAAH

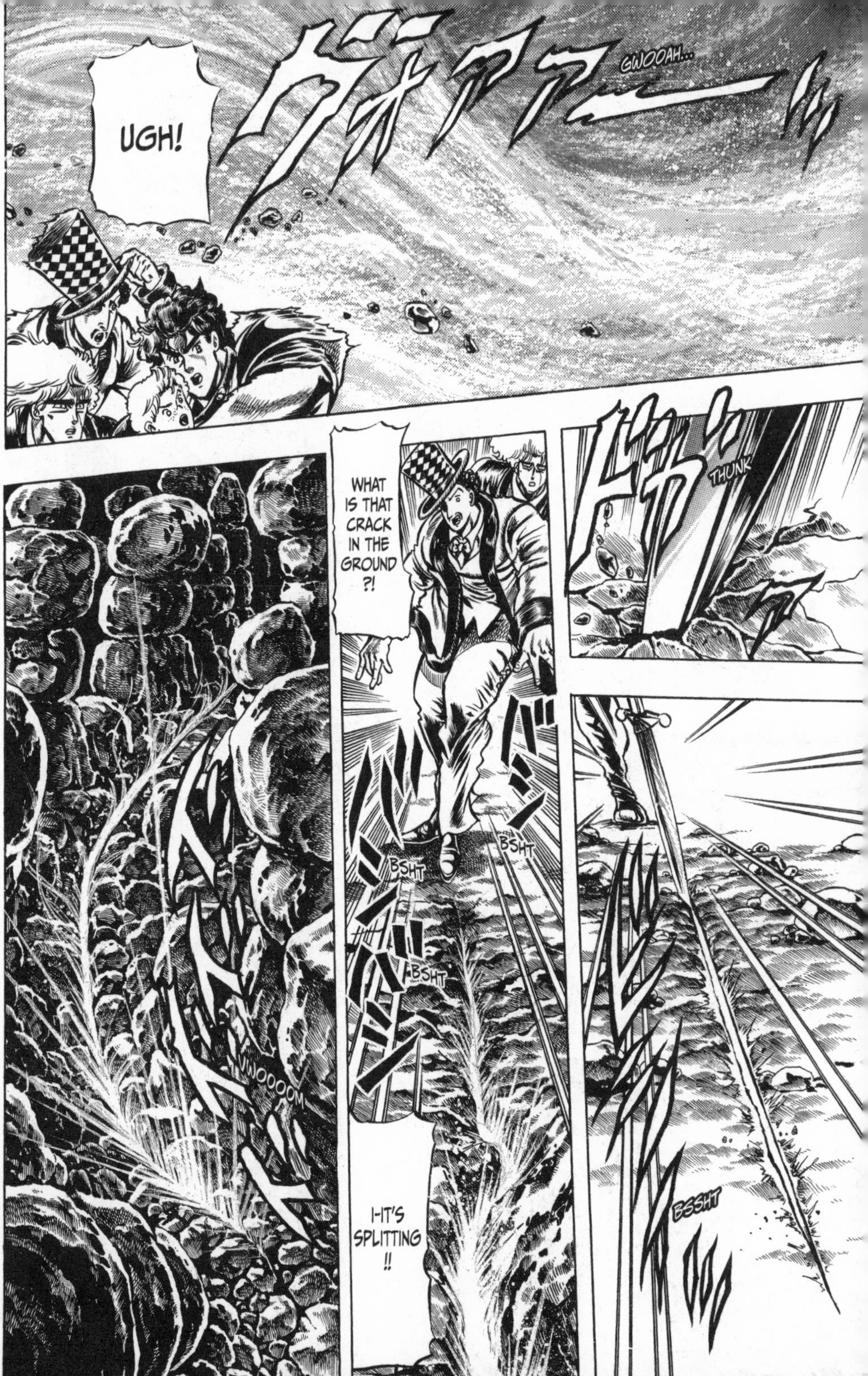
GWOOAH...
UGH!
THUNK
BSSHT
WHAT IS THAT CRACK IN THE GROUND ?!
BSHT
BSHT
BSHT
I-IT'S SPLITTING !!
WWOOOOM

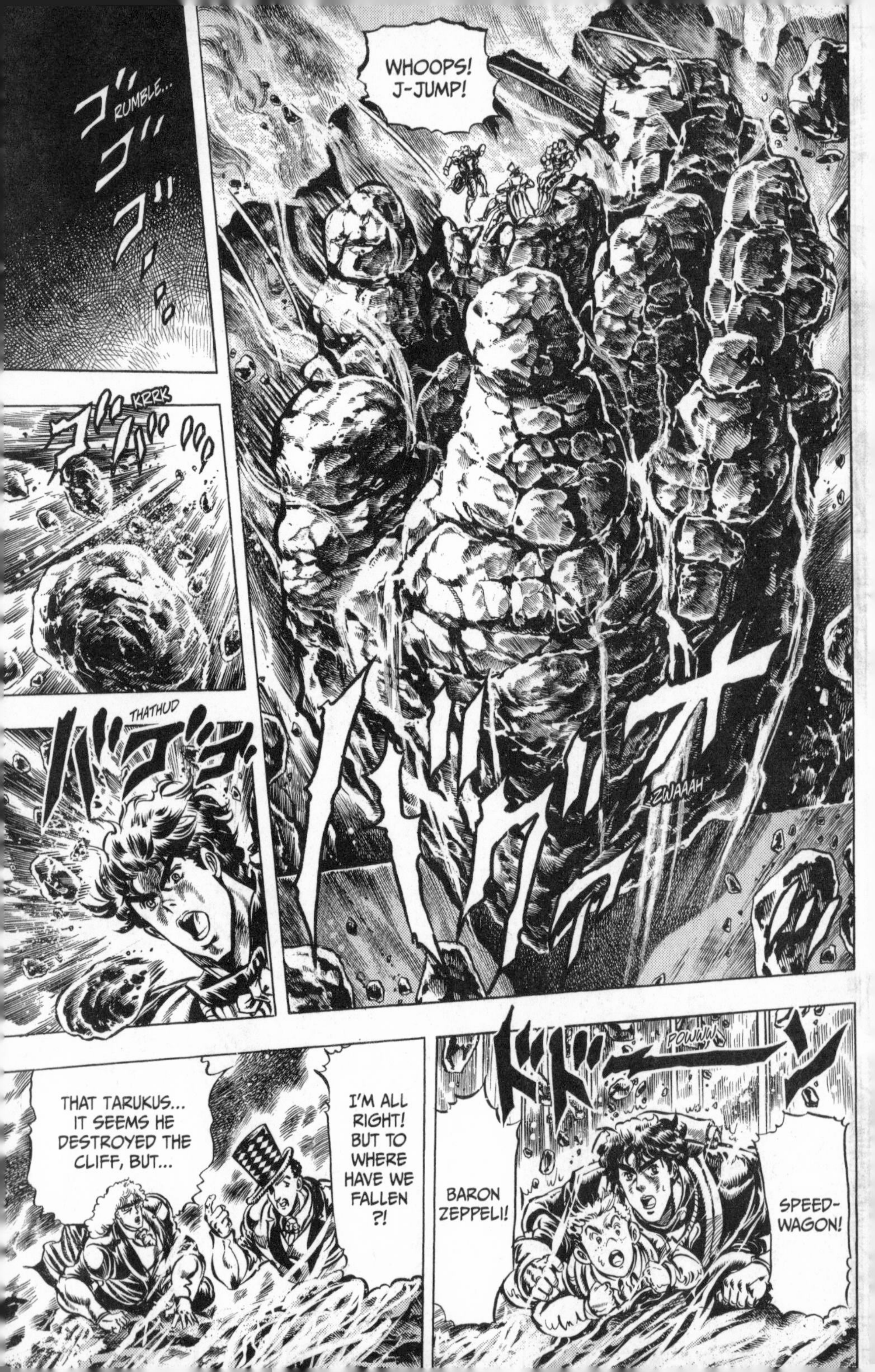
WHOOPS! J-JUMP!
ZWAAAH
RUMBLE...
KRRK
THATHUD
POWWW
SPEED-WAGON!
BARON ZEPPELI!
I'M ALL RIGHT! BUT TO WHERE HAVE WE FALLEN?!
THAT TARUKUS... IT SEEMS HE DESTROYED THE CLIFF, BUT...

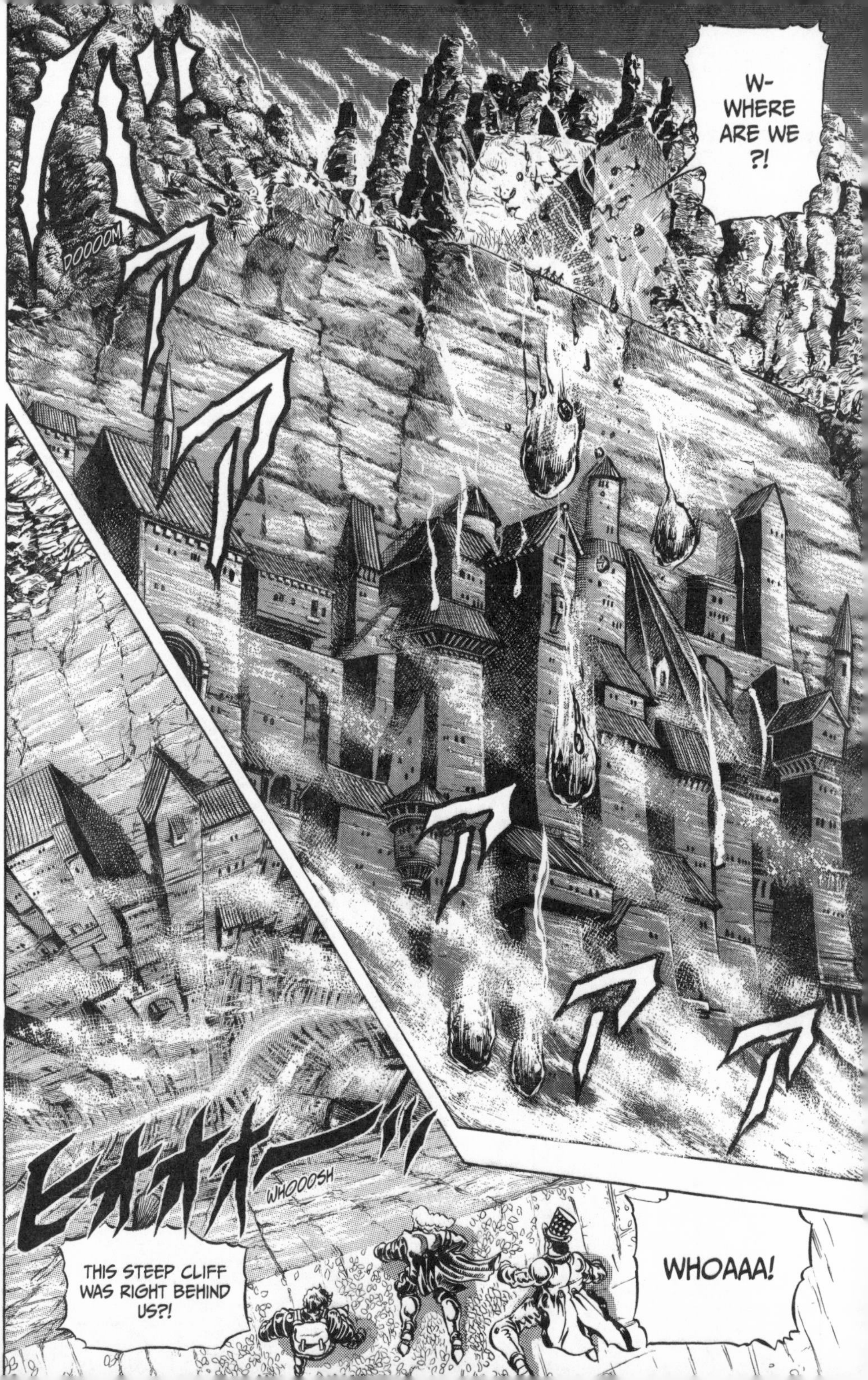
W- WHERE ARE WE ?!
DOOOOM
WHOOOSH
WHOAAA!
THIS STEEP CLIFF WAS RIGHT BEHIND US?!

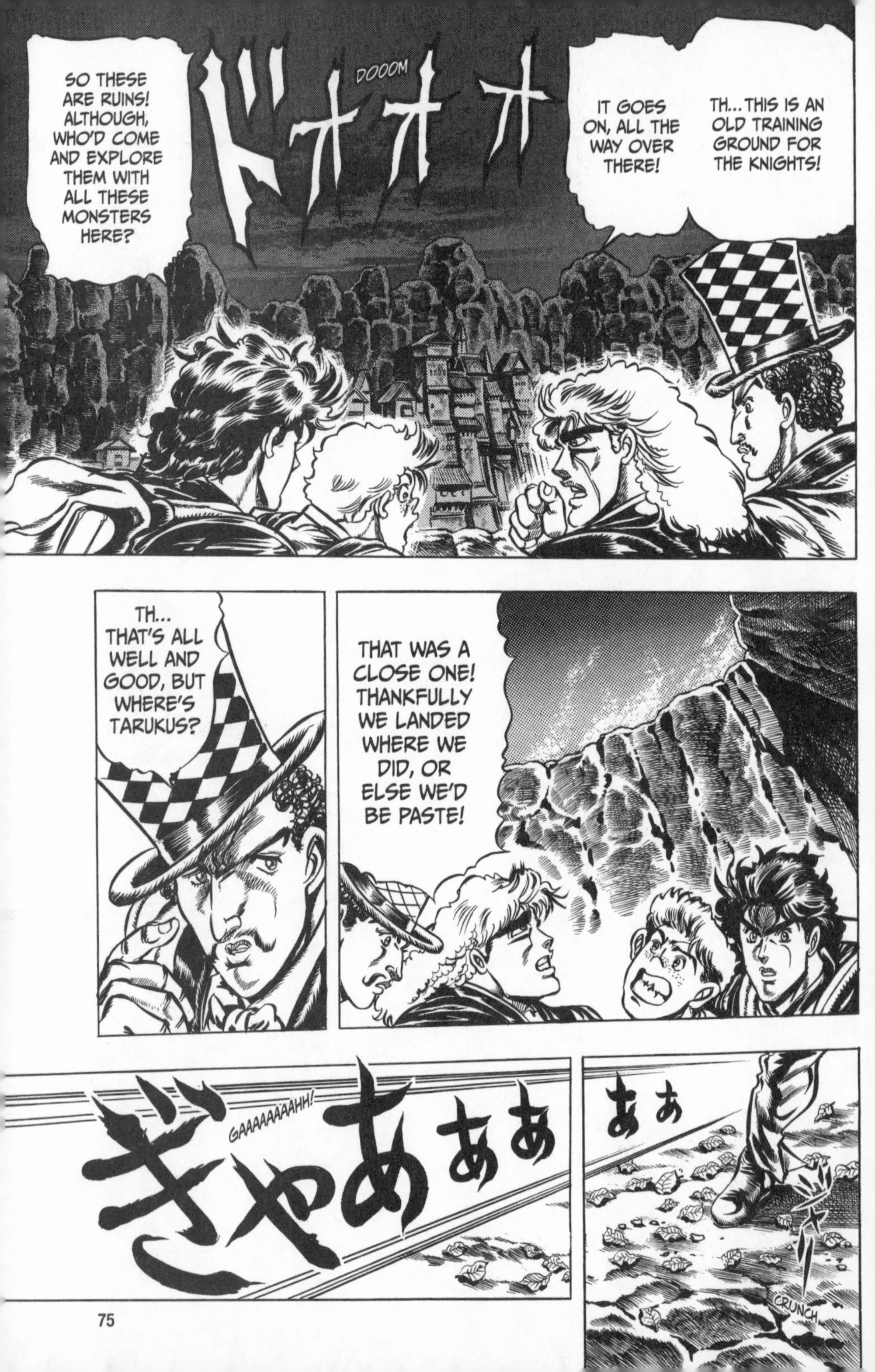
TH... THIS IS AN OLD TRAINING GROUND FOR THE KNIGHTS!
IT GOES ON, ALL THE WAY OVER THERE!
ドォオオ
DOOOM
SO THESE ARE RUINS! ALTHOUGH, WHO'D COME AND EXPLORE THEM WITH ALL THESE MONSTERS HERE?
THAT WAS A CLOSE ONE! THANKFULLY WE LANDED WHERE WE DID, OR ELSE WE'D BE PASTE!
TH... THAT'S ALL WELL AND GOOD, BUT WHERE'S TARUKUS?
CRUNCH
ぎやあぁぁぁ
GAAAAAAAAHH!

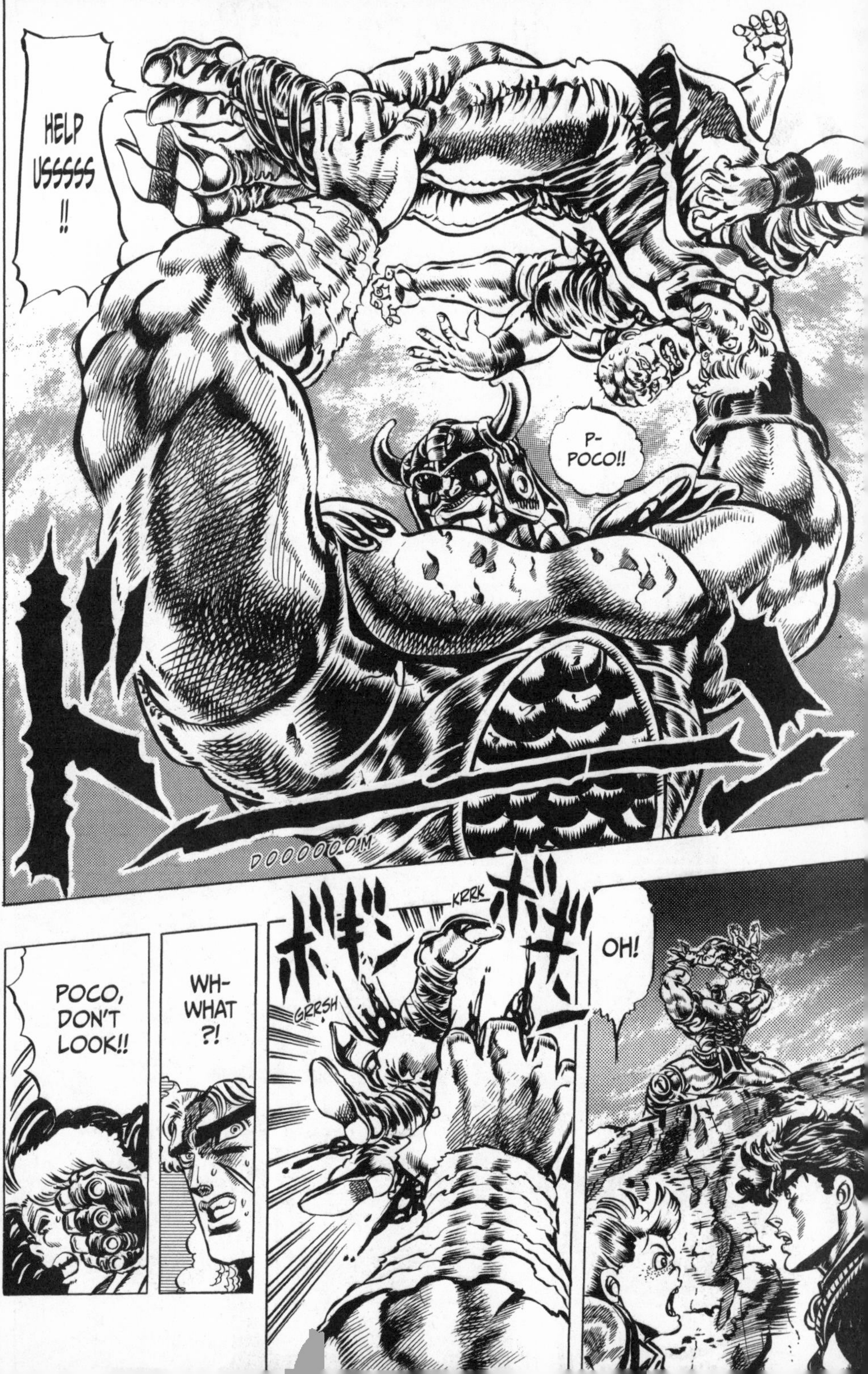
HELP USSSSS!!
P-POCO!!
DOOOOOOOM
OH!
KRRK
GRRSH
WH-WHAT?!
POCO, DON'T LOOK!!

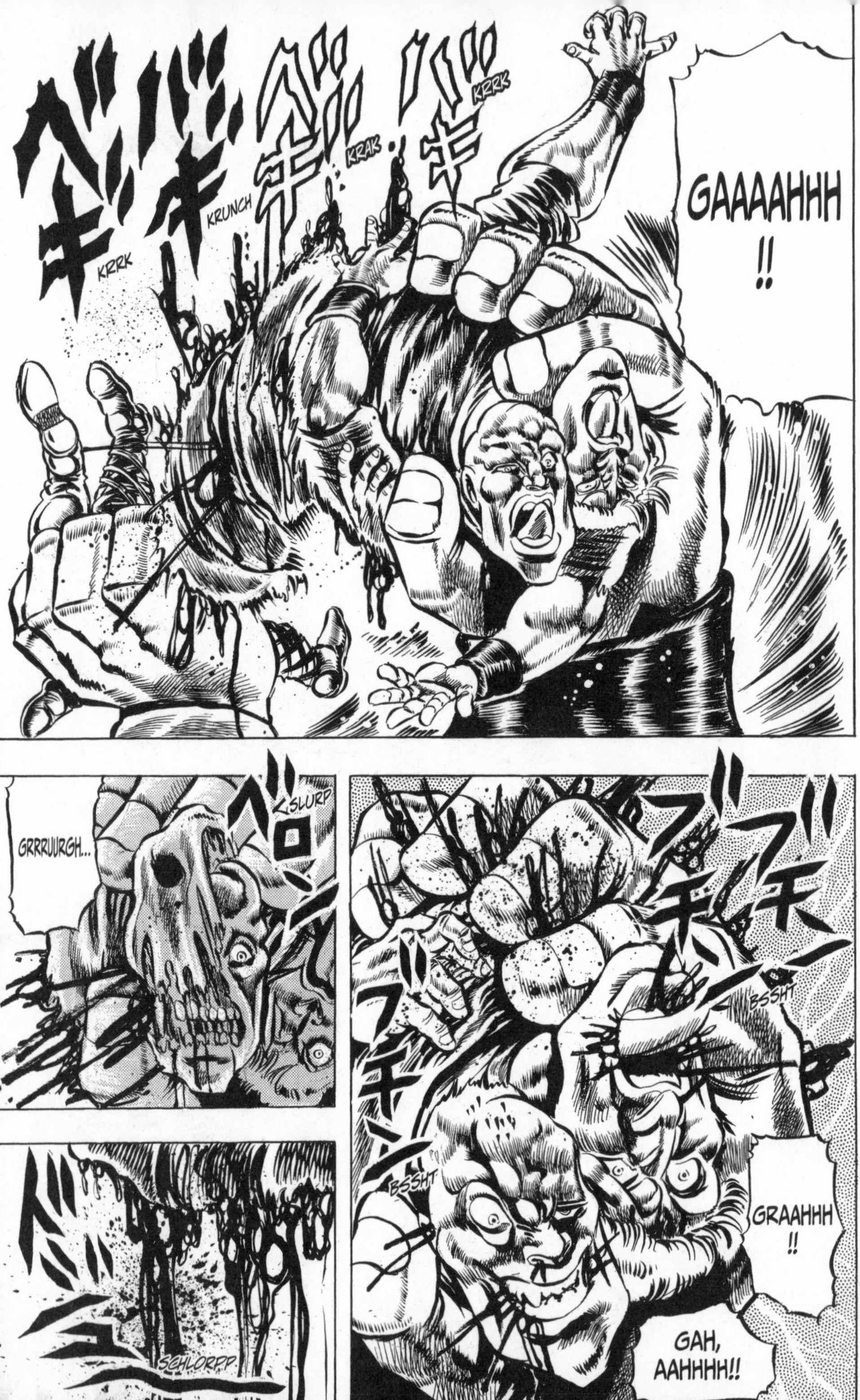
GAAAAHHH!!
KRRK
KRAK
KRUNCH
KRRK
BSSHT
GRAAHHH!!
GAH, AAHHHH!!
BSSHT
SLURP
GRRRUURGH...
SCHLORPP

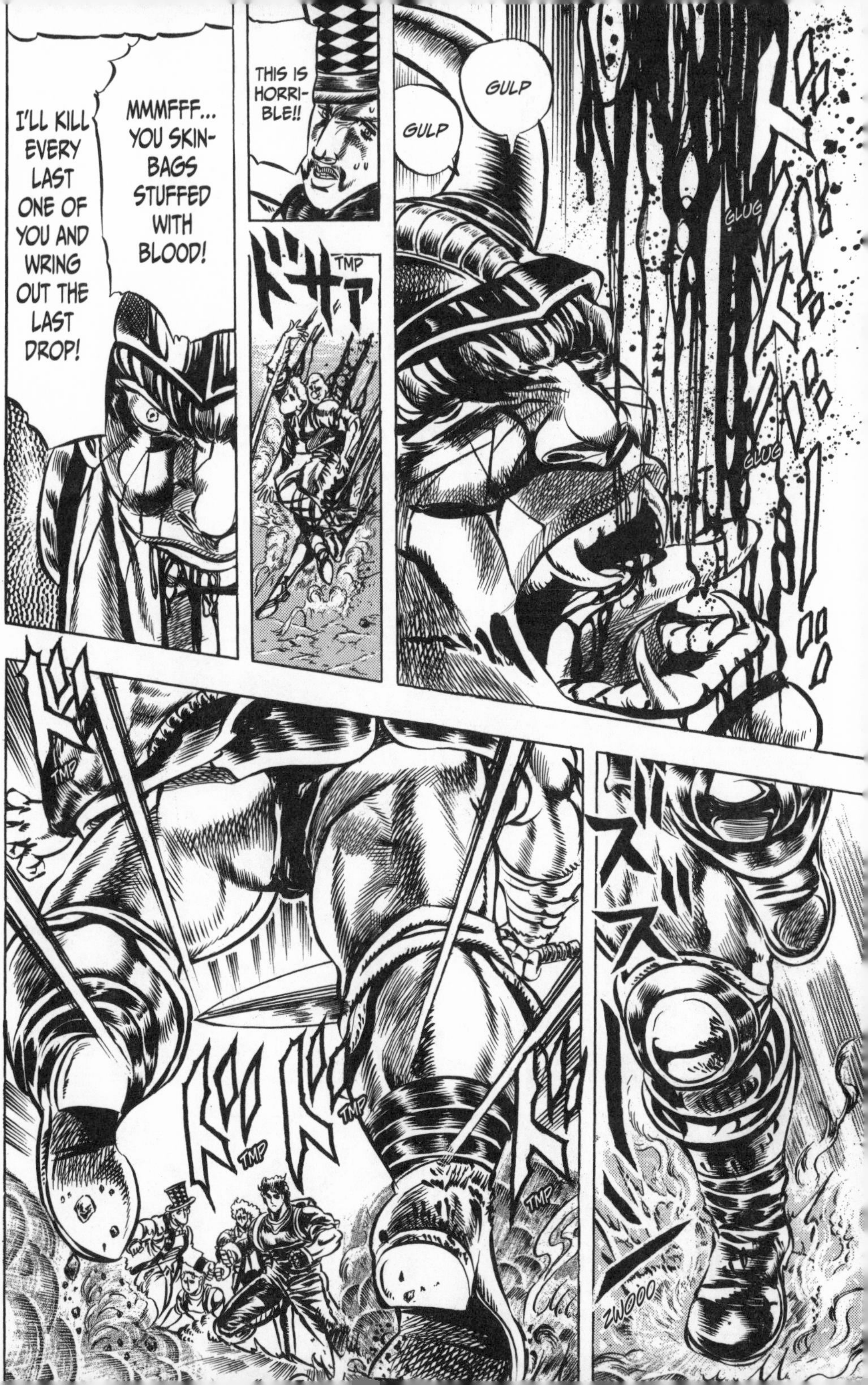
GULP
GULP
GLUG
GLUG
THIS IS HORRI-BLE!!
TMP
MMMFFF... YOU SKIN-BAGS STUFFED WITH BLOOD!
I'LL KILL EVERY LAST ONE OF YOU AND WRING OUT THE LAST DROP!
ZWOOO
TMP
TMP
TMP
TMP

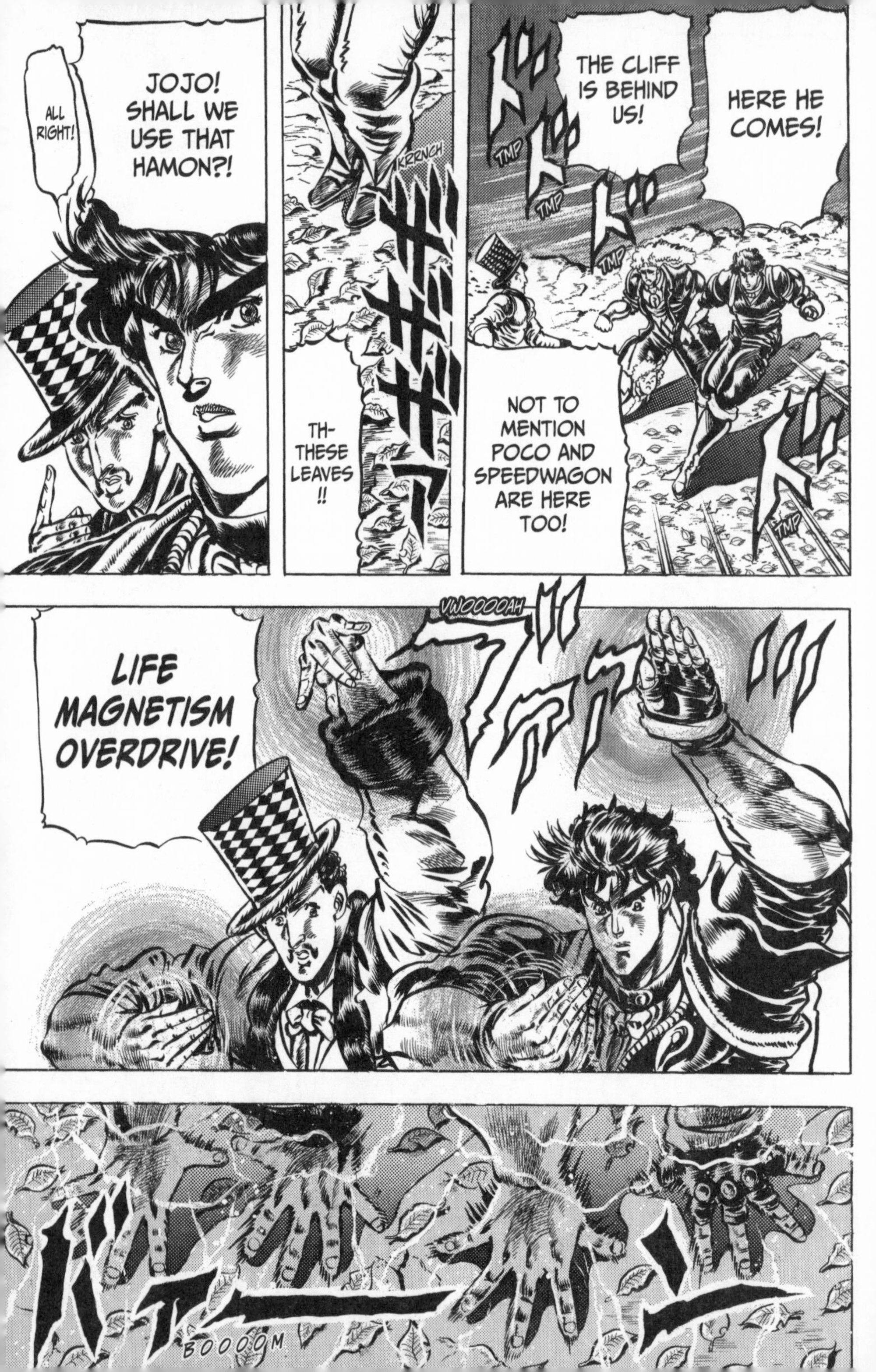
HERE HE COMES!
THE CLIFF IS BEHIND US!
TMP
TMP
TMP
NOT TO MENTION POCO AND SPEEDWAGON ARE HERE TOO!
TMP
KRRNCH
TH-THESE LEAVES!!
JOJO! SHALL WE USE THAT HAMON?!
ALL RIGHT!
VWOOOOAH
LIFE MAGNETISM OVERDRIVE!
BOOOOM

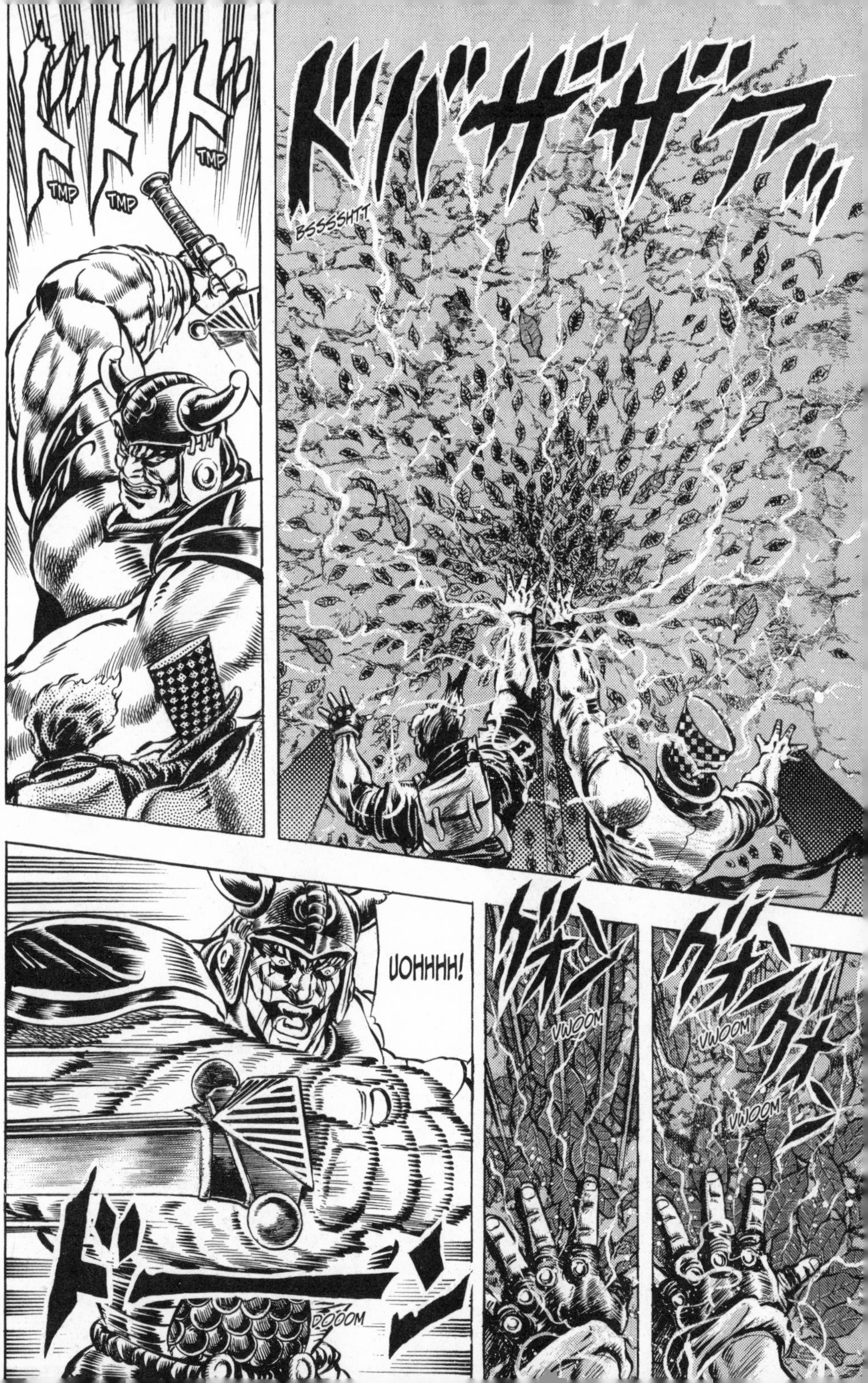
BSSSSHTT
TMP
TMP
TMP
TMP
VWOOM
VWOOM
VWOOM
UOHHHH!
DOOOM

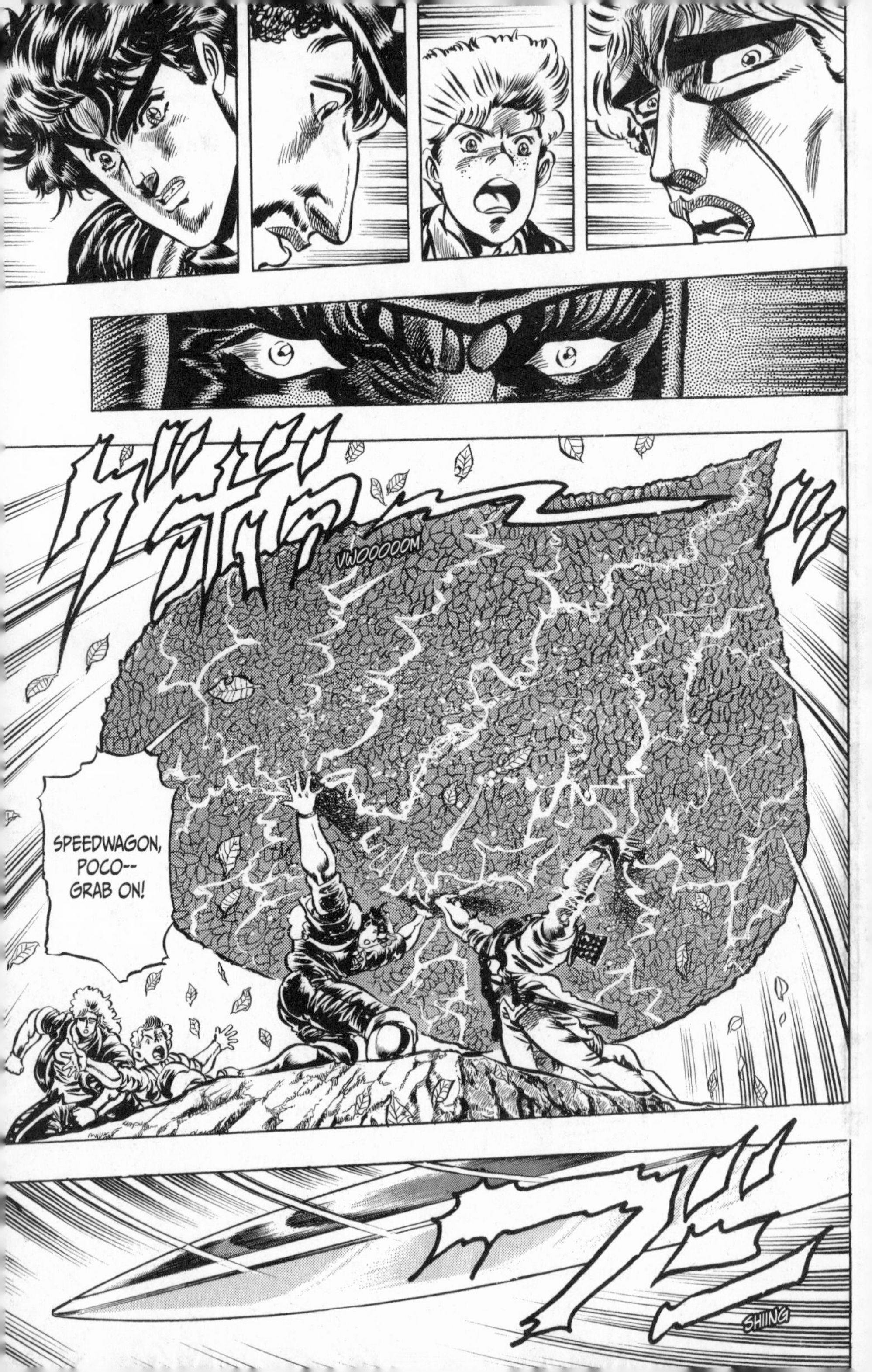
VWOOOOOM
SPEEDWAGON, POCO-- GRAB ON!
SHING

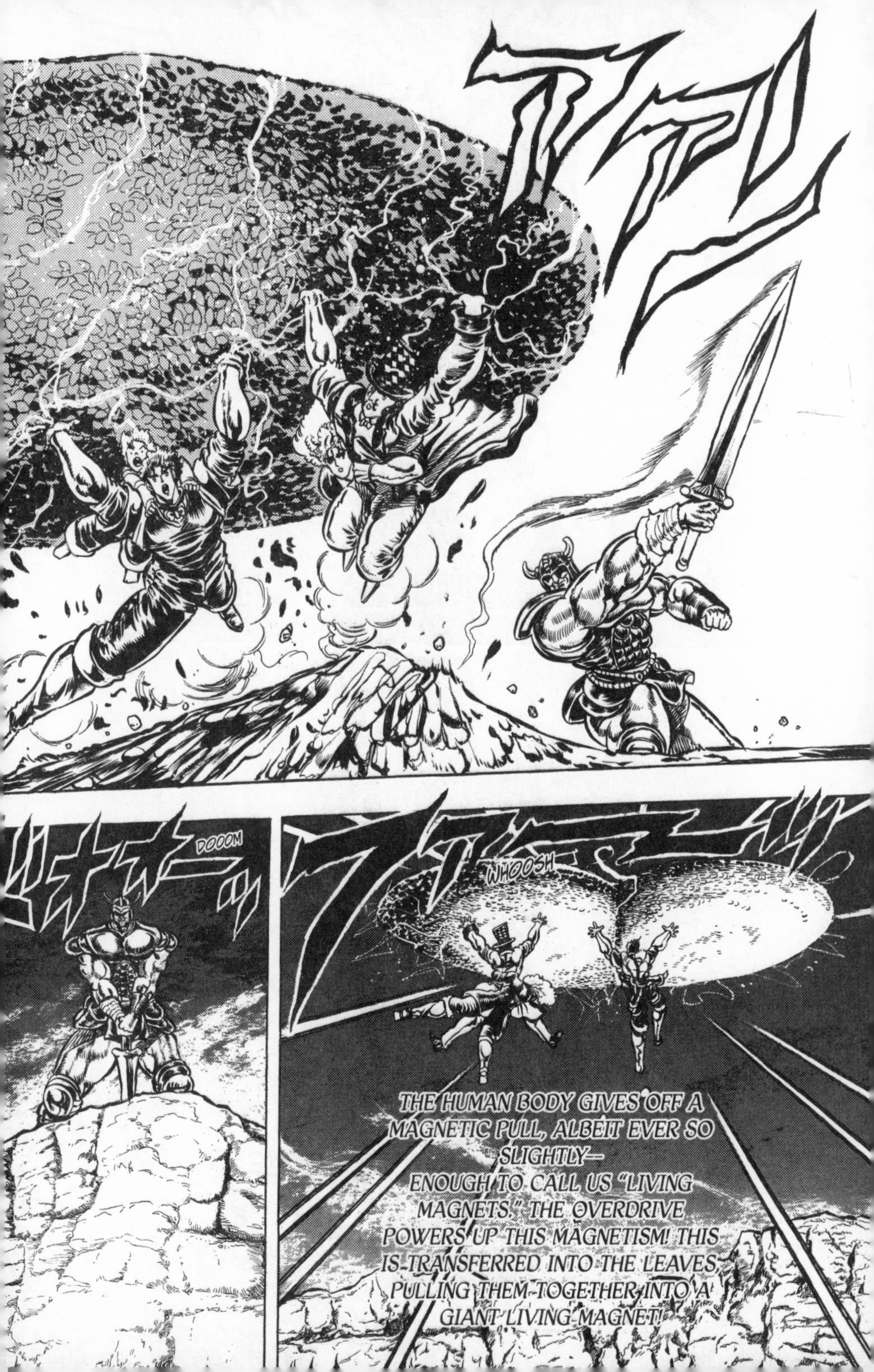
WHOOSH
THE HUMAN BODY GIVES OFF A MAGNETIC PULL, ALBEIT EVER SO SLIGHTLY— ENOUGH TO CALL US "LIVING MAGNETS." THE OVERDRIVE POWERS UP THIS MAGNETISM! THIS IS TRANSFERRED INTO THE LEAVES, PULLING THEM TOGETHER INTO A GIANT LIVING MAGNET!
DOOOM

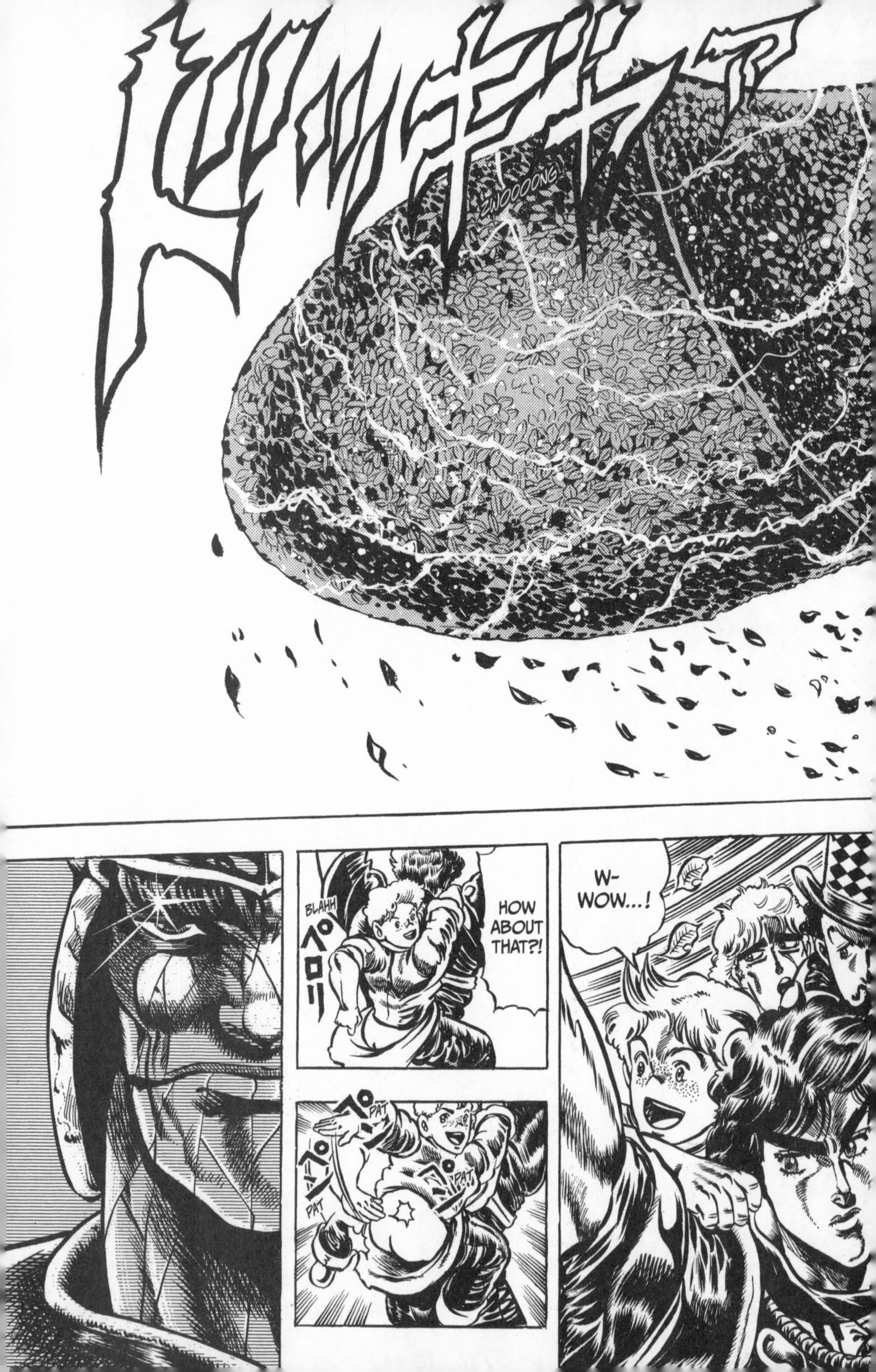
ZWOOOONG
W-
WOW...!
BLAHH
HOW ABOUT THAT?!
PAT
PAT
PAT

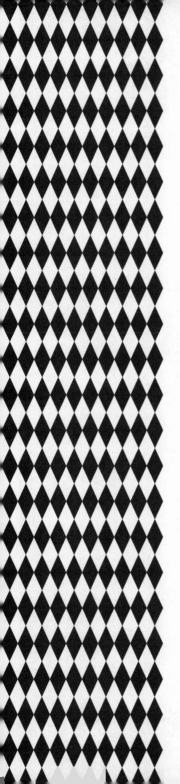

JoJo's
BIZARRE ADVENTURE

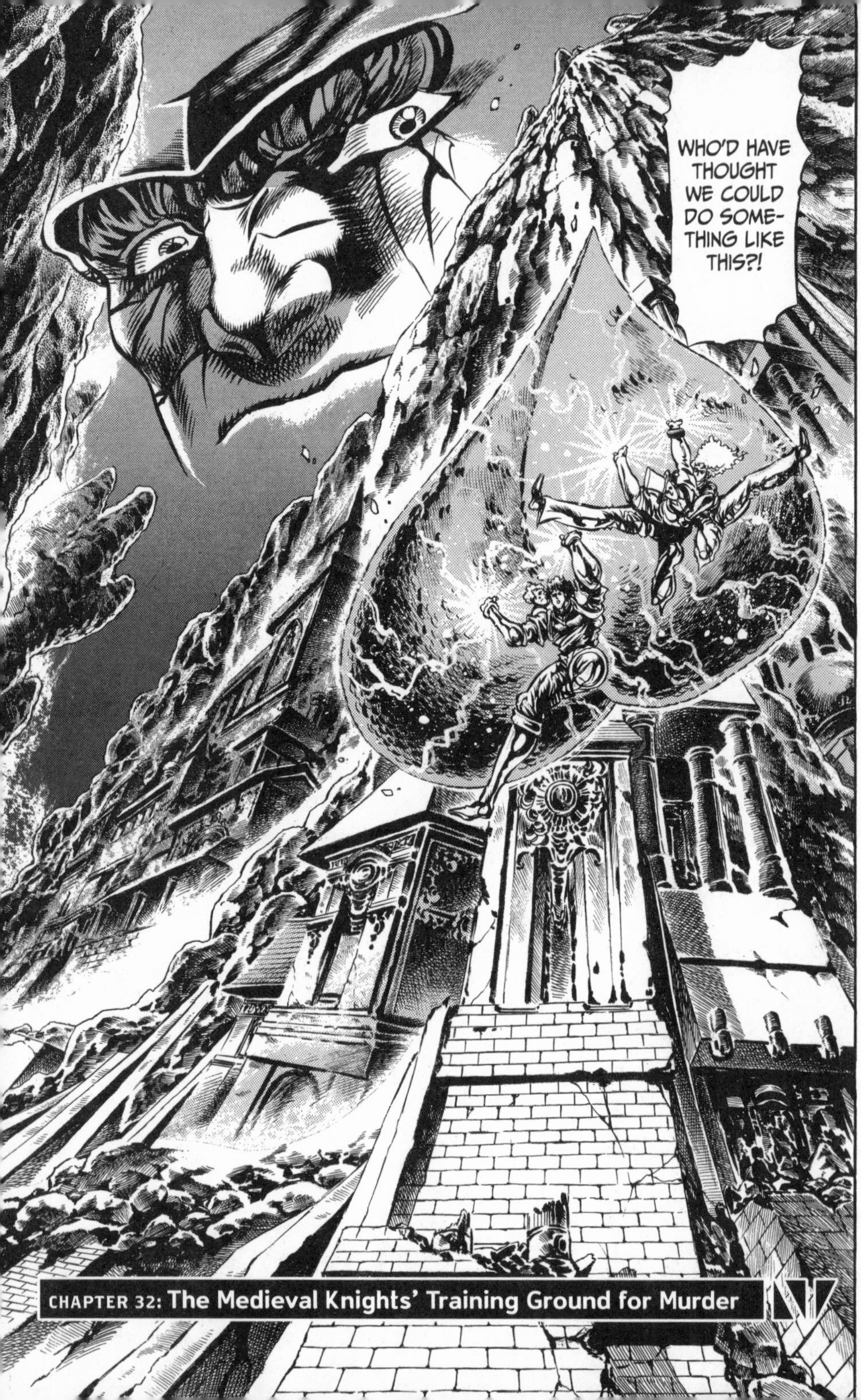
WHO'D HAVE THOUGHT WE COULD DO SOME-THING LIKE THIS?!
CHAPTER 32: The Medieval Knights' Training Ground for Murder

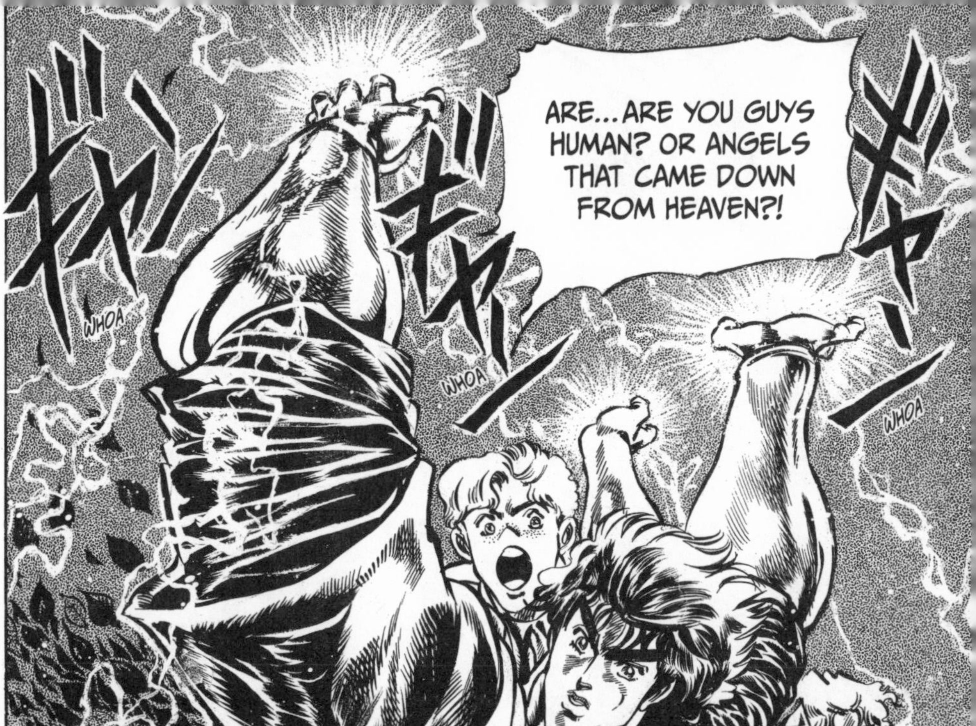
WHOA
ARE...ARE YOU GUYS HUMAN? OR ANGELS THAT CAME DOWN FROM HEAVEN?!
WHOA
WHOA

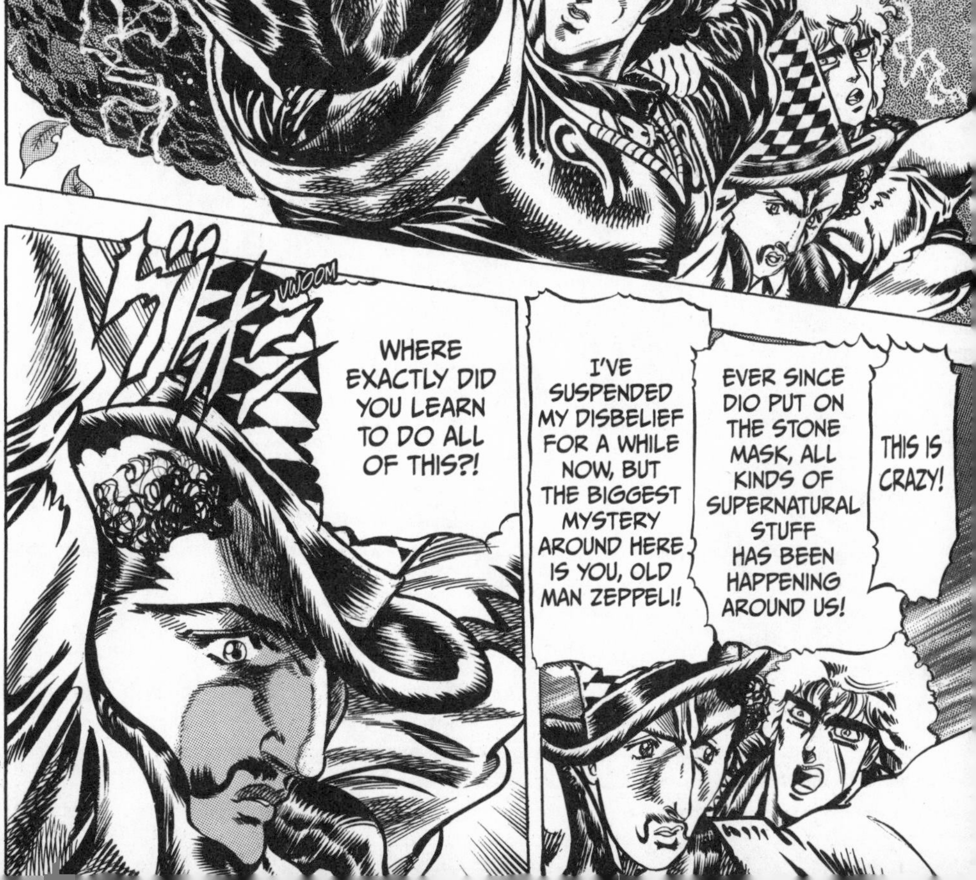
THIS IS CRAZY!
EVER SINCE DIO PUT ON THE STONE MASK, ALL KINDS OF SUPERNATURAL STUFF HAS BEEN HAPPENING AROUND US!
I'VE SUSPENDED MY DISBELIEF FOR A WHILE NOW, BUT THE BIGGEST MYSTERY AROUND HERE IS YOU, OLD MAN ZEPPELI!
VWOOM
WHERE EXACTLY DID YOU LEARN TO DO ALL OF THIS?!

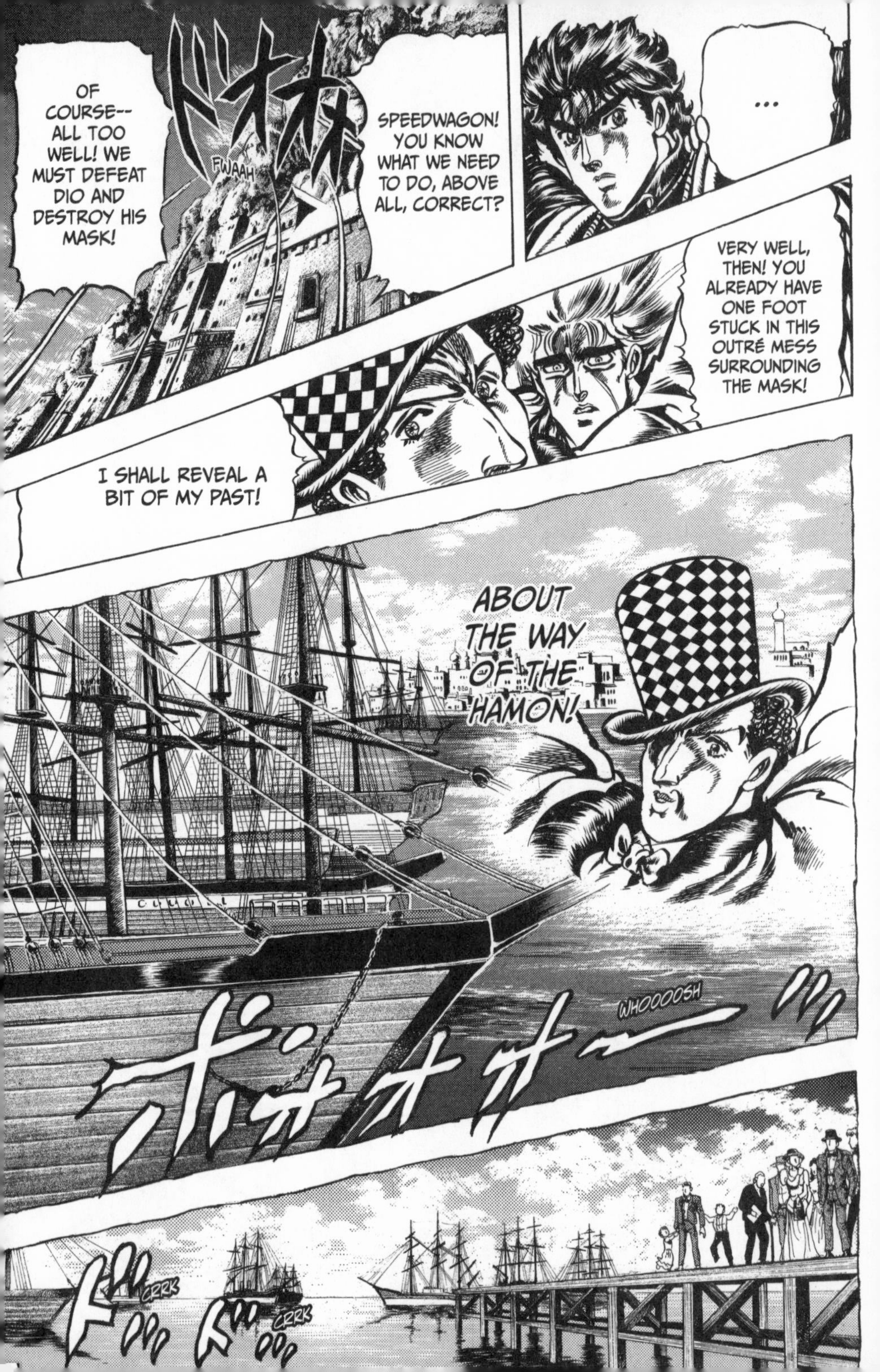
...
SPEEDWAGON! YOU KNOW WHAT WE NEED TO DO, ABOVE ALL, CORRECT?
ドオオオ
FWAAH
OF COURSE-- ALL TOO WELL! WE MUST DEFEAT DIO AND DESTROY HIS MASK!
VERY WELL, THEN! YOU ALREADY HAVE ONE FOOT STUCK IN THIS OUTRÉ MESS SURROUNDING THE MASK!
I SHALL REVEAL A BIT OF MY PAST!
ABOUT THE WAY OF THE HAMON!
ボォオォー
WHOOOOSH
ド
CRRK
ド
CRRK

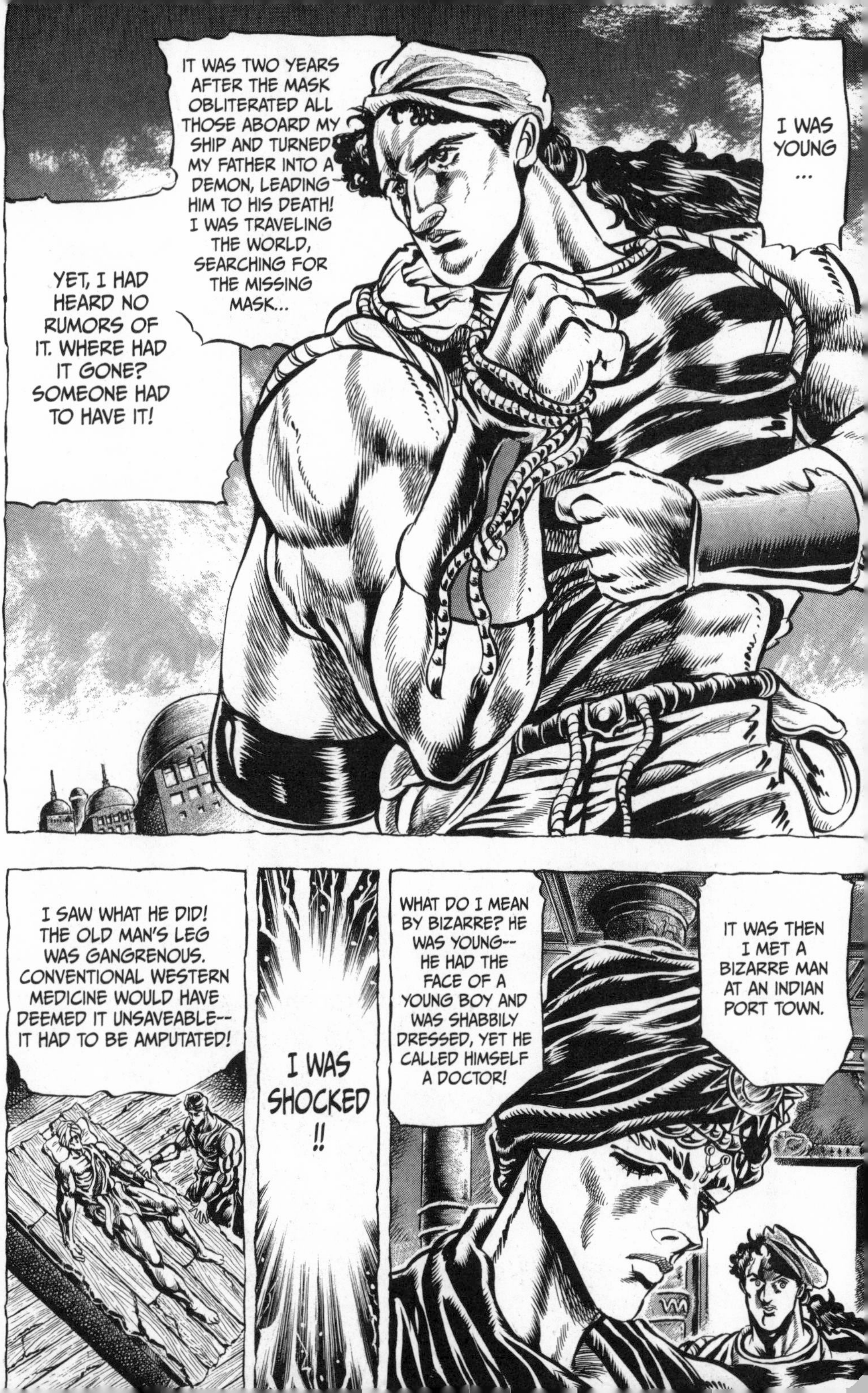
I WAS YOUNG ...
IT WAS TWO YEARS AFTER THE MASK OBLITERATED ALL THOSE ABOARD MY SHIP AND TURNED MY FATHER INTO A DEMON, LEADING HIM TO HIS DEATH! I WAS TRAVELING THE WORLD, SEARCHING FOR THE MISSING MASK...
YET, I HAD HEARD NO RUMORS OF IT. WHERE HAD IT GONE? SOMEONE HAD TO HAVE IT!
IT WAS THEN I MET A BIZARRE MAN AT AN INDIAN PORT TOWN.
WHAT DO I MEAN BY BIZARRE? HE WAS YOUNG-- HE HAD THE FACE OF A YOUNG BOY AND WAS SHABBILY DRESSED, YET HE CALLED HIMSELF A DOCTOR!
I WAS SHOCKED !!
I SAW WHAT HE DID! THE OLD MAN'S LEG WAS GANGRENOUS. CONVENTIONAL WESTERN MEDICINE WOULD HAVE DEEMED IT UNSAVEABLE-- IT HAD TO BE AMPUTATED!

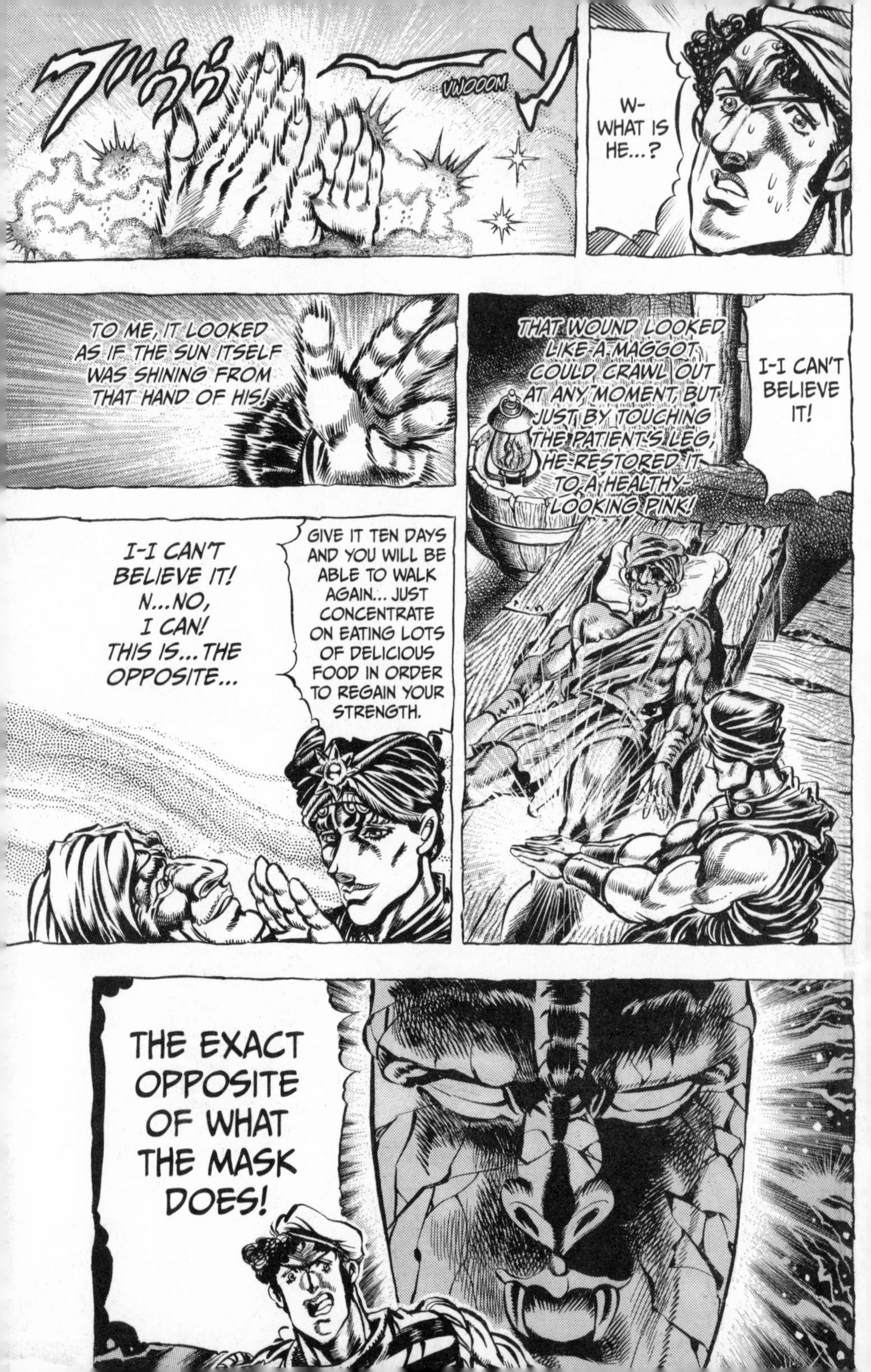
W-
WHAT IS
HE...?
VWOOOM
I-I CAN'T BELIEVE IT!
THAT WOUND LOOKED LIKE A MAGGOT COULD CRAWL OUT AT ANY MOMENT, BUT JUST BY TOUCHING THE PATIENT'S LEG, HE RESTORED IT TO A HEALTHY-LOOKING PINK!
TO ME, IT LOOKED AS IF THE SUN ITSELF WAS SHINING FROM THAT HAND OF HIS!
GIVE IT TEN DAYS AND YOU WILL BE ABLE TO WALK AGAIN... JUST CONCENTRATE ON EATING LOTS OF DELICIOUS FOOD IN ORDER TO REGAIN YOUR STRENGTH.
I-I CAN'T BELIEVE IT! N...NO, I CAN! THIS IS...THE OPPOSITE...
THE EXACT OPPOSITE OF WHAT THE MASK DOES!

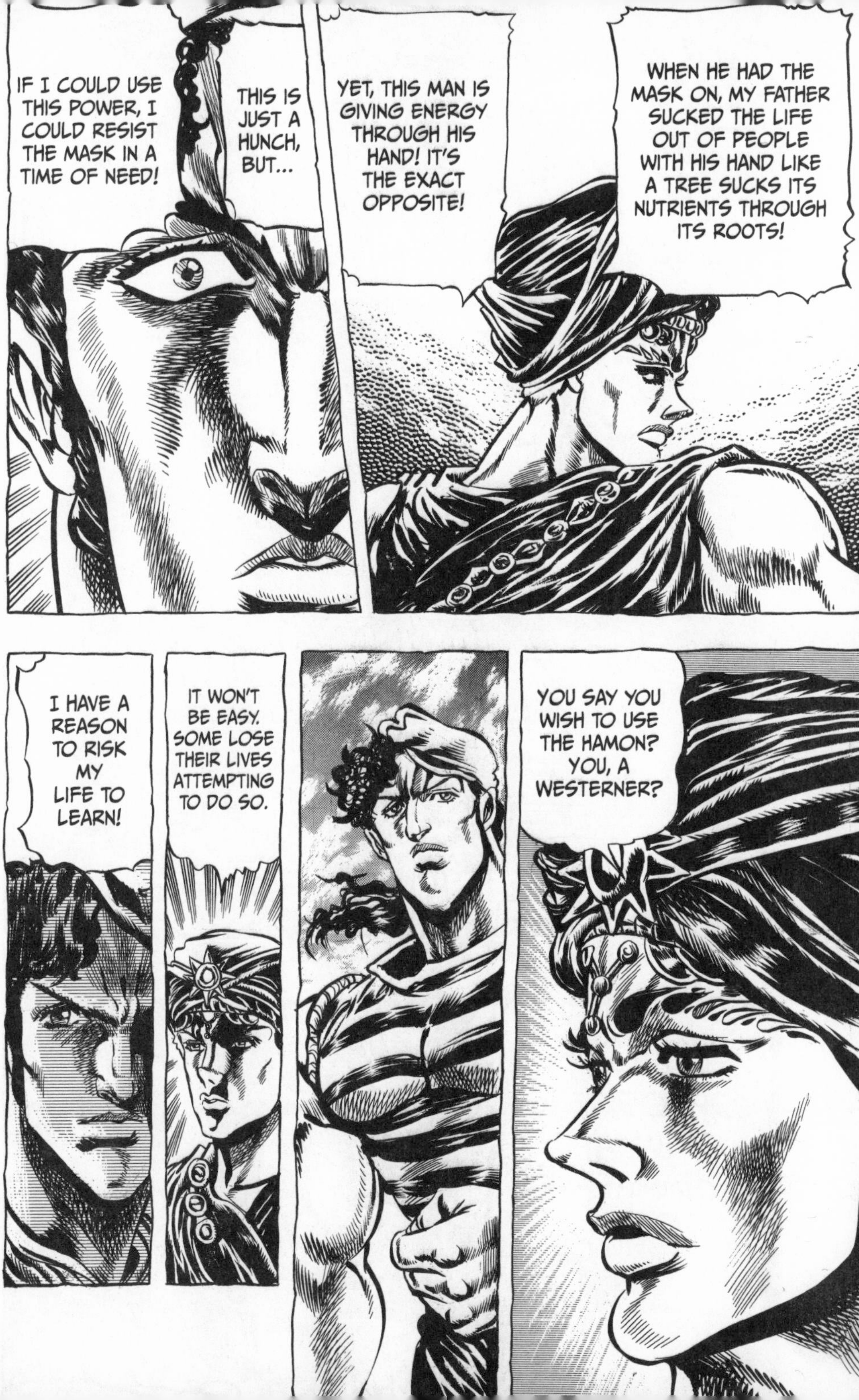
WHEN HE HAD THE MASK ON, MY FATHER SUCKED THE LIFE OUT OF PEOPLE WITH HIS HAND LIKE A TREE SUCKS ITS NUTRIENTS THROUGH ITS ROOTS!
YET, THIS MAN IS GIVING ENERGY THROUGH HIS HAND! IT'S THE EXACT OPPOSITE!
THIS IS JUST A HUNCH, BUT...
IF I COULD USE THIS POWER, I COULD RESIST THE MASK IN A TIME OF NEED!
YOU SAY YOU WISH TO USE THE HAMON? YOU, A WESTERNER?
IT WON'T BE EASY. SOME LOSE THEIR LIVES ATTEMPTING TO DO SO.
I HAVE A REASON TO RISK MY LIFE TO LEARN!

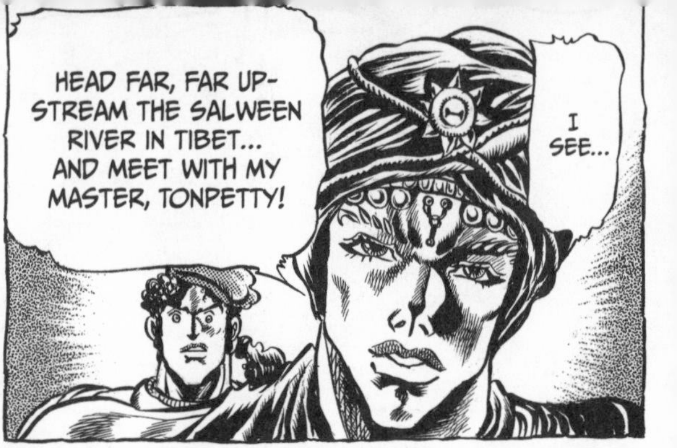
HEAD FAR, FAR UP-STREAM THE SALWEEN RIVER IN TIBET... AND MEET WITH MY MASTER, TONPETTY!
I SEE...
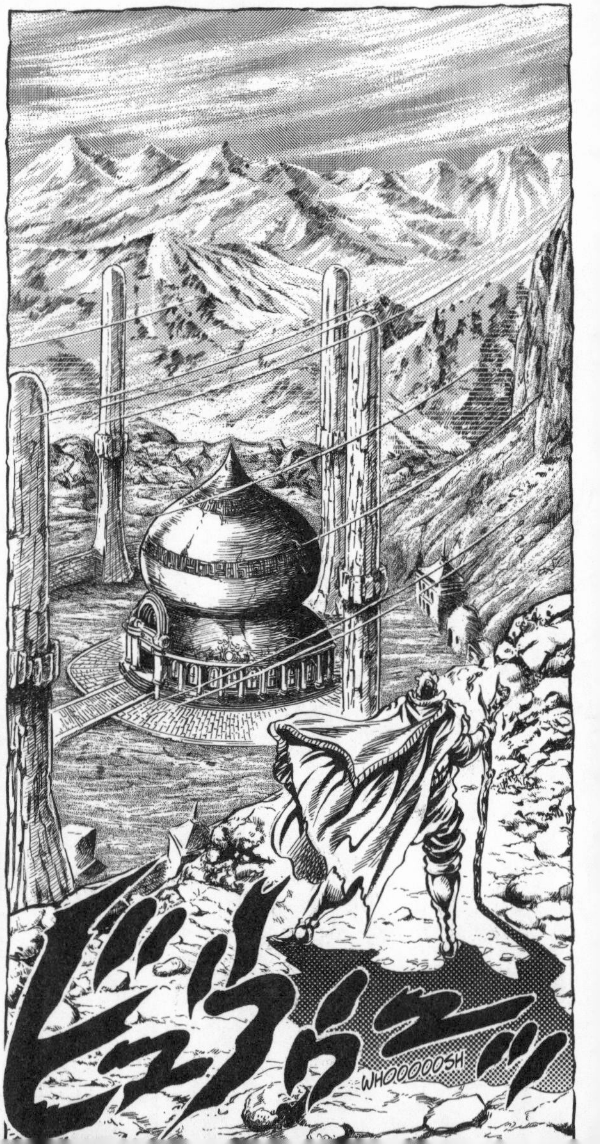
WHOOOOOSH
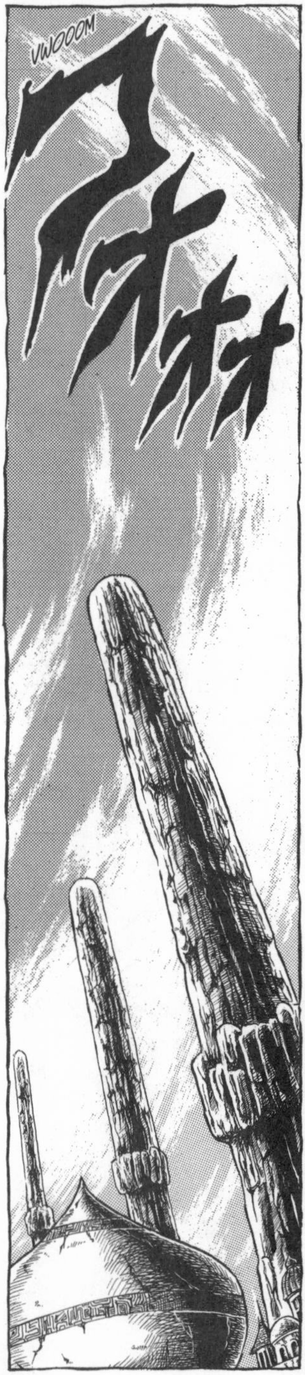
VWOOOM

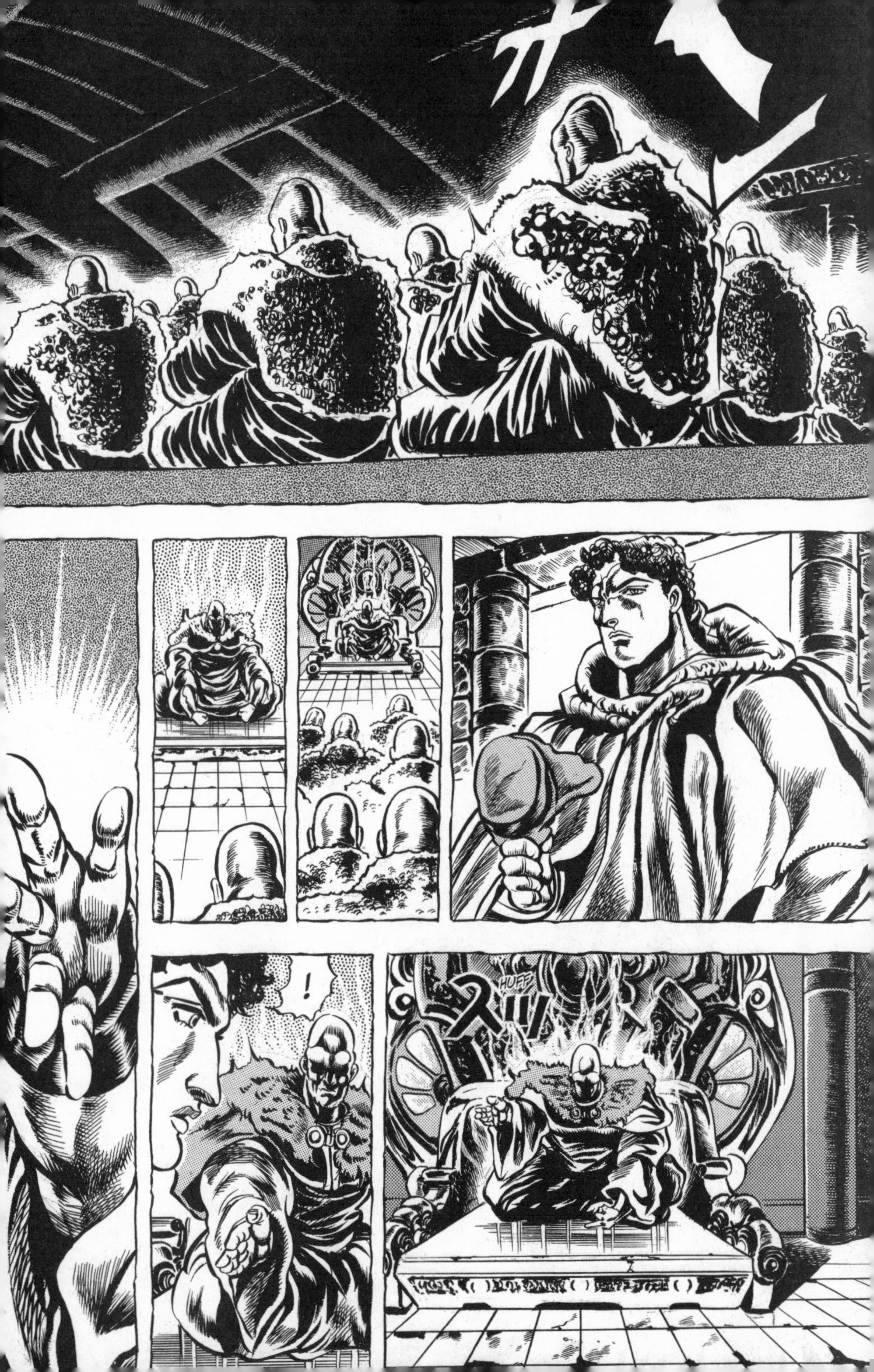
HUFF
!

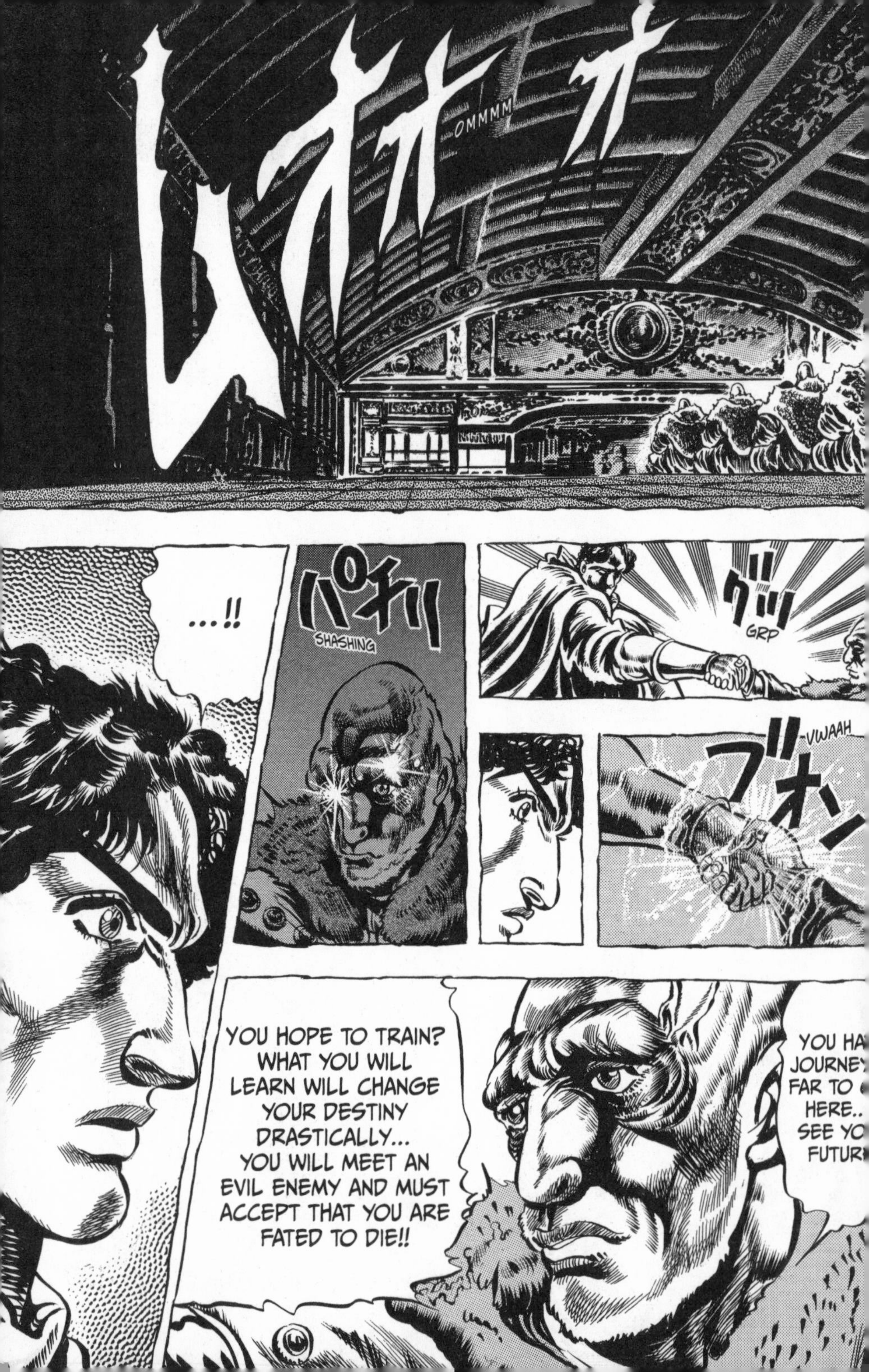
OMMMM
GRP
VWAAH
SHASHING
...!!
YOU HA
JOURNEY
FAR TO
HERE..
SEE YO
FUTUR
YOU HOPE TO TRAIN? WHAT YOU WILL LEARN WILL CHANGE YOUR DESTINY DRASTICALLY... YOU WILL MEET AN EVIL ENEMY AND MUST ACCEPT THAT YOU ARE FATED TO DIE!!

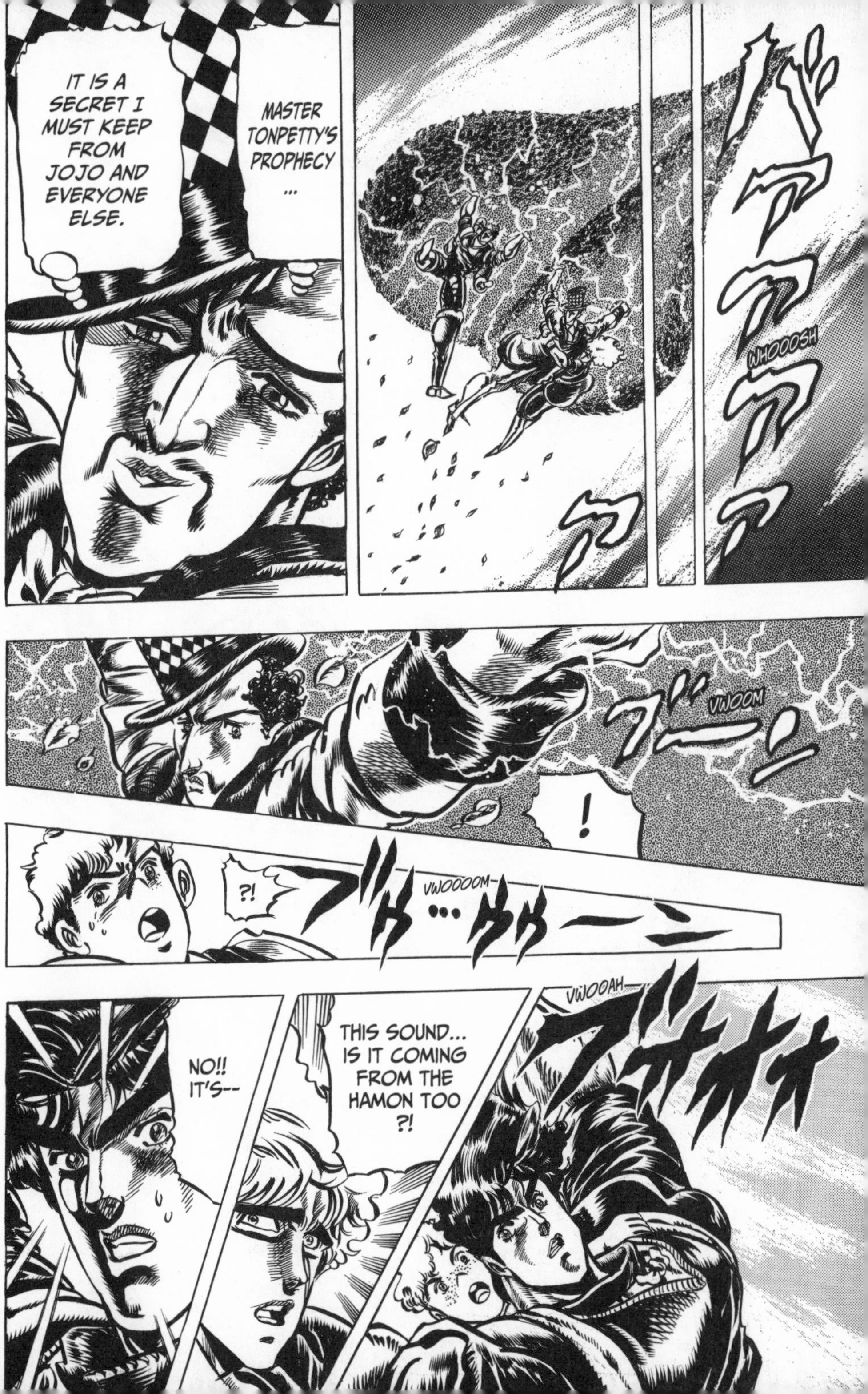
WHOOOSH
MASTER TONPETTY'S PROPHECY ...
IT IS A SECRET I MUST KEEP FROM JOJO AND EVERYONE ELSE.
VWOOM
!
VWOOOOM-
?!
VWOOAH
THIS SOUND... IS IT COMING FROM THE HAMON TOO ?!
NO!! IT'S--

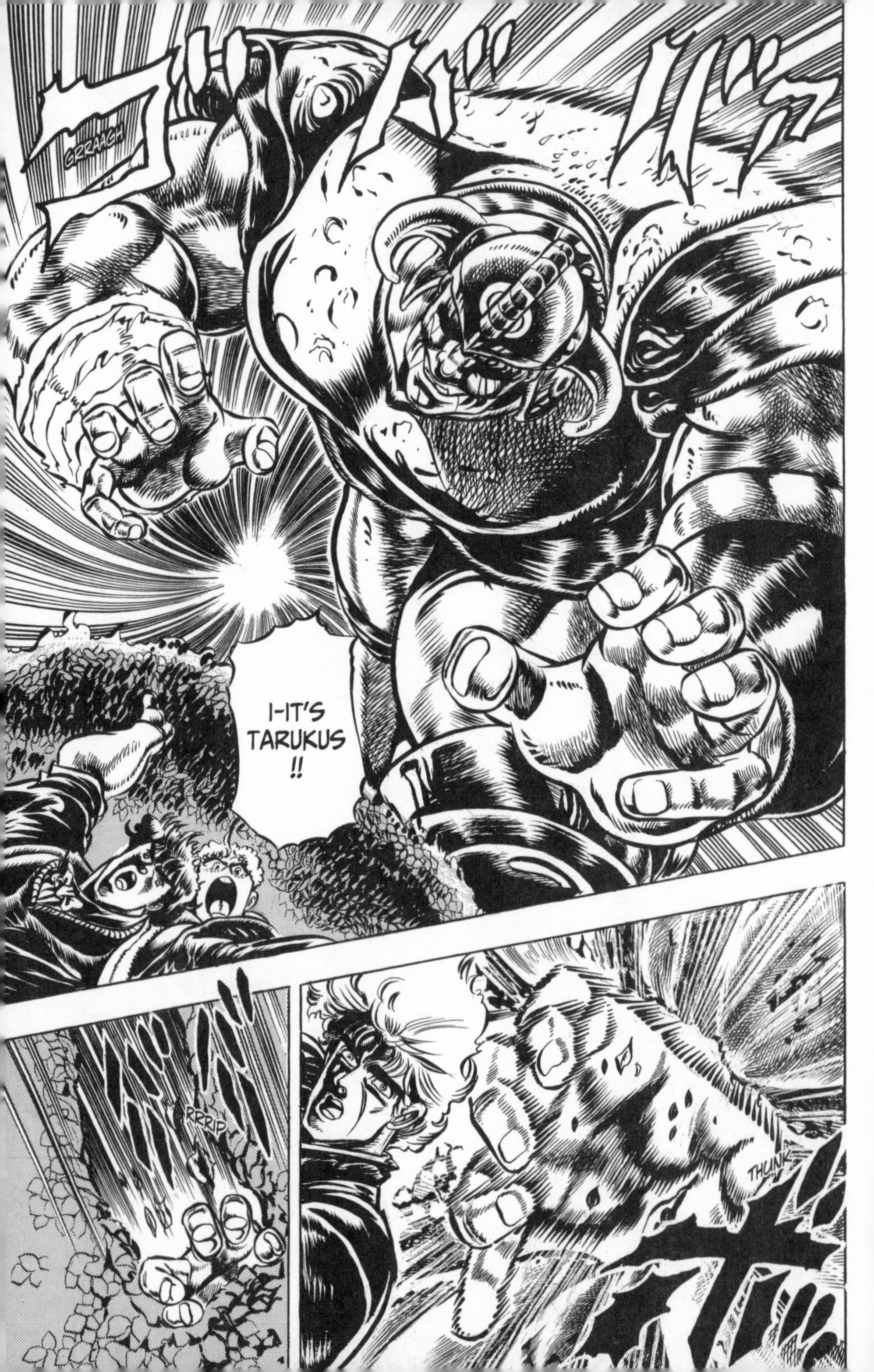
GRRAAGH
I-IT'S TARUKUS !!
THUNK
RRRIP

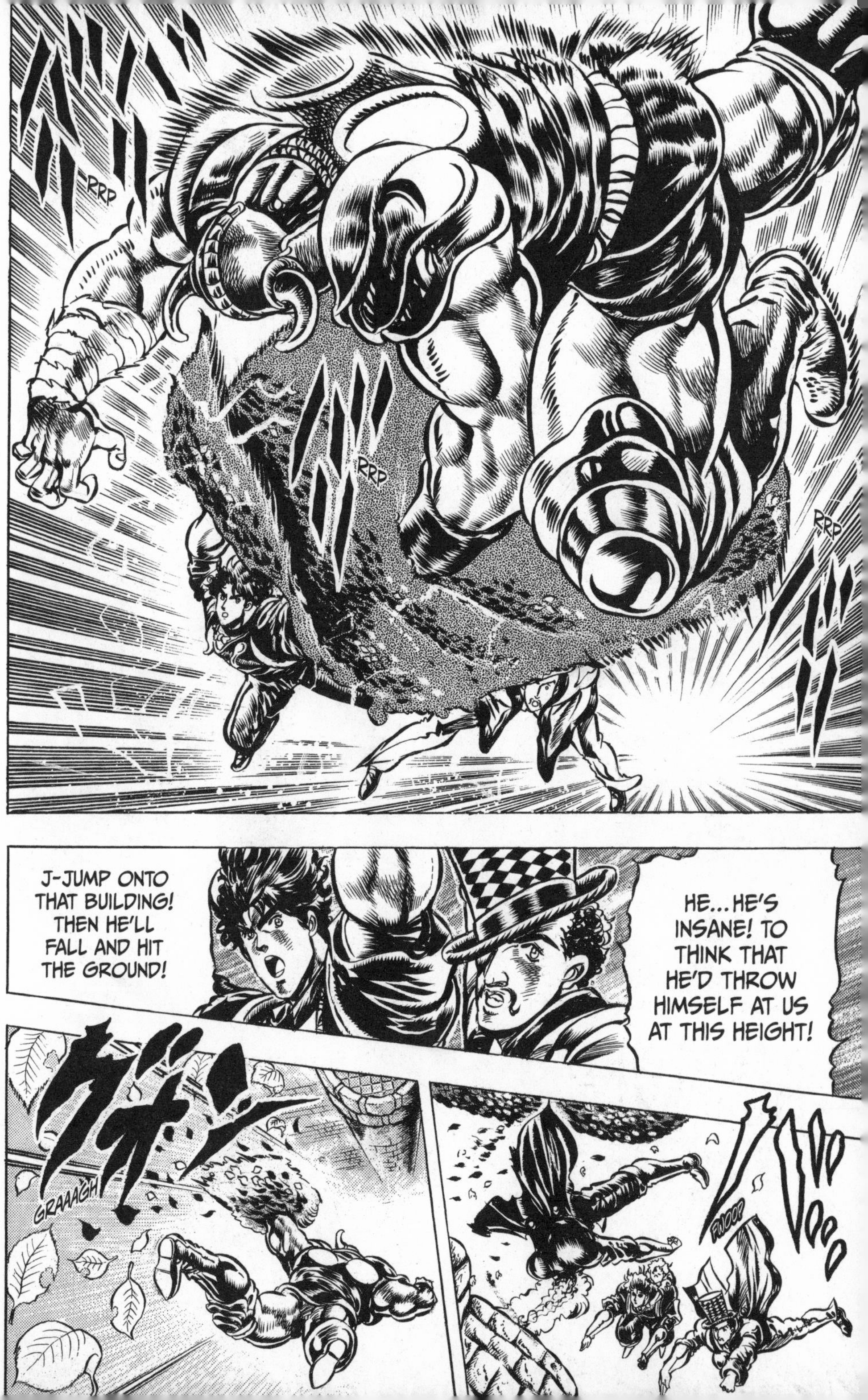
RRP
RRP
RRP
HE...HE'S INSANE! TO THINK THAT HE'D THROW HIMSELF AT US AT THIS HEIGHT!
J-JUMP ONTO THAT BUILDING! THEN HE'LL FALL AND HIT THE GROUND!
FWOOP
GRAAAGH

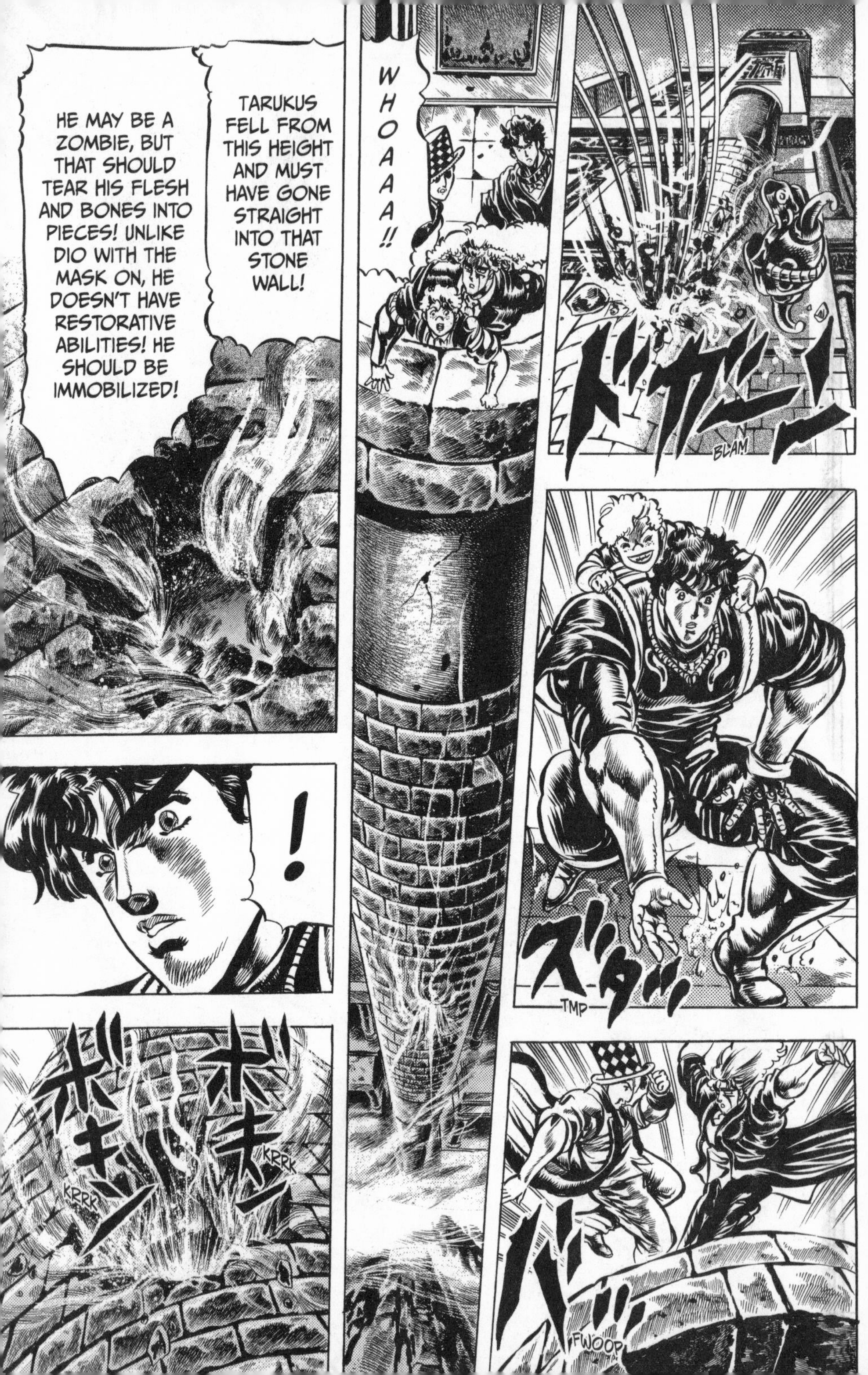
BLAM
WHOAAAA!!
TARUKUS FELL FROM THIS HEIGHT AND MUST HAVE GONE STRAIGHT INTO THAT STONE WALL!
HE MAY BE A ZOMBIE, BUT THAT SHOULD TEAR HIS FLESH AND BONES INTO PIECES! UNLIKE DIO WITH THE MASK ON, HE DOESN'T HAVE RESTORATIVE ABILITIES! HE SHOULD BE IMMOBILIZED!
TMP
!
FWOOP
KRRK
KRRK

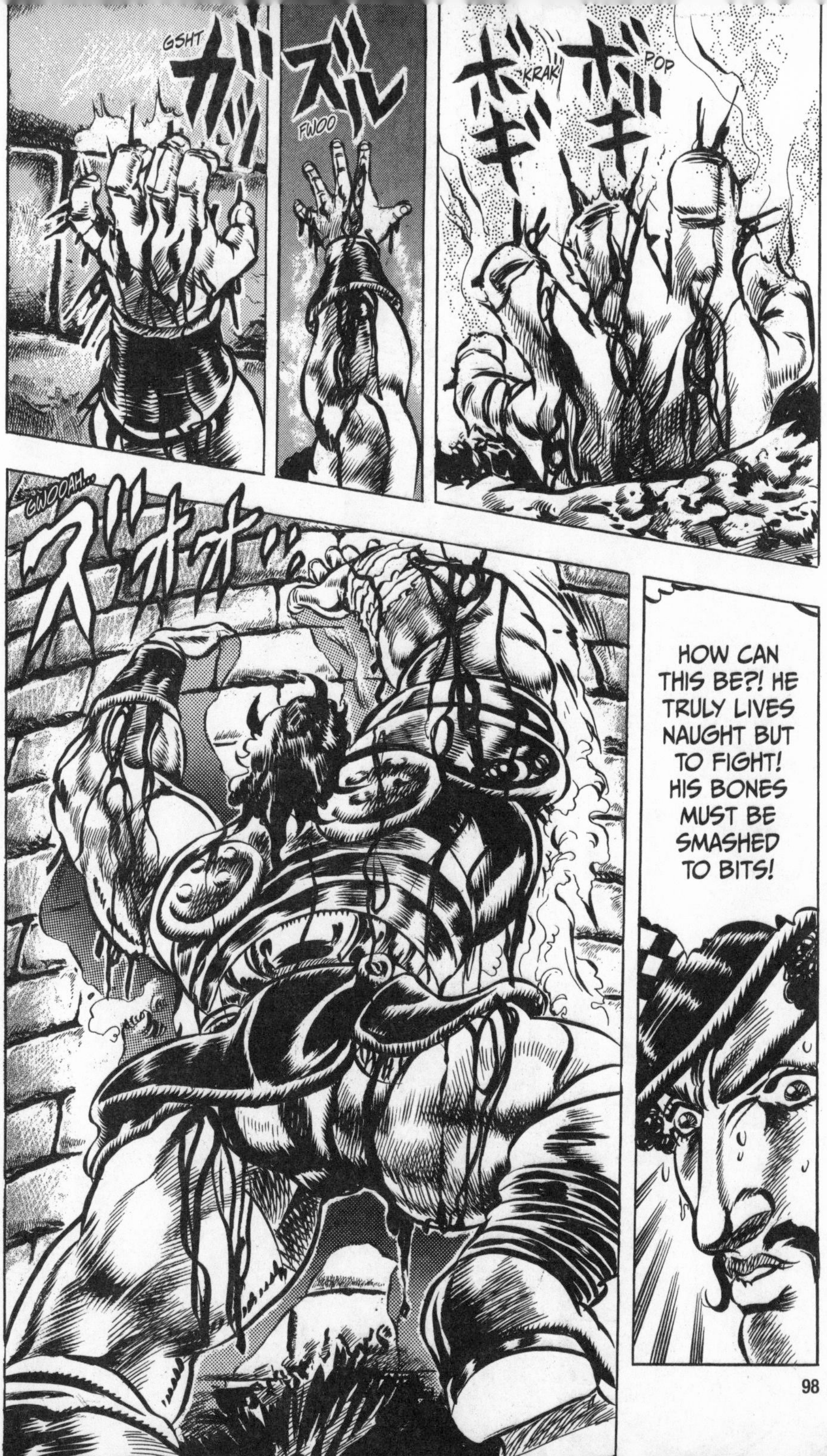
POP
ボギ
KRAK
ボギ
ズル
FWOO
GSHT
ガッ
HOW CAN THIS BE?! HE TRULY LIVES NAUGHT BUT TO FIGHT! HIS BONES MUST BE SMASHED TO BITS!
GWOOAH...
ズオオッ

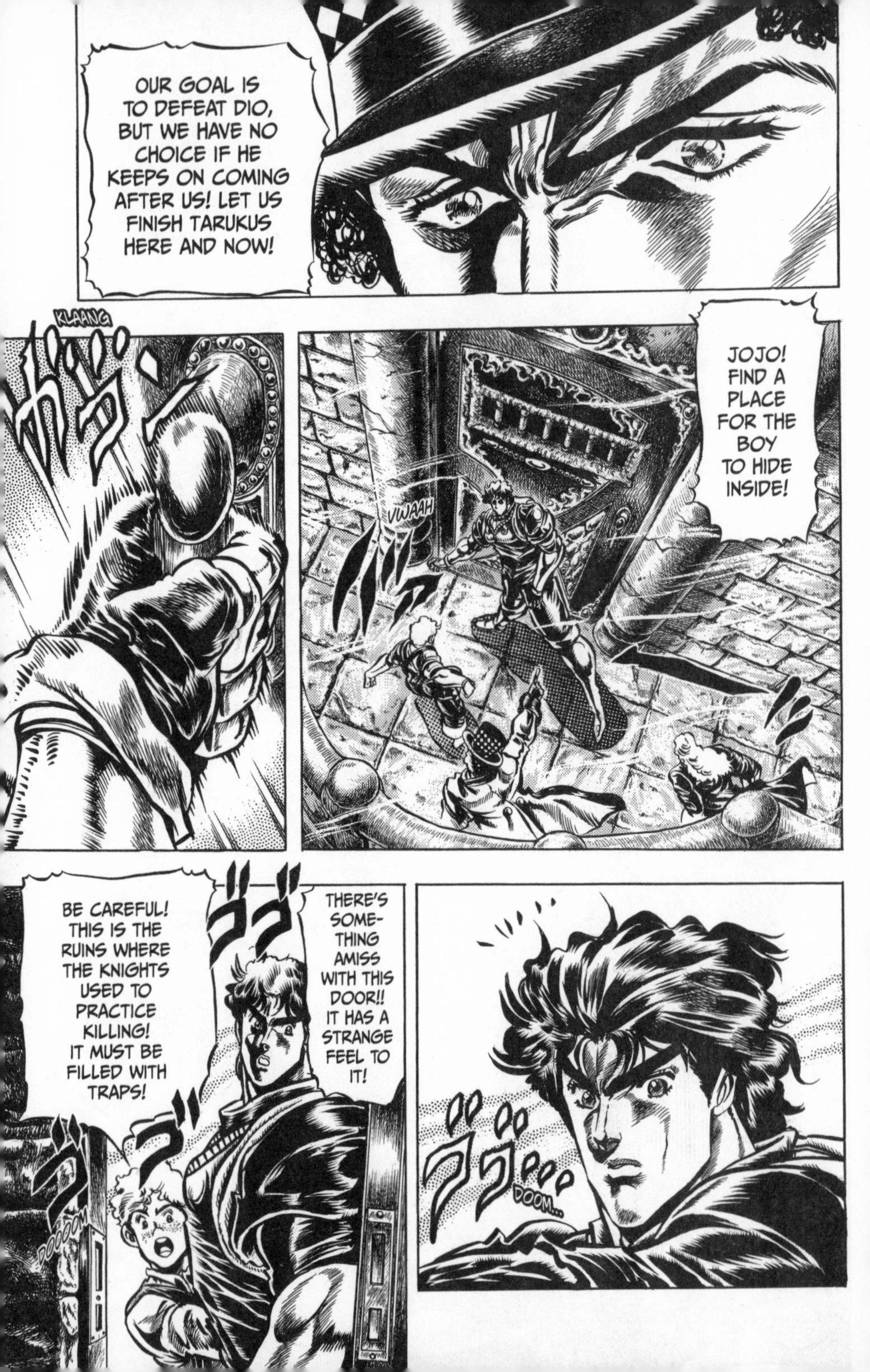
OUR GOAL IS TO DEFEAT DIO, BUT WE HAVE NO CHOICE IF HE KEEPS ON COMING AFTER US! LET US FINISH TARUKUS HERE AND NOW!
JOJO! FIND A PLACE FOR THE BOY TO HIDE INSIDE!
VWAAH
KLAANG
DOOM...
THERE'S SOME-THING AMISS WITH THIS DOOR!! IT HAS A STRANGE FEEL TO IT!
BE CAREFUL! THIS IS THE RUINS WHERE THE KNIGHTS USED TO PRACTICE KILLING! IT MUST BE FILLED WITH TRAPS!
DOOOOM

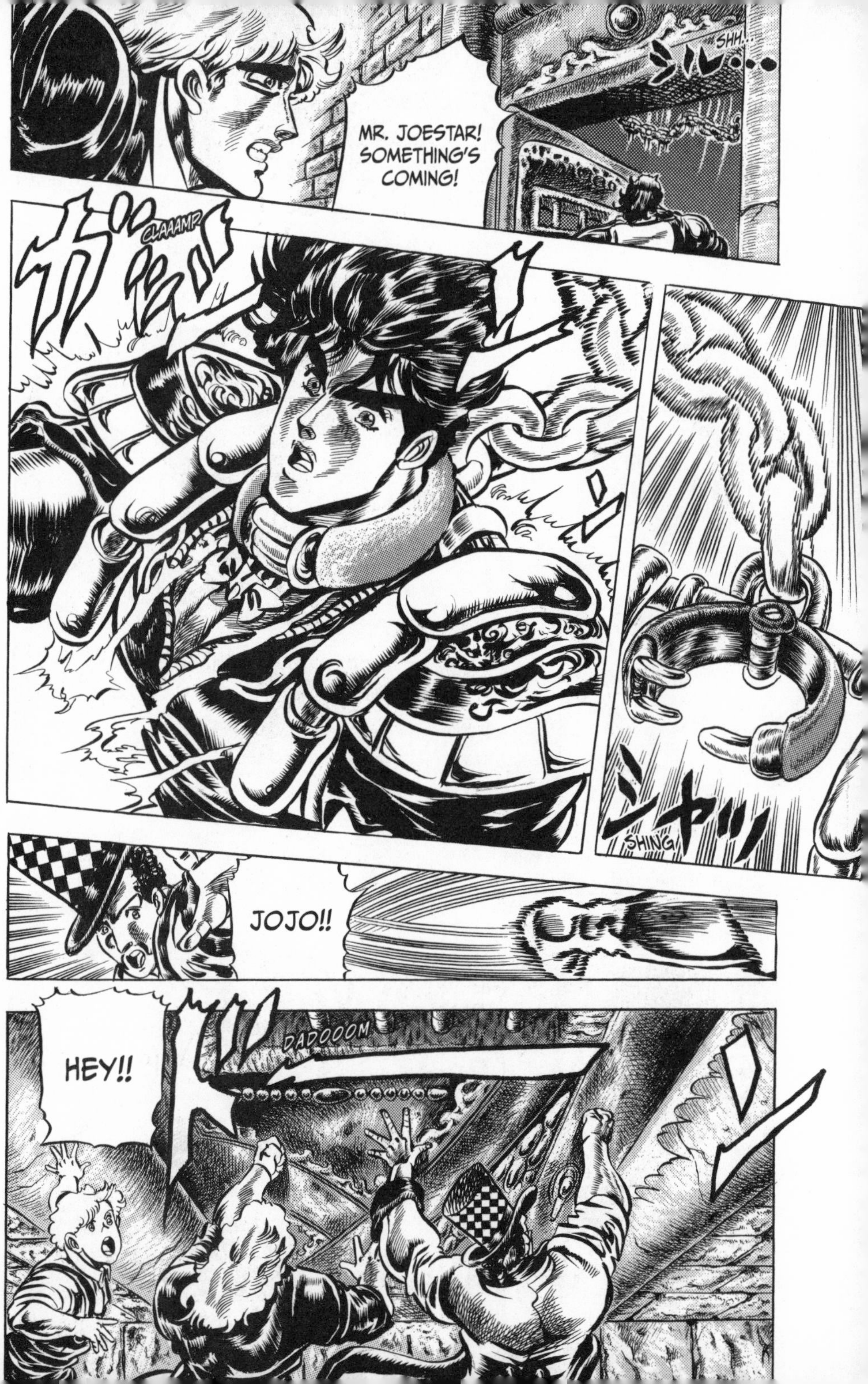
SHH...
シル…
MR. JOESTAR! SOMETHING'S COMING!
シャッ
SHING
CLAAAMP
JOJO!!
HEY!!
DADOOOM

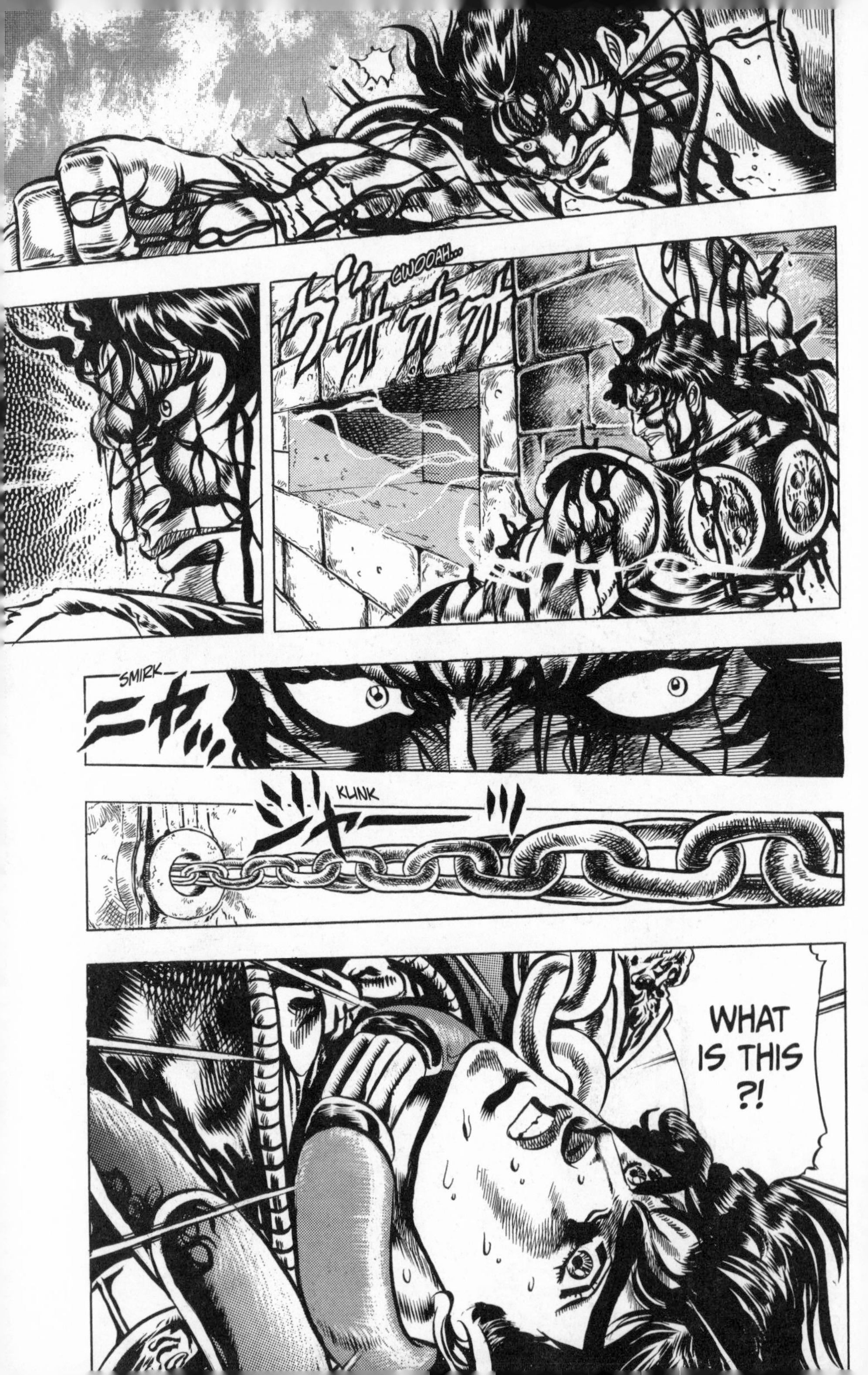
GWOOAH...
SMIRK
KLUNK
WHAT IS THIS ?!

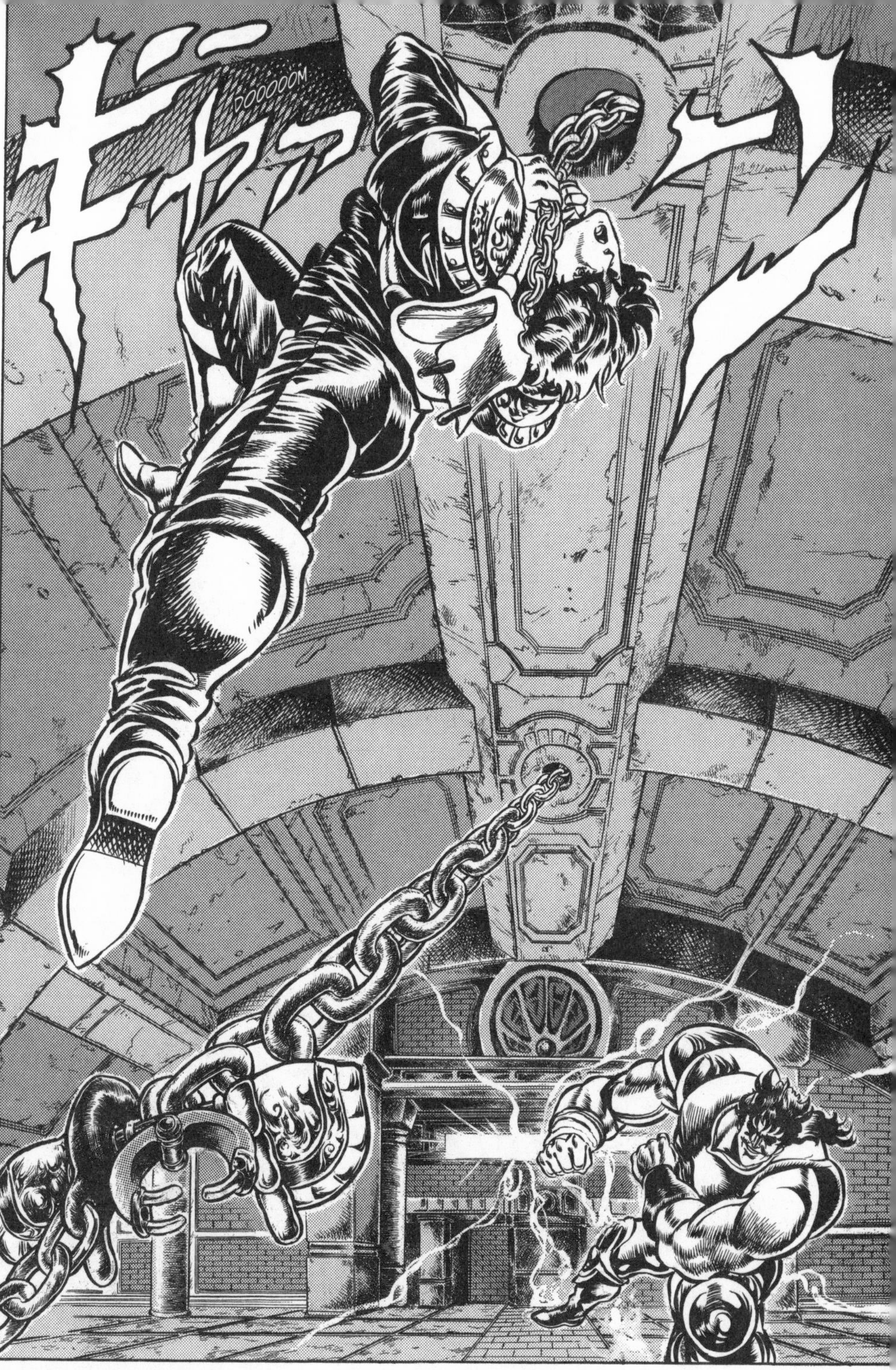
ギャァァーン
DOOOOOM

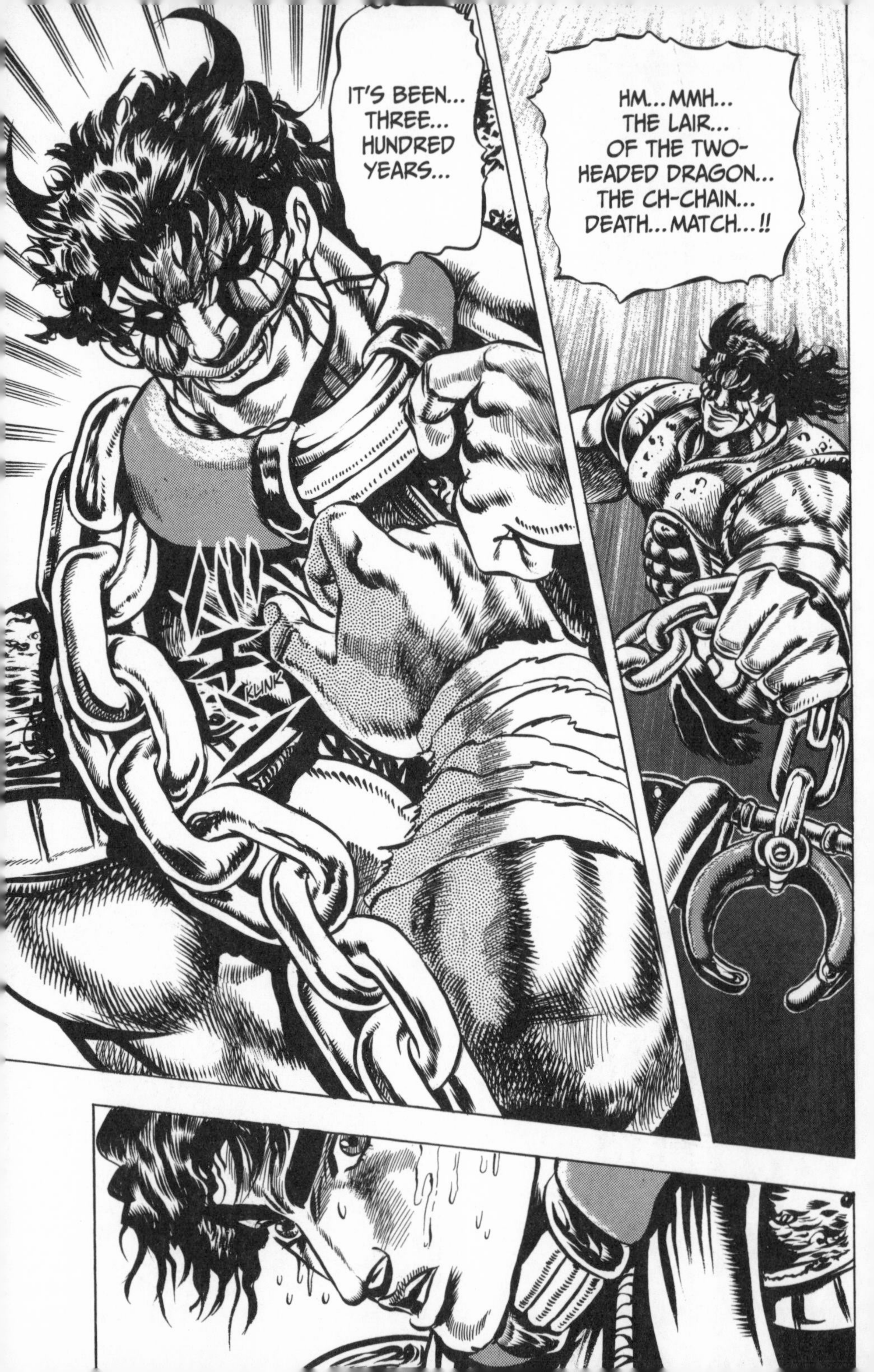
HM...MMH... THE LAIR... OF THE TWO-HEADED DRAGON... THE CH-CHAIN... DEATH...MATCH...!!
IT'S BEEN... THREE... HUNDRED YEARS...
KLUNK

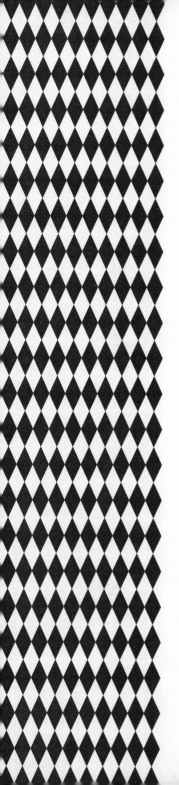

JoJo's
BIZARRE ADVENTURE

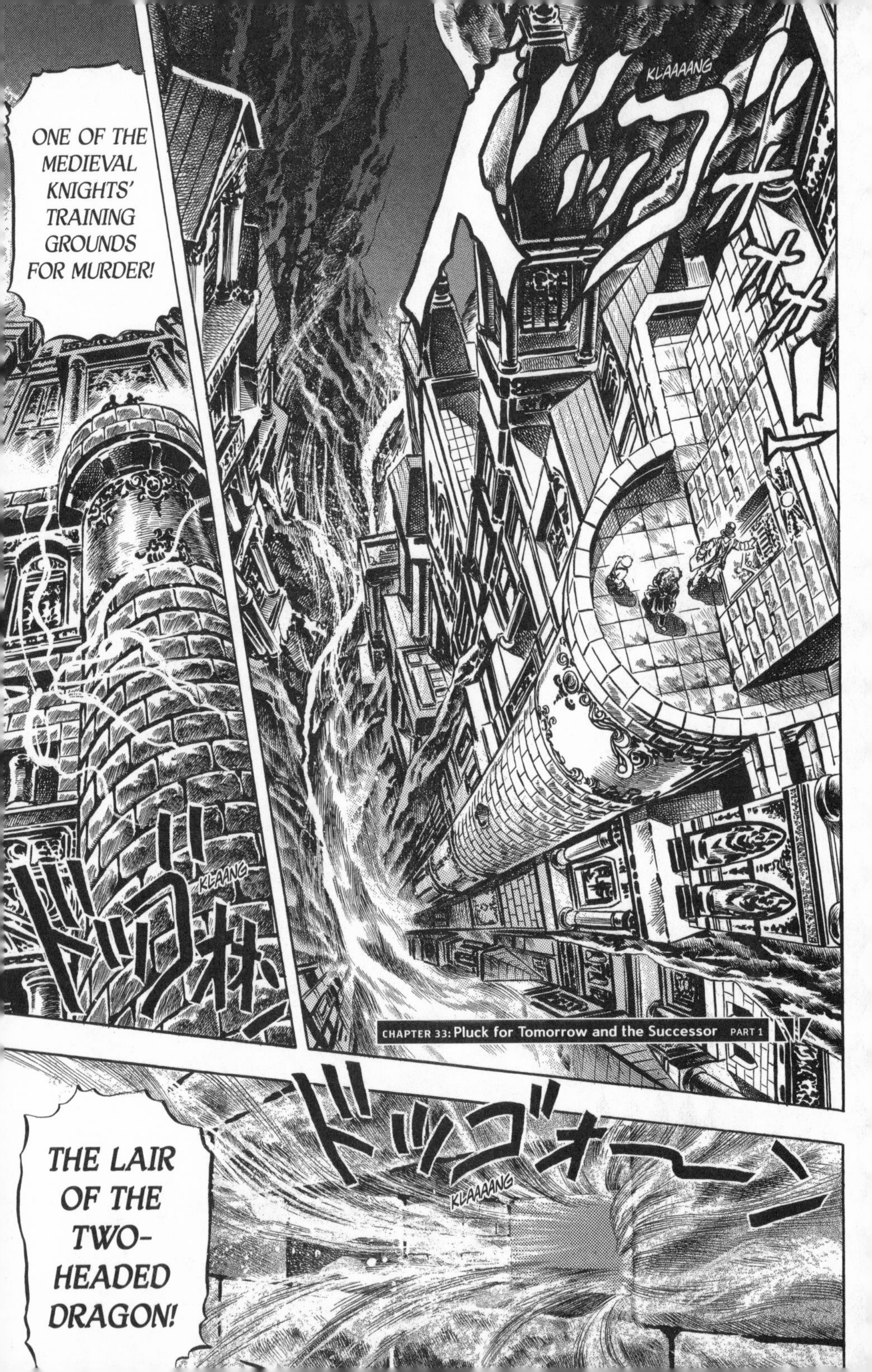
KLAAAANG
CHAPTER 33: Pluck for Tomorrow and the Successor PART 1
ONE OF THE MEDIEVAL KNIGHTS' TRAINING GROUNDS FOR MURDER!
KLAANG
THE LAIR OF THE TWO-HEADED DRAGON!
KLAAAANG

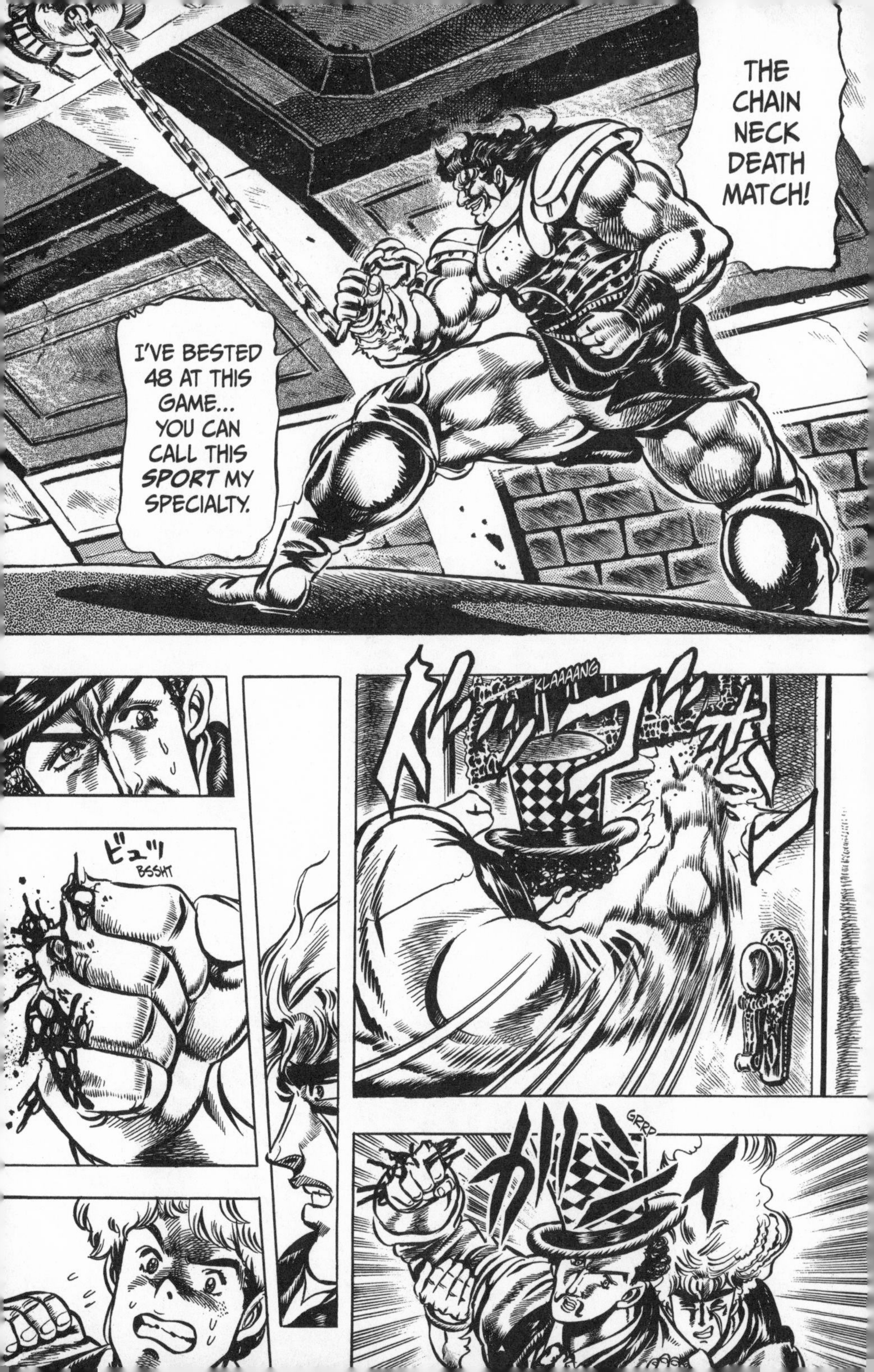
THE CHAIN NECK DEATH MATCH!
I'VE BESTED 48 AT THIS GAME... YOU CAN CALL THIS *SPORT* MY SPECIALTY.
KLAAAANG
GRRP
ビュッ
BSSHT

CHAPTER 33: Pluck for Tomorrow and the Successor PART 1

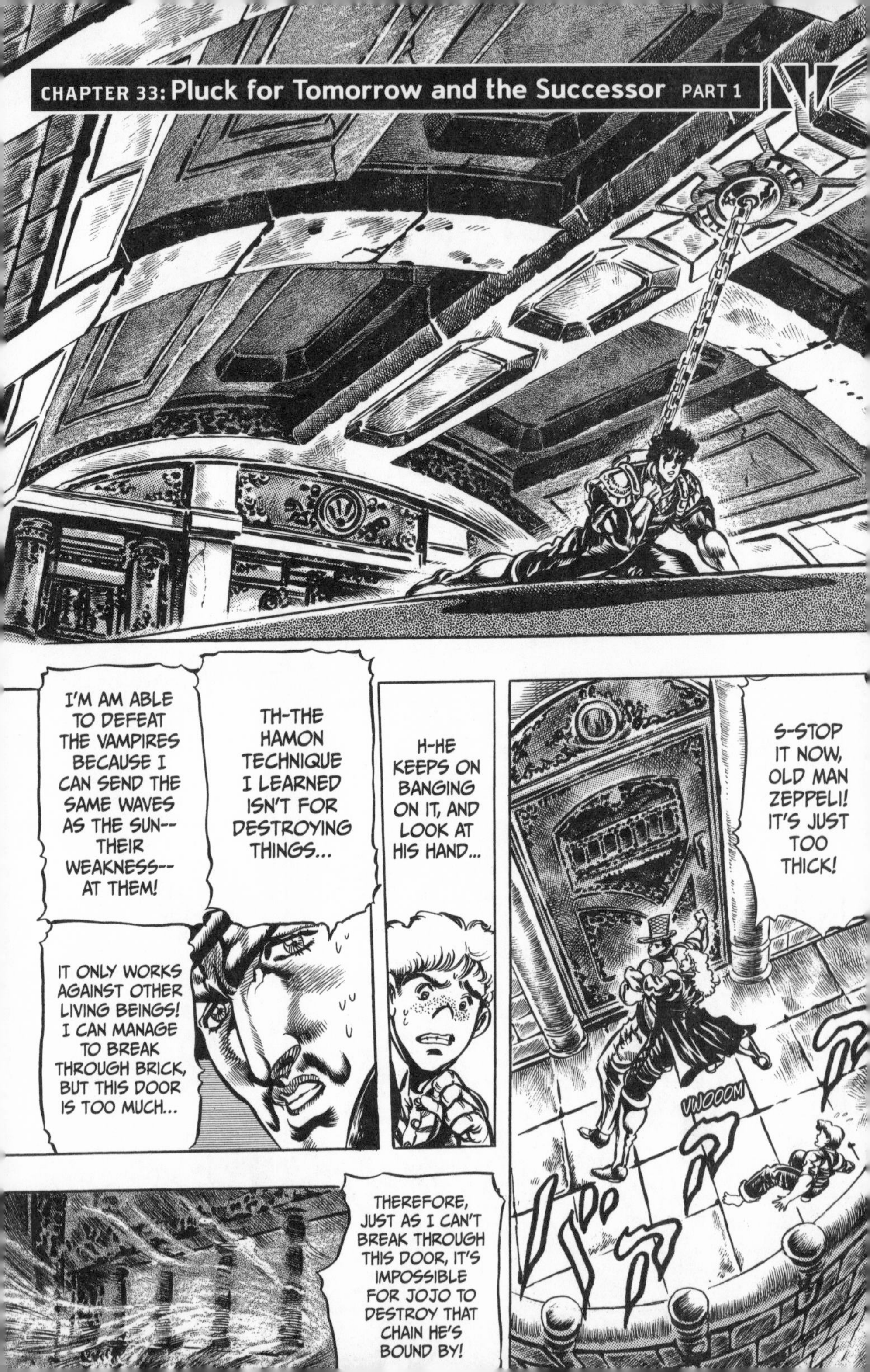
S-STOP IT NOW, OLD MAN ZEPPELI! IT'S JUST TOO THICK!
VWOOOM
DO
H-HE KEEPS ON BANGING ON IT, AND LOOK AT HIS HAND...
TH-THE HAMON TECHNIQUE I LEARNED ISN'T FOR DESTROYING THINGS...
I'M AM ABLE TO DEFEAT THE VAMPIRES BECAUSE I CAN SEND THE SAME WAVES AS THE SUN--THEIR WEAKNESS--AT THEM!
IT ONLY WORKS AGAINST OTHER LIVING BEINGS! I CAN MANAGE TO BREAK THROUGH BRICK, BUT THIS DOOR IS TOO MUCH...
THEREFORE, JUST AS I CAN'T BREAK THROUGH THIS DOOR, IT'S IMPOSSIBLE FOR JOJO TO DESTROY THAT CHAIN HE'S BOUND BY!

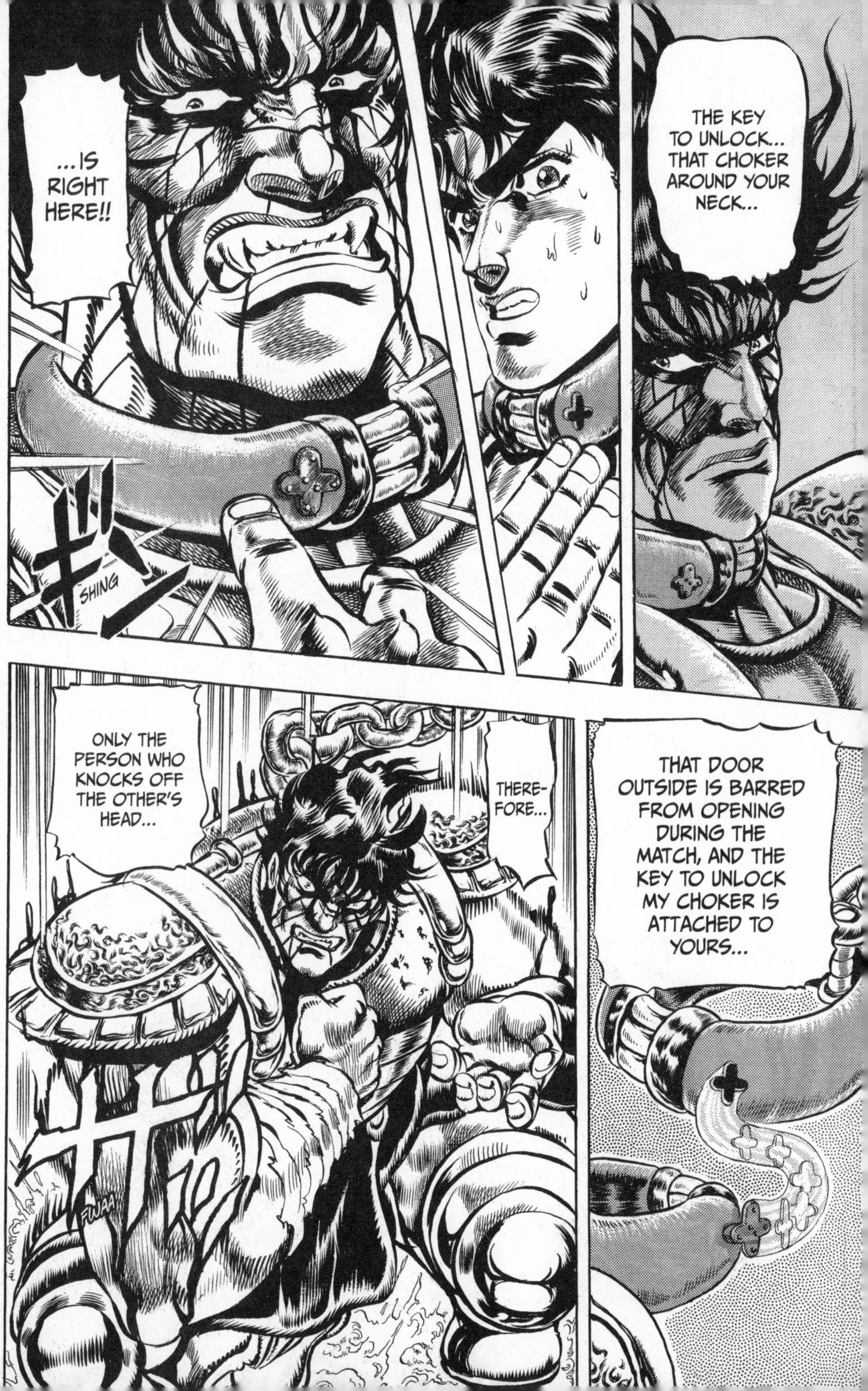
THE KEY TO UNLOCK... THAT CHOKER AROUND YOUR NECK...
...IS RIGHT HERE!!
SHING
THAT DOOR OUTSIDE IS BARRED FROM OPENING DURING THE MATCH, AND THE KEY TO UNLOCK MY CHOKER IS ATTACHED TO YOURS...
THERE-FORE...
ONLY THE PERSON WHO KNOCKS OFF THE OTHER'S HEAD...
FWAA

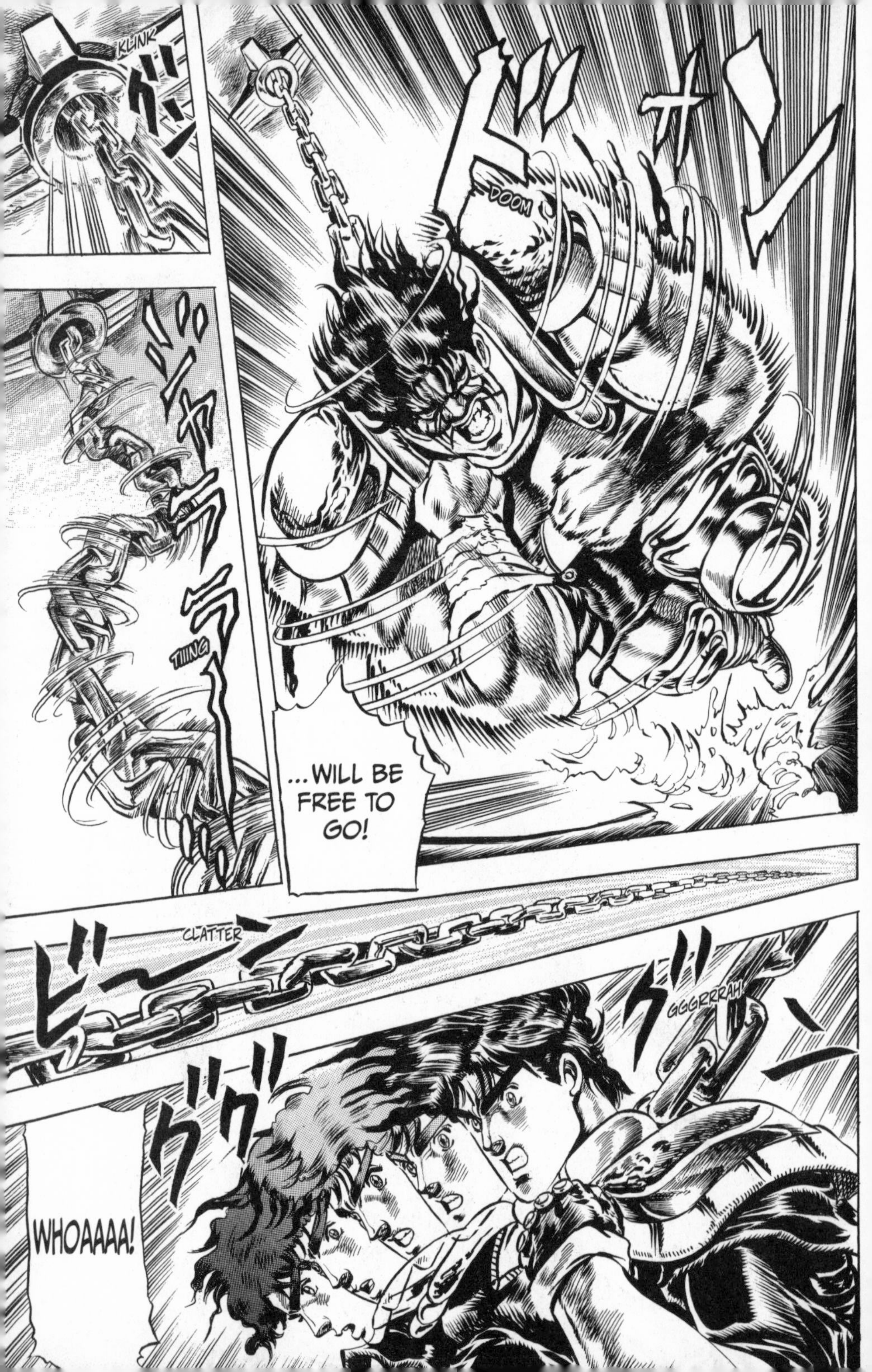
DOOM
...WILL BE FREE TO GO!
KLINK
TIING
GGGRRRAH!
CLATTER
WHOAAAA!

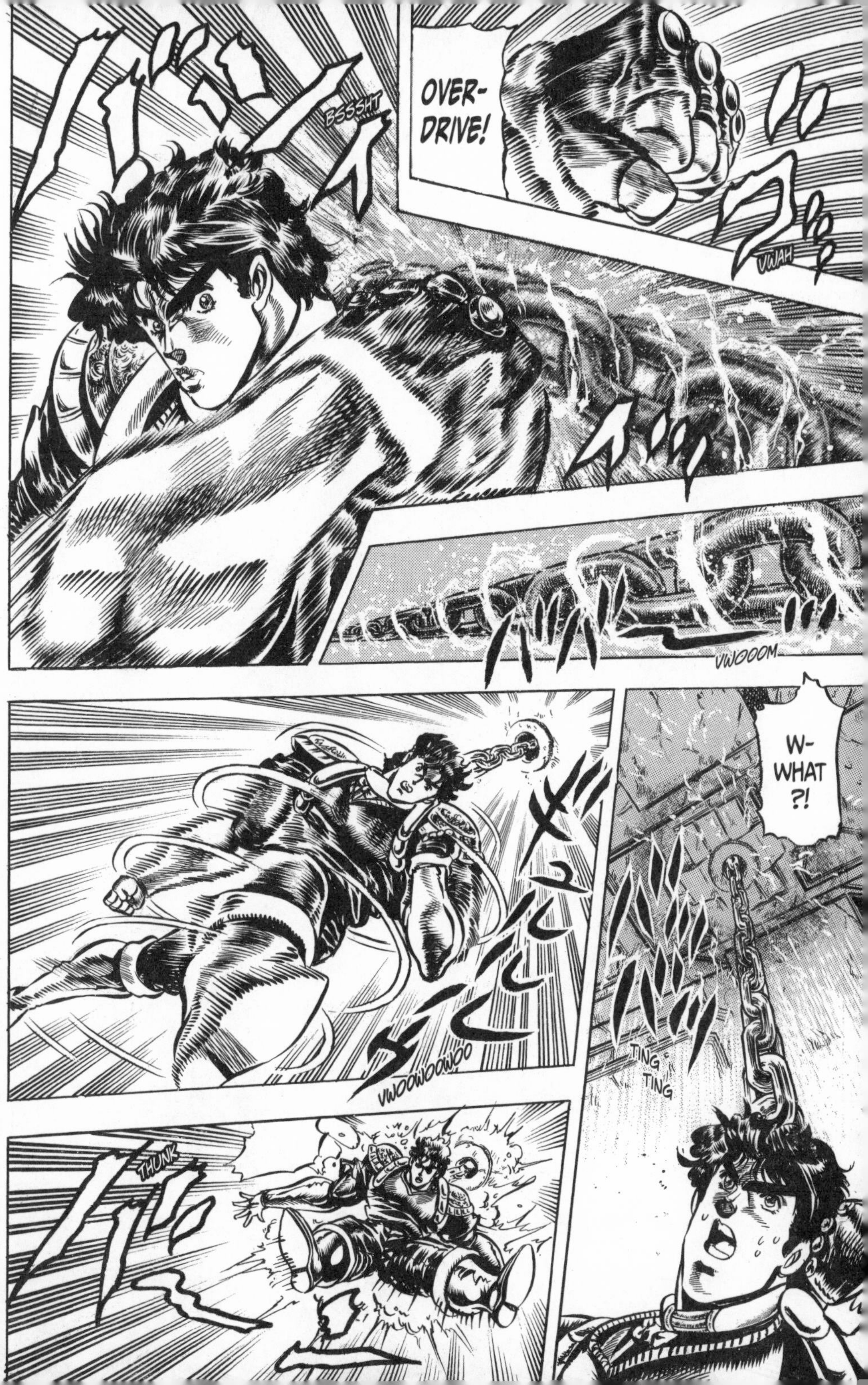
OVER-DRIVE!
VWAH
BSSSHT
VWOOOM
W-WHAT?!
TING TING
VWOOWOOWOO
THUNK

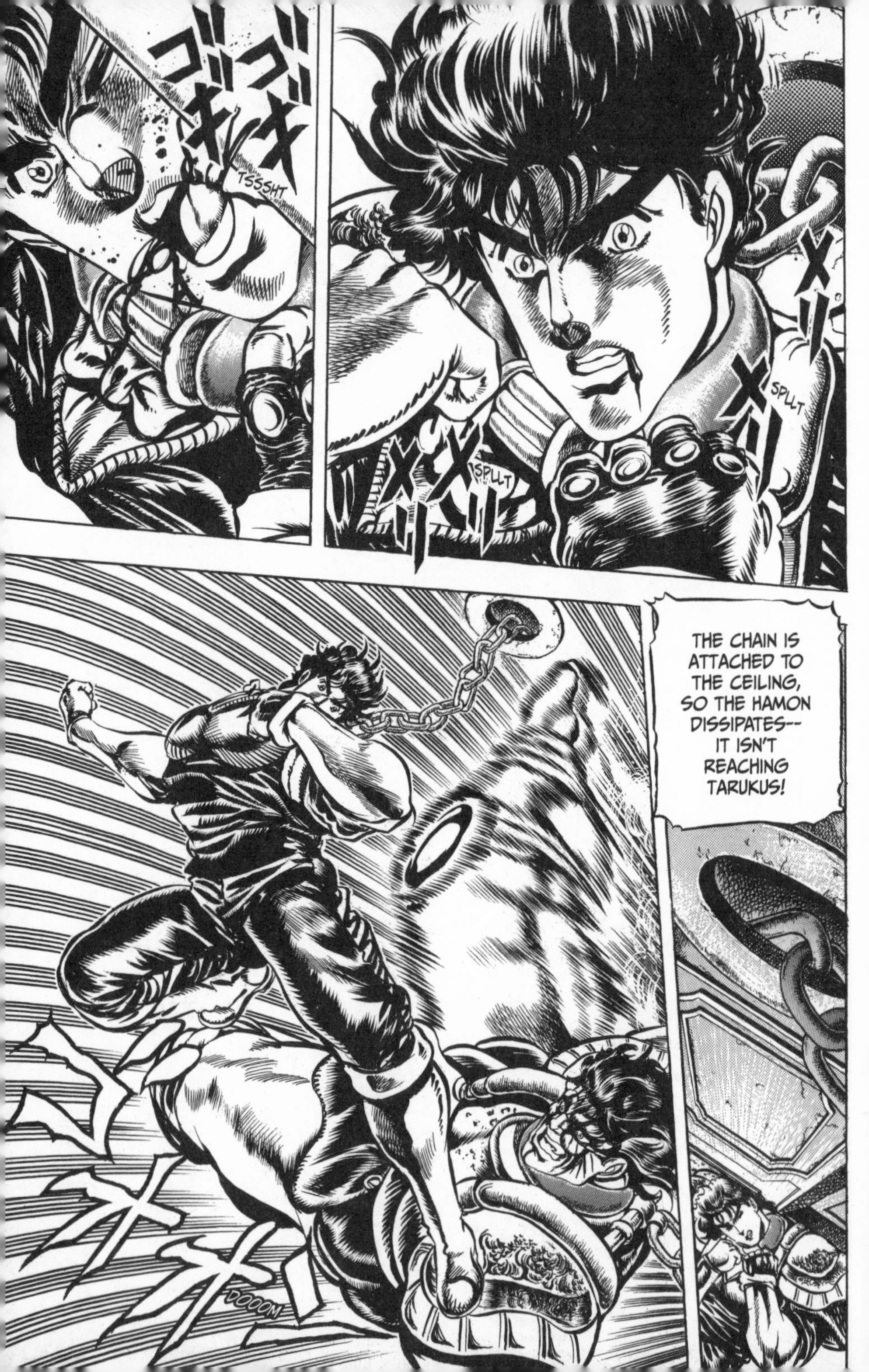
SPLLT
SPLLT
TSSSHT
THE CHAIN IS ATTACHED TO THE CEILING, SO THE HAMON DISSIPATES-- IT ISN'T REACHING TARUKUS!
DOOOM

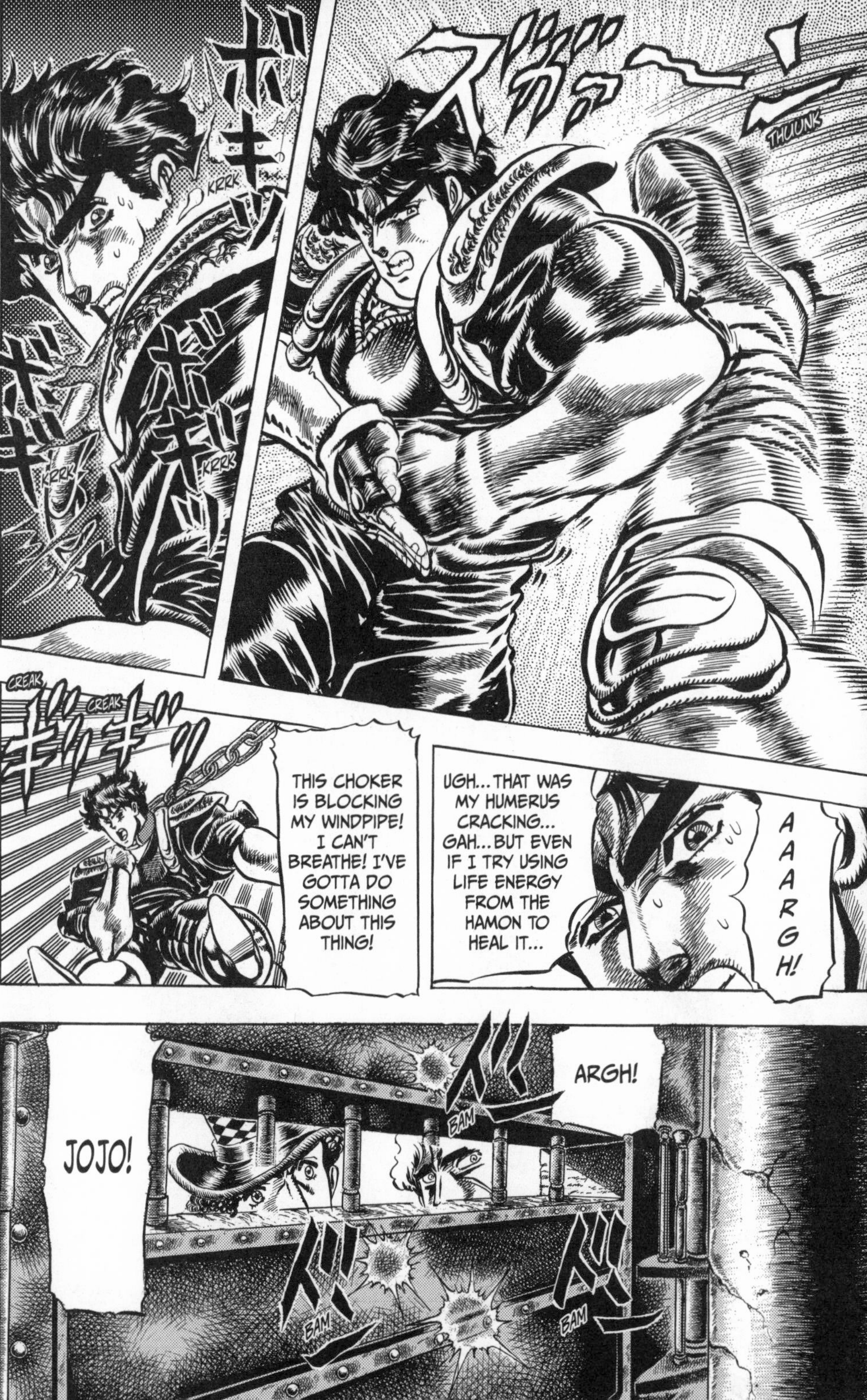
THUUNK
KRRK
KRRK
KRRK
AAAARGH!
UGH... THAT WAS MY HUMERUS CRACKING... GAH... BUT EVEN IF I TRY USING LIFE ENERGY FROM THE HAMON TO HEAL IT...
THIS CHOKER IS BLOCKING MY WINDPIPE! I CAN'T BREATHE! I'VE GOTTA DO SOMETHING ABOUT THIS THING!
CREAK
CREAK
BAM
ARGH!
JOJO!
BAM
BAM

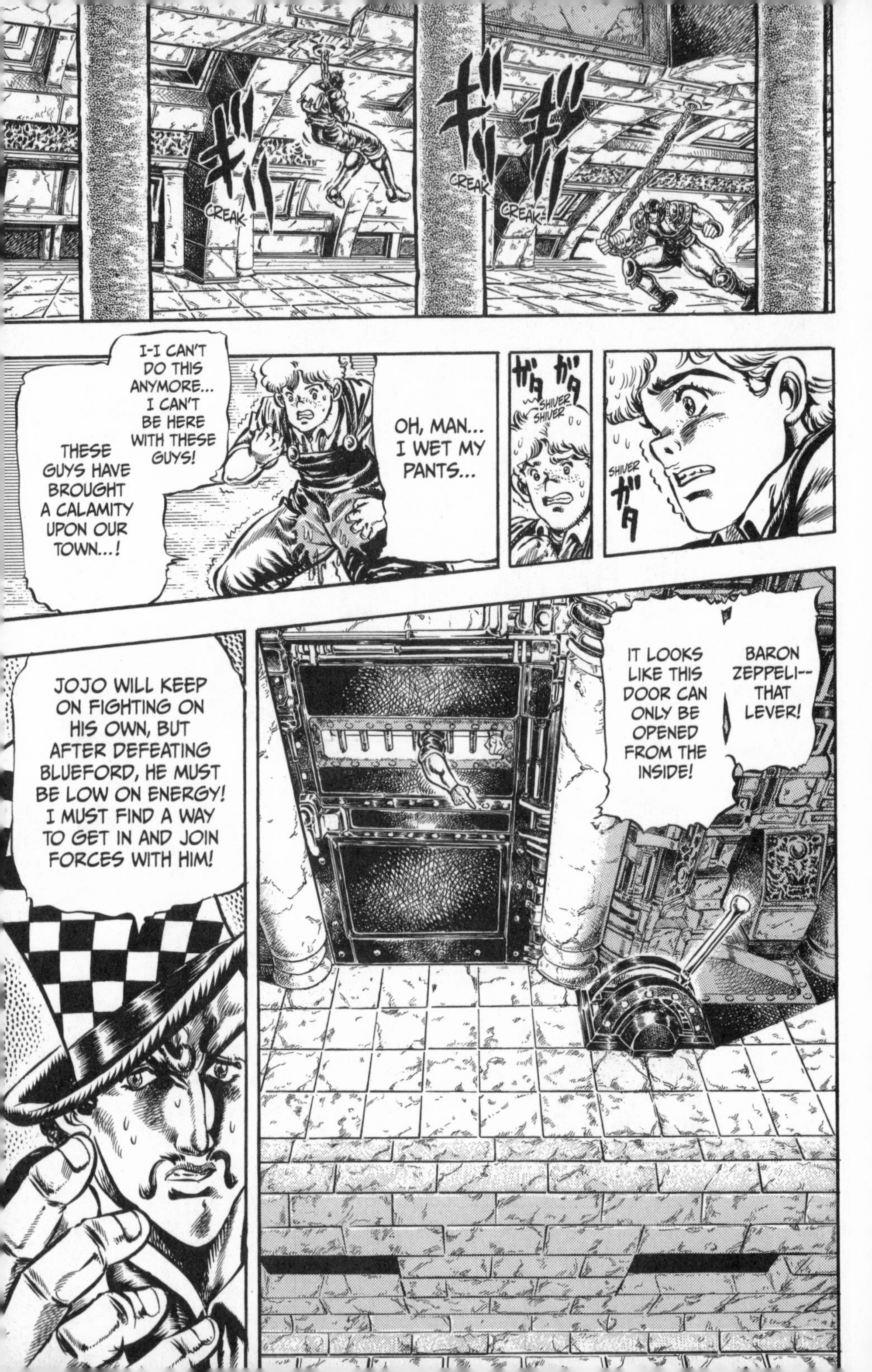
ギ ギ
CREAK
CREAK
ギ
CREAK
SHIVER
ガタ
ガタ ガタ
SHIVER SHIVER
OH, MAN... I WET MY PANTS...
I-I CAN'T DO THIS ANYMORE... I CAN'T BE HERE WITH THESE GUYS!
THESE GUYS HAVE BROUGHT A CALAMITY UPON OUR TOWN...!
BARON ZEPPELI-- THAT LEVER!
IT LOOKS LIKE THIS DOOR CAN ONLY BE OPENED FROM THE INSIDE!
JOJO WILL KEEP ON FIGHTING ON HIS OWN, BUT AFTER DEFEATING BLUEFORD, HE MUST BE LOW ON ENERGY! I MUST FIND A WAY TO GET IN AND JOIN FORCES WITH HIM!

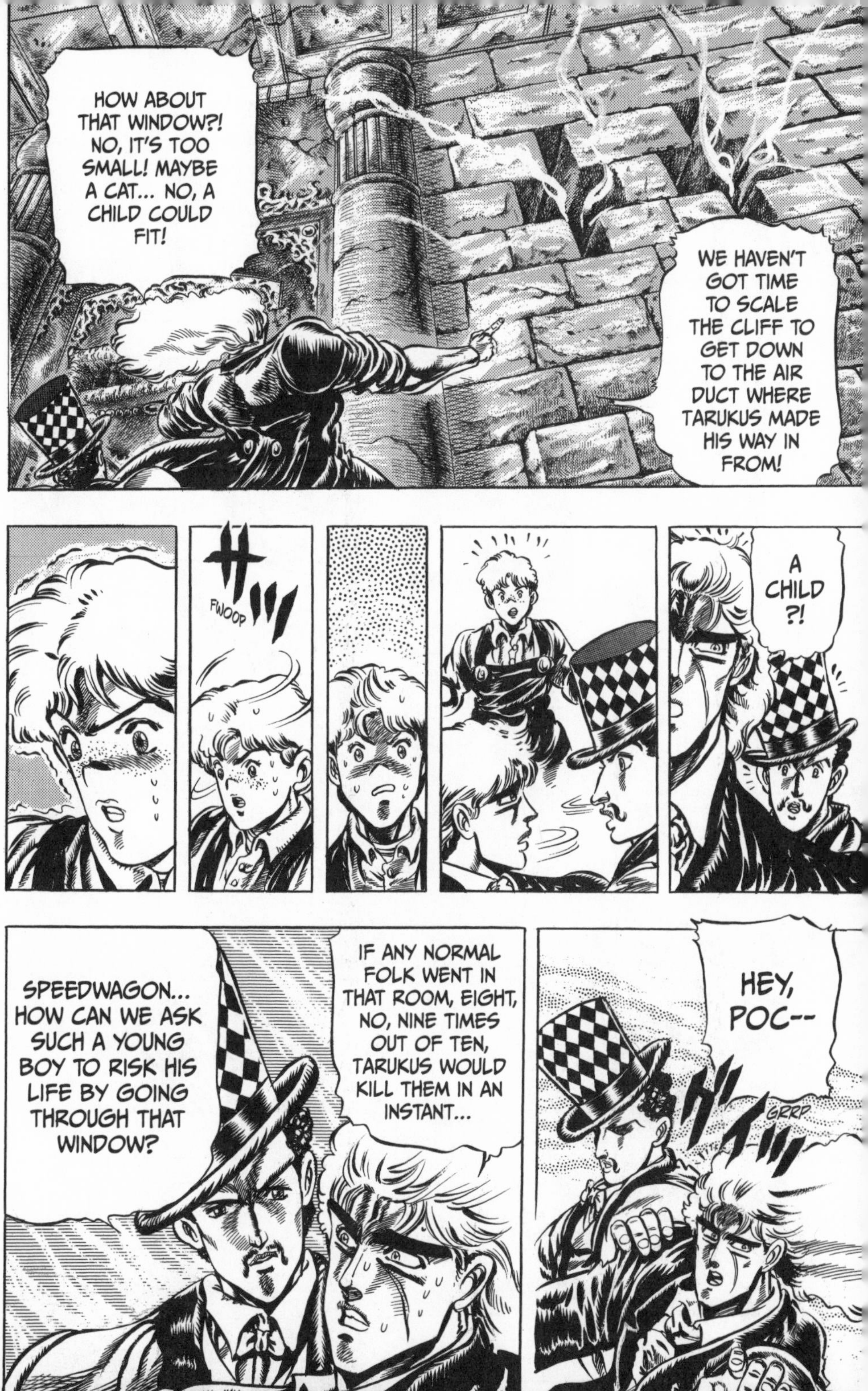
WE HAVEN'T GOT TIME TO SCALE THE CLIFF TO GET DOWN TO THE AIR DUCT WHERE TARUKUS MADE HIS WAY IN FROM!
HOW ABOUT THAT WINDOW?! NO, IT'S TOO SMALL! MAYBE A CAT... NO, A CHILD COULD FIT!
A CHILD ?!
FWOOP
HEY, POC--
GRRP
IF ANY NORMAL FOLK WENT IN THAT ROOM, EIGHT, NO, NINE TIMES OUT OF TEN, TARUKUS WOULD KILL THEM IN AN INSTANT...
SPEEDWAGON... HOW CAN WE ASK SUCH A YOUNG BOY TO RISK HIS LIFE BY GOING THROUGH THAT WINDOW?

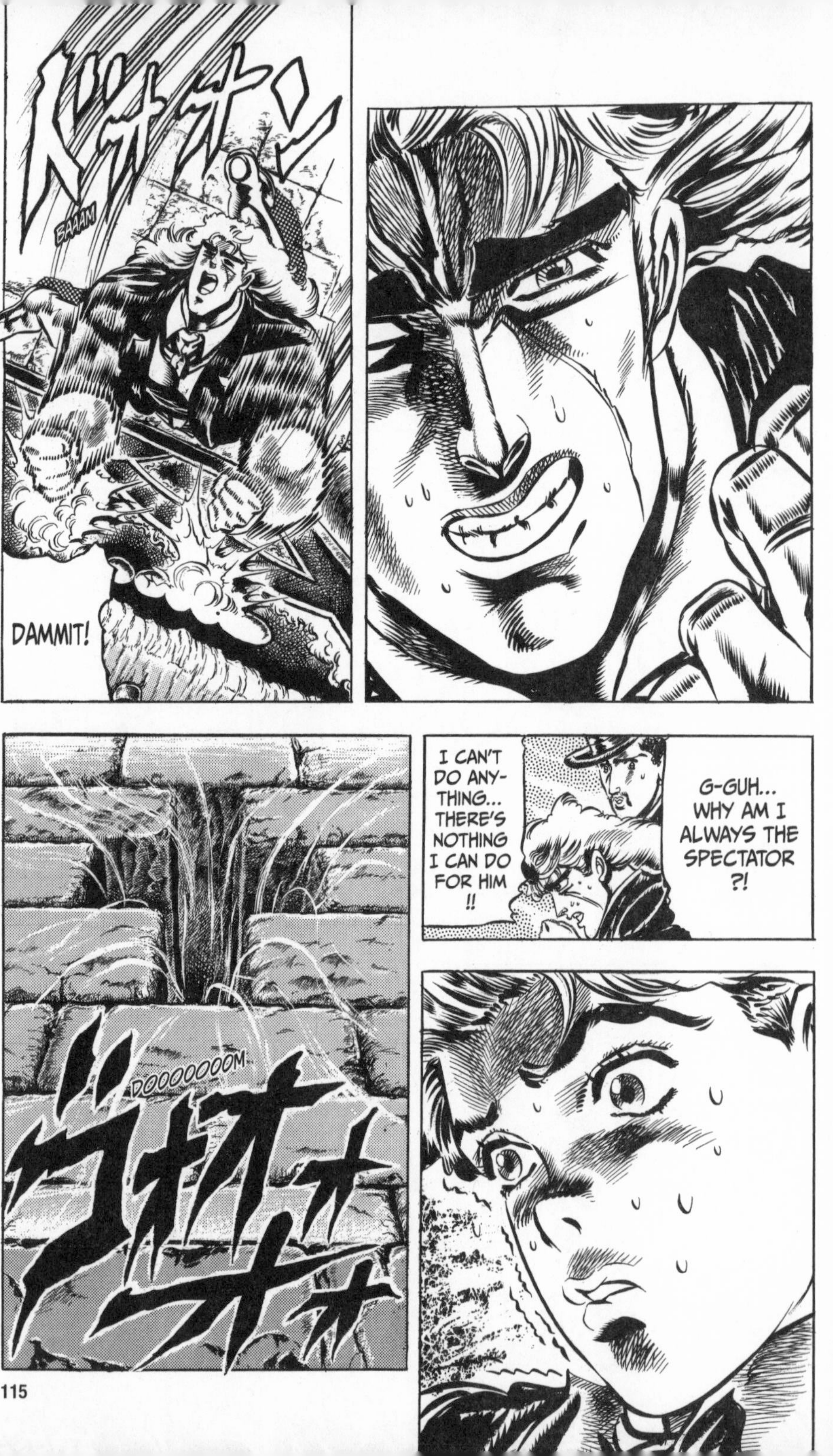
BAAAM
DAMMIT!
G-GUH... WHY AM I ALWAYS THE SPECTATOR ?!
I CAN'T DO ANY-THING... THERE'S NOTHING I CAN DO FOR HIM !!
DOOOOOOOM

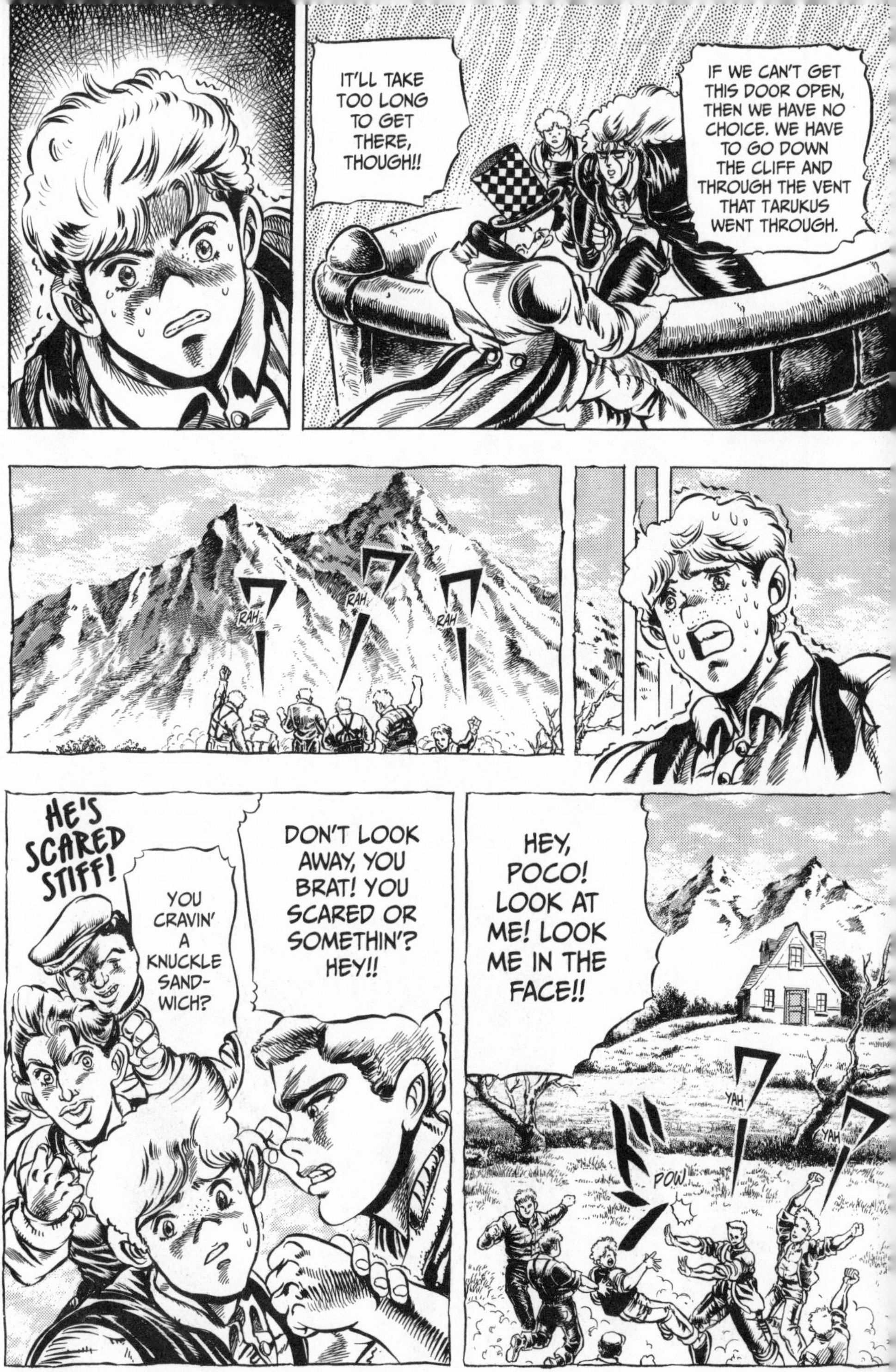
IF WE CAN'T GET THIS DOOR OPEN, THEN WE HAVE NO CHOICE. WE HAVE TO GO DOWN THE CLIFF AND THROUGH THE VENT THAT TARUKUS WENT THROUGH.
IT'LL TAKE TOO LONG TO GET THERE, THOUGH!!
RAH
RAH
RAH
HEY, POCO! LOOK AT ME! LOOK ME IN THE FACE!!
YAH
YAH
POW
DON'T LOOK AWAY, YOU BRAT! YOU SCARED OR SOMETHIN'? HEY!!
YOU CRAVIN' A KNUCKLE SAND-WICH?
HE'S SCARED STIFF!

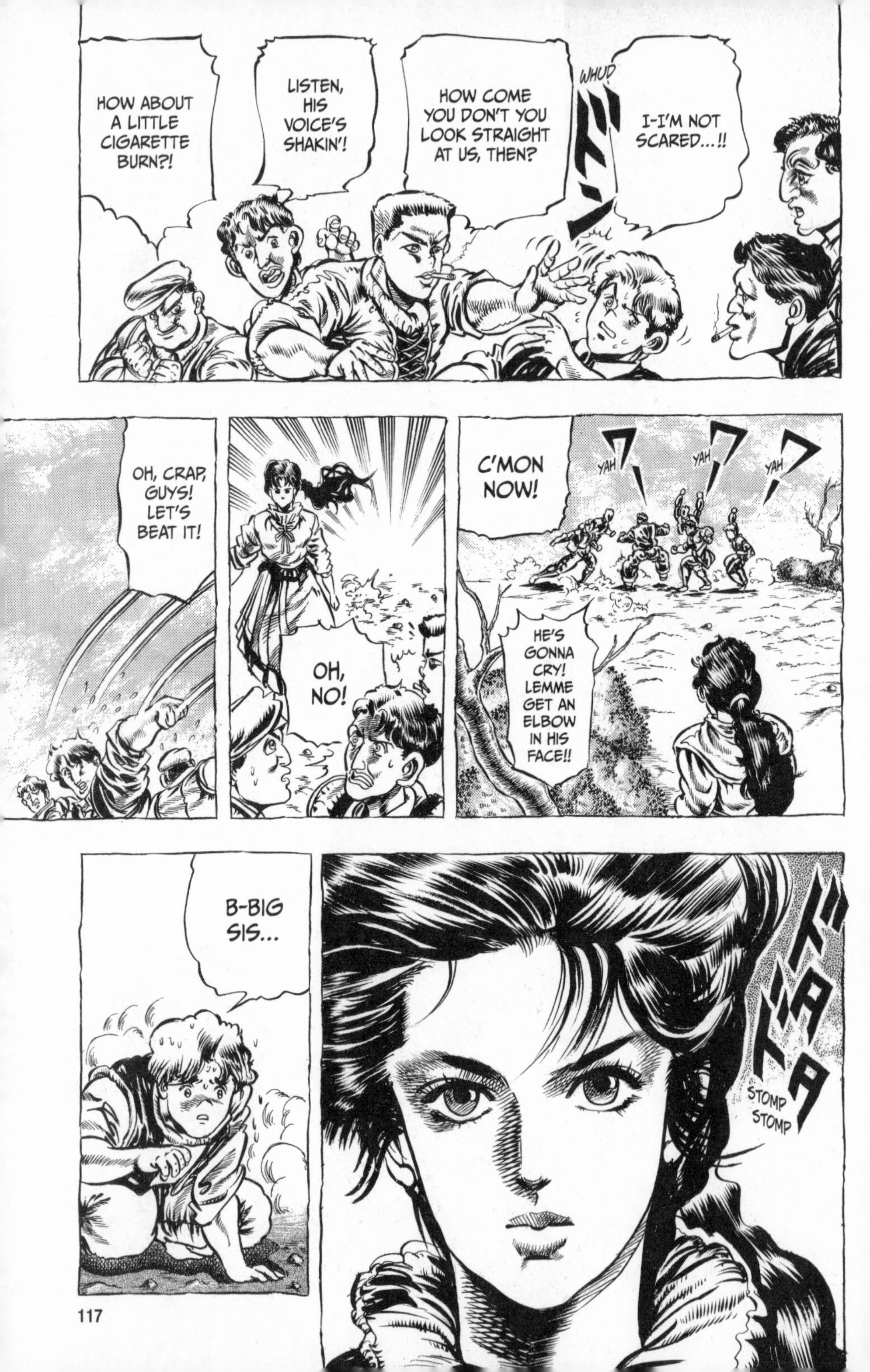

WHUD
I-I'M NOT SCARED...!!
HOW COME YOU DON'T YOU LOOK STRAIGHT AT US, THEN?
LISTEN, HIS VOICE'S SHAKIN'!
HOW ABOUT A LITTLE CIGARETTE BURN?!
YAH
YAH
YAH
C'MON NOW!
HE'S GONNA CRY! LEMME GET AN ELBOW IN HIS FACE!!
OH, NO!
OH, CRAP, GUYS! LET'S BEAT IT!
STOMP STOMP
B-BIG SIS...

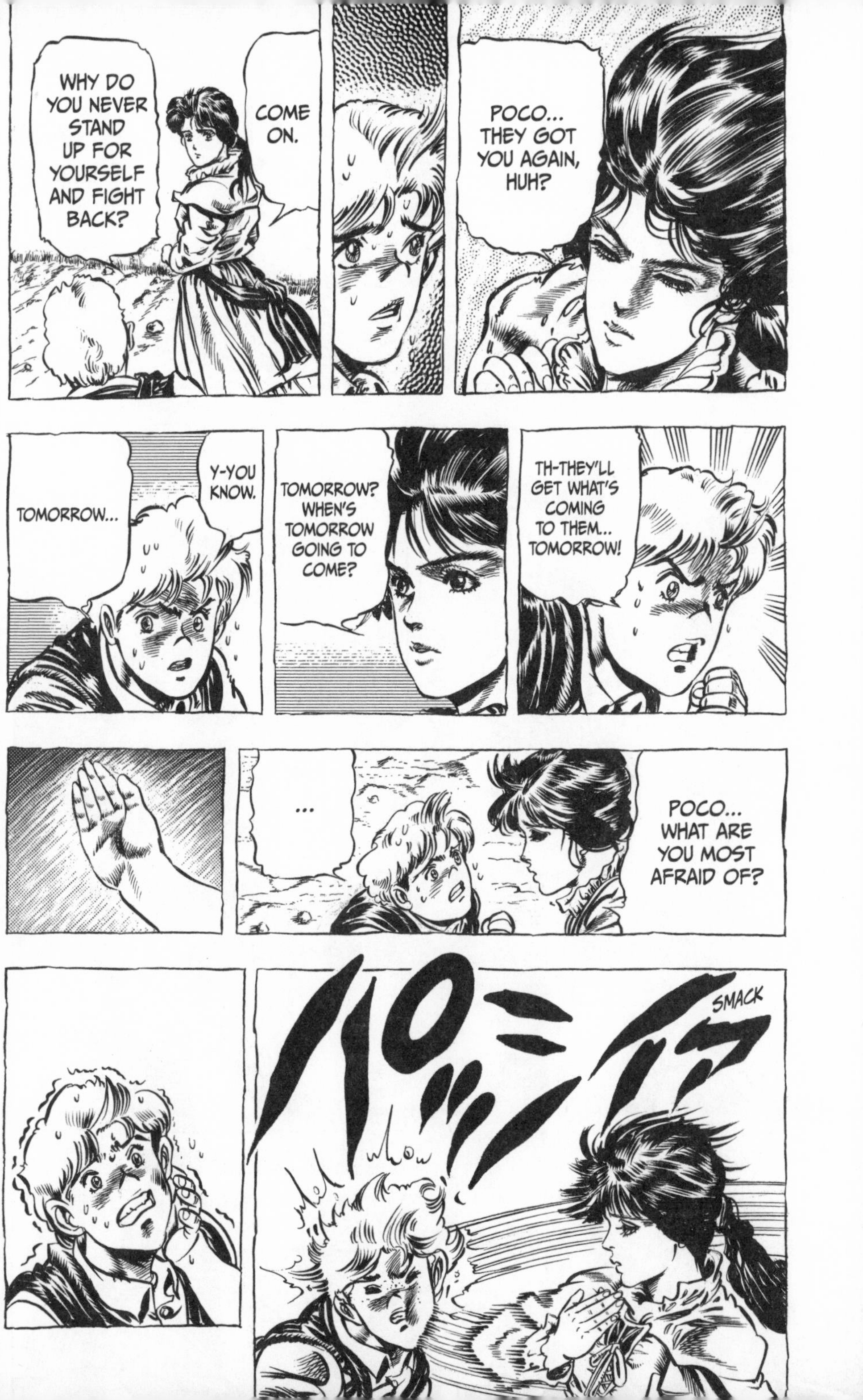
POCO... THEY GOT YOU AGAIN, HUH?
COME ON.
WHY DO YOU NEVER STAND UP FOR YOURSELF AND FIGHT BACK?
TH-THEY'LL GET WHAT'S COMING TO THEM... TOMORROW!
TOMORROW? WHEN'S TOMORROW GOING TO COME?
Y-YOU KNOW.
TOMORROW...
POCO... WHAT ARE YOU MOST AFRAID OF?
...
パーン
SMACK

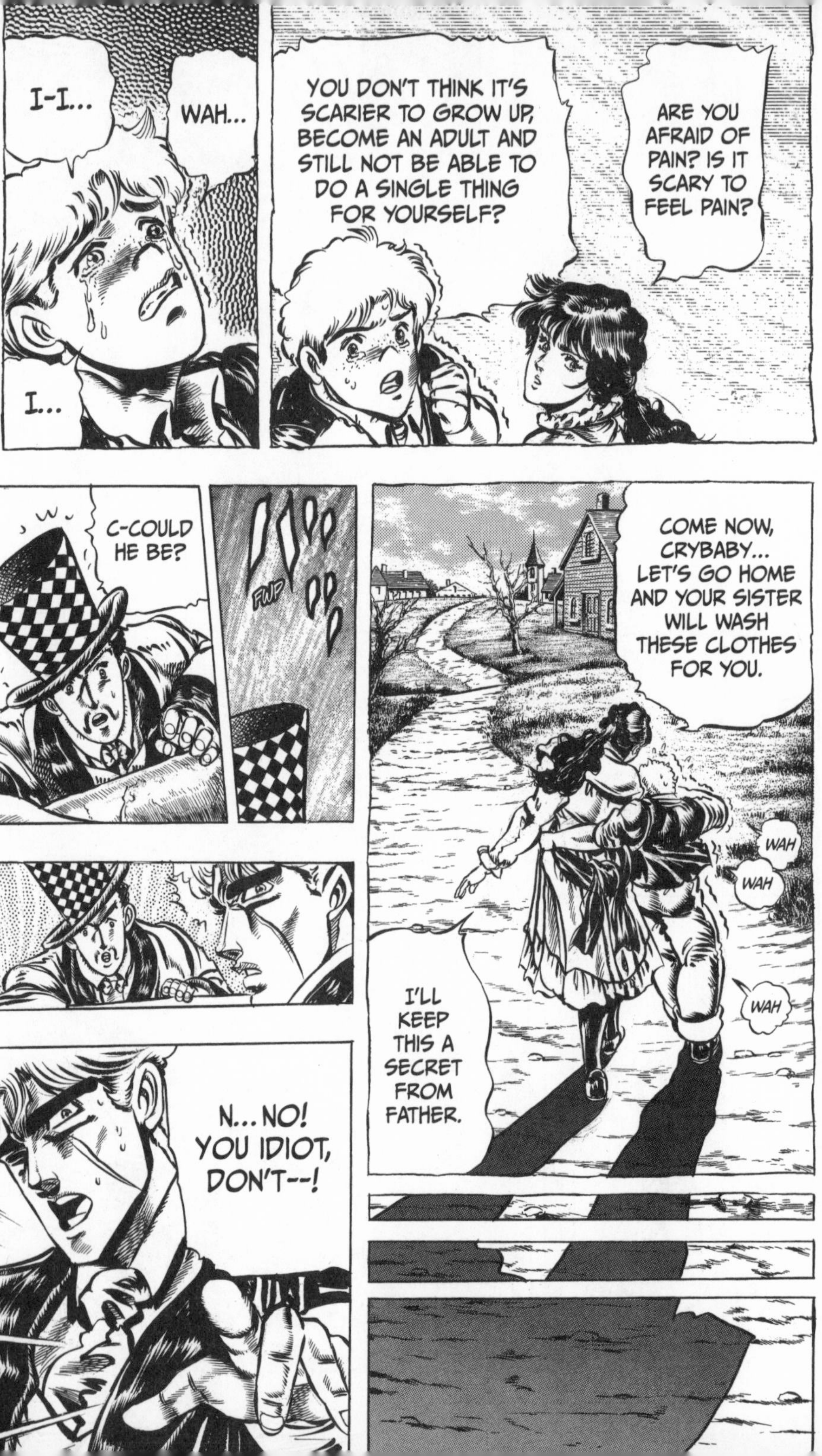
ARE YOU AFRAID OF PAIN? IS IT SCARY TO FEEL PAIN?
YOU DON'T THINK IT'S SCARIER TO GROW UP, BECOME AN ADULT AND STILL NOT BE ABLE TO DO A SINGLE THING FOR YOURSELF?
WAH...
I-I...
I...
COME NOW, CRYBABY... LET'S GO HOME AND YOUR SISTER WILL WASH THESE CLOTHES FOR YOU.
WAH
WAH
I'LL KEEP THIS A SECRET FROM FATHER.
WAH
FWP
C-COULD HE BE?
N...NO! YOU IDIOT, DON'T--!

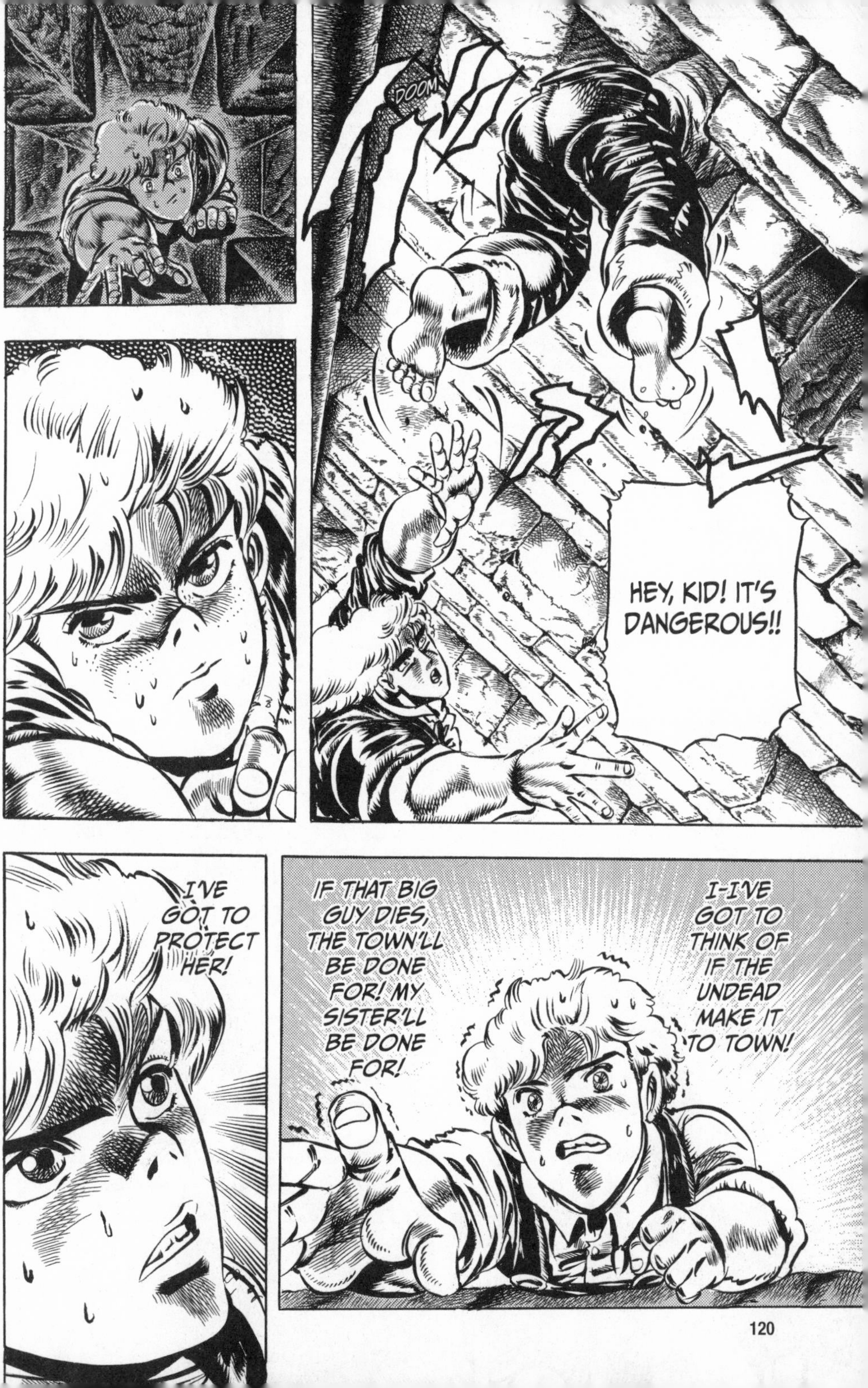
DOOM
HEY, KID! IT'S DANGEROUS!!
I-I'VE GOT TO THINK OF IF THE UNDEAD MAKE IT TO TOWN!
IF THAT BIG GUY DIES, THE TOWN'LL BE DONE FOR! MY SISTER'LL BE DONE FOR!
I'VE GOT TO PROTECT HER!

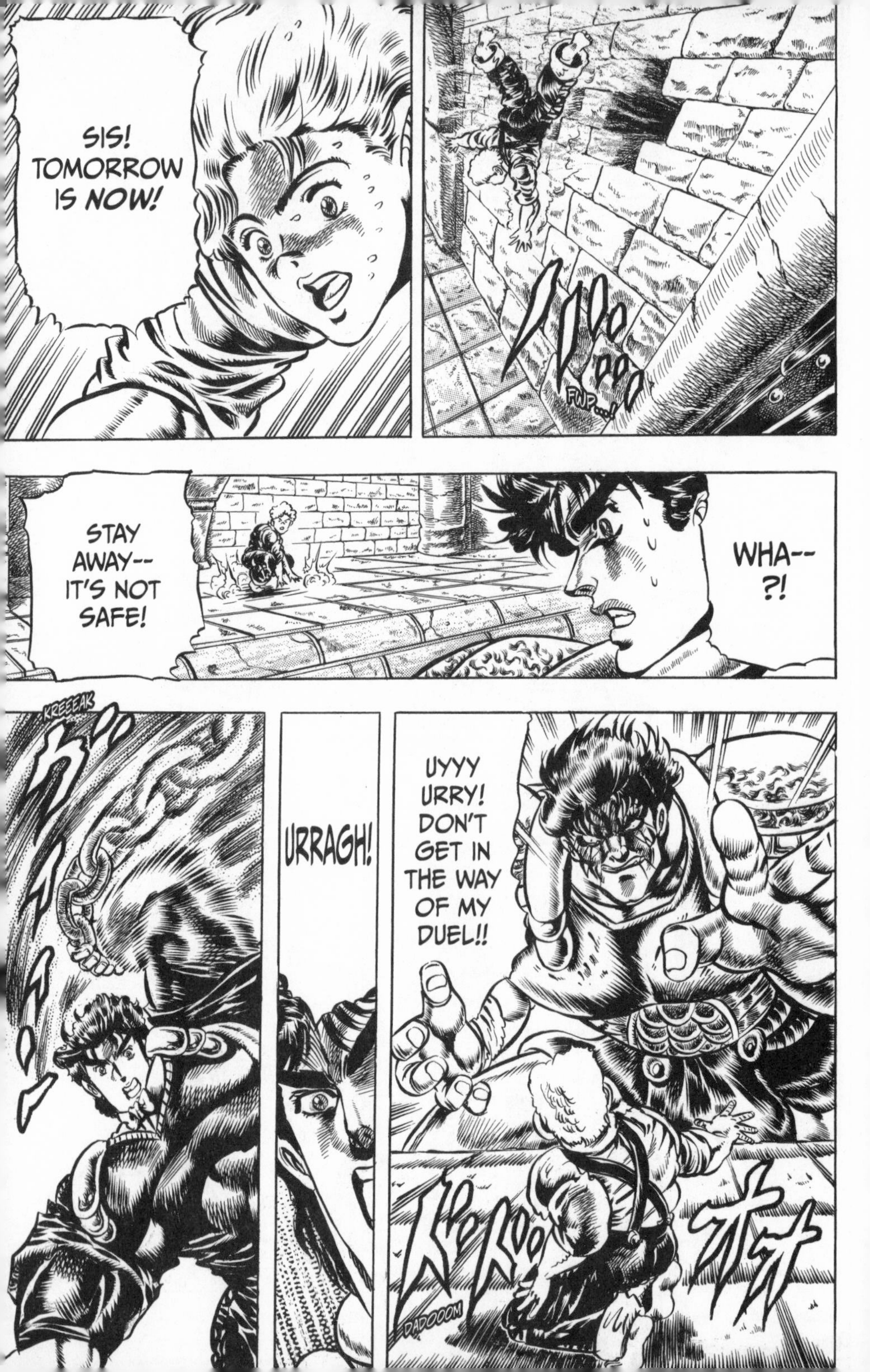
FWP...!
SIS! TOMORROW IS NOW!
WHA--?!
STAY AWAY-- IT'S NOT SAFE!
UYYY URRY! DON'T GET IN THE WAY OF MY DUEL!!
DADOOOM
URRAGH!
KREEEAK

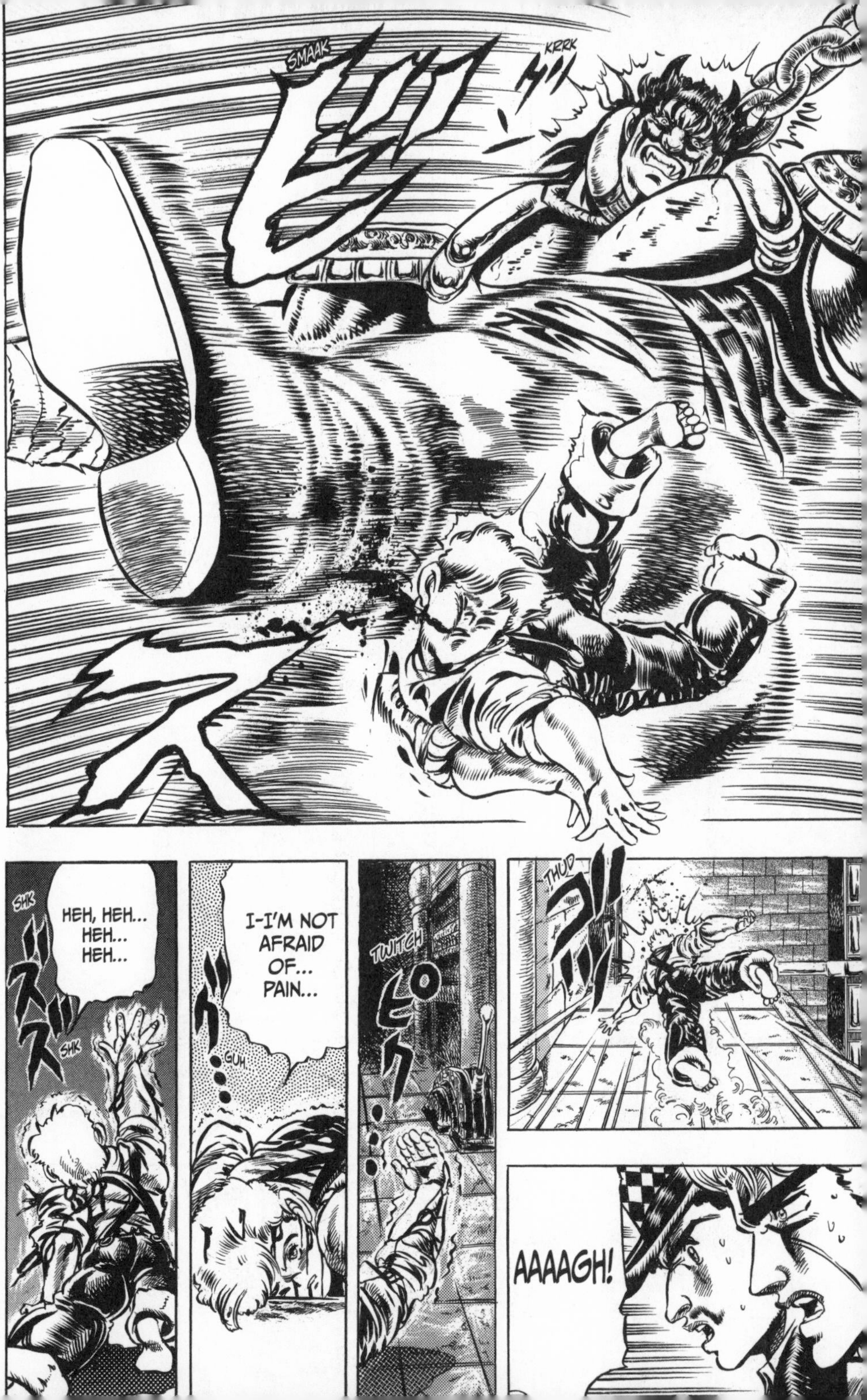
KRRK
SMAAK
THUD
AAAAGH!
TWITCH
I-I'M NOT AFRAID OF... PAIN...
GUH
SHK
HEH, HEH... HEH... HEH...
SHK

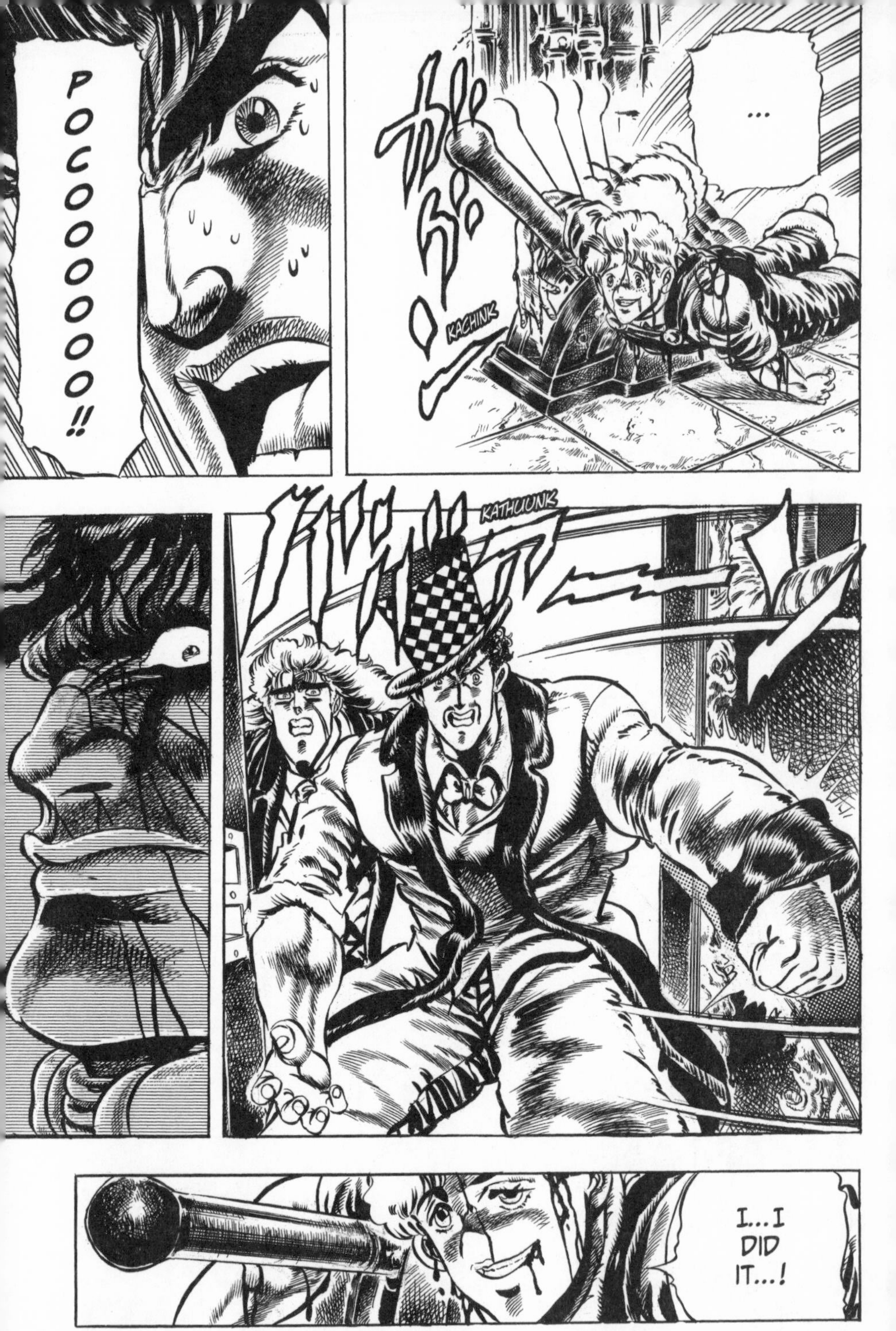
...
KACHINK
POCOOOOOOOOO!!
KATHUUNK
I...I DID IT...!

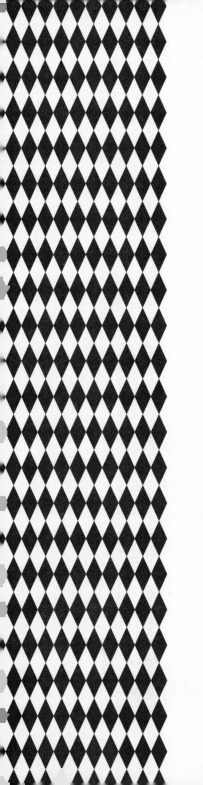

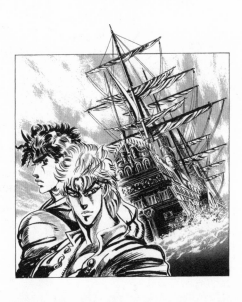

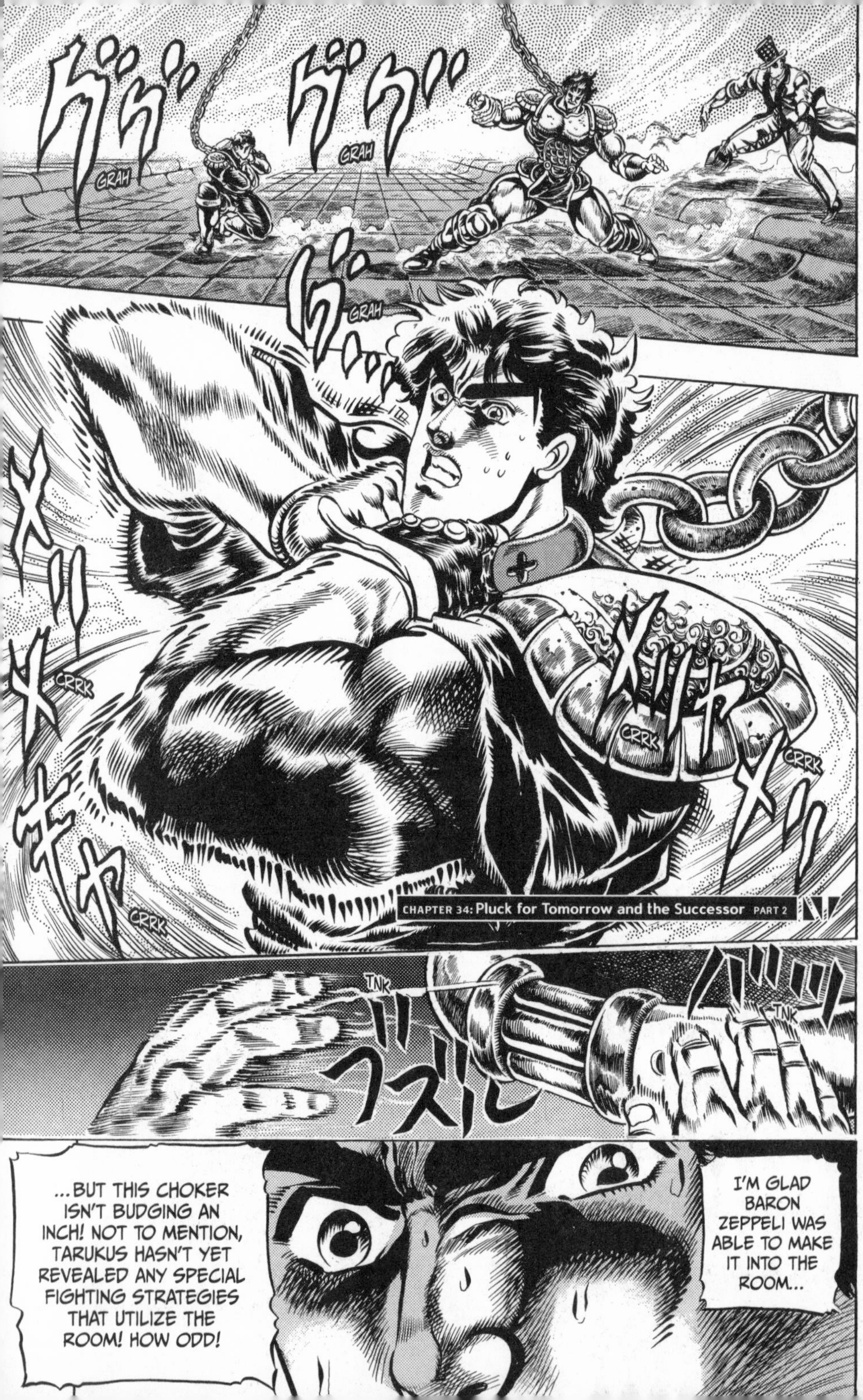
GRAH
GRAH
GRAH
CRRK
CRRK
CRRK
CHAPTER 34: Pluck for Tomorrow and the Successor PART 2
TNK
TNK
I'M GLAD BARON ZEPPELI WAS ABLE TO MAKE IT INTO THE ROOM...
...BUT THIS CHOKER ISN'T BUDGING AN INCH! NOT TO MENTION, TARUKUS HASN'T YET REVEALED ANY SPECIAL FIGHTING STRATEGIES THAT UTILIZE THE ROOM! HOW ODD!

CHAPTER 34: Pluck for Tomorrow and the Successor PART 2

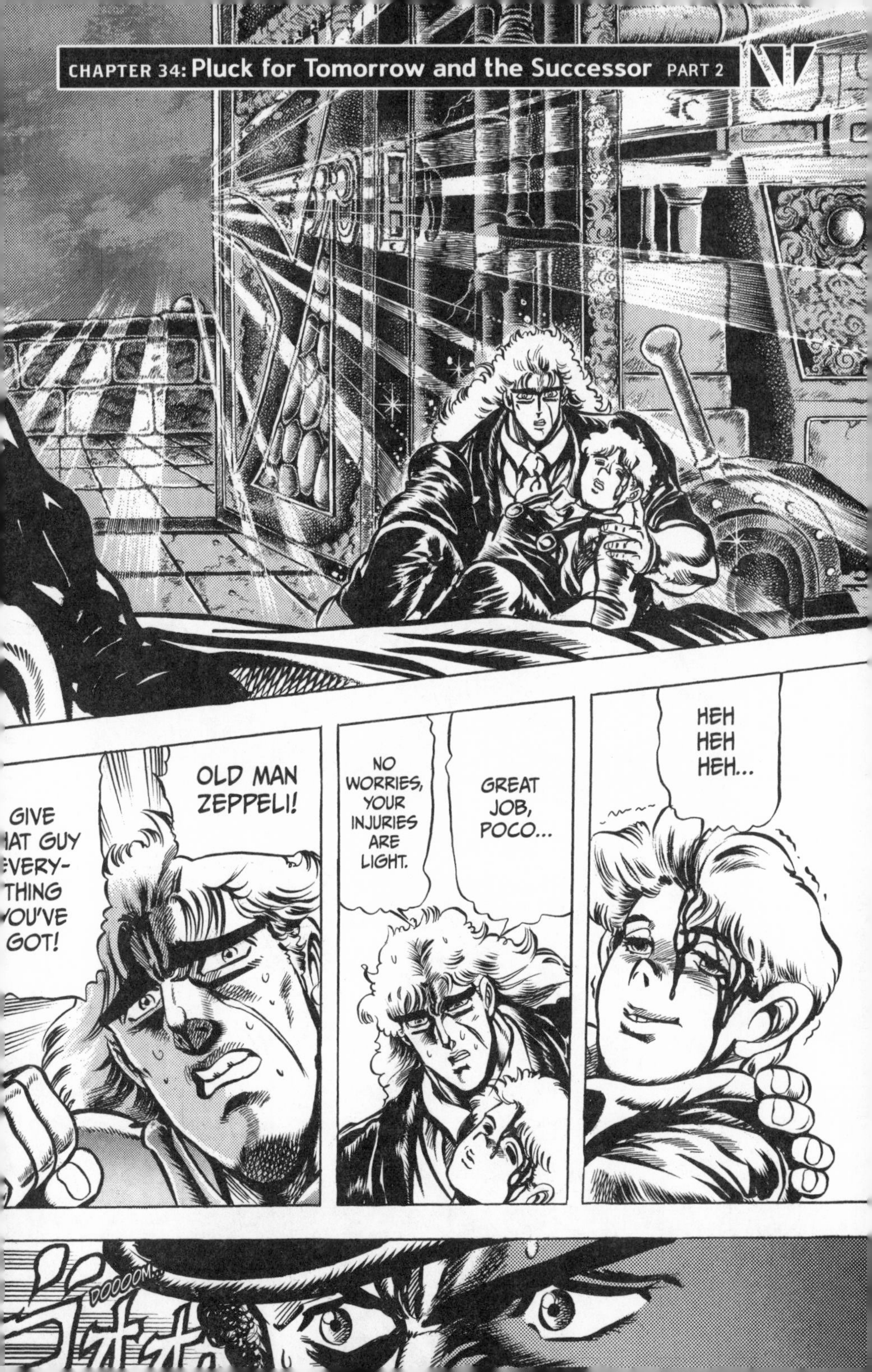
HEH HEH HEH...
GREAT JOB, POCO...
NO WORRIES, YOUR INJURIES ARE LIGHT.
OLD MAN ZEPPELI!
GIVE HAT GUY VERY-THING OU'VE GOT!
DOOOOM

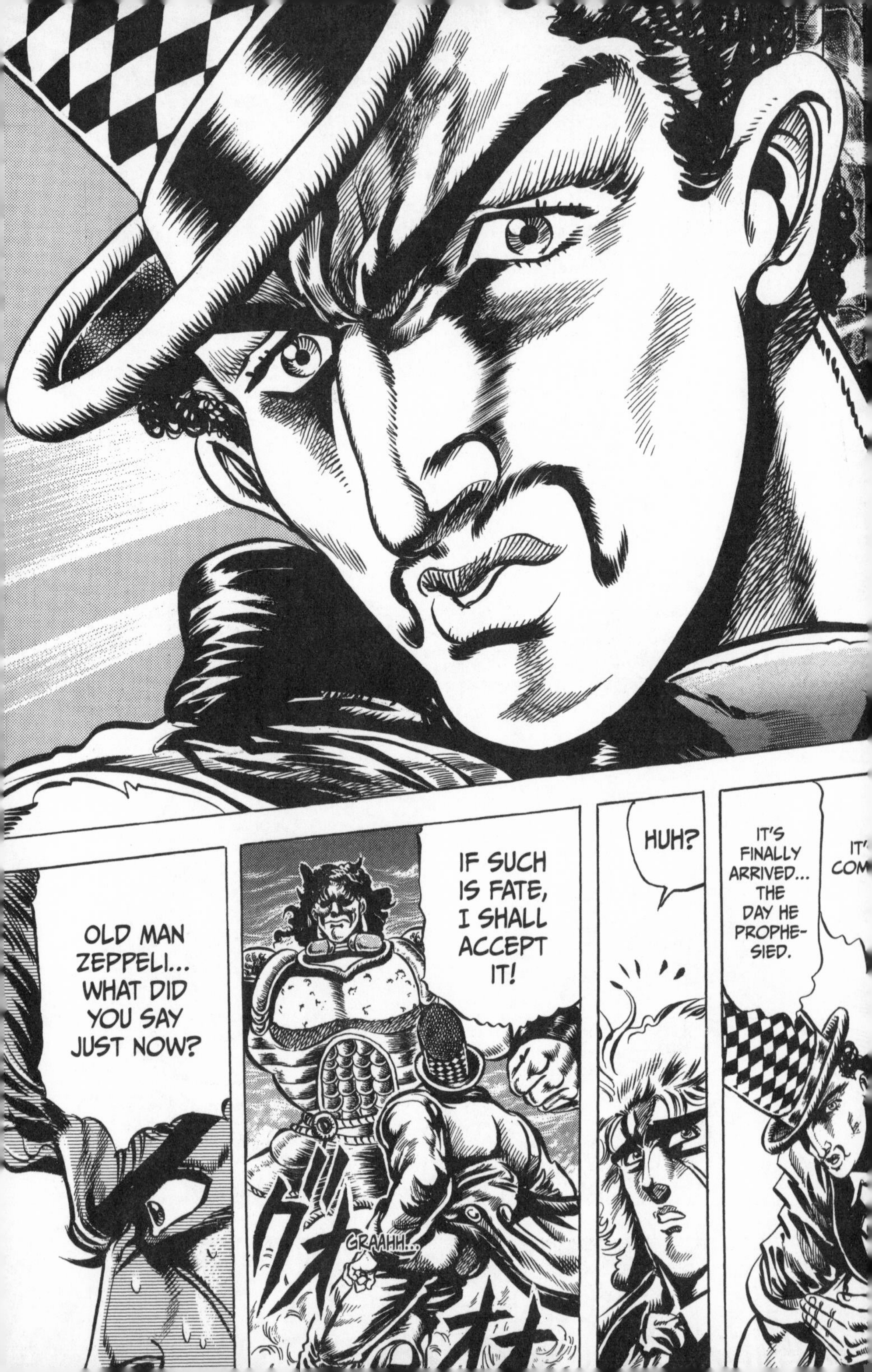
IT'S FINALLY ARRIVED... THE DAY HE PROPHESIED.
HUH?
IF SUCH IS FATE, I SHALL ACCEPT IT!
GRAAHH...
OLD MAN ZEPPELI... WHAT DID YOU SAY JUST NOW?

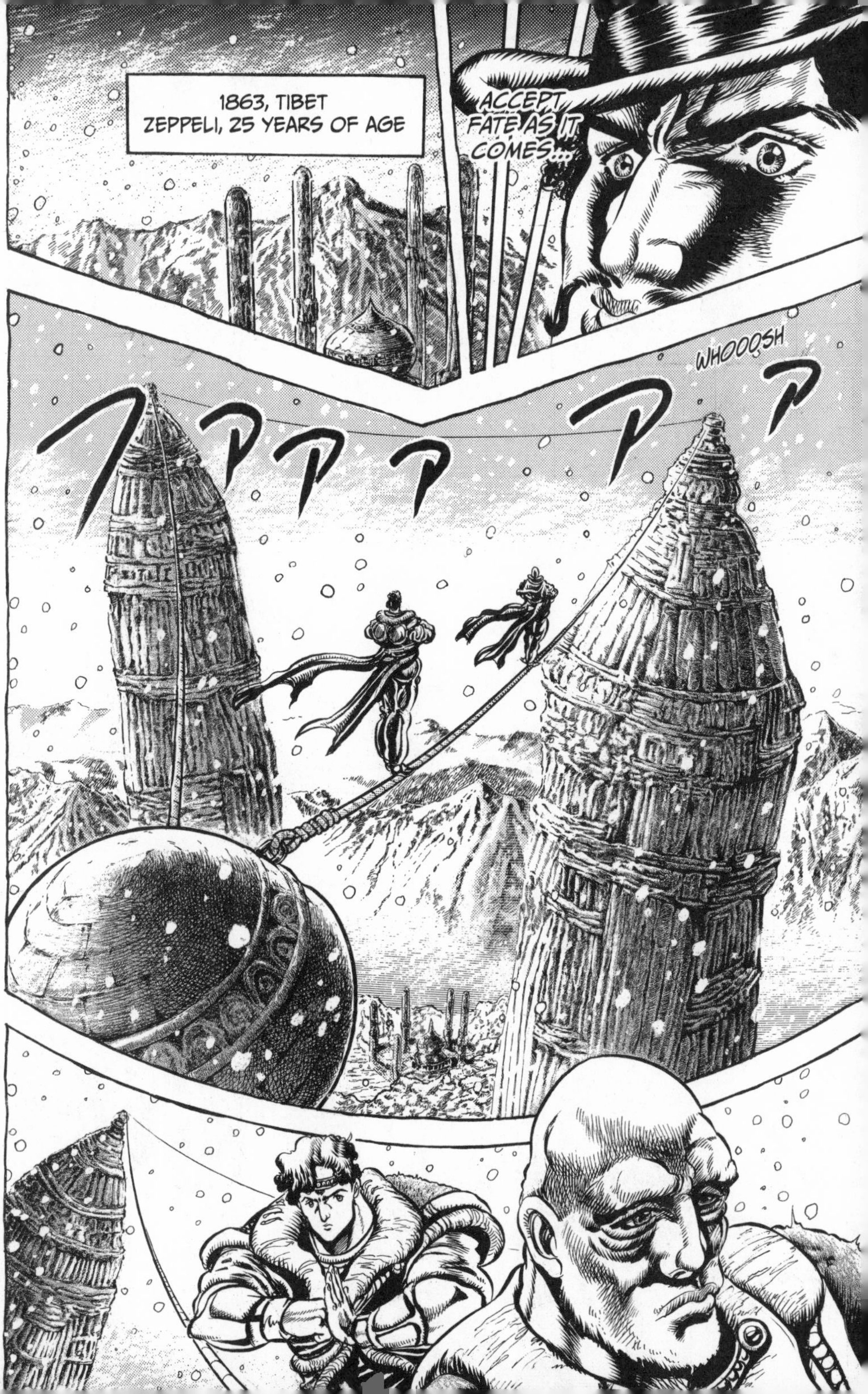
ACCEPT FATE AS IT COMES...
1863, TIBET
ZEPPELI, 25 YEARS OF AGE
WHOOOSH

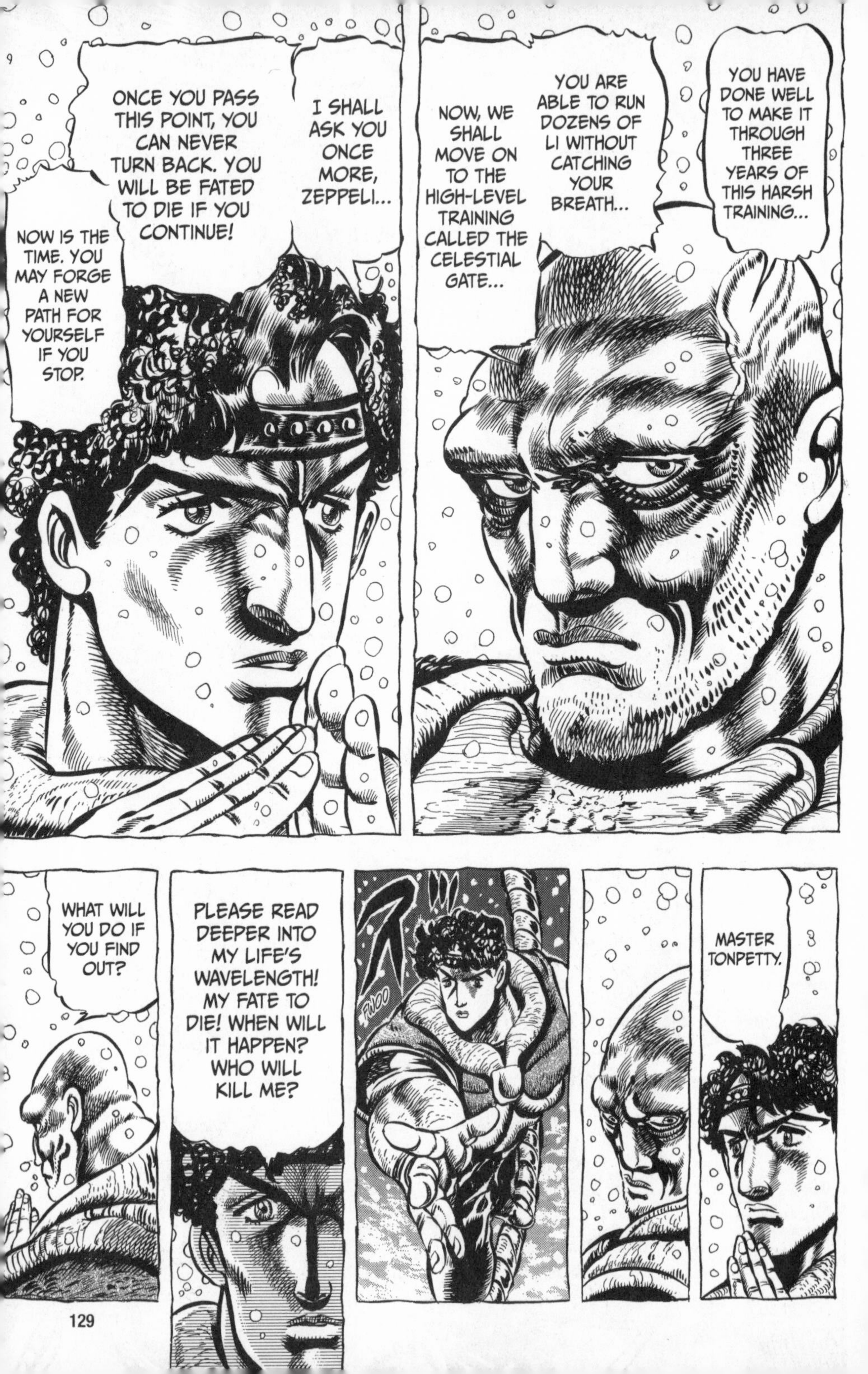
YOU HAVE DONE WELL TO MAKE IT THROUGH THREE YEARS OF THIS HARSH TRAINING...
YOU ARE ABLE TO RUN DOZENS OF LI WITHOUT CATCHING YOUR BREATH...
NOW, WE SHALL MOVE ON TO THE HIGH-LEVEL TRAINING CALLED THE CELESTIAL GATE...
I SHALL ASK YOU ONCE MORE, ZEPPELI...
ONCE YOU PASS THIS POINT, YOU CAN NEVER TURN BACK. YOU WILL BE FATED TO DIE IF YOU CONTINUE!
NOW IS THE TIME. YOU MAY FORGE A NEW PATH FOR YOURSELF IF YOU STOP.
MASTER TONPETTY.
FWOO
PLEASE READ DEEPER INTO MY LIFE'S WAVELENGTH! MY FATE TO DIE! WHEN WILL IT HAPPEN? WHO WILL KILL ME?
WHAT WILL YOU DO IF YOU FIND OUT?

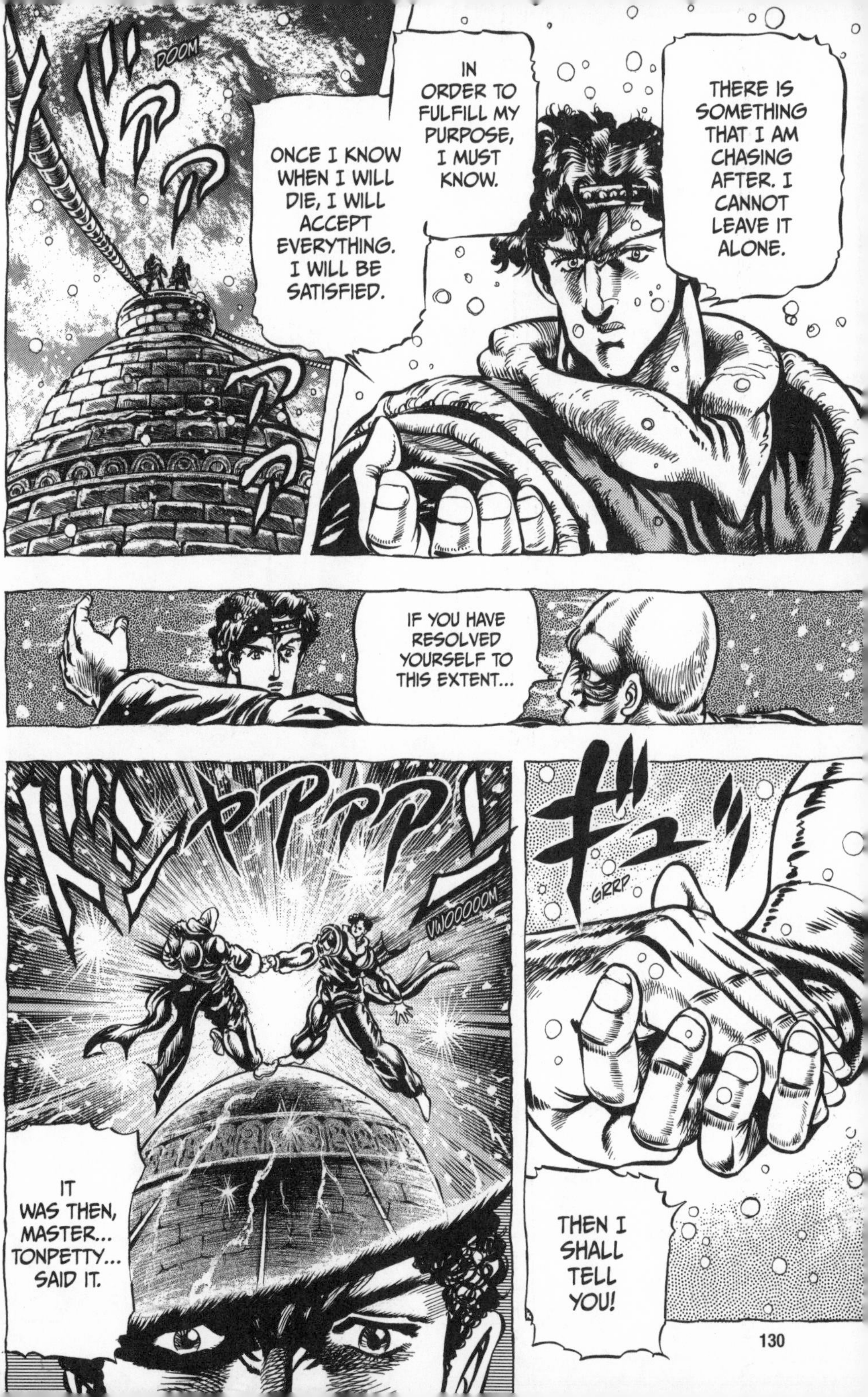
THERE IS SOMETHING THAT I AM CHASING AFTER. I CANNOT LEAVE IT ALONE.
IN ORDER TO FULFILL MY PURPOSE, I MUST KNOW.
ONCE I KNOW WHEN I WILL DIE, I WILL ACCEPT EVERYTHING. I WILL BE SATISFIED.
DOOM
IF YOU HAVE RESOLVED YOURSELF TO THIS EXTENT...
GRRP
THEN I SHALL TELL YOU!
VWOOOOOM
IT WAS THEN, MASTER... TONPETTY... SAID IT.

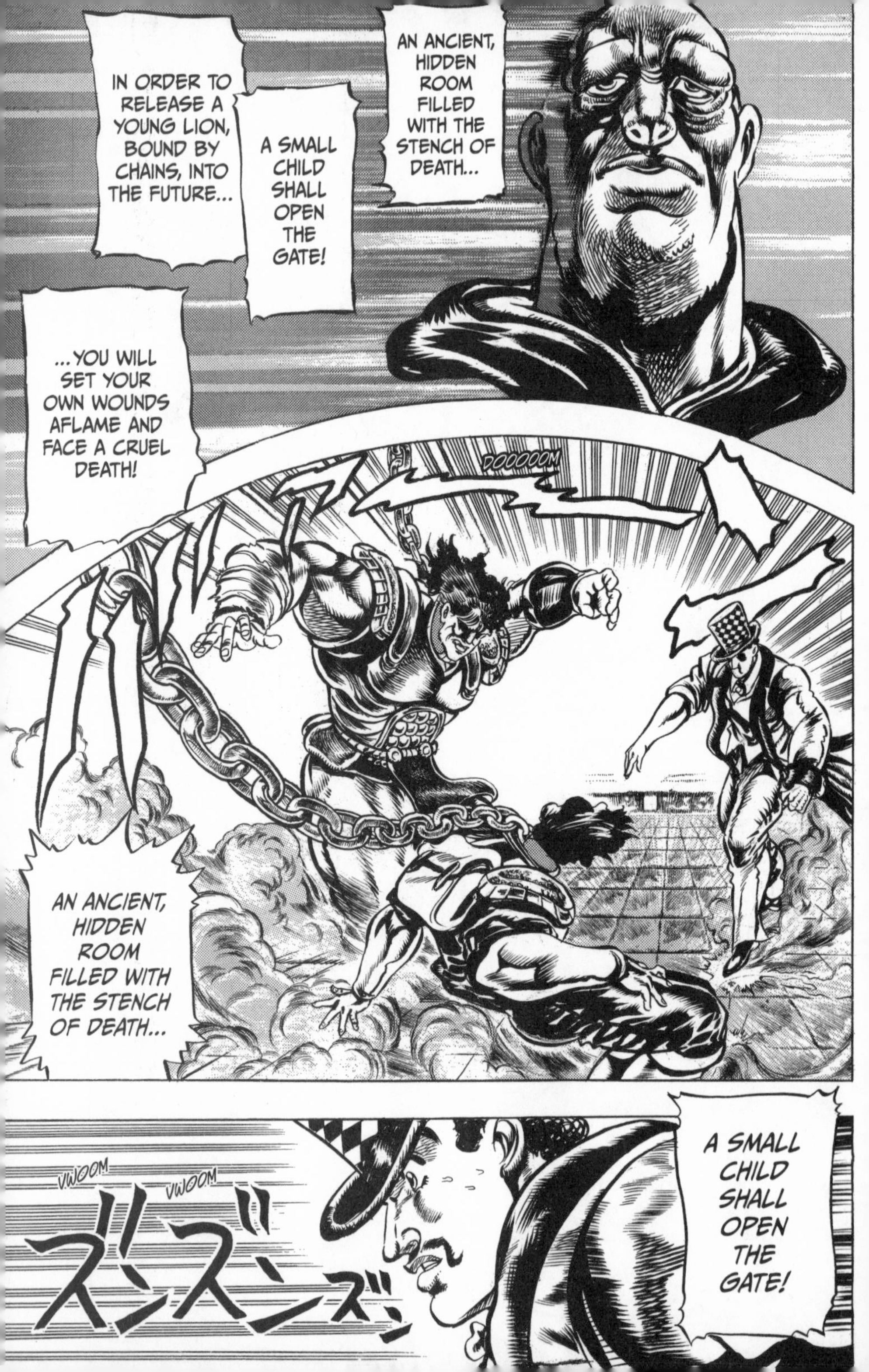
AN ANCIENT, HIDDEN ROOM FILLED WITH THE STENCH OF DEATH...
A SMALL CHILD SHALL OPEN THE GATE!
IN ORDER TO RELEASE A YOUNG LION, BOUND BY CHAINS, INTO THE FUTURE...
...YOU WILL SET YOUR OWN WOUNDS AFLAME AND FACE A CRUEL DEATH!
DOOOOOM
AN ANCIENT, HIDDEN ROOM FILLED WITH THE STENCH OF DEATH...
A SMALL CHILD SHALL OPEN THE GATE!
VWOOM
VWOOM
ズンズンズン

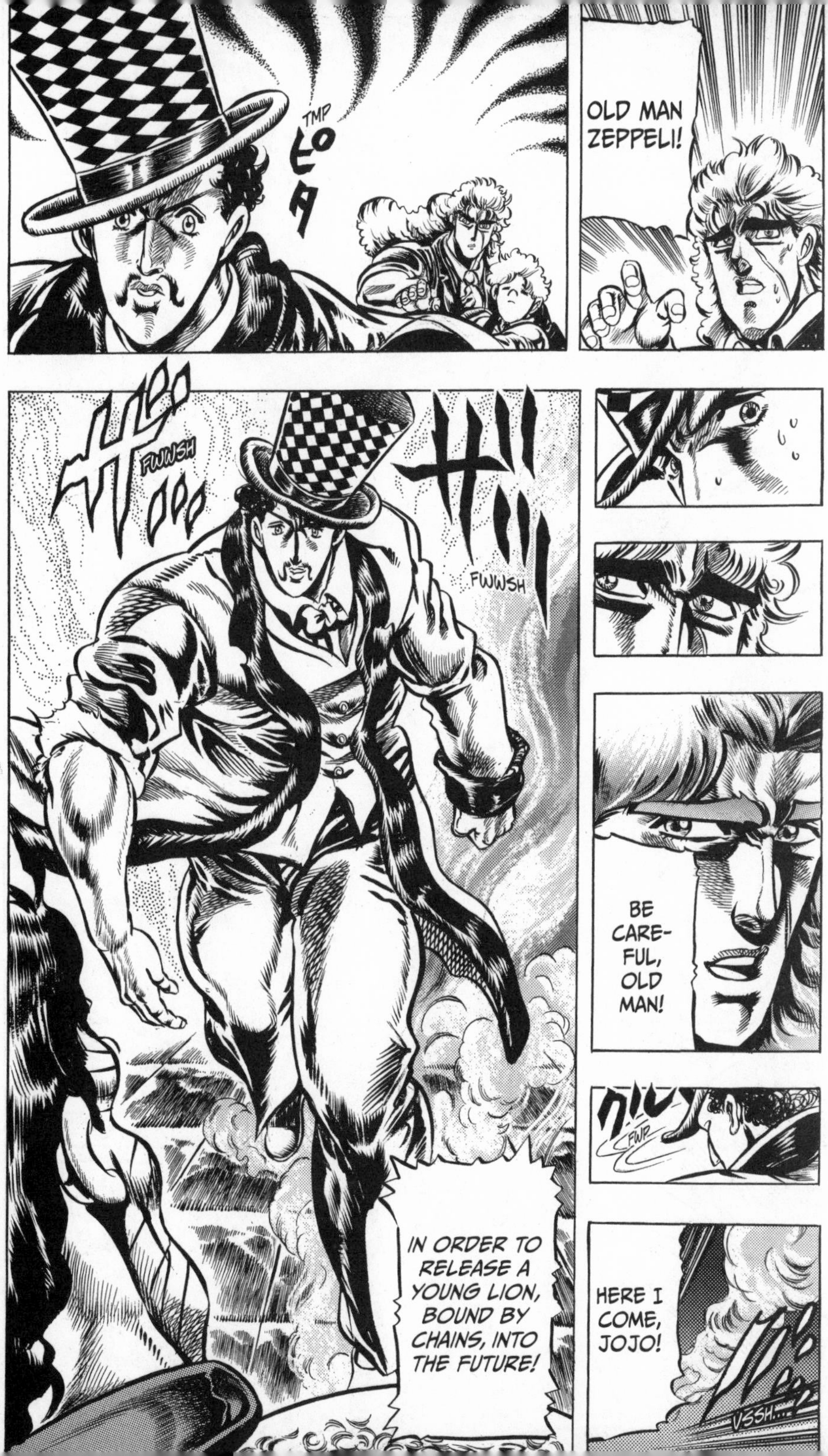
OLD MAN ZEPPELI!
TMP
BE CARE-FUL, OLD MAN!
CFWP
HERE I COME, JOJO!
VSSH...
FWWSH
FWWSH
IN ORDER TO RELEASE A YOUNG LION, BOUND BY CHAINS, INTO THE FUTURE!

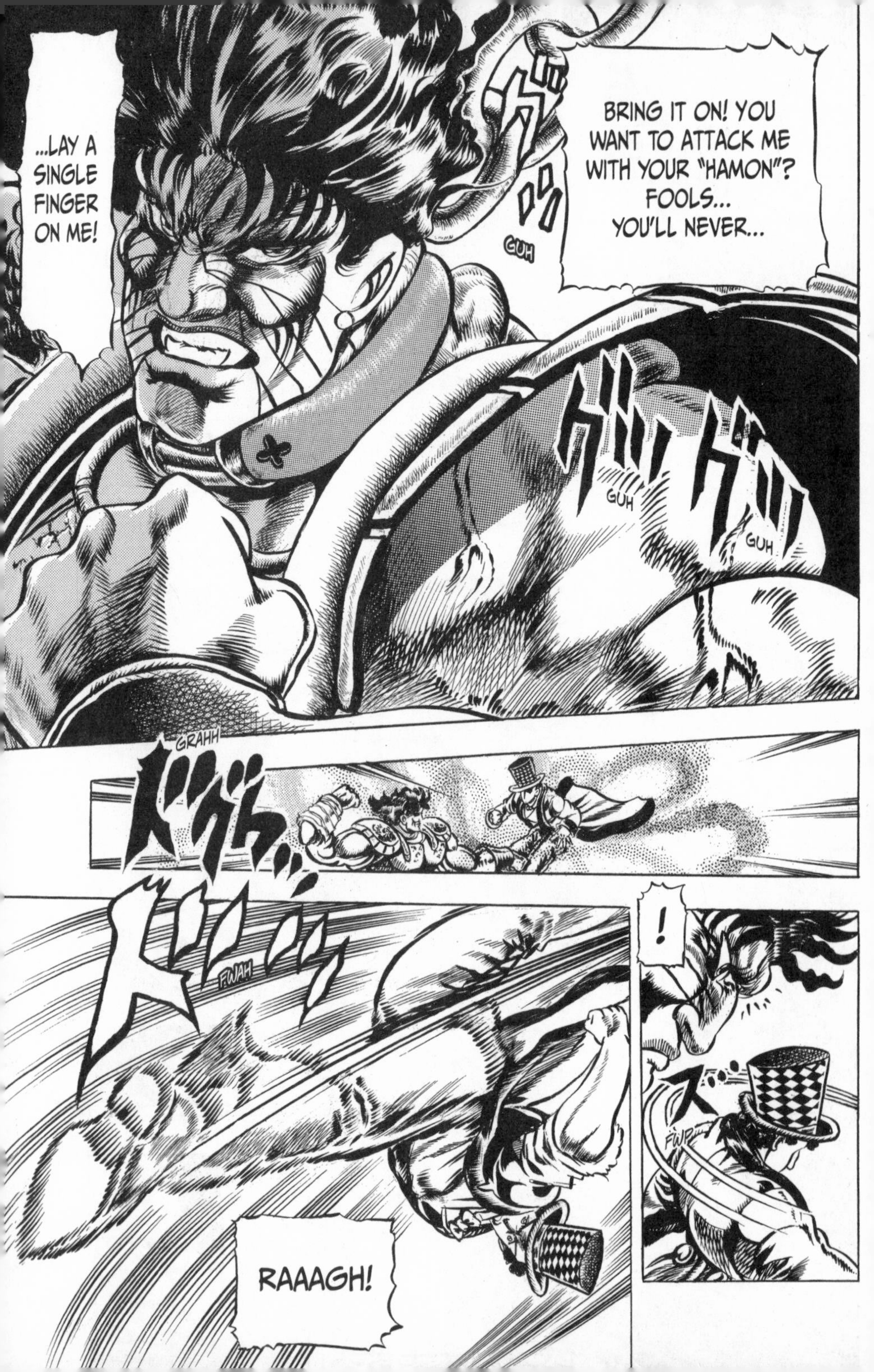
BRING IT ON! YOU WANT TO ATTACK ME WITH YOUR "HAMON"? FOOLS... YOU'LL NEVER...
GUH
...LAY A SINGLE FINGER ON ME!
GUH
GUH
GRAHH
!
FWP
FWAH
RAAAGH!

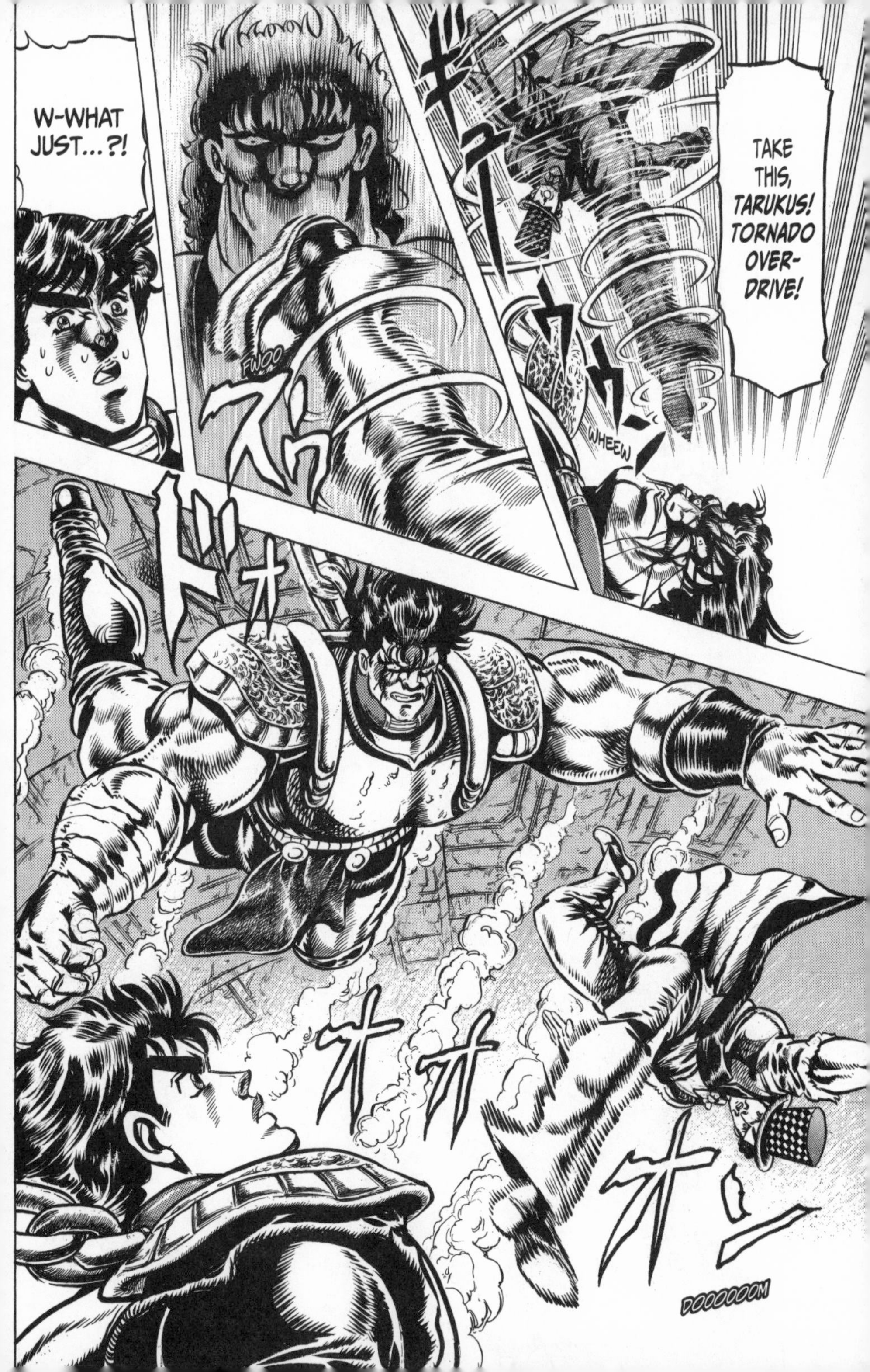
TAKE THIS, TARUKUS! TORNADO OVER-DRIVE!
WHEEW
FWOO
W-WHAT JUST...?!
DOOOOOOM

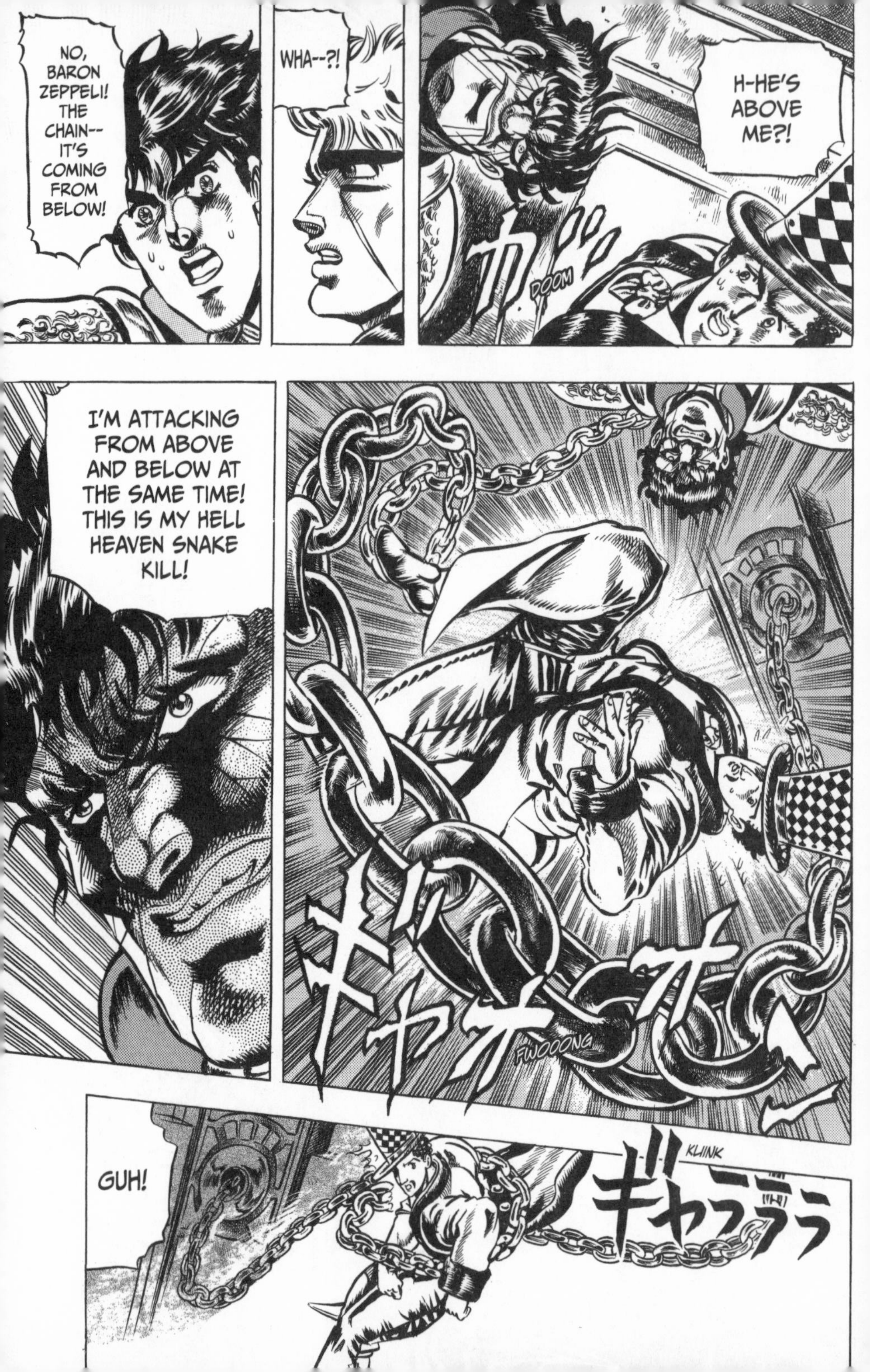
H-HE'S ABOVE ME?!
DOOM
WHA--?!
NO, BARON ZEPPELI! THE CHAIN-- IT'S COMING FROM BELOW!
FWOOOONG
I'M ATTACKING FROM ABOVE AND BELOW AT THE SAME TIME! THIS IS MY HELL HEAVEN SNAKE KILL!
KLIINK
GUH!

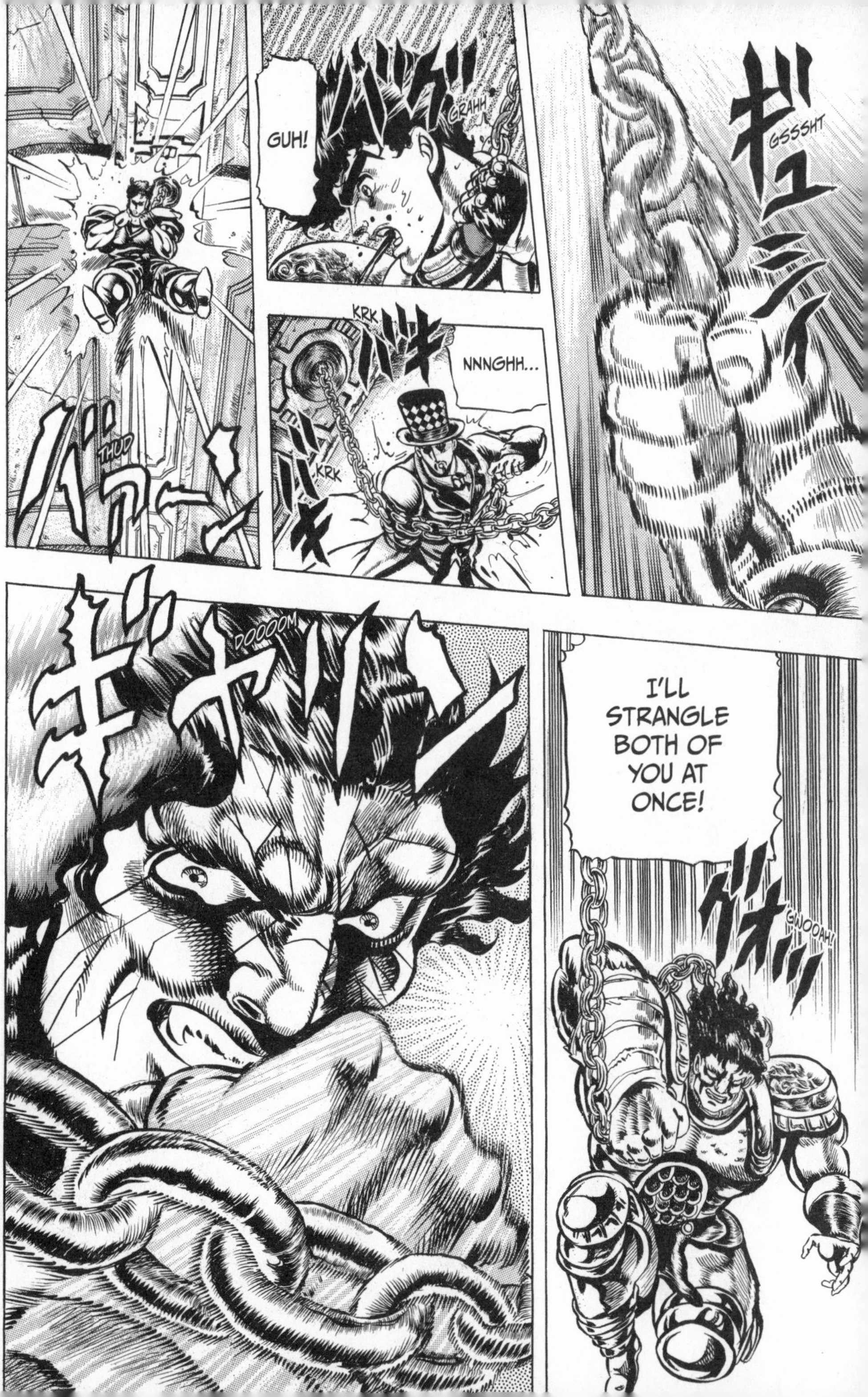
GSSSHT
GUH!
GRAHH
KRK
NNNGHH...
KRK
THUD
I'LL STRANGLE BOTH OF YOU AT ONCE!
GWOOAH!
DOOOOM

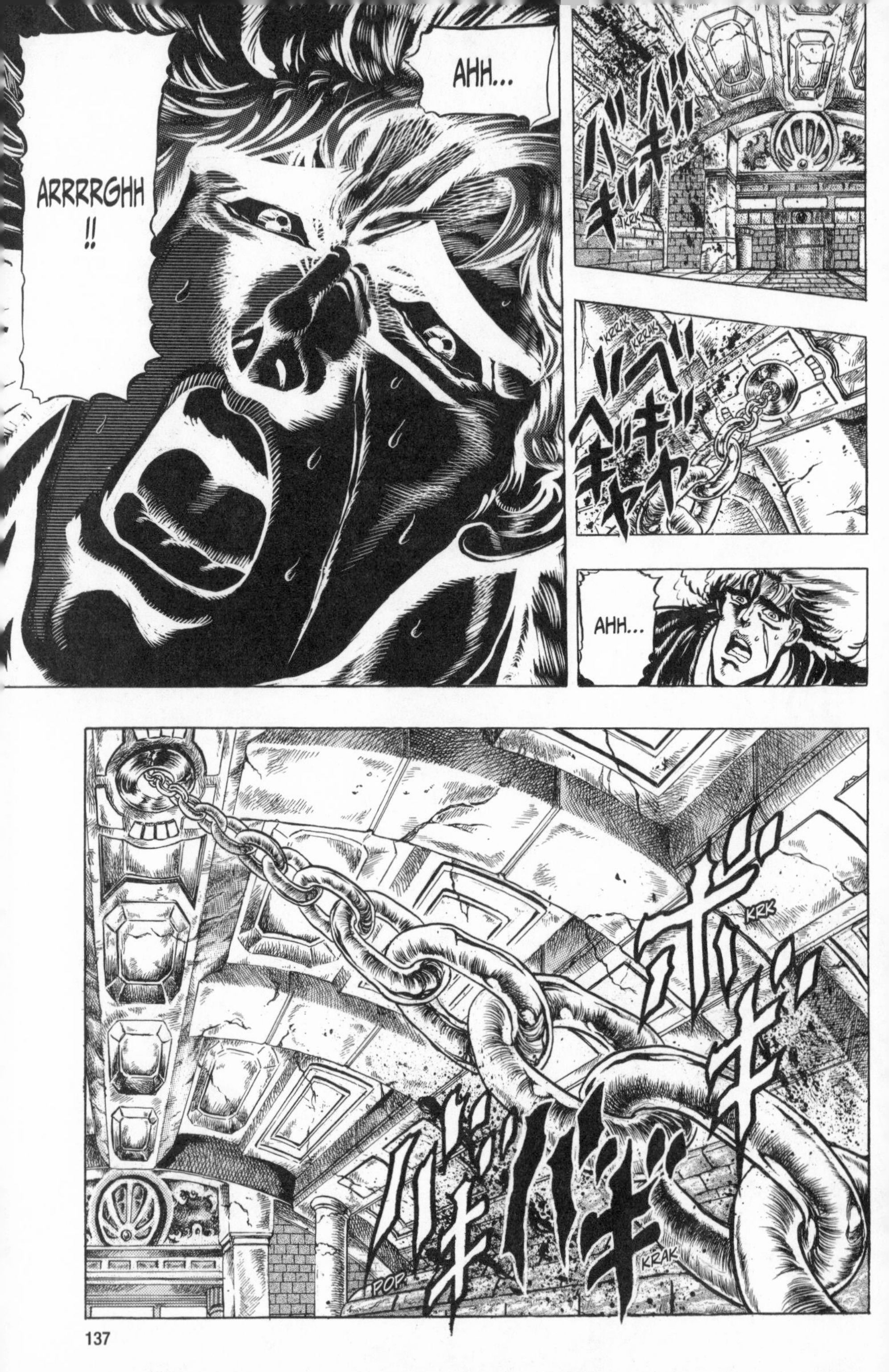
KRK
KRK
KRRAK
KRRAK
AHH...
AHH...
ARRRGHH !!
KRK
KRAK
POP

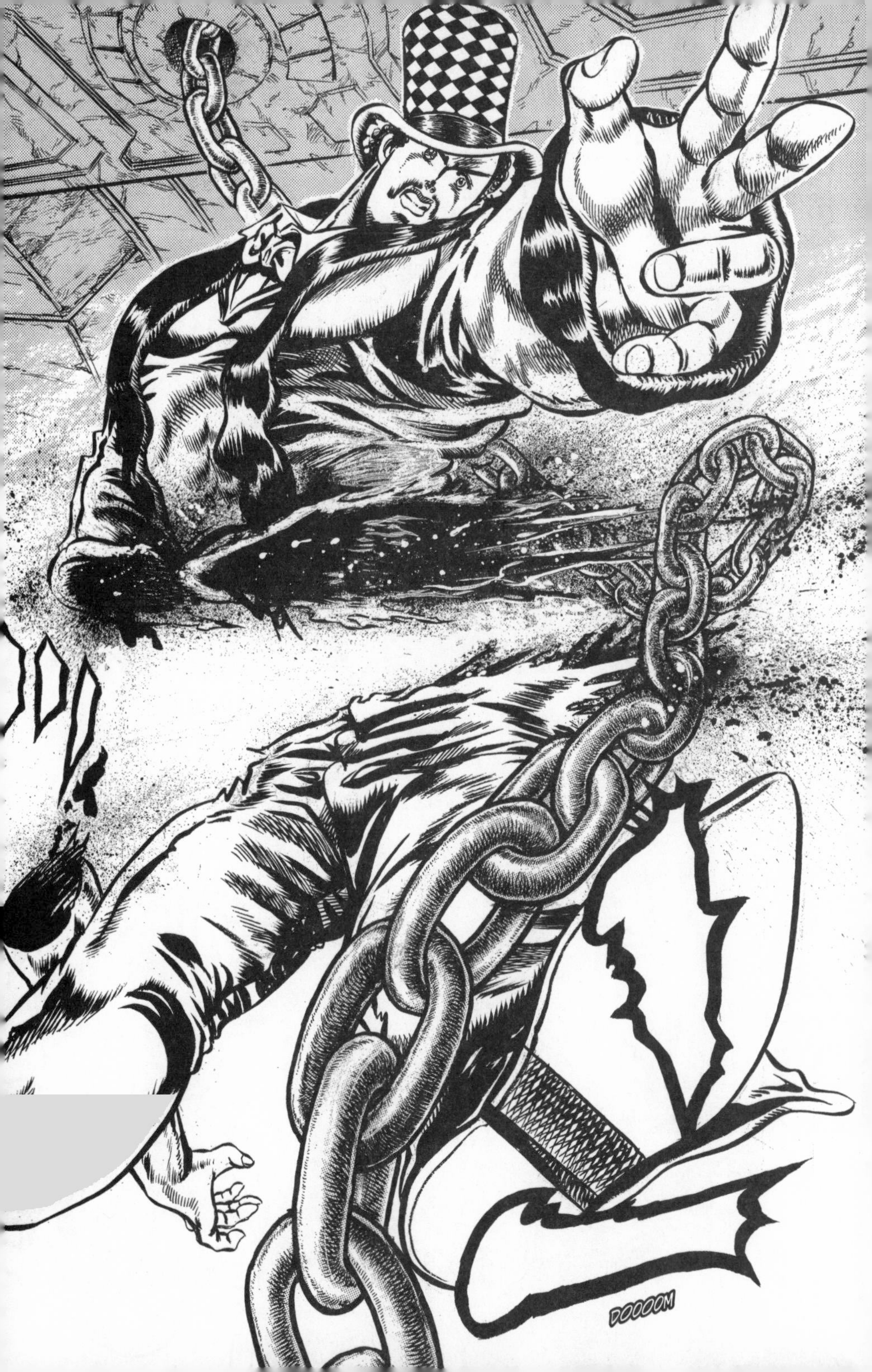
DOOOOM

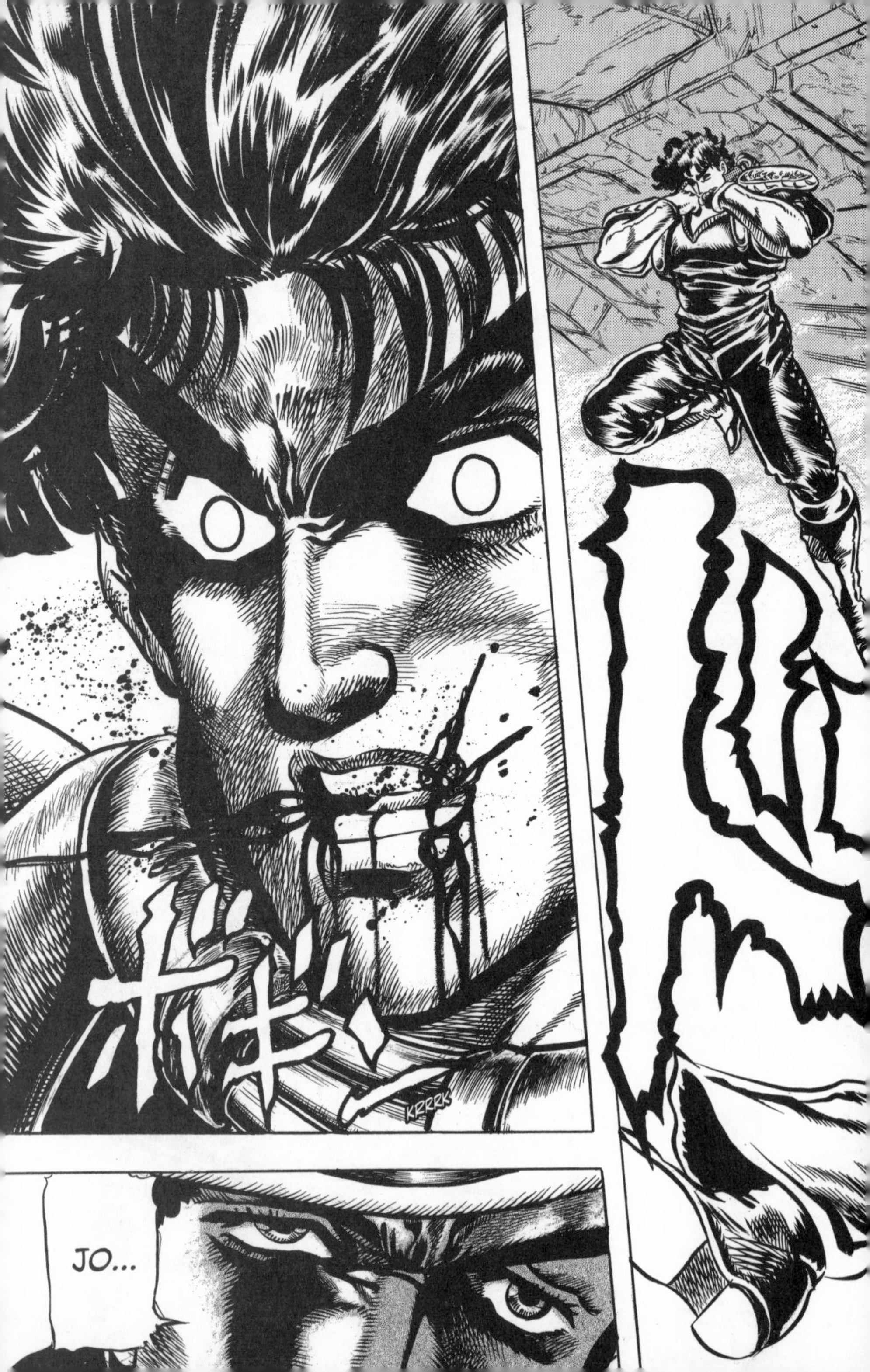
KRRRK
JO...

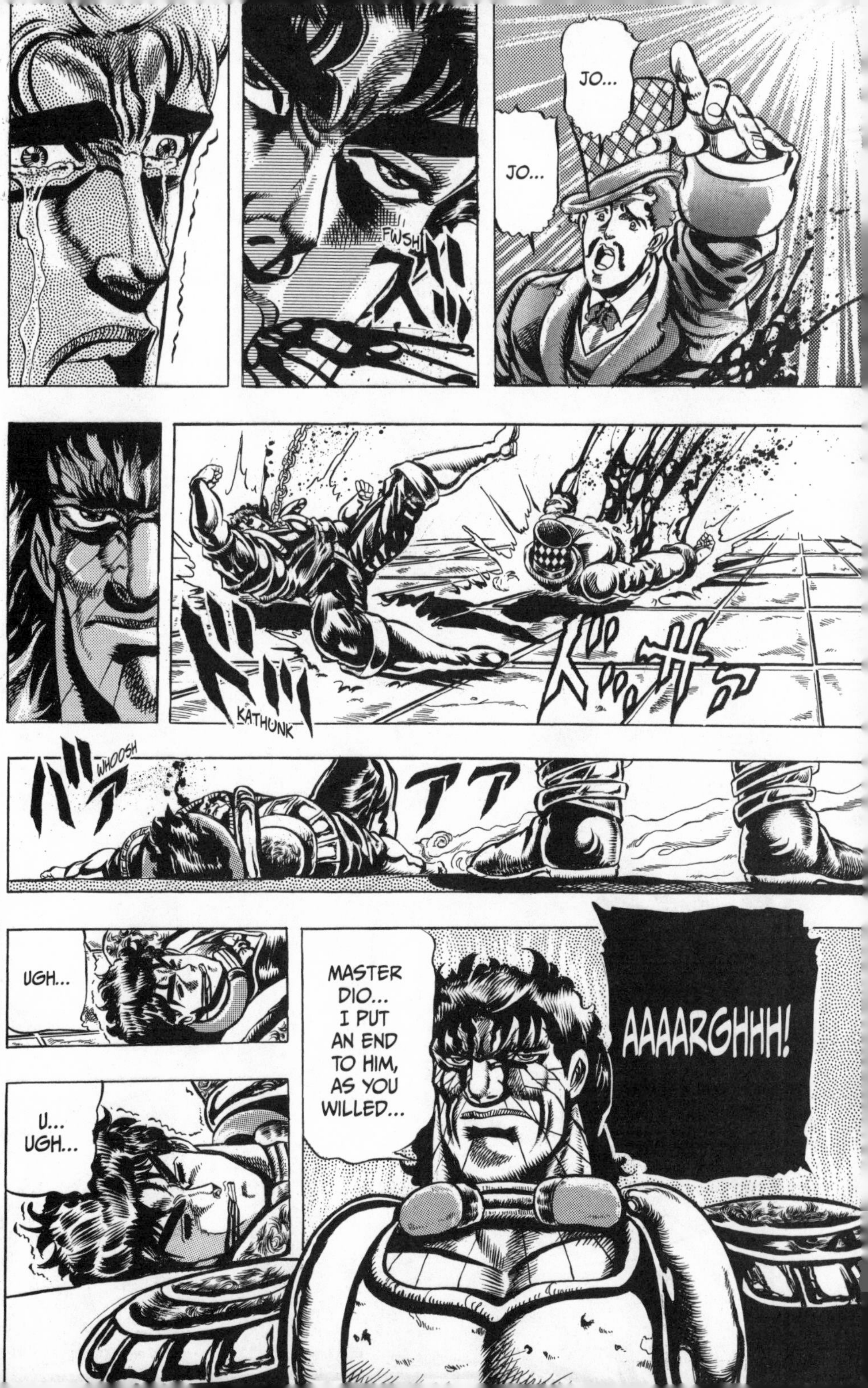
JO...
JO...
FWSH
KATHUNK
WHOOSH
AAAARGHHH!
MASTER DIO... I PUT AN END TO HIM, AS YOU WILLED...
UGH...
U... UGH...

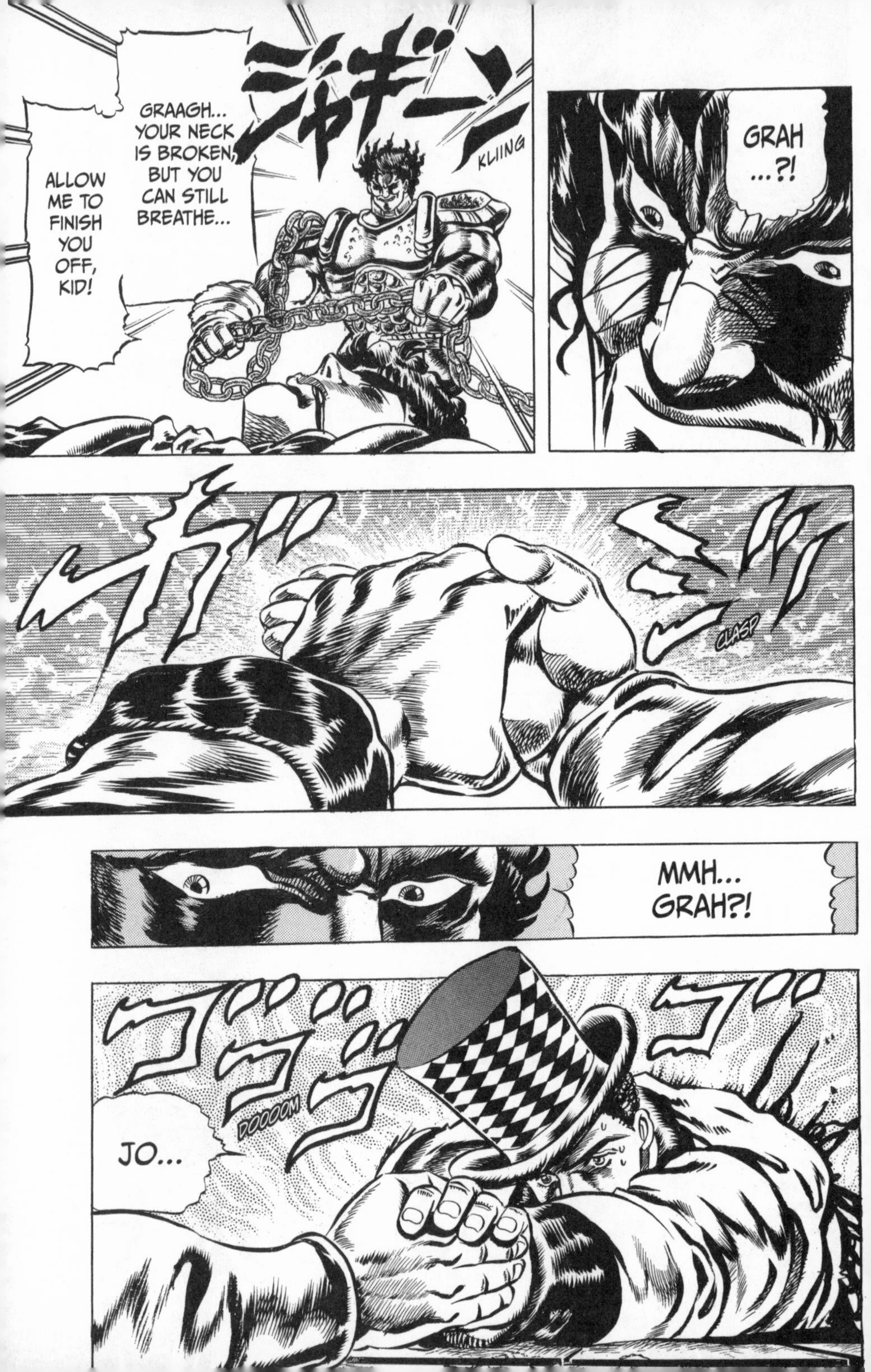
GRAH ...?!
ジャギーン
KLIING
GRAAGH... YOUR NECK IS BROKEN, BUT YOU CAN STILL BREATHE...
ALLOW ME TO FINISH YOU OFF, KID!
CLASP
MMH... GRAH?!
ゴゴゴゴ
DOOOOM
JO...

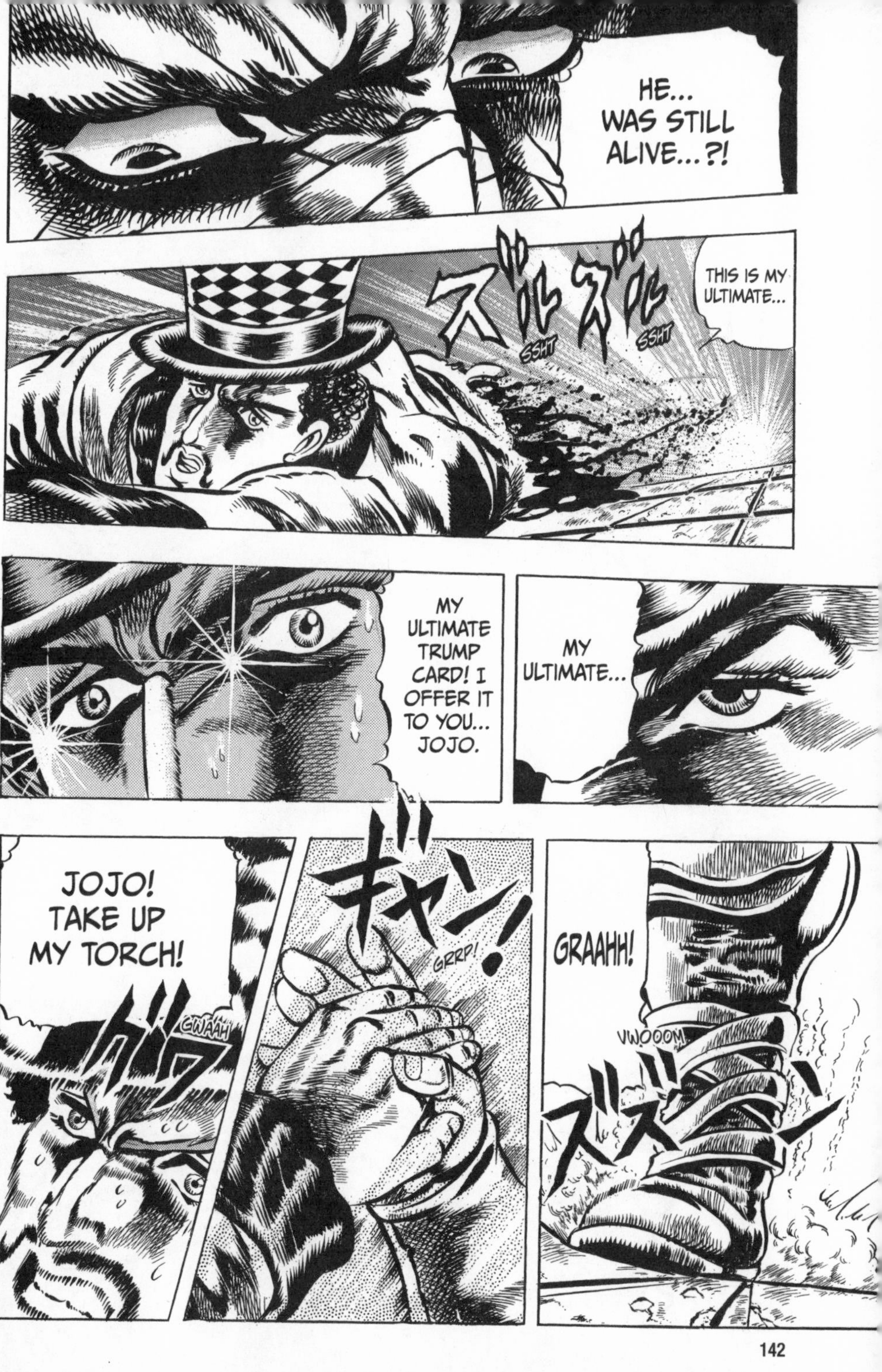
HE... WAS STILL ALIVE...?!
THIS IS MY ULTIMATE...
SSHT
SSHT
MY ULTIMATE...
MY ULTIMATE TRUMP CARD! I OFFER IT TO YOU... JOJO.
GRAAHH!
VWOOOM
GRRP!
JOJO! TAKE UP MY TORCH!
GWAAH

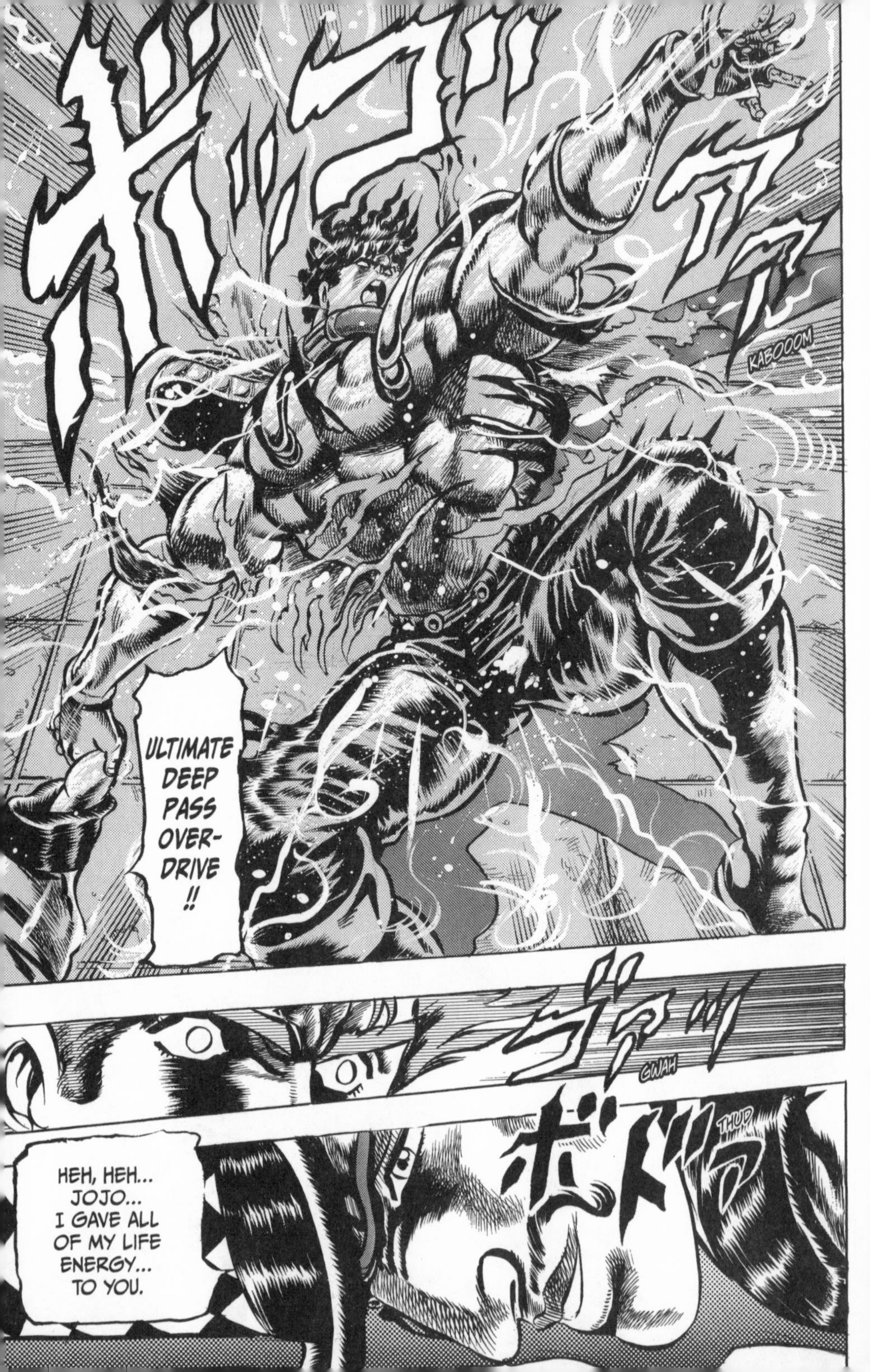
KABOOOM
ULTIMATE DEEP PASS OVER-DRIVE!!
GWAH
THUD
HEH, HEH... JOJO... I GAVE ALL OF MY LIFE ENERGY... TO YOU.

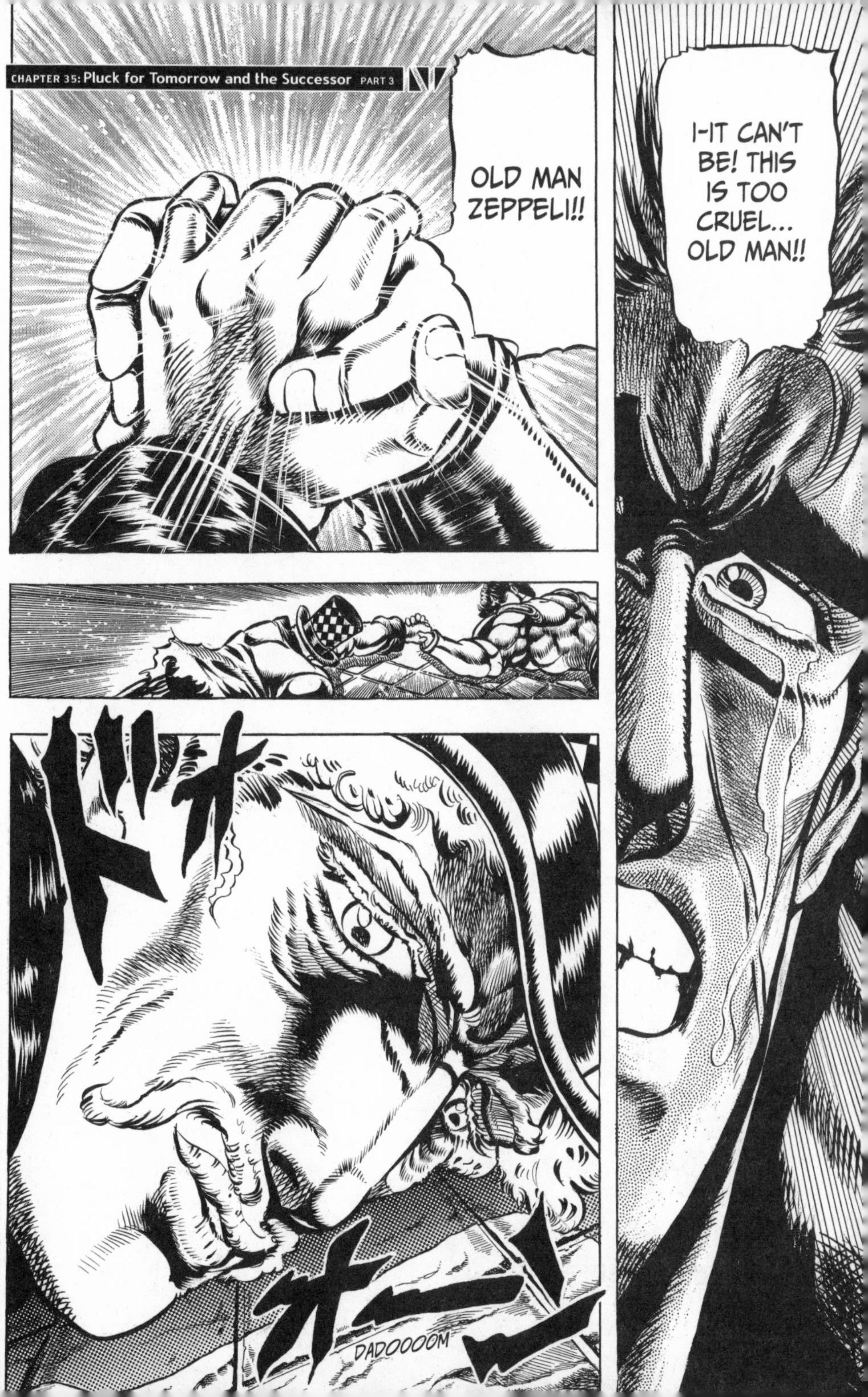
I-IT CAN'T BE! THIS IS TOO CRUEL... OLD MAN!!
CHAPTER 35: Pluck for Tomorrow and the Successor PART 3
OLD MAN ZEPPELI!!
DADOOOOM

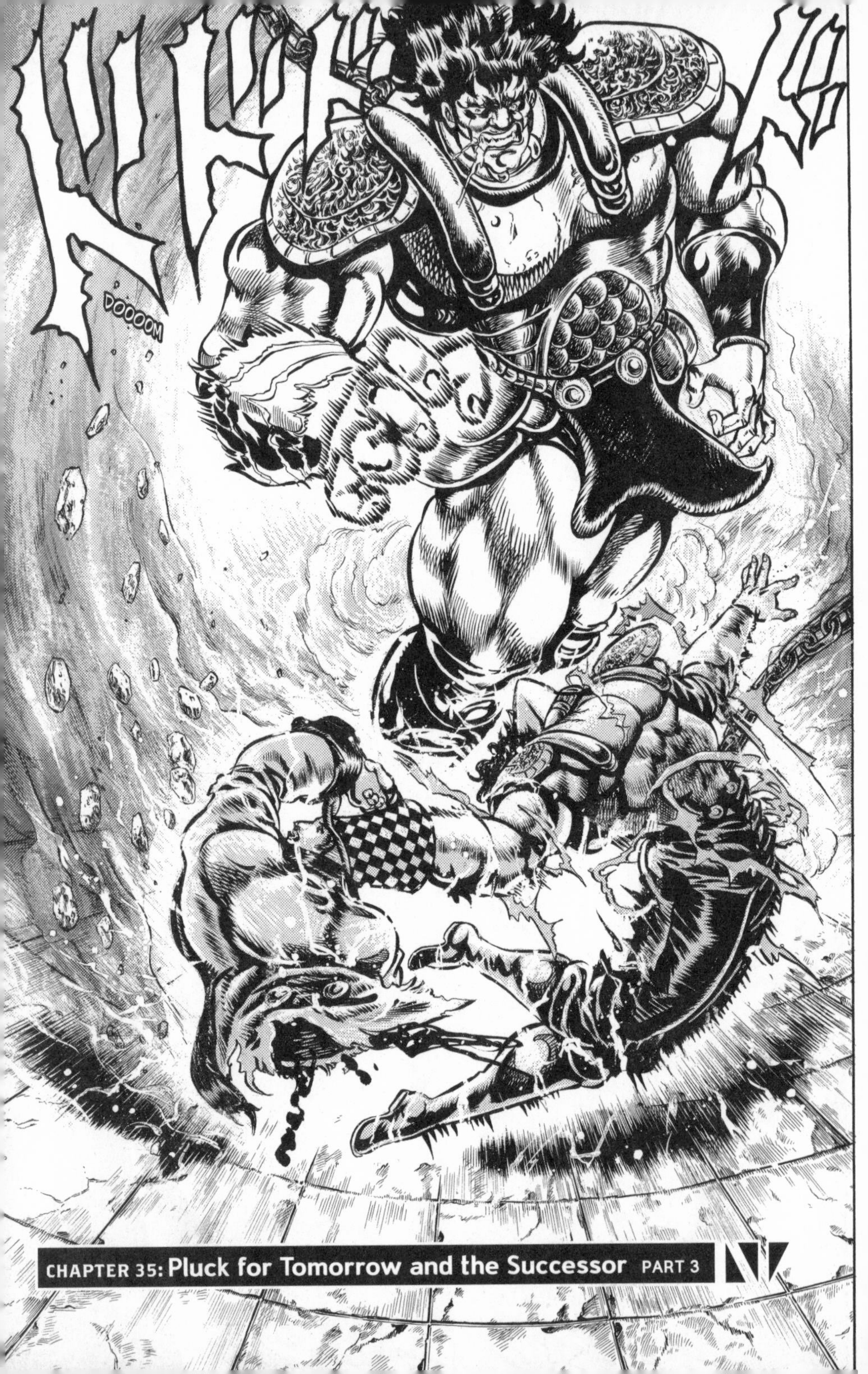
DOOOOM

CHAPTER 35: Pluck for Tomorrow and the Successor PART 3

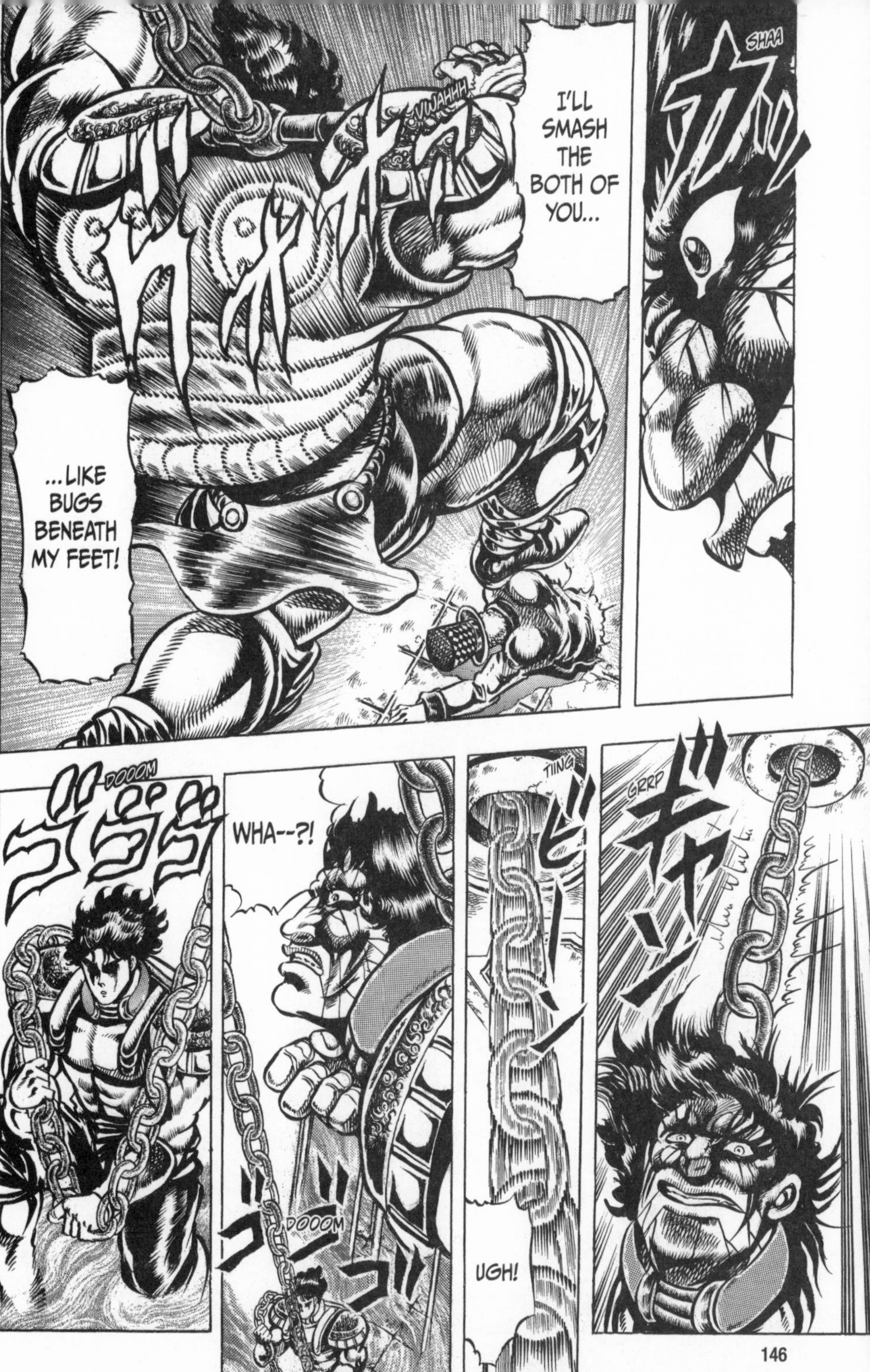
SHAA
VWAHHH
I'LL SMASH THE BOTH OF YOU...
...LIKE BUGS BENEATH MY FEET!
GRRP
TIING
UGH!
WHA--?!
DOOOM
DOOOM

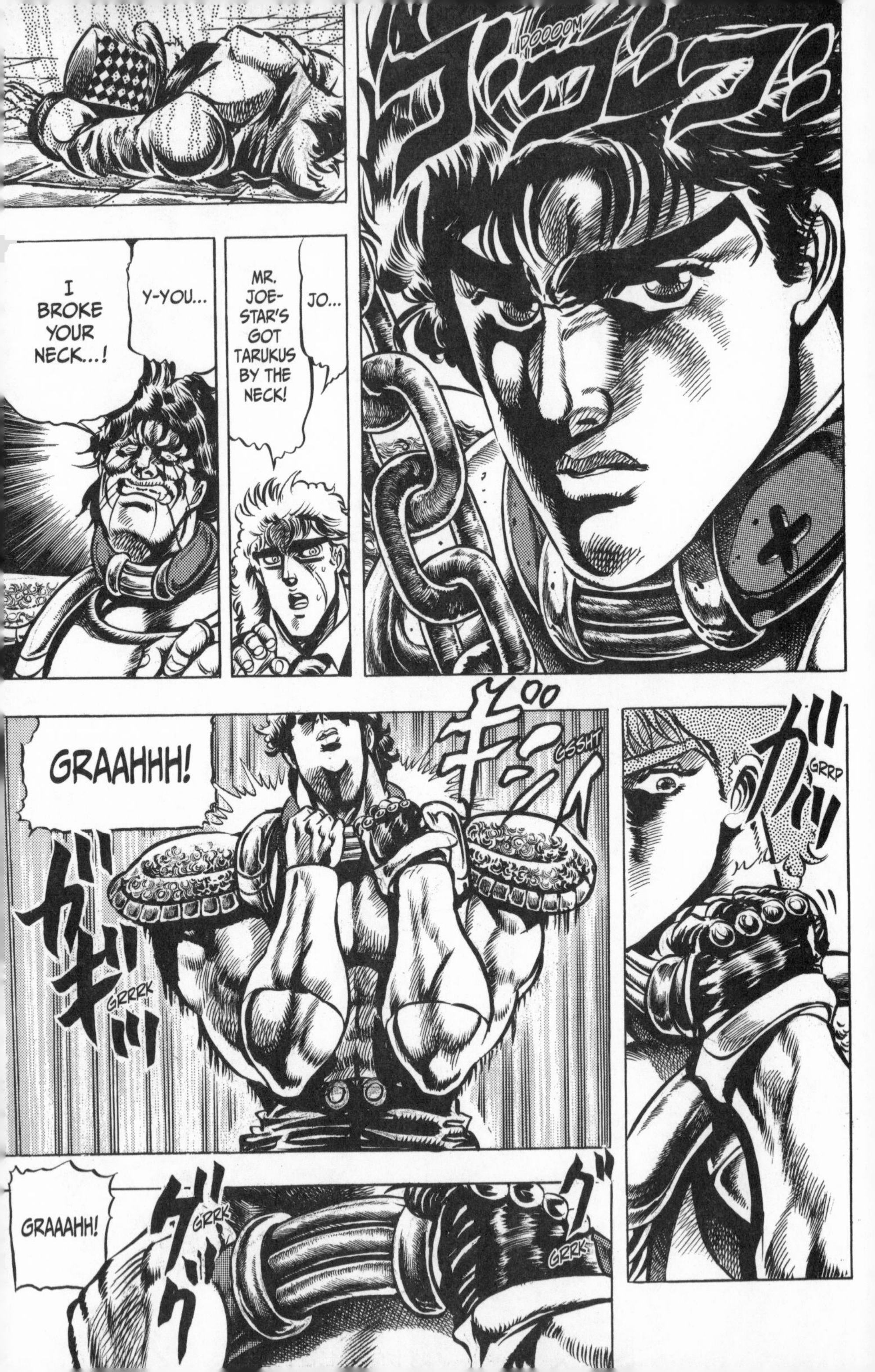
DOOOOM
JO...
MR. JOE-STAR'S GOT TARUKUS BY THE NECK!
Y-YOU...
I BROKE YOUR NECK...!
GRRP
ZOOO
GSSHT
GRAAHHH!
GRRRK
GRRK
GRRK
GRAAAHH!

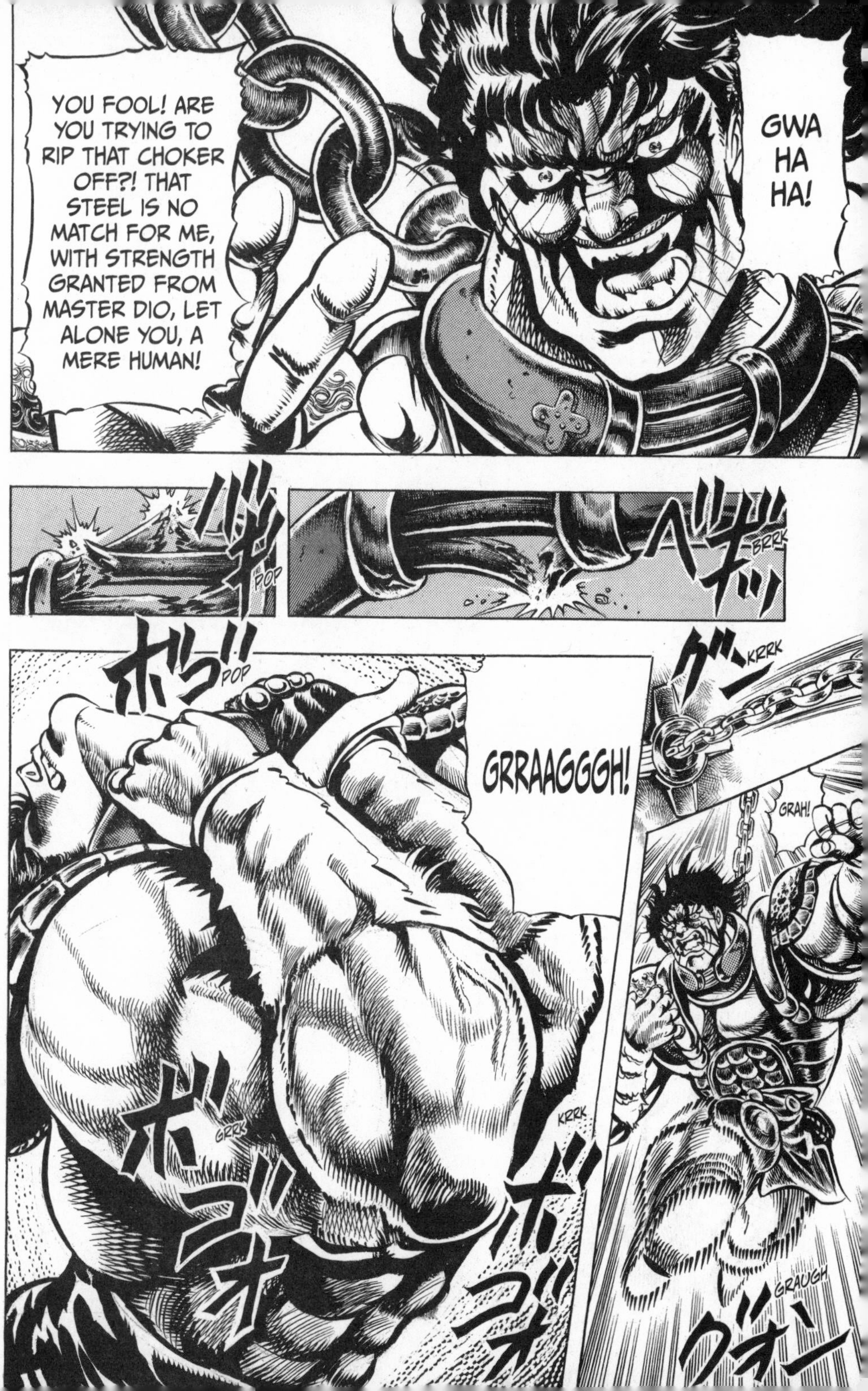
GWA HA HA!
YOU FOOL! ARE YOU TRYING TO RIP THAT CHOKER OFF?! THAT STEEL IS NO MATCH FOR ME, WITH STRENGTH GRANTED FROM MASTER DIO, LET ALONE YOU, A MERE HUMAN!
BRRK
POP
KRRK
GRAH!
GRAUGH
GRRAAGGGH!
POP
KRRK
GRRK

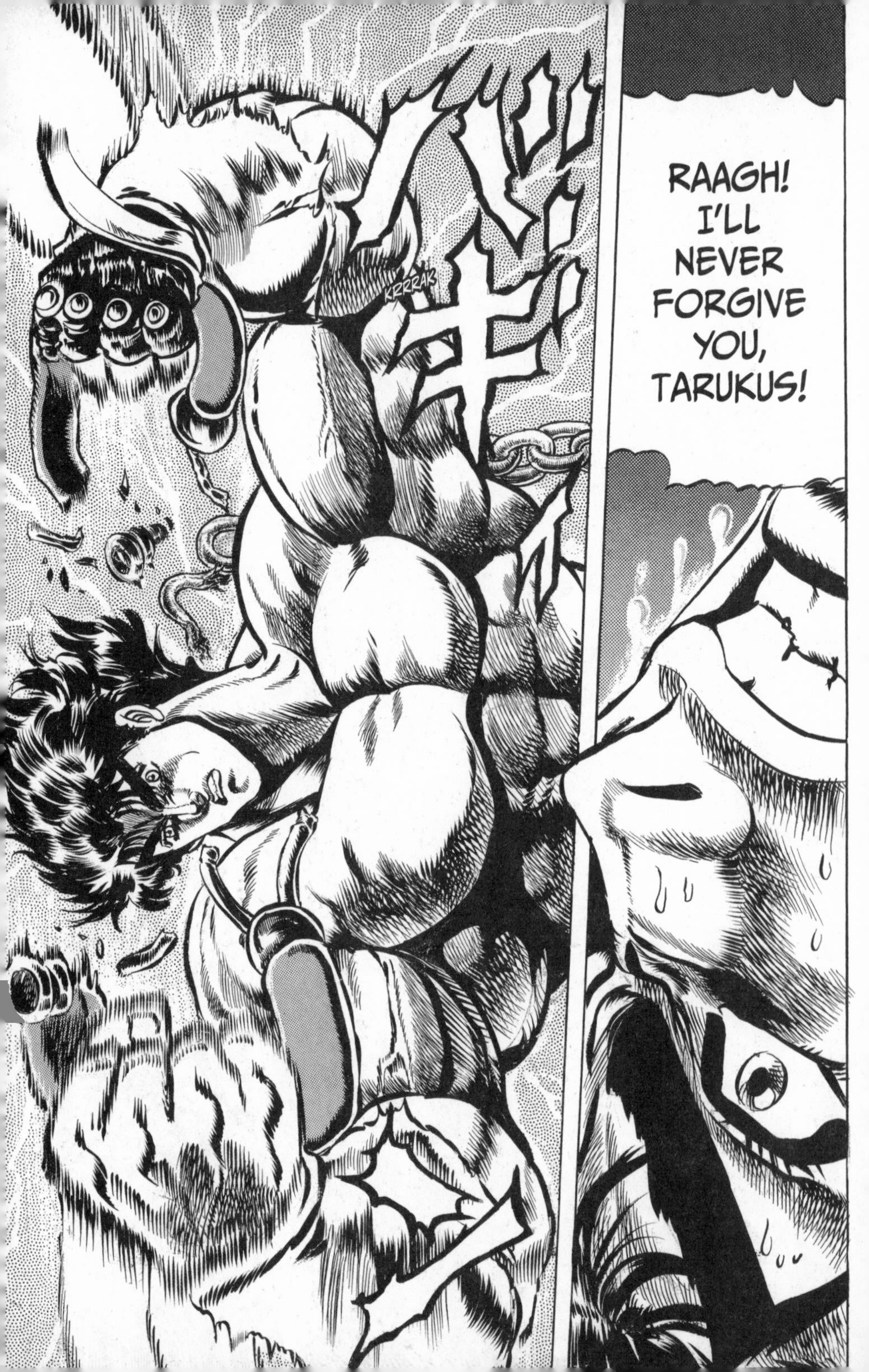
RAAGH! I'LL NEVER FORGIVE YOU, TARUKUS!
KRRRAK

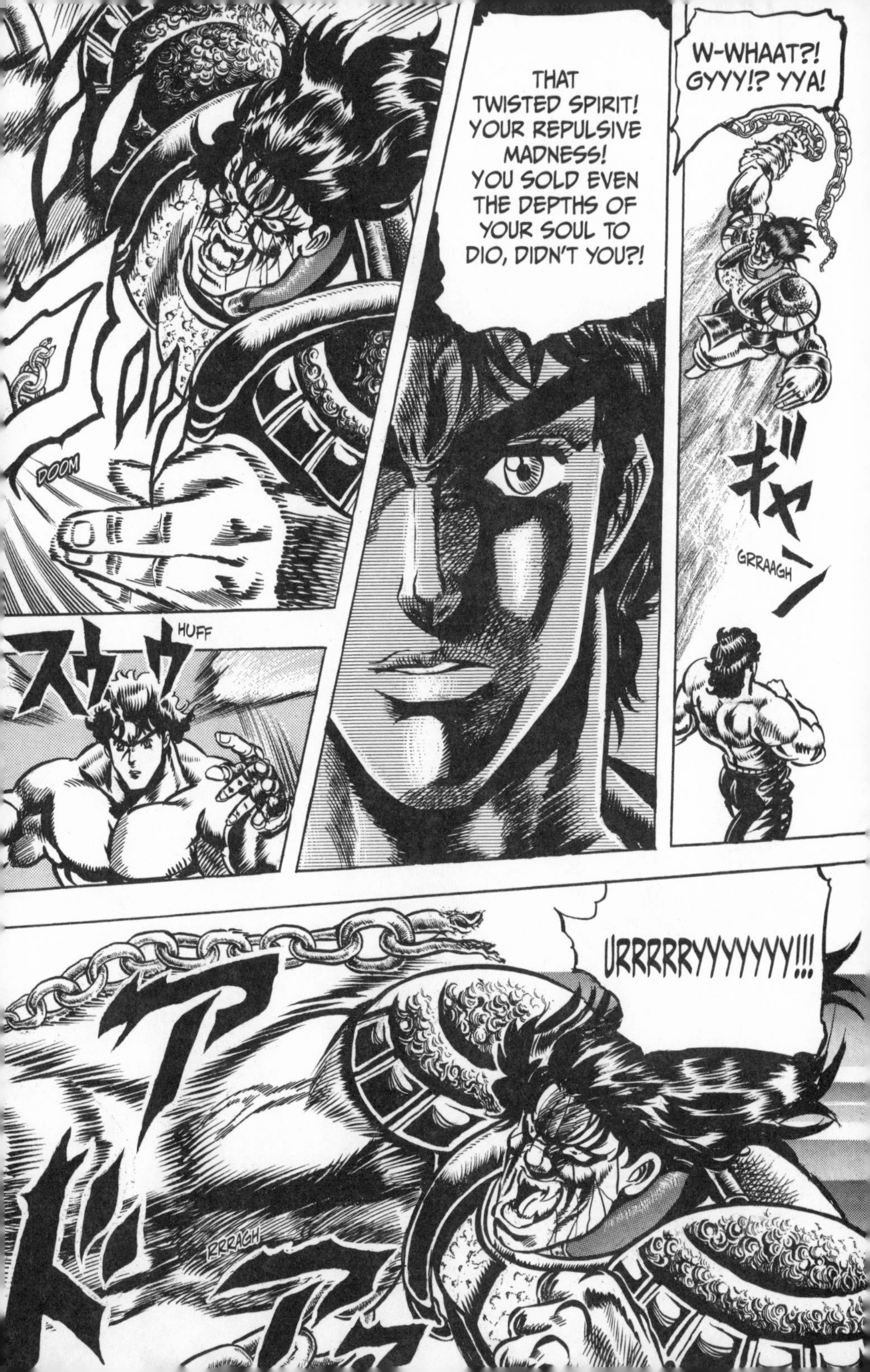
W-WHAAT?! GYYY!? YYA!
ギャーン
GRRAAGH
THAT TWISTED SPIRIT! YOUR REPULSIVE MADNESS! YOU SOLD EVEN THE DEPTHS OF YOUR SOUL TO DIO, DIDN'T YOU?!
DOOM
HUFF
URRRRRYYYYYY!!!
RRRAGH

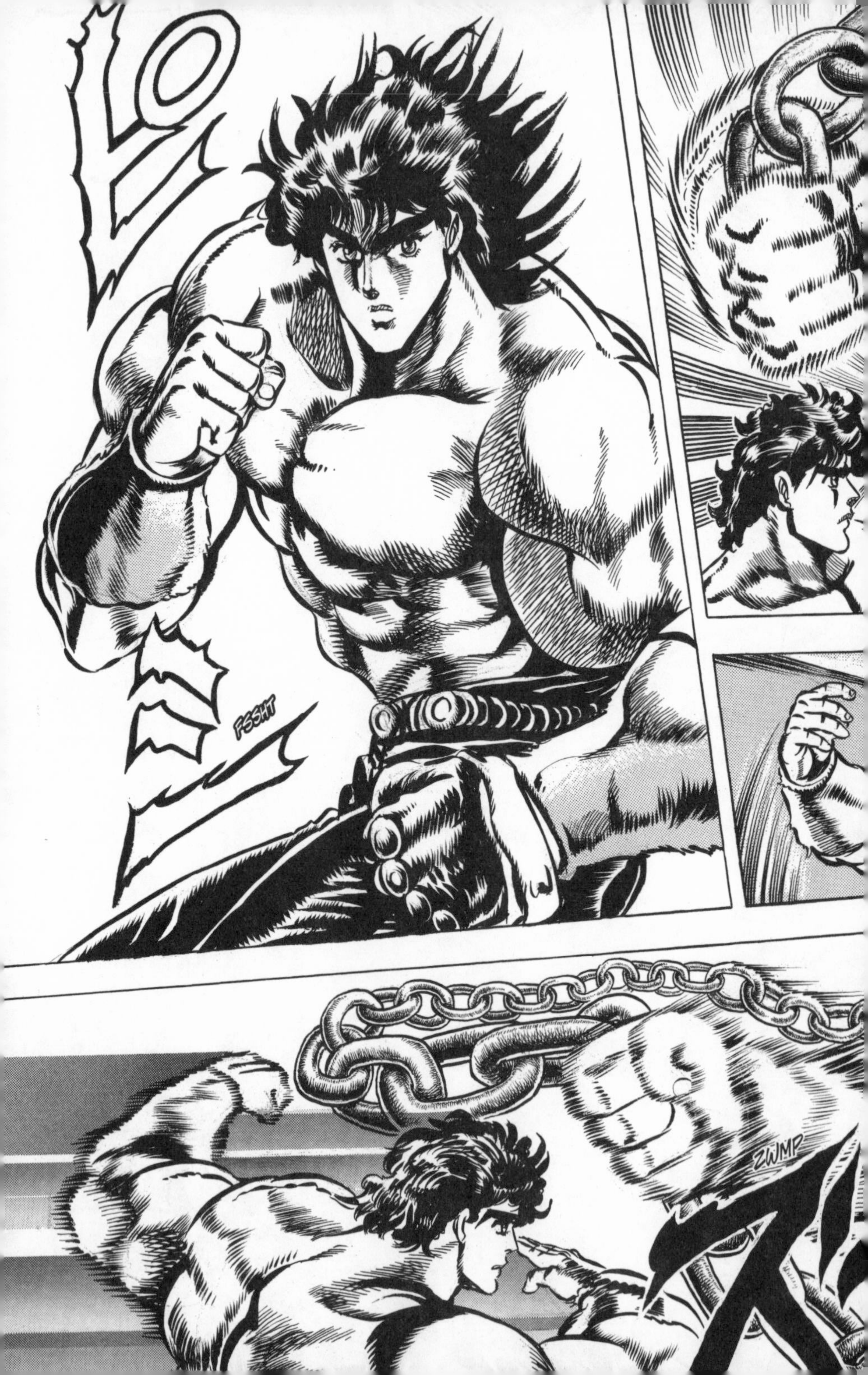
PSSHT
ZWMP

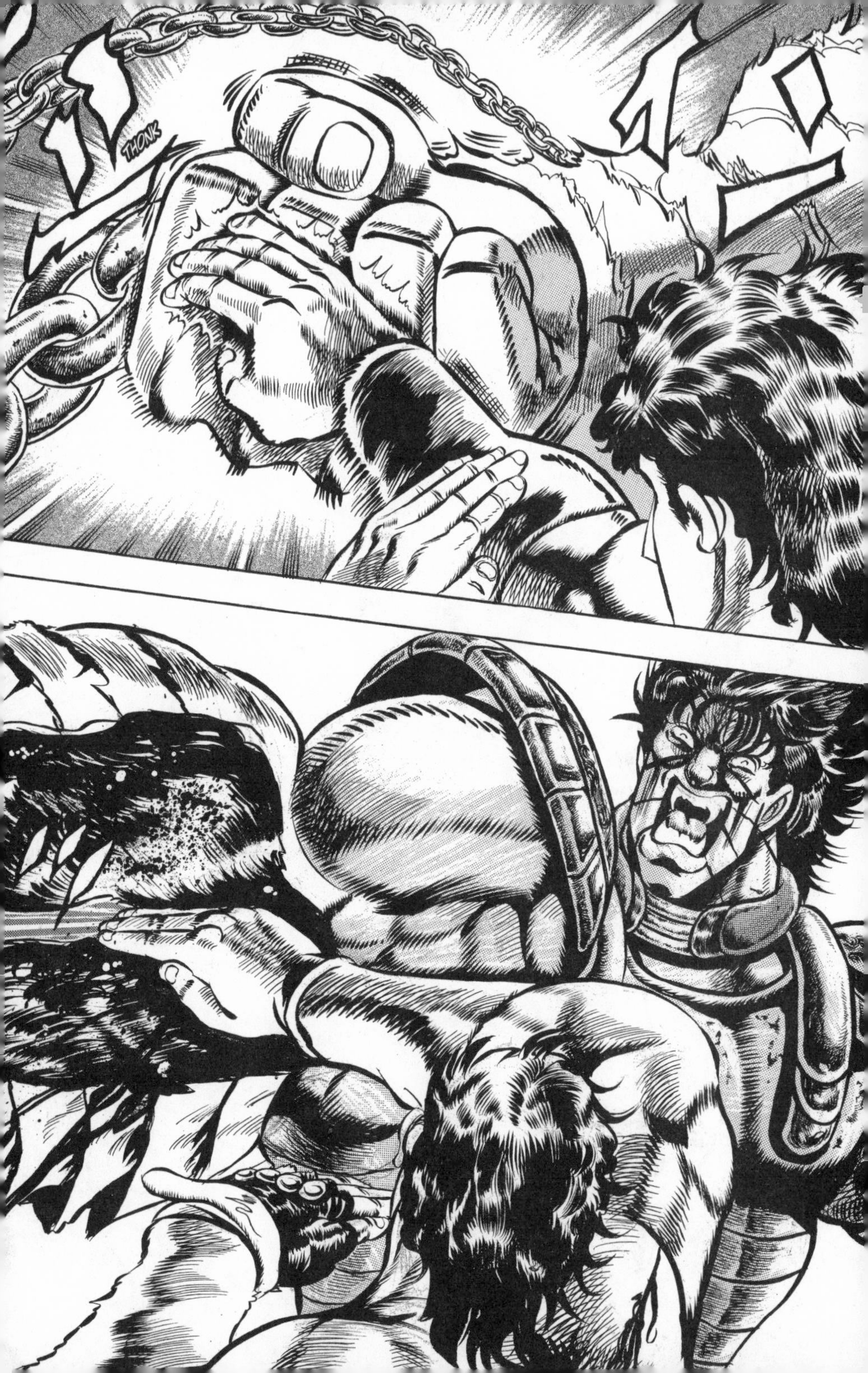
THONK

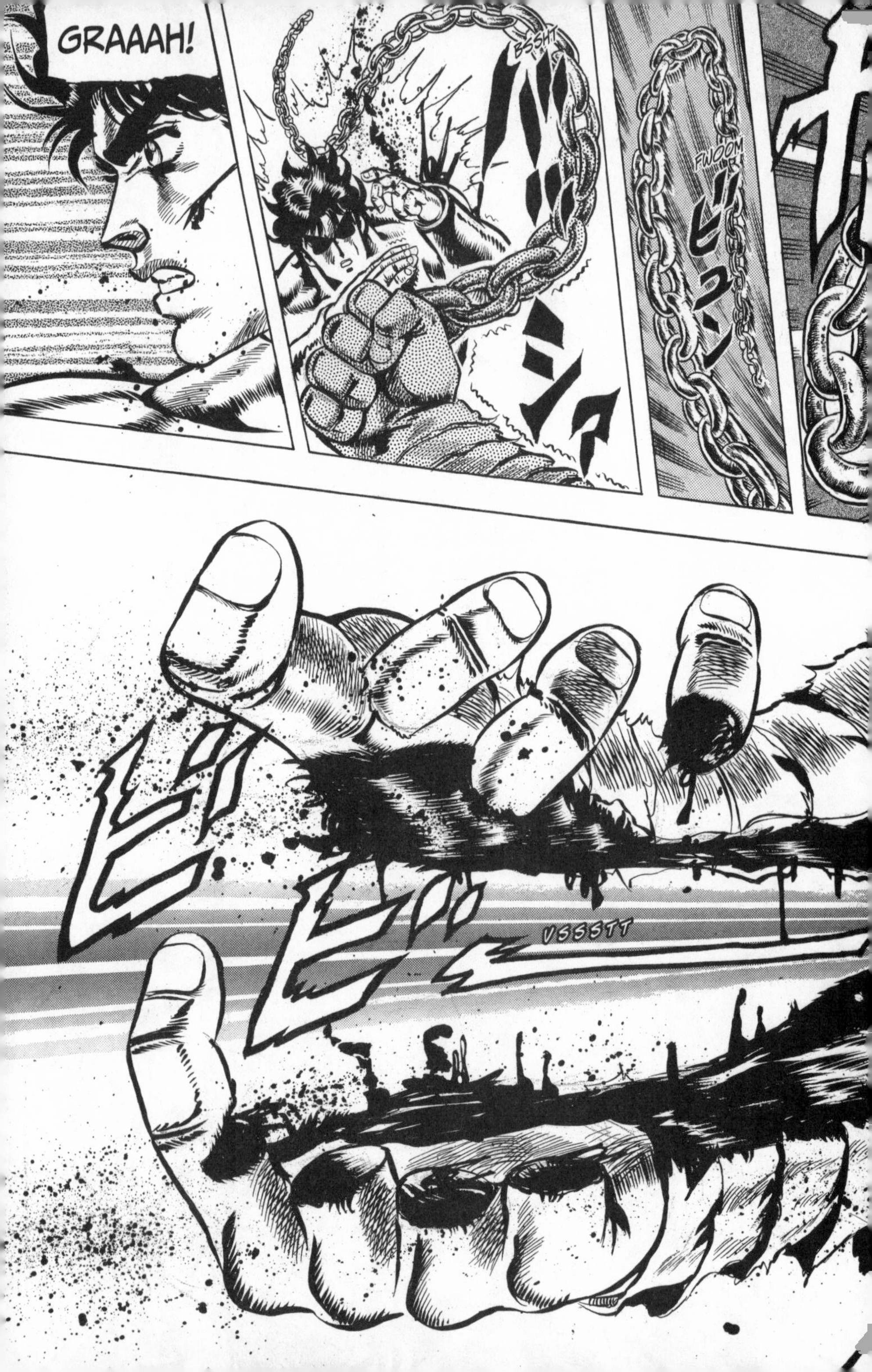
FWOOM
BSSHT
GRAAAH!
VSSSTT

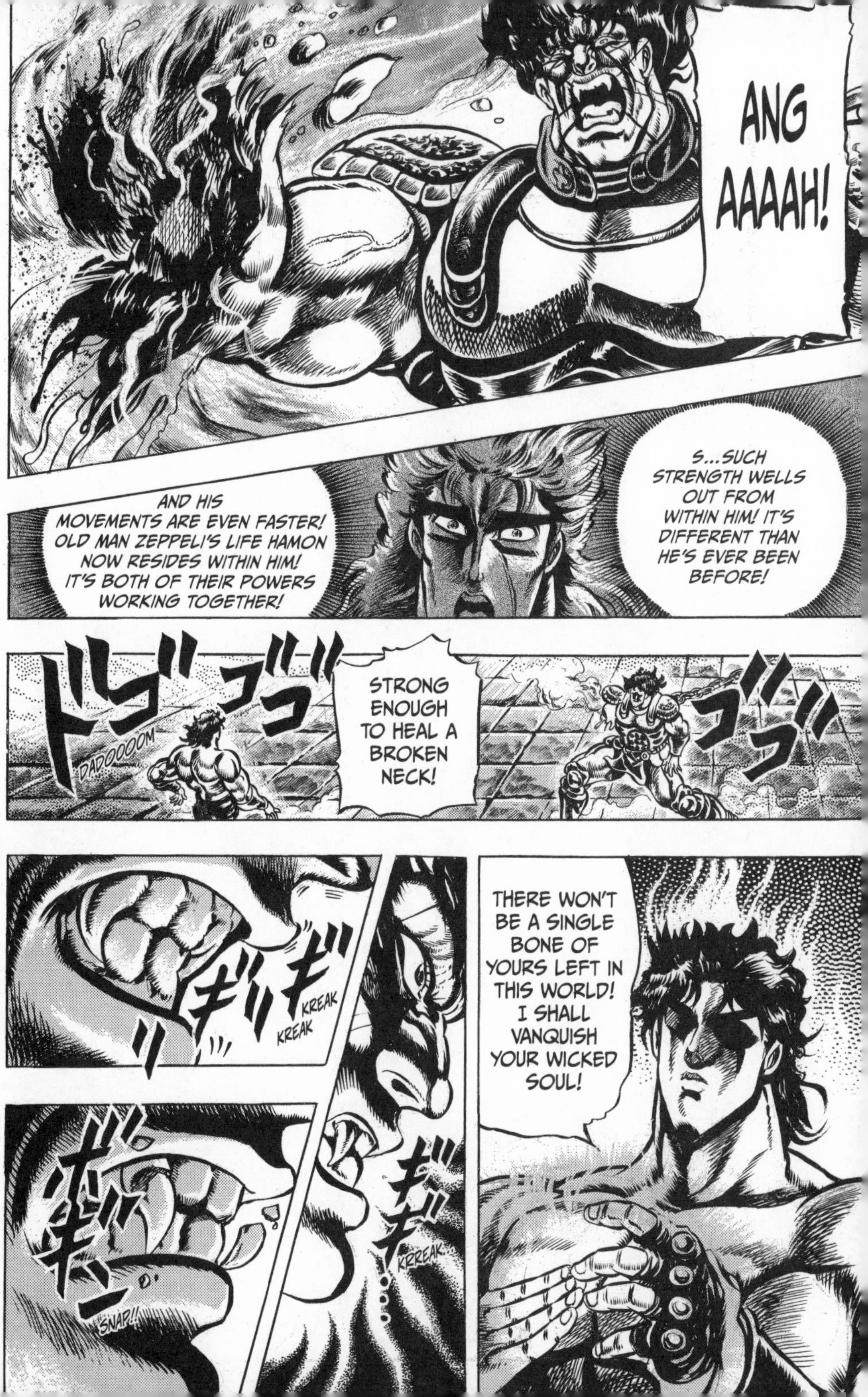
ANG AAAAH!
S...SUCH STRENGTH WELLS OUT FROM WITHIN HIM! IT'S DIFFERENT THAN HE'S EVER BEEN BEFORE!
AND HIS MOVEMENTS ARE EVEN FASTER! OLD MAN ZEPPELI'S LIFE HAMON NOW RESIDES WITHIN HIM! IT'S BOTH OF THEIR POWERS WORKING TOGETHER!
STRONG ENOUGH TO HEAL A BROKEN NECK!
DADOOOOM
THERE WON'T BE A SINGLE BONE OF YOURS LEFT IN THIS WORLD! I SHALL VANQUISH YOUR WICKED SOUL!
KRREAK
KREAK KREAK
SNAP!!

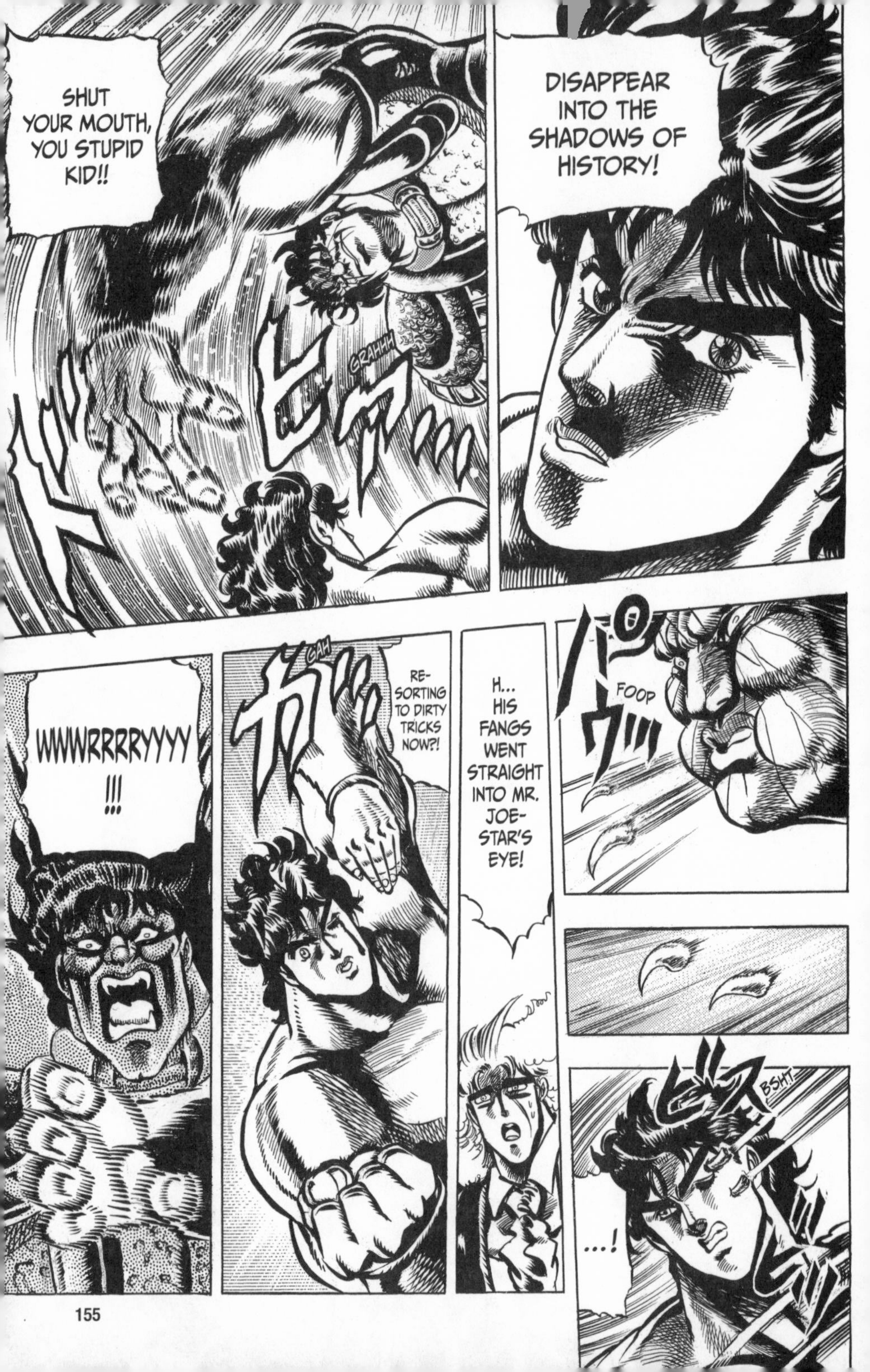
DISAPPEAR INTO THE SHADOWS OF HISTORY!
SHUT YOUR MOUTH, YOU STUPID KID!!
GRAHHH
FOOP
BSHT
...!
H... HIS FANGS WENT STRAIGHT INTO MR. JOE-STAR'S EYE!
GAH
RE-SORTING TO DIRTY TRICKS NOW?!
WWWRRRRYYYY!!!

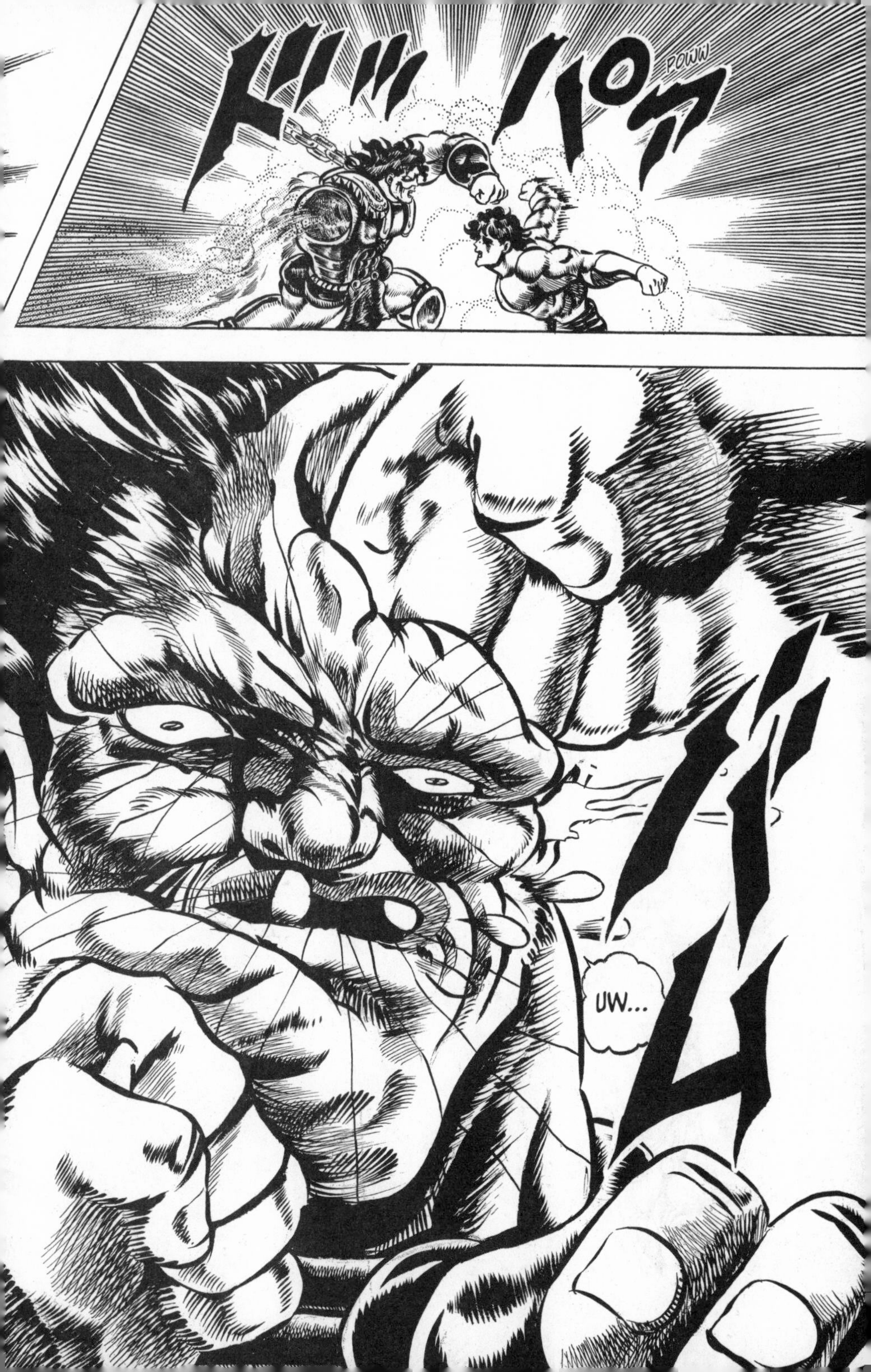
POWW
UW...

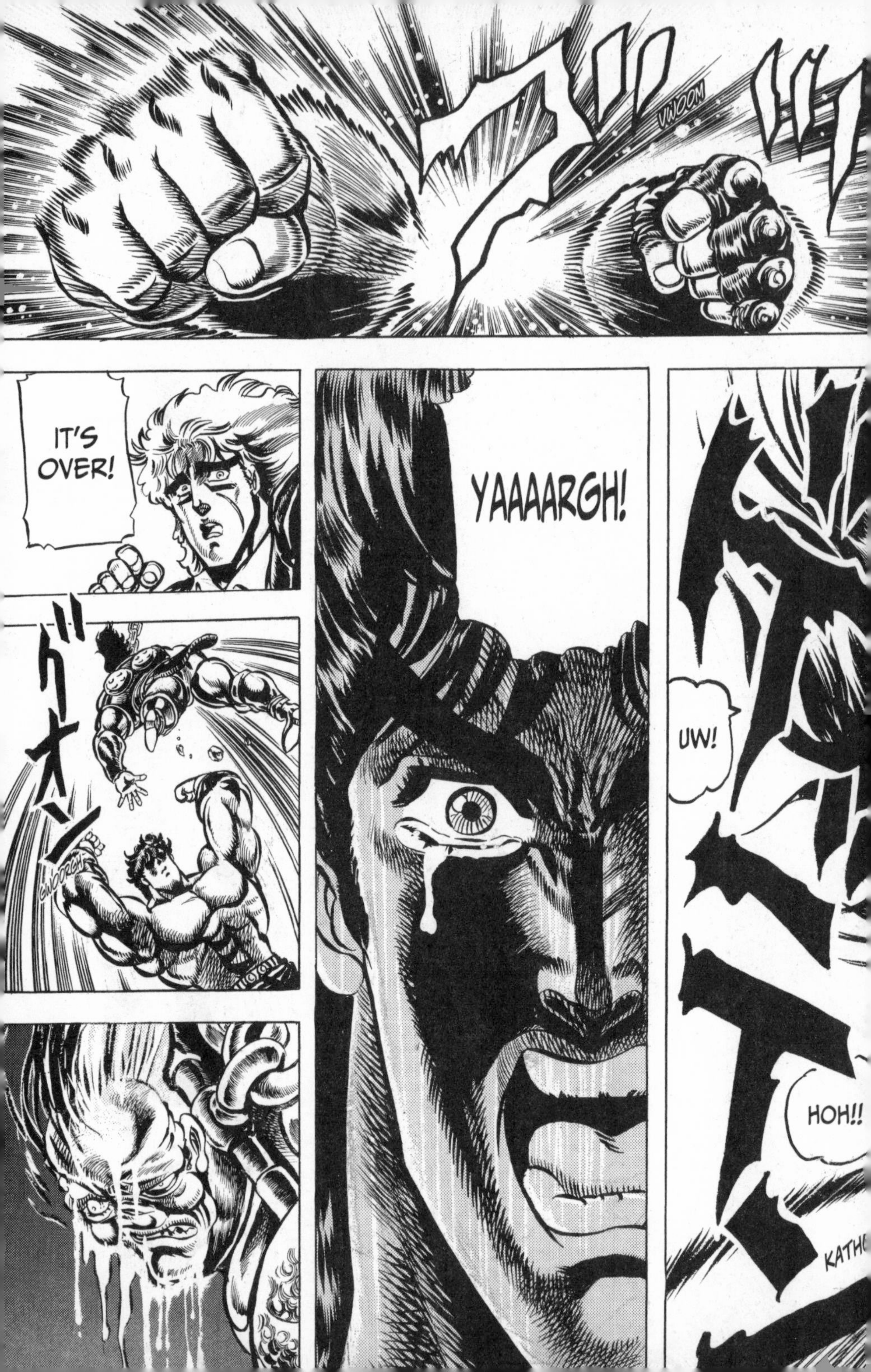
VWOOM
UW!
HOH!!
KATH
YAAAARGH!
IT'S OVER!
GWOORGH

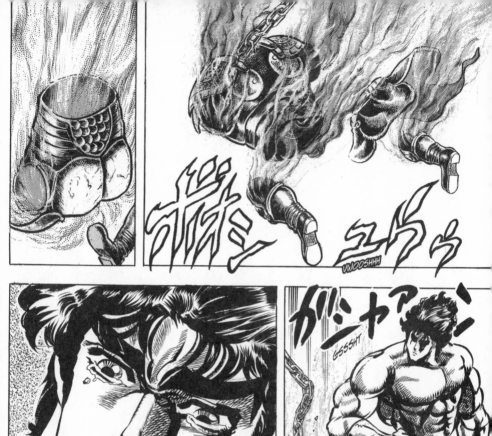

ゴオオオシ

VWOOSHH ユラララ

ガシャアン
GSSSHT

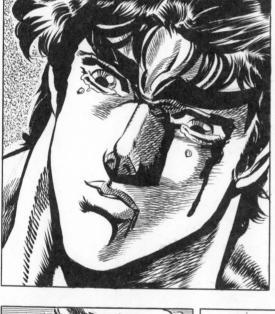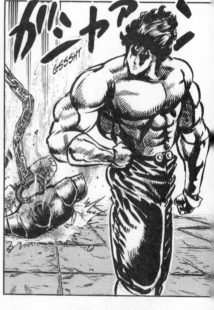

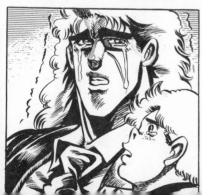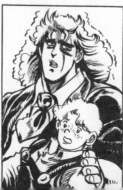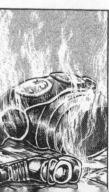

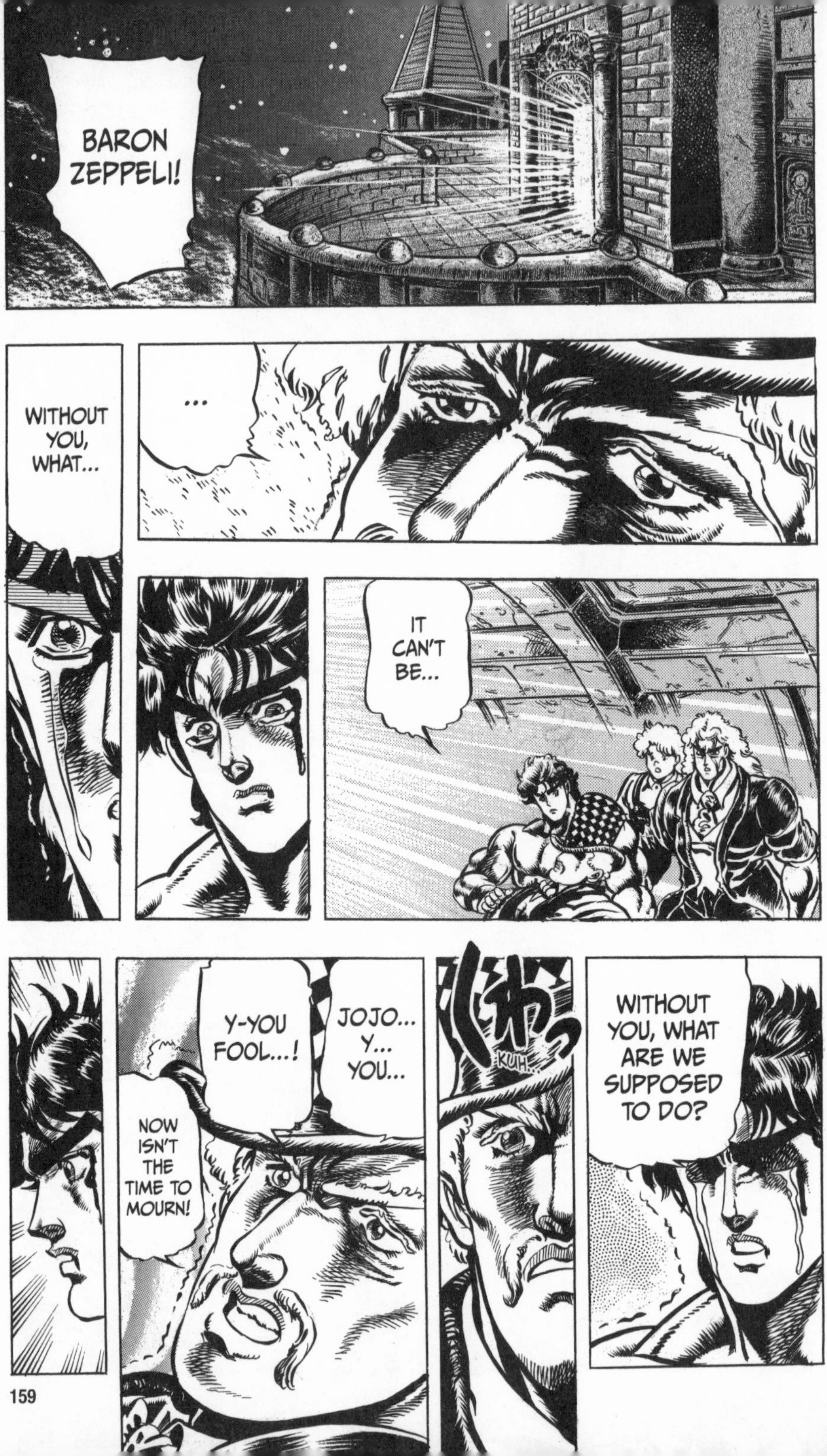
BARON ZEPPELI!
...
IT CAN'T BE...
WITHOUT YOU, WHAT...
WITHOUT YOU, WHAT ARE WE SUPPOSED TO DO?
KUH...
JOJO... Y... YOU...
Y-YOU FOOL...!
NOW ISN'T THE TIME TO MOURN!

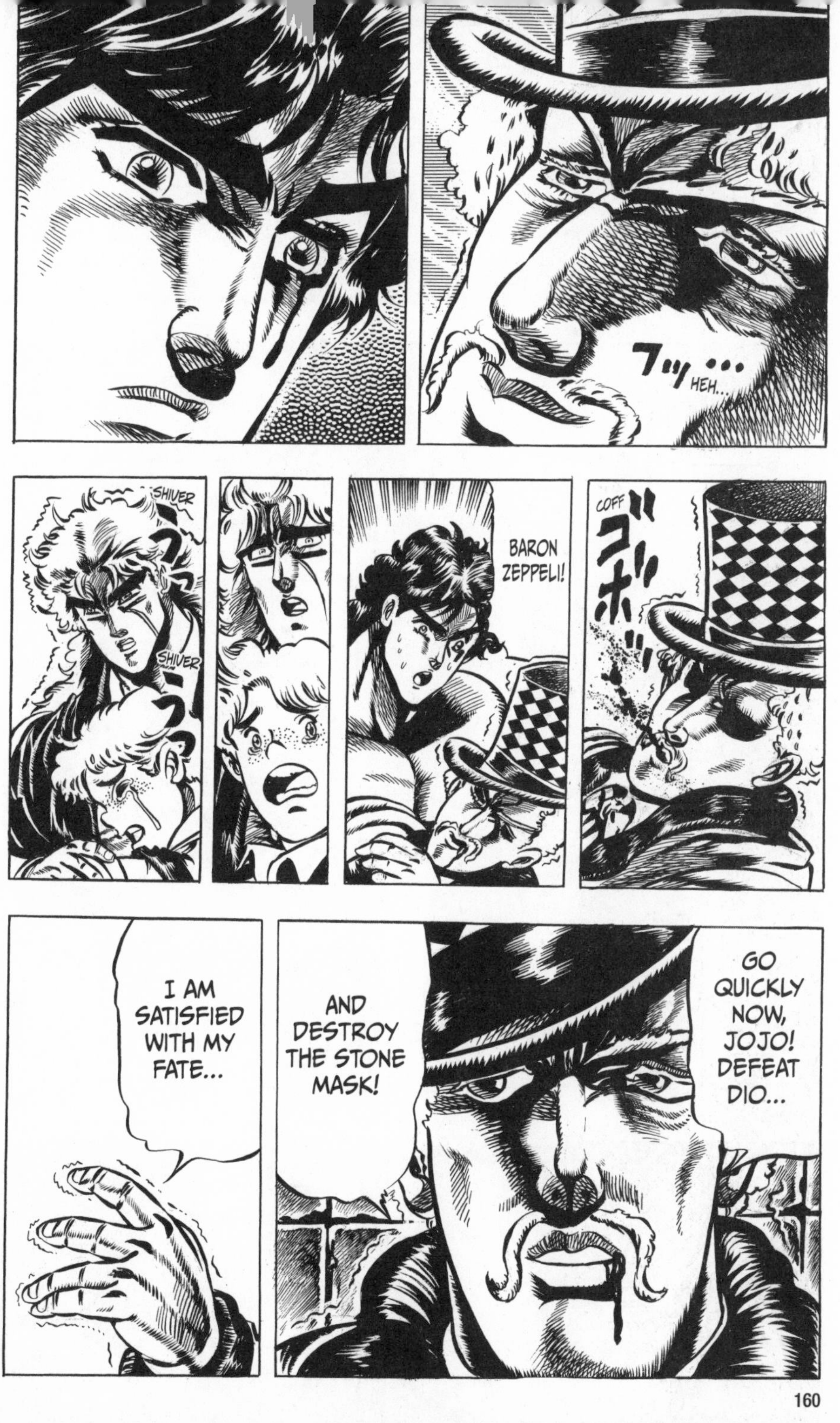
フッ…
HEH...
COFF
ゴボッ
BARON ZEPPELI!
SHIVER
SHIVER
GO QUICKLY NOW, JOJO! DEFEAT DIO...
AND DESTROY THE STONE MASK!
I AM SATISFIED WITH MY FATE...

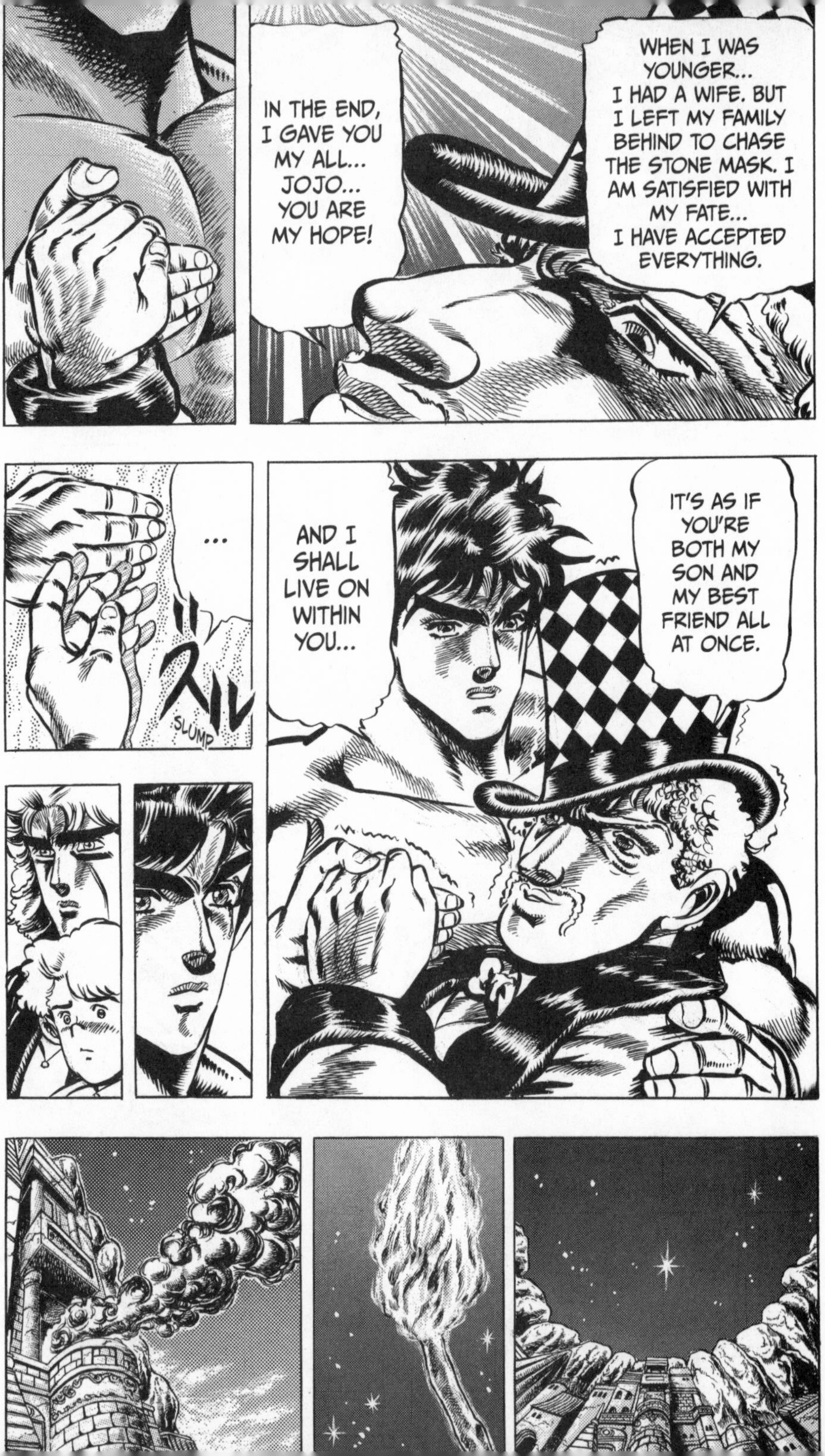
WHEN I WAS YOUNGER... I HAD A WIFE. BUT I LEFT MY FAMILY BEHIND TO CHASE THE STONE MASK. I AM SATISFIED WITH MY FATE... I HAVE ACCEPTED EVERYTHING.
IN THE END, I GAVE YOU MY ALL... JOJO... YOU ARE MY HOPE!
IT'S AS IF YOU'RE BOTH MY SON AND MY BEST FRIEND ALL AT ONCE.
AND I SHALL LIVE ON WITHIN YOU...
...
ズル
SLUMP

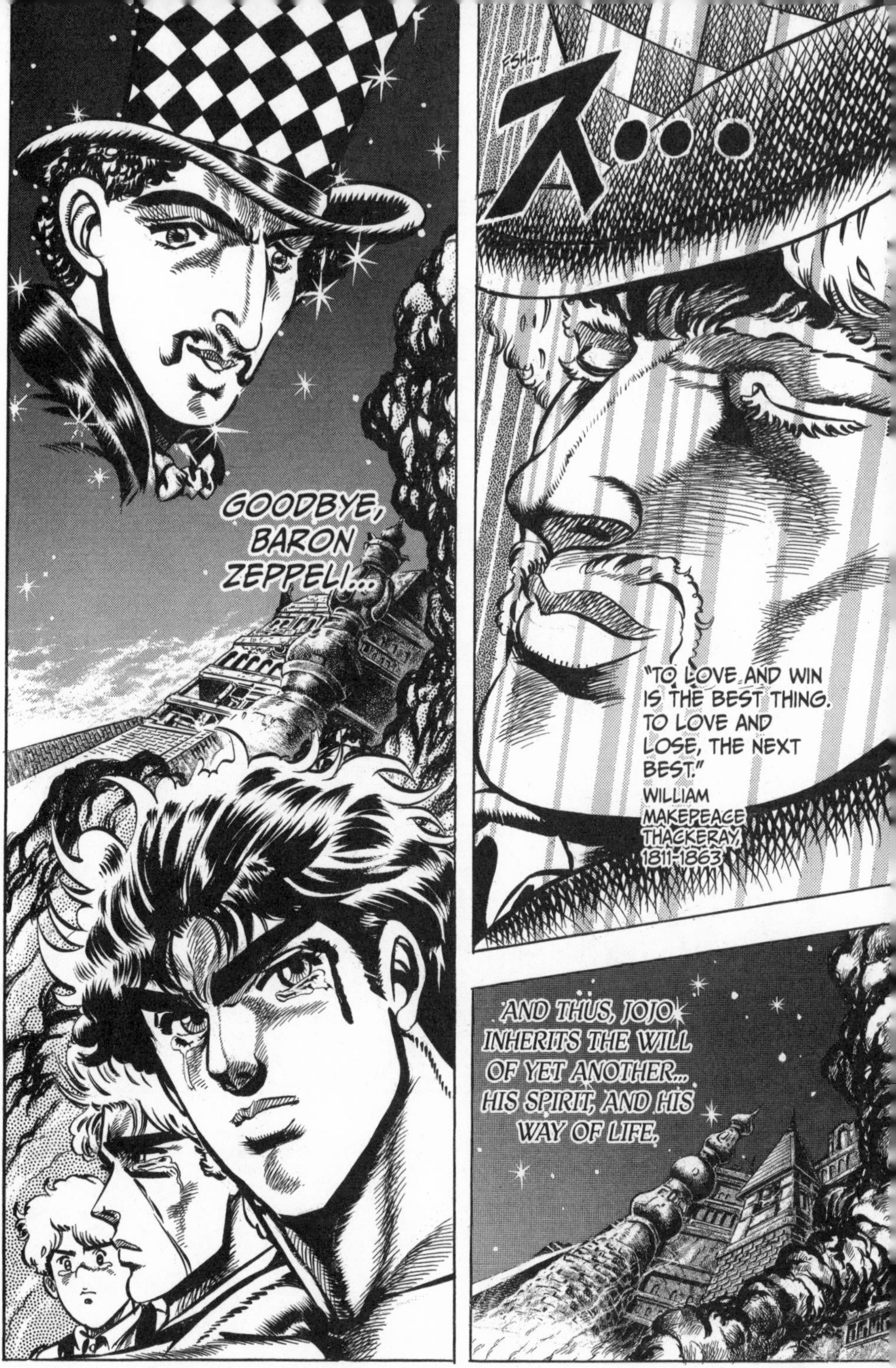
FSH...
ス...
"TO LOVE AND WIN IS THE BEST THING. TO LOVE AND LOSE, THE NEXT BEST."
WILLIAM MAKEPEACE THACKERAY, 1811-1863
AND THUS, JOJO INHERITS THE WILL OF YET ANOTHER... HIS SPIRIT, AND HIS WAY OF LIFE.
GOODBYE, BARON ZEPPELI...

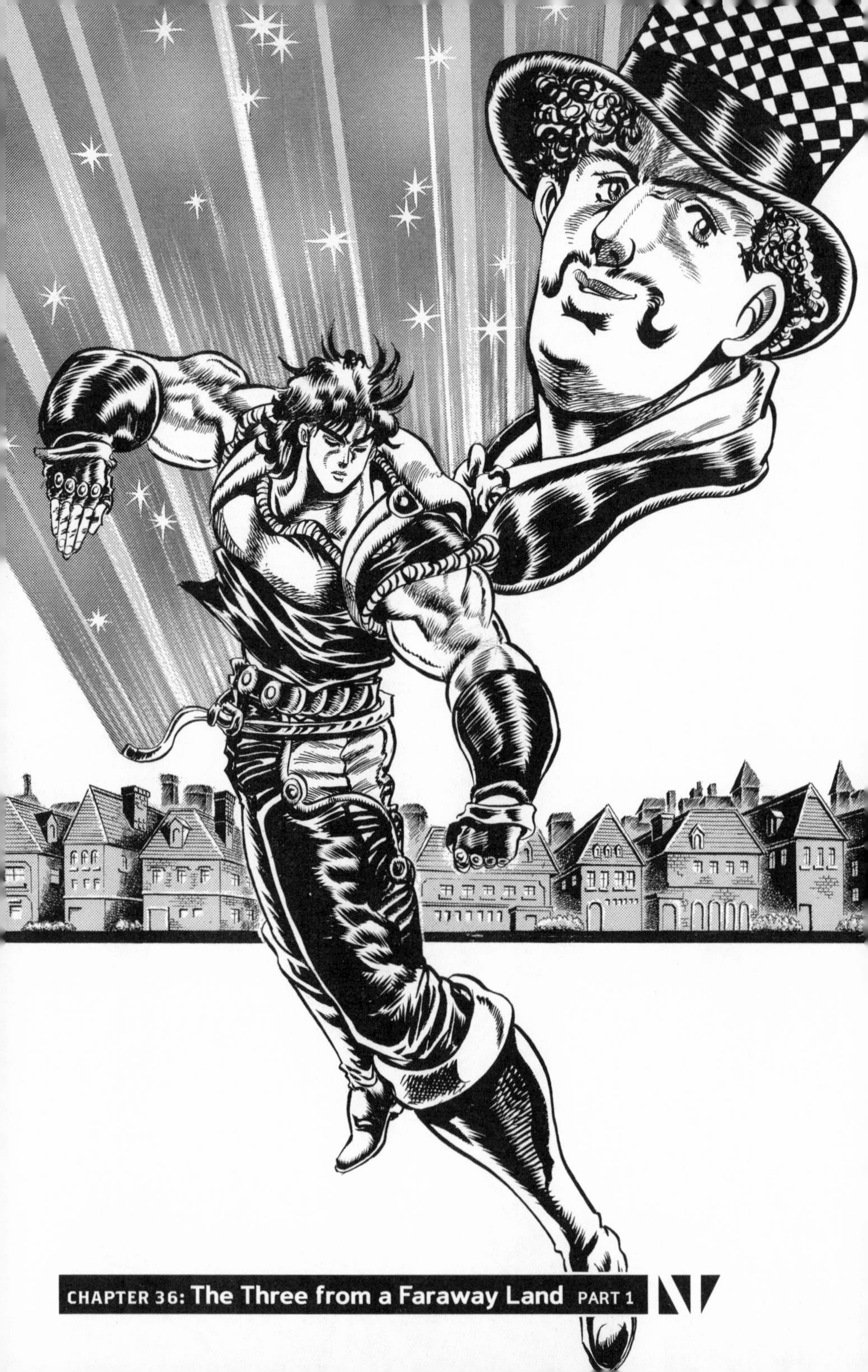

CHAPTER 36: The Three from a Faraway Land PART 1

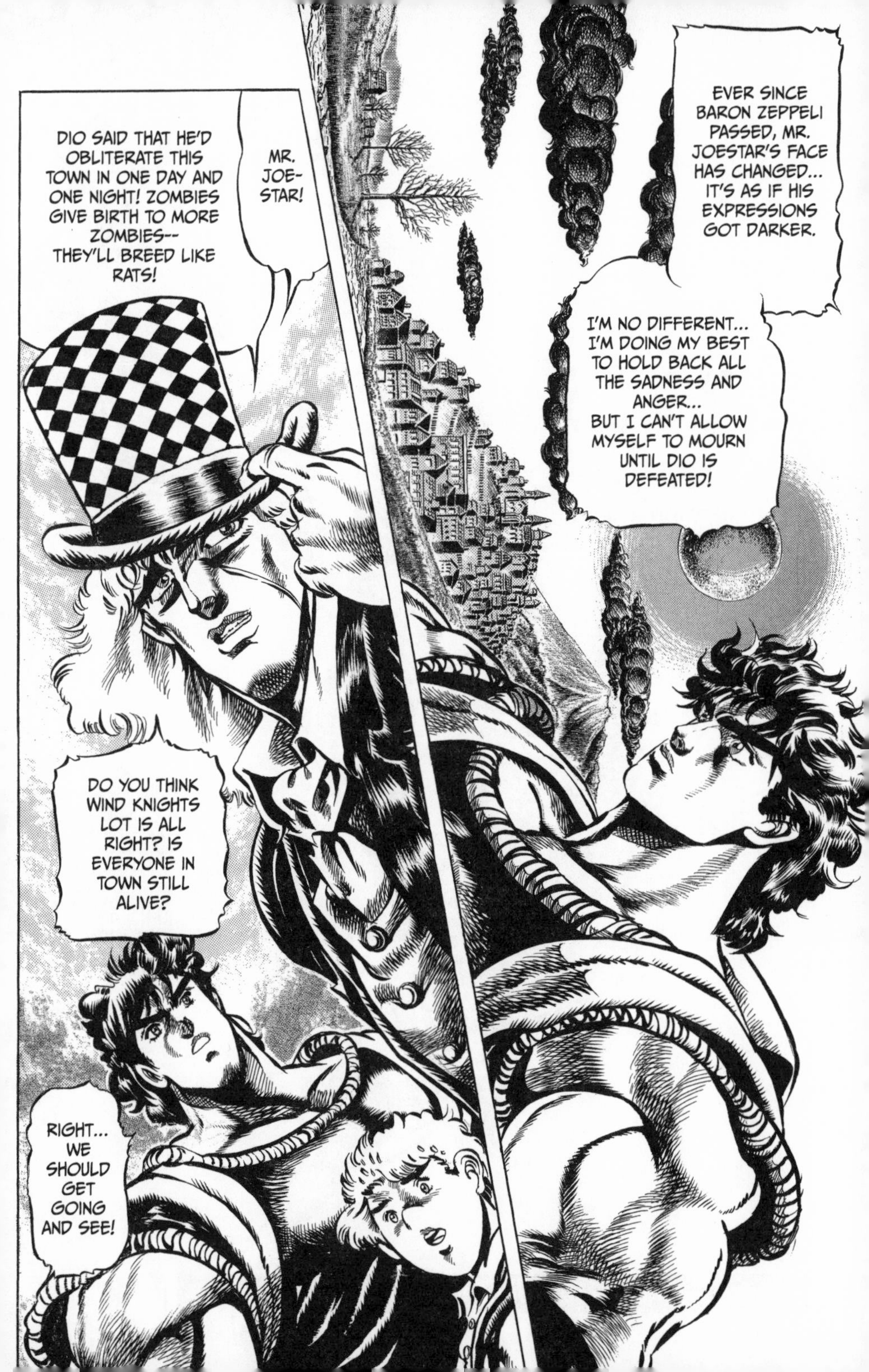
EVER SINCE BARON ZEPPELI PASSED, MR. JOESTAR'S FACE HAS CHANGED... IT'S AS IF HIS EXPRESSIONS GOT DARKER.
I'M NO DIFFERENT... I'M DOING MY BEST TO HOLD BACK ALL THE SADNESS AND ANGER... BUT I CAN'T ALLOW MYSELF TO MOURN UNTIL DIO IS DEFEATED!
MR. JOE-STAR!
DIO SAID THAT HE'D OBLITERATE THIS TOWN IN ONE DAY AND ONE NIGHT! ZOMBIES GIVE BIRTH TO MORE ZOMBIES-- THEY'LL BREED LIKE RATS!
DO YOU THINK WIND KNIGHTS LOT IS ALL RIGHT? IS EVERYONE IN TOWN STILL ALIVE?
RIGHT... WE SHOULD GET GOING AND SEE!

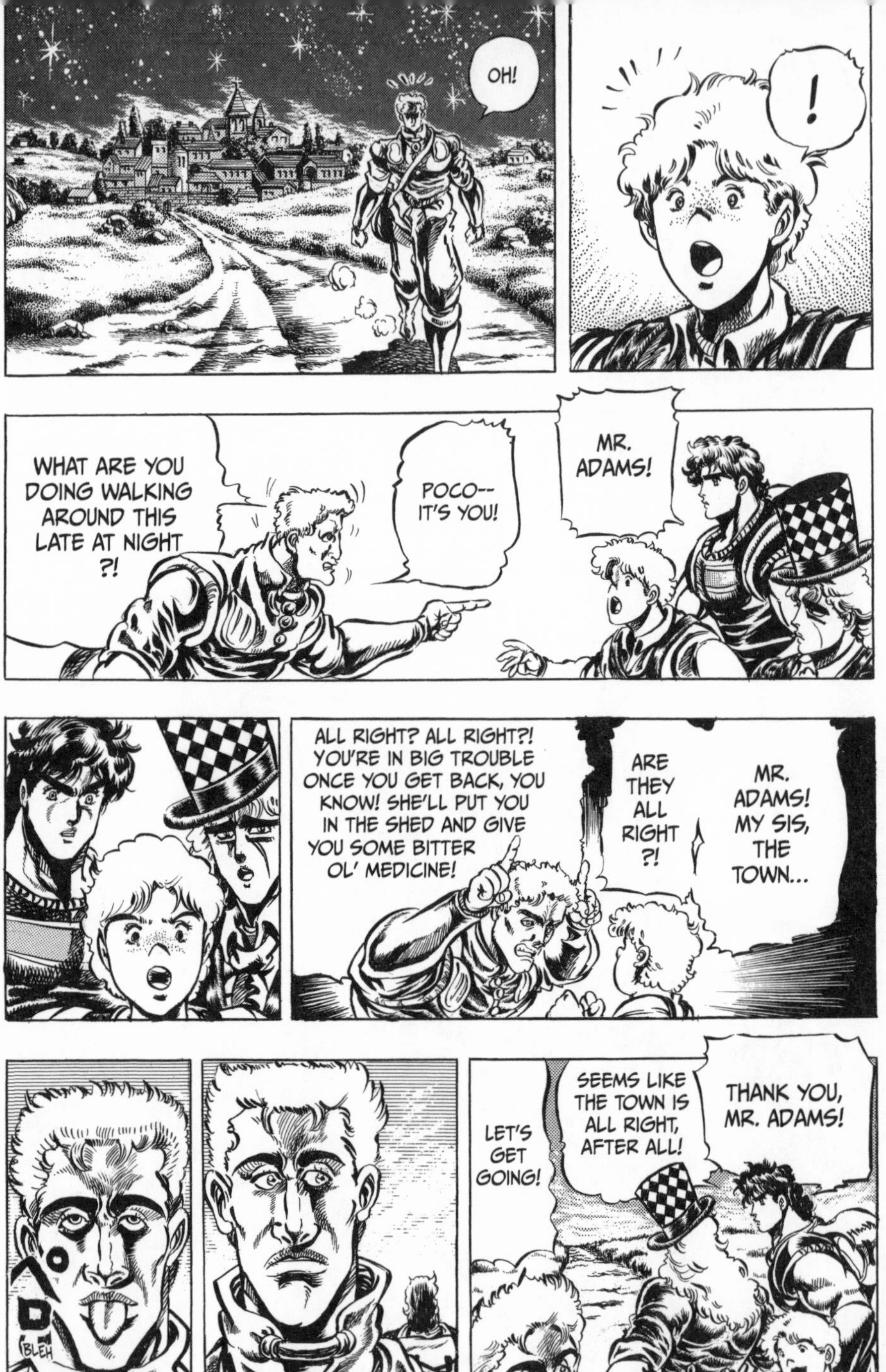
!
OH!
MR. ADAMS!
POCO--
IT'S YOU!
WHAT ARE YOU DOING WALKING AROUND THIS LATE AT NIGHT ?!
MR. ADAMS! MY SIS, THE TOWN...
ARE THEY ALL RIGHT ?!
ALL RIGHT? ALL RIGHT?! YOU'RE IN BIG TROUBLE ONCE YOU GET BACK, YOU KNOW! SHE'LL PUT YOU IN THE SHED AND GIVE YOU SOME BITTER OL' MEDICINE!
THANK YOU, MR. ADAMS!
SEEMS LIKE THE TOWN IS ALL RIGHT, AFTER ALL!
LET'S GET GOING!
BLEH

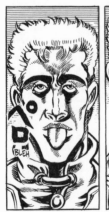

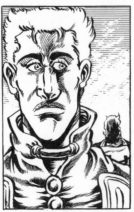

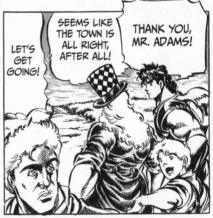

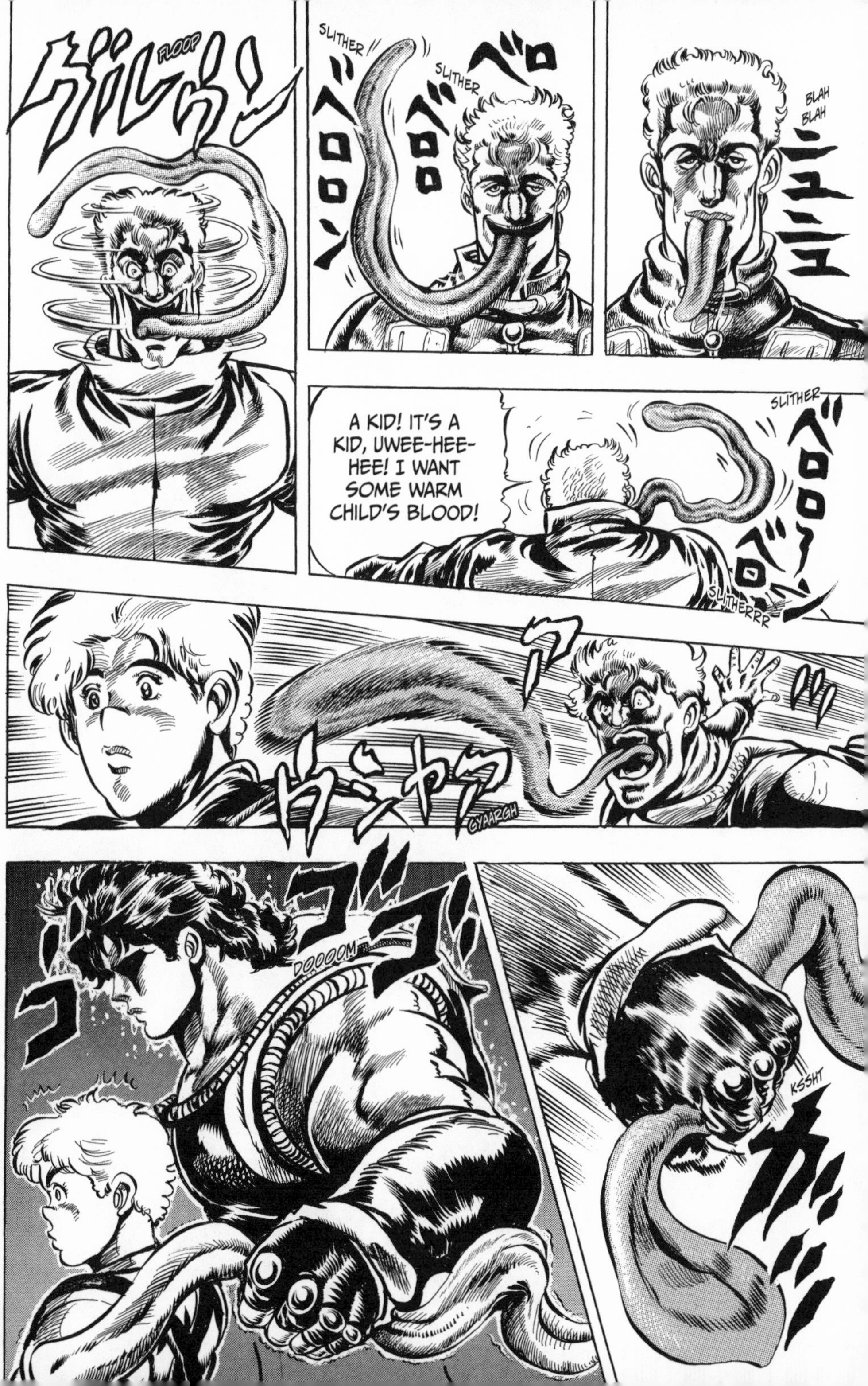
BLAH BLAH
SLITHER
SLITHER
SLITHER
A KID! IT'S A KID, UWEE-HEE-HEE! I WANT SOME WARM CHILD'S BLOOD!
SLITHERRR
FLOOP
GYAARGH
KSSHT
DOOOOM

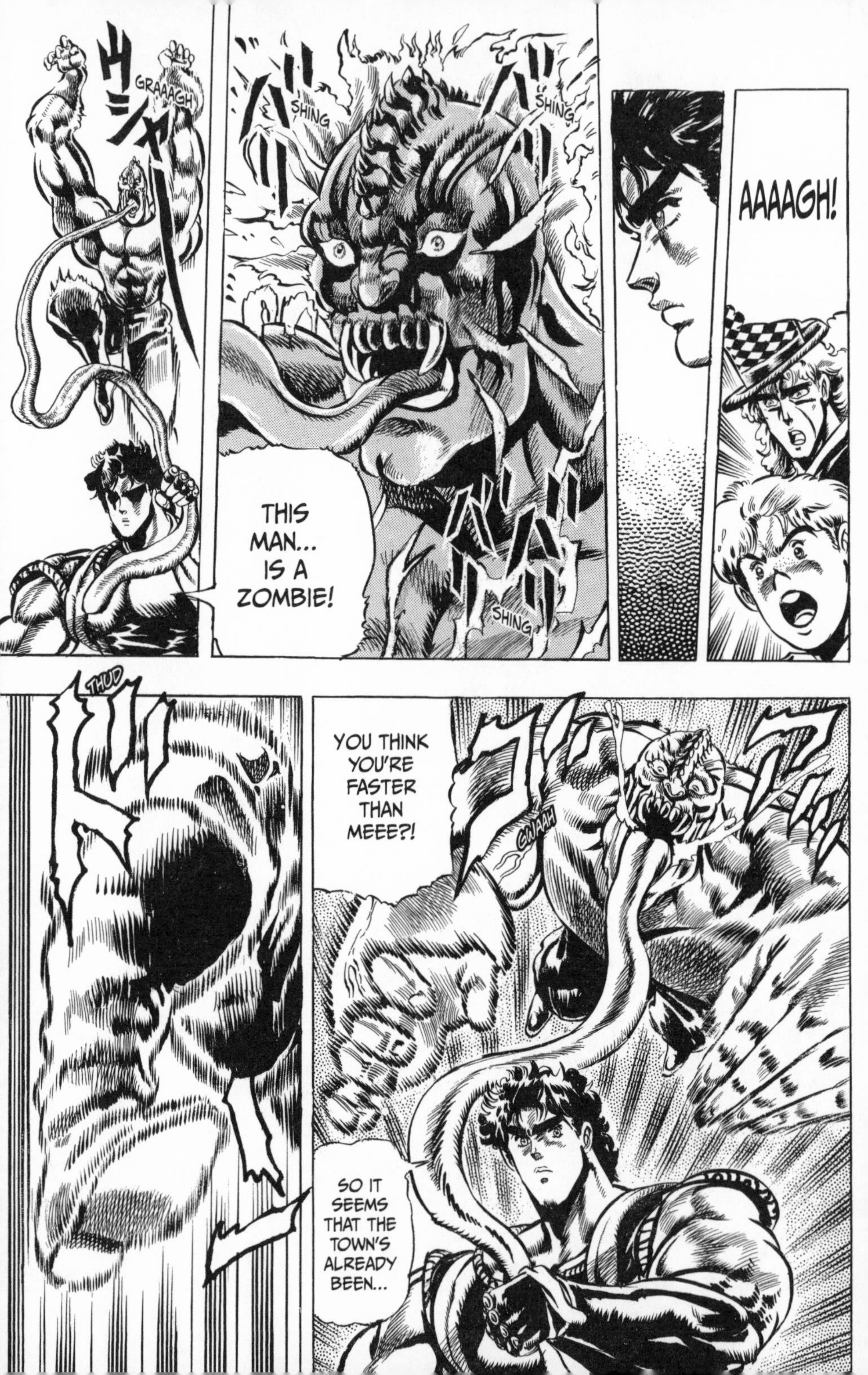
AAAAGH!
SHING
SHING
THIS MAN... IS A ZOMBIE!
SHING
GRAAAGH
YOU THINK YOU'RE FASTER THAN MEEE?!
GWAAH
SO IT SEEMS THAT THE TOWN'S ALREADY BEEN...
THUD

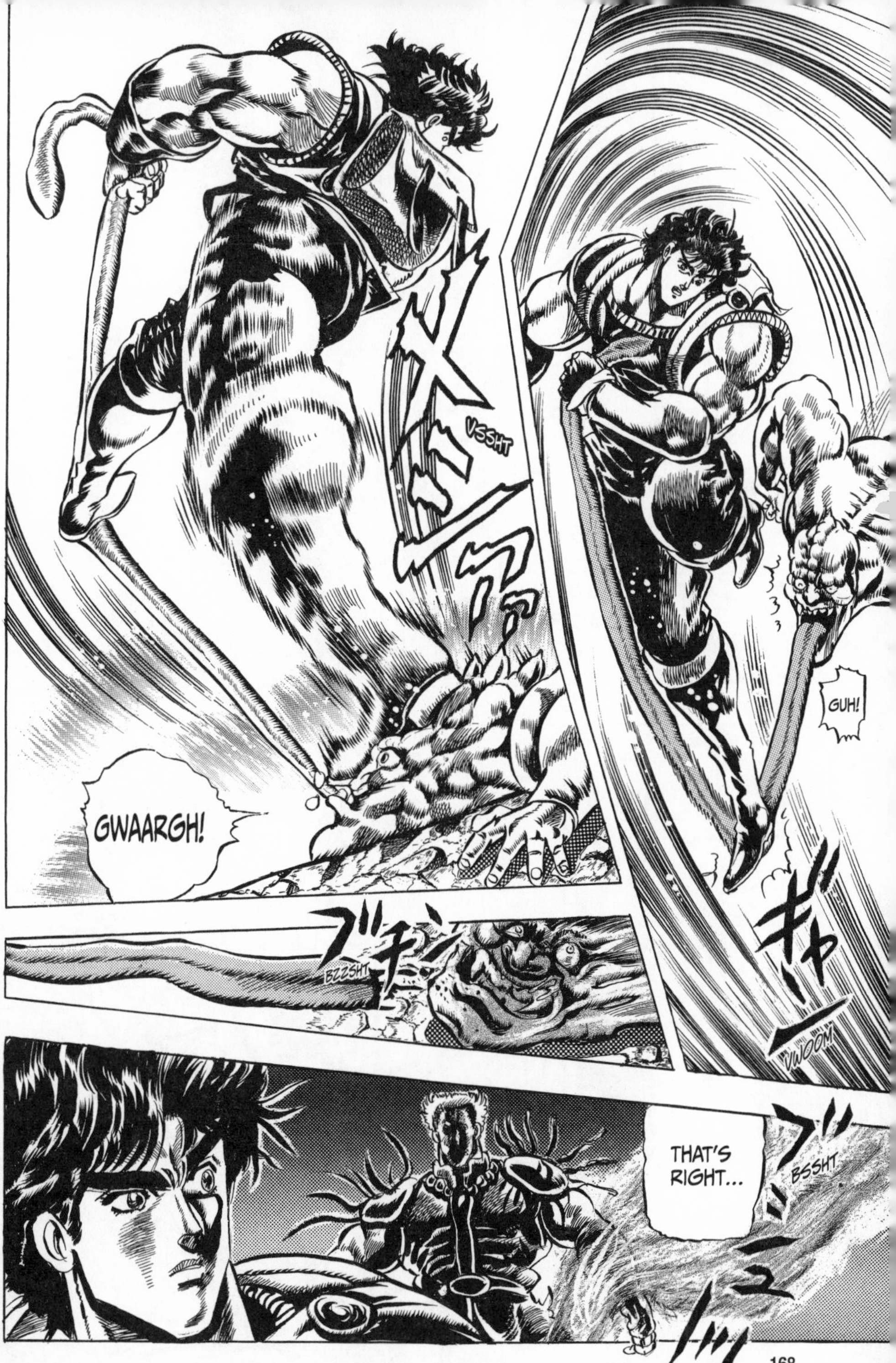
GUH!
VWOOM
VSSHT
GWAARGH!
BZZSHT
BSSHT
THAT'S RIGHT...

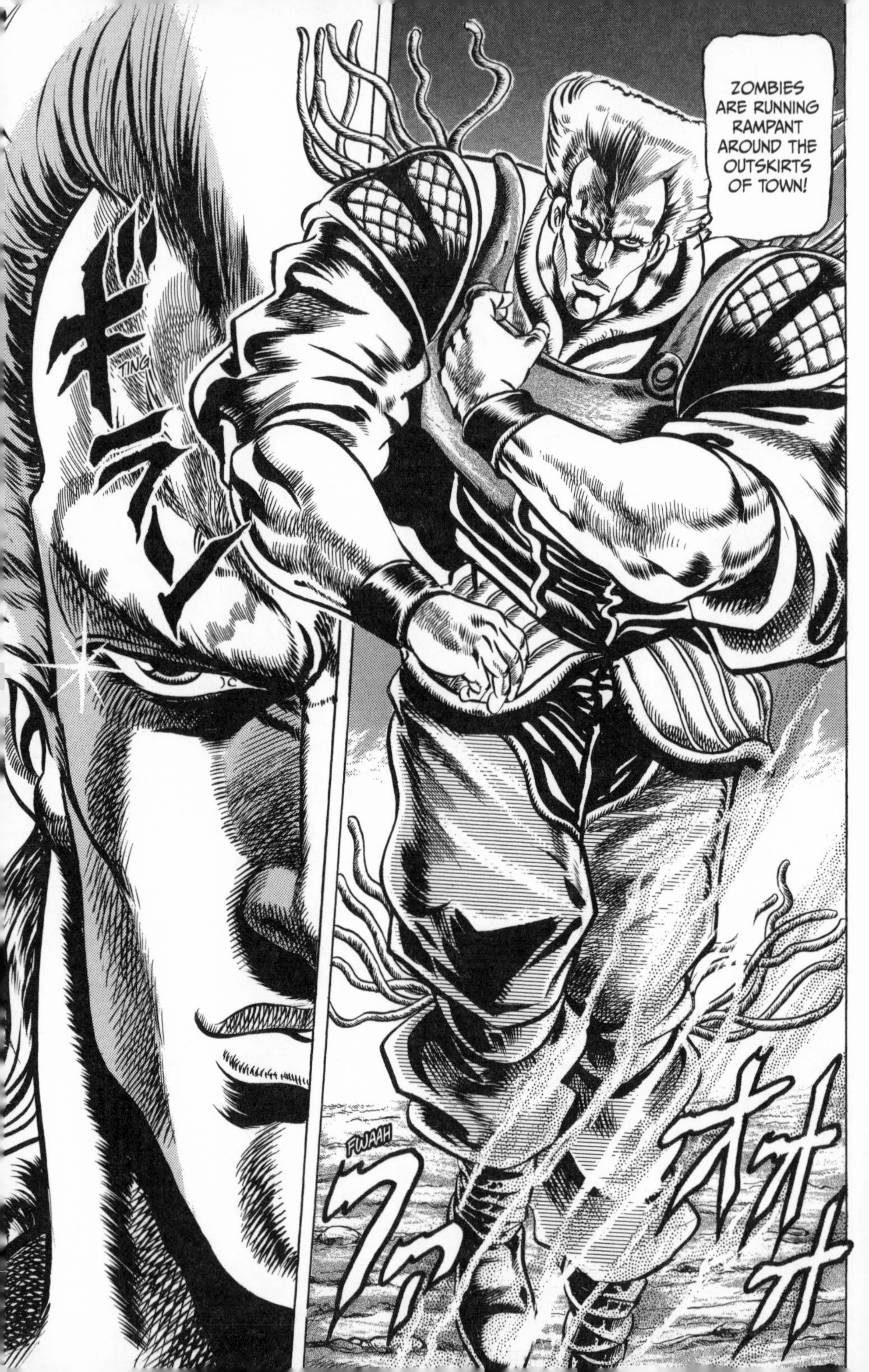
ZOMBIES ARE RUNNING RAMPANT AROUND THE OUTSKIRTS OF TOWN!
FWAAH
TING

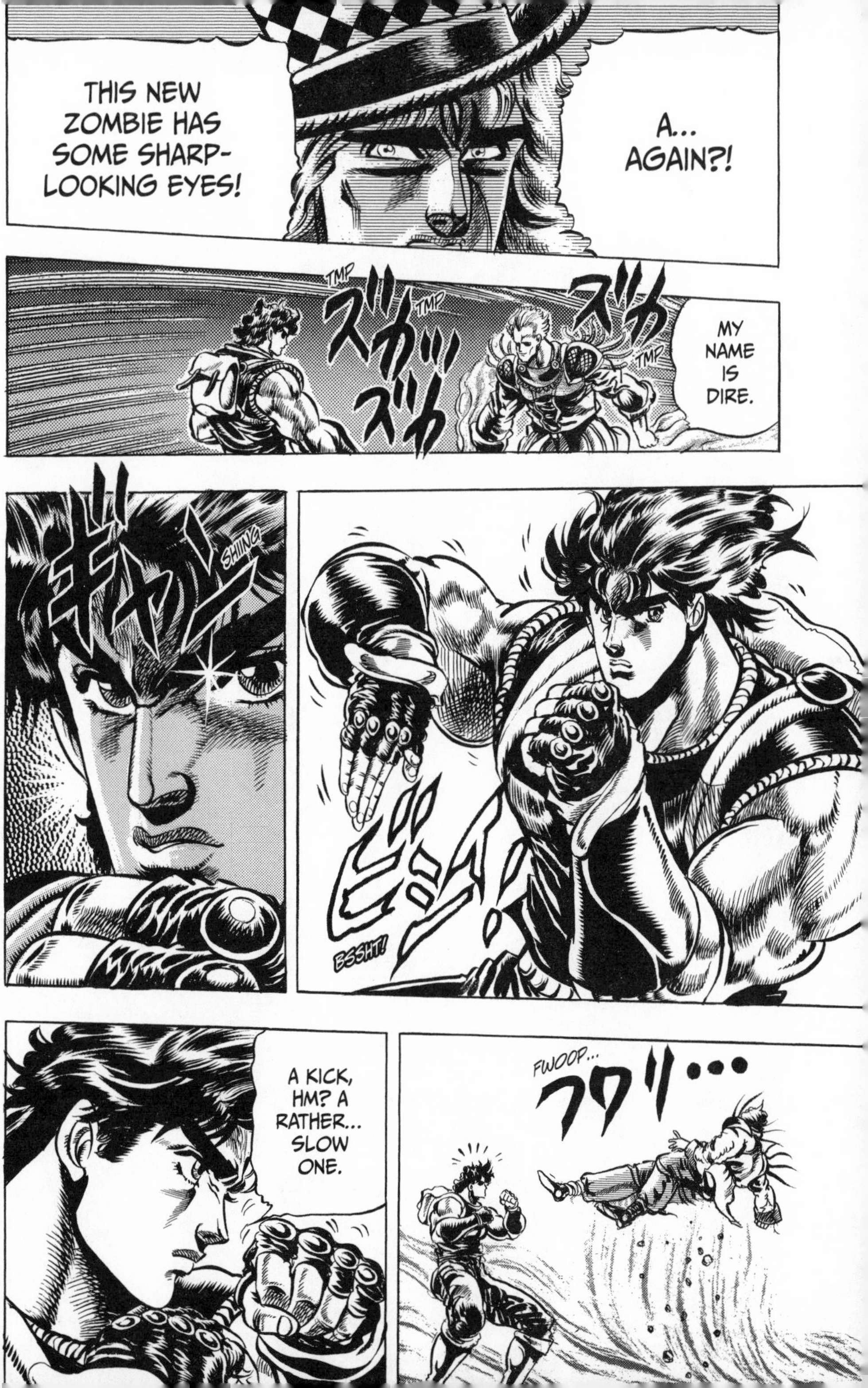
A...
AGAIN?!
THIS NEW ZOMBIE HAS SOME SHARP-LOOKING EYES!
MY NAME IS DIRE.
TMP
TMP
TMP
BSSHT!
SHIING
FWOOP...
フワリ•••
A KICK, HM? A RATHER... SLOW ONE.

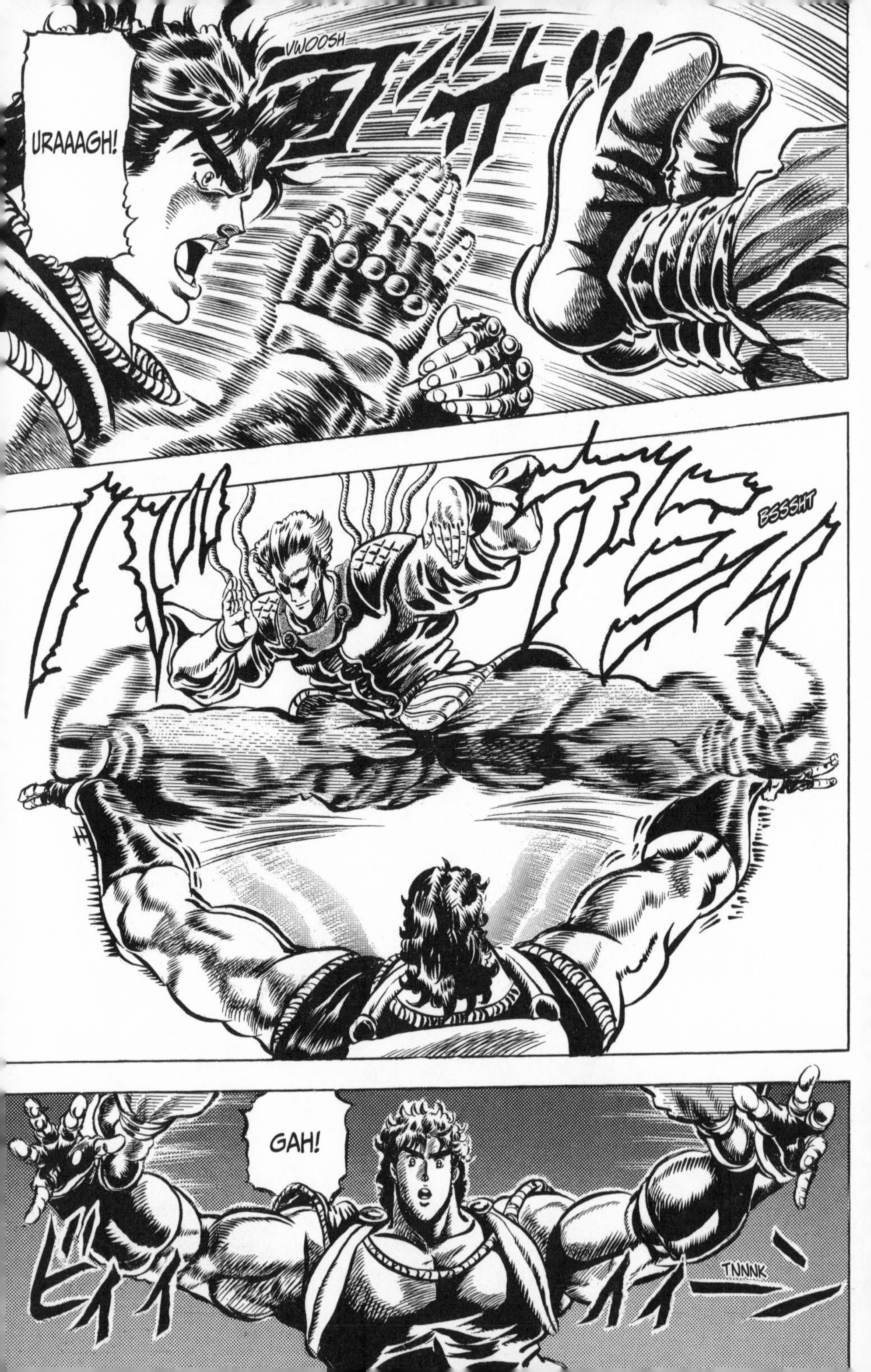
VWOOSH
URAAAGH!
BSSSHT
GAH!
TNNNK

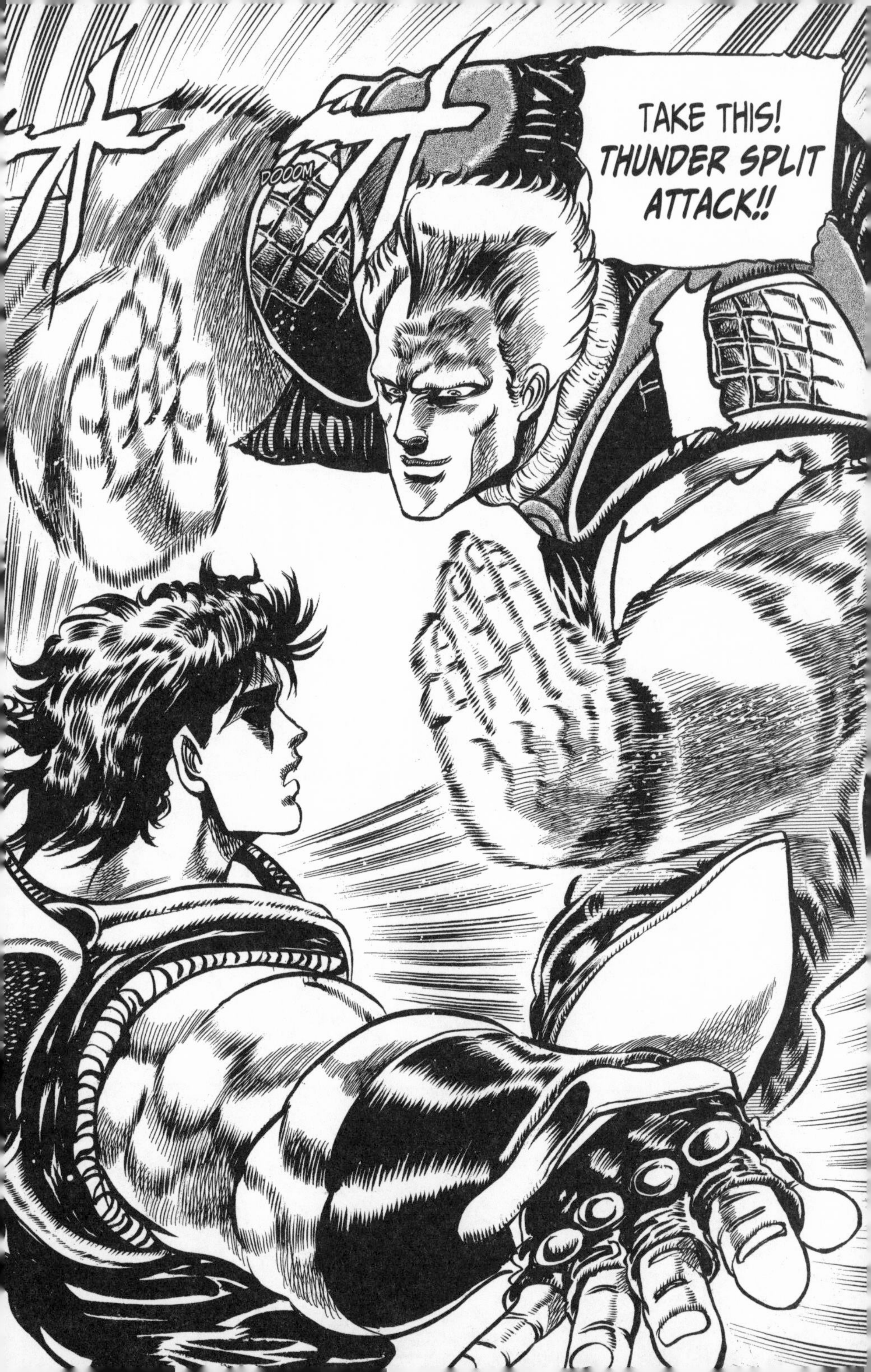
DOOOM
TAKE THIS! THUNDER SPLIT ATTACK!!

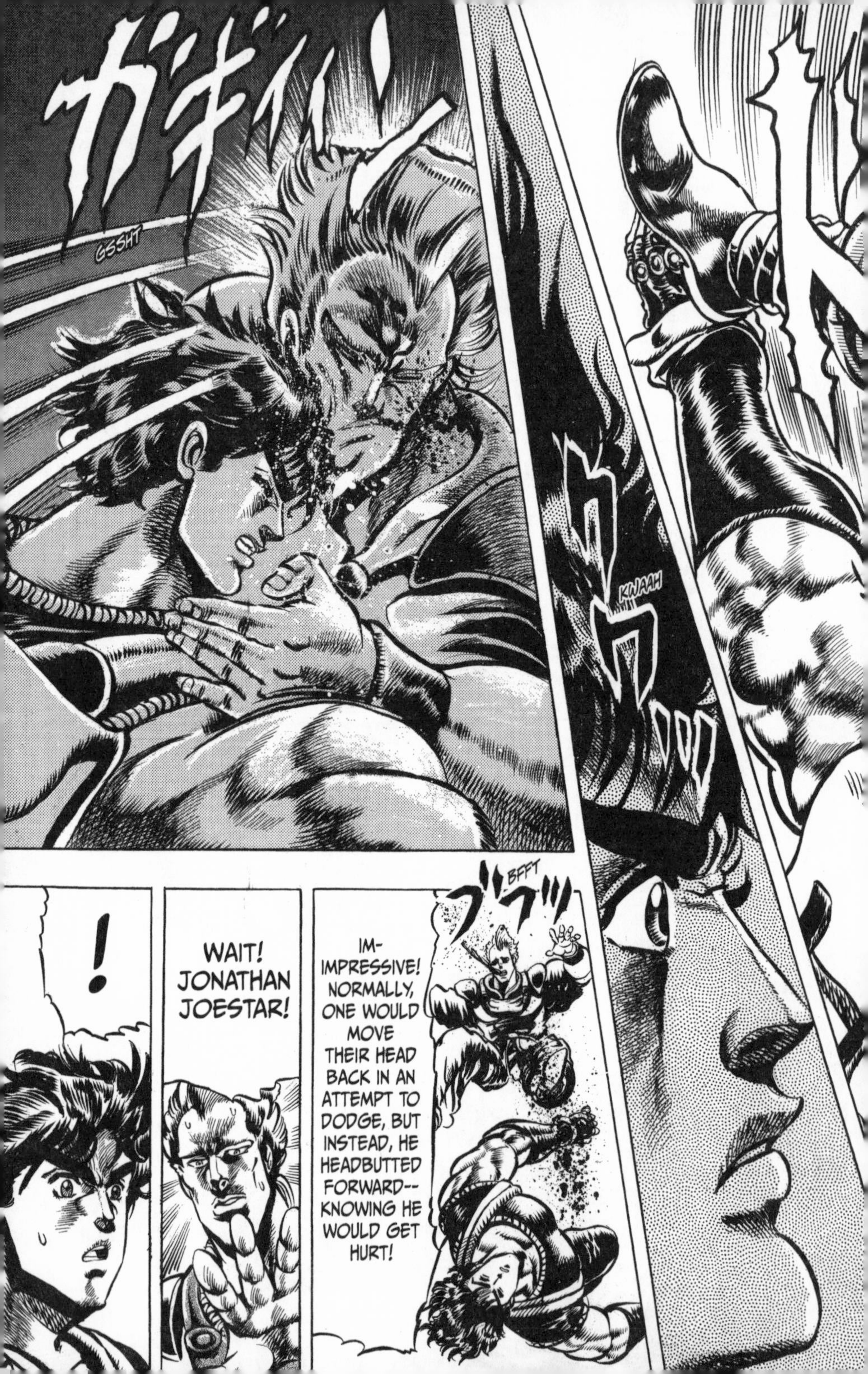
KWAAH
GSSHT
BFFT
IM-IMPRESSIVE! NORMALLY, ONE WOULD MOVE THEIR HEAD BACK IN AN ATTEMPT TO DODGE, BUT INSTEAD, HE HEADBUTTED FORWARD-- KNOWING HE WOULD GET HURT!
WAIT! JONATHAN JOESTAR!
!

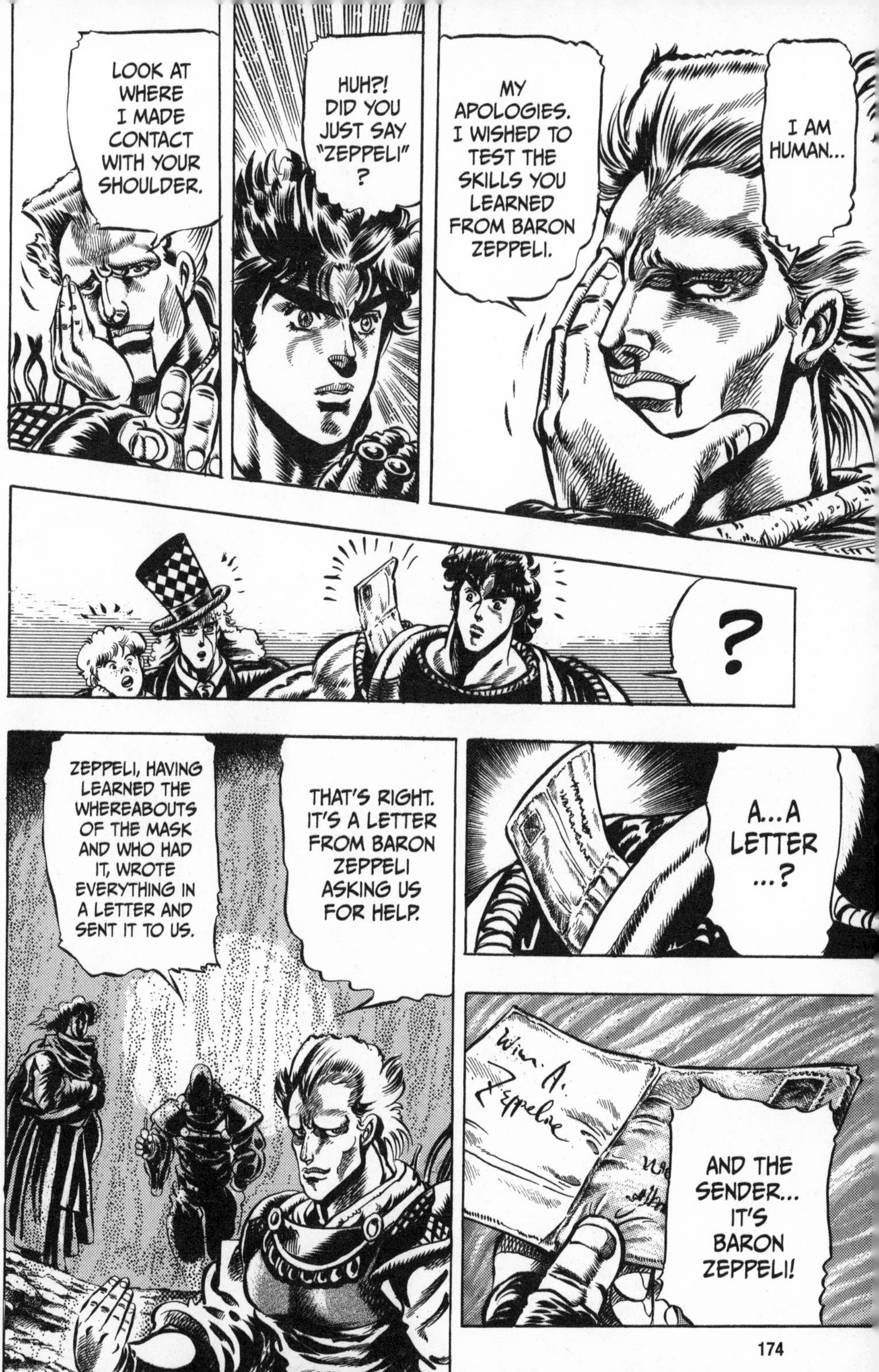
I AM HUMAN...
MY APOLOGIES. I WISHED TO TEST THE SKILLS YOU LEARNED FROM BARON ZEPPELI.
HUH?! DID YOU JUST SAY "ZEPPELI" ?
LOOK AT WHERE I MADE CONTACT WITH YOUR SHOULDER.
?
A...A LETTER ...?
AND THE SENDER... IT'S BARON ZEPPELI!
Wm. A. Zeppeloe
THAT'S RIGHT. IT'S A LETTER FROM BARON ZEPPELI ASKING US FOR HELP.
ZEPPELI, HAVING LEARNED THE WHEREABOUTS OF THE MASK AND WHO HAD IT, WROTE EVERYTHING IN A LETTER AND SENT IT TO US.

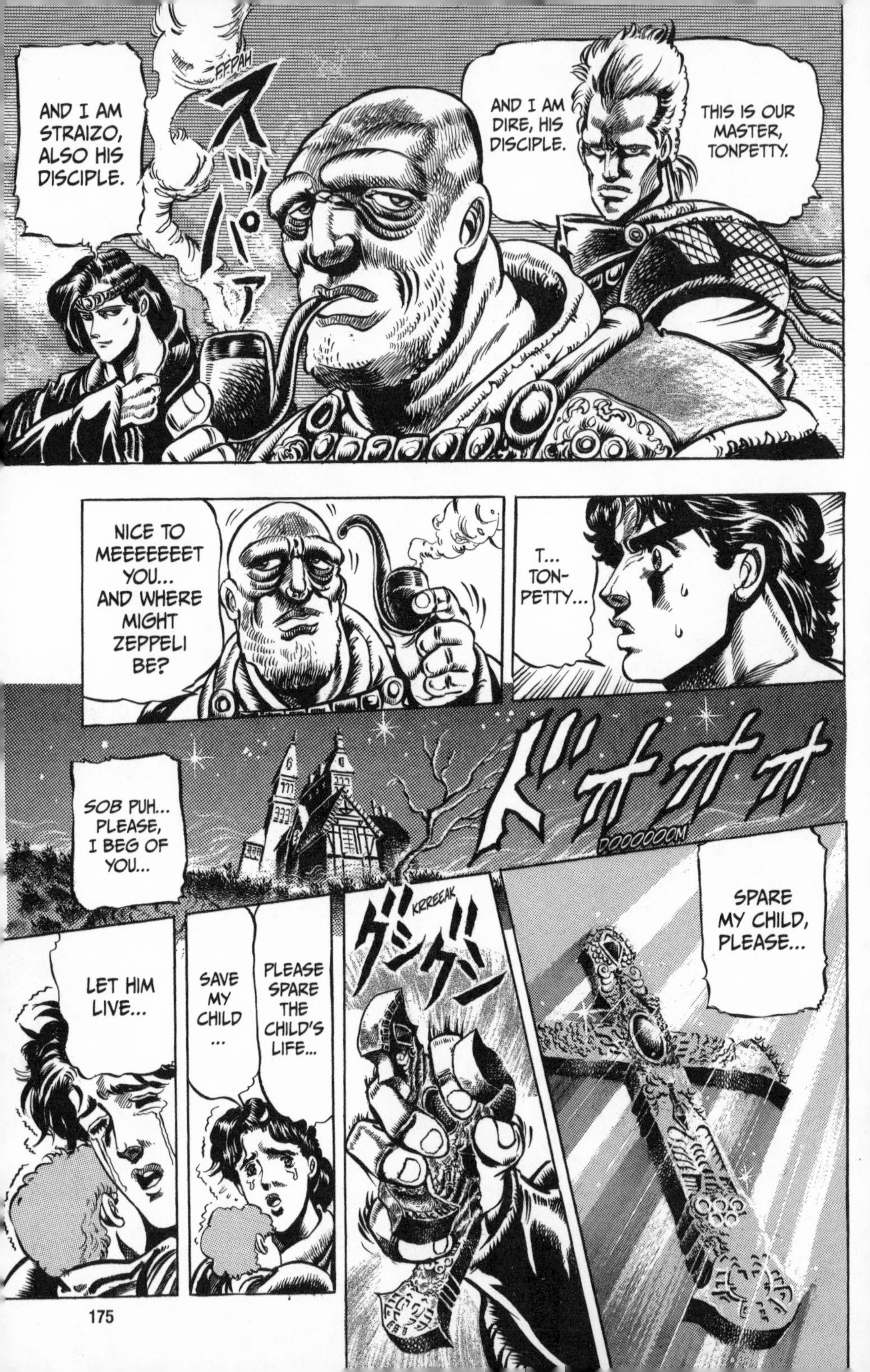
THIS IS OUR MASTER, TONPETTY.
AND I AM DIRE, HIS DISCIPLE.
FFPAH
AND I AM STRAIZO, ALSO HIS DISCIPLE.
T... TON-PETTY...
NICE TO MEEEEEEET YOU... AND WHERE MIGHT ZEPPELI BE?
DOOOOOOOM
SOB PUH... PLEASE, I BEG OF YOU...
SPARE MY CHILD, PLEASE...
KRREEAK
PLEASE SPARE THE CHILD'S LIFE...
SAVE MY CHILD ...
LET HIM LIVE...

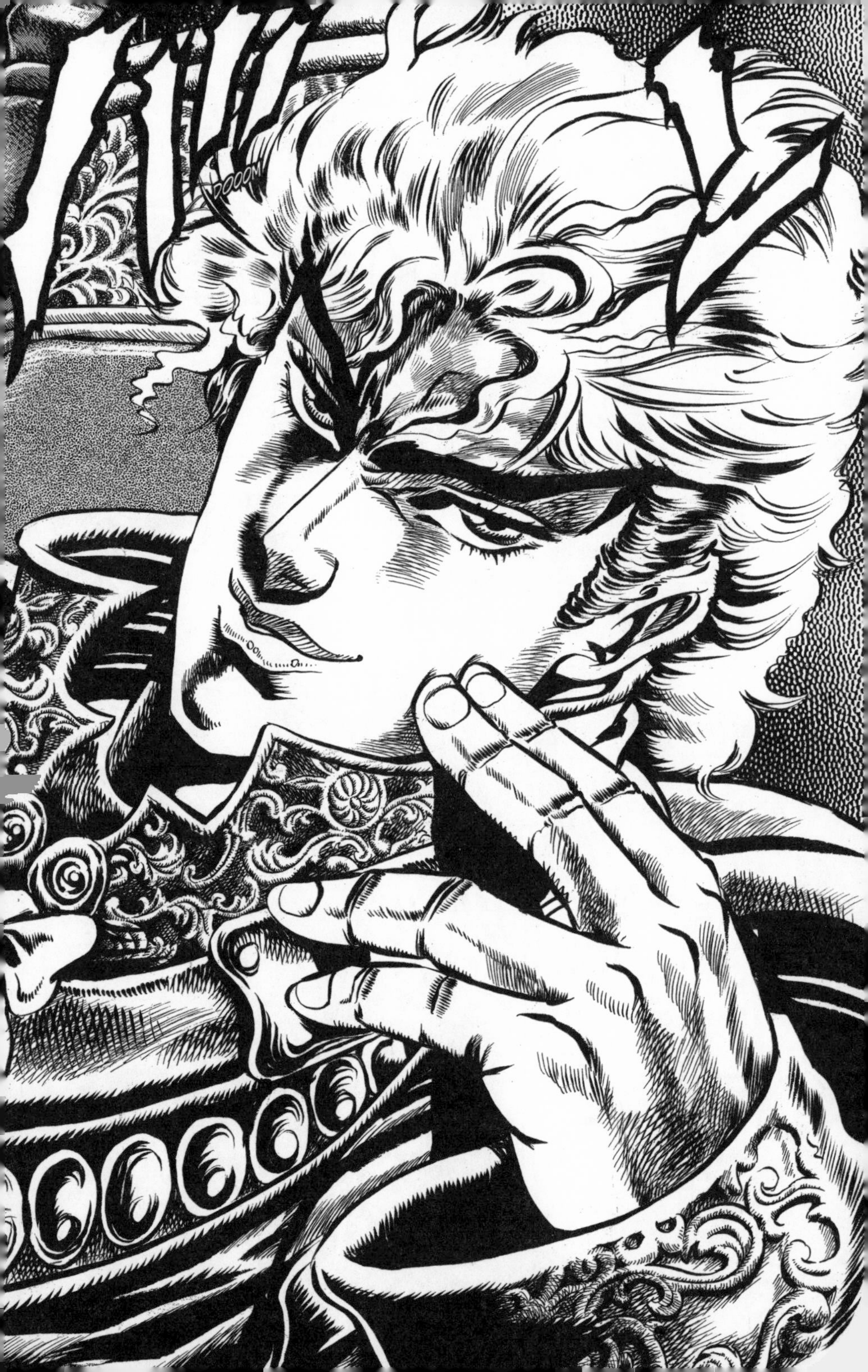
DOOOM

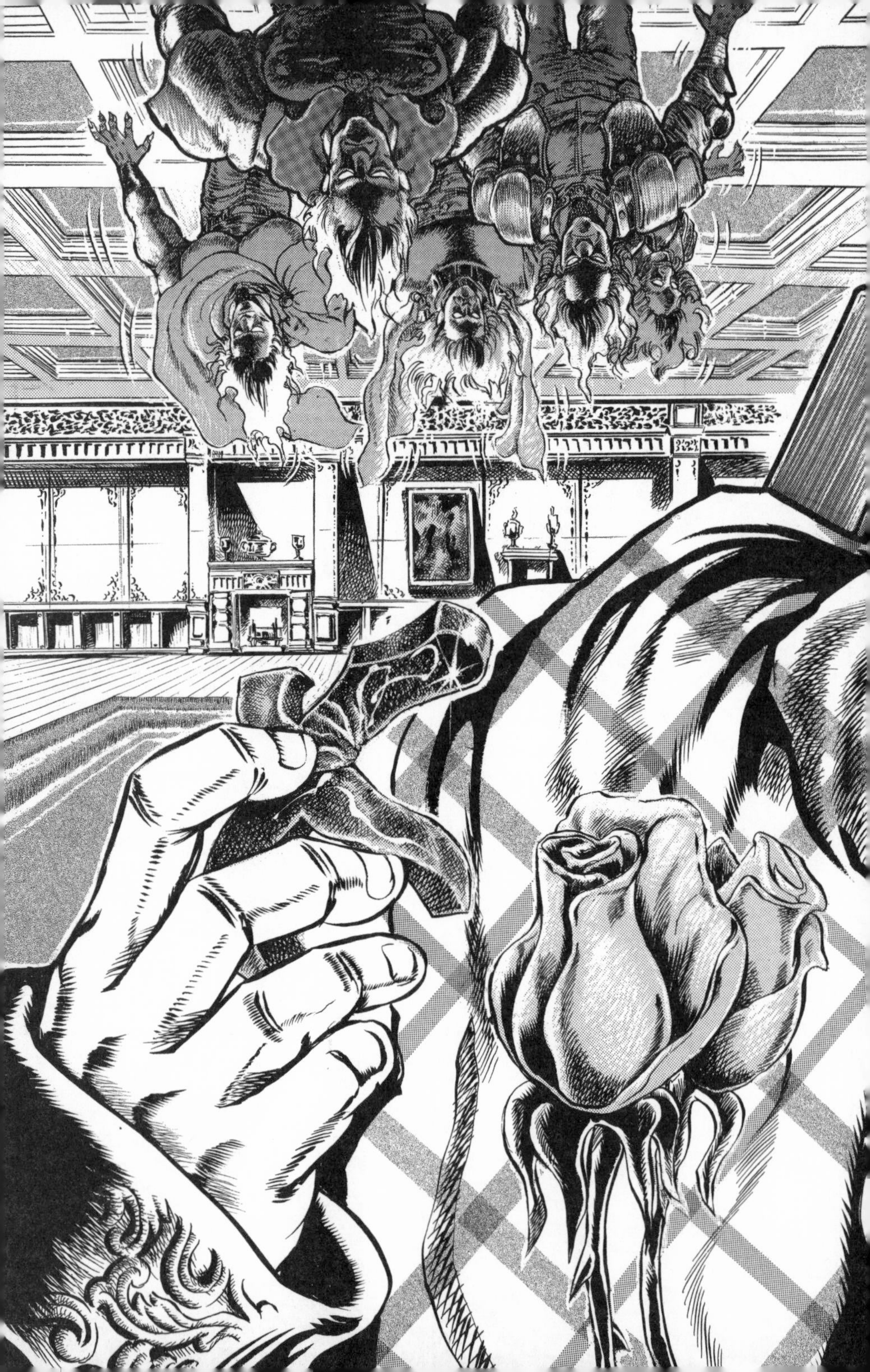

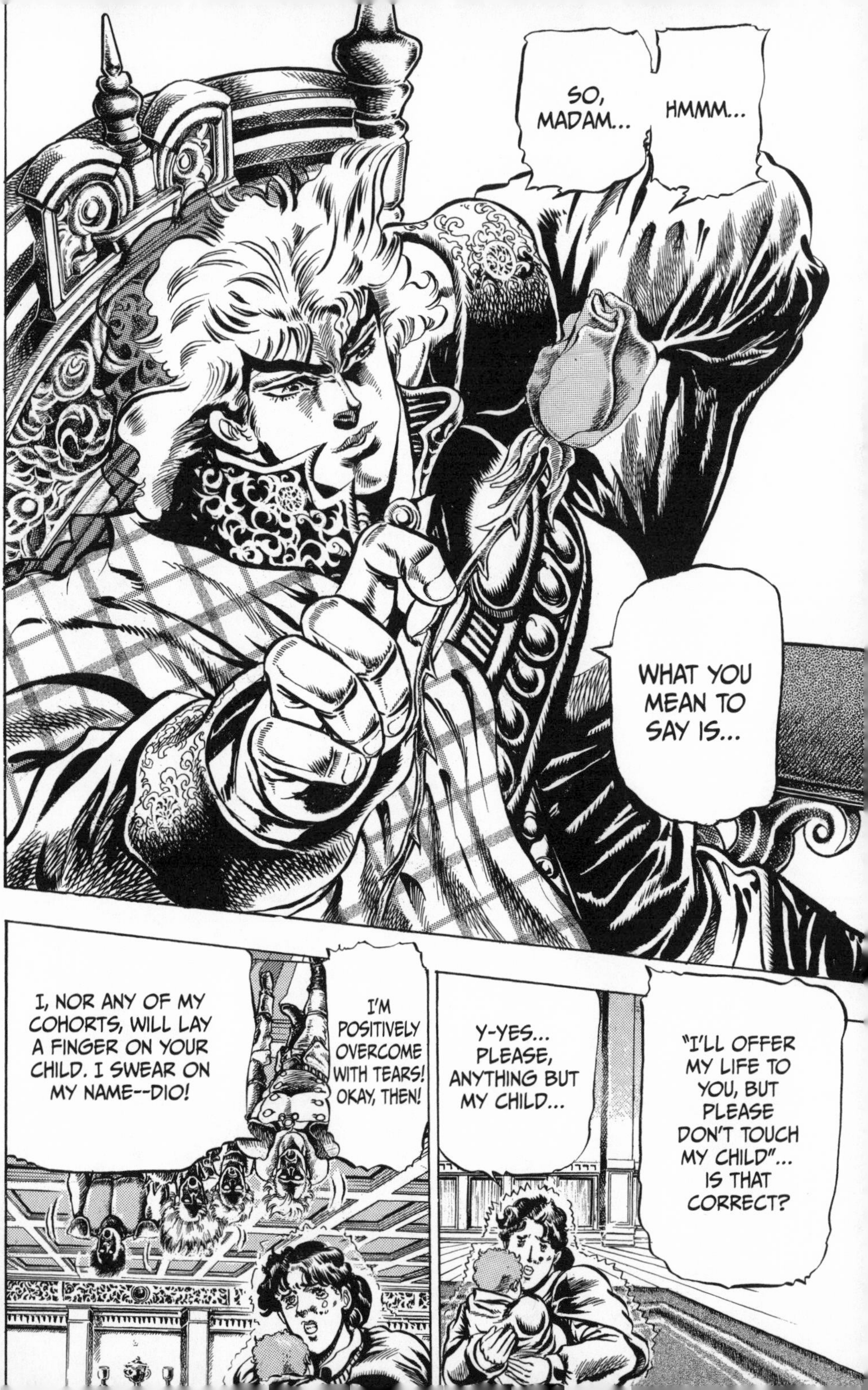
HMMM...
SO, MADAM...
WHAT YOU MEAN TO SAY IS...
"I'LL OFFER MY LIFE TO YOU, BUT PLEASE DON'T TOUCH MY CHILD"... IS THAT CORRECT?
Y-YES... PLEASE, ANYTHING BUT MY CHILD...
I'M POSITIVELY OVERCOME WITH TEARS! OKAY, THEN!
I, NOR ANY OF MY COHORTS, WILL LAY A FINGER ON YOUR CHILD. I SWEAR ON MY NAME--DIO!

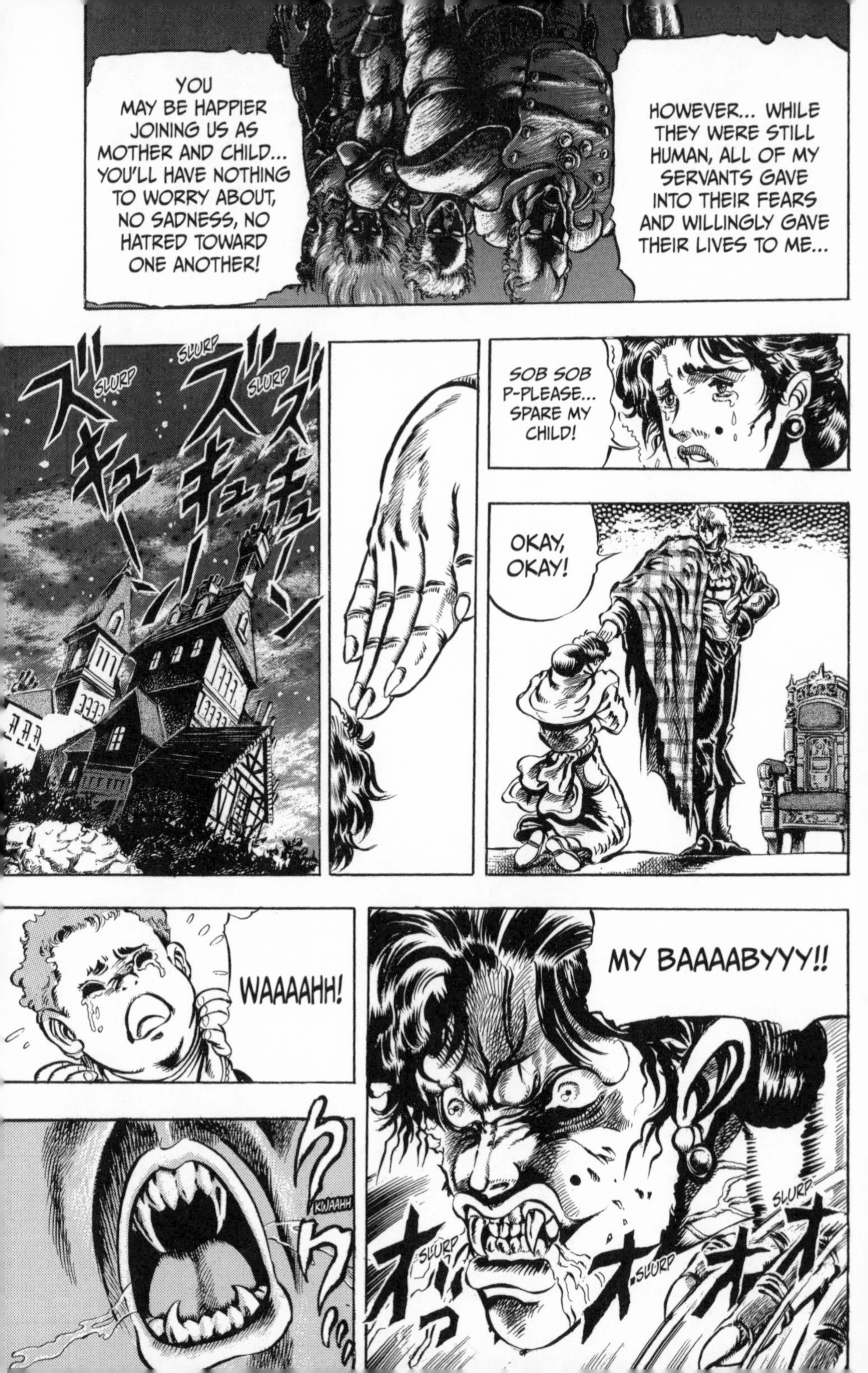
HOWEVER... WHILE THEY WERE STILL HUMAN, ALL OF MY SERVANTS GAVE INTO THEIR FEARS AND WILLINGLY GAVE THEIR LIVES TO ME...
YOU MAY BE HAPPIER JOINING US AS MOTHER AND CHILD... YOU'LL HAVE NOTHING TO WORRY ABOUT, NO SADNESS, NO HATRED TOWARD ONE ANOTHER!
SOB SOB P-PLEASE... SPARE MY CHILD!
OKAY, OKAY!
SLURP
SLURP
SLURP
MY BAAAABYYY!!
SLURP
SLURP
SLURP
WAAAAHH!
KWAAHH

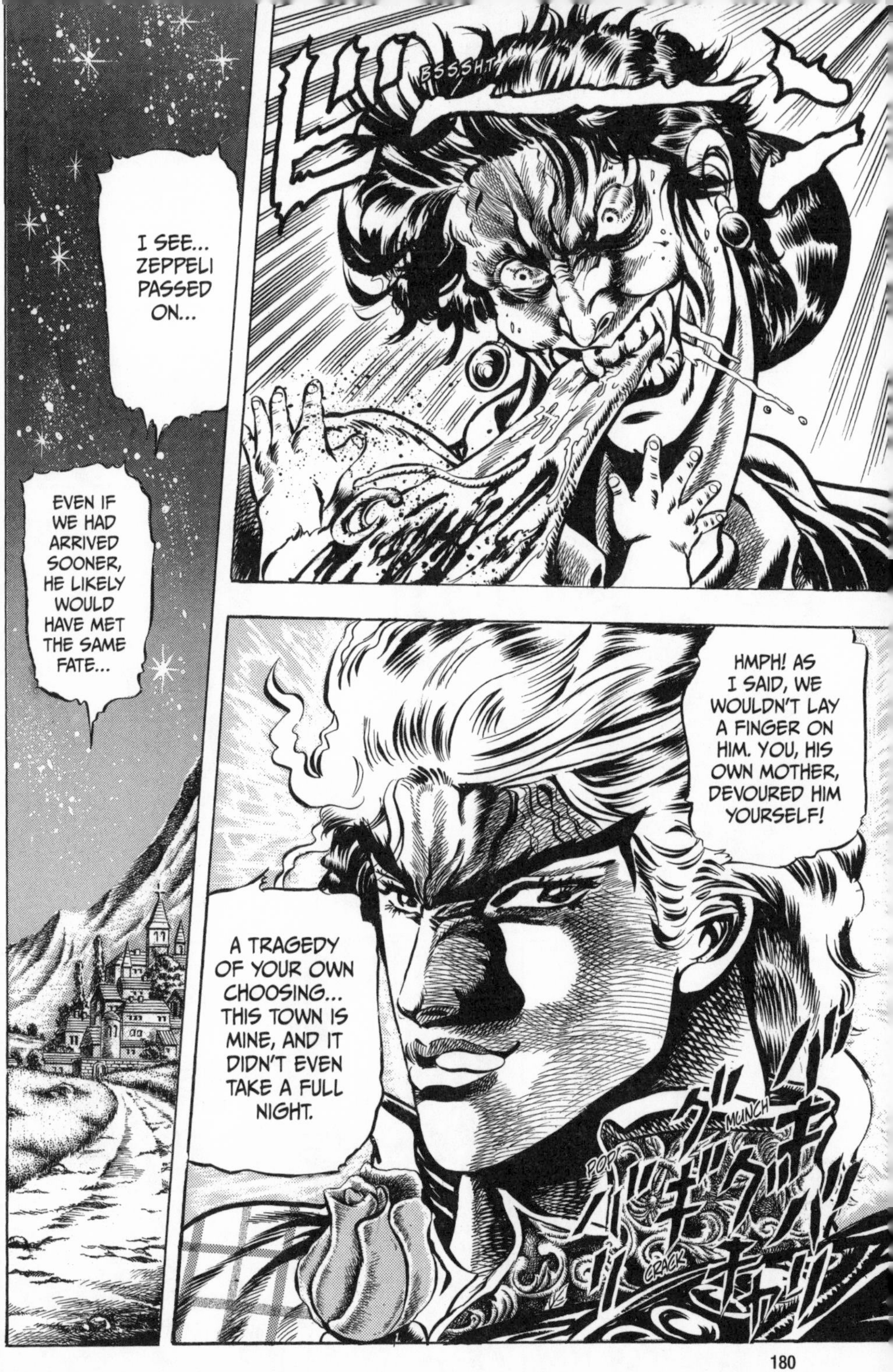
BSSSHT
HMPH! AS I SAID, WE WOULDN'T LAY A FINGER ON HIM. YOU, HIS OWN MOTHER, DEVOURED HIM YOURSELF!
A TRAGEDY OF YOUR OWN CHOOSING... THIS TOWN IS MINE, AND IT DIDN'T EVEN TAKE A FULL NIGHT.
MUNCH
POP
CRACK
I SEE... ZEPPELI PASSED ON...
EVEN IF WE HAD ARRIVED SOONER, HE LIKELY WOULD HAVE MET THE SAME FATE...

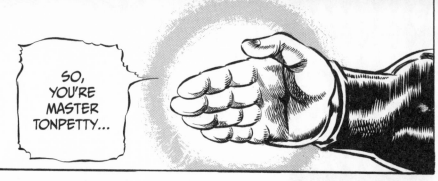

SO, YOU'RE MASTER TONPETTY...

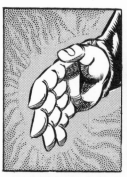

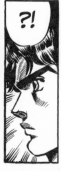

?!

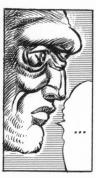

...

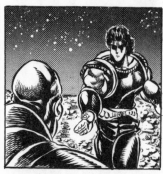

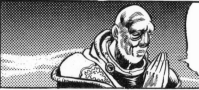

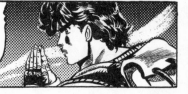

WE DON'T HAVE SUCH CUSTOMS... THIS IS OUR FORM OF GREETING.

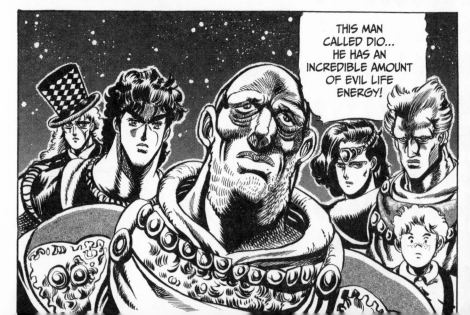

THIS MAN CALLED DIO... HE HAS AN INCREDIBLE AMOUNT OF EVIL LIFE ENERGY!

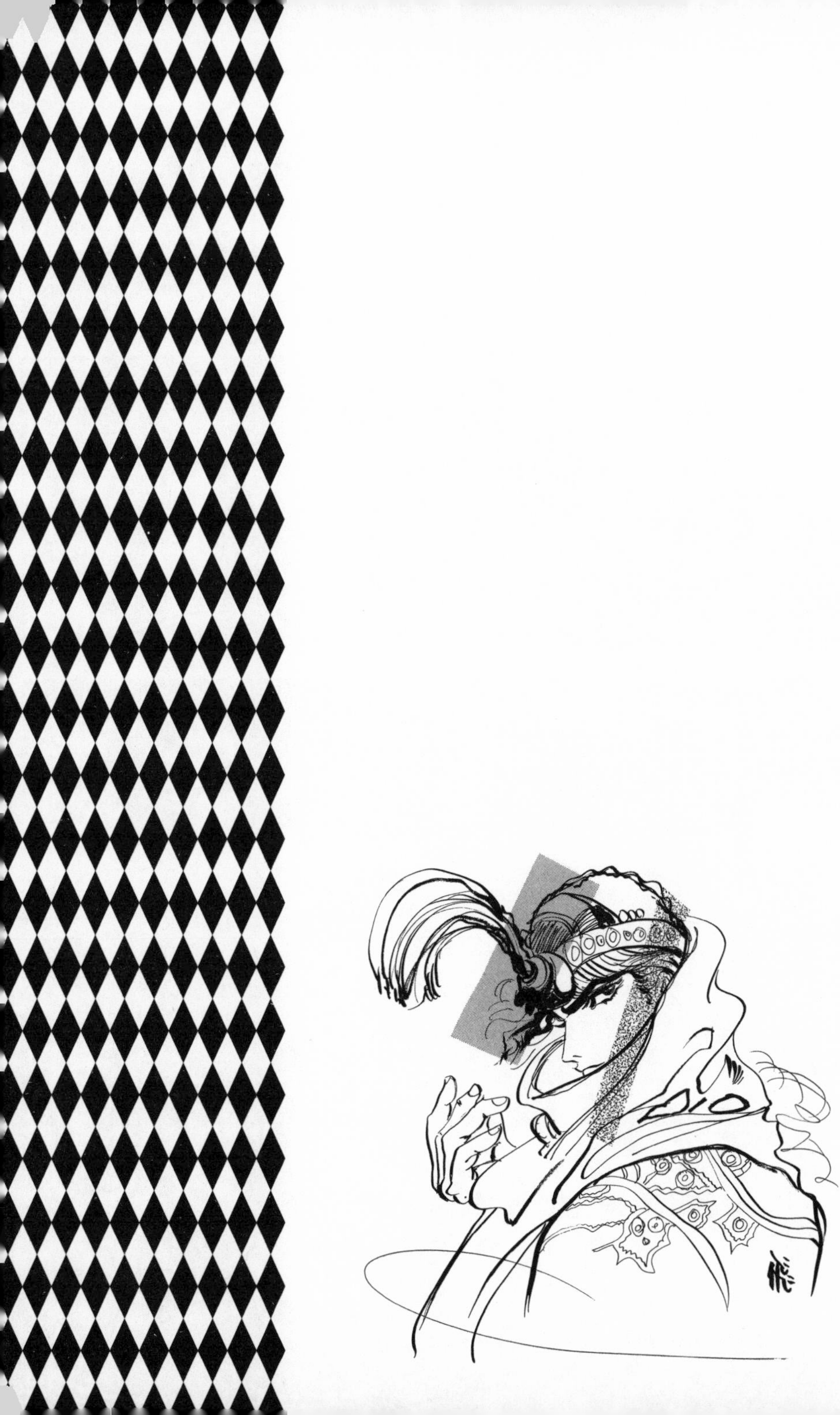
DIO

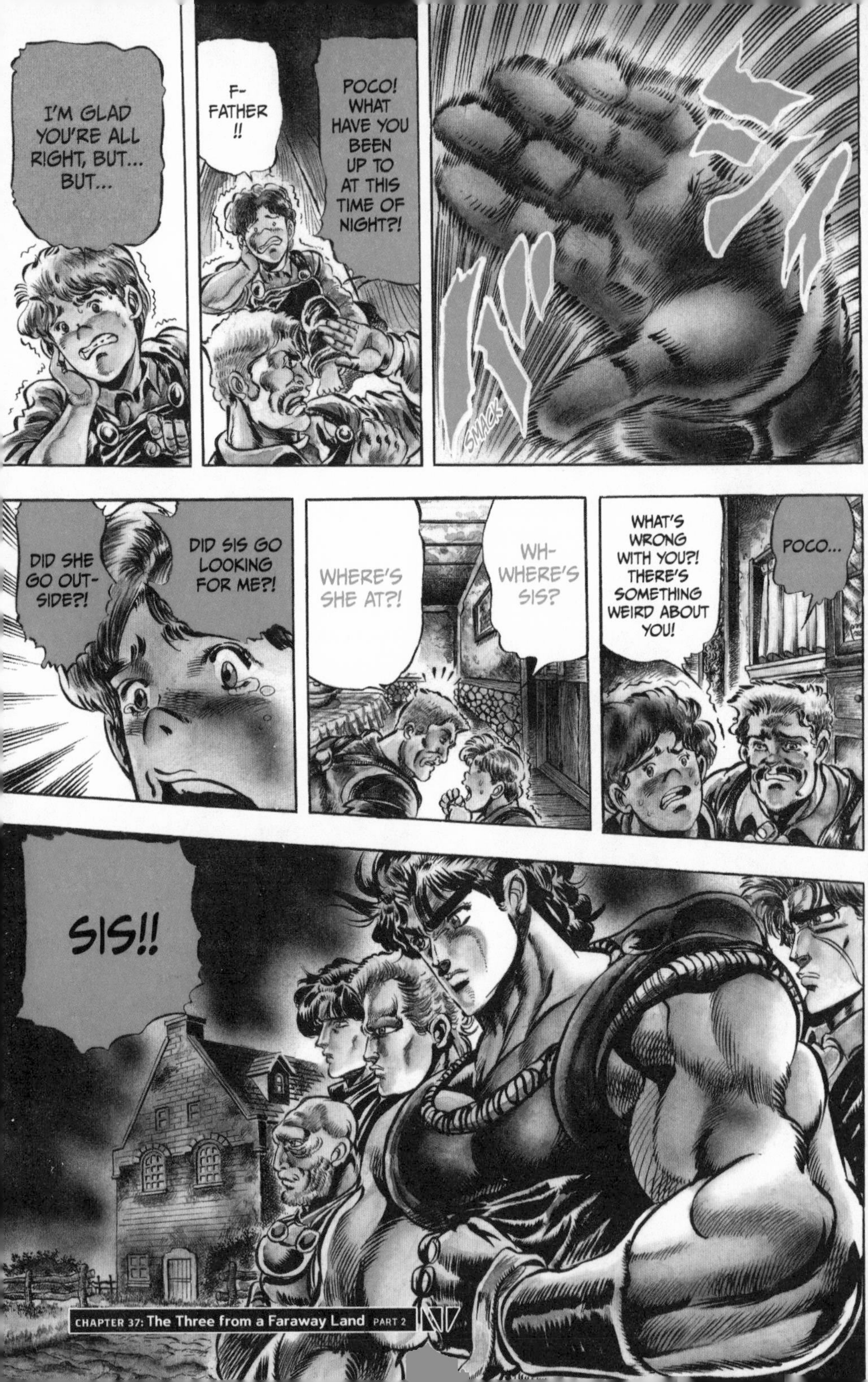
SMACK
POCO! WHAT HAVE YOU BEEN UP TO AT THIS TIME OF NIGHT?!
F-FATHER!!
I'M GLAD YOU'RE ALL RIGHT, BUT... BUT...
POCO...
WHAT'S WRONG WITH YOU?! THERE'S SOMETHING WEIRD ABOUT YOU!
WH-WHERE'S SIS?
WHERE'S SHE AT?!
DID SIS GO LOOKING FOR ME?!
DID SHE GO OUT-SIDE?!
SIS!!
CHAPTER 37: The Three from a Faraway Land PART 2

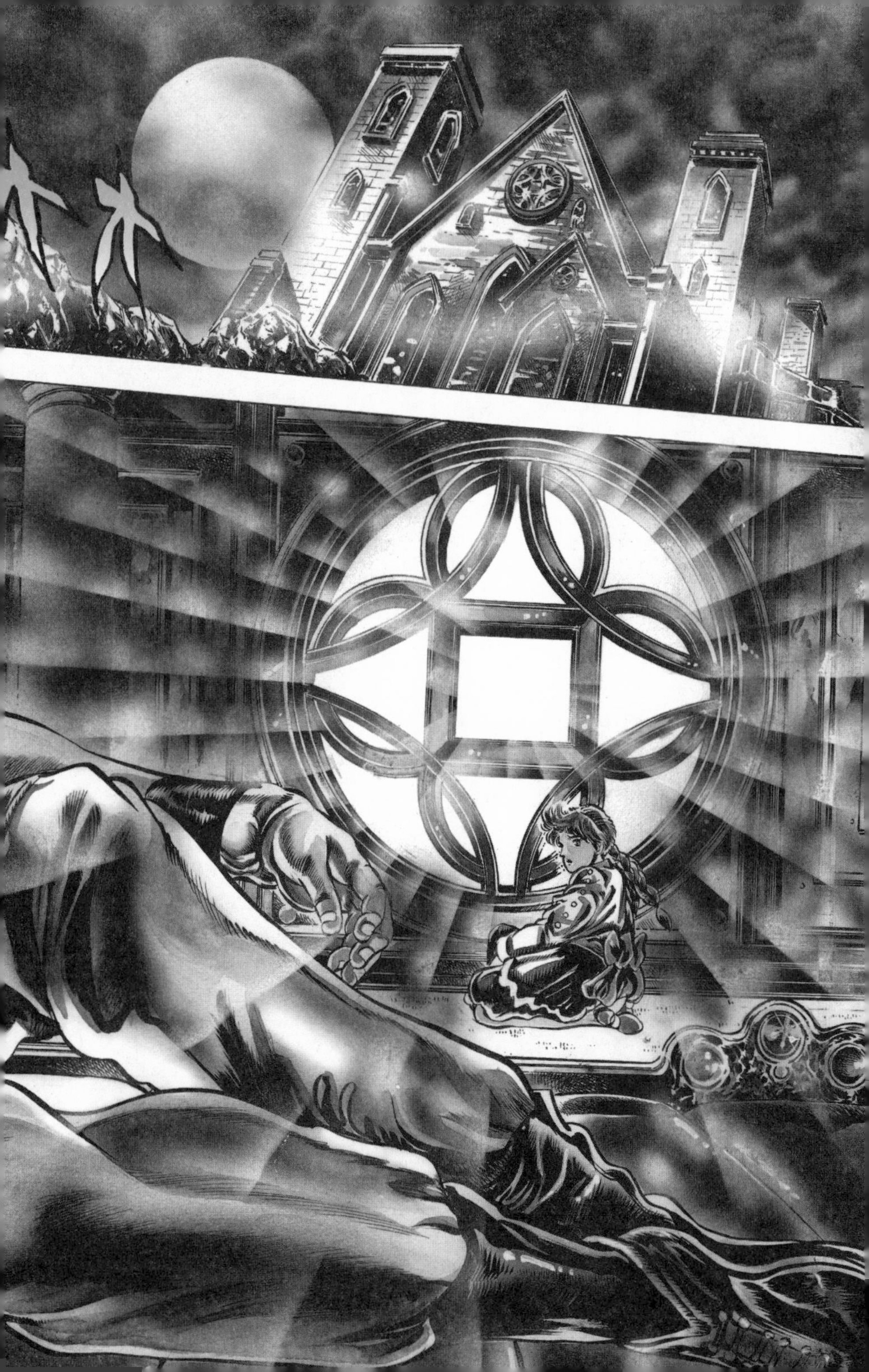

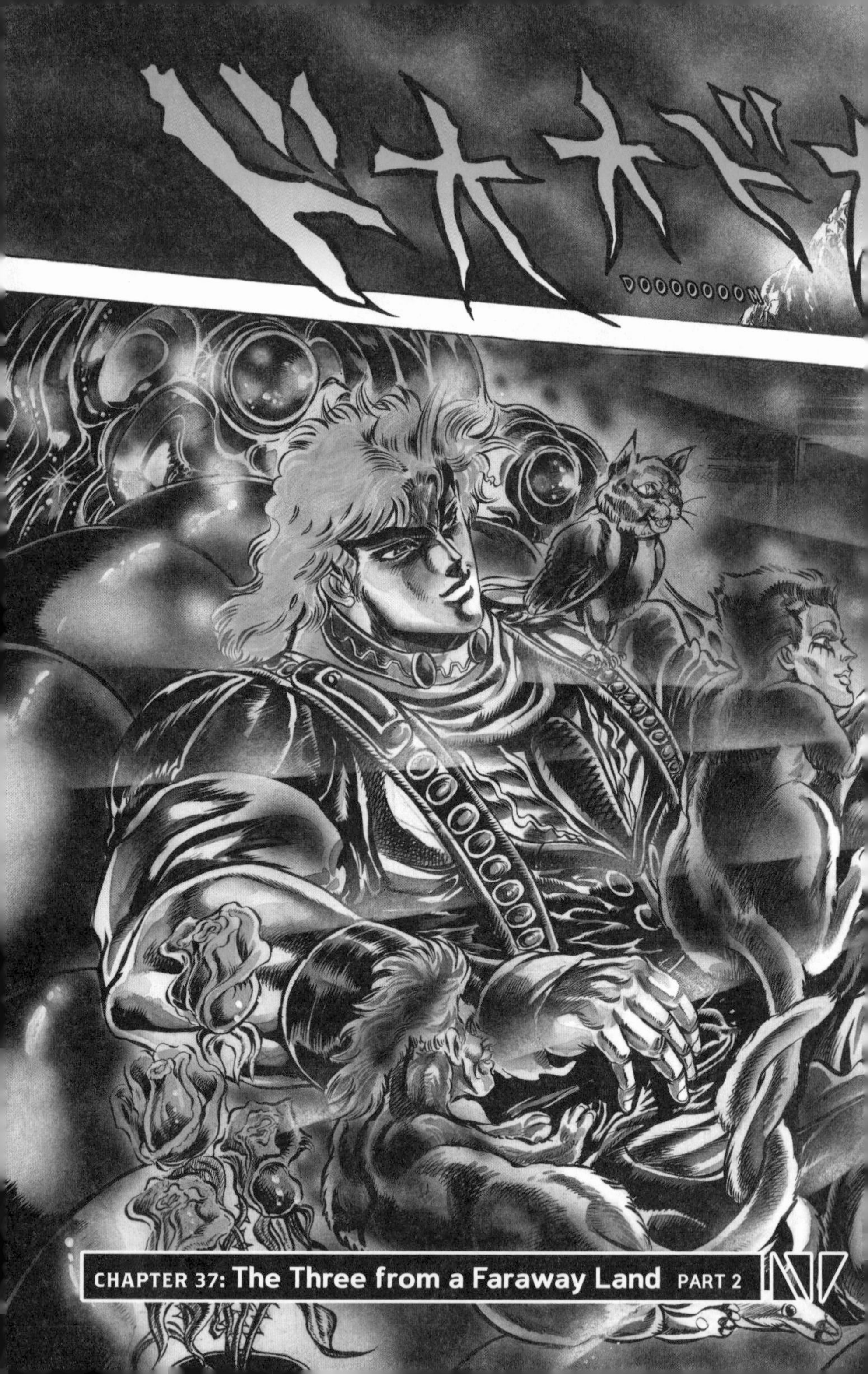
DOOOOOOOM
CHAPTER 37: The Three from a Faraway Land PART 2

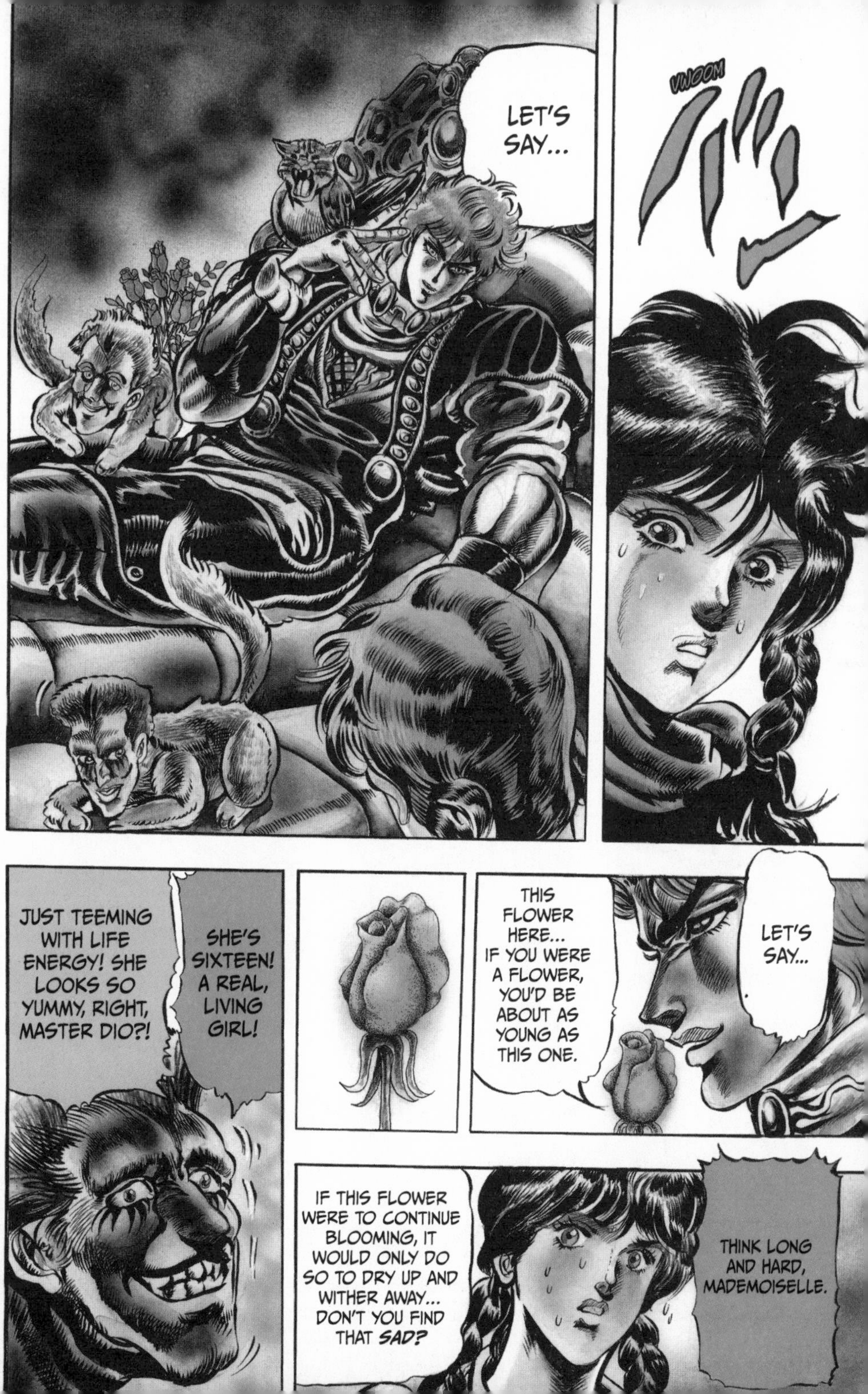
VWOOM
LET'S SAY...
LET'S SAY...
THIS FLOWER HERE... IF YOU WERE A FLOWER, YOU'D BE ABOUT AS YOUNG AS THIS ONE.
THINK LONG AND HARD, MADEMOISELLE.
IF THIS FLOWER WERE TO CONTINUE BLOOMING, IT WOULD ONLY DO SO TO DRY UP AND WITHER AWAY... DON'T YOU FIND THAT *SAD?*
SHE'S SIXTEEN! A REAL, LIVING GIRL!
JUST TEEMING WITH LIFE ENERGY! SHE LOOKS SO YUMMY, RIGHT, MASTER DIO?!

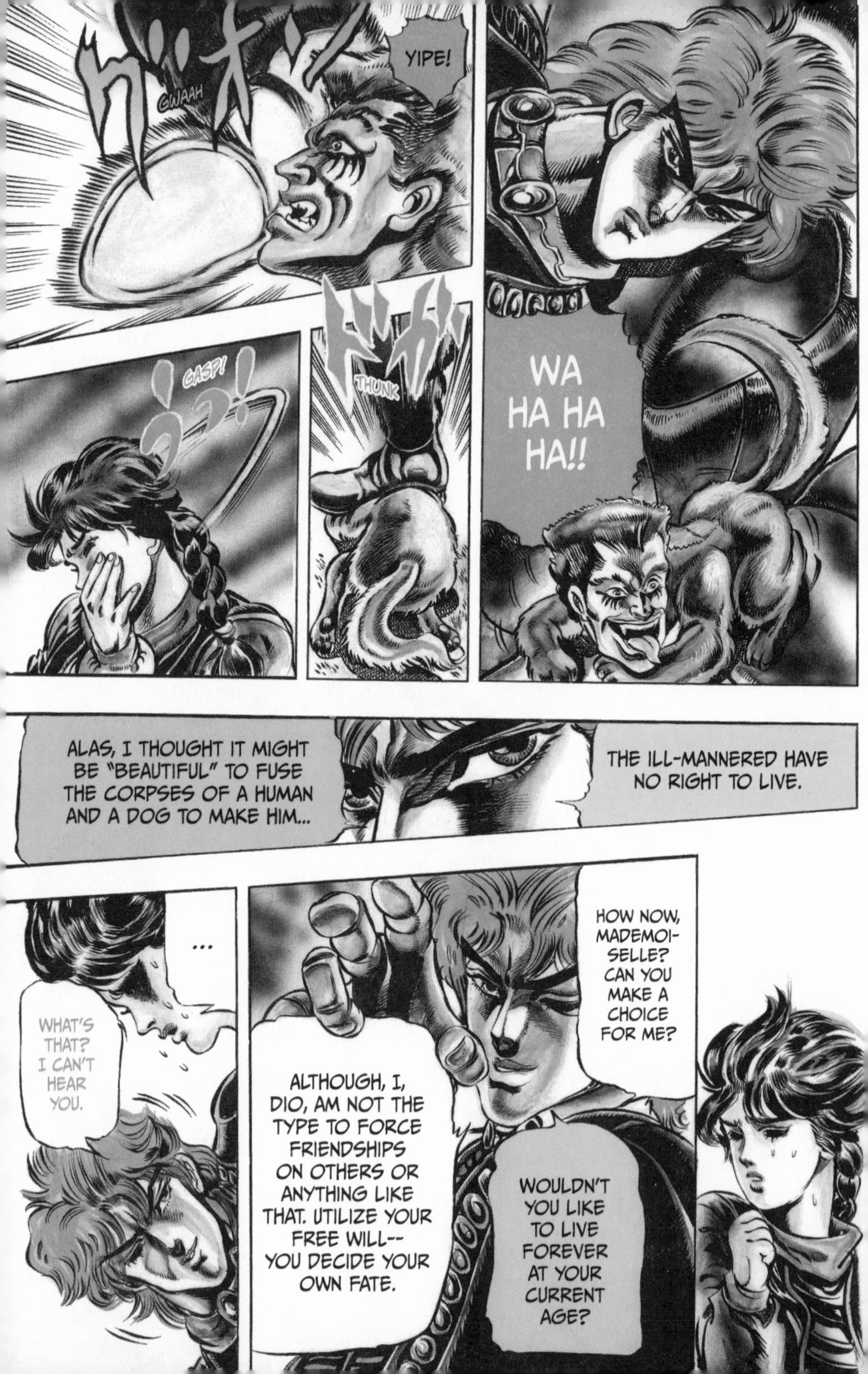
WA HA HA HA!!
YIPE!
GWAAH
THUNK
GASP!
THE ILL-MANNERED HAVE NO RIGHT TO LIVE.
ALAS, I THOUGHT IT MIGHT BE "BEAUTIFUL" TO FUSE THE CORPSES OF A HUMAN AND A DOG TO MAKE HIM...
HOW NOW, MADEMOI-SELLE? CAN YOU MAKE A CHOICE FOR ME?
ALTHOUGH, I, DIO, AM NOT THE TYPE TO FORCE FRIENDSHIPS ON OTHERS OR ANYTHING LIKE THAT. UTILIZE YOUR FREE WILL-- YOU DECIDE YOUR OWN FATE.
WOULDN'T YOU LIKE TO LIVE FOREVER AT YOUR CURRENT AGE?
...
WHAT'S THAT? I CAN'T HEAR YOU.

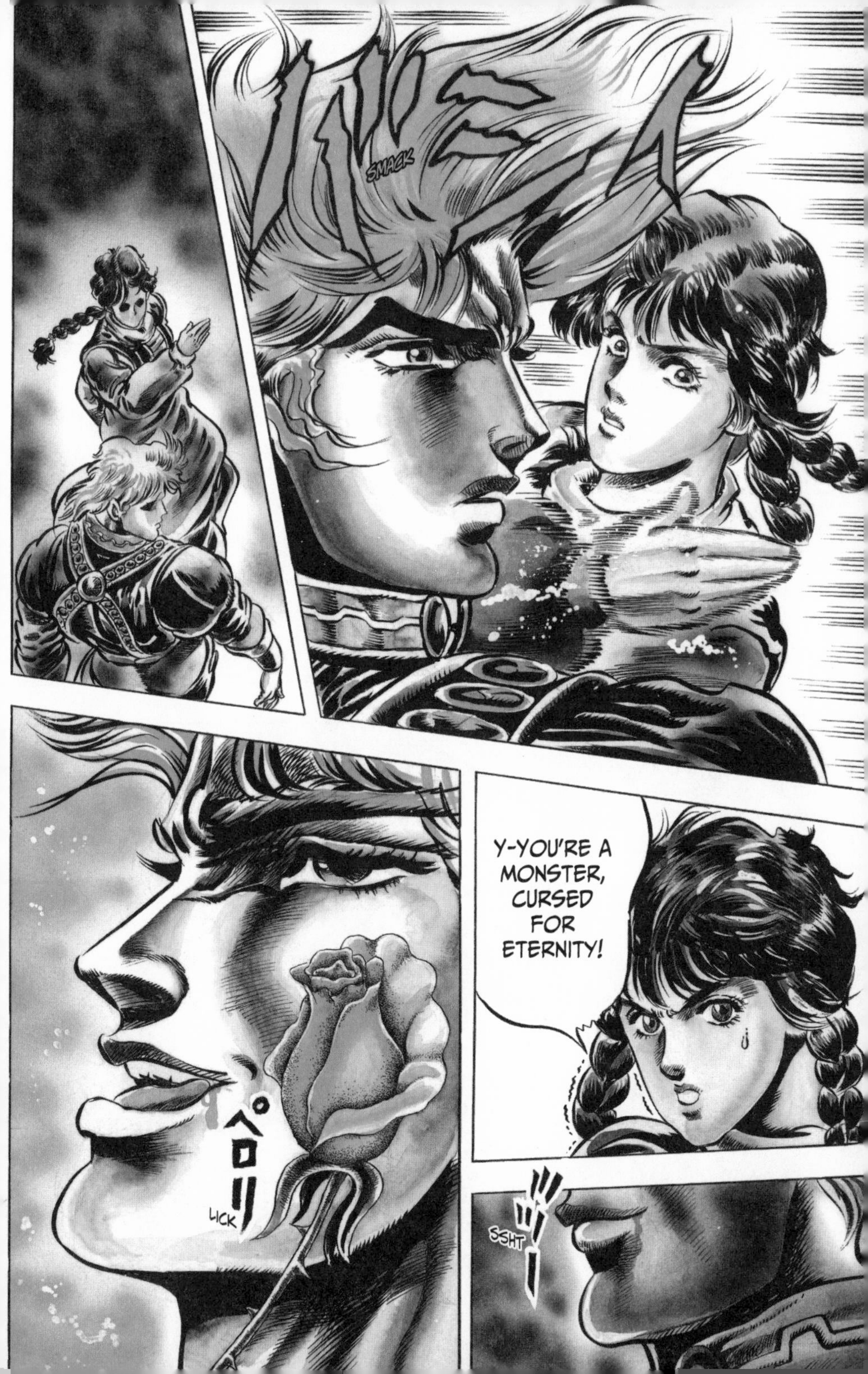
SMACK
Y-YOU'RE A MONSTER, CURSED FOR ETERNITY!
SSHT
ペロリ
LICK

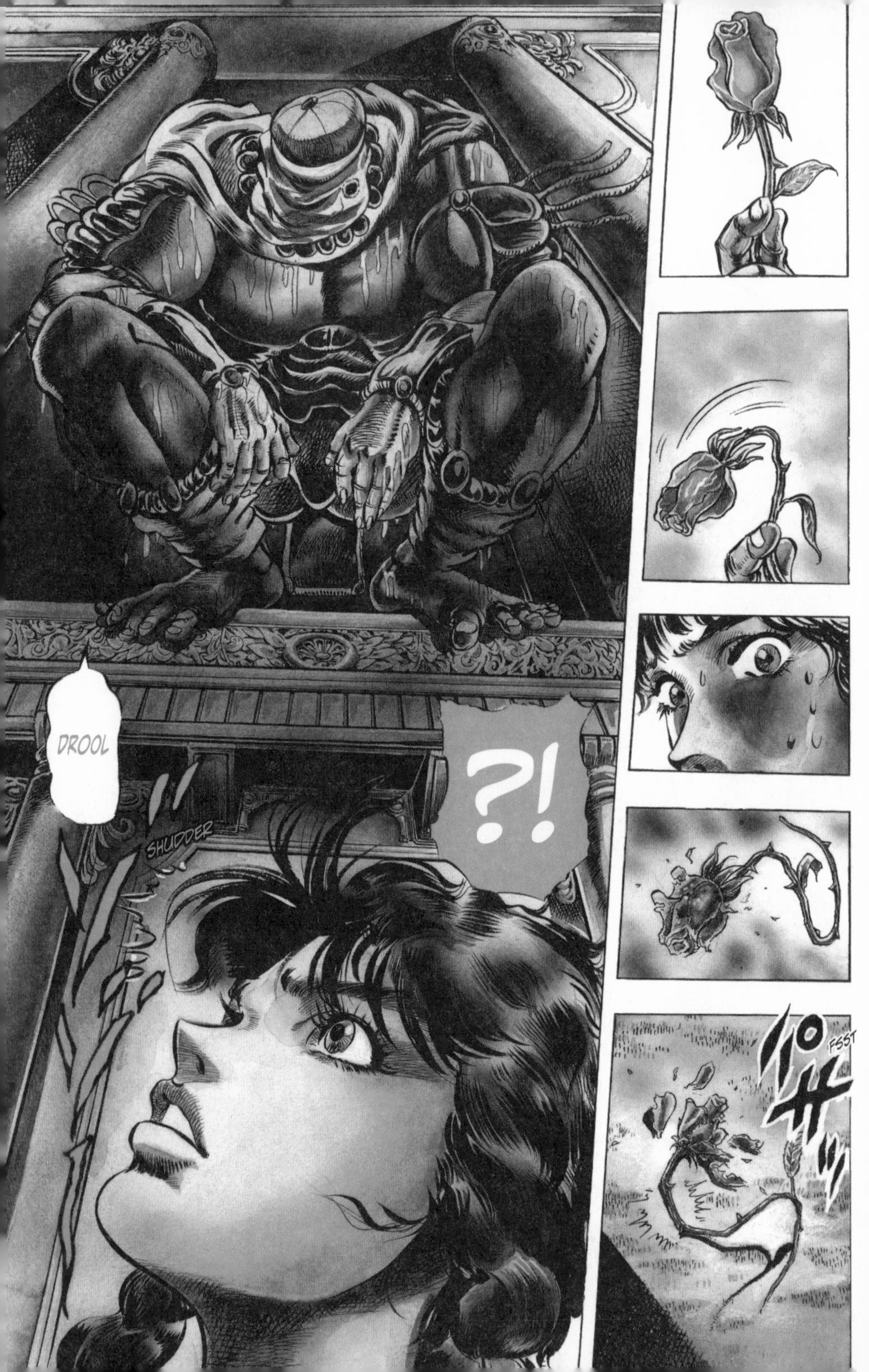
パサッ
FSST
DROOL
SHUDDER
?!

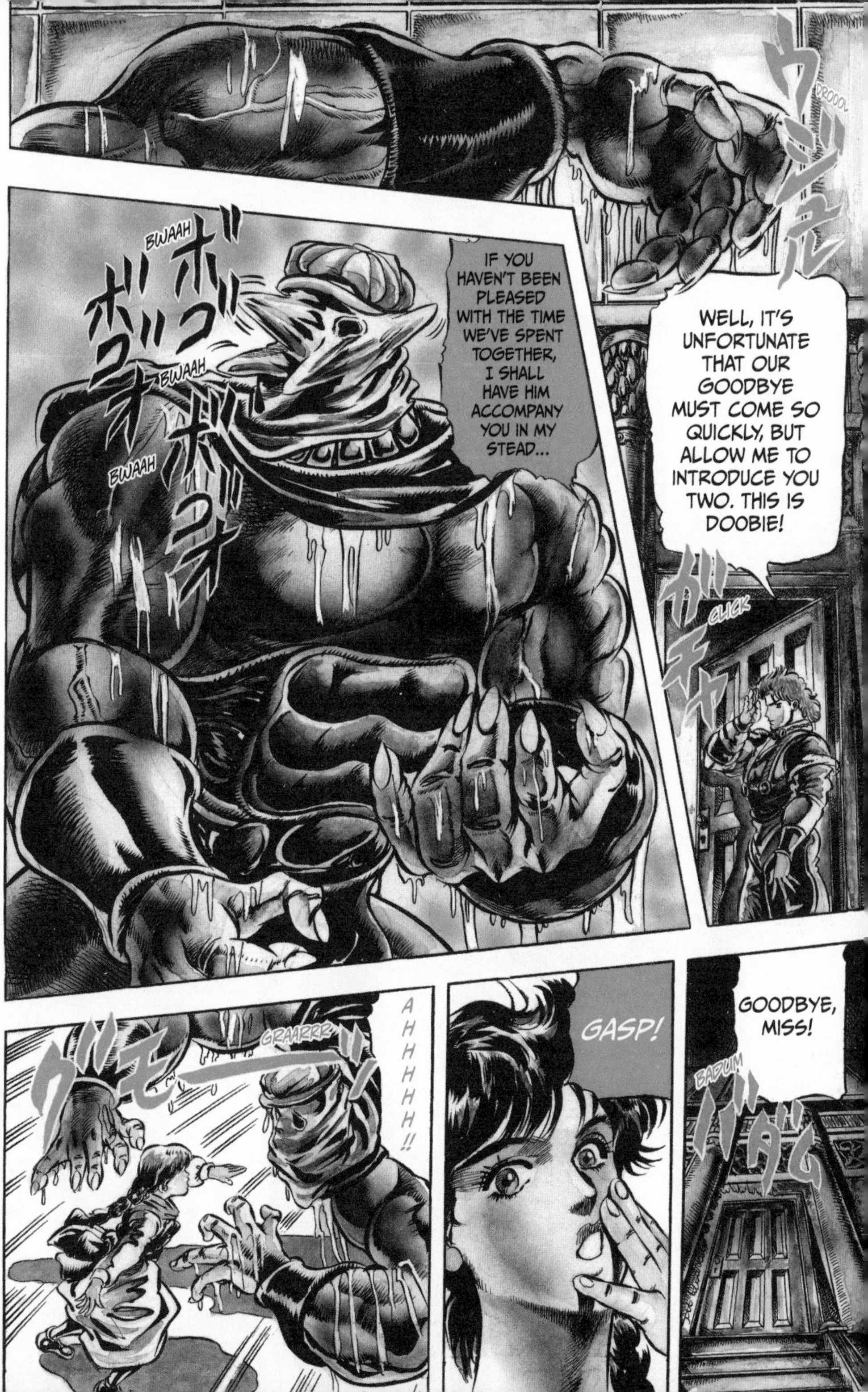
DROOOL
WELL, IT'S UNFORTUNATE THAT OUR GOODBYE MUST COME SO QUICKLY, BUT ALLOW ME TO INTRODUCE YOU TWO. THIS IS DOOBIE!
CLICK
IF YOU HAVEN'T BEEN PLEASED WITH THE TIME WE'VE SPENT TOGETHER, I SHALL HAVE HIM ACCOMPANY YOU IN MY STEAD...
BWAAH
BWAAH
BWAAH
GOODBYE, MISS!
BADUM
GASP!
AHHHHHH!!
GRAARRR

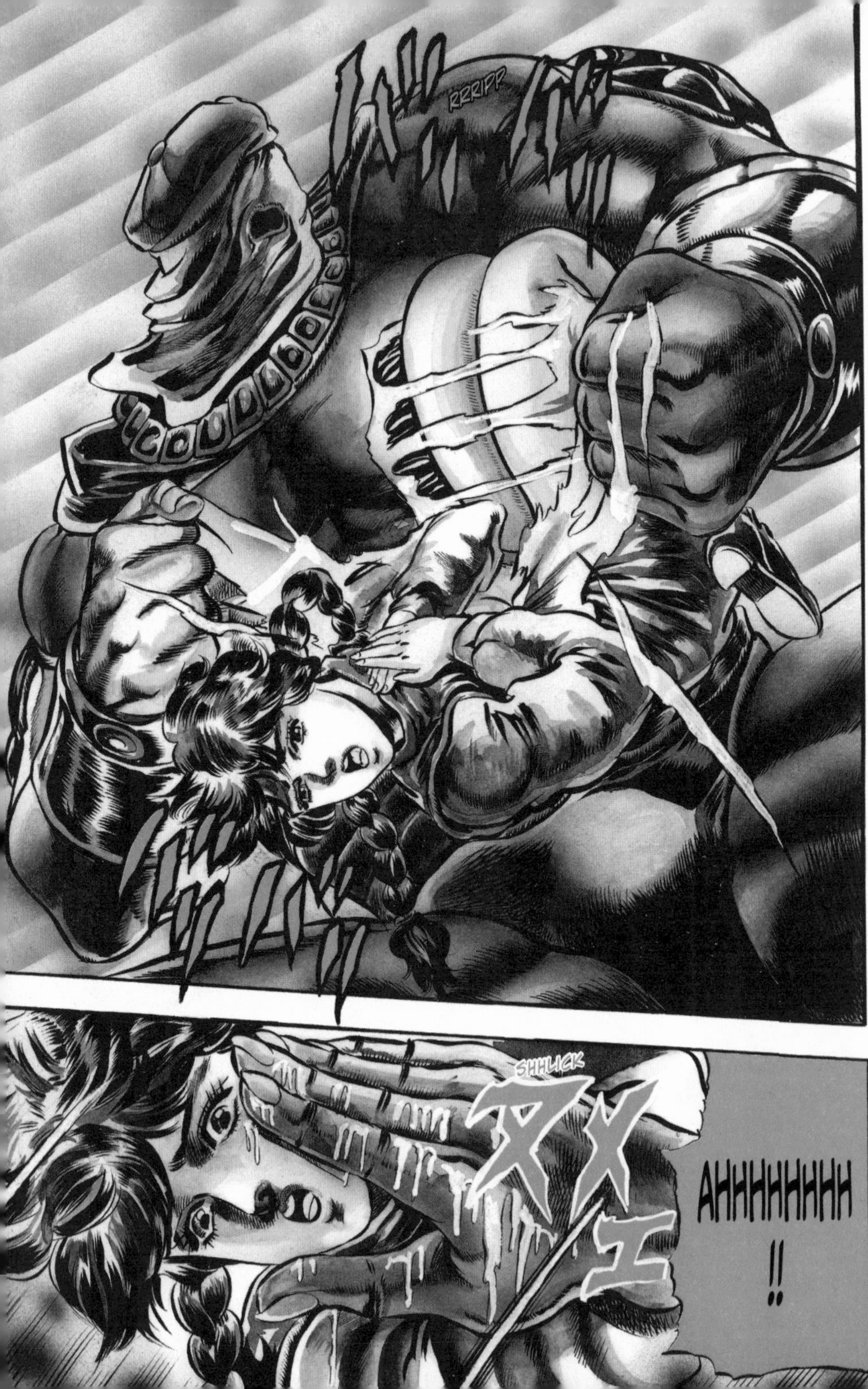
RRRIPP
SHHLICK
AHHHHHHHH !!

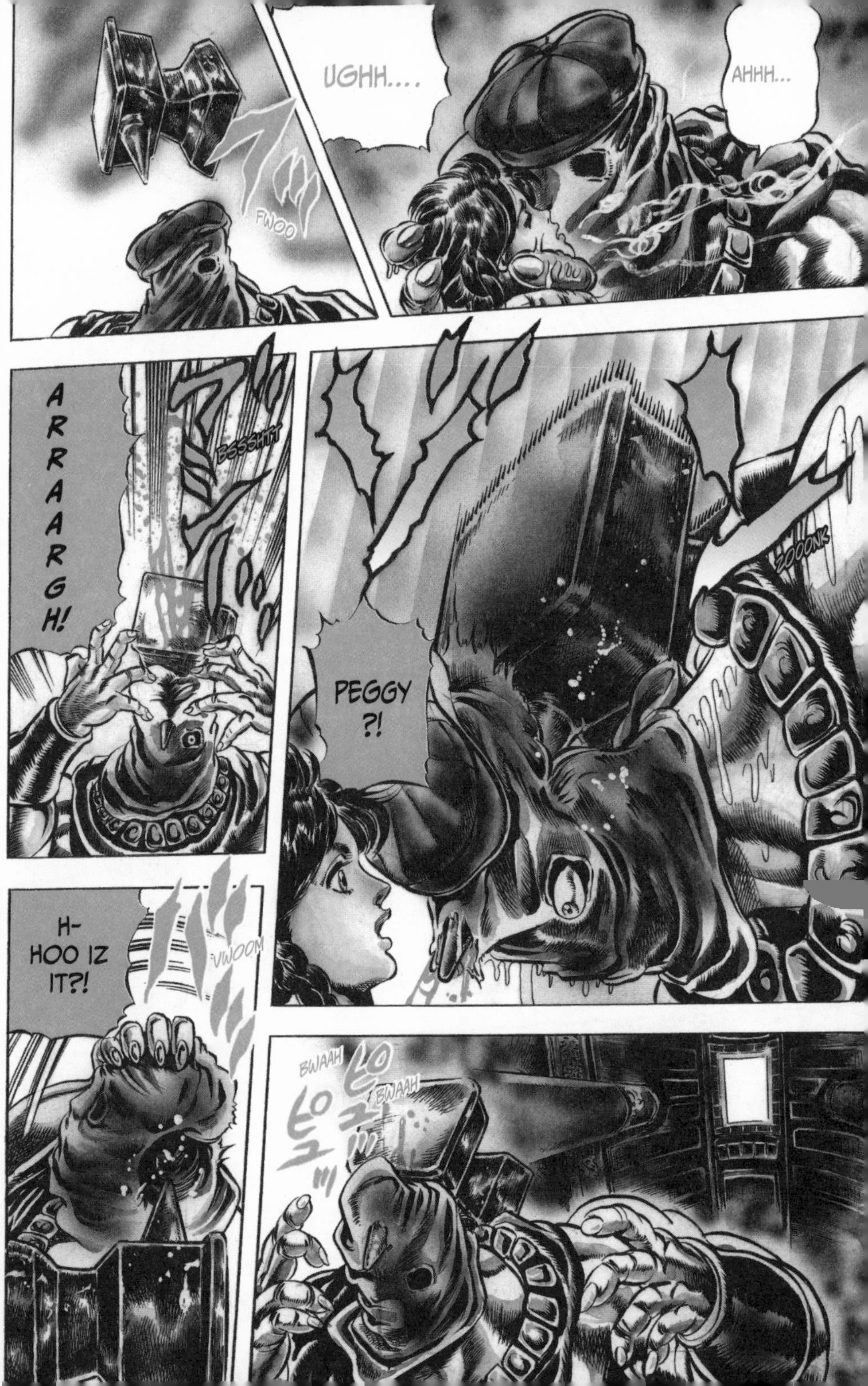
AHHH...
UGHH....
FWOO
ZOOONK
PEGGY ?!
ARRRAARGH!
BSSSHTTT
H-HOO IZ IT?!
VWOOM
BWAAH
BWAAH

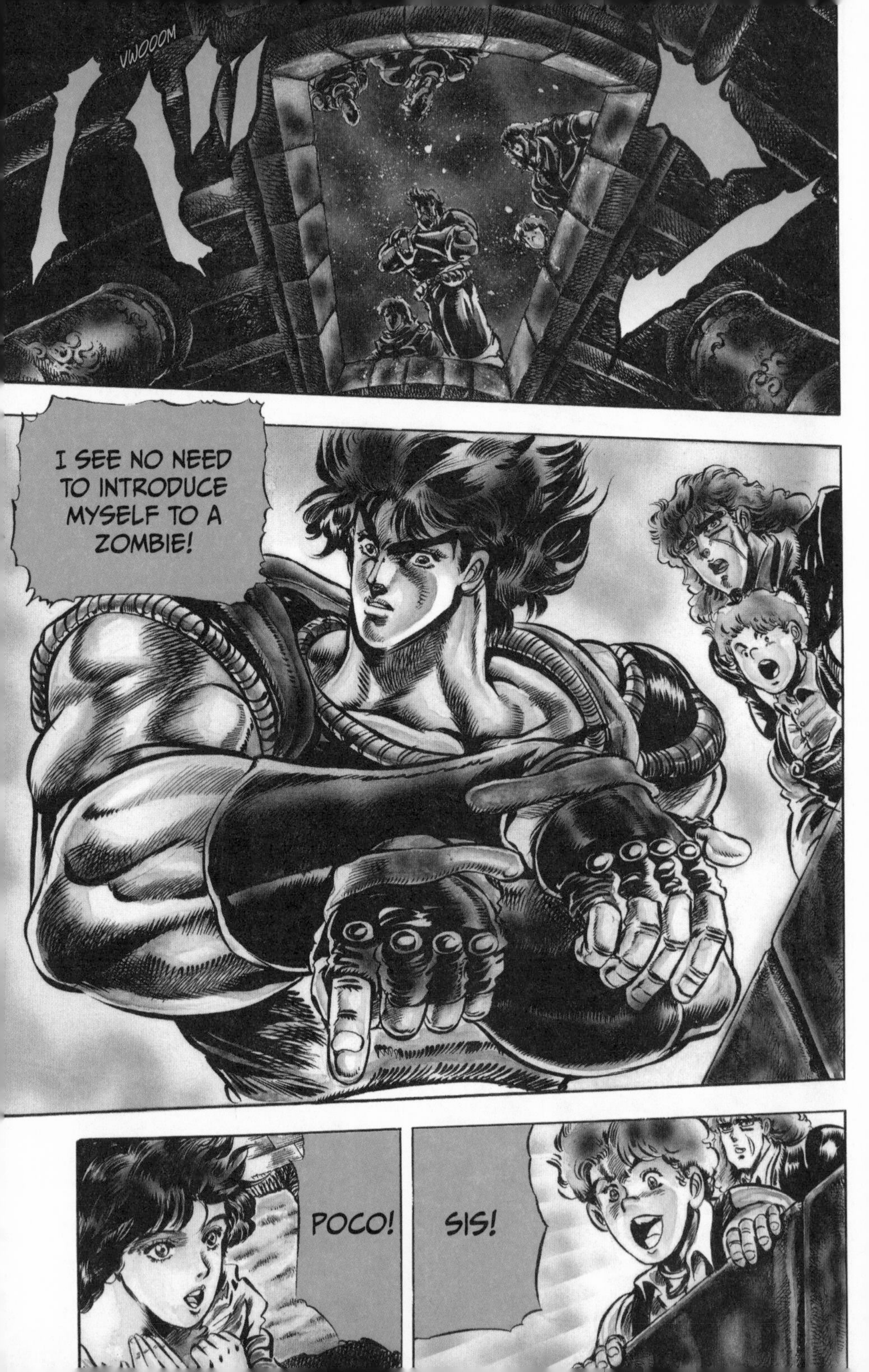
VWOOOM
I SEE NO NEED TO INTRODUCE MYSELF TO A ZOMBIE!
SIS!
POCO!

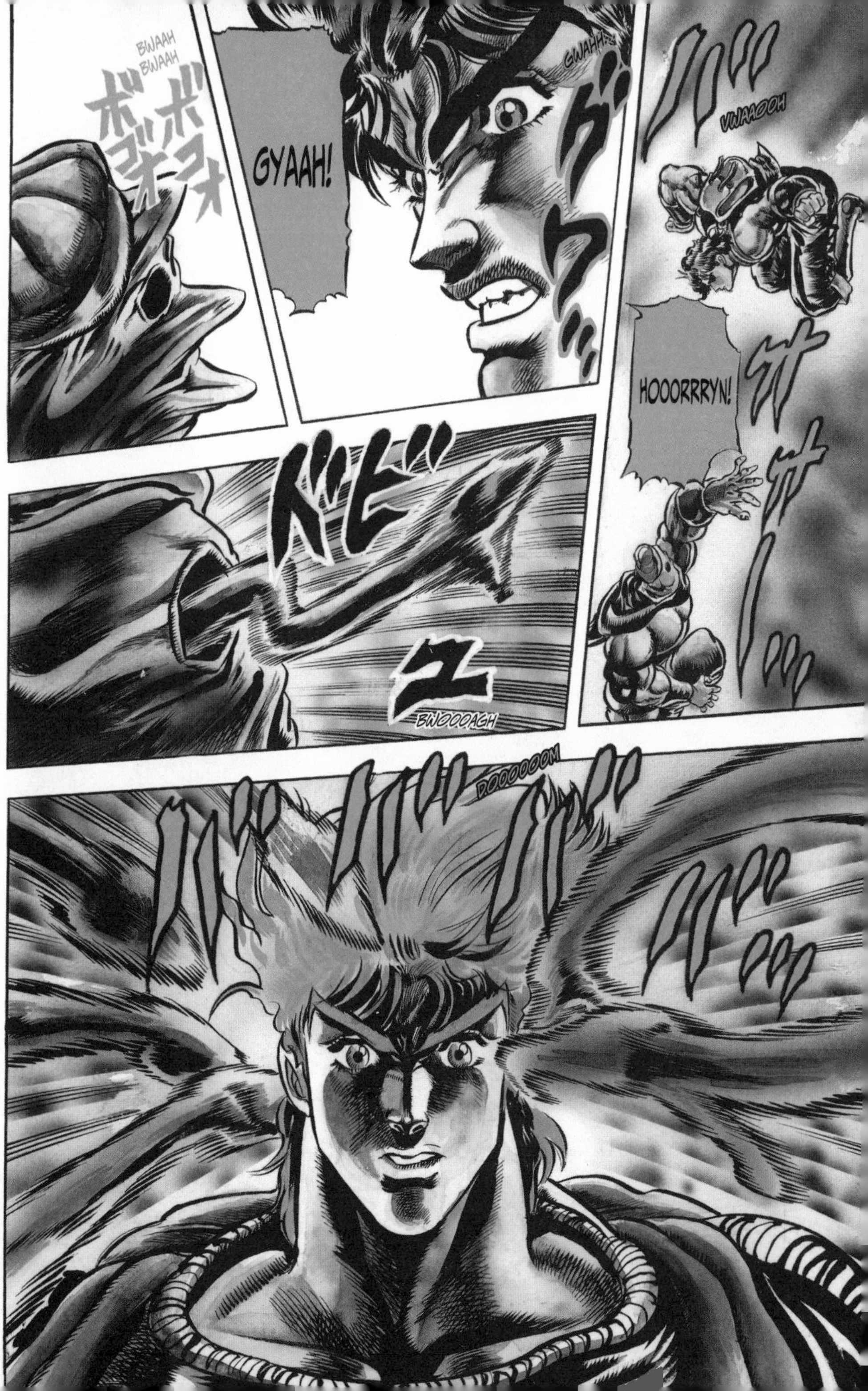
VWAAOOH
HOOORRRYN!
GWAHH
GYAAH!
BWAAH
BWAAH
BWOOOAGH
DOOOOOOM

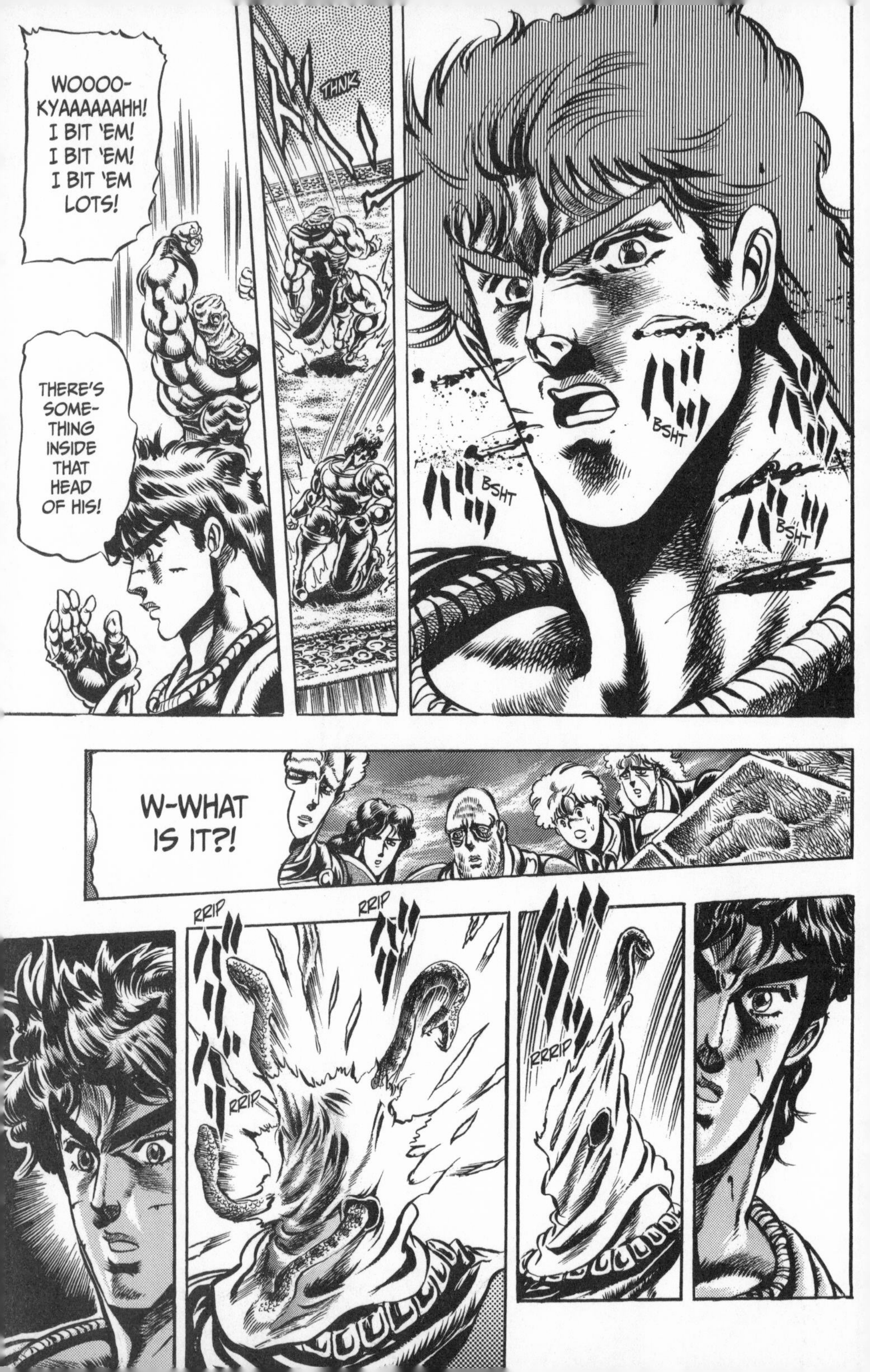
BSHT
BSHT
BSHT
THNK
WOOOO-KYAAAAAAHH! I BIT 'EM! I BIT 'EM! I BIT 'EM LOTS!
THERE'S SOME-THING INSIDE THAT HEAD OF HIS!
W-WHAT IS IT?!
RRRIP
RRIP
RRIP
RRIP

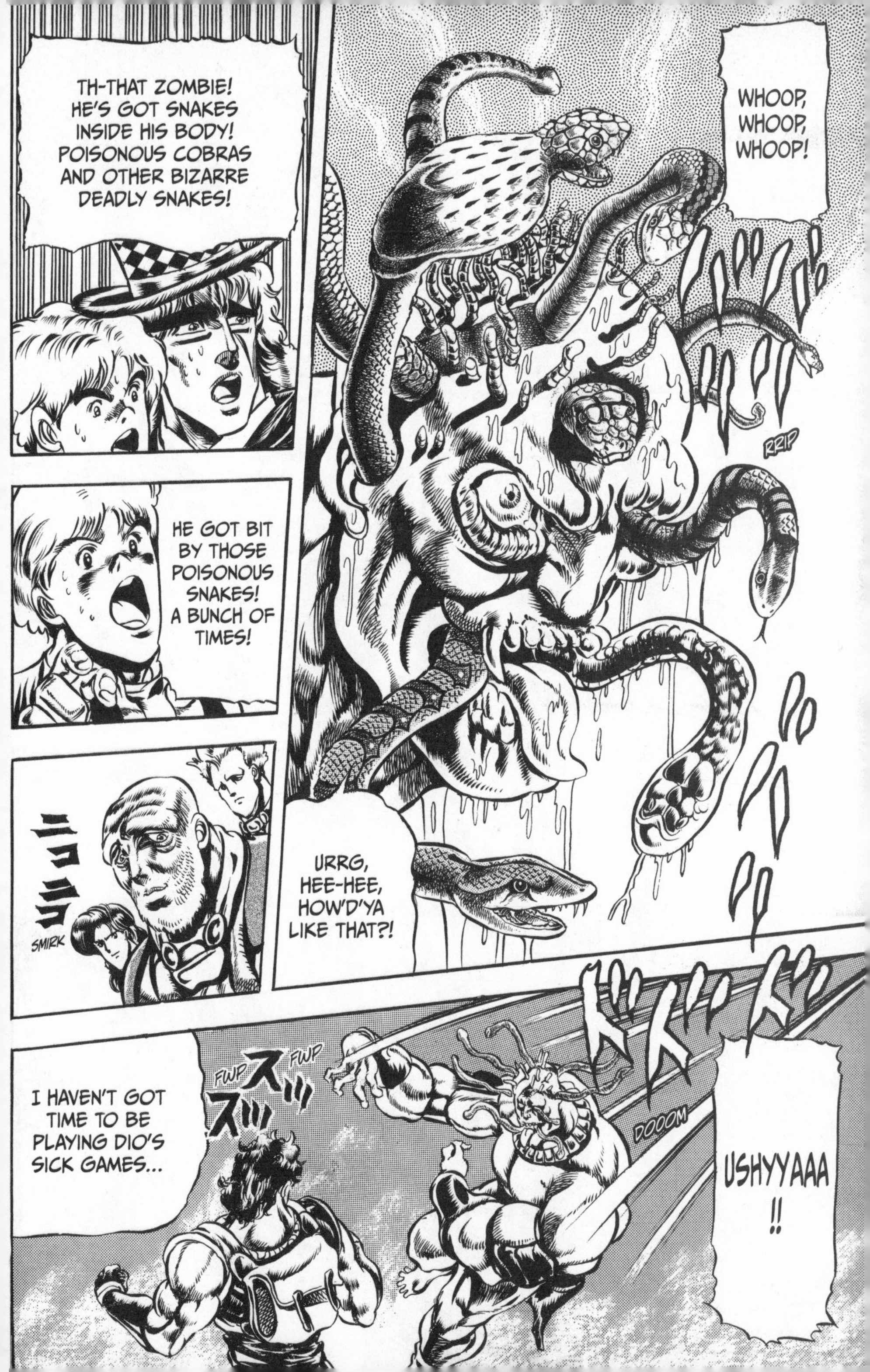
WHOOP, WHOOP, WHOOP!
RRIP
URRG, HEE-HEE, HOW'D'YA LIKE THAT?!
TH-THAT ZOMBIE! HE'S GOT SNAKES INSIDE HIS BODY! POISONOUS COBRAS AND OTHER BIZARRE DEADLY SNAKES!
HE GOT BIT BY THOSE POISONOUS SNAKES! A BUNCH OF TIMES!
SMIRK
USHYYAAA !!
DOOOM
FWP
FWP
I HAVEN'T GOT TIME TO BE PLAYING DIO'S SICK GAMES...

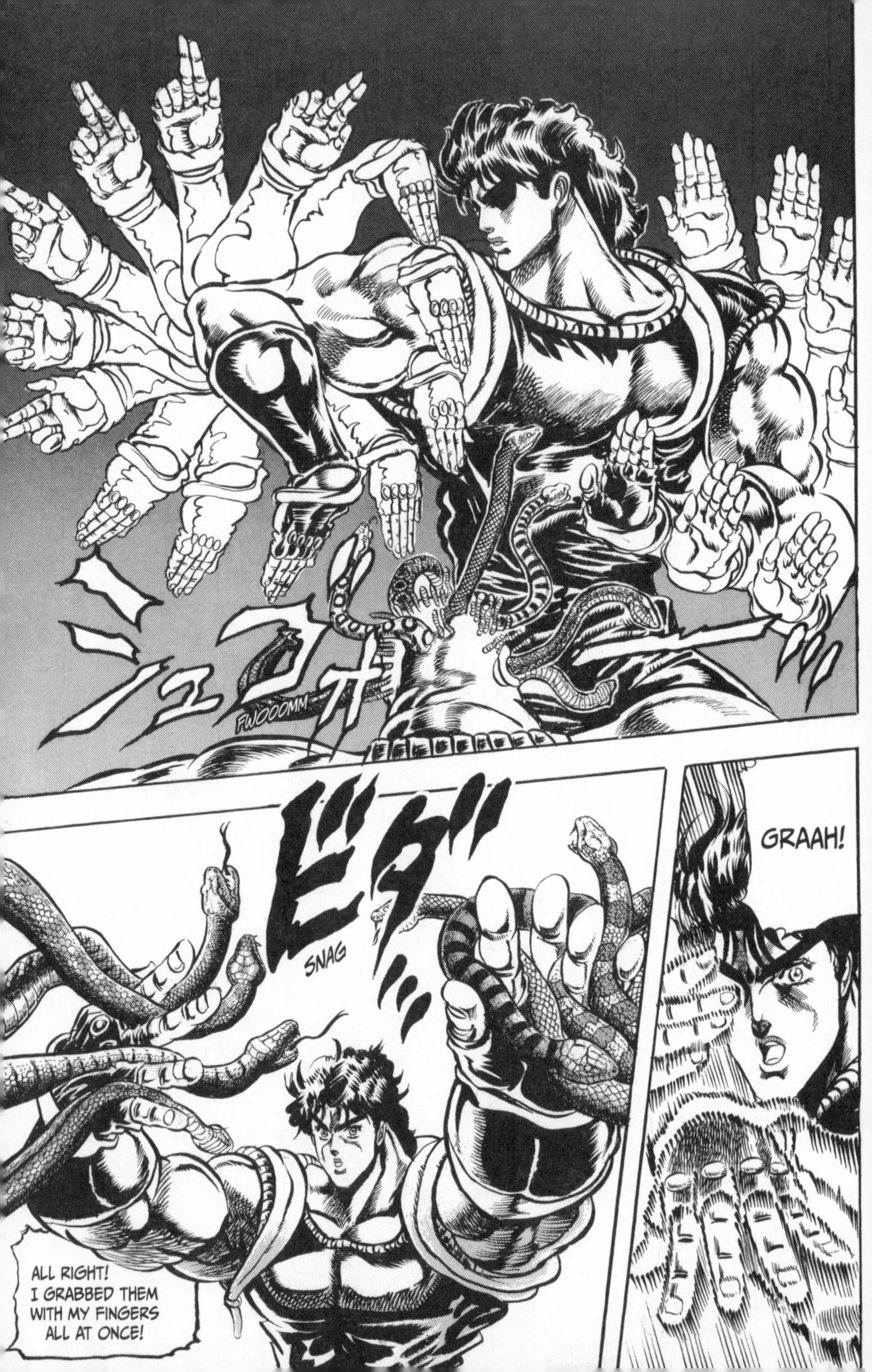
FWOOOMM
GRAAH!
SNAG
ALL RIGHT! I GRABBED THEM WITH MY FINGERS ALL AT ONCE!

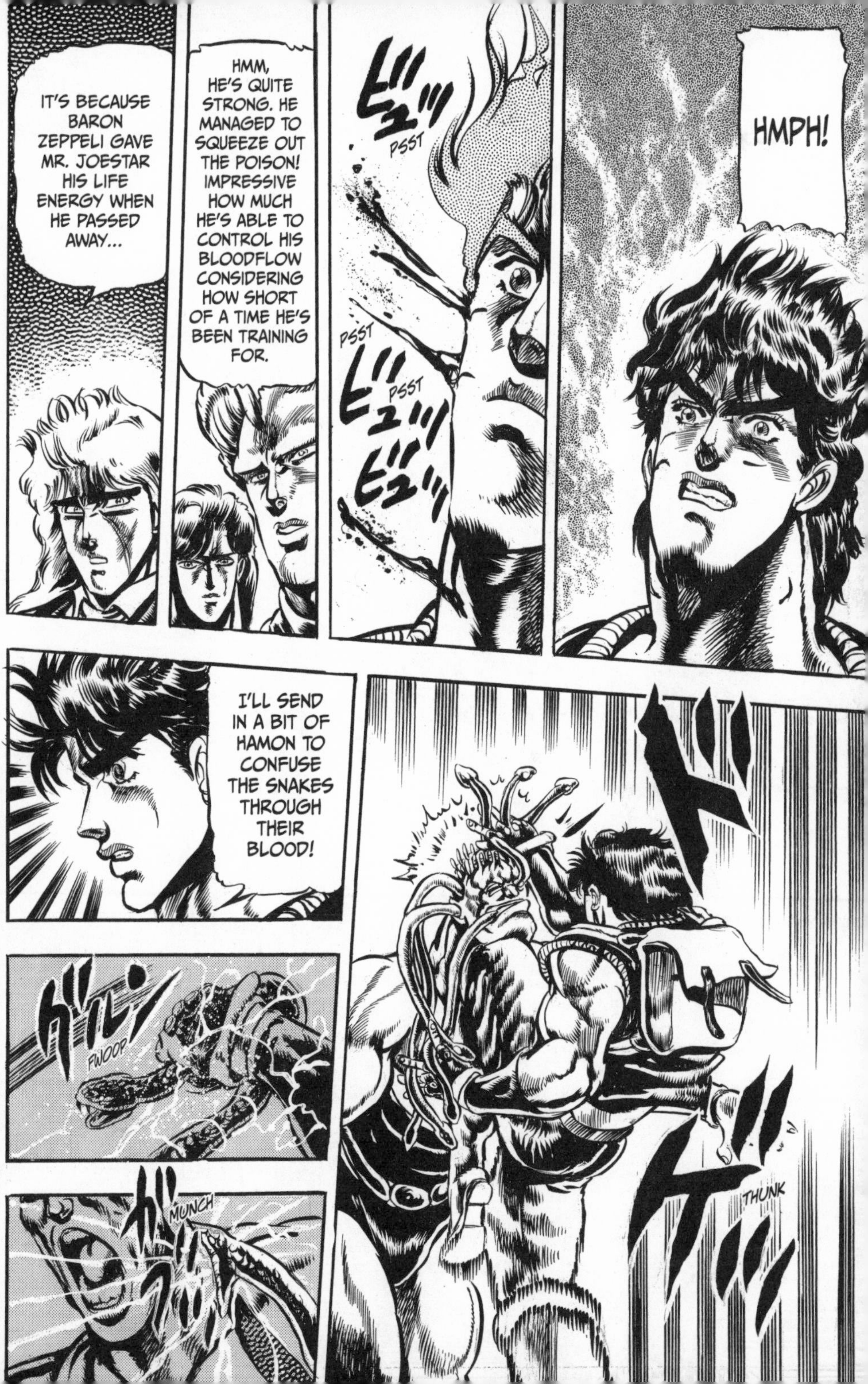
HMPH!
PSST
PSST
PSST
HMM, HE'S QUITE STRONG. HE MANAGED TO SQUEEZE OUT THE POISON! IMPRESSIVE HOW MUCH HE'S ABLE TO CONTROL HIS BLOODFLOW CONSIDERING HOW SHORT OF A TIME HE'S BEEN TRAINING FOR.
IT'S BECAUSE BARON ZEPPELI GAVE MR. JOESTAR HIS LIFE ENERGY WHEN HE PASSED AWAY...
THUNK
I'LL SEND IN A BIT OF HAMON TO CONFUSE THE SNAKES THROUGH THEIR BLOOD!
FWOOP
MUNCH

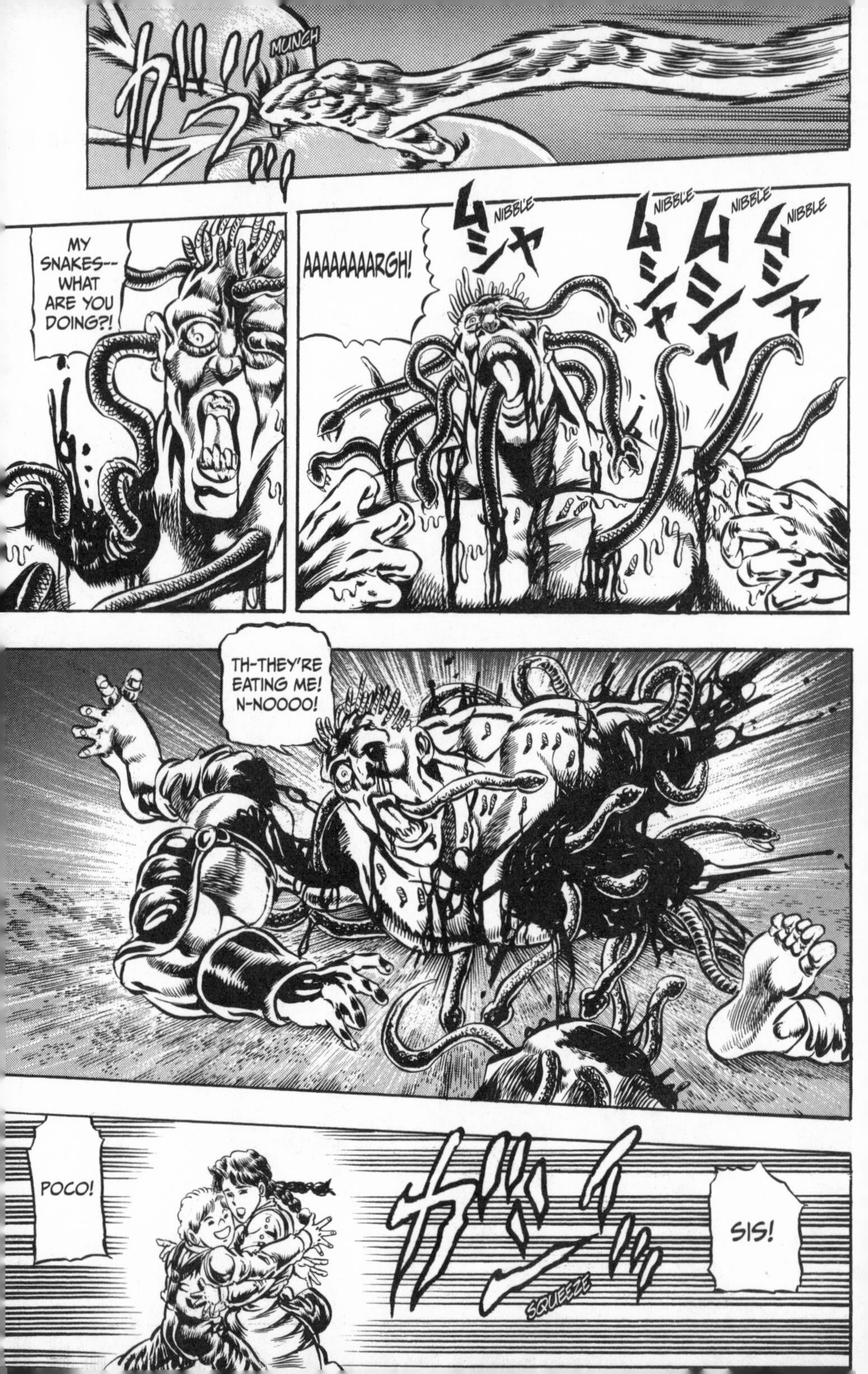
MUNCH
ムシャ NIBBLE
ムシャ NIBBLE
ムシャ NIBBLE
ムシャ NIBBLE
AAAAAAAARGH!
MY SNAKES-- WHAT ARE YOU DOING?!
TH-THEY'RE EATING ME! N-NOOOO!
SIS!
SQUEEZE
POCO!

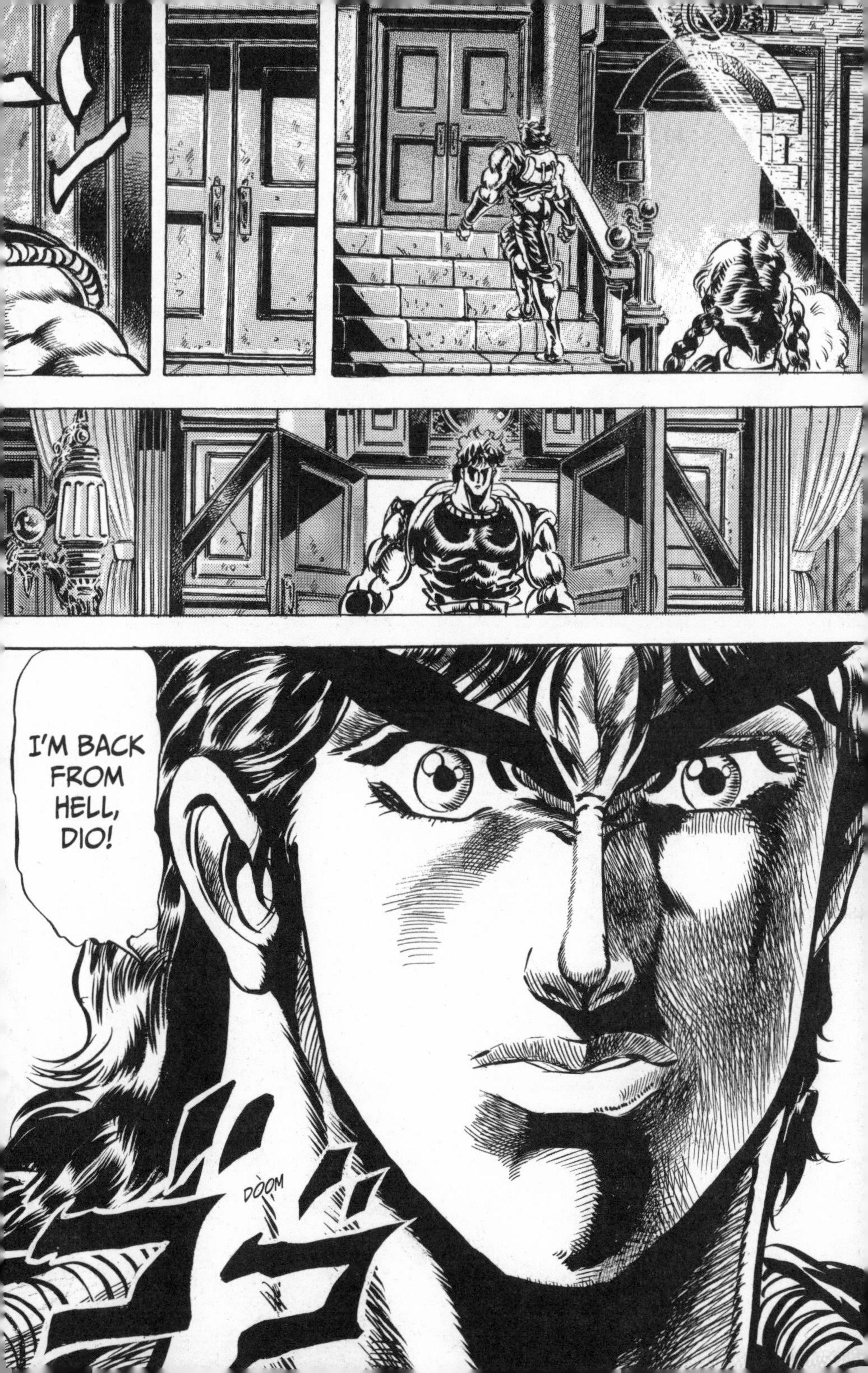
I'M BACK FROM HELL, DIO!
DOOM

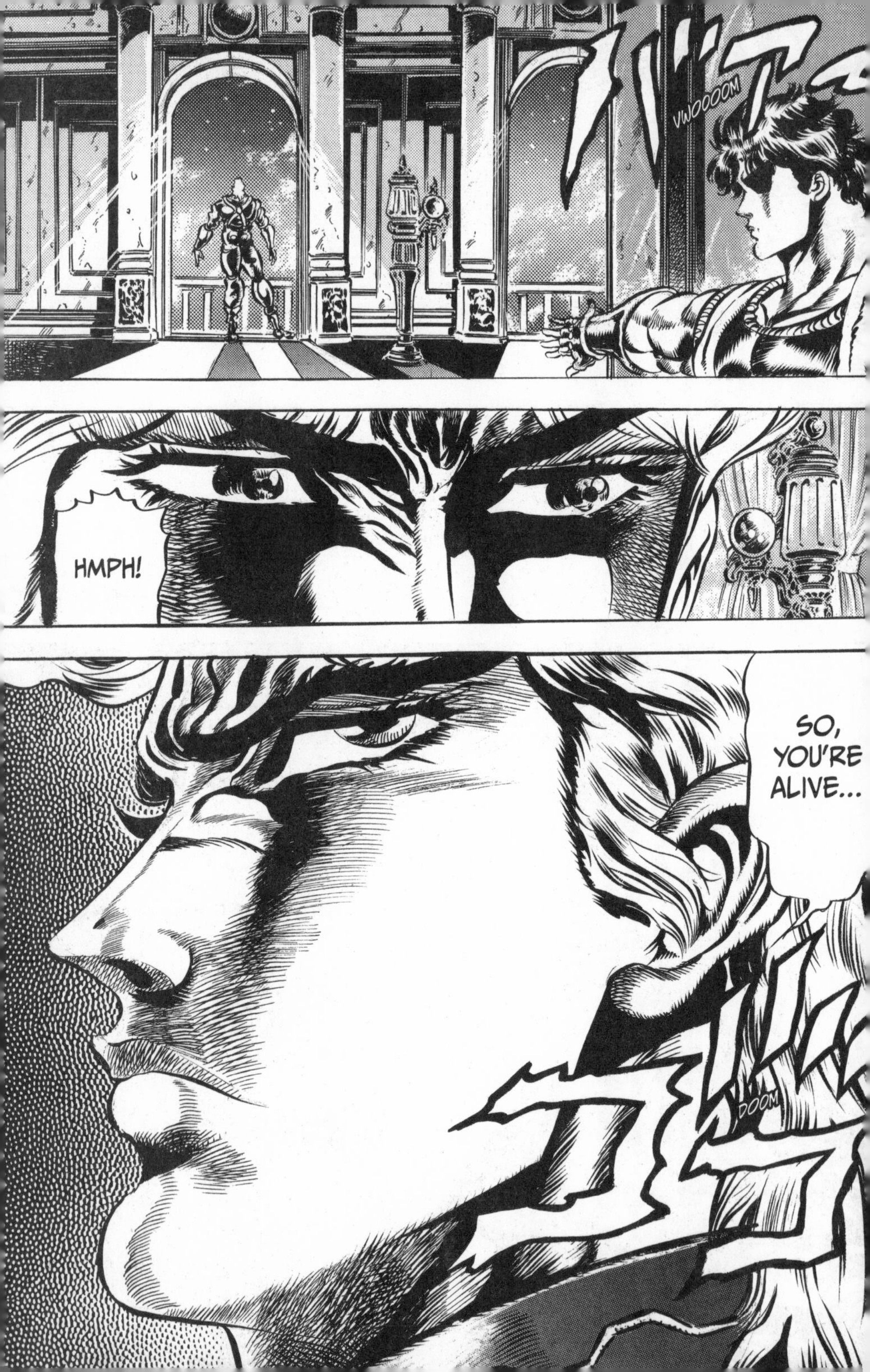
VWOOOOM
HMPH!
SO, YOU'RE ALIVE...
DOOM

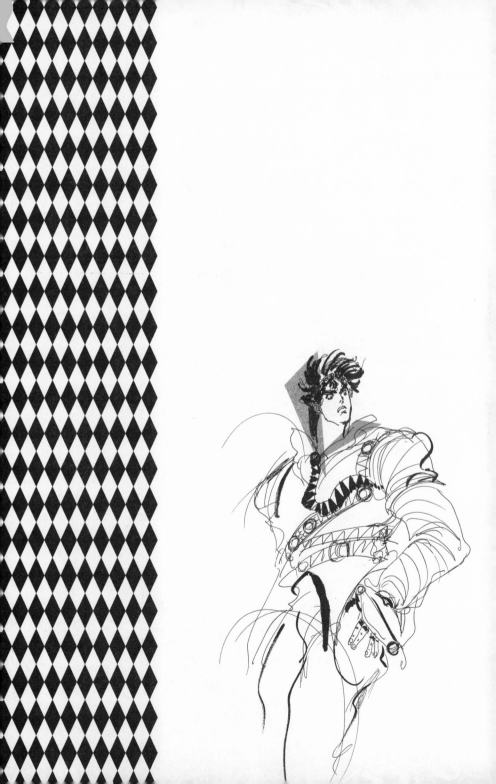

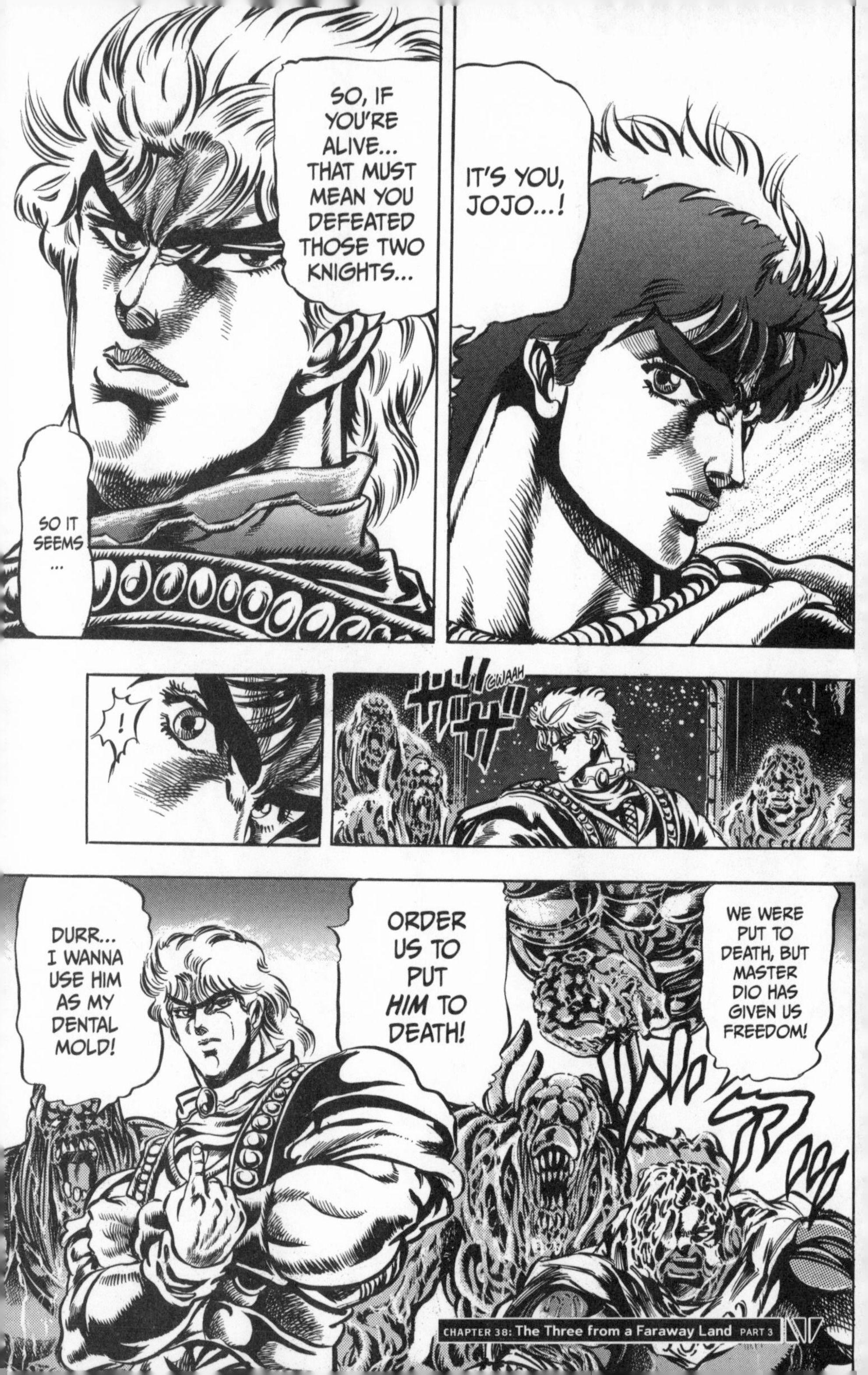
IT'S YOU, JOJO...!
SO, IF YOU'RE ALIVE... THAT MUST MEAN YOU DEFEATED THOSE TWO KNIGHTS...
SO IT SEEMS ...
GWAAH
!
WE WERE PUT TO DEATH, BUT MASTER DIO HAS GIVEN US FREEDOM!
ORDER US TO PUT *HIM* TO DEATH!
DURR... I WANNA USE HIM AS MY DENTAL MOLD!
CHAPTER 38: The Three from a Faraway Land PART 3

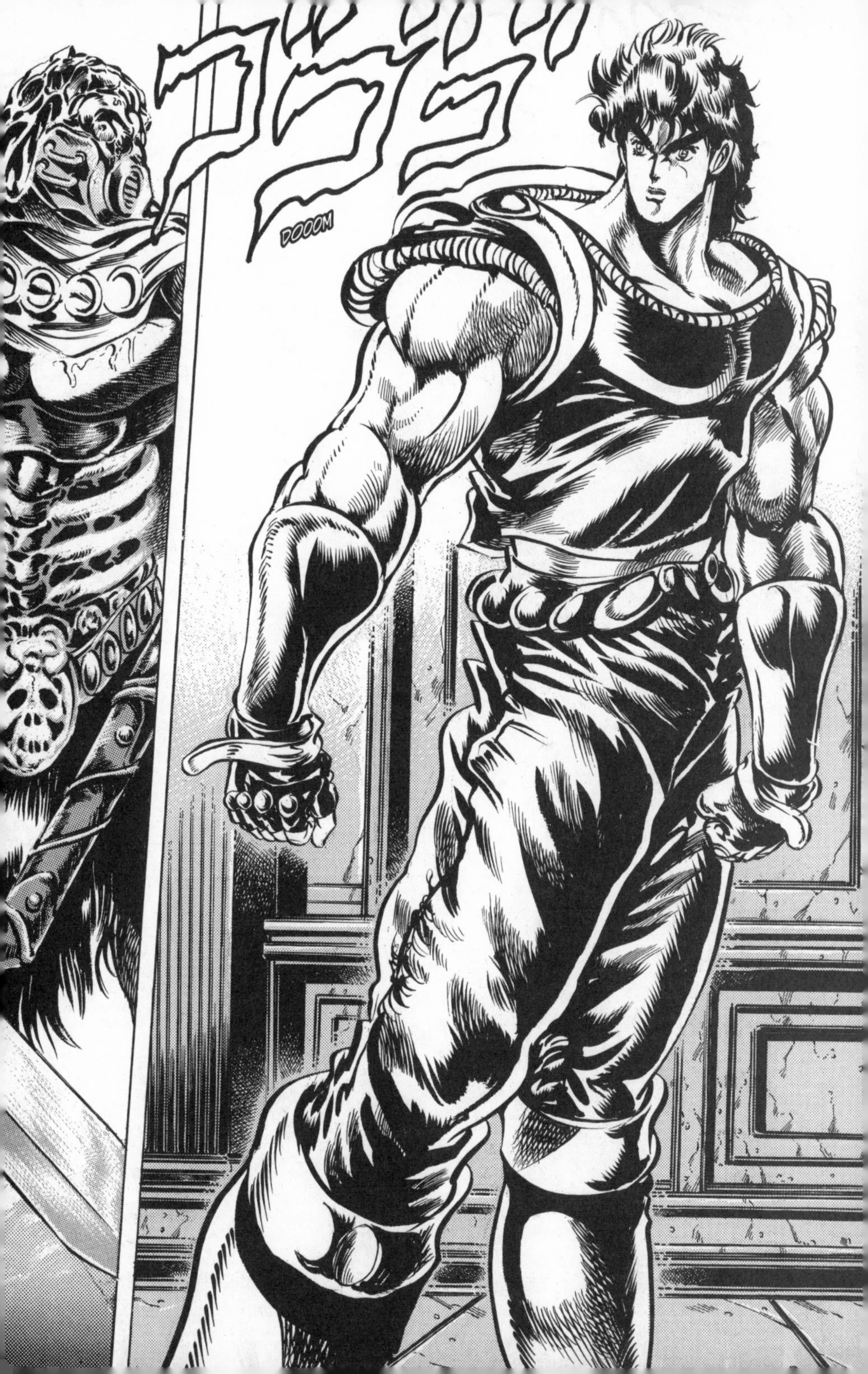
DOOOM

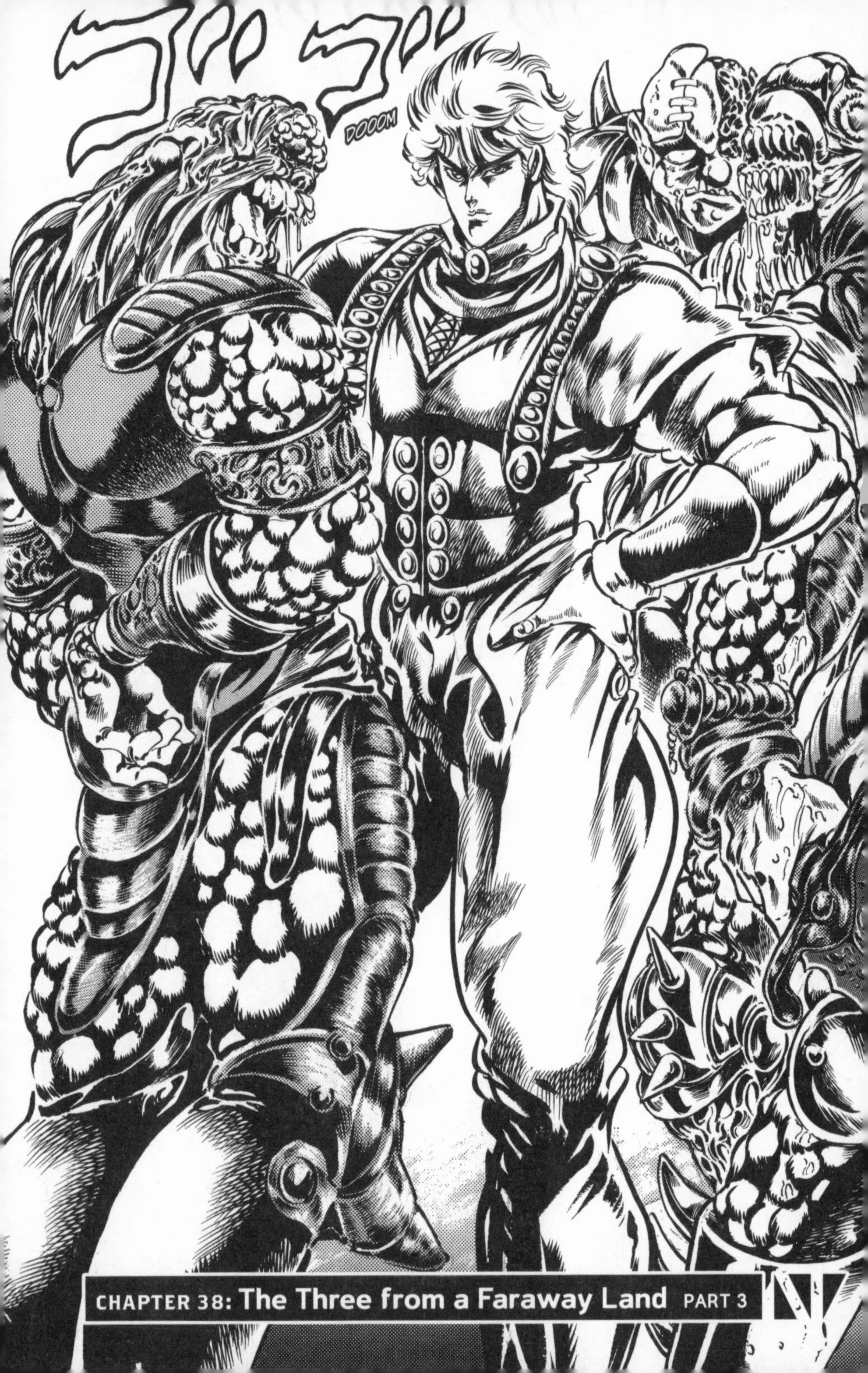
DOOOM

CHAPTER 38: The Three from a Faraway Land PART 3

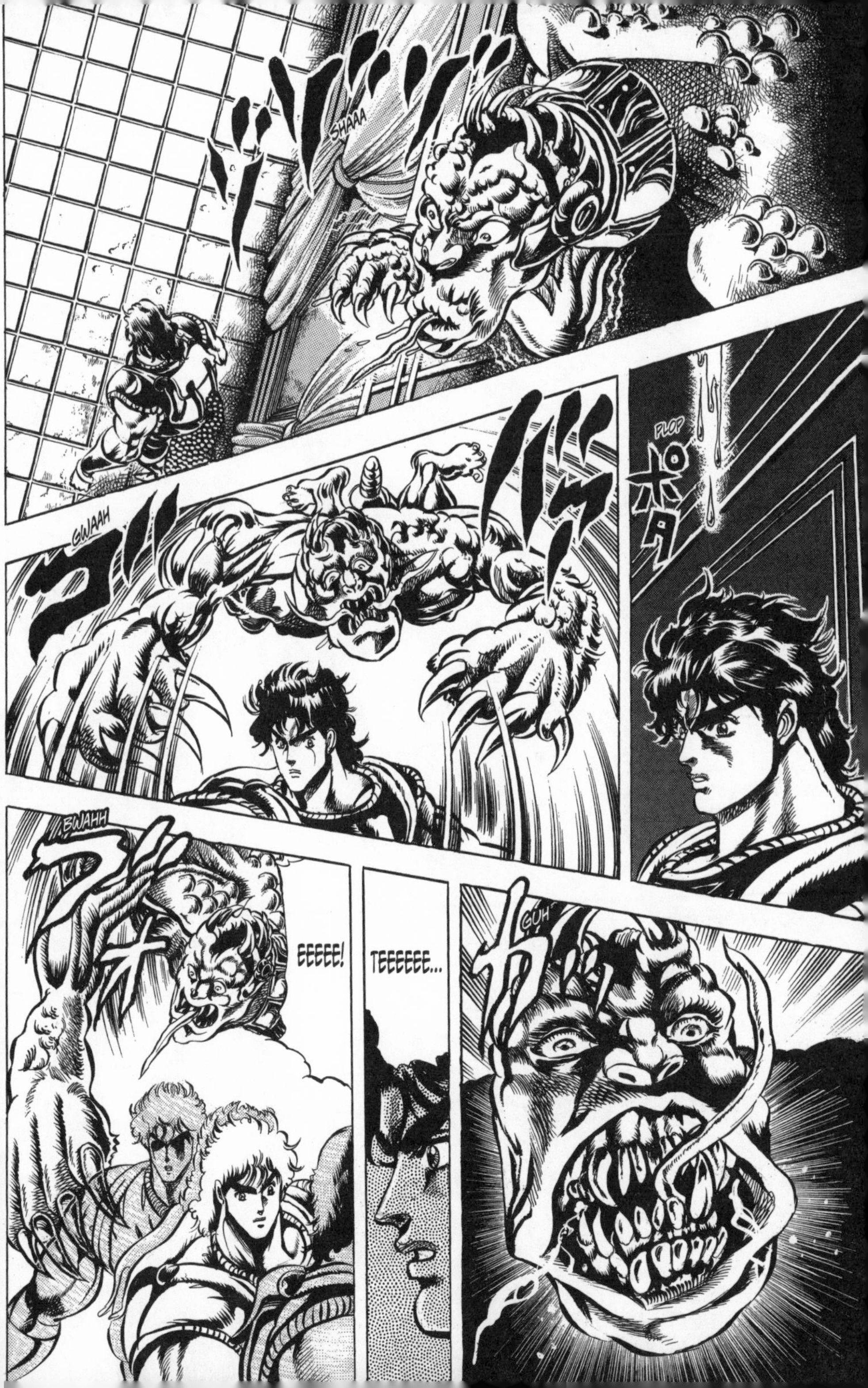
SHAAA
PLOP
GWAAH
GUH
TEEEEEE...
BWAHH
EEEEE!

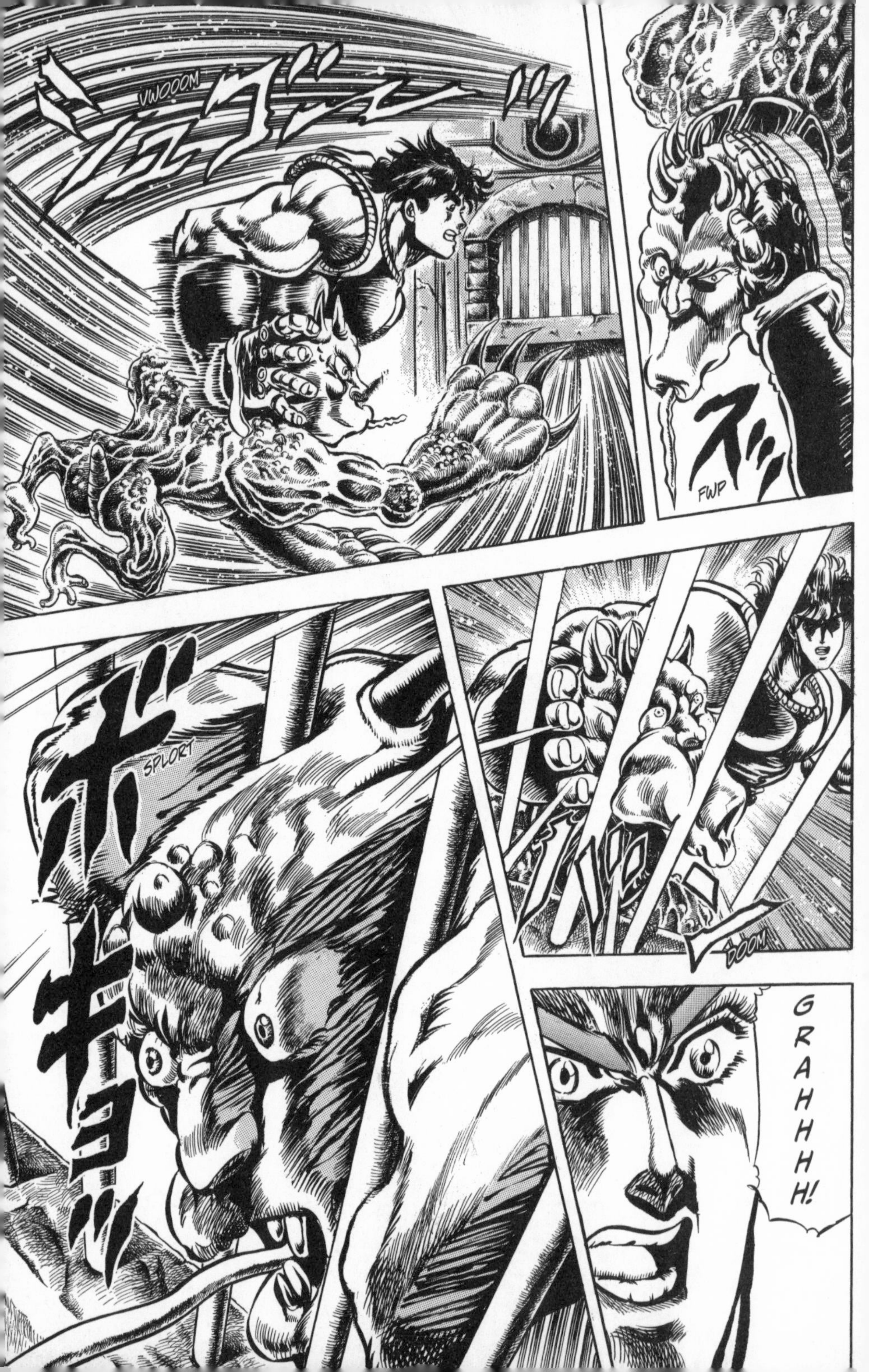
FWP
VWOOOM
DOOM
GRAHHHHH!
SPLORT

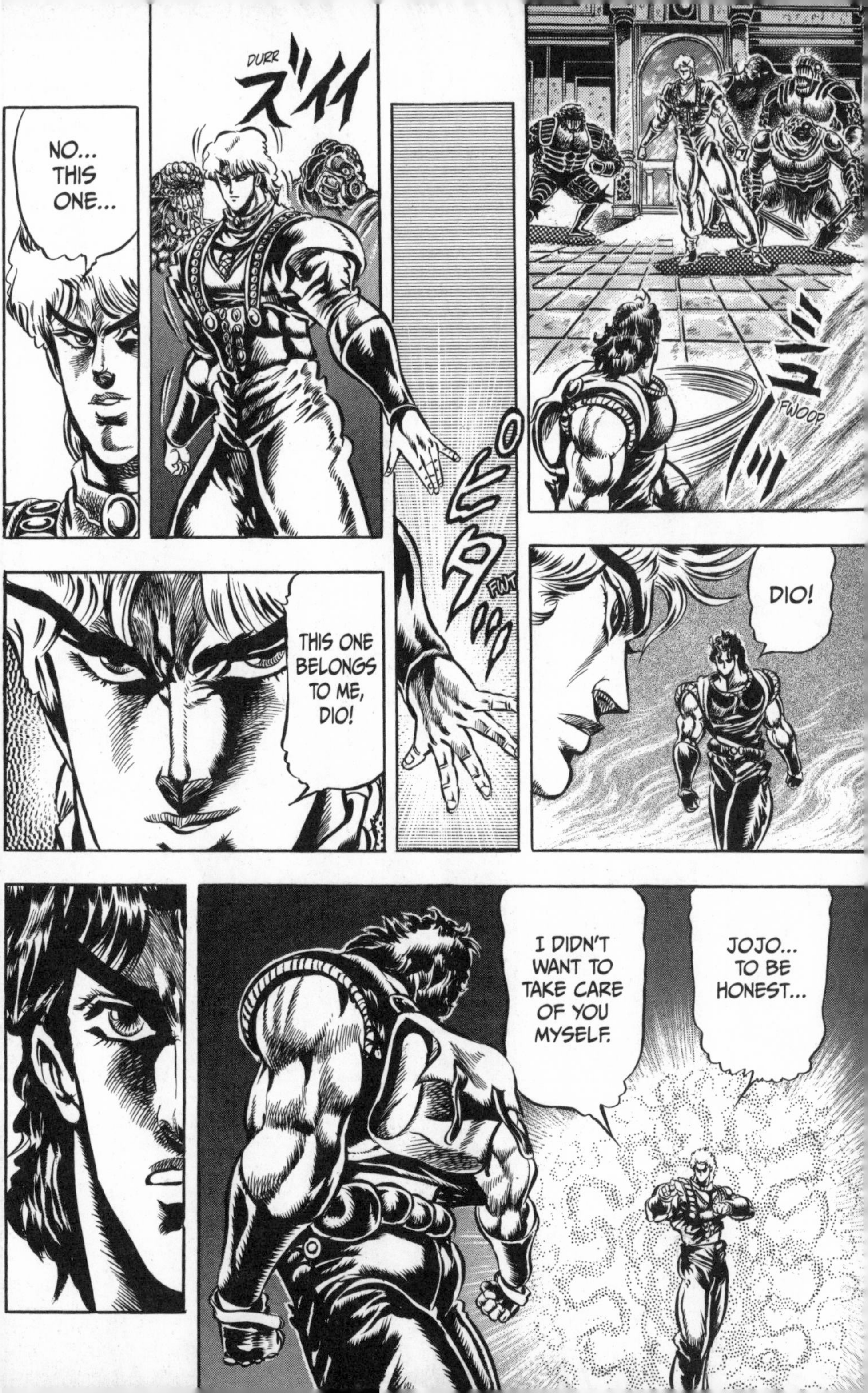
FWOOP
DIO!
FWT
DURR
ズイイ
NO... THIS ONE...
THIS ONE BELONGS TO ME, DIO!
JOJO... TO BE HONEST...
I DIDN'T WANT TO TAKE CARE OF YOU MYSELF.

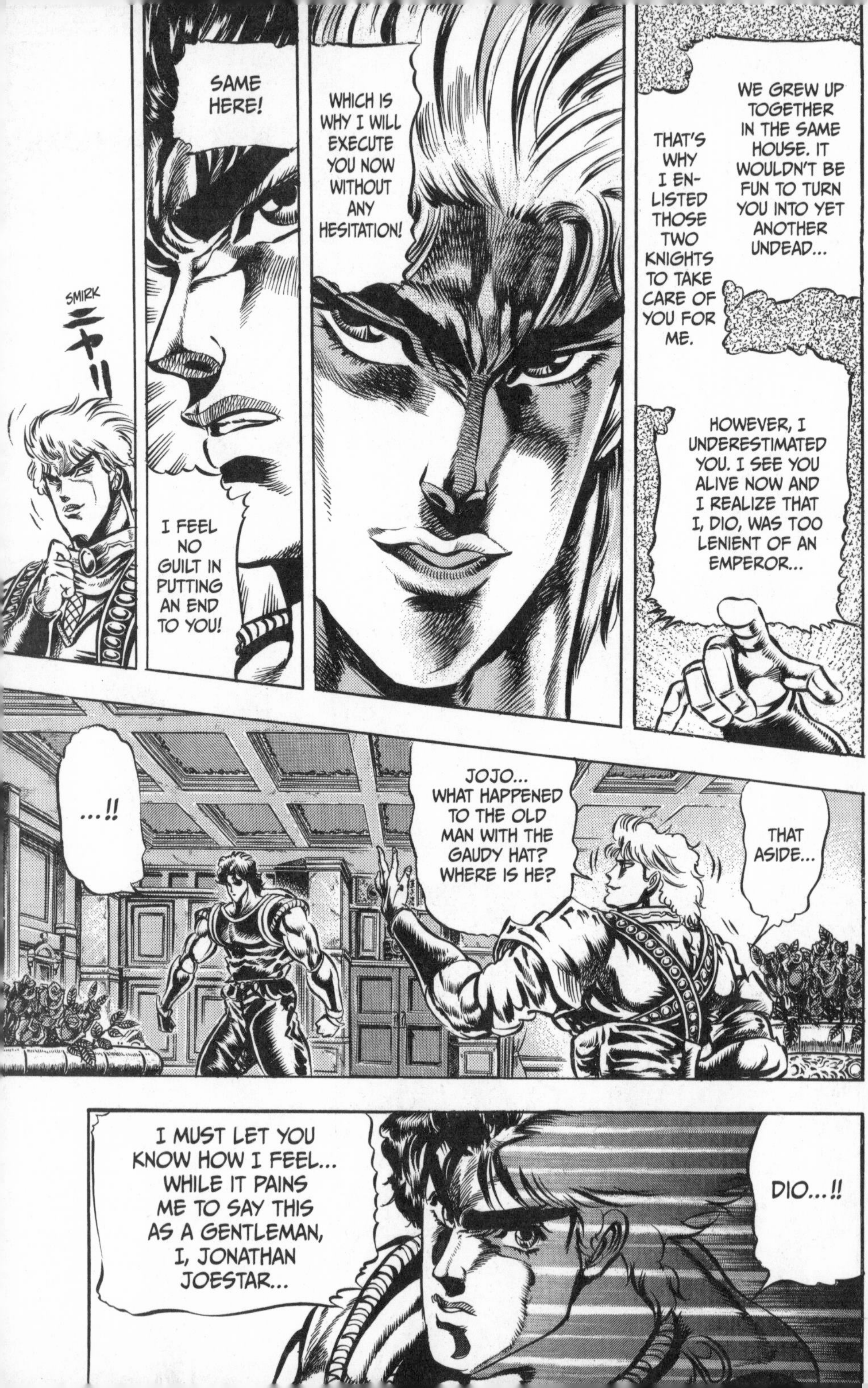
WE GREW UP TOGETHER IN THE SAME HOUSE. IT WOULDN'T BE FUN TO TURN YOU INTO YET ANOTHER UNDEAD...
THAT'S WHY I EN-LISTED THOSE TWO KNIGHTS TO TAKE CARE OF YOU FOR ME.
HOWEVER, I UNDERESTIMATED YOU. I SEE YOU ALIVE NOW AND I REALIZE THAT I, DIO, WAS TOO LENIENT OF AN EMPEROR...
WHICH IS WHY I WILL EXECUTE YOU NOW WITHOUT ANY HESITATION!
SAME HERE!
I FEEL NO GUILT IN PUTTING AN END TO YOU!
SMIRK
THAT ASIDE...
JOJO... WHAT HAPPENED TO THE OLD MAN WITH THE GAUDY HAT? WHERE IS HE?
...!!
DIO...!!
I MUST LET YOU KNOW HOW I FEEL... WHILE IT PAINS ME TO SAY THIS AS A GENTLEMAN, I, JONATHAN JOESTAR...

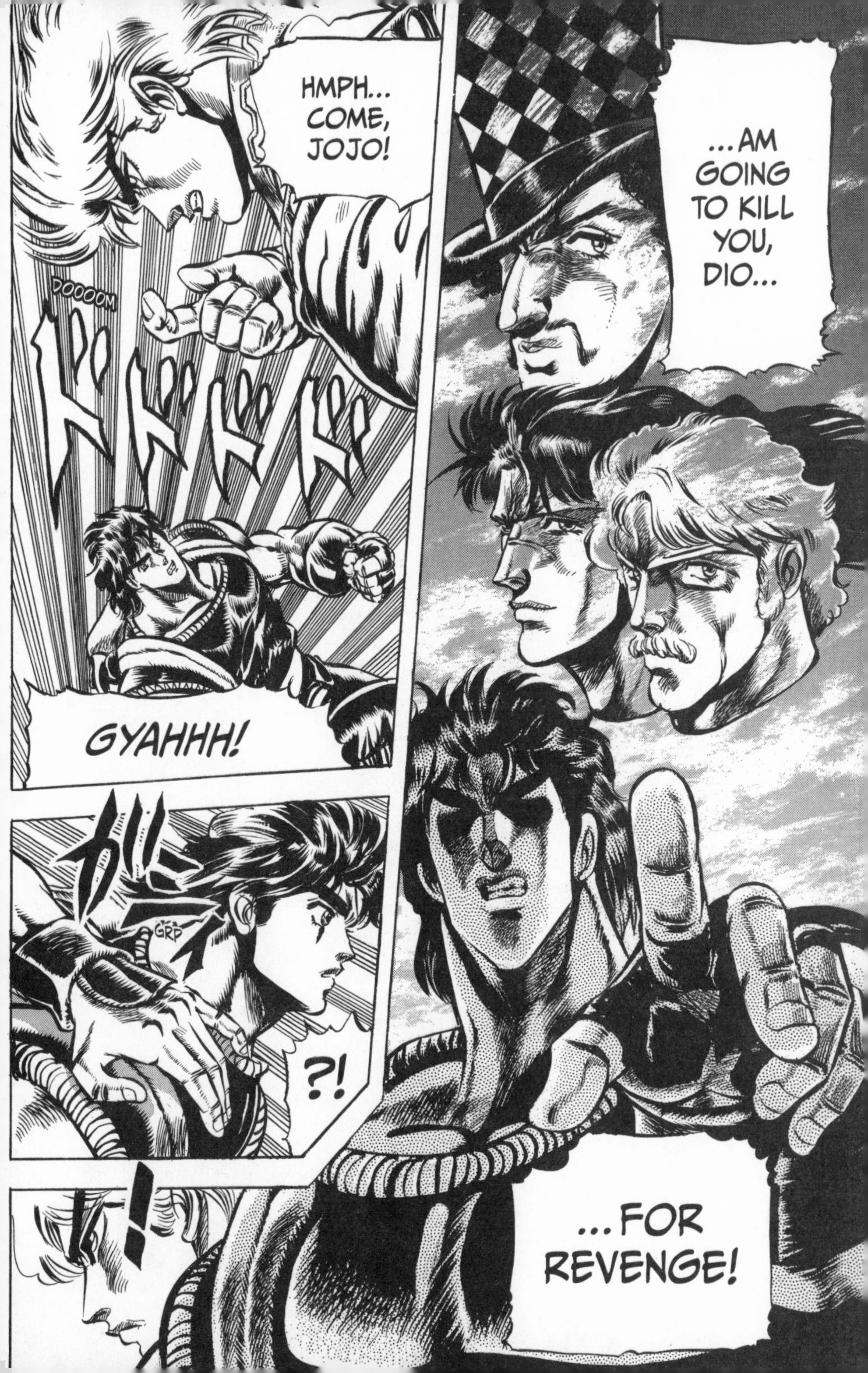
...AM GOING TO KILL YOU, DIO...
...FOR REVENGE!
HMPH... COME, JOJO!
DOOOOM
GYAHHH!
GRP
?!

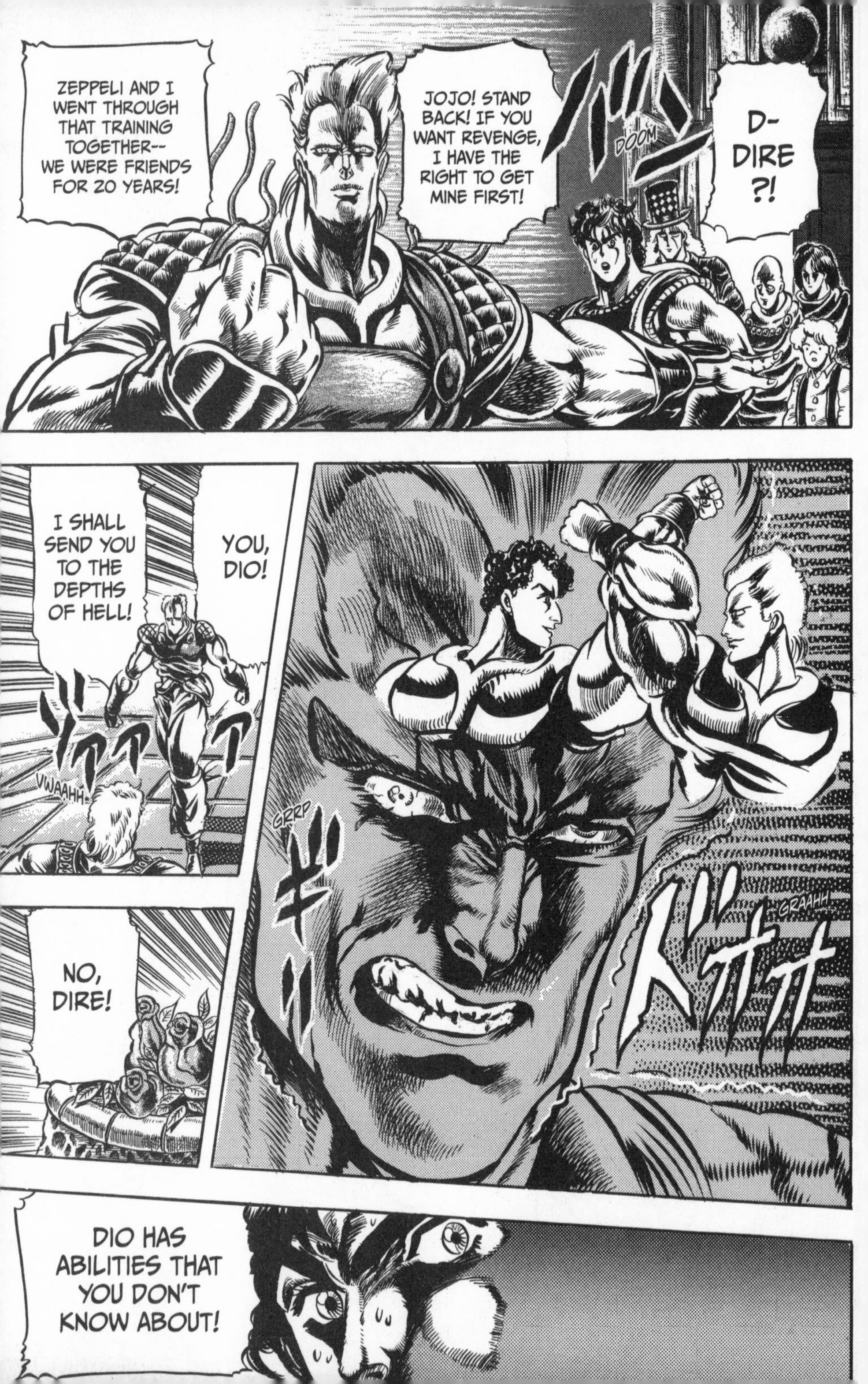
D-DIRE?!
DOOM
JOJO! STAND BACK! IF YOU WANT REVENGE, I HAVE THE RIGHT TO GET MINE FIRST!
ZEPPELI AND I WENT THROUGH THAT TRAINING TOGETHER-- WE WERE FRIENDS FOR 20 YEARS!
GRAAHH
GRRP
YOU, DIO!
I SHALL SEND YOU TO THE DEPTHS OF HELL!
VWAAHH
NO, DIRE!
DIO HAS ABILITIES THAT YOU DON'T KNOW ABOUT!

HMM... INTERESTING MOVEMENTS... IT SEEMS THAT GIVEN ENOUGH TRAINING, HUMANS CAN LEARN TO LIGHTEN THEIR BODIES AND MOVE IN SUCH A MYSTERIOUS WAY.

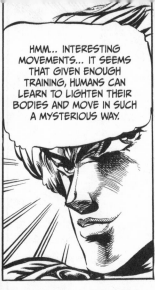

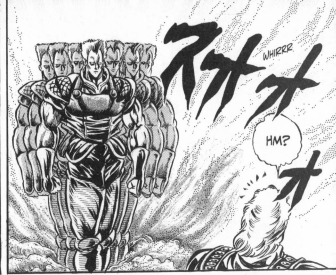

WHIRRR

HM?

HMPH! HOWEVER... IN ONE NIGHT, I HAVE FAR SURPASSED THE ABILITIES OF ANY MAN!

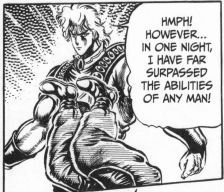

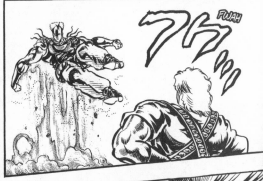

FWAH

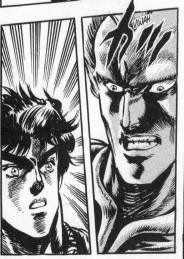

FUWAH

UREYYYYY! YOU THINK YOU CAN DEFEAT ME WITH THAT SLEEP-INDUCING DANCE OF YOURS?!

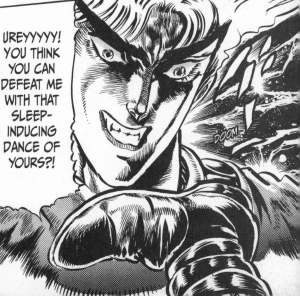

DOOM

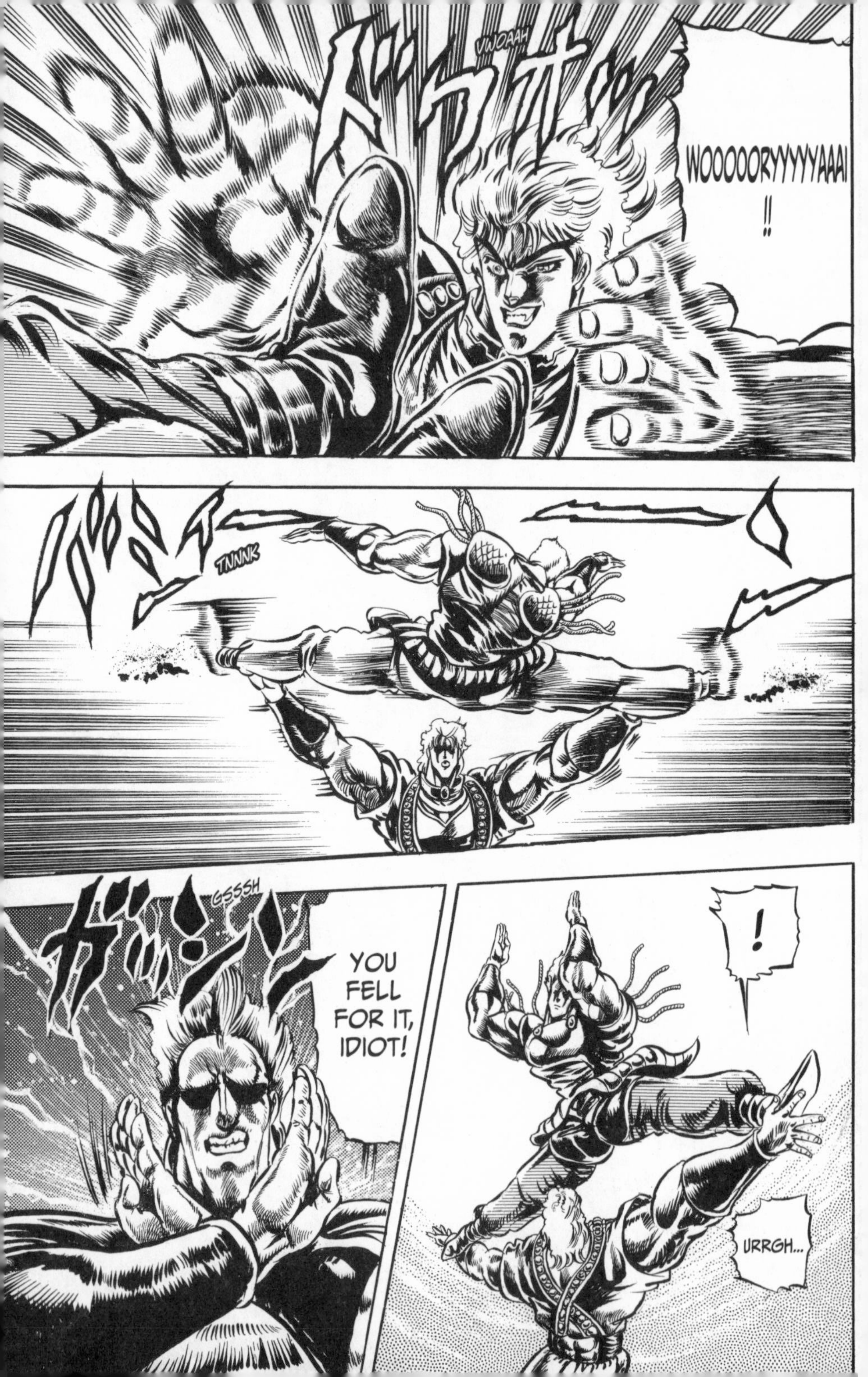
VWOAAH
WOOOOORYYYYYAAAI !!
TNNNK
!
URRGH...
GSSSH
YOU FELL FOR IT, IDIOT!

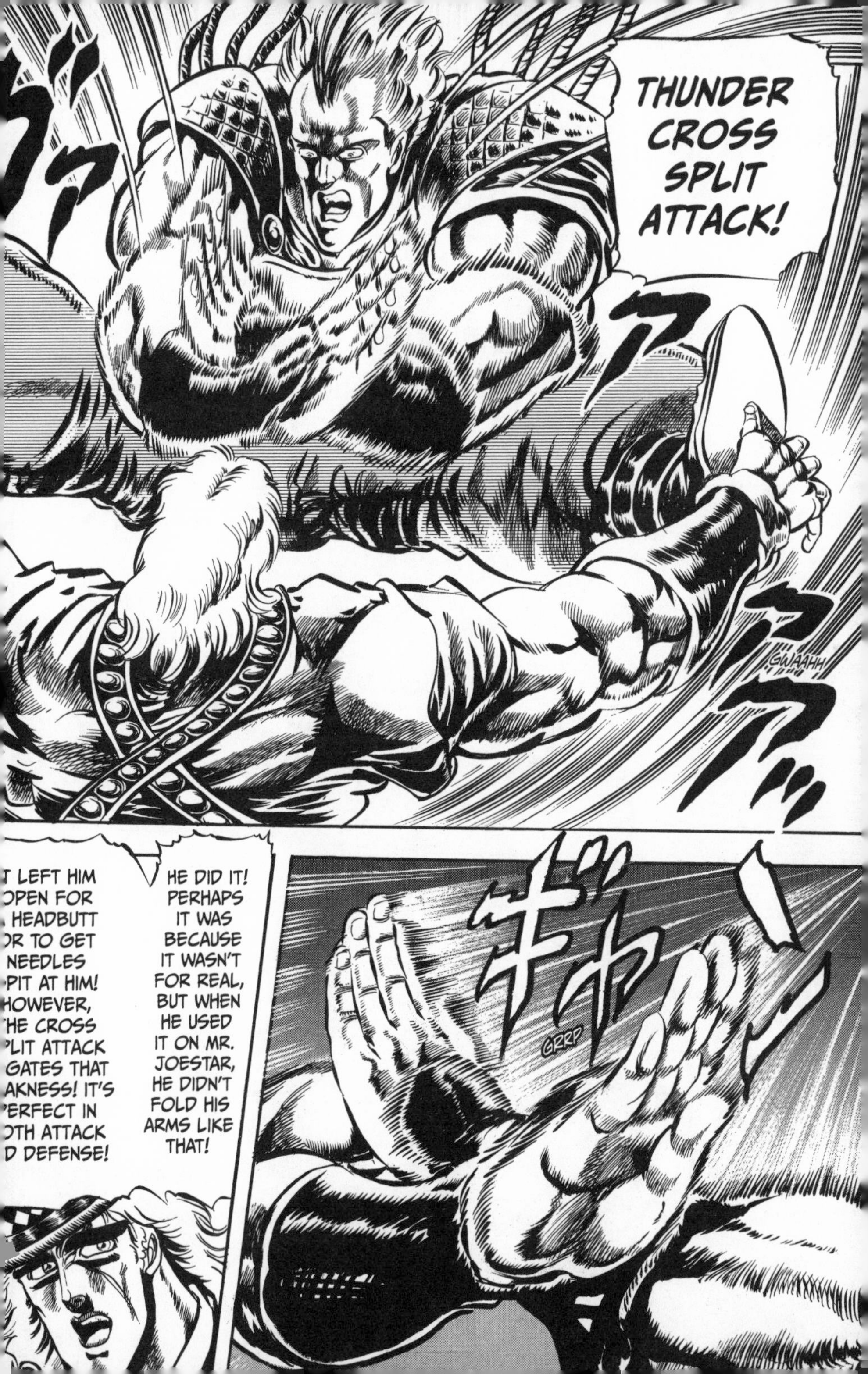
THUNDER CROSS SPLIT ATTACK!
GWAAHH
GRRP
HE DID IT! PERHAPS IT WAS BECAUSE IT WASN'T FOR REAL, BUT WHEN HE USED IT ON MR. JOESTAR, HE DIDN'T FOLD HIS ARMS LIKE THAT!
T LEFT HIM OPEN FOR HEADBUTT OR TO GET NEEDLES PIT AT HIM! HOWEVER, HE CROSS PLIT ATTACK GATES THAT AKNESS! IT'S ERFECT IN OTH ATTACK D DEFENSE!

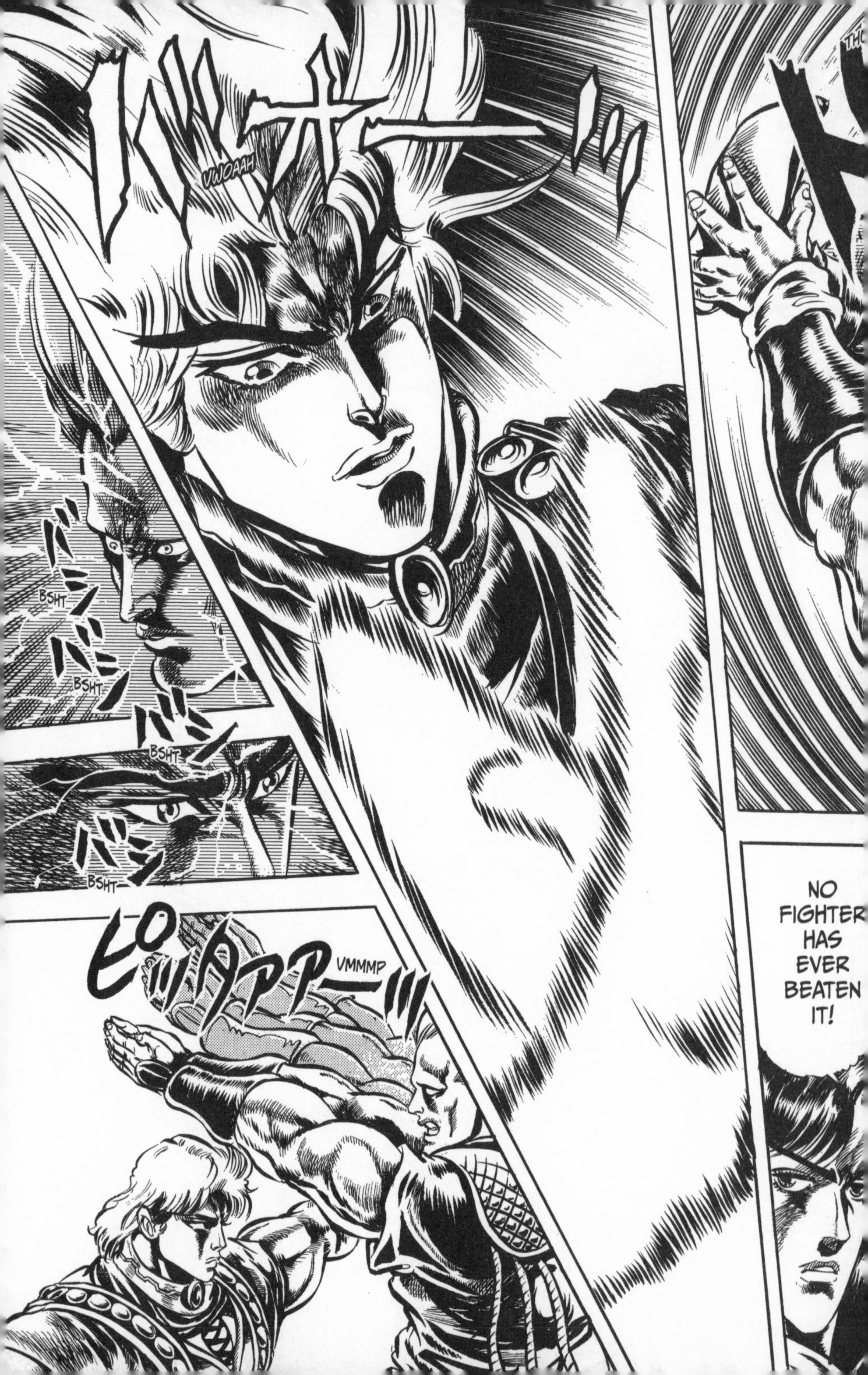
NO FIGHTER HAS EVER BEATEN IT!
UWOAAH
BSHT
BSHT
BSHT
BSHT
VMMMP

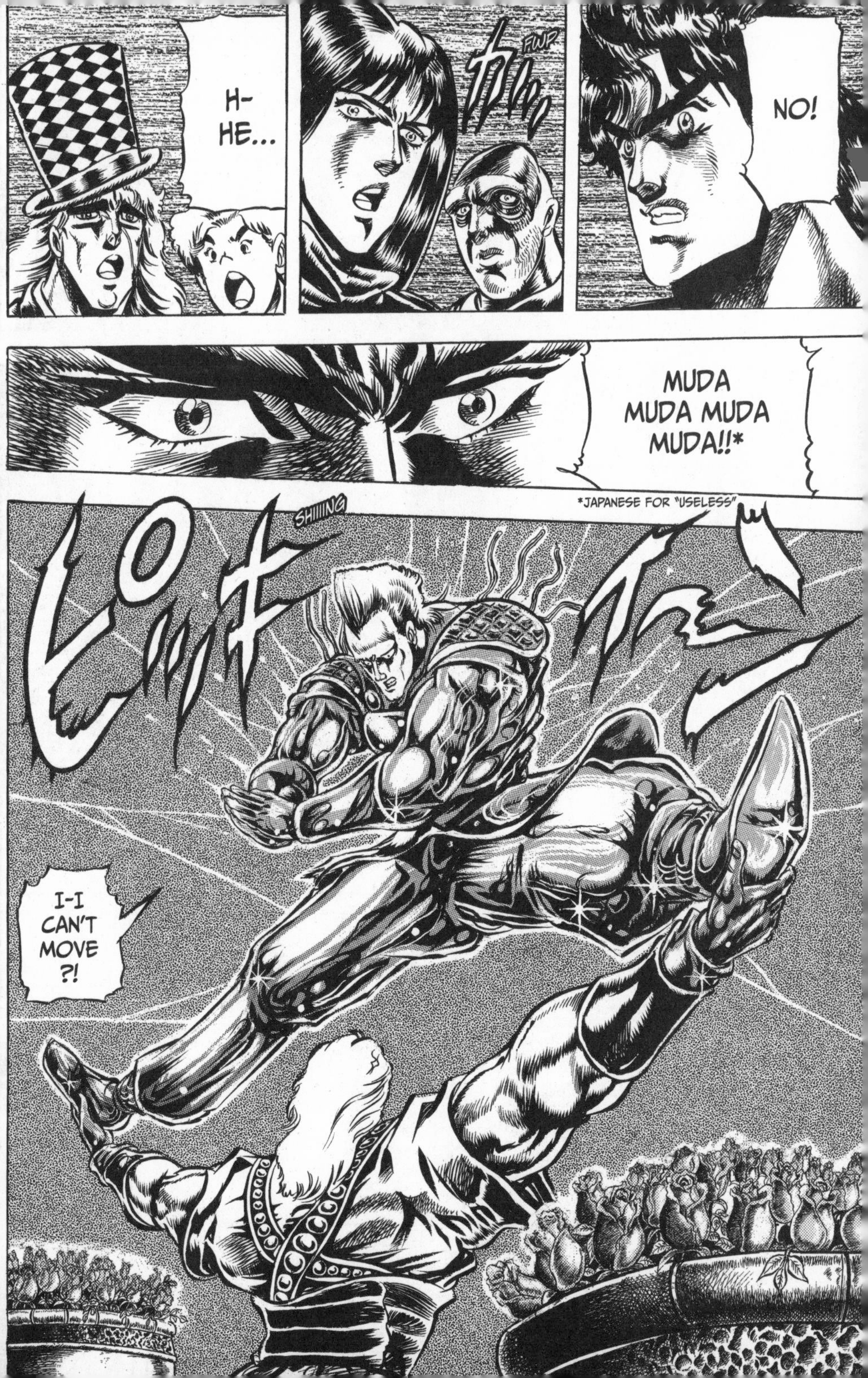
NO!
FWP
H-
HE...
MUDA
MUDA MUDA
MUDA!!*
*JAPANESE FOR "USELESS"
SHIIING
I-I
CAN'T
MOVE
?!

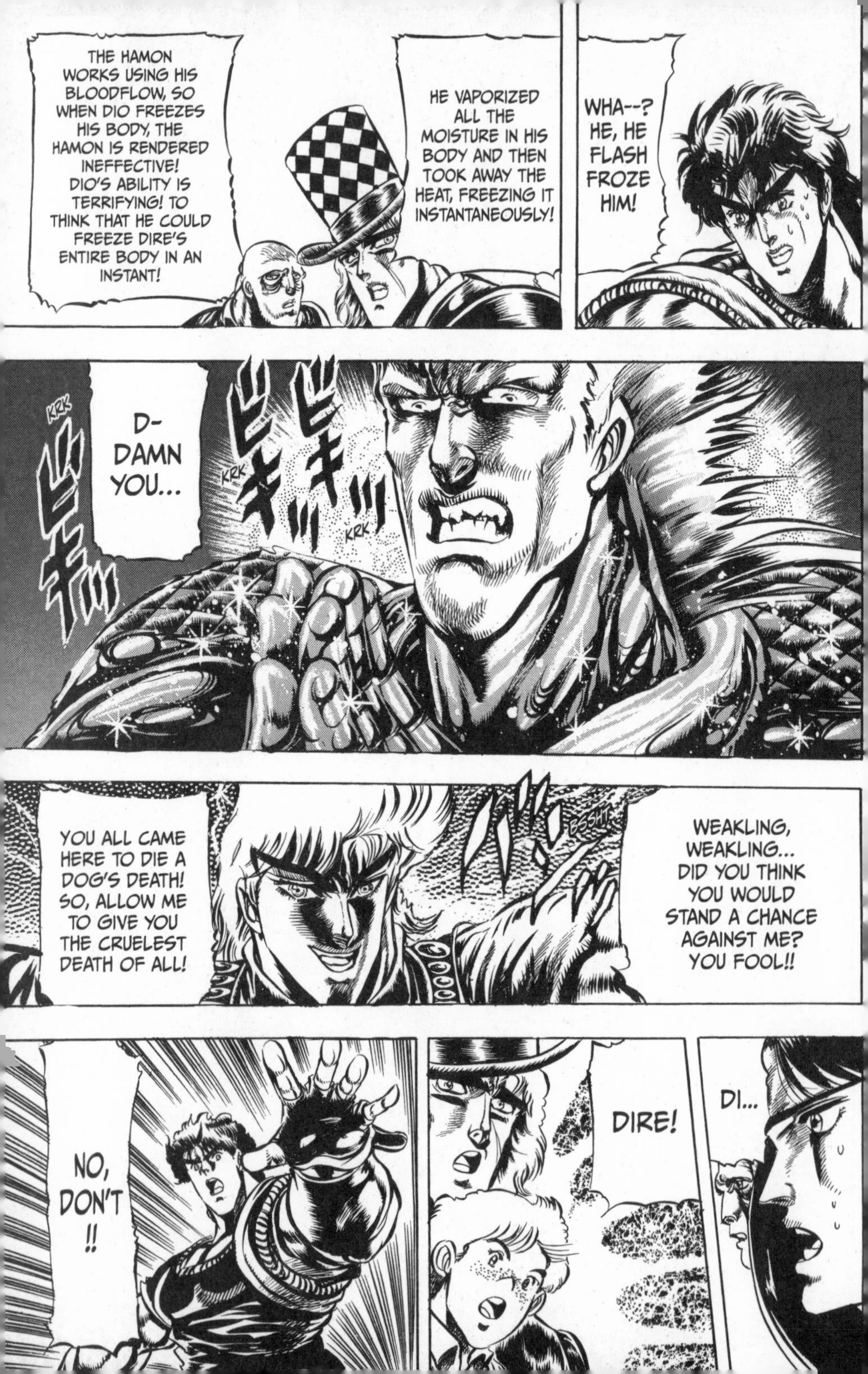
WHA--? HE, HE FLASH FROZE HIM!
HE VAPORIZED ALL THE MOISTURE IN HIS BODY AND THEN TOOK AWAY THE HEAT, FREEZING IT INSTANTANEOUSLY!
THE HAMON WORKS USING HIS BLOODFLOW, SO WHEN DIO FREEZES HIS BODY, THE HAMON IS RENDERED INEFFECTIVE! DIO'S ABILITY IS TERRIFYING! TO THINK THAT HE COULD FREEZE DIRE'S ENTIRE BODY IN AN INSTANT!
KRK
KRK
D-DAMN YOU...
KRK
WEAKLING, WEAKLING... DID YOU THINK YOU WOULD STAND A CHANCE AGAINST ME? YOU FOOL!!
BSSHT
YOU ALL CAME HERE TO DIE A DOG'S DEATH! SO, ALLOW ME TO GIVE YOU THE CRUELEST DEATH OF ALL!
DI...
DIRE!
NO, DON'T !!

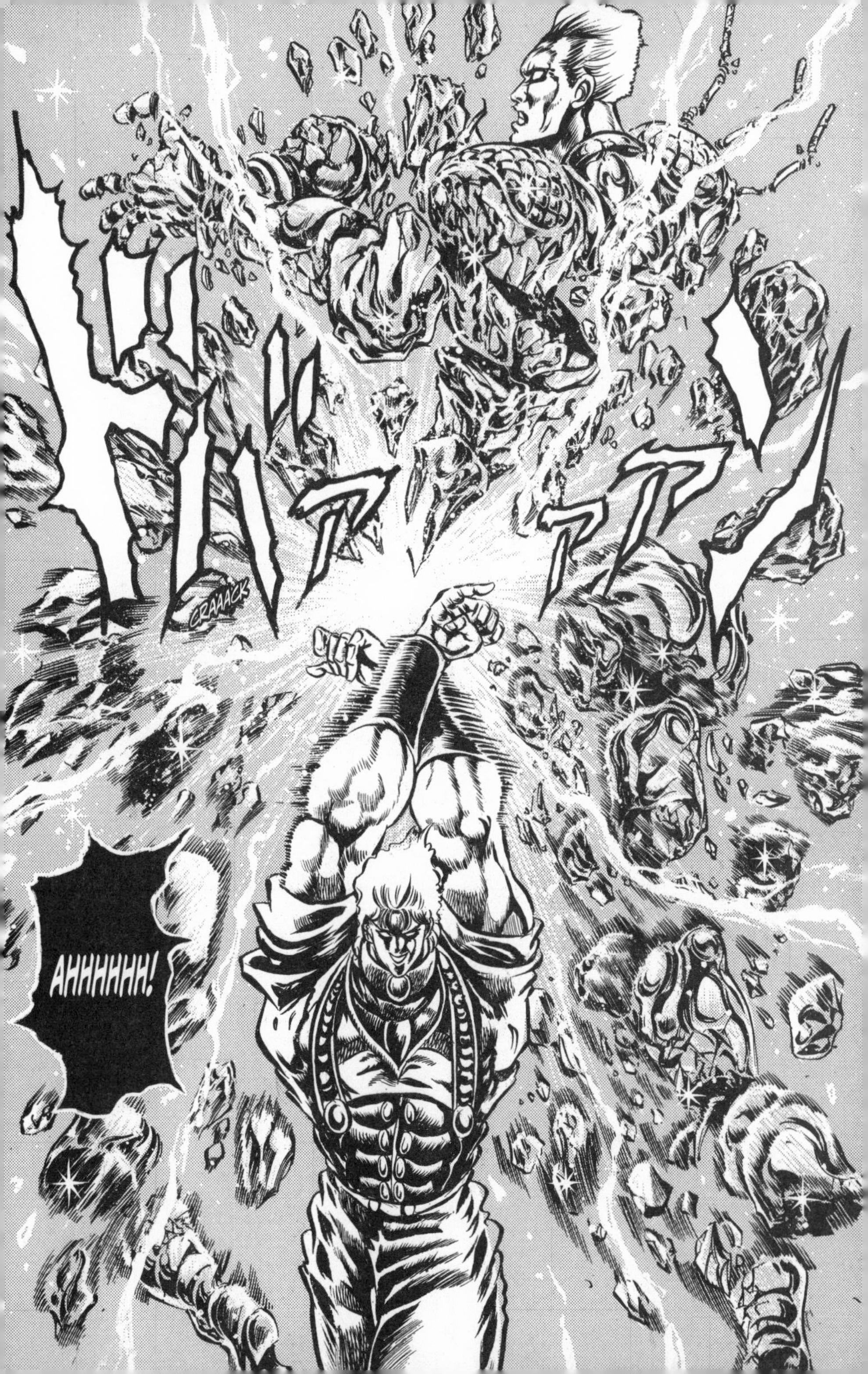
CRAAACK
AHHHHHH!

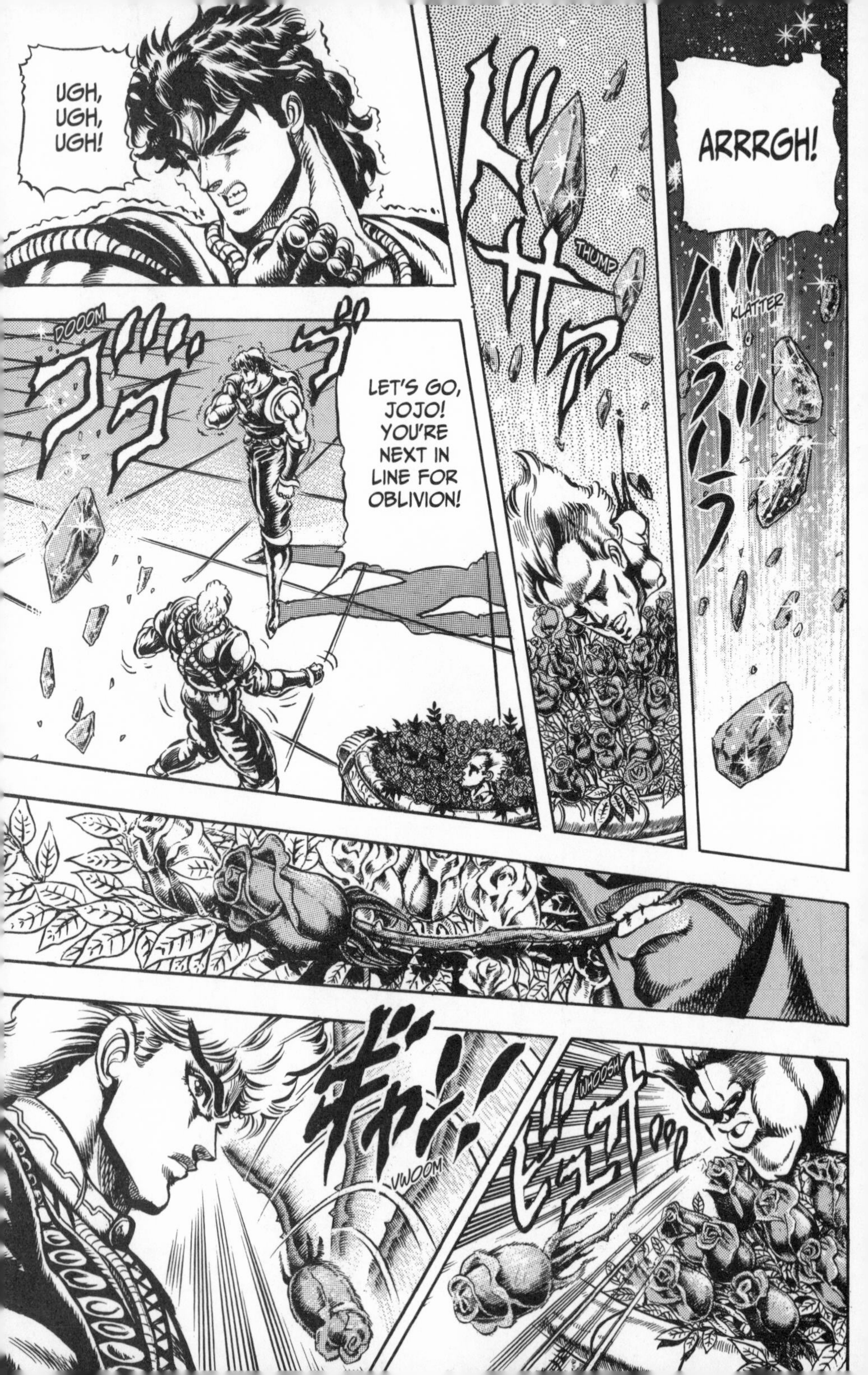
ARRRGH!
KLATTER
THUMP
UGH, UGH, UGH!
DOOOM
LET'S GO, JOJO! YOU'RE NEXT IN LINE FOR OBLIVION!
WHOOSH
VWOOM

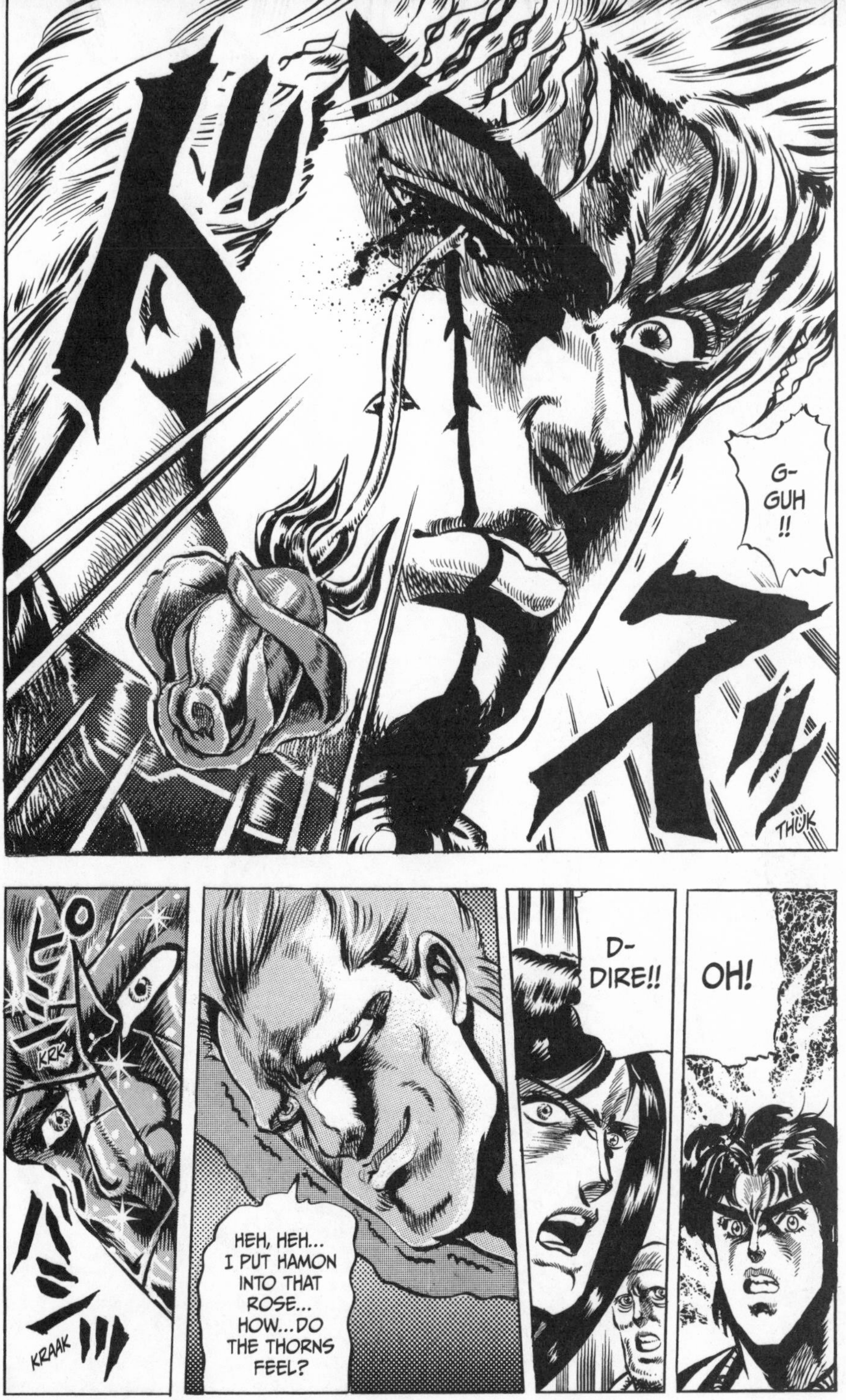
G-GUH!!
THUK
OH!
D-DIRE!!
HEH, HEH... I PUT HAMON INTO THAT ROSE... HOW...DO THE THORNS FEEL?
KRK
KRAAK

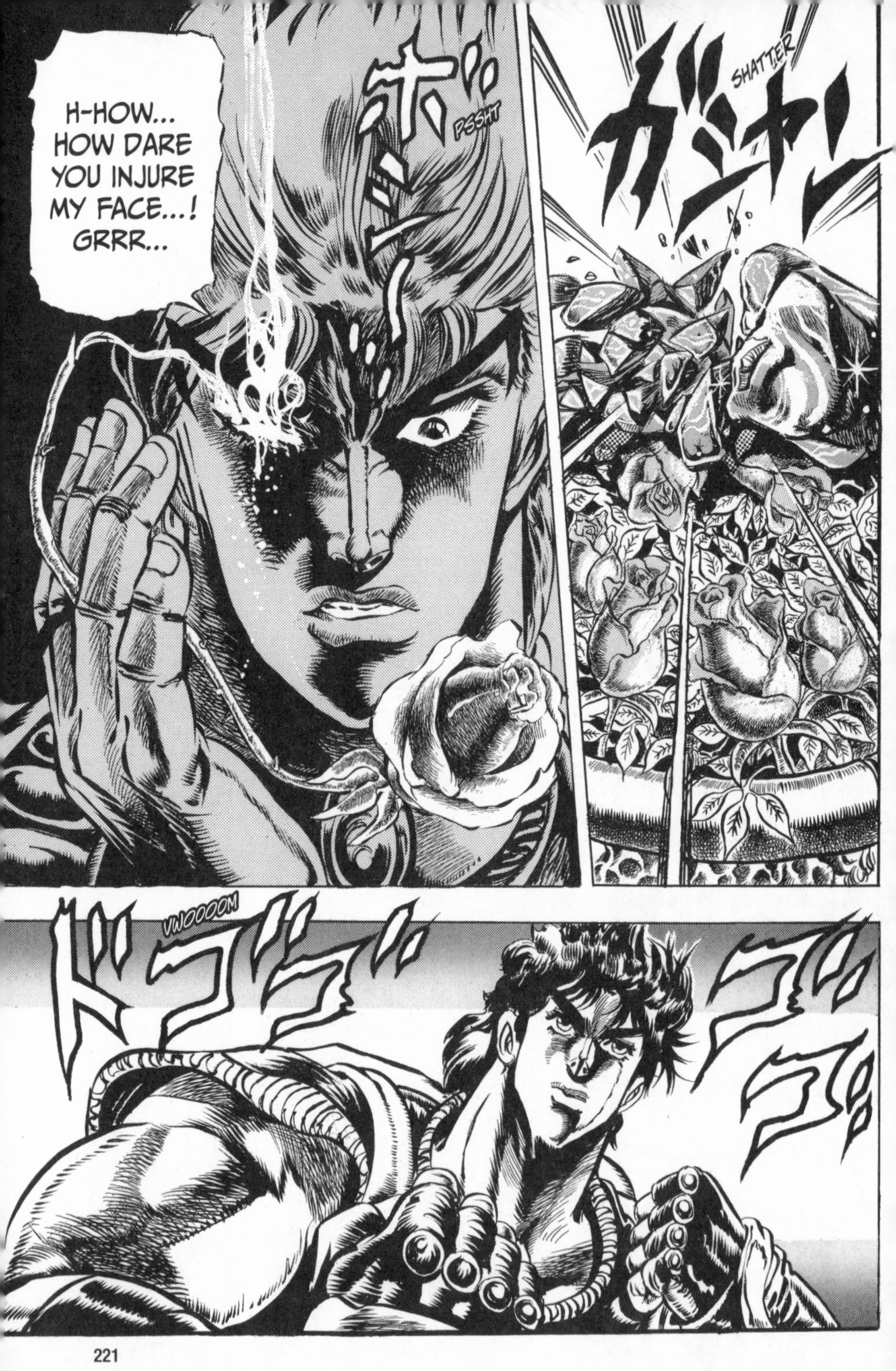
SHATTER
PSSHT
H-HOW... HOW DARE YOU INJURE MY FACE...! GRRR...
VWOOOOM

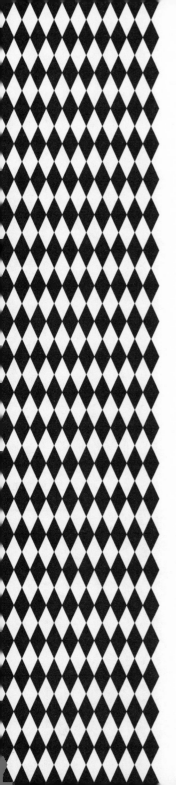

JoJo's
BIZARRE ADVENTURE

CHAPTER 39: Fire and Ice, Jonathan and Dio PART 1

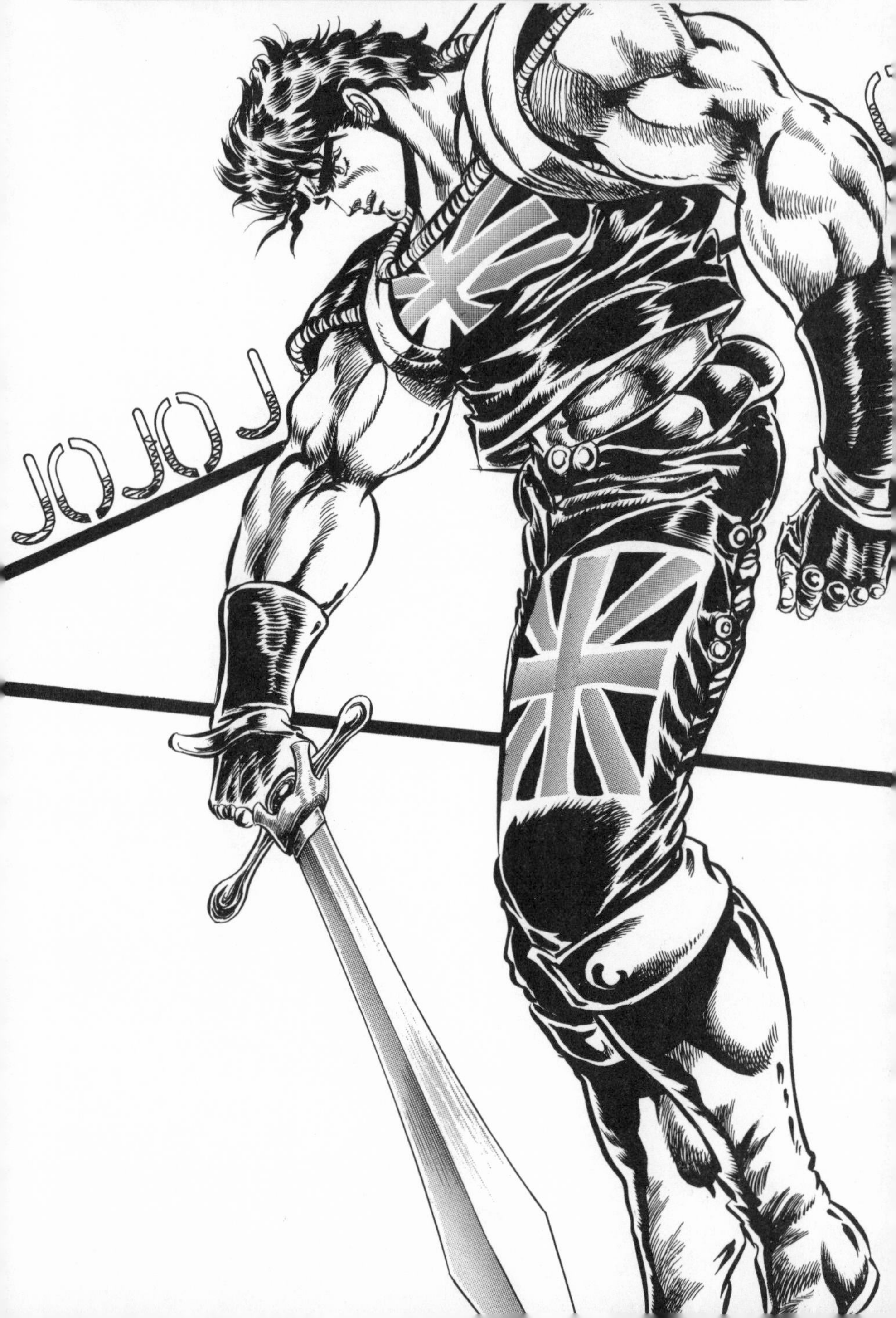

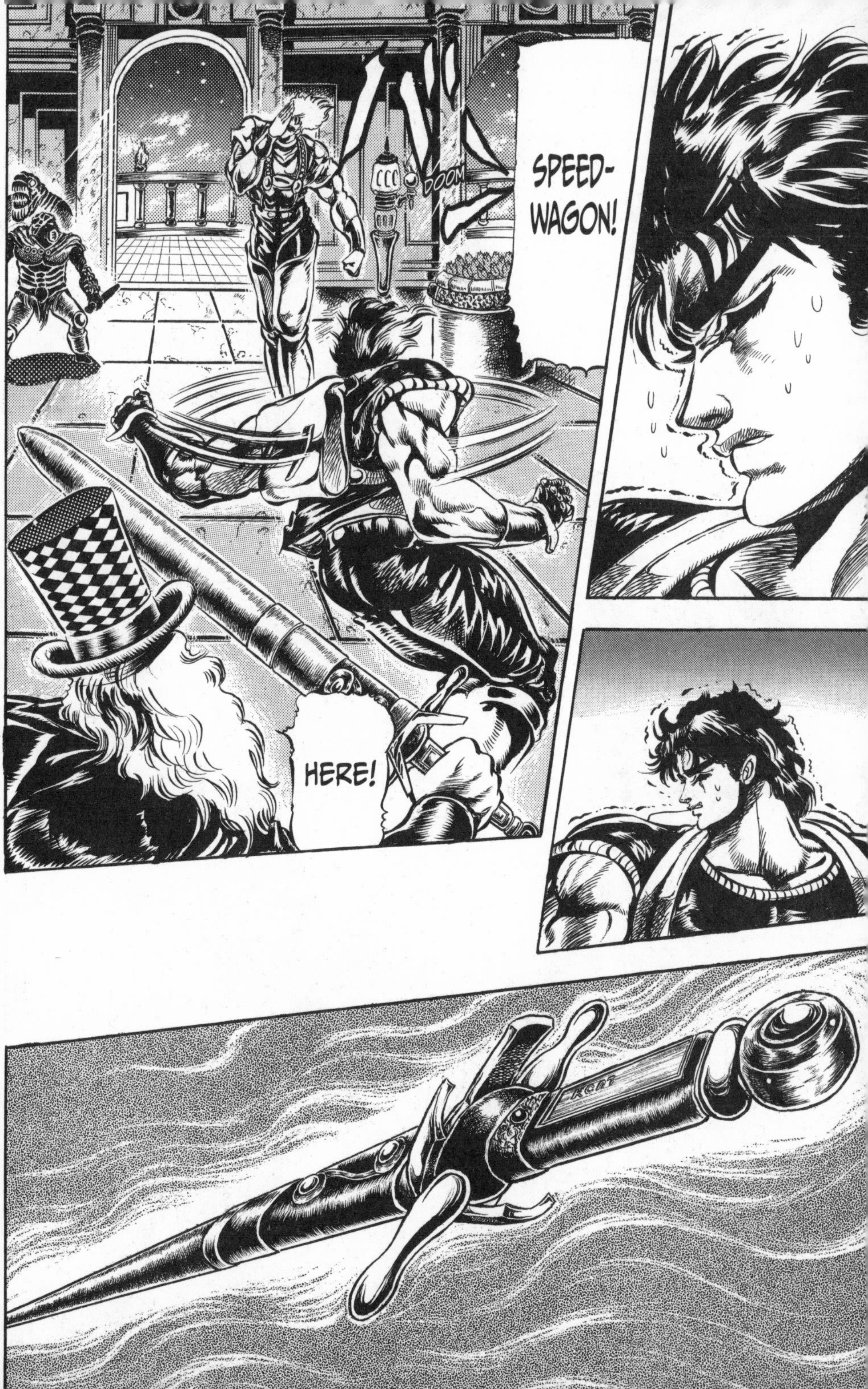
SPEED-
WAGON!
DOOM
HERE!

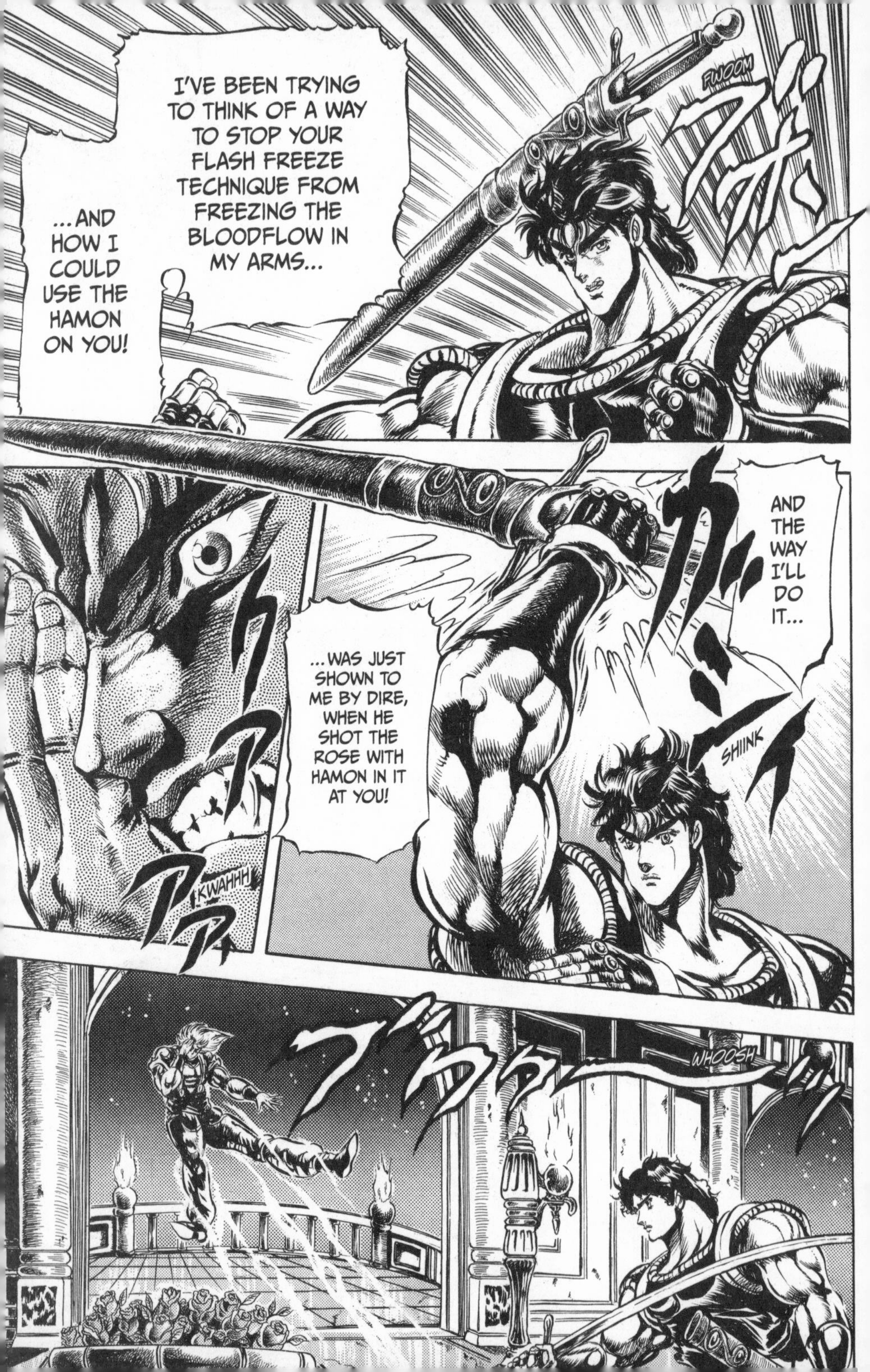
FWOOM
I'VE BEEN TRYING TO THINK OF A WAY TO STOP YOUR FLASH FREEZE TECHNIQUE FROM FREEZING THE BLOODFLOW IN MY ARMS...
...AND HOW I COULD USE THE HAMON ON YOU!
AND THE WAY I'LL DO IT...
SHIINK
...WAS JUST SHOWN TO ME BY DIRE, WHEN HE SHOT THE ROSE WITH HAMON IN IT AT YOU!
KWAHHH
WHOOSH

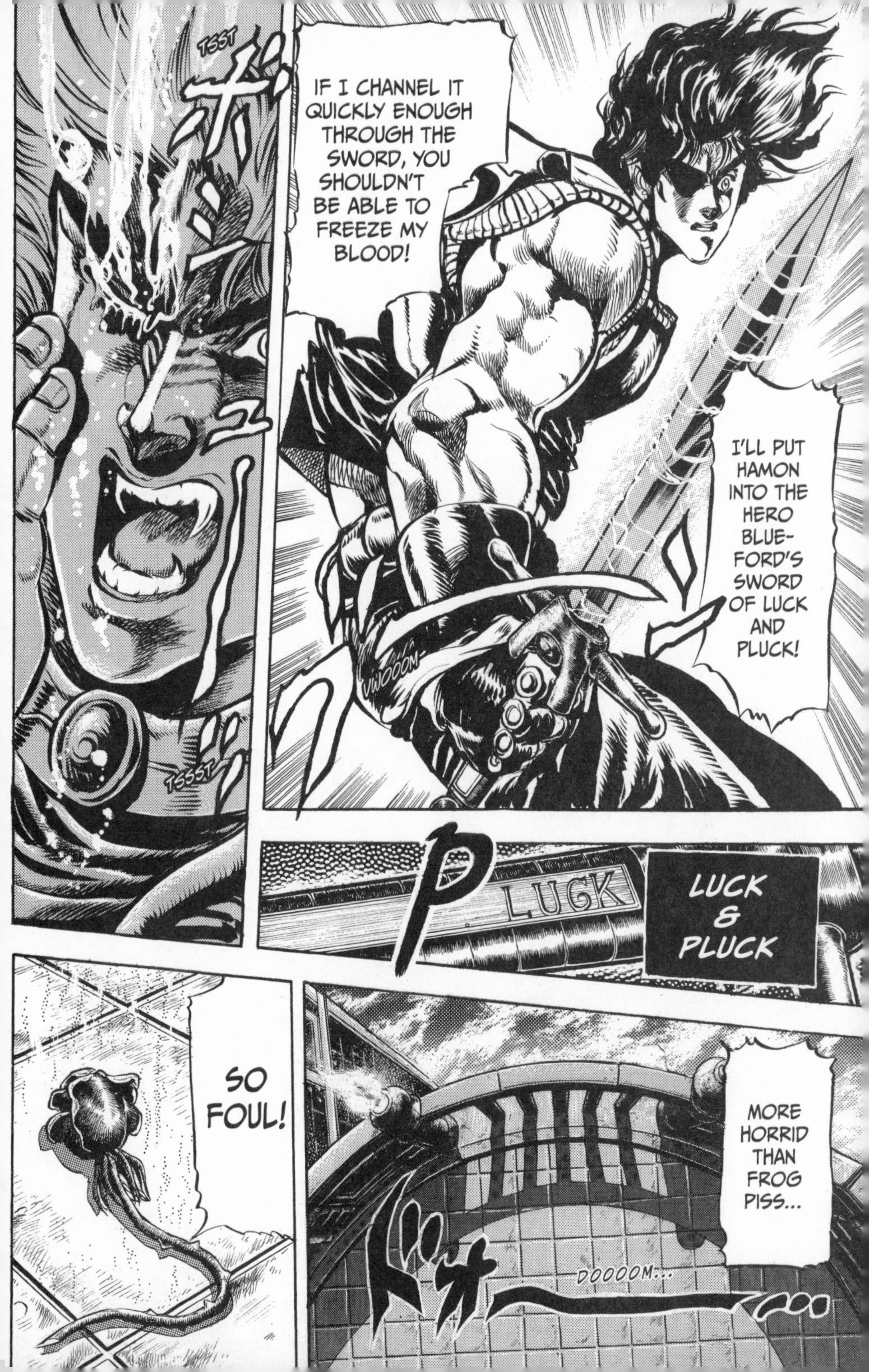
I'LL PUT HAMON INTO THE HERO BLUE-FORD'S SWORD OF LUCK AND PLUCK!
IF I CHANNEL IT QUICKLY ENOUGH THROUGH THE SWORD, YOU SHOULDN'T BE ABLE TO FREEZE MY BLOOD!
VWOOOM
LUCK
LUCK & PLUCK
TSST
TSSST
MORE HORRID THAN FROG PISS...
DOOOOM...
SO FOUL!

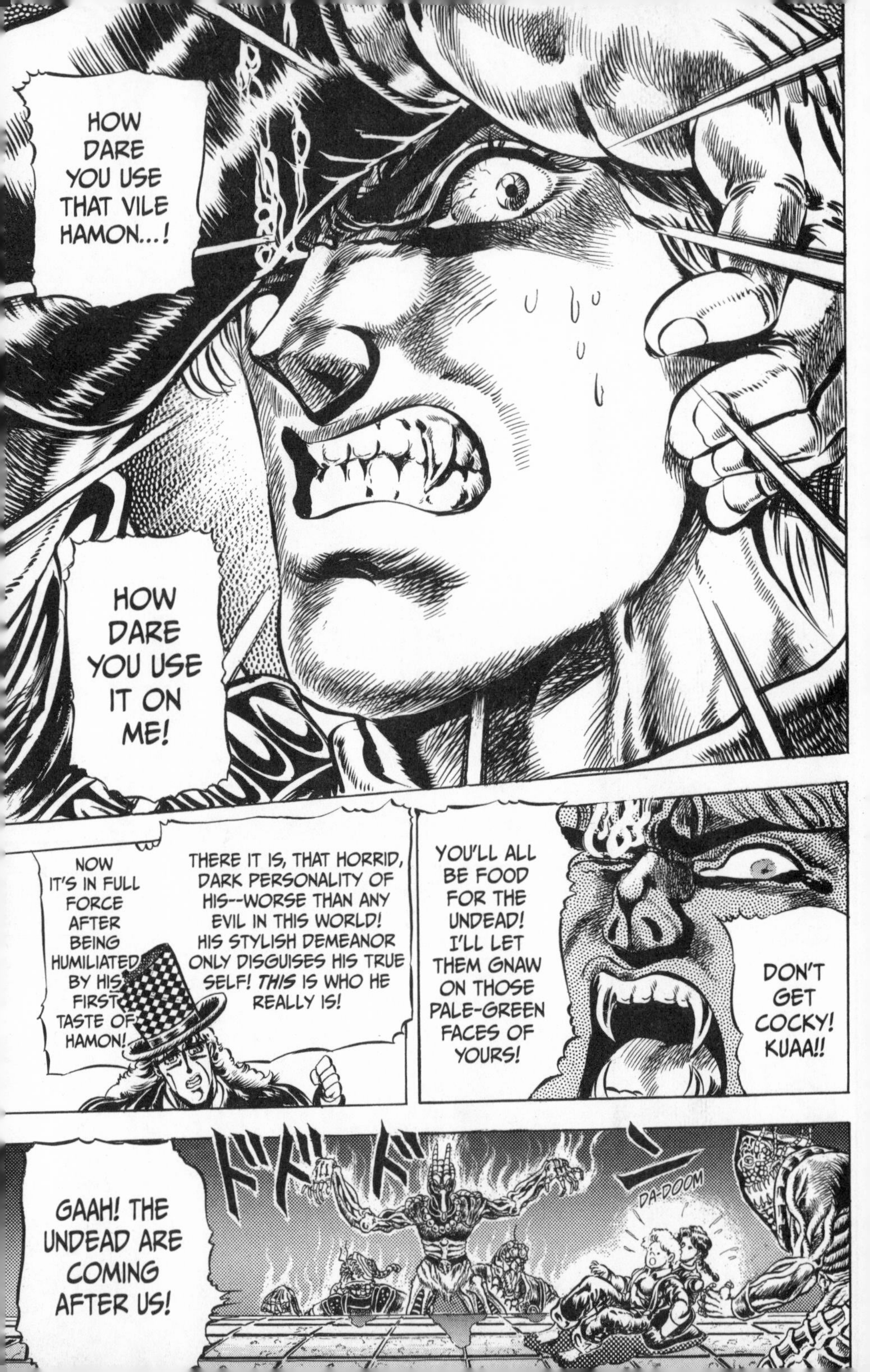
HOW DARE YOU USE THAT VILE HAMON...!
HOW DARE YOU USE IT ON ME!
DON'T GET COCKY! KUAA!!
YOU'LL ALL BE FOOD FOR THE UNDEAD! I'LL LET THEM GNAW ON THOSE PALE-GREEN FACES OF YOURS!
THERE IT IS, THAT HORRID, DARK PERSONALITY OF HIS--WORSE THAN ANY EVIL IN THIS WORLD! HIS STYLISH DEMEANOR ONLY DISGUISES HIS TRUE SELF! *THIS* IS WHO HE REALLY IS!
NOW IT'S IN FULL FORCE AFTER BEING HUMILIATED BY HIS FIRST TASTE OF HAMON!
ドドドン
DA-DOOM
GAAH! THE UNDEAD ARE COMING AFTER US!

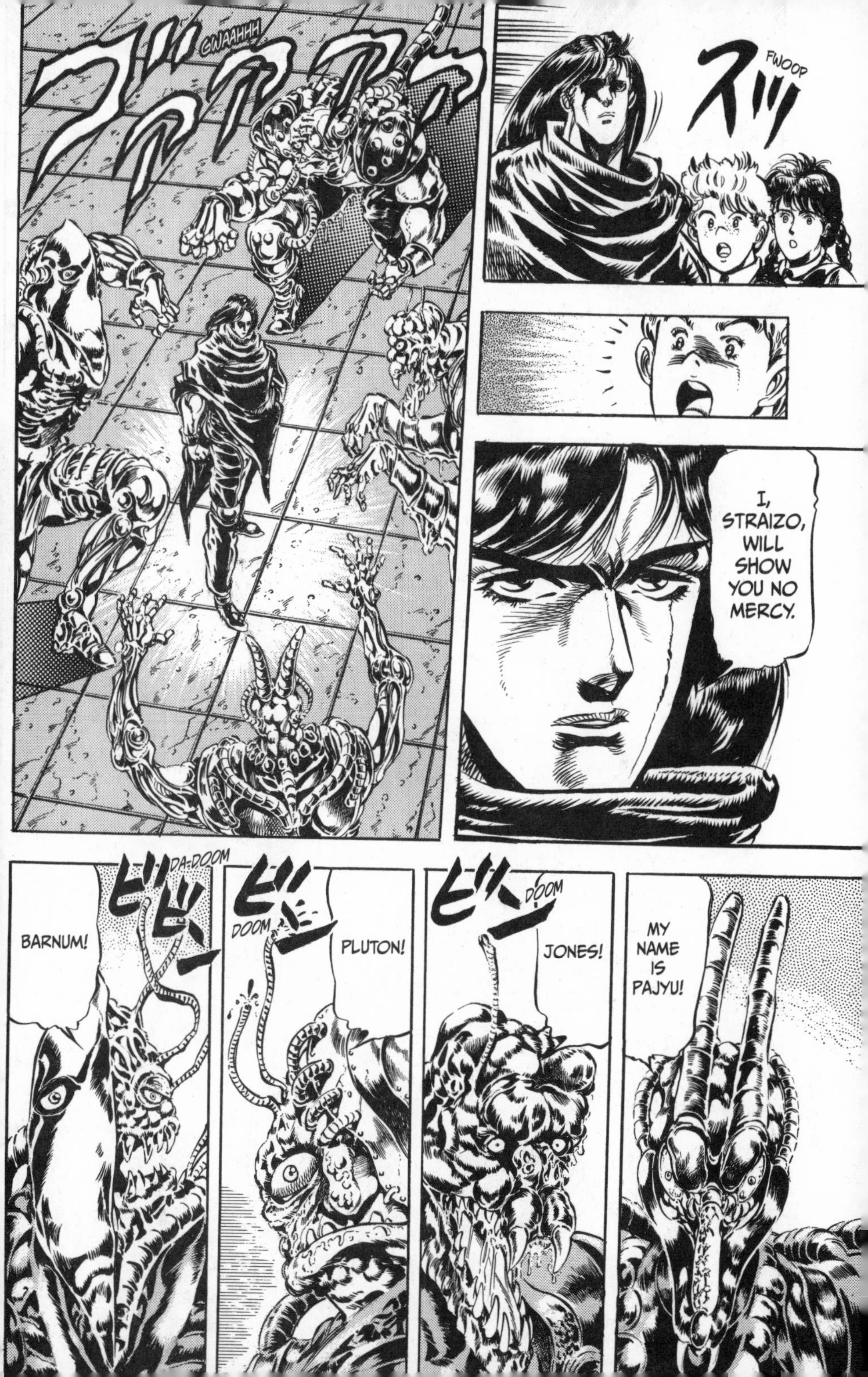
FWOOP
I, STRAIZO, WILL SHOW YOU NO MERCY.
GWAAHHH
MY NAME IS PAJYU!
DOOM
JONES!
DOOM
PLUTON!
DA-DOOM
BARNUM!

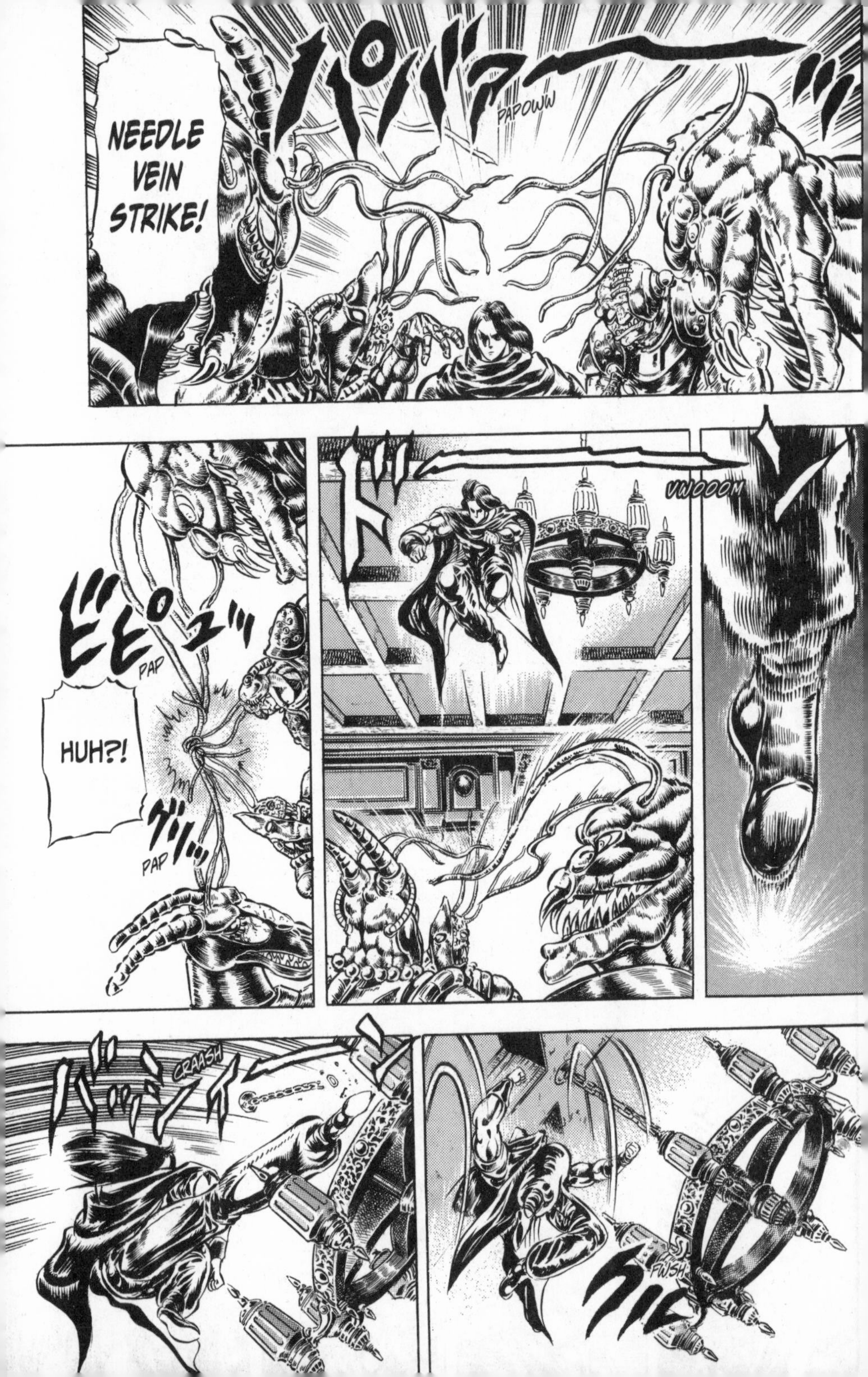
NEEDLE VEIN STRIKE!
PAPOWW
VWOOOM
PAP
HUH?!
PAP
FWSH
CRAASH

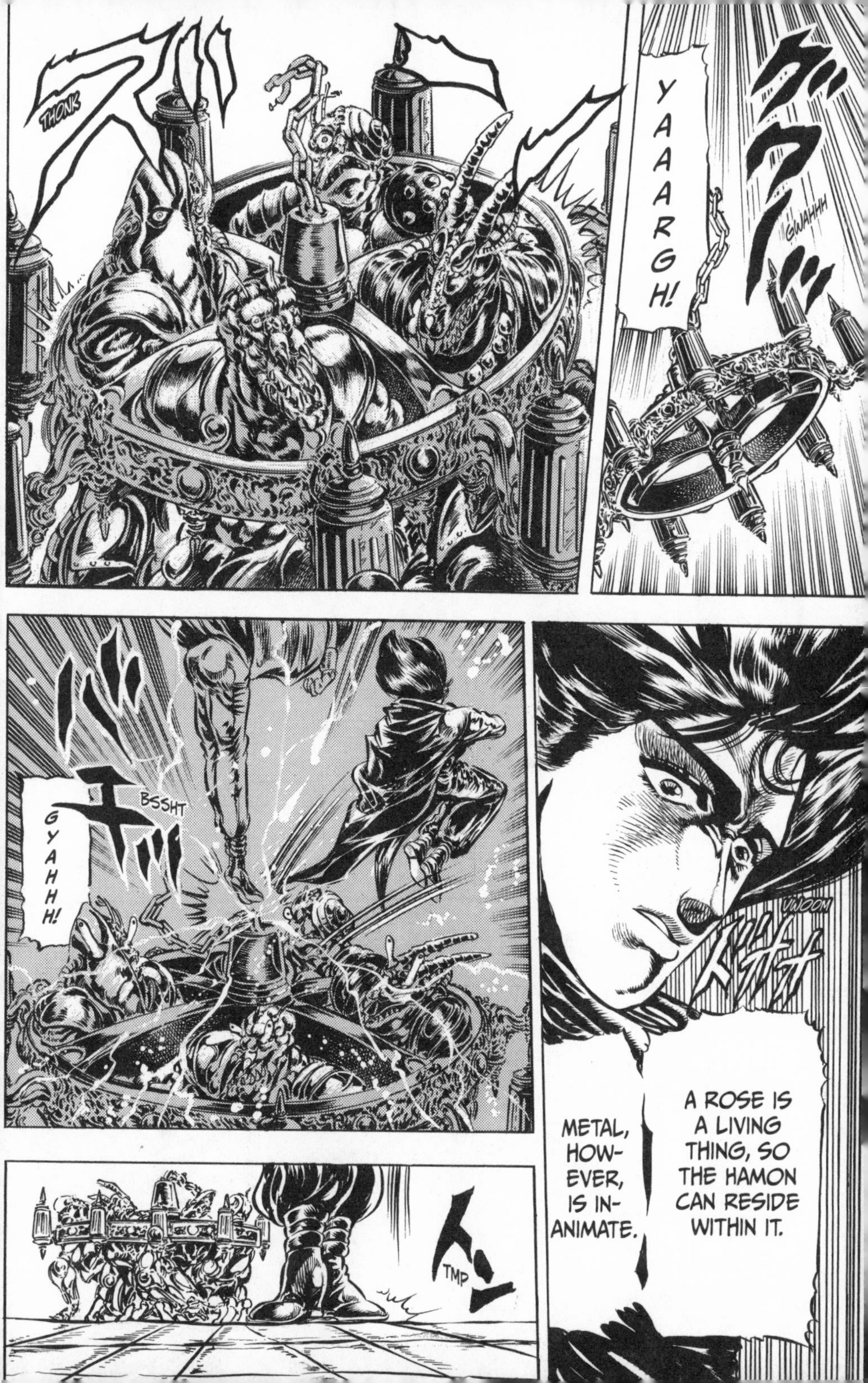
YAAAARGH!
GWAHHH
THONK
UWOON
BSSHT
GYAHHH!
A ROSE IS A LIVING THING, SO THE HAMON CAN RESIDE WITHIN IT.
METAL, HOW-EVER, IS IN-ANIMATE.
TMP

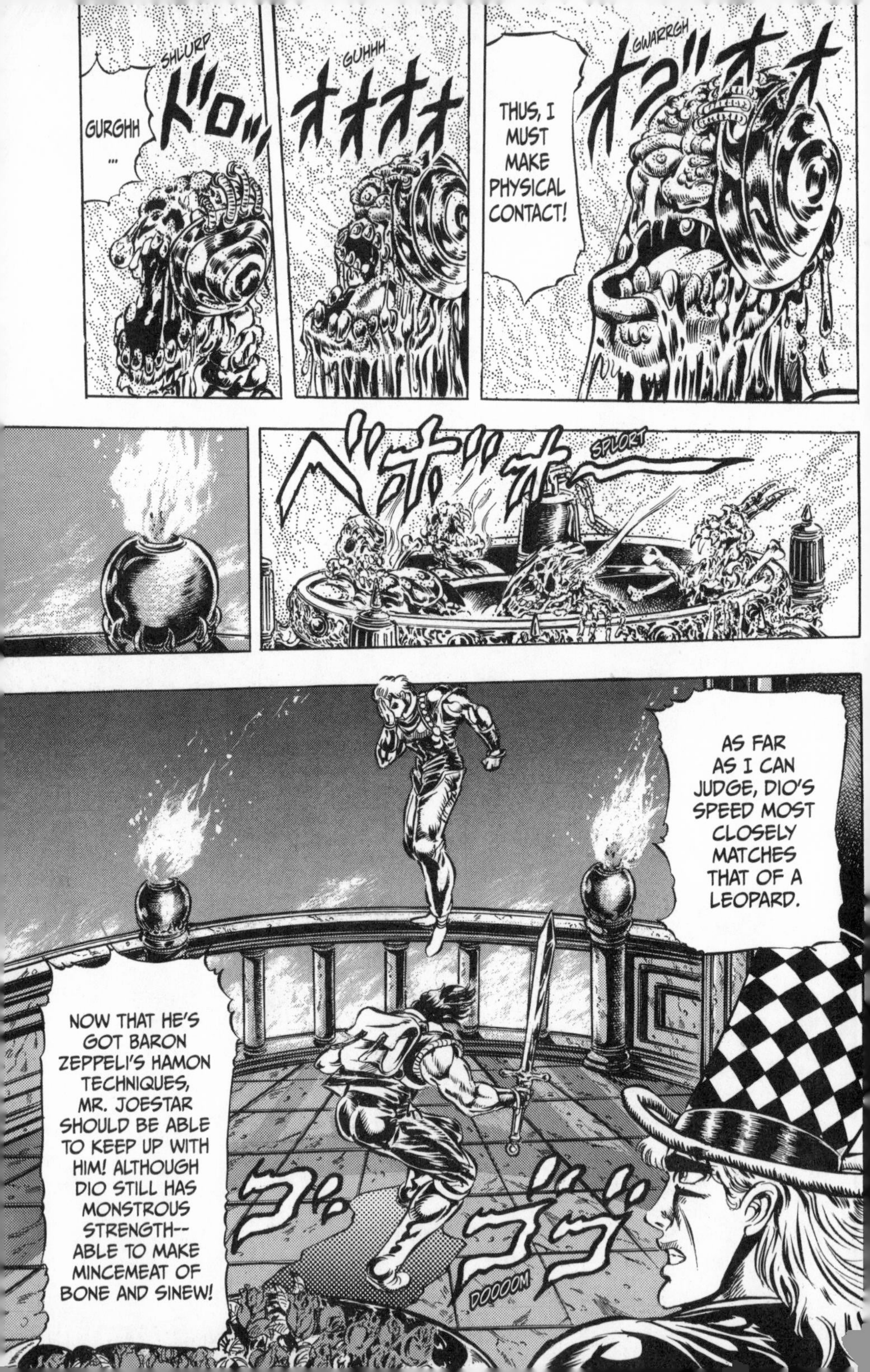

GWARRGH
THUS, I MUST MAKE PHYSICAL CONTACT!
GUHHH
SHLURP
GURGHH ...
SPLORT
AS FAR AS I CAN JUDGE, DIO'S SPEED MOST CLOSELY MATCHES THAT OF A LEOPARD.
NOW THAT HE'S GOT BARON ZEPPELI'S HAMON TECHNIQUES, MR. JOESTAR SHOULD BE ABLE TO KEEP UP WITH HIM! ALTHOUGH DIO STILL HAS MONSTROUS STRENGTH-- ABLE TO MAKE MINCEMEAT OF BONE AND SINEW!
DOOOOM

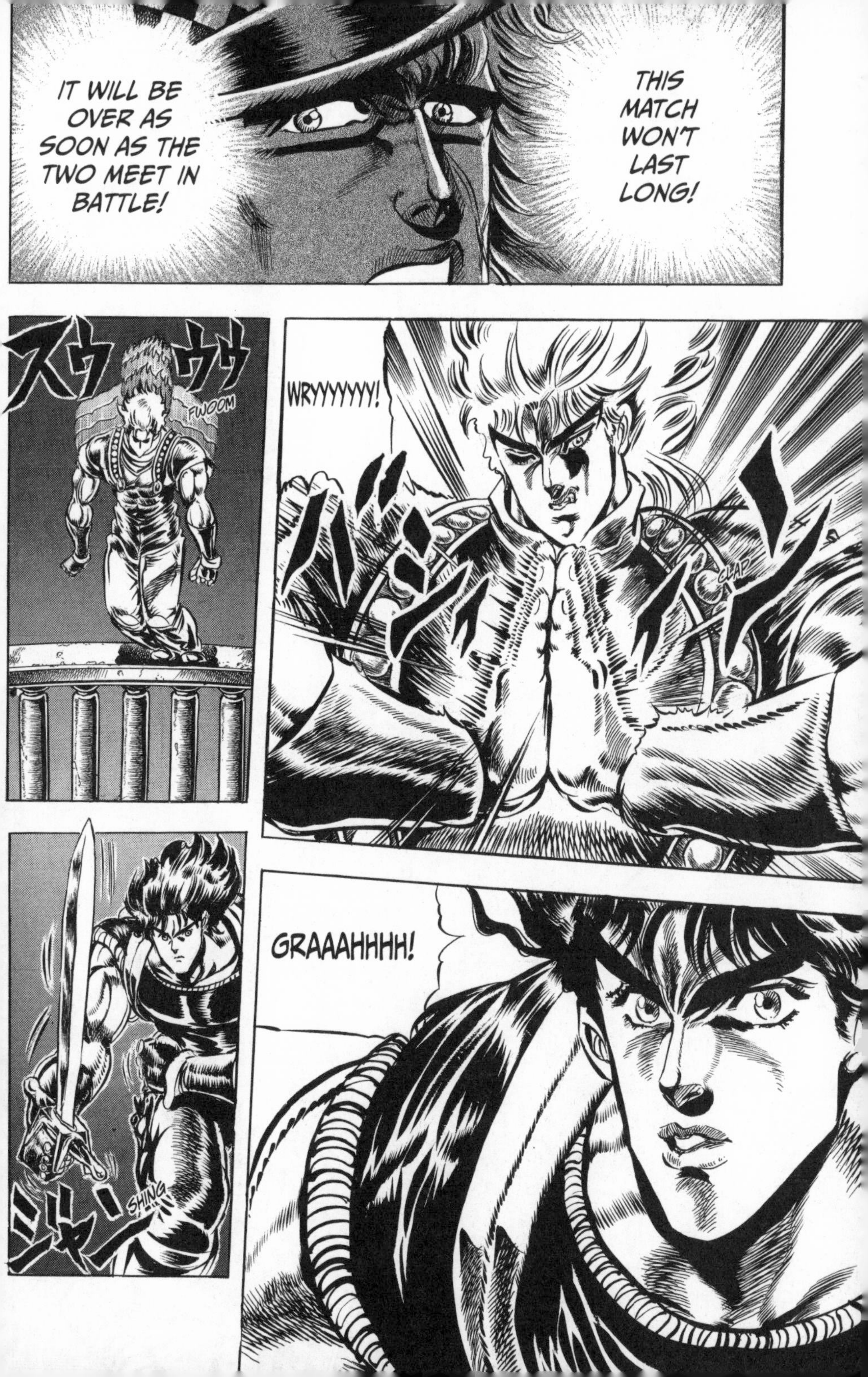
THIS MATCH WON'T LAST LONG!
IT WILL BE OVER AS SOON AS THE TWO MEET IN BATTLE!
WRYYYYYYY!
CLAP
スウウ
FWOOM
GRAAAHHHH!
SHING

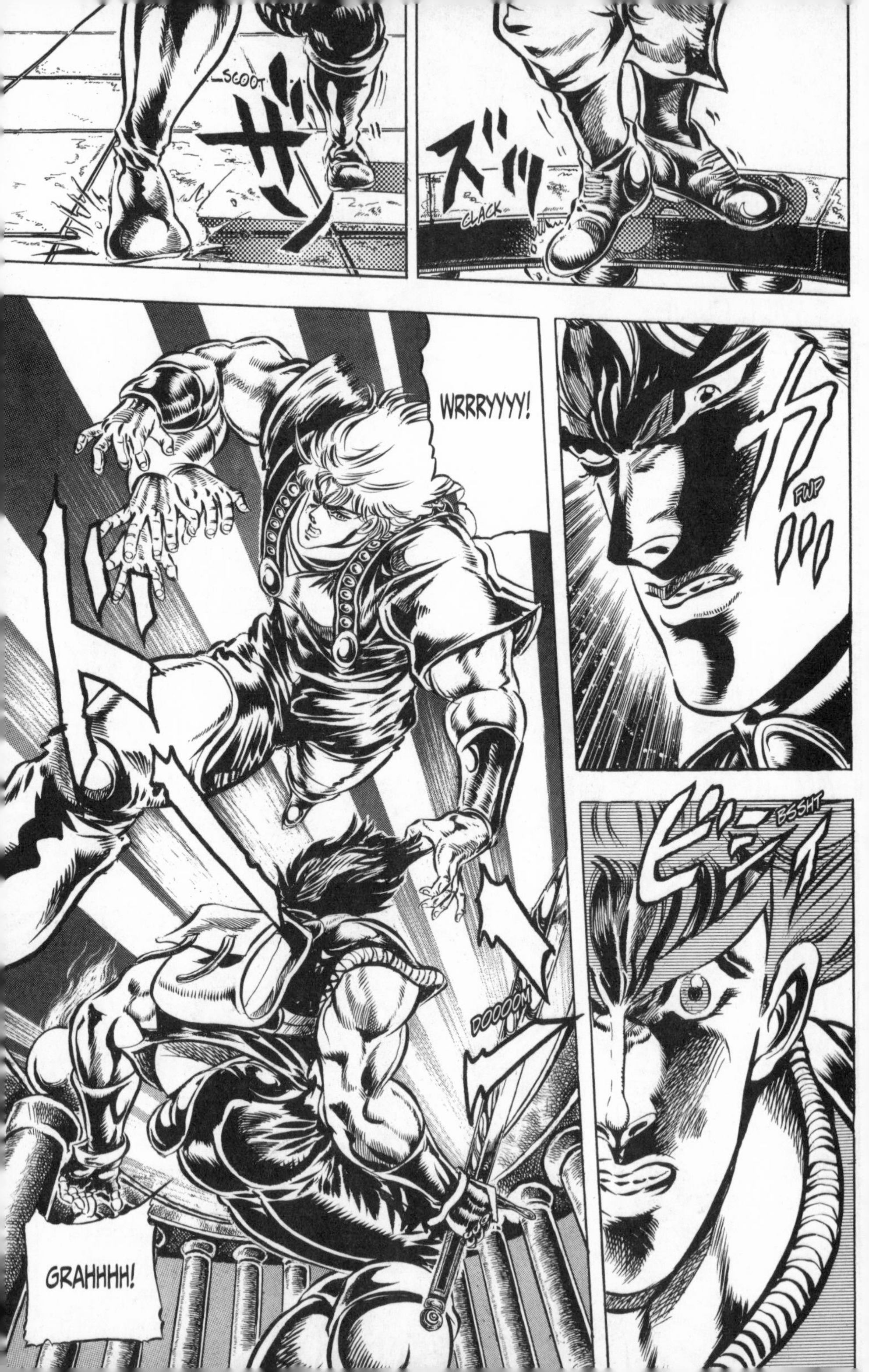
CLACK
SCOOT
FWP
BSSHT
WRRRYYYY!
DOOOOM
GRAHHHH!

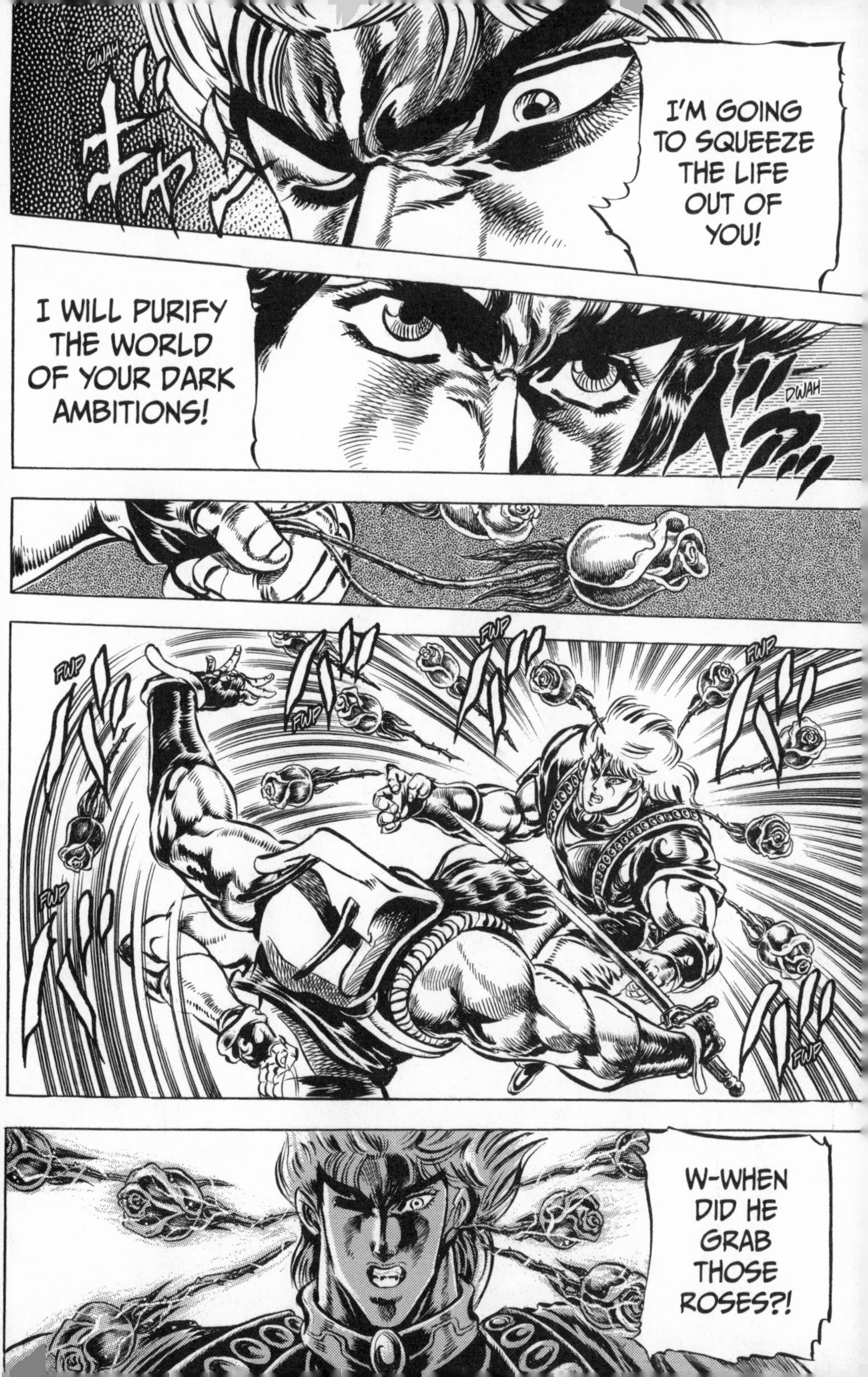
GWAH
I'M GOING TO SQUEEZE THE LIFE OUT OF YOU!
DWAH
I WILL PURIFY THE WORLD OF YOUR DARK AMBITIONS!
FWP
FWP
FWP
FWP
FWP
FWP
FWP
W-WHEN DID HE GRAB THOSE ROSES?!

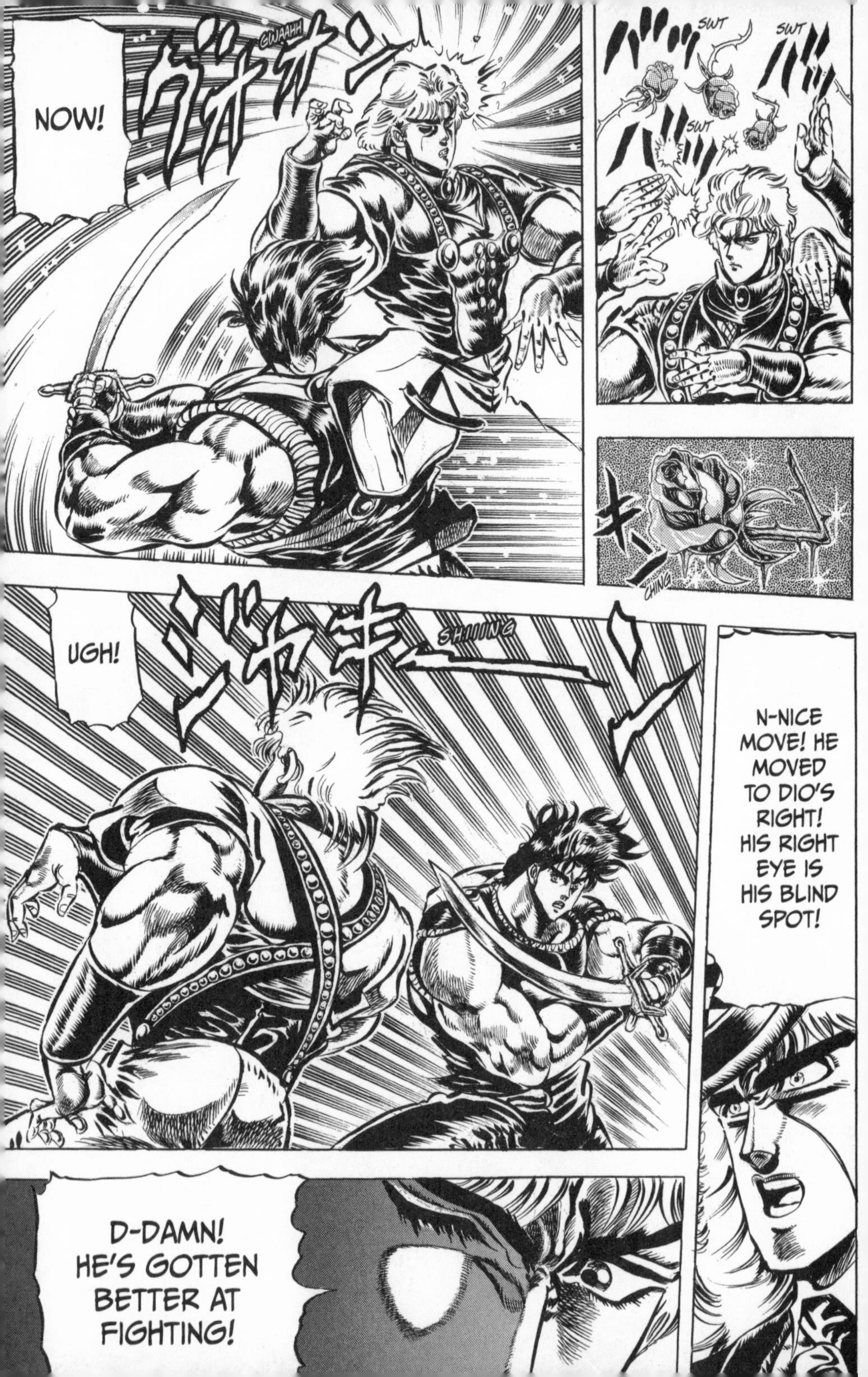
SWT
SWT
SWT
CHING
GWAAHH
NOW!
N-NICE MOVE! HE MOVED TO DIO'S RIGHT! HIS RIGHT EYE IS HIS BLIND SPOT!
SHIIING
UGH!
D-DAMN! HE'S GOTTEN BETTER AT FIGHTING!

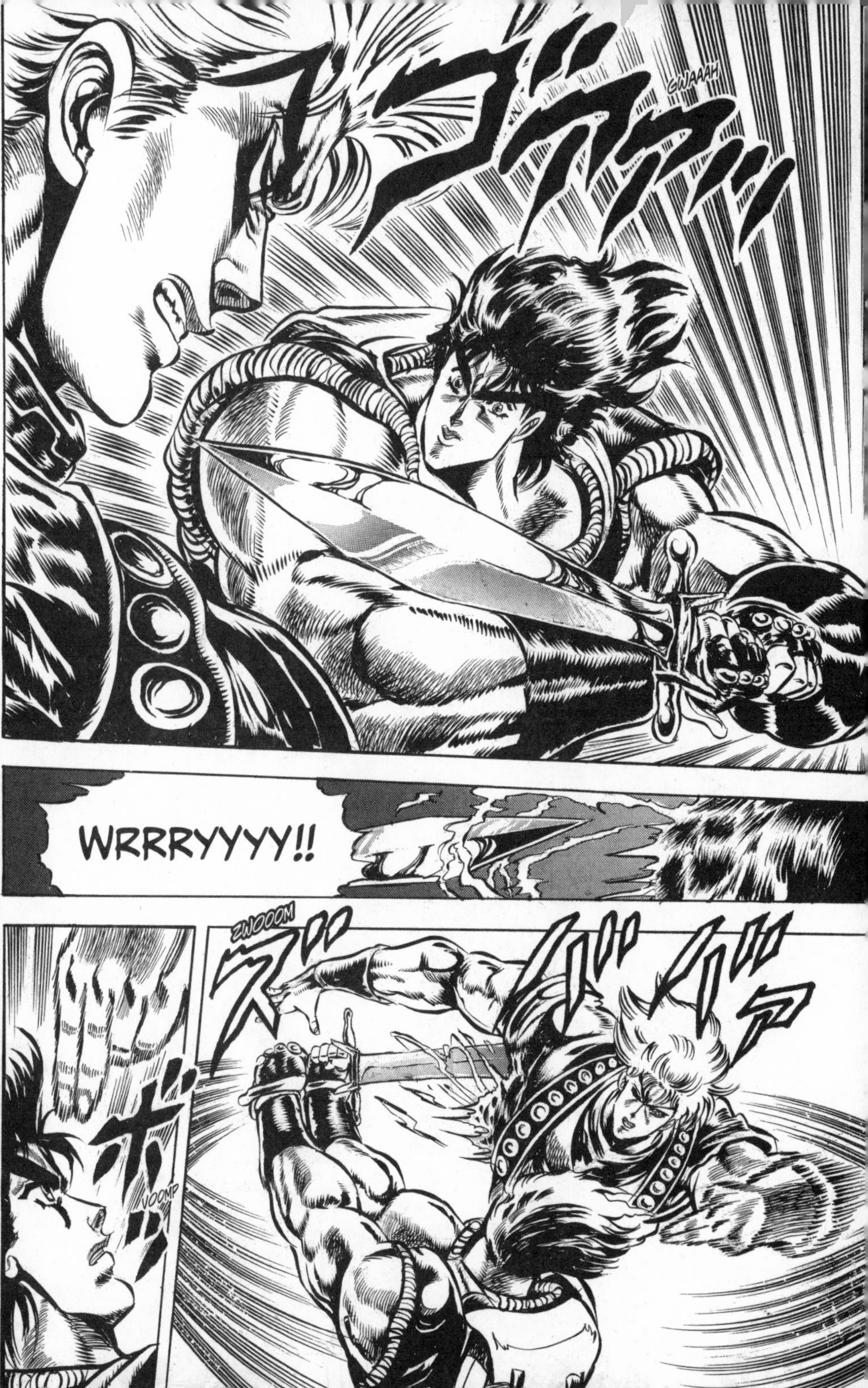
GWAAAH
WRRRYYYY!!
ZWOOOM
VOOMP

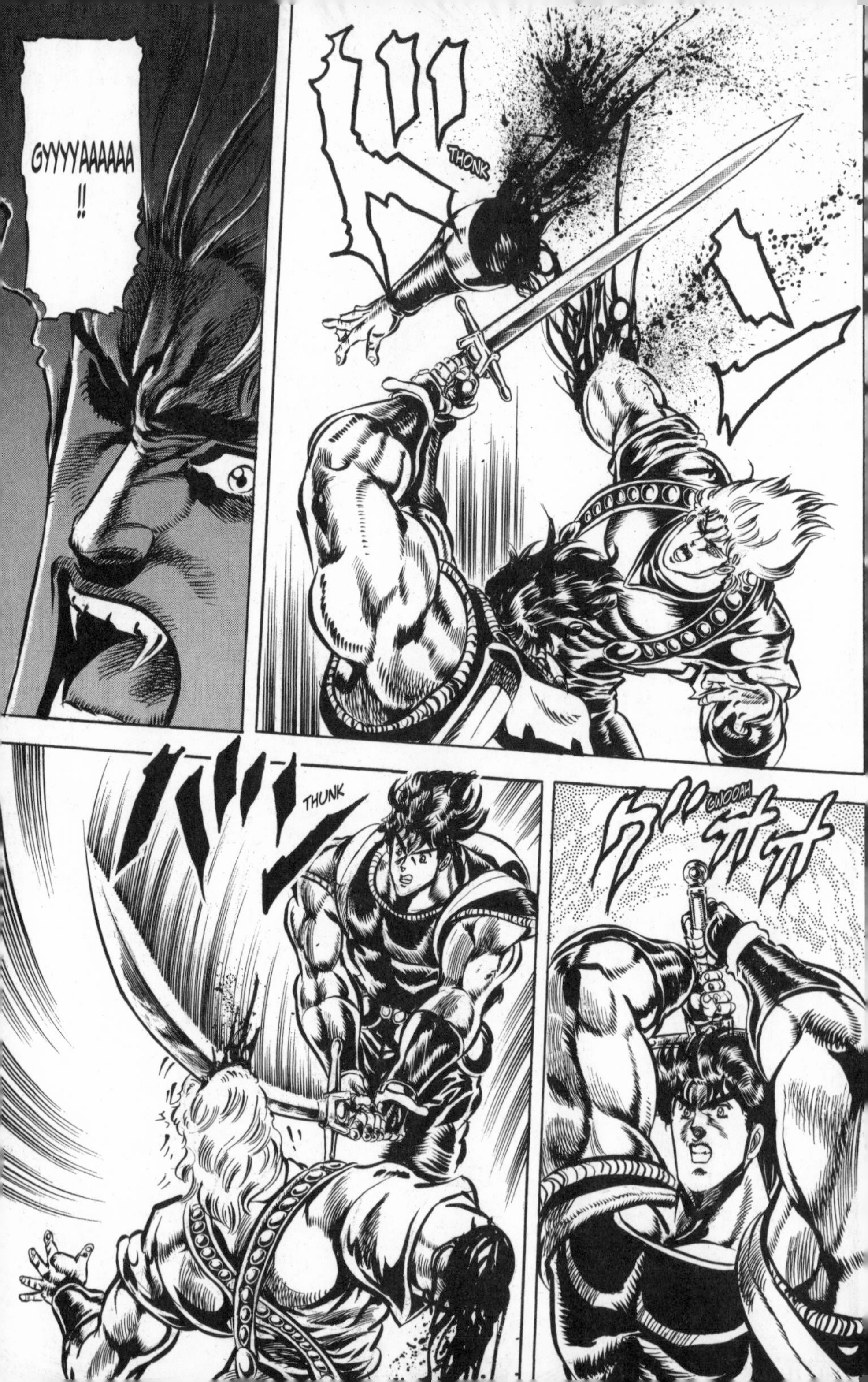
THONK
GYYYYAAAAAA!!
GWOOAH
THUNK

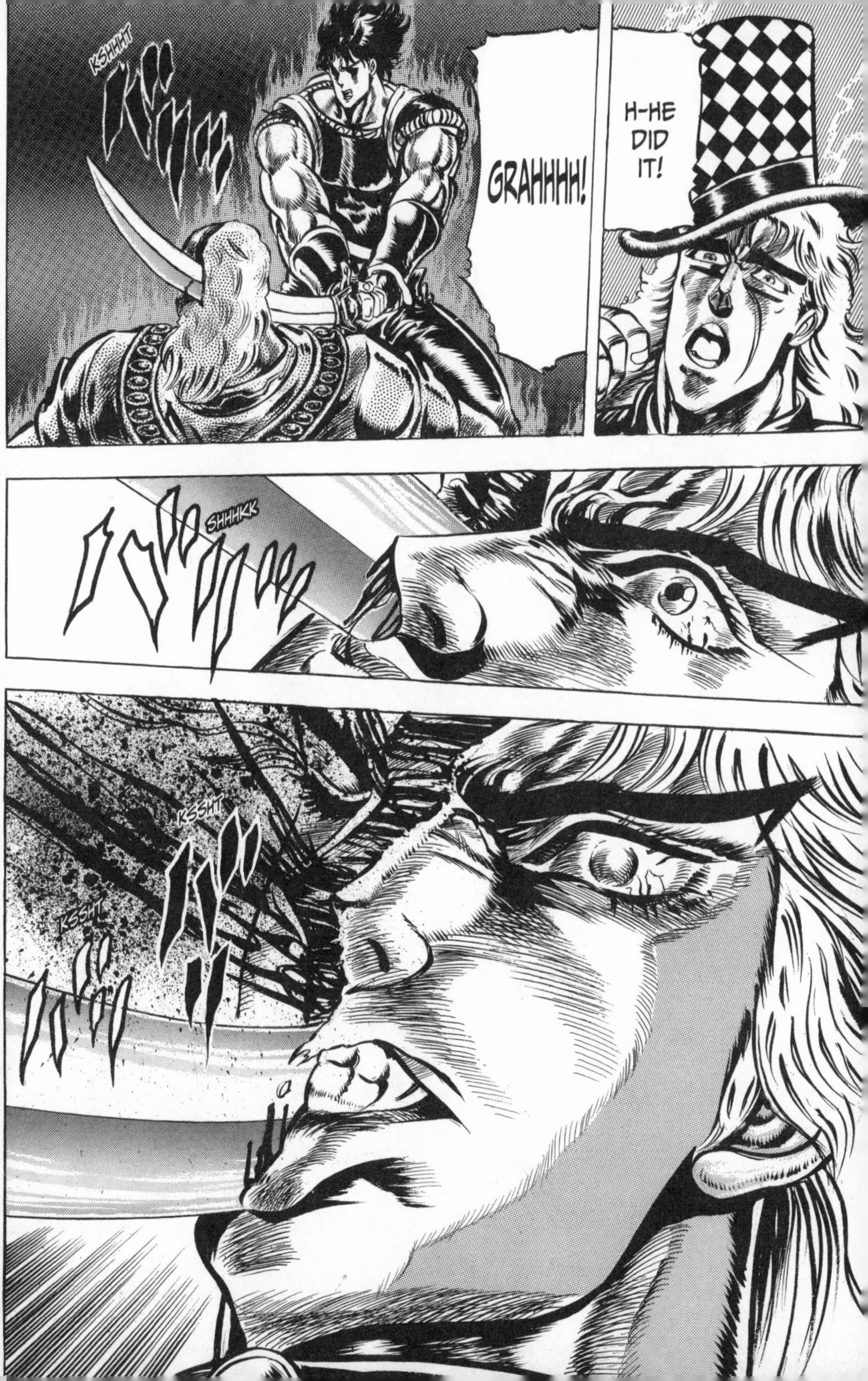
H-HE DID IT!
GRAHHHH!
KSHHHT
SHHHKK
KSSHT
KSSHT

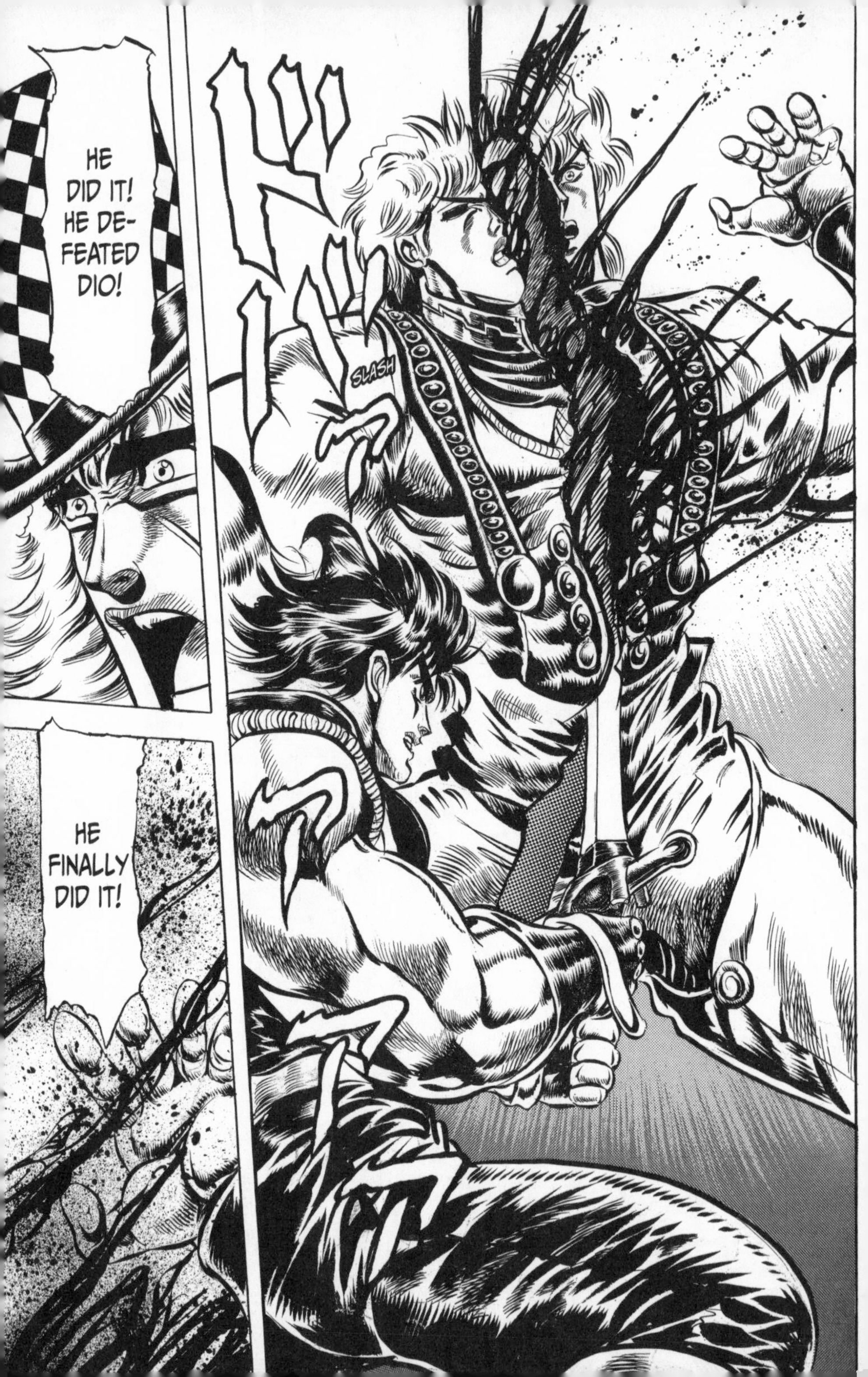
SLASH
HE DID IT! HE DEFEATED DIO!
HE FINALLY DID IT!

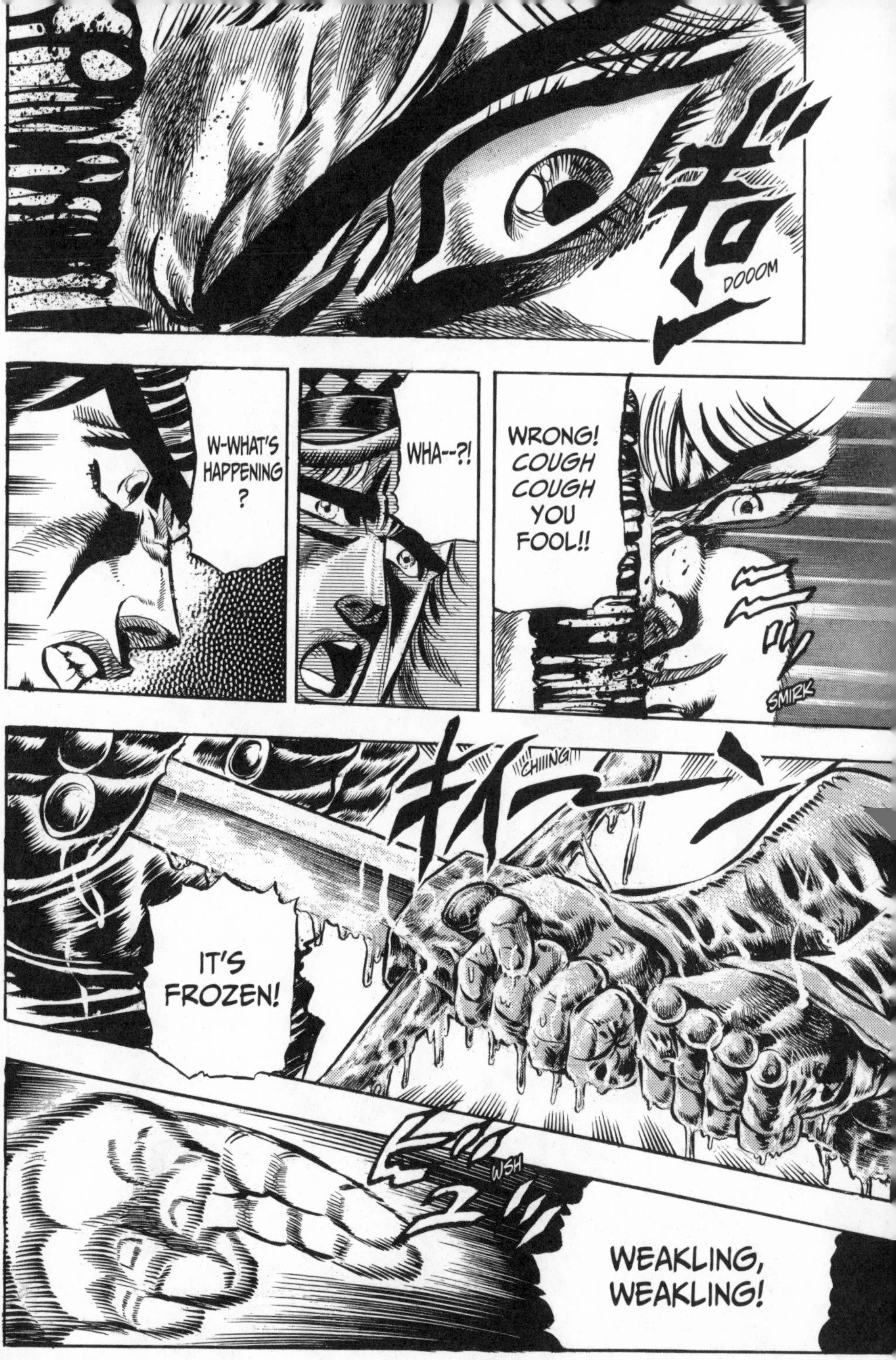
DOOOM
WRONG! COUGH COUGH YOU FOOL!!
SMIRK
WHA--?!
W-WHAT'S HAPPENING?
CHIING
IT'S FROZEN!
WEAKLING, WEAKLING!
WSH

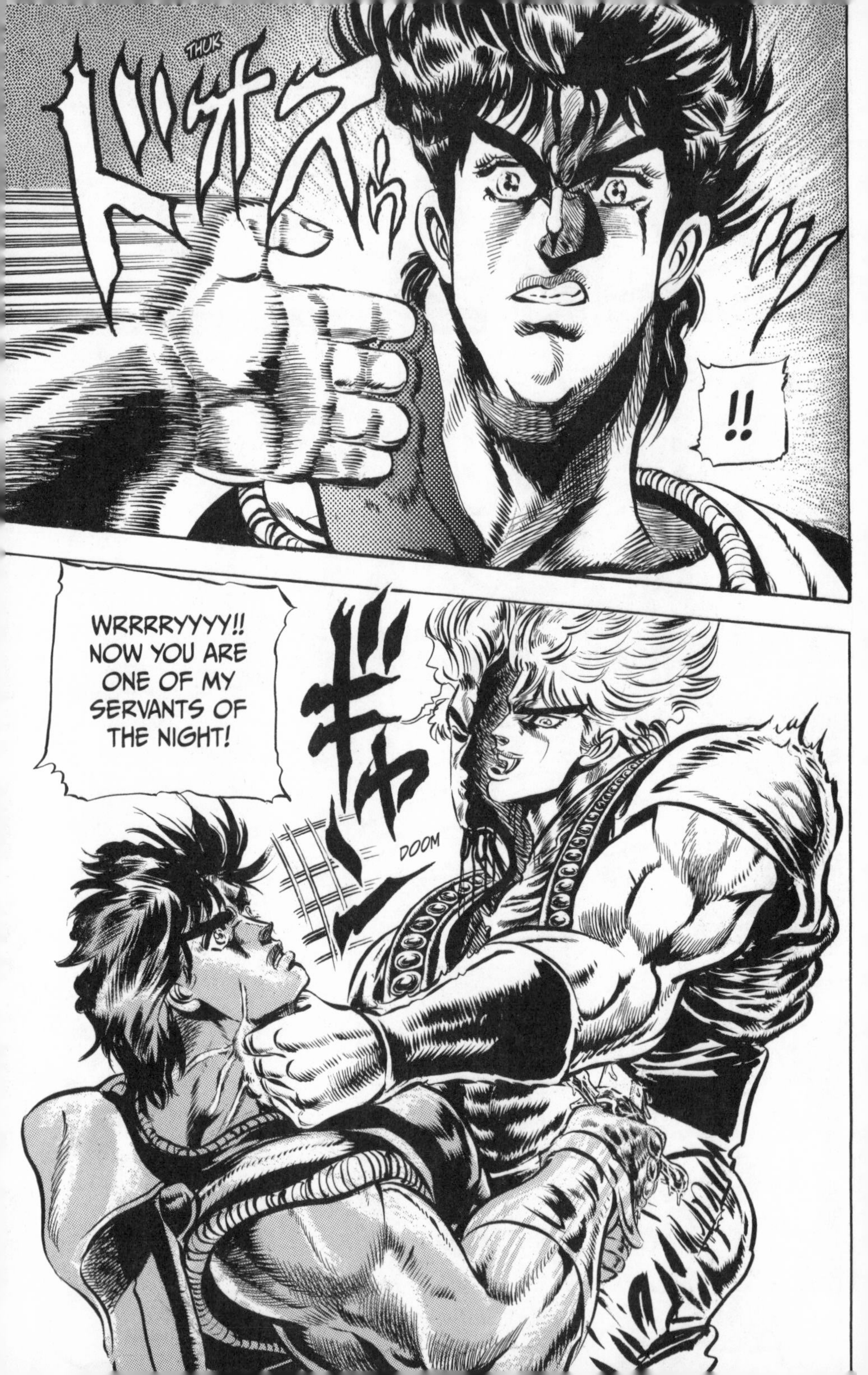
THUK
!!
WRRRRYYYY!! NOW YOU ARE ONE OF MY SERVANTS OF THE NIGHT!
DOOM

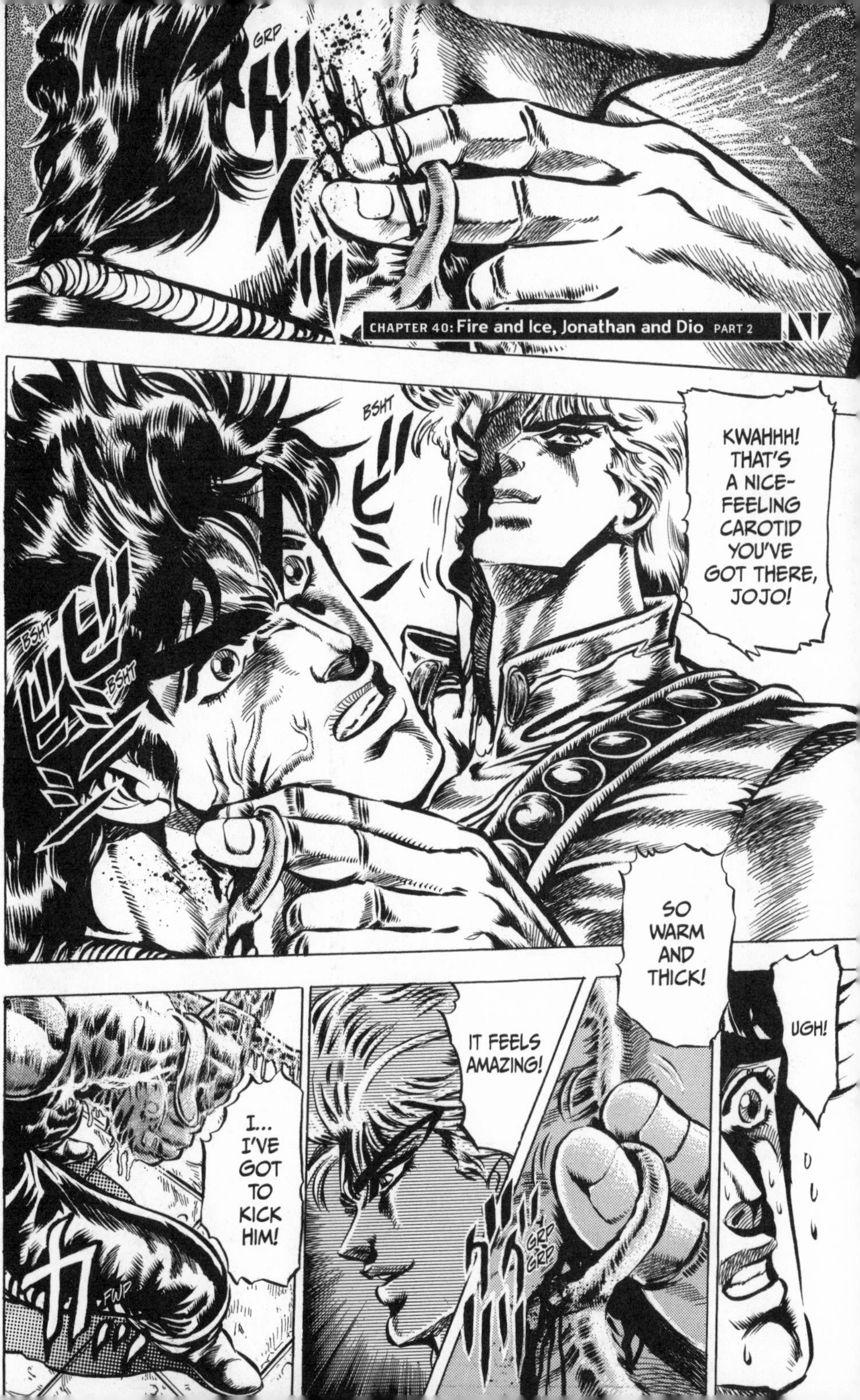
GRP
CHAPTER 40: Fire and Ice, Jonathan and Dio PART 2
KWAHHH! THAT'S A NICE-FEELING CAROTID YOU'VE GOT THERE, JOJO!
BSHT
BSHT
BSHT
SO WARM AND THICK!
UGH!
IT FEELS AMAZING!
GRP GRP
I... I'VE GOT TO KICK HIM!
FWP

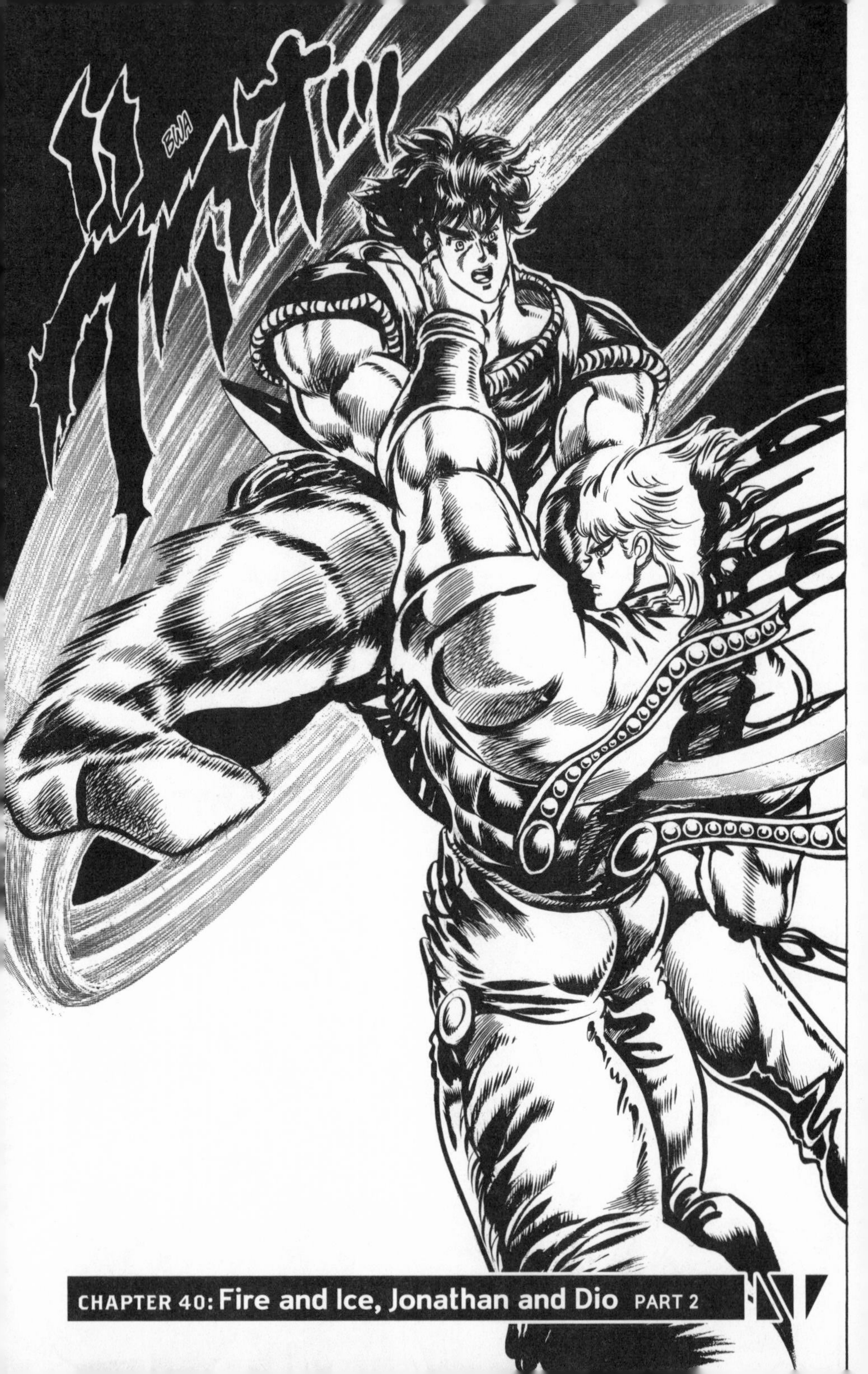
BWA

CHAPTER 40: Fire and Ice, Jonathan and Dio PART 2

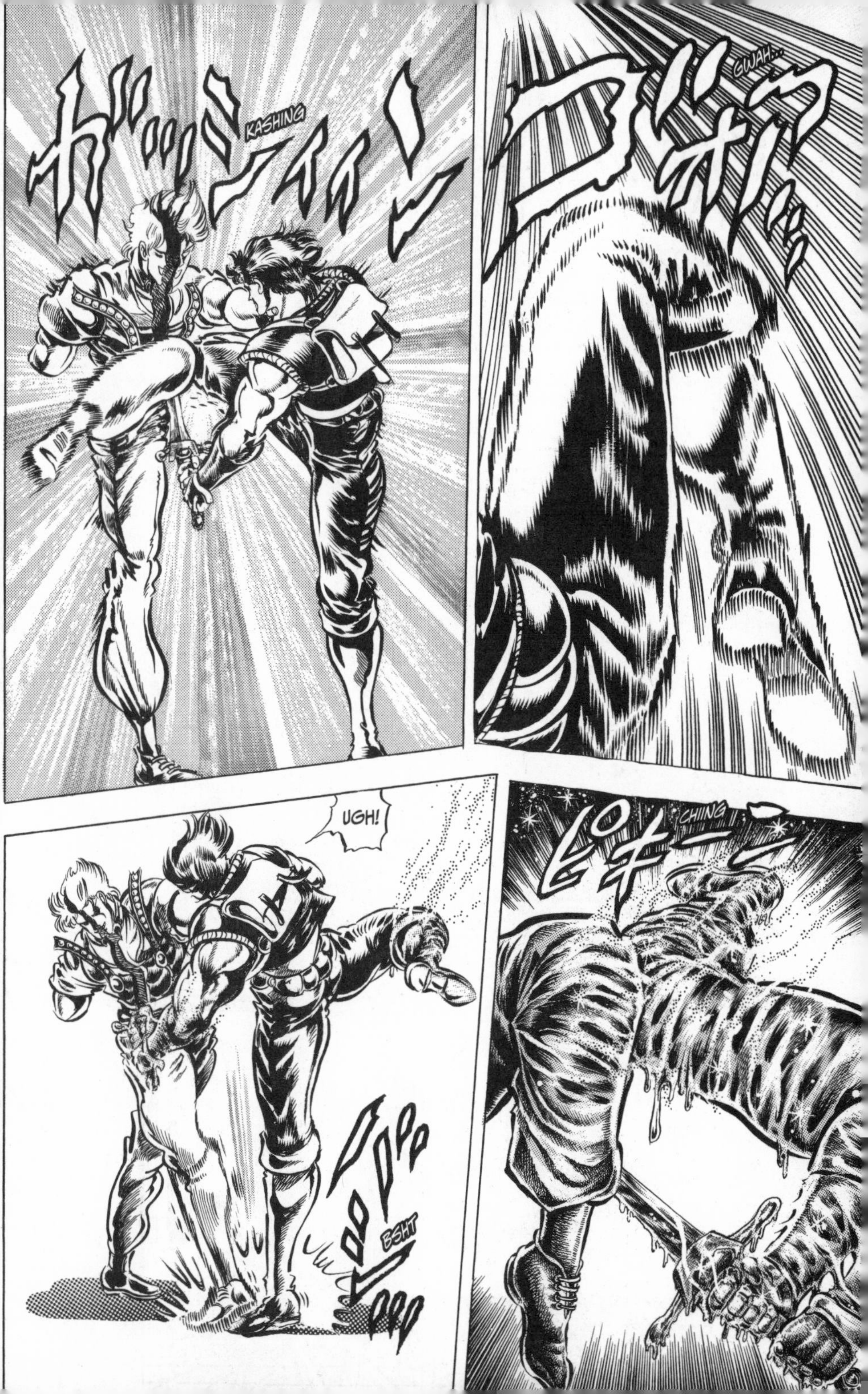
GWAH...
KASHING
CHING
UGH!
BSHT

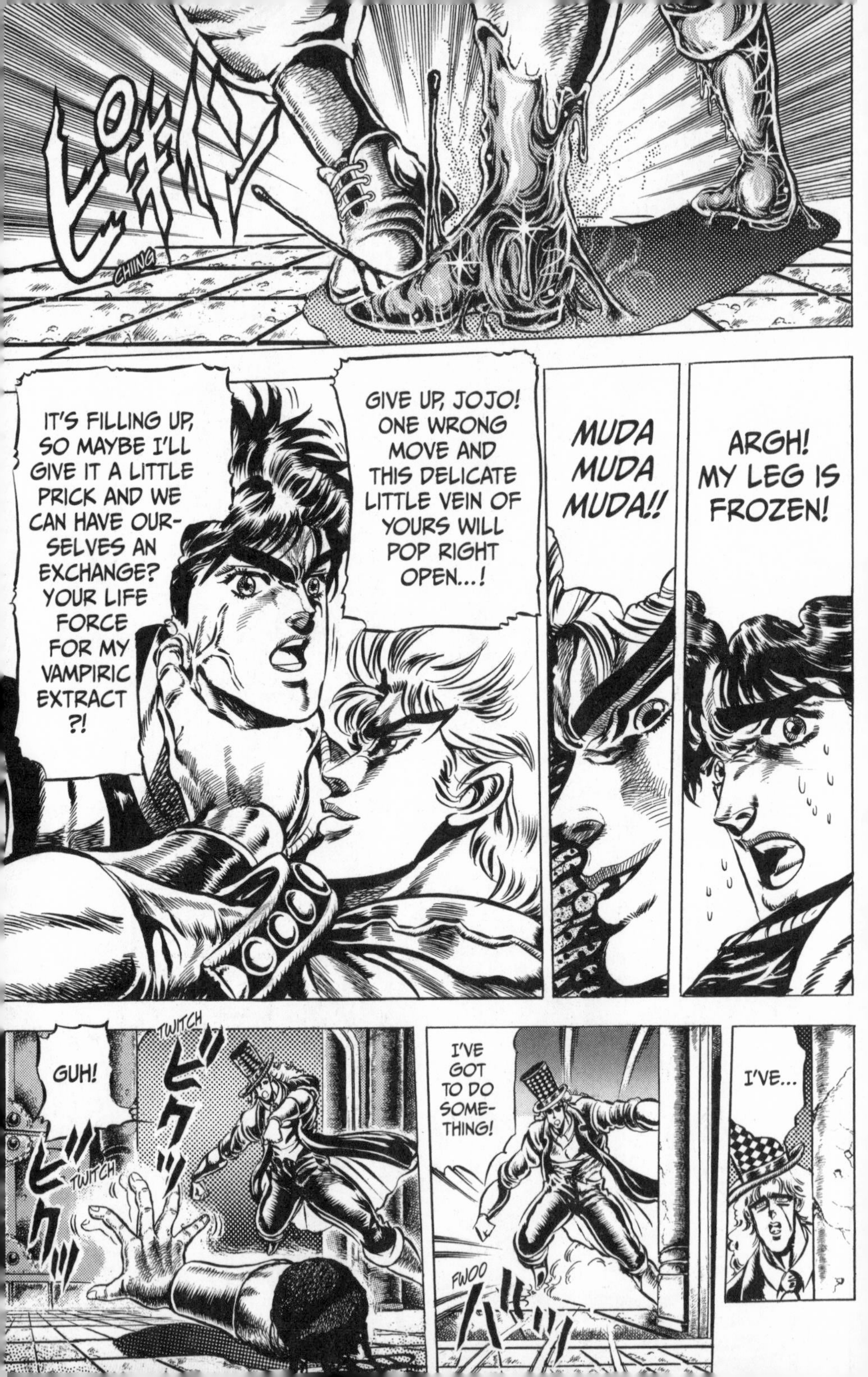
CHING
ARGH! MY LEG IS FROZEN!
MUDA MUDA MUDA!!
GIVE UP, JOJO! ONE WRONG MOVE AND THIS DELICATE LITTLE VEIN OF YOURS WILL POP RIGHT OPEN...!
IT'S FILLING UP, SO MAYBE I'LL GIVE IT A LITTLE PRICK AND WE CAN HAVE OUR-SELVES AN EXCHANGE? YOUR LIFE FORCE FOR MY VAMPIRIC EXTRACT ?!
I'VE...
I'VE GOT TO DO SOME-THING!
FWOO
TWITCH
GUH!
TWITCH

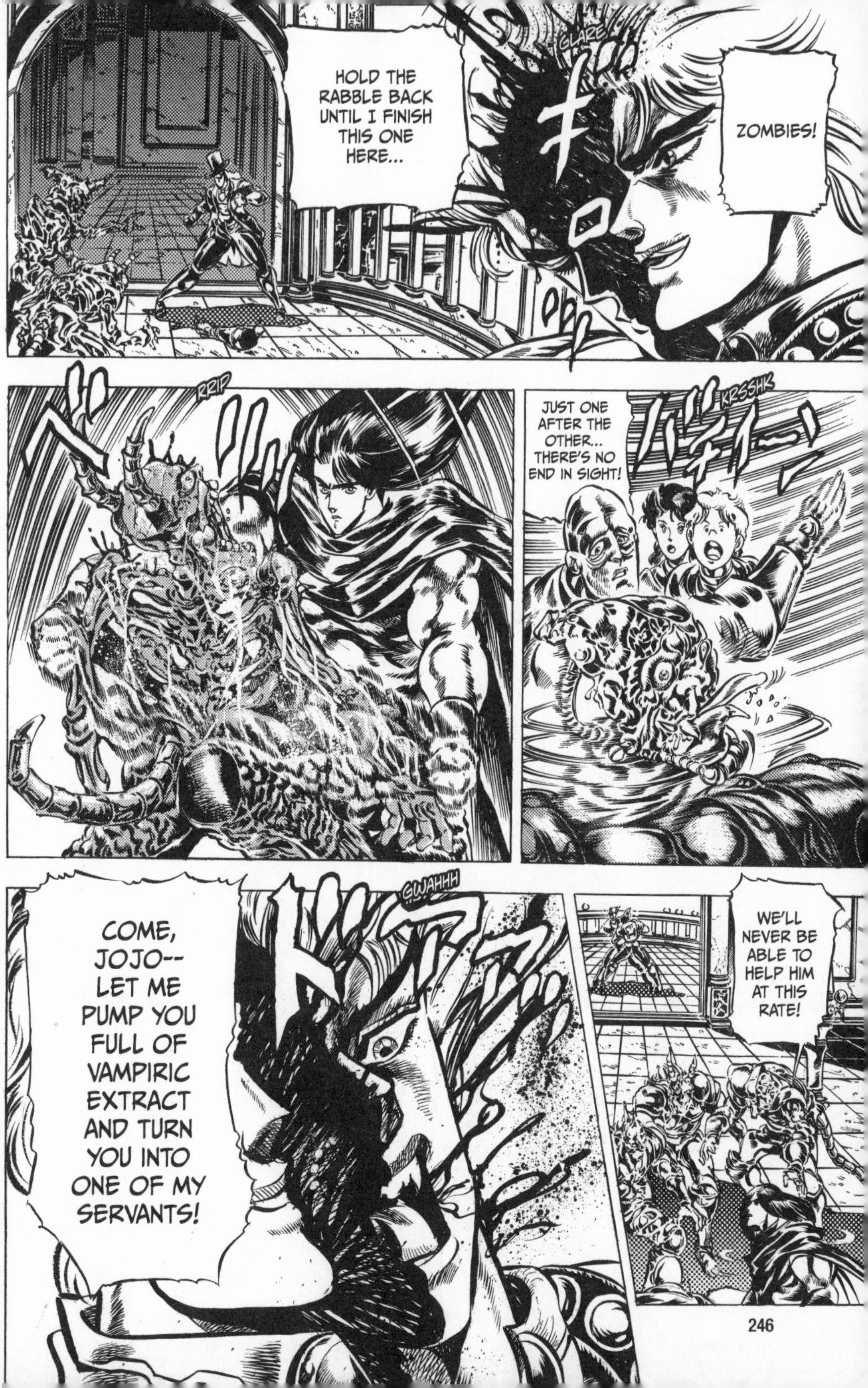
GLARE
ZOMBIES!
HOLD THE RABBLE BACK UNTIL I FINISH THIS ONE HERE...
KRSSHK
JUST ONE AFTER THE OTHER... THERE'S NO END IN SIGHT!
RRIP
WE'LL NEVER BE ABLE TO HELP HIM AT THIS RATE!
GWAHHH
COME, JOJO-- LET ME PUMP YOU FULL OF VAMPIRIC EXTRACT AND TURN YOU INTO ONE OF MY SERVANTS!

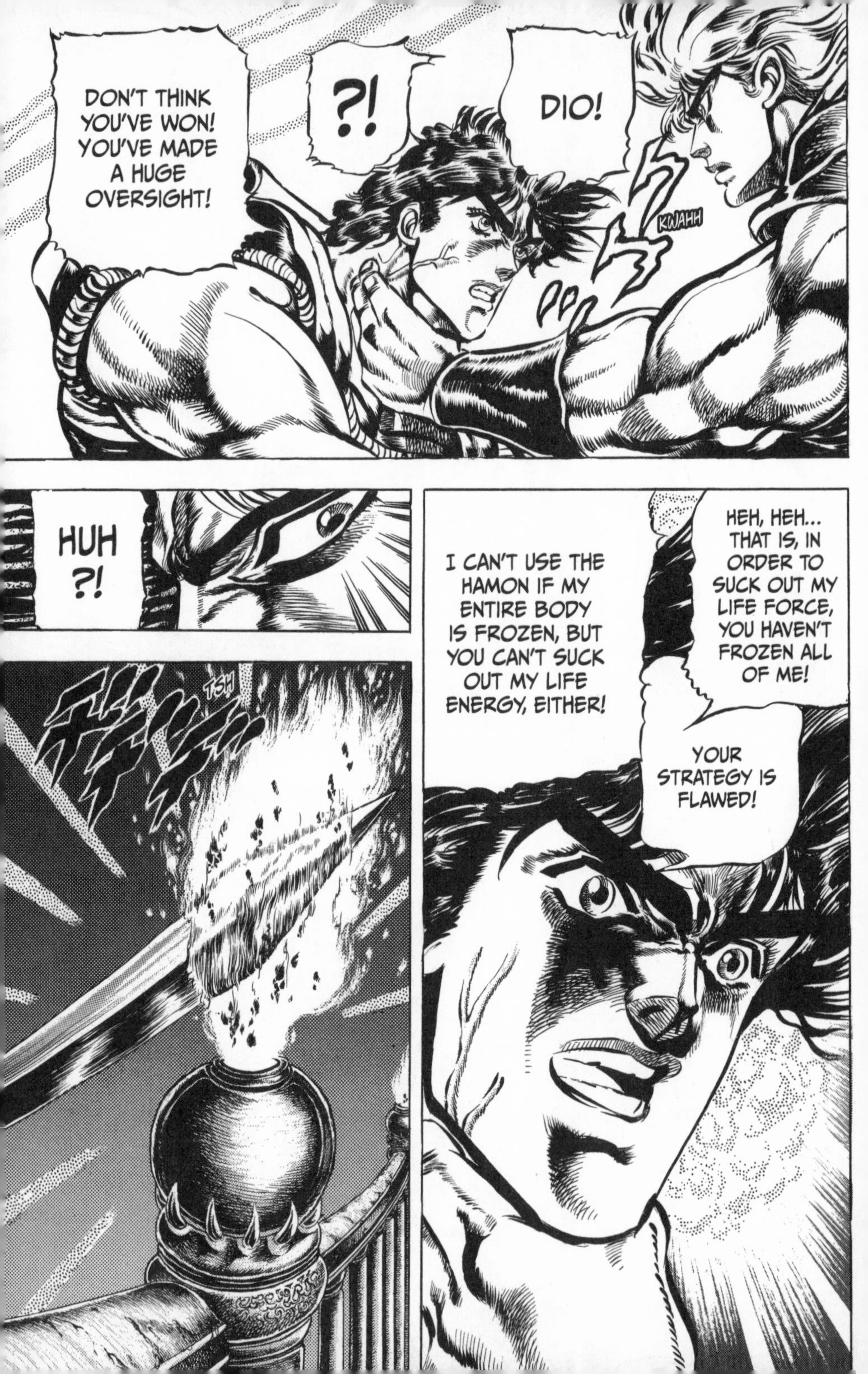
DIO!
KWAHH
?!
DON'T THINK YOU'VE WON! YOU'VE MADE A HUGE OVERSIGHT!
HEH, HEH... THAT IS, IN ORDER TO SUCK OUT MY LIFE FORCE, YOU HAVEN'T FROZEN ALL OF ME!
I CAN'T USE THE HAMON IF MY ENTIRE BODY IS FROZEN, BUT YOU CAN'T SUCK OUT MY LIFE ENERGY, EITHER!
YOUR STRATEGY IS FLAWED!
HUH ?!
TSH

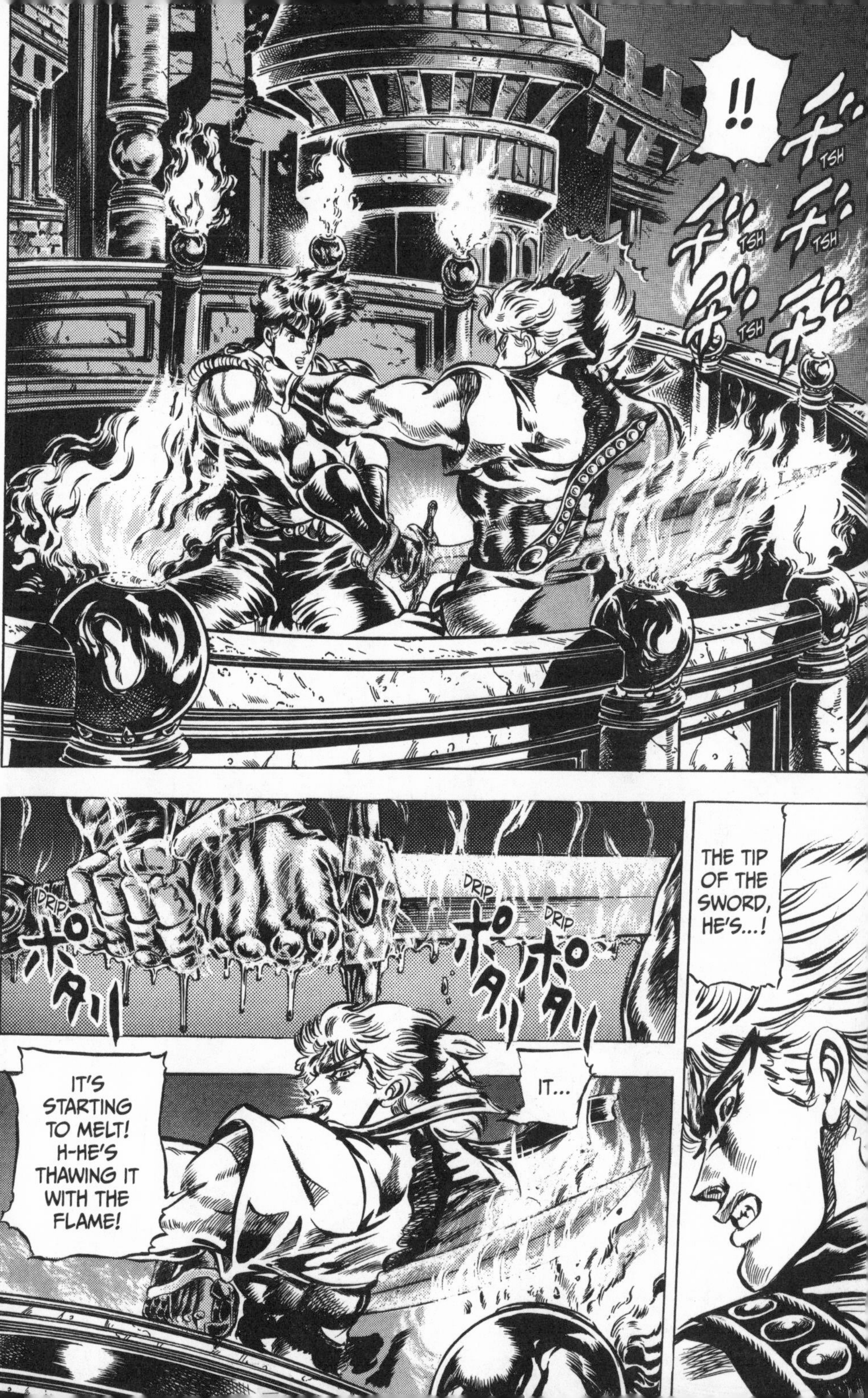
!!
TSH
TSH
TSH
TSH
TSH
THE TIP OF THE SWORD, HE'S...!
DRIP
DRIP
DRIP
IT...
IT'S STARTING TO MELT! H-HE'S THAWING IT WITH THE FLAME!

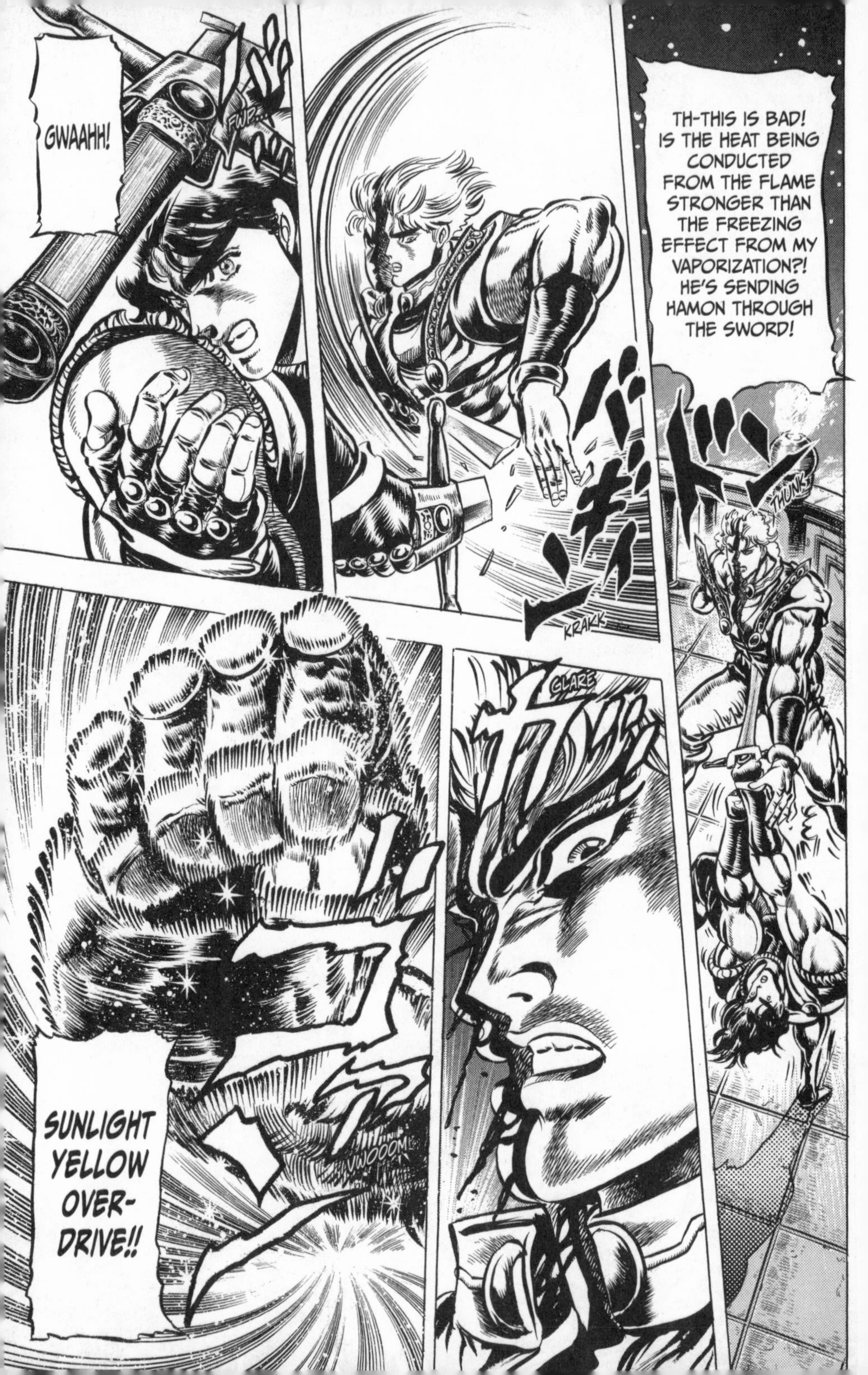
TH-THIS IS BAD! IS THE HEAT BEING CONDUCTED FROM THE FLAME STRONGER THAN THE FREEZING EFFECT FROM MY VAPORIZATION?! HE'S SENDING HAMON THROUGH THE SWORD!
THUNK
KRAKK
FWP...
GWAAHH!
GLARE
VWOOOM
SUNLIGHT YELLOW OVER-DRIVE!!

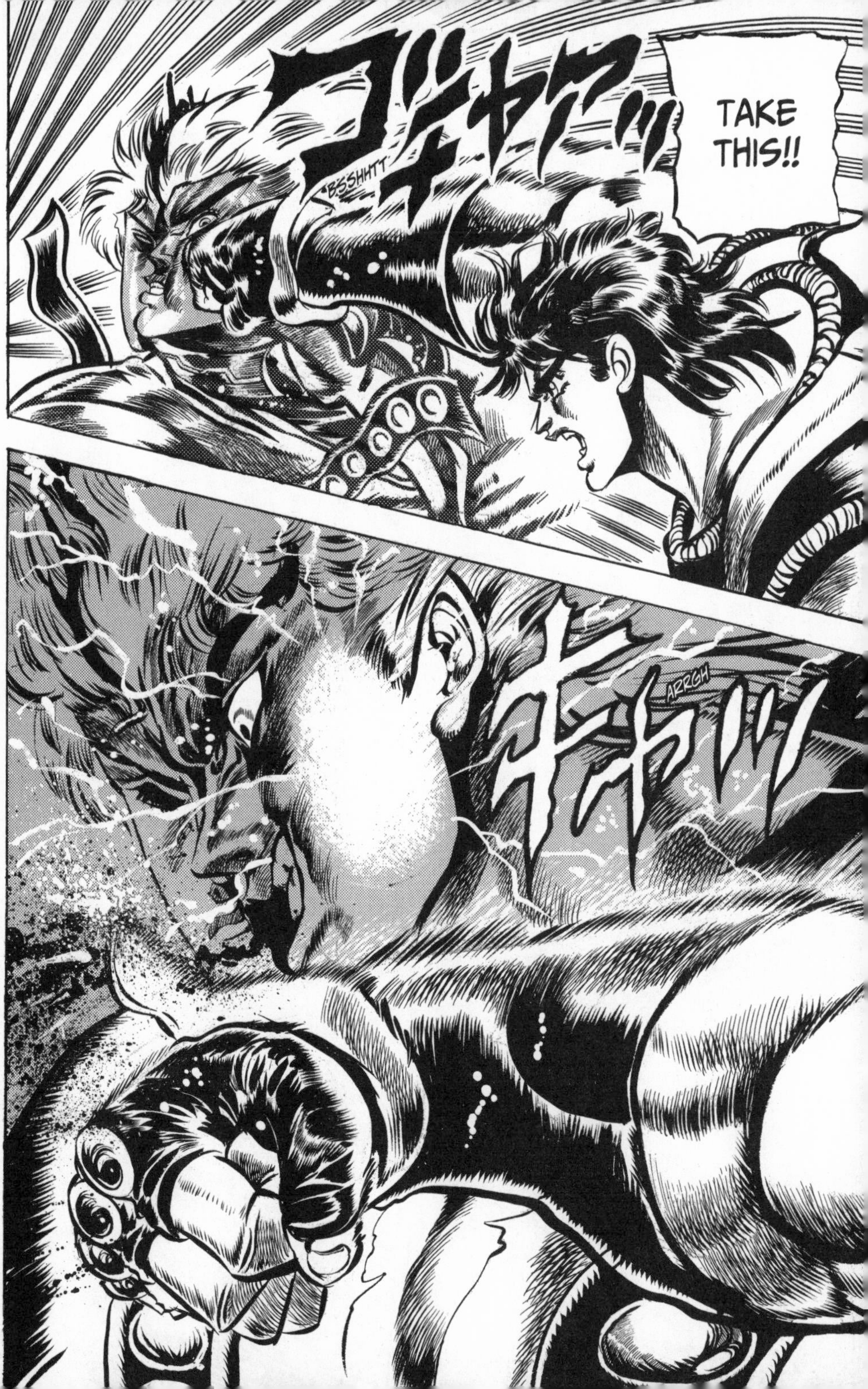
TAKE THIS!!
BSSHHTT
ARRGH

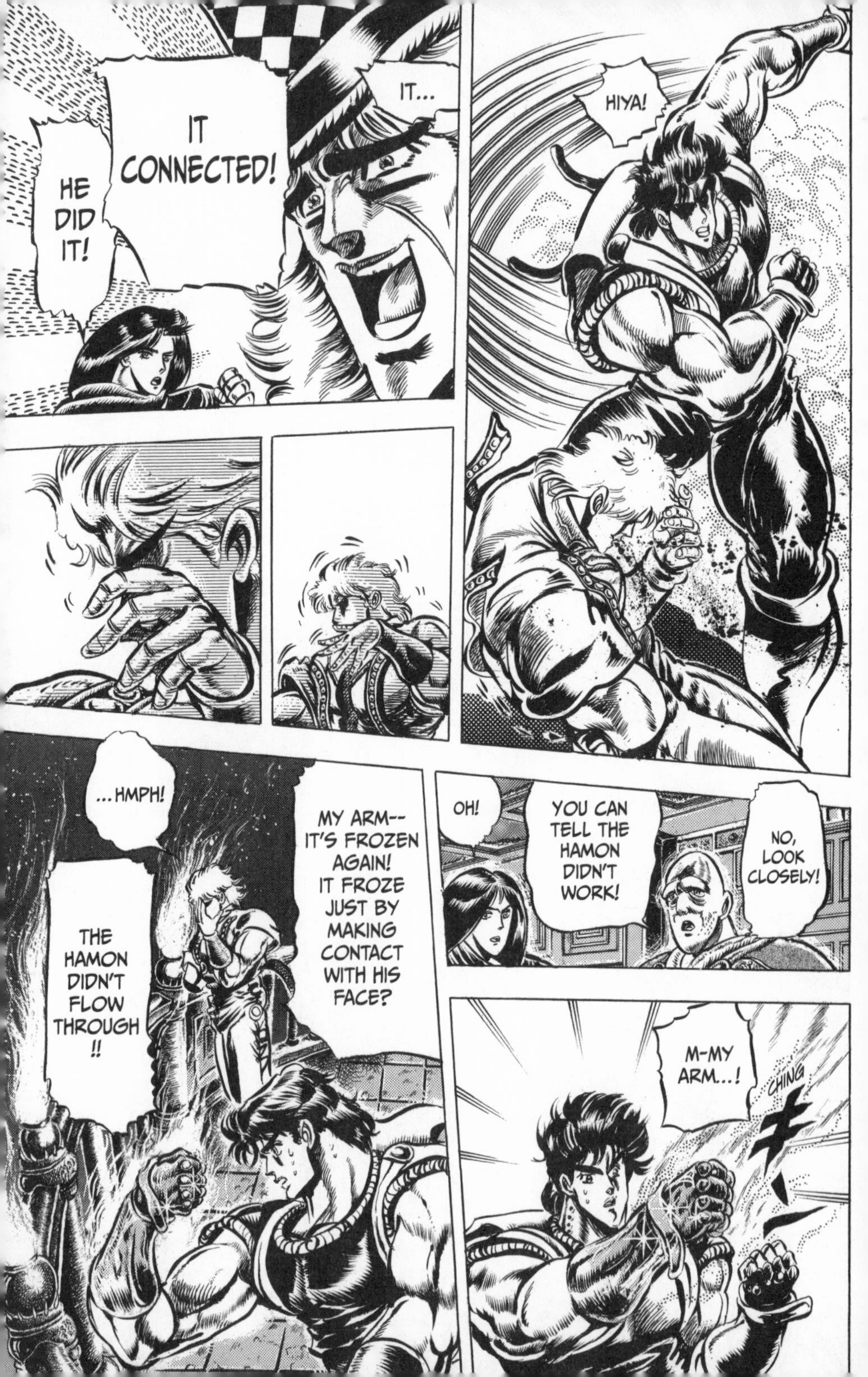
HIYA!
IT...
IT CONNECTED!
HE DID IT!
NO, LOOK CLOSELY!
YOU CAN TELL THE HAMON DIDN'T WORK!
OH!
M-MY ARM...!
CHING
MY ARM-- IT'S FROZEN AGAIN! IT FROZE JUST BY MAKING CONTACT WITH HIS FACE?
...HMPH!
THE HAMON DIDN'T FLOW THROUGH !!

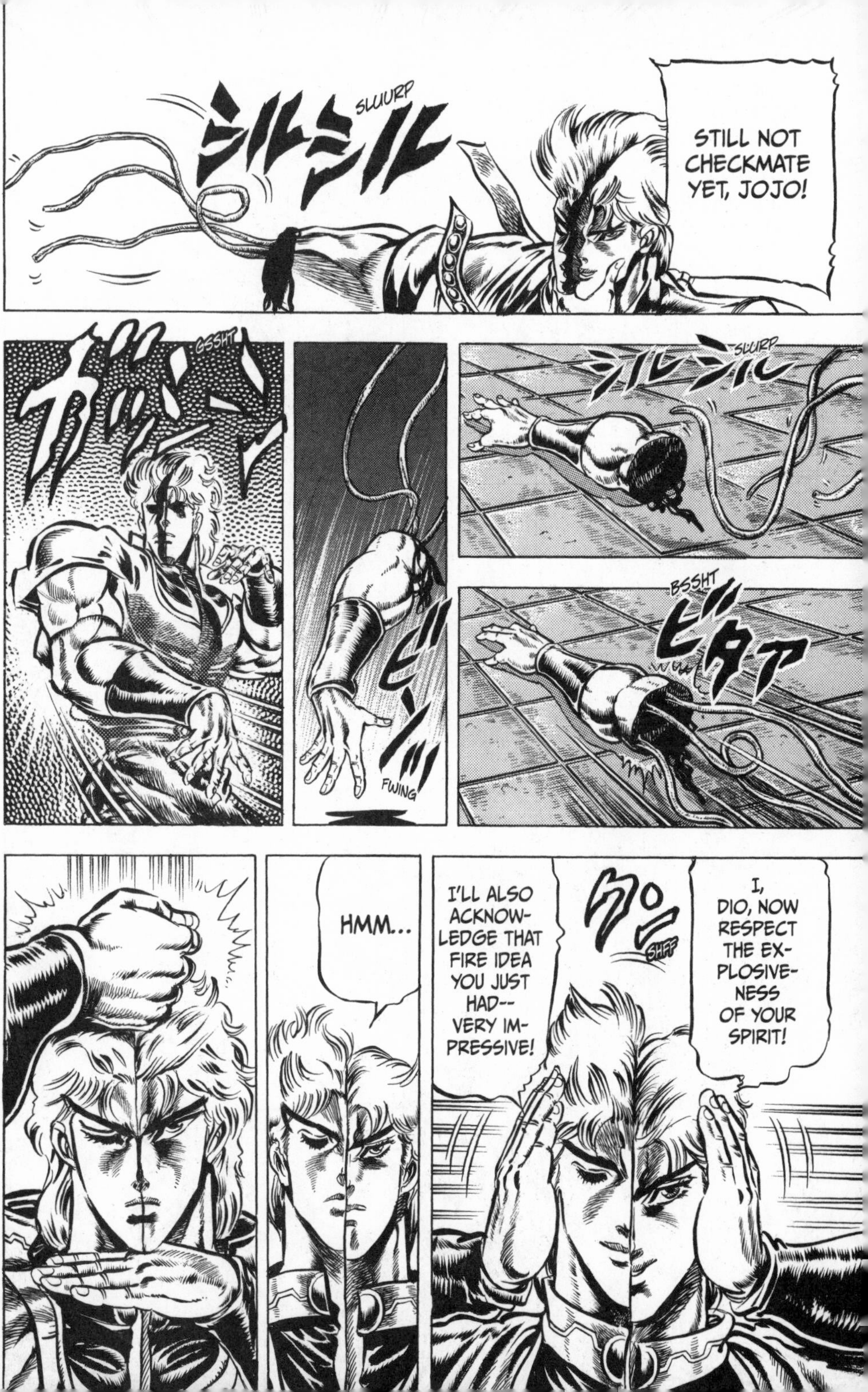
STILL NOT CHECKMATE YET, JOJO!
SLUURP
SLUURP
BSSHT
FWING
GSSHT
I, DIO, NOW RESPECT THE EXPLOSIVENESS OF YOUR SPIRIT!
SHFF
I'LL ALSO ACKNOWLEDGE THAT FIRE IDEA YOU JUST HAD-- VERY IMPRESSIVE!
HMM...

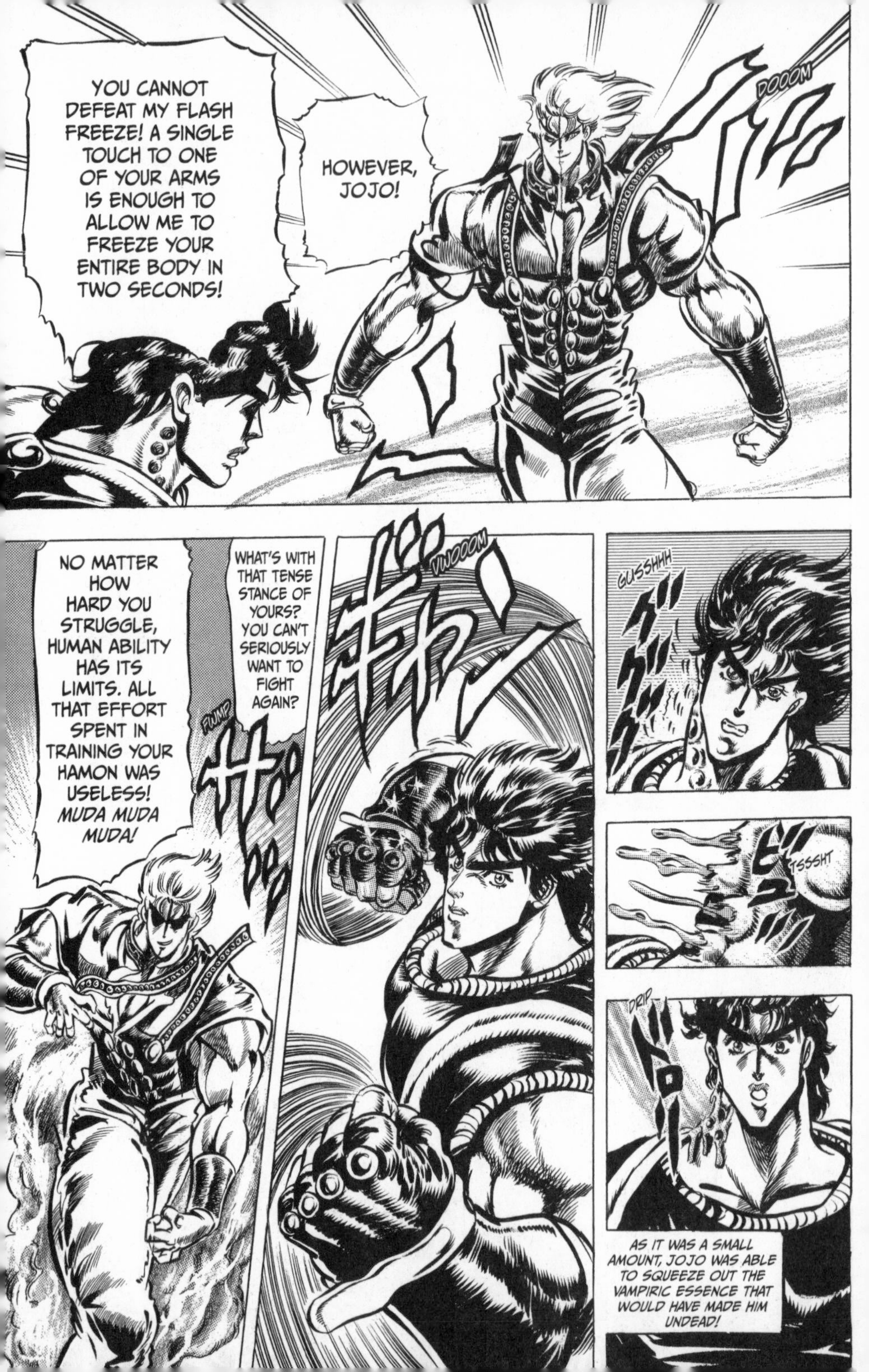
DOOOM
HOWEVER, JOJO!
YOU CANNOT DEFEAT MY FLASH FREEZE! A SINGLE TOUCH TO ONE OF YOUR ARMS IS ENOUGH TO ALLOW ME TO FREEZE YOUR ENTIRE BODY IN TWO SECONDS!
GUSSHHH
TSSSHT
DRIP
AS IT WAS A SMALL AMOUNT, JOJO WAS ABLE TO SQUEEZE OUT THE VAMPIRIC ESSENCE THAT WOULD HAVE MADE HIM UNDEAD!
VWOOOM
WHAT'S WITH THAT TENSE STANCE OF YOURS? YOU CAN'T SERIOUSLY WANT TO FIGHT AGAIN?
FWMP
NO MATTER HOW HARD YOU STRUGGLE, HUMAN ABILITY HAS ITS LIMITS. ALL THAT EFFORT SPENT IN TRAINING YOUR HAMON WAS USELESS! *MUDA MUDA MUDA!*

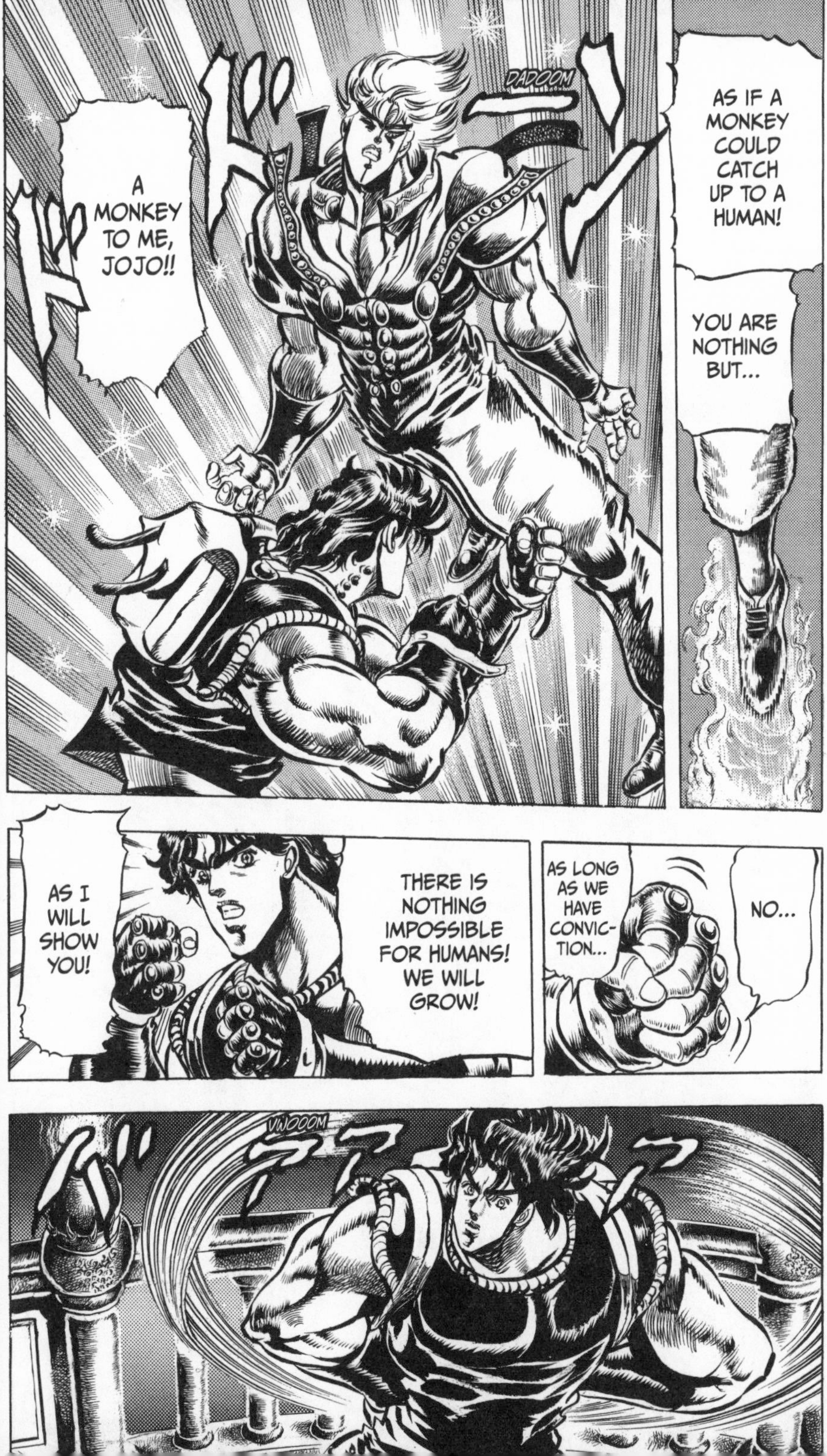
AS IF A MONKEY COULD CATCH UP TO A HUMAN!
YOU ARE NOTHING BUT...
DADOOM
A MONKEY TO ME, JOJO!!
NO...
AS LONG AS WE HAVE CONVIC-TION...
THERE IS NOTHING IMPOSSIBLE FOR HUMANS! WE WILL GROW!
AS I WILL SHOW YOU!
VWOOOM

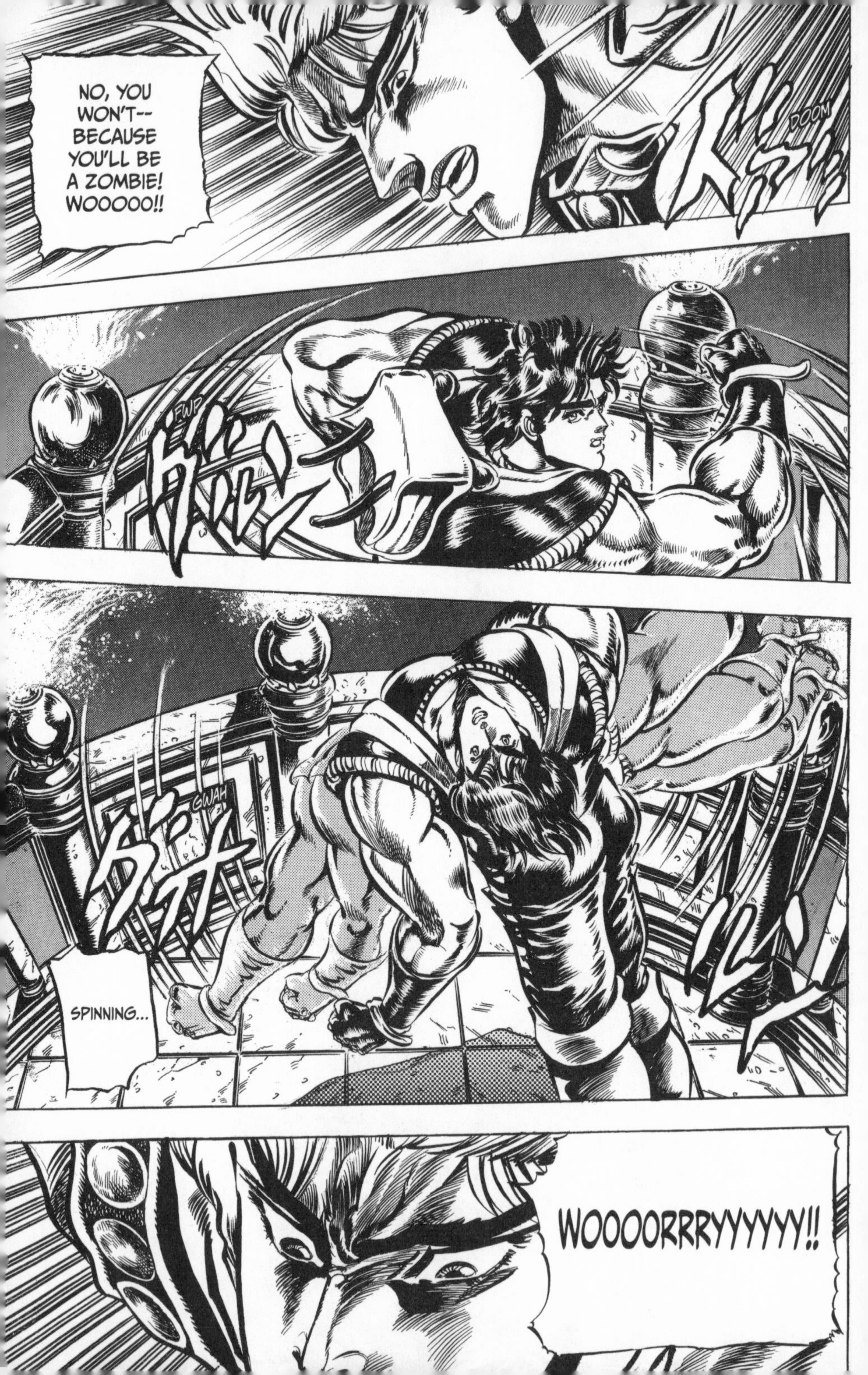
DOOM
NO, YOU WON'T-- BECAUSE YOU'LL BE A ZOMBIE! WOOOOO!!
FWP
GWAH
SPINNING...
WOOOORRRYYYYYY!!

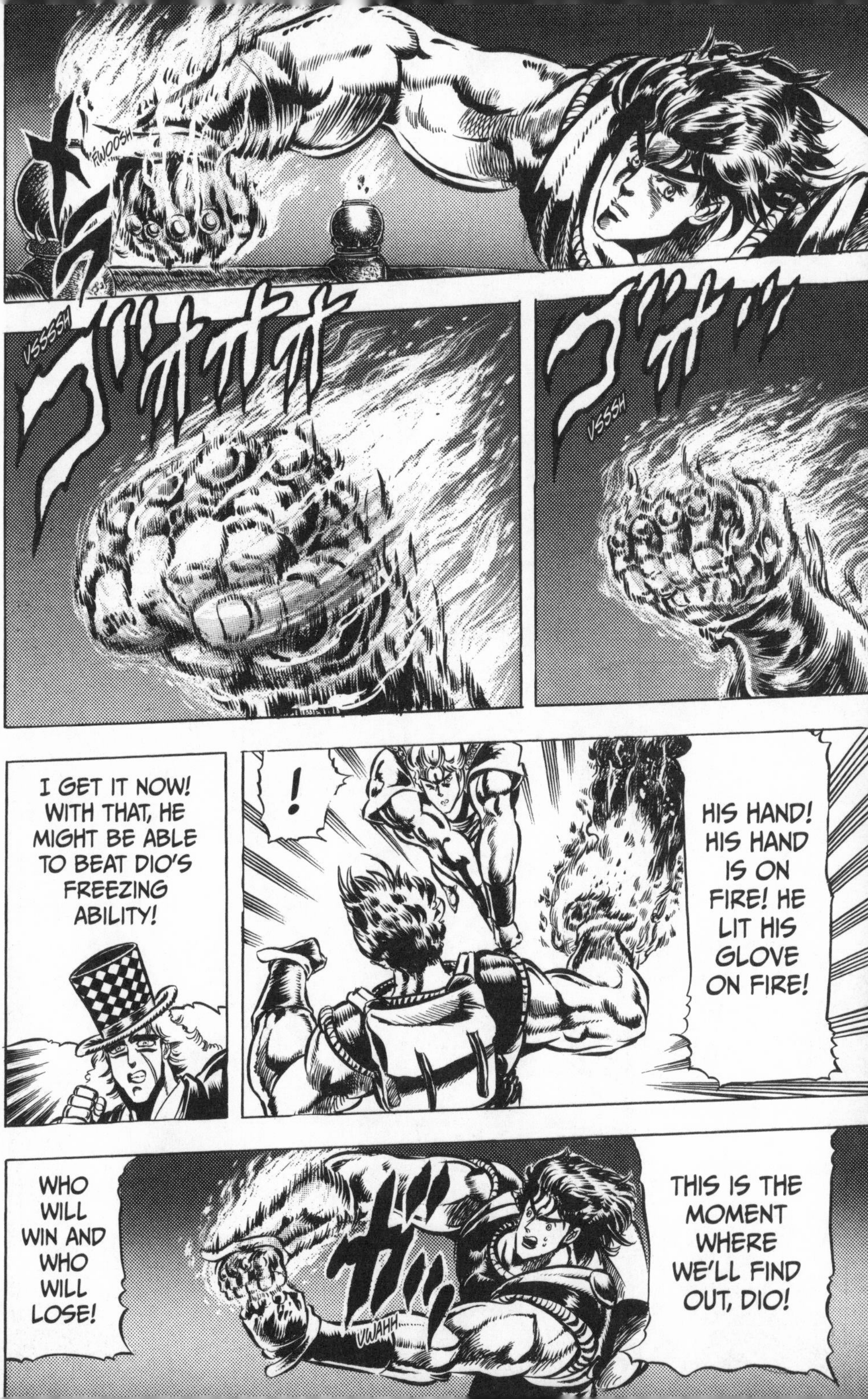
FWOOSH
VSSSH
VSSSSH
HIS HAND! HIS HAND IS ON FIRE! HE LIT HIS GLOVE ON FIRE!
!
I GET IT NOW! WITH THAT, HE MIGHT BE ABLE TO BEAT DIO'S FREEZING ABILITY!
THIS IS THE MOMENT WHERE WE'LL FIND OUT, DIO!
WHO WILL WIN AND WHO WILL LOSE!
VWAHH

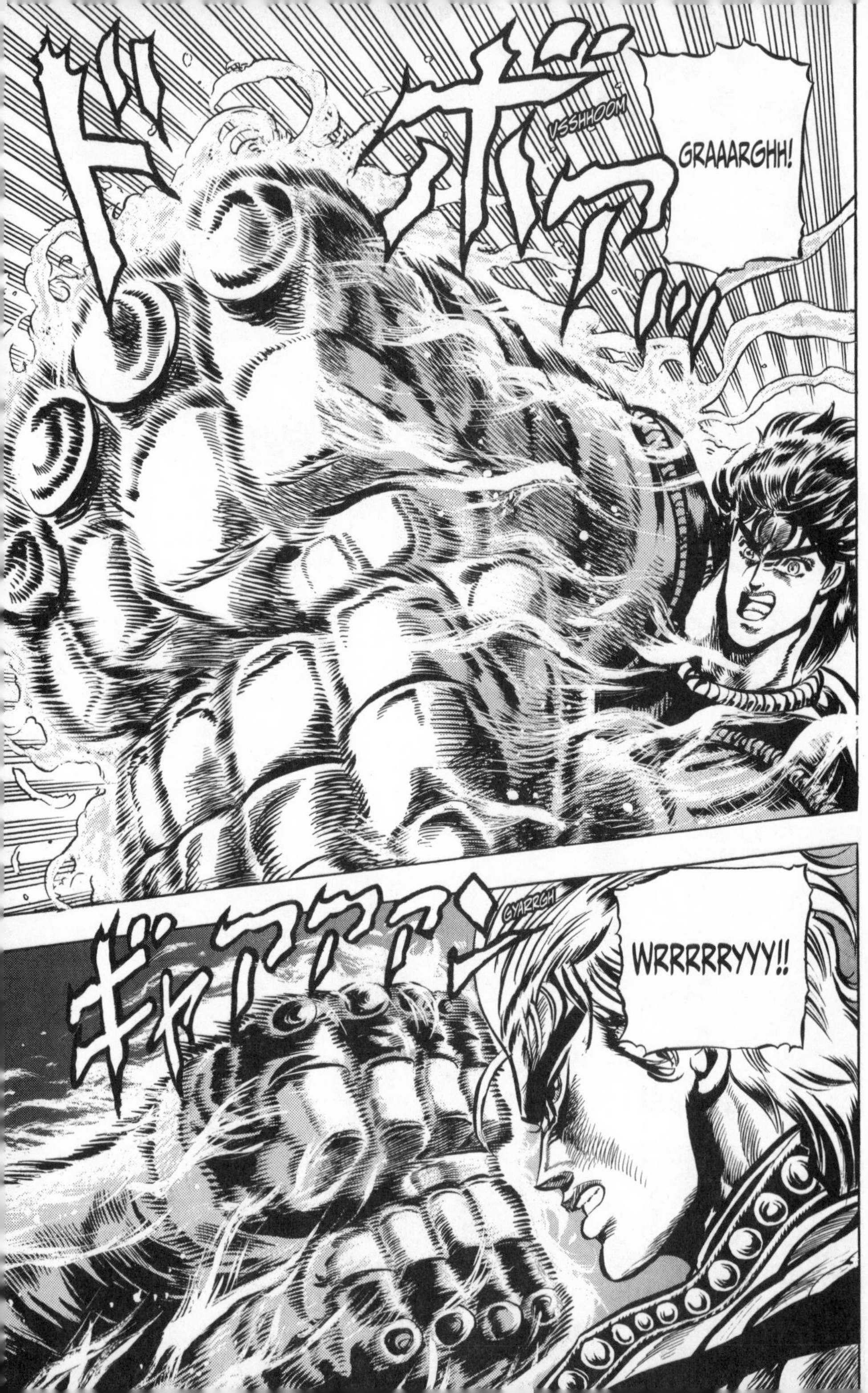
GRAAARGHH!
VSSHHOOM
WRRRRRYYY!!
GYARRGH

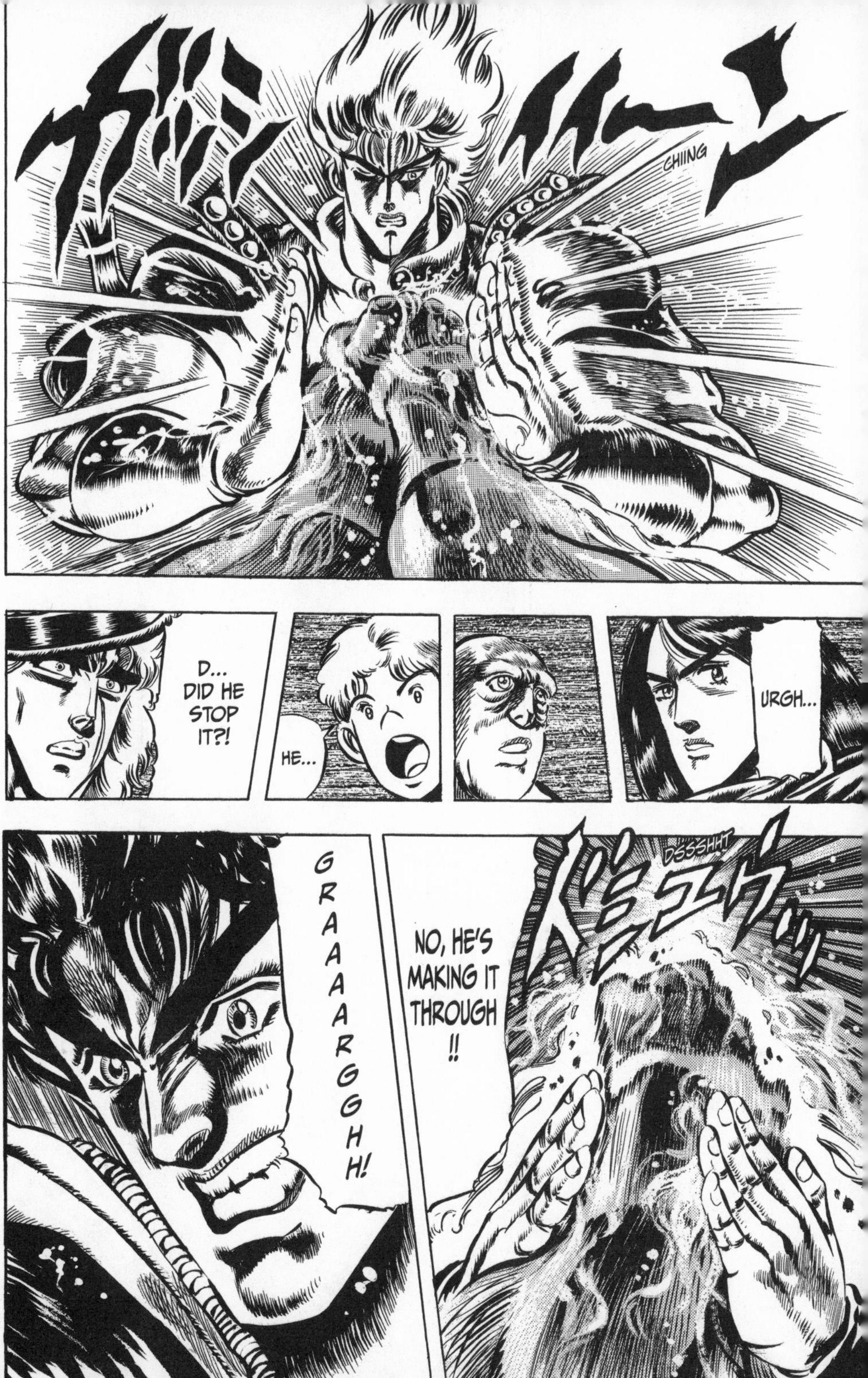
CHIING
URGH...
HE...
D... DID HE STOP IT?!
DSSSHHT
NO, HE'S MAKING IT THROUGH !!
GRAAAARGGHH!

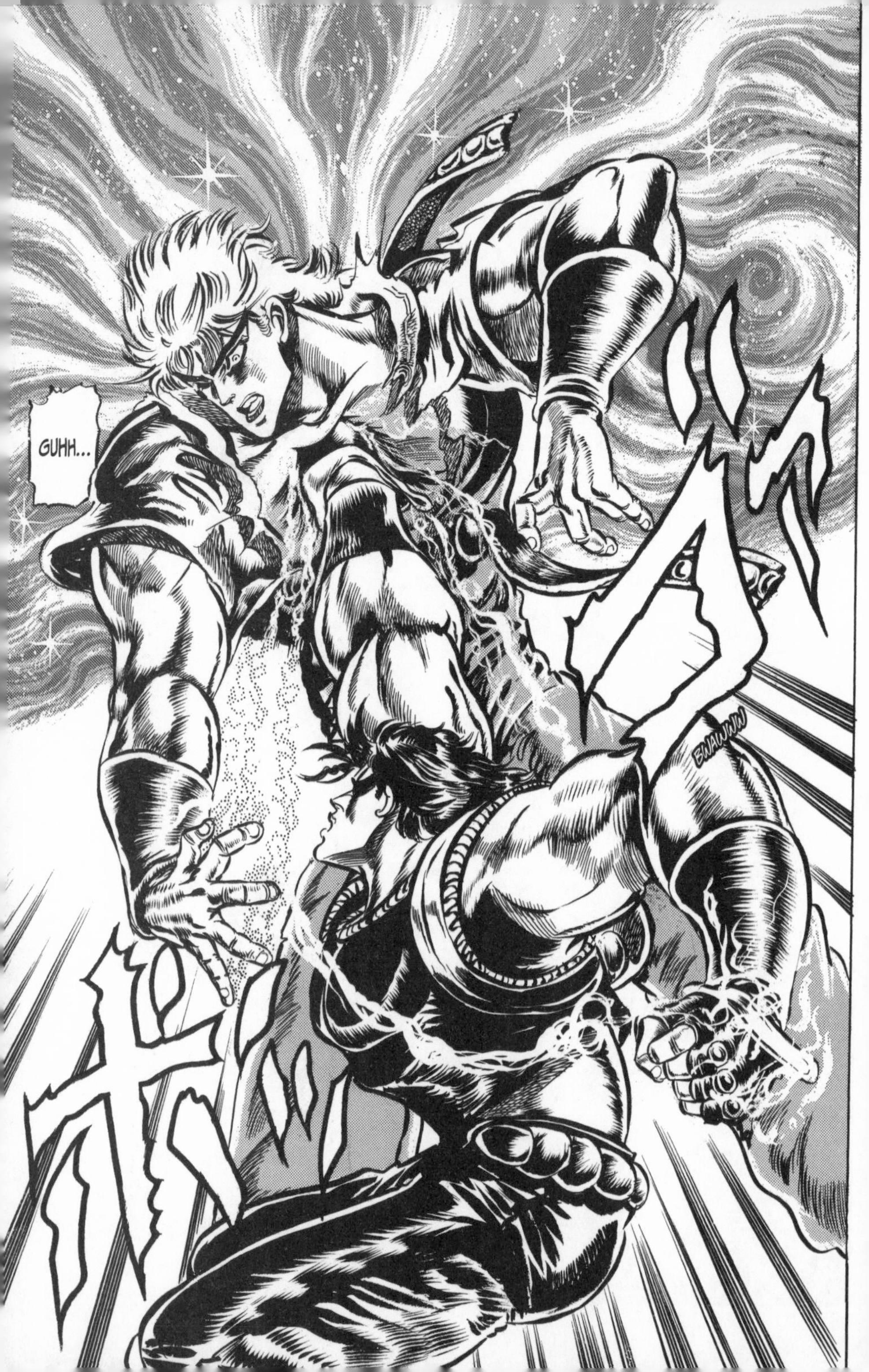
BWAWWW
GUHH...

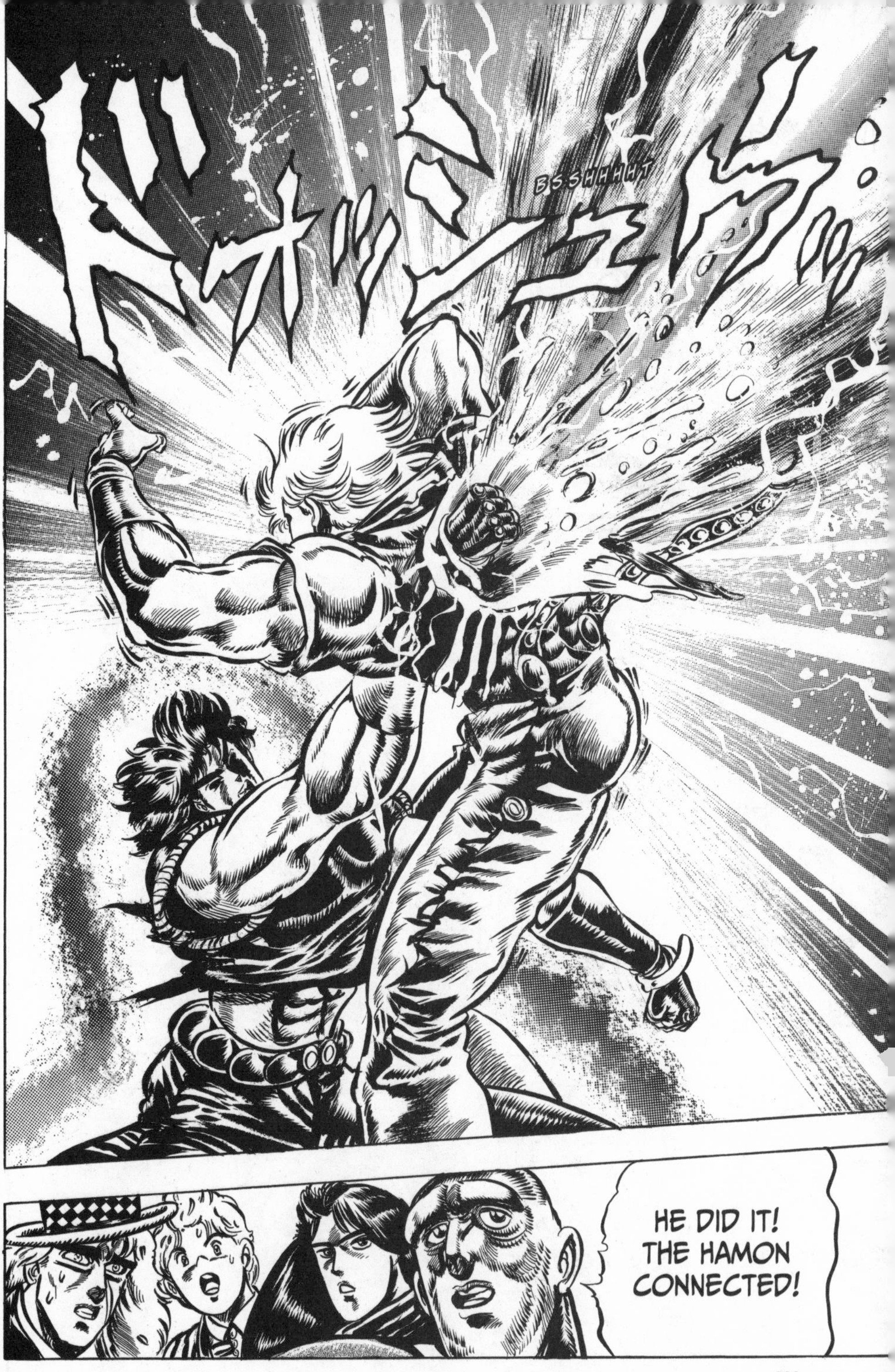
BSSHHHHT
HE DID IT! THE HAMON CONNECTED!

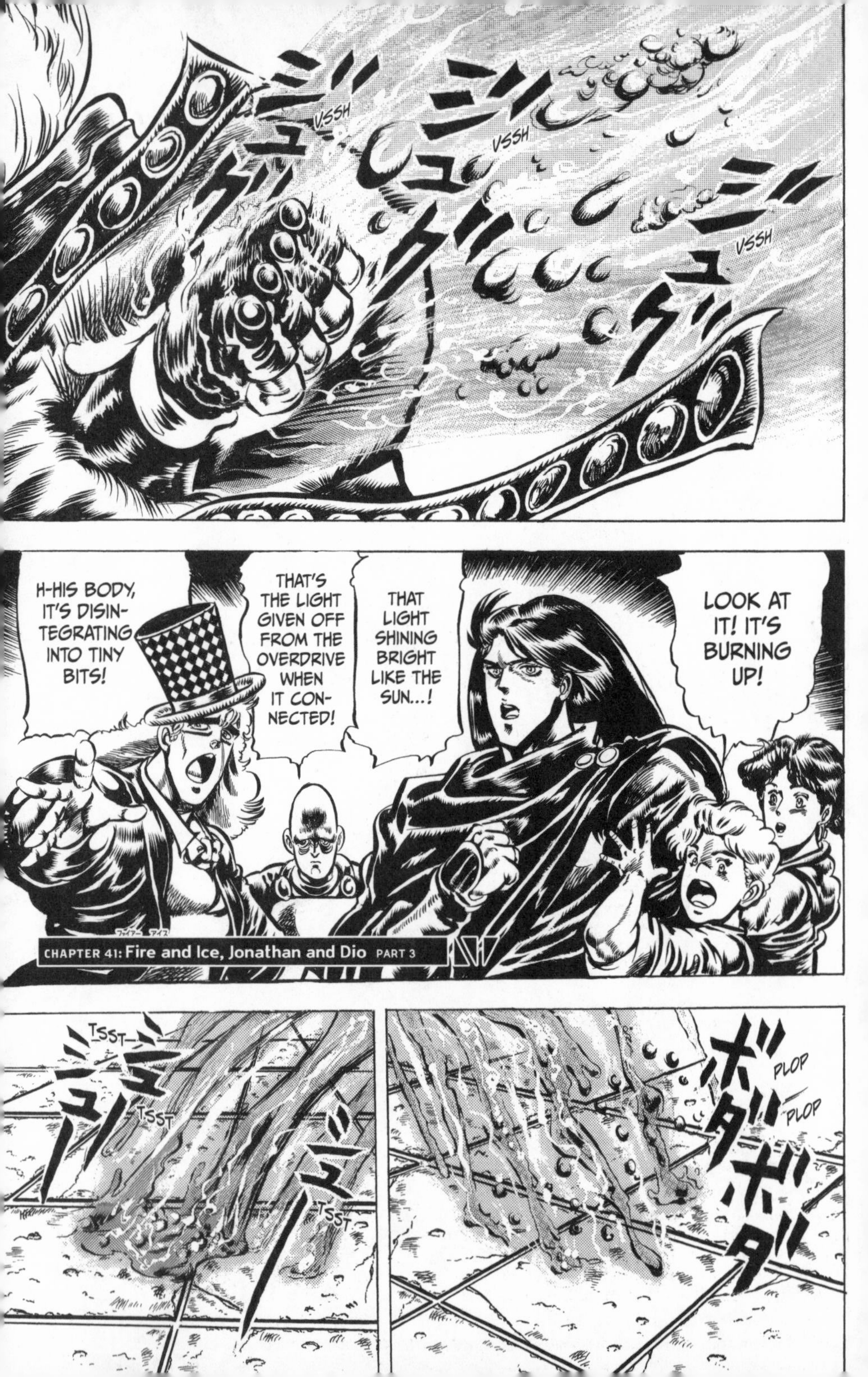
VSSH
VSSH
VSSH
LOOK AT IT! IT'S BURNING UP!
THAT LIGHT SHINING BRIGHT LIKE THE SUN...!
THAT'S THE LIGHT GIVEN OFF FROM THE OVERDRIVE WHEN IT CONNECTED!
H-HIS BODY, IT'S DISINTEGRATING INTO TINY BITS!
CHAPTER 41: Fire and Ice, Jonathan and Dio PART 3
PLOP
PLOP
TSST
TSST
TSST

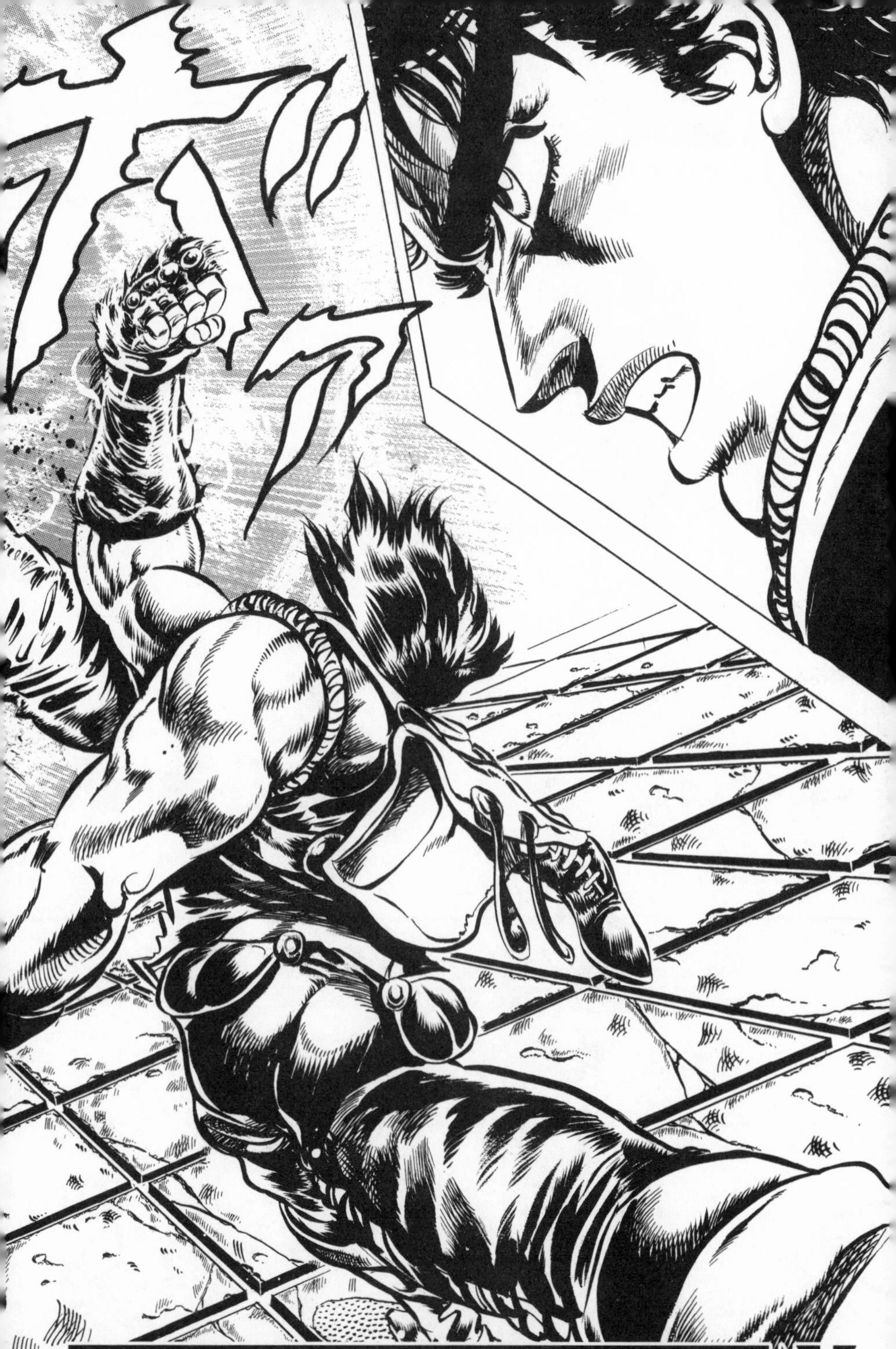

CHAPTER 41: Fire and Ice, Jonathan and Dio PART 3

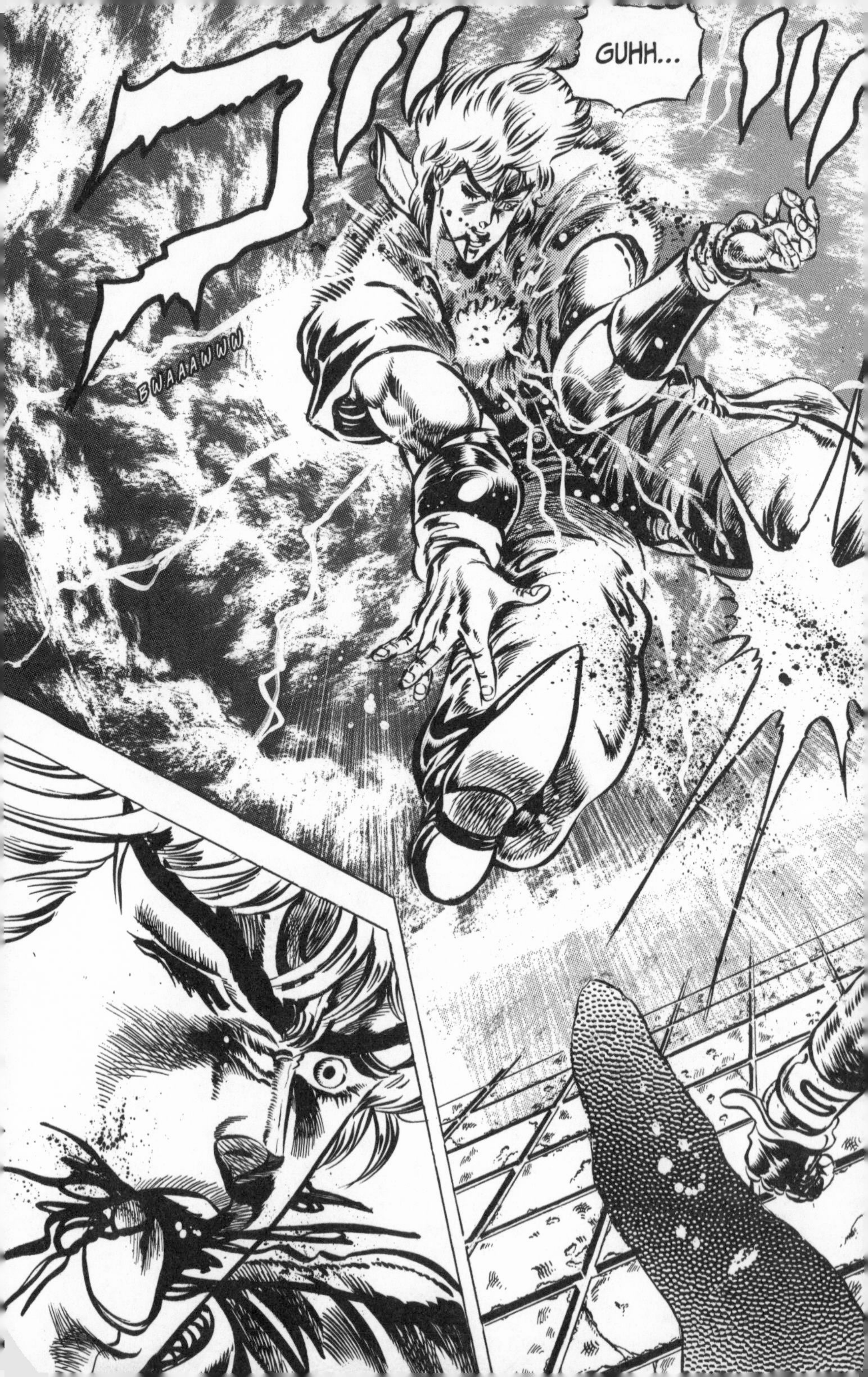
GUHH...
BWAAAAWWW

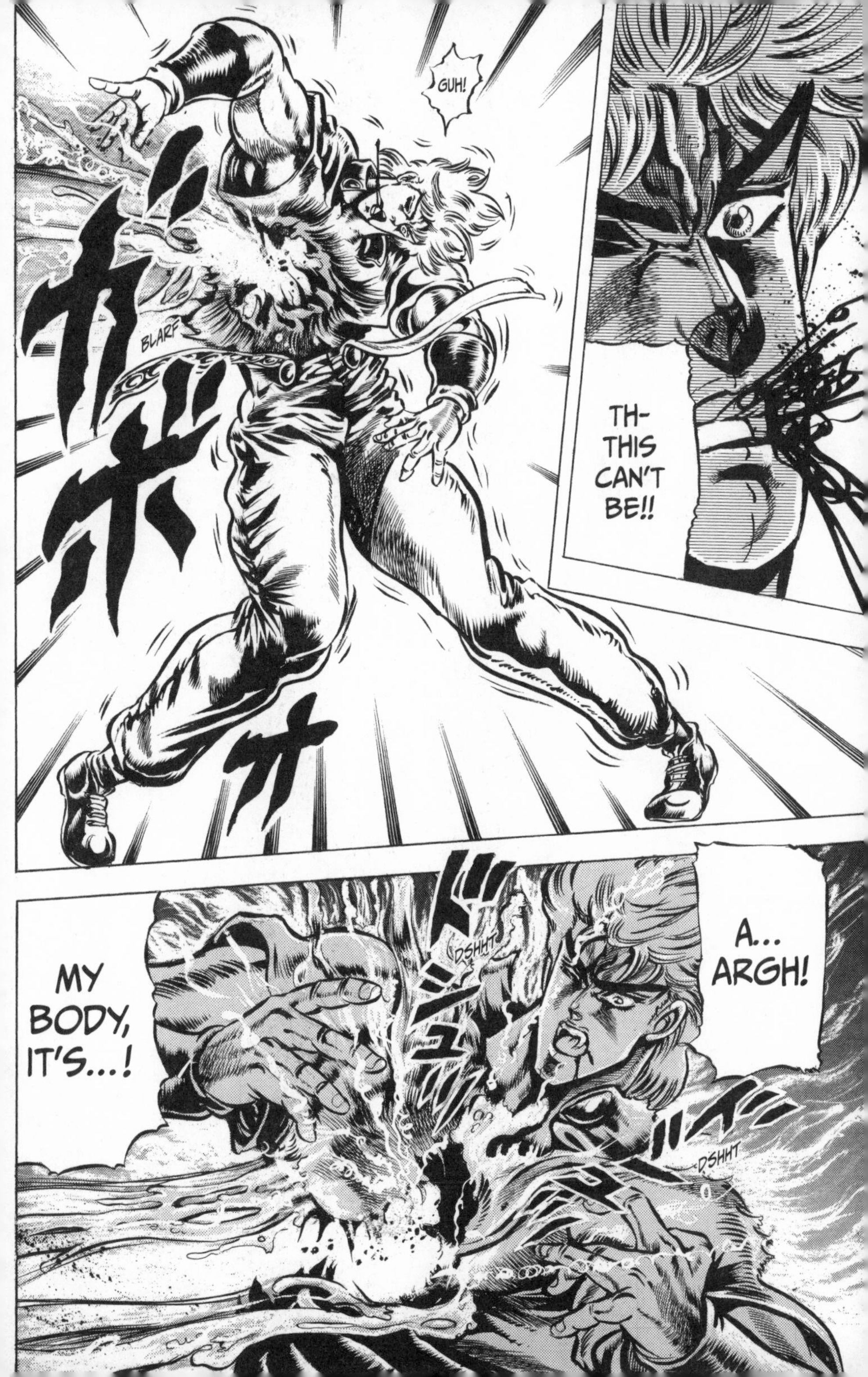
TH- THIS CAN'T BE!!
GUH!
BLARF
A... ARGH!
DSHHT
DSHHT
MY BODY, IT'S...!

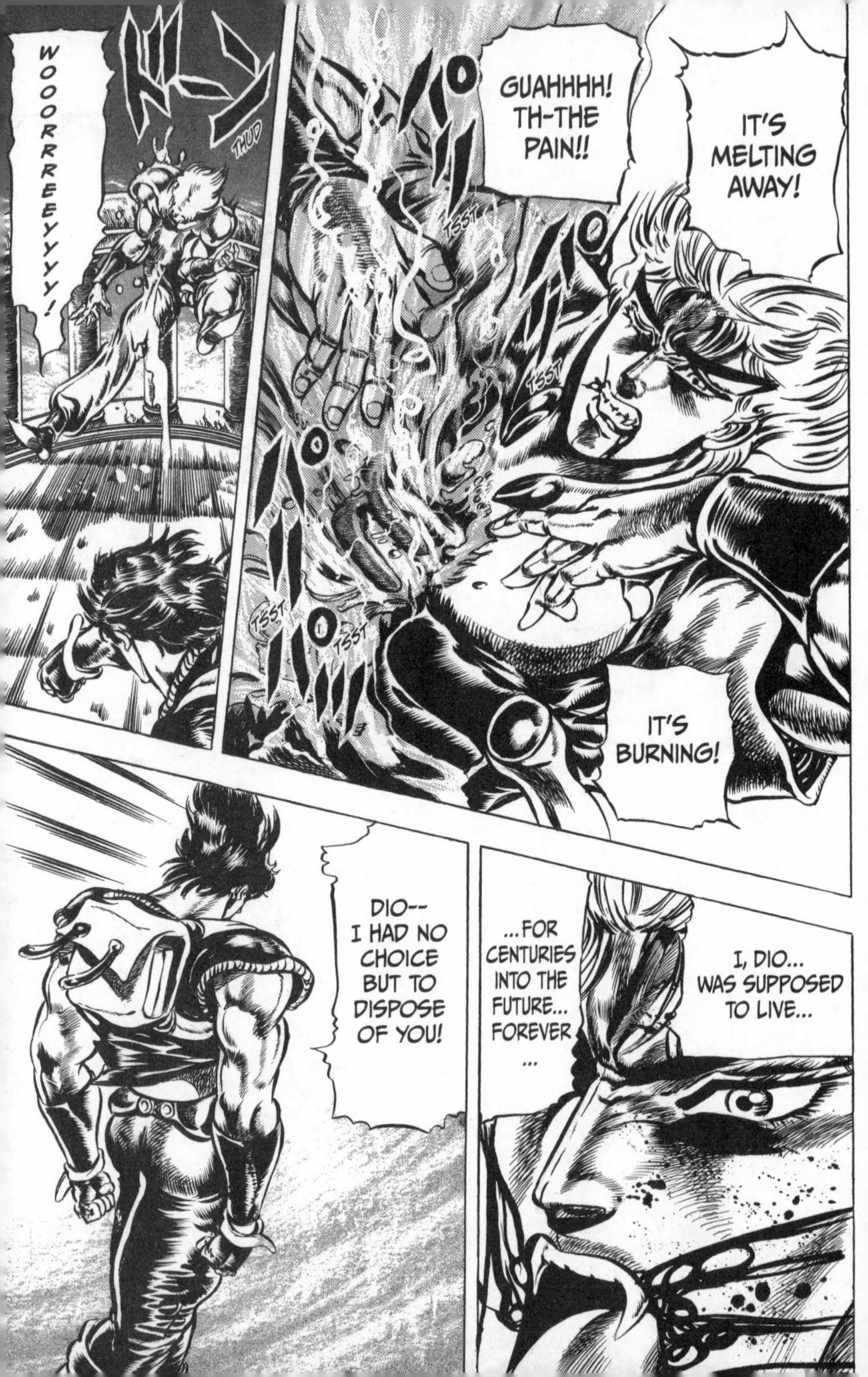
IT'S MELTING AWAY!
GUAHHHH! TH-THE PAIN!!
TSST
TSST
TSST
TSST
IT'S BURNING!
WOOORRRREEYYYY!
THUD
I, DIO... WAS SUPPOSED TO LIVE...
...FOR CENTURIES INTO THE FUTURE... FOREVER ...
DIO-- I HAD NO CHOICE BUT TO DISPOSE OF YOU!

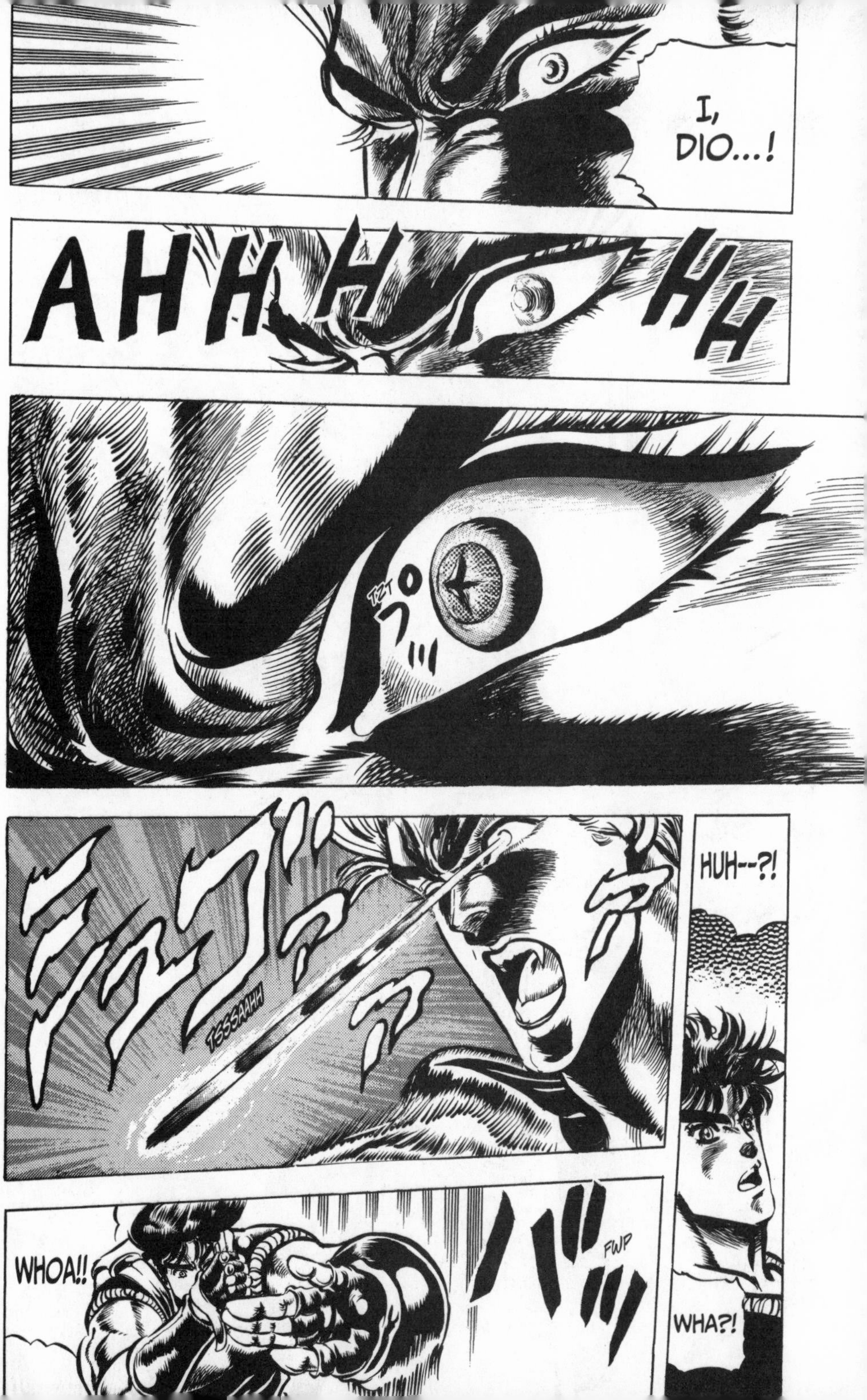
I,
DIO...!
AHHHHHH
TZT
プッ
HUH--?!
WHA?!
TSSSAAHH
FWP
バッ
WHOA!!

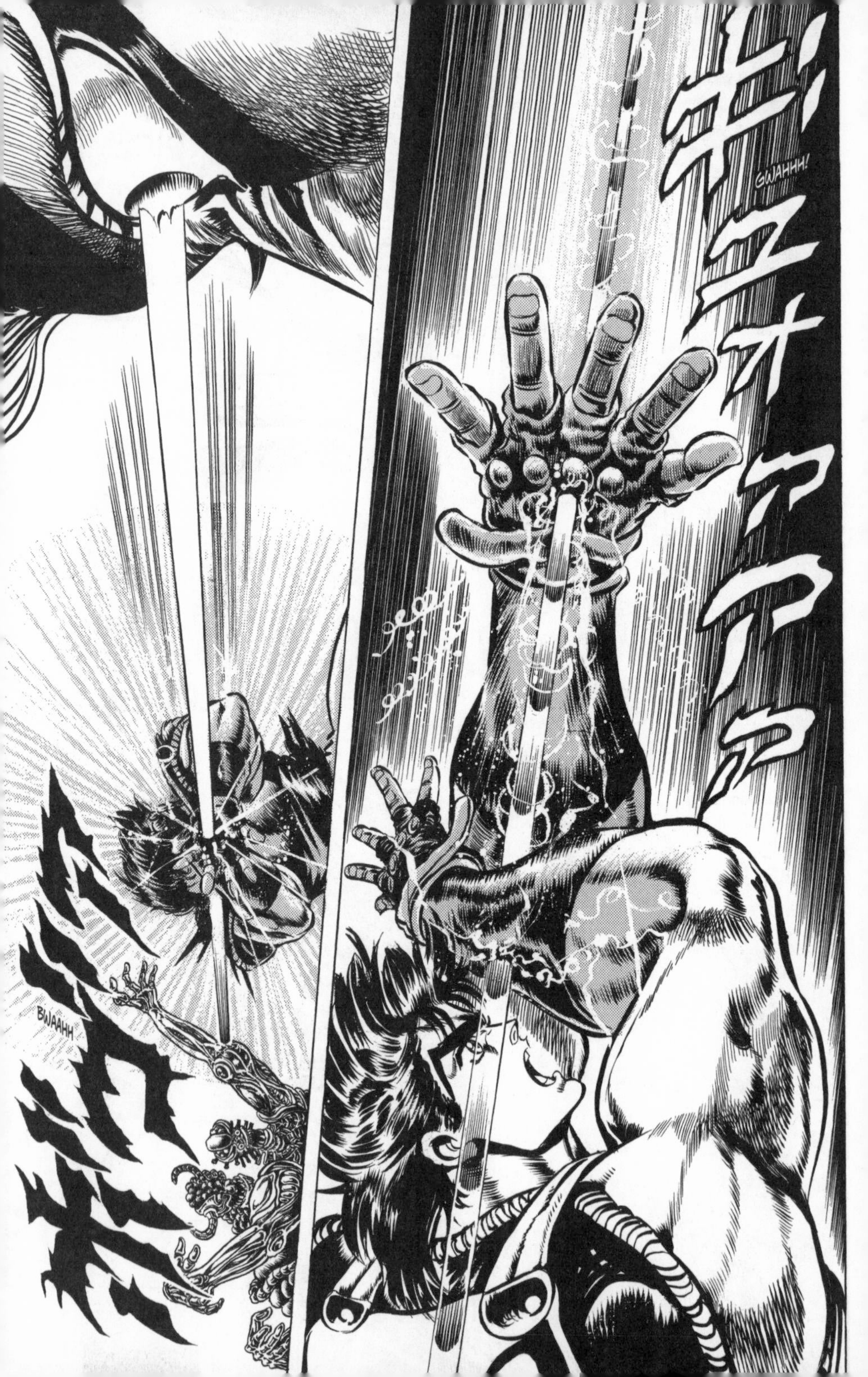
GWAHHH!
BWAAHH

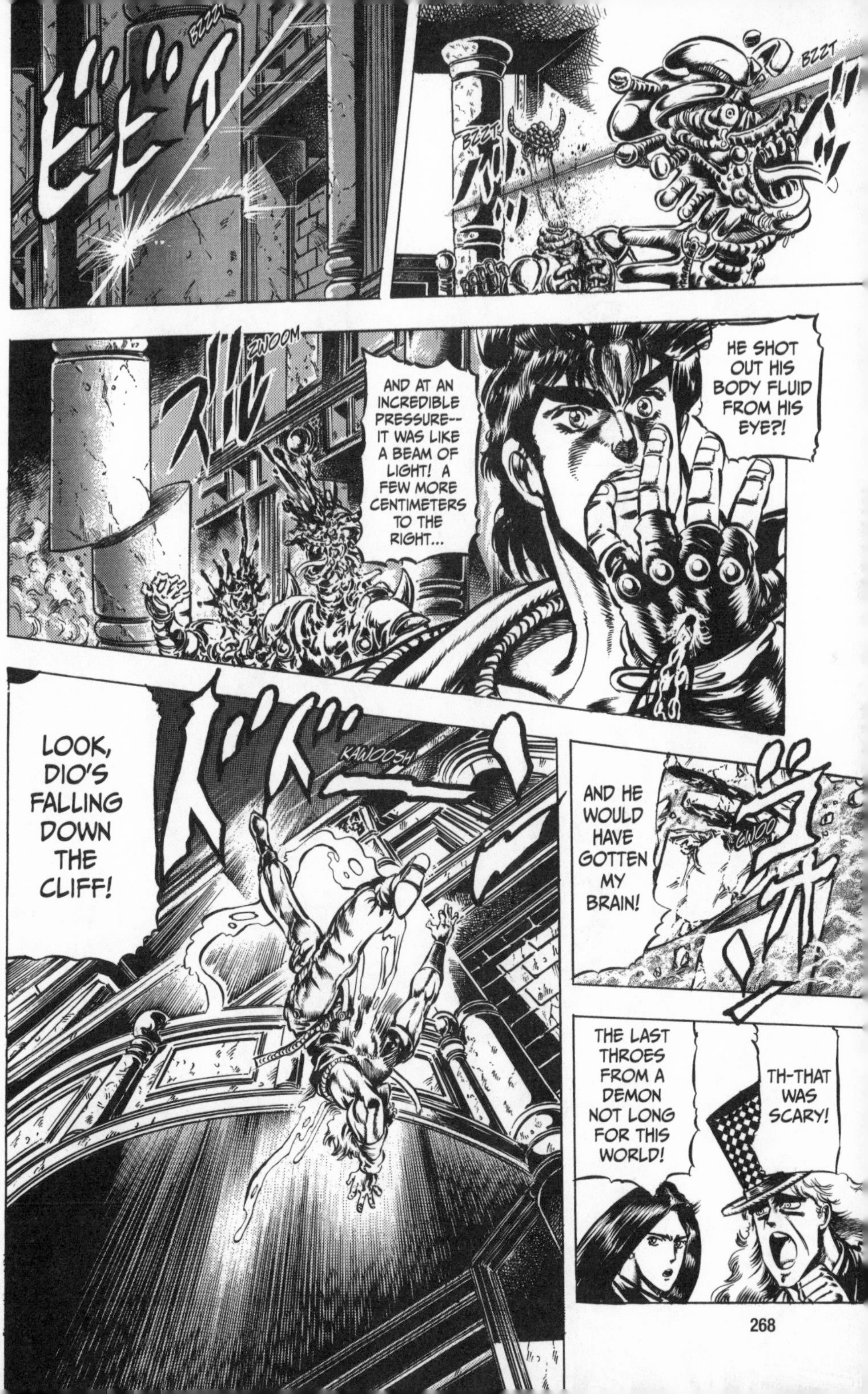
BZZT
BZZT
BZZT
HE SHOT OUT HIS BODY FLUID FROM HIS EYE?!
AND AT AN INCREDIBLE PRESSURE-- IT WAS LIKE A BEAM OF LIGHT! A FEW MORE CENTIMETERS TO THE RIGHT...
ZWOOM
AND HE WOULD HAVE GOTTEN MY BRAIN!
GWOO
TH-THAT WAS SCARY!
THE LAST THROES FROM A DEMON NOT LONG FOR THIS WORLD!
KAWOOSH
LOOK, DIO'S FALLING DOWN THE CLIFF!

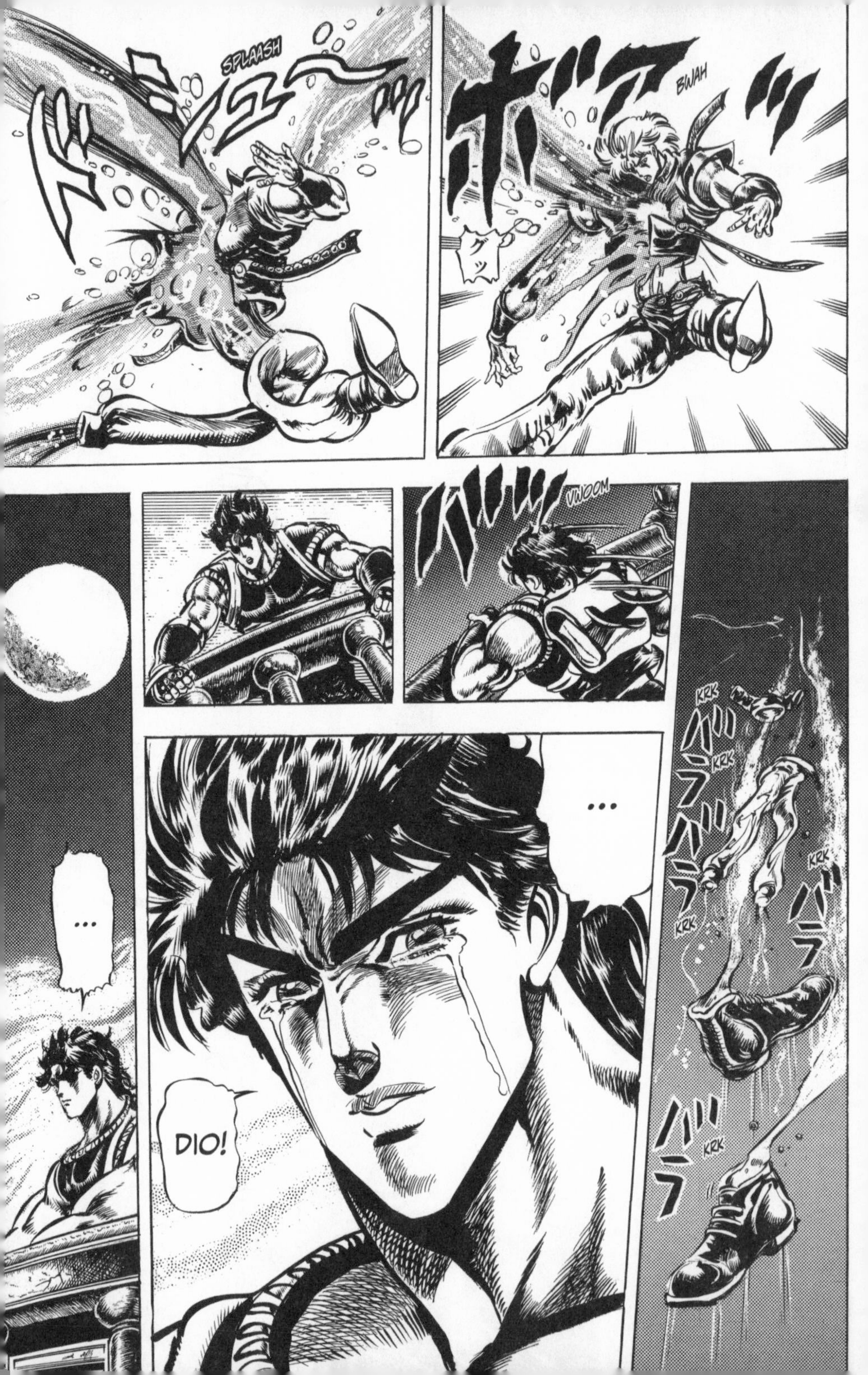
BWAH
グッ
SPLAASH
KRK
KRK
KRK
KRK
KRK
VWOOM
...
DIO!
...

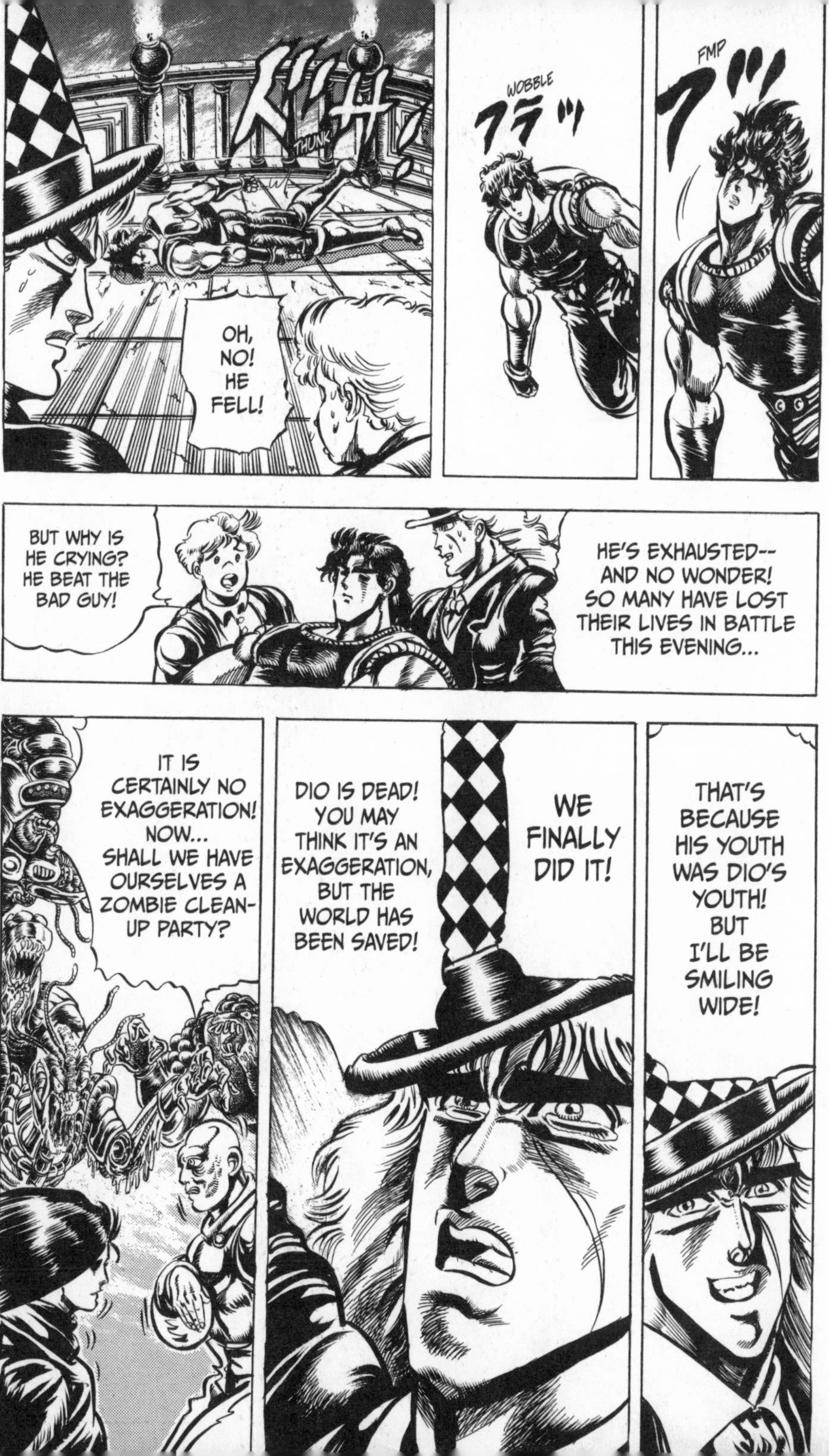
FMP
WOBBLE
フラッ
THUNK
OH, NO! HE FELL!
HE'S EXHAUSTED-- AND NO WONDER! SO MANY HAVE LOST THEIR LIVES IN BATTLE THIS EVENING...
BUT WHY IS HE CRYING? HE BEAT THE BAD GUY!
THAT'S BECAUSE HIS YOUTH WAS DIO'S YOUTH! BUT I'LL BE SMILING WIDE!
WE FINALLY DID IT!
DIO IS DEAD! YOU MAY THINK IT'S AN EXAGGERATION, BUT THE WORLD HAS BEEN SAVED!
IT IS CERTAINLY NO EXAGGERATION! NOW... SHALL WE HAVE OURSELVES A ZOMBIE CLEAN-UP PARTY?

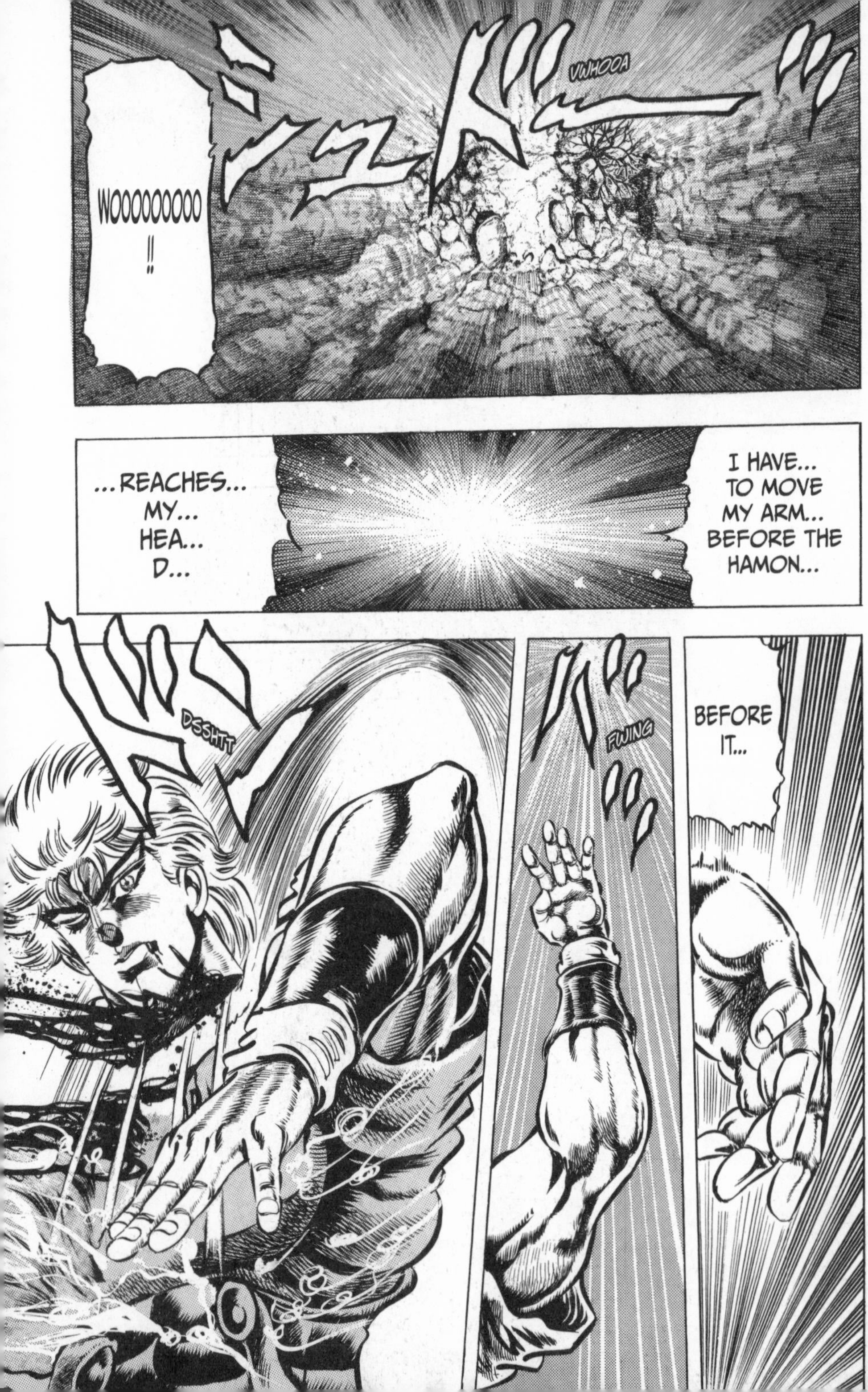
WOOOOOOOOO!!
VWHOOA
I HAVE... TO MOVE MY ARM... BEFORE THE HAMON...
...REACHES... MY... HEA... D...
BEFORE IT...
FWING
DSSHTT

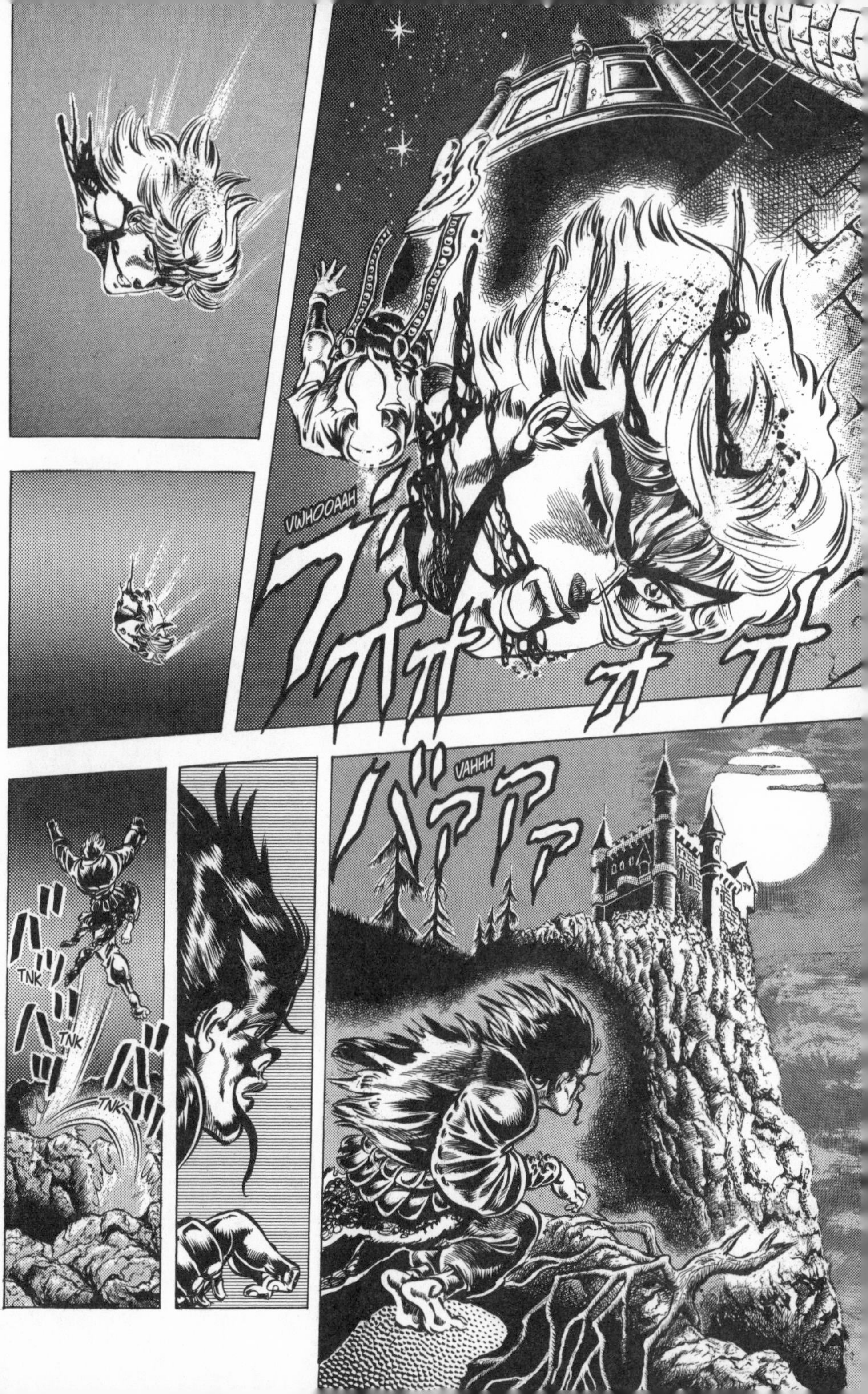
VWHOOAAH
フォオオオ
VAHHH
バァアア
TNK
TNK
TNK
バッバッバッ

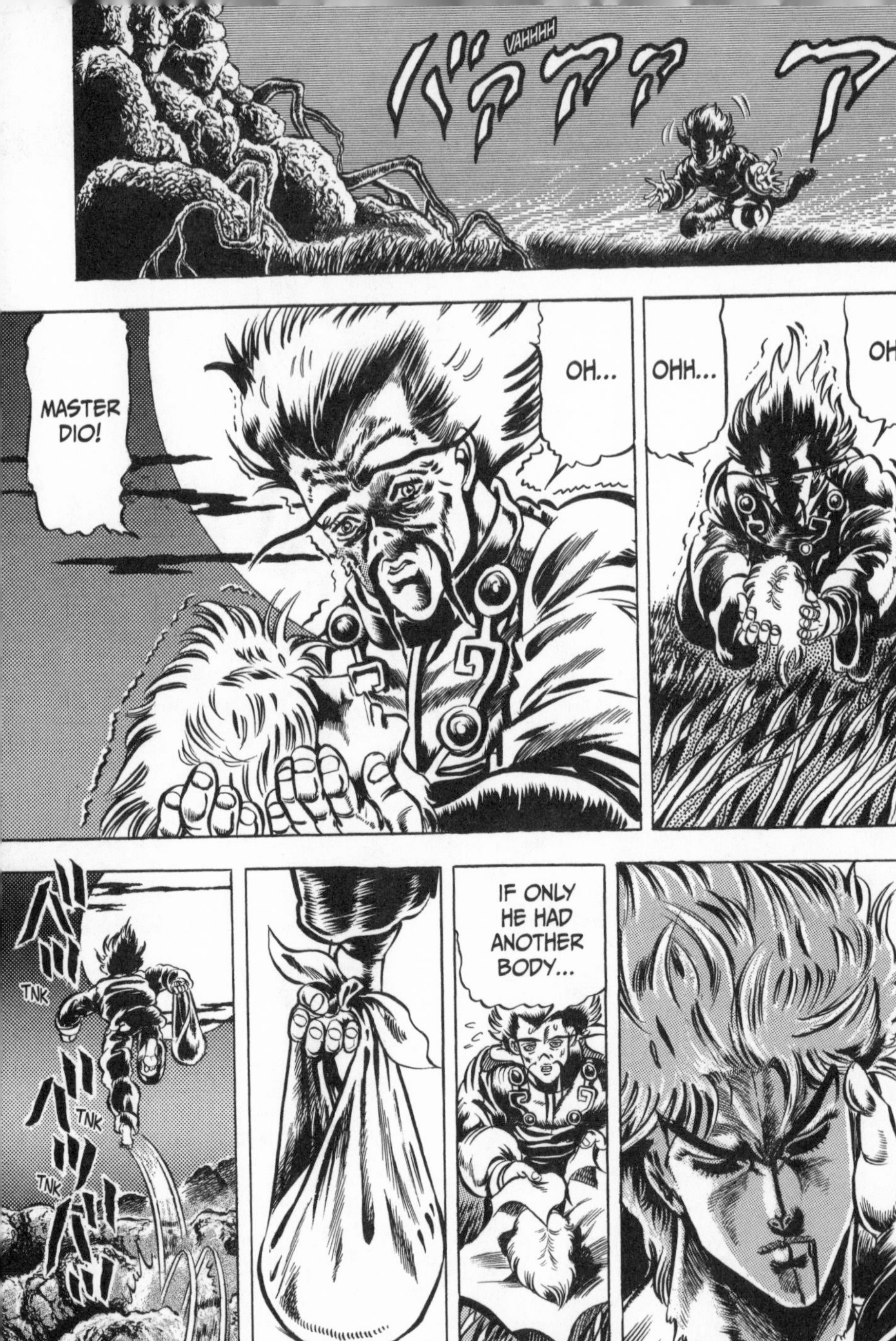
バァアア ア
VAHHHH
OH...
OHH...
OH...
MASTER DIO!
IF ONLY HE HAD ANOTHER BODY...
TNK
TNK
TNK

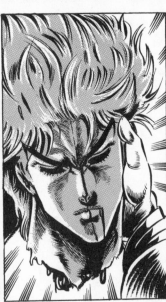

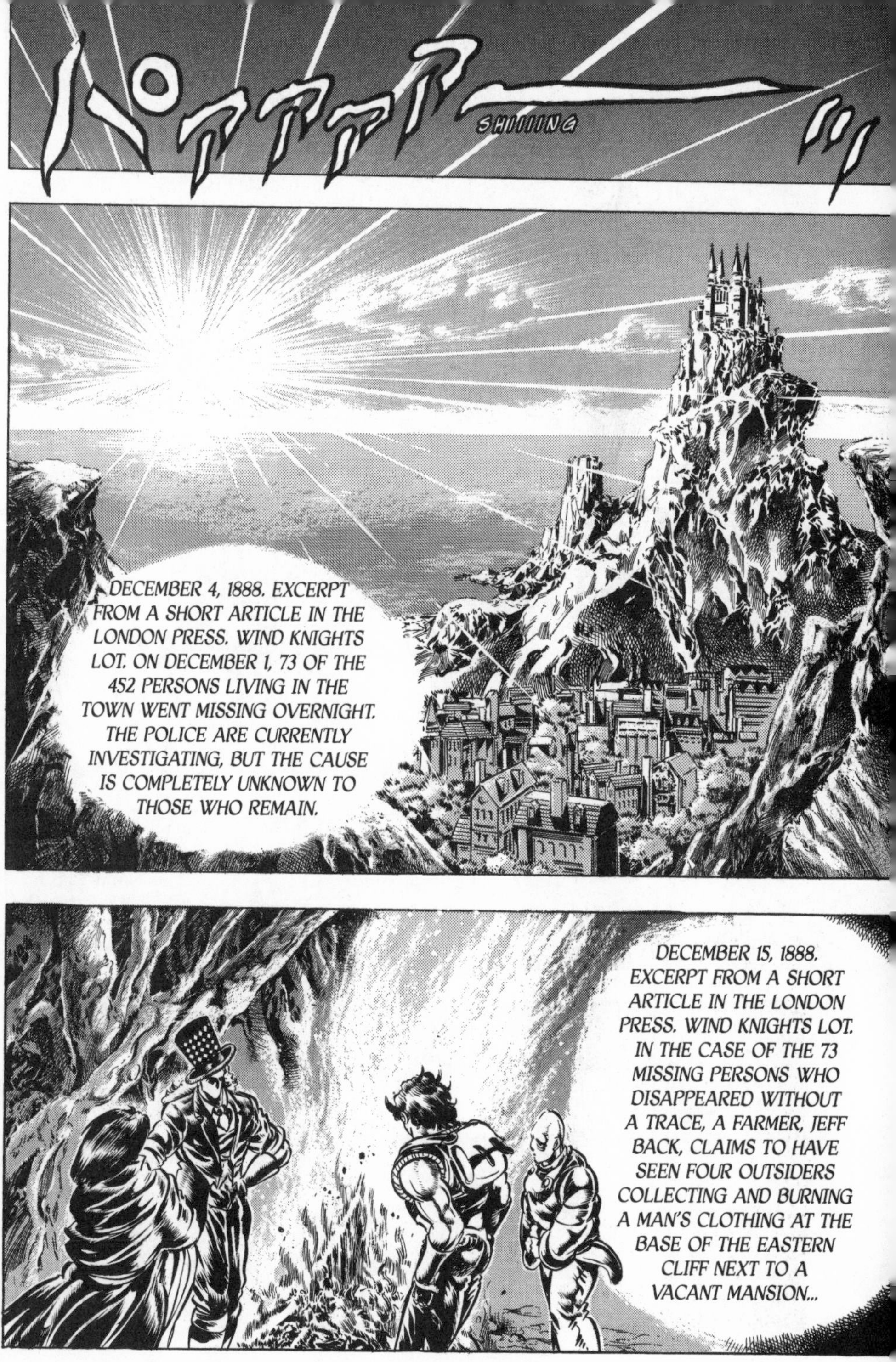
パァァァアーーーッ
SHIIIING
DECEMBER 4, 1888. EXCERPT FROM A SHORT ARTICLE IN THE LONDON PRESS. WIND KNIGHTS LOT. ON DECEMBER 1, 73 OF THE 452 PERSONS LIVING IN THE TOWN WENT MISSING OVERNIGHT. THE POLICE ARE CURRENTLY INVESTIGATING, BUT THE CAUSE IS COMPLETELY UNKNOWN TO THOSE WHO REMAIN.
DECEMBER 15, 1888. EXCERPT FROM A SHORT ARTICLE IN THE LONDON PRESS. WIND KNIGHTS LOT. IN THE CASE OF THE 73 MISSING PERSONS WHO DISAPPEARED WITHOUT A TRACE, A FARMER, JEFF BACK, CLAIMS TO HAVE SEEN FOUR OUTSIDERS COLLECTING AND BURNING A MAN'S CLOTHING AT THE BASE OF THE EASTERN CLIFF NEXT TO A VACANT MANSION...

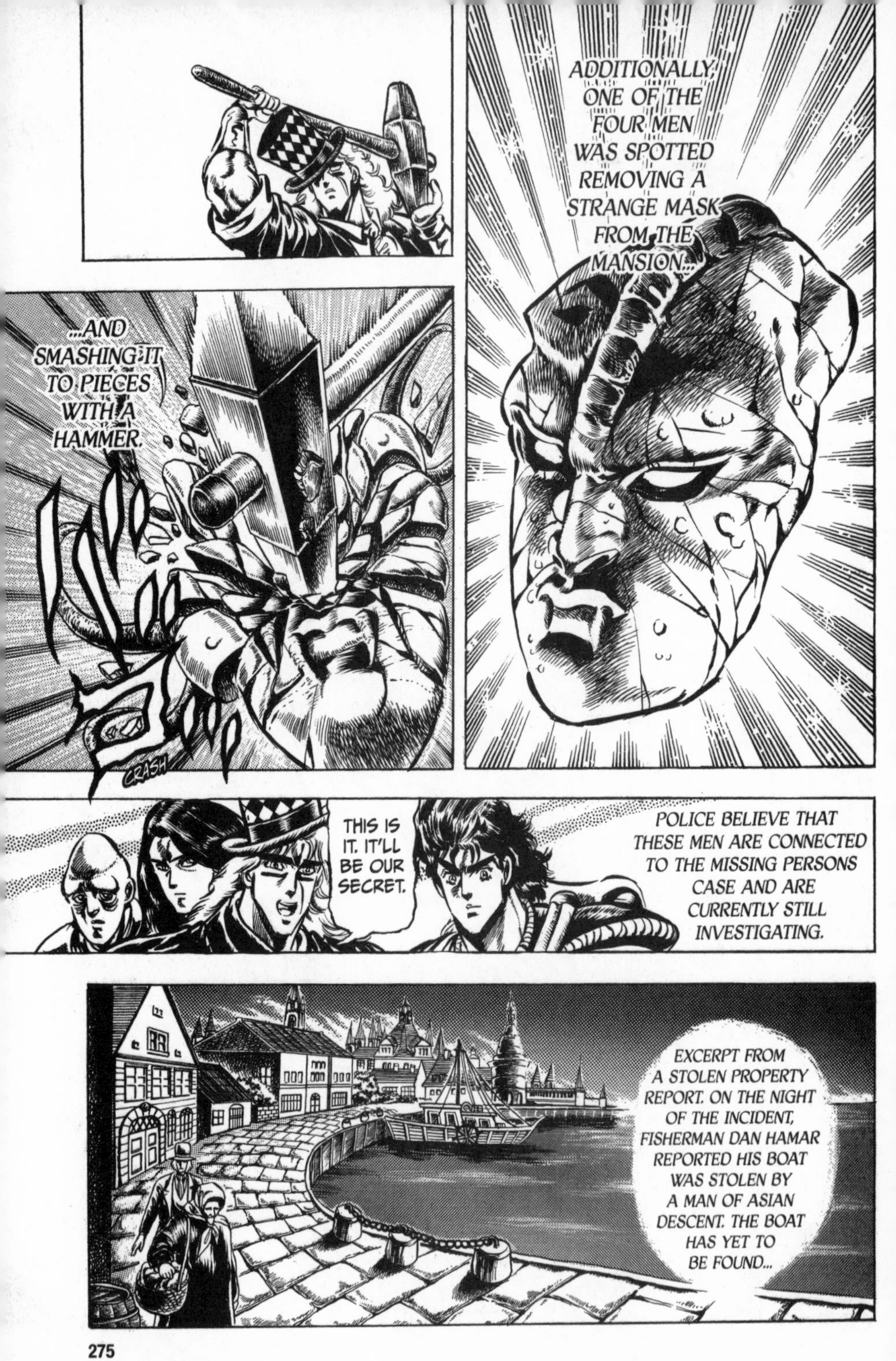
ADDITIONALLY, ONE OF THE FOUR MEN WAS SPOTTED REMOVING A STRANGE MASK FROM THE MANSION...
...AND SMASHING IT TO PIECES WITH A HAMMER.
CRASH
POLICE BELIEVE THAT THESE MEN ARE CONNECTED TO THE MISSING PERSONS CASE AND ARE CURRENTLY STILL INVESTIGATING.
THIS IS IT. IT'LL BE OUR SECRET.
EXCERPT FROM A STOLEN PROPERTY REPORT. ON THE NIGHT OF THE INCIDENT, FISHERMAN DAN HAMAR REPORTED HIS BOAT WAS STOLEN BY A MAN OF ASIAN DESCENT. THE BOAT HAS YET TO BE FOUND...

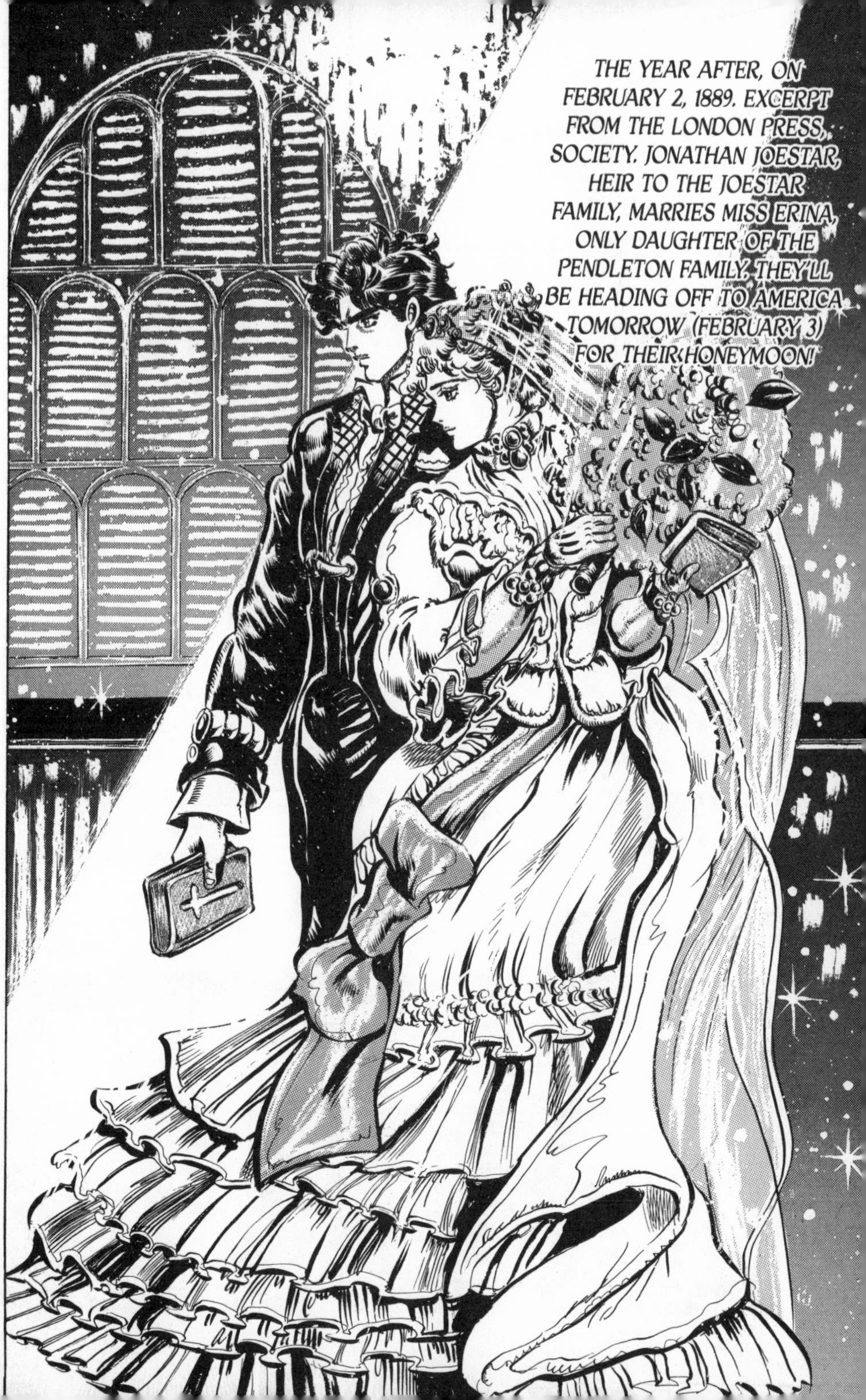
THE YEAR AFTER, ON FEBRUARY 2, 1889. EXCERPT FROM THE LONDON PRESS, SOCIETY. JONATHAN JOESTAR, HEIR TO THE JOESTAR FAMILY, MARRIES MISS ERINA, ONLY DAUGHTER OF THE PENDLETON FAMILY. THEY'LL BE HEADING OFF TO AMERICA TOMORROW (FEBRUARY 3) FOR THEIR HONEYMOON!

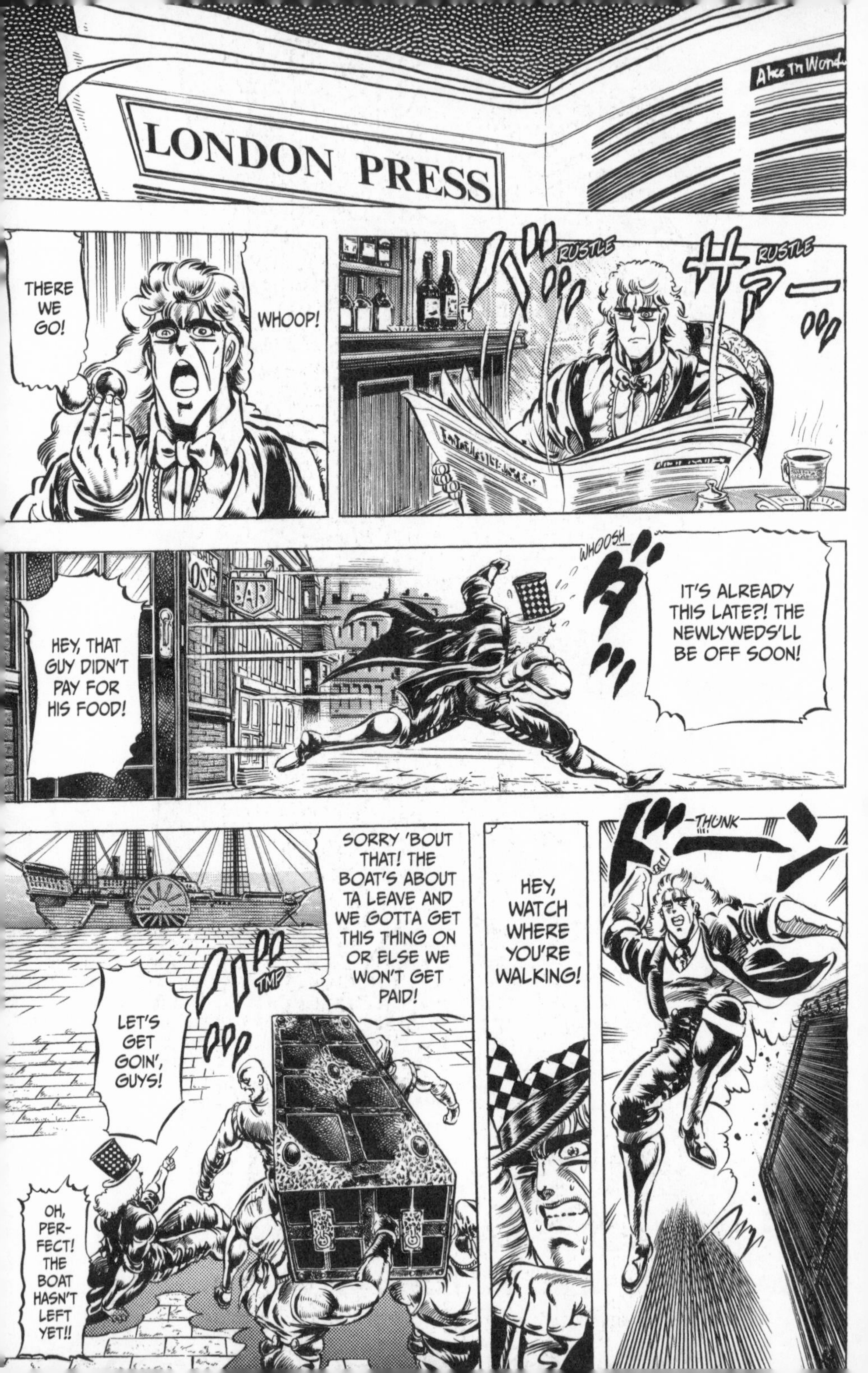
LONDON PRESS
RUSTLE
RUSTLE
THERE WE GO!
WHOOP!
WHOOSH
IT'S ALREADY THIS LATE?! THE NEWLYWEDS'LL BE OFF SOON!
HEY, THAT GUY DIDN'T PAY FOR HIS FOOD!
THUNK
HEY, WATCH WHERE YOU'RE WALKING!
SORRY 'BOUT THAT! THE BOAT'S ABOUT TA LEAVE AND WE GOTTA GET THIS THING ON OR ELSE WE WON'T GET PAID!
TMP
LET'S GET GOIN', GUYS!
OH, PER-FECT! THE BOAT HASN'T LEFT YET!!

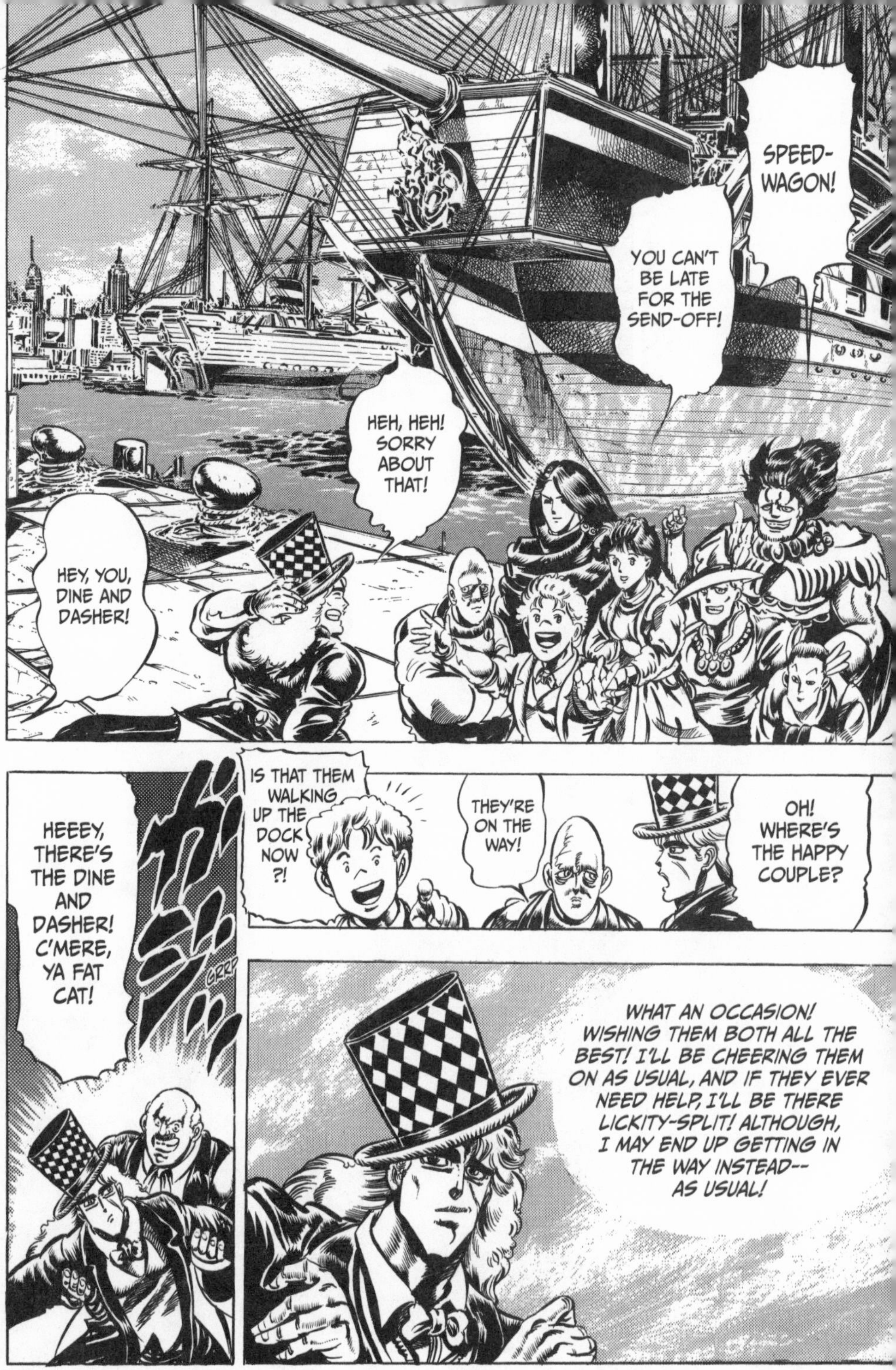
SPEED-WAGON!
YOU CAN'T BE LATE FOR THE SEND-OFF!
HEH, HEH! SORRY ABOUT THAT!
HEY, YOU, DINE AND DASHER!
OH! WHERE'S THE HAPPY COUPLE?
THEY'RE ON THE WAY!
IS THAT THEM WALKING UP THE DOCK NOW ?!
WHAT AN OCCASION! WISHING THEM BOTH ALL THE BEST! I'LL BE CHEERING THEM ON AS USUAL, AND IF THEY EVER NEED HELP, I'LL BE THERE LICKITY-SPLIT! ALTHOUGH, I MAY END UP GETTING IN THE WAY INSTEAD-- AS USUAL!
HEEEY, THERE'S THE DINE AND DASHER! C'MERE, YA FAT CAT!
GRRP

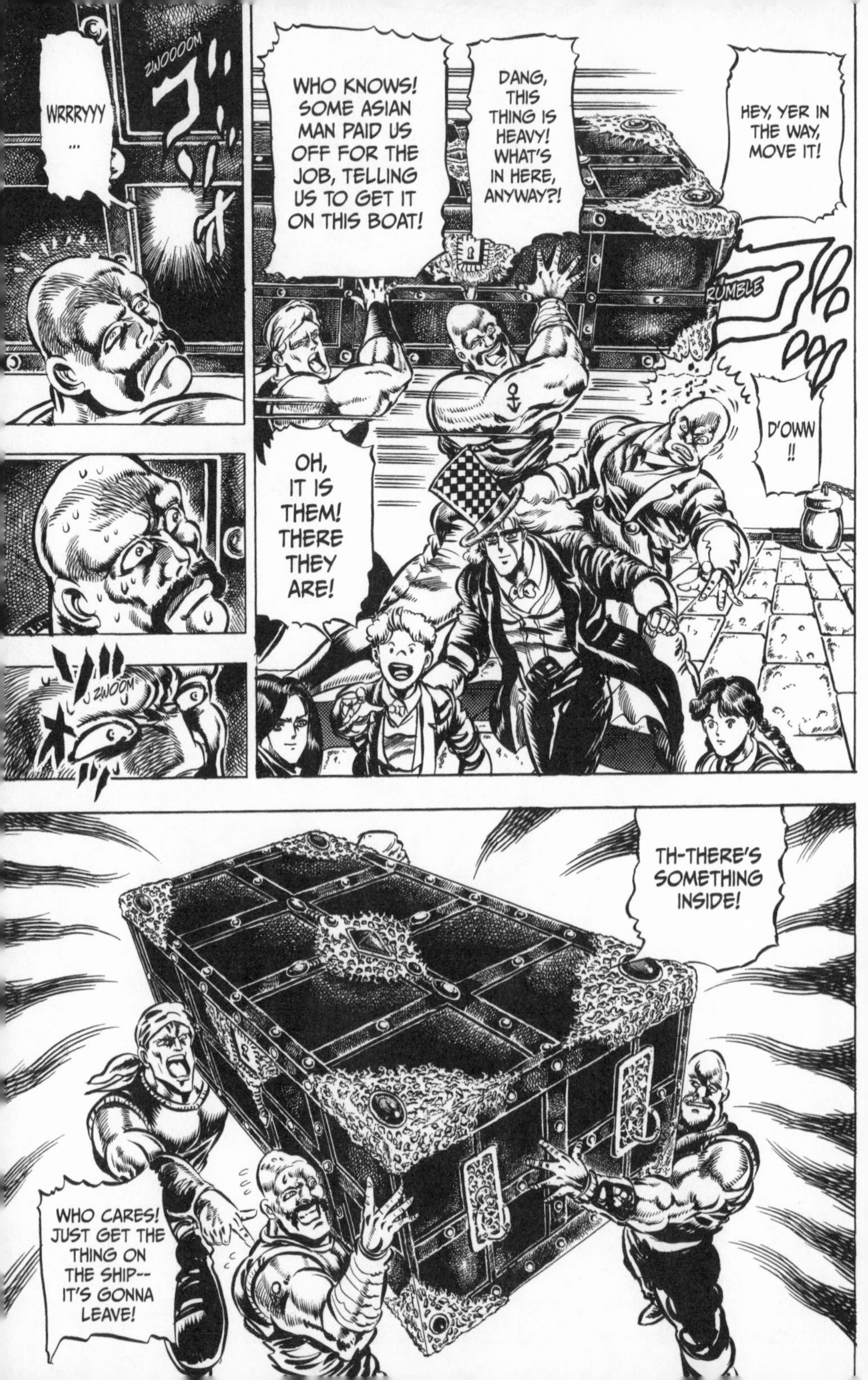
HEY, YER IN THE WAY, MOVE IT!
DANG, THIS THING IS HEAVY! WHAT'S IN HERE, ANYWAY?!
WHO KNOWS! SOME ASIAN MAN PAID US OFF FOR THE JOB, TELLING US TO GET IT ON THIS BOAT!
RUMBLE
D'OWW !!
OH, IT IS THEM! THERE THEY ARE!
WRRRYYY ...
ZWOOOOM
ZWOOM
TH-THERE'S SOMETHING INSIDE!
WHO CARES! JUST GET THE THING ON THE SHIP-- IT'S GONNA LEAVE!

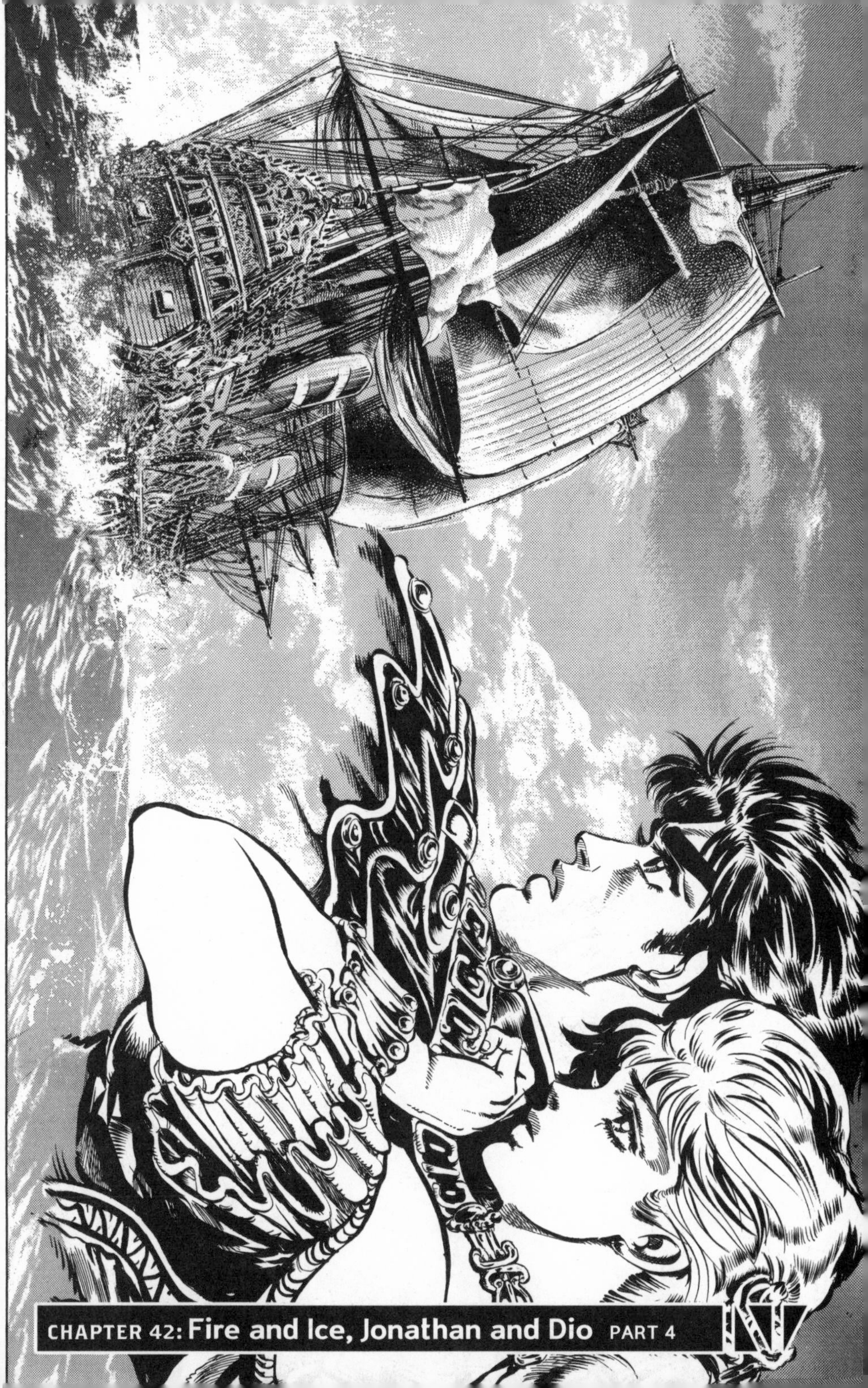

CHAPTER 42: Fire and Ice, Jonathan and Dio PART 4

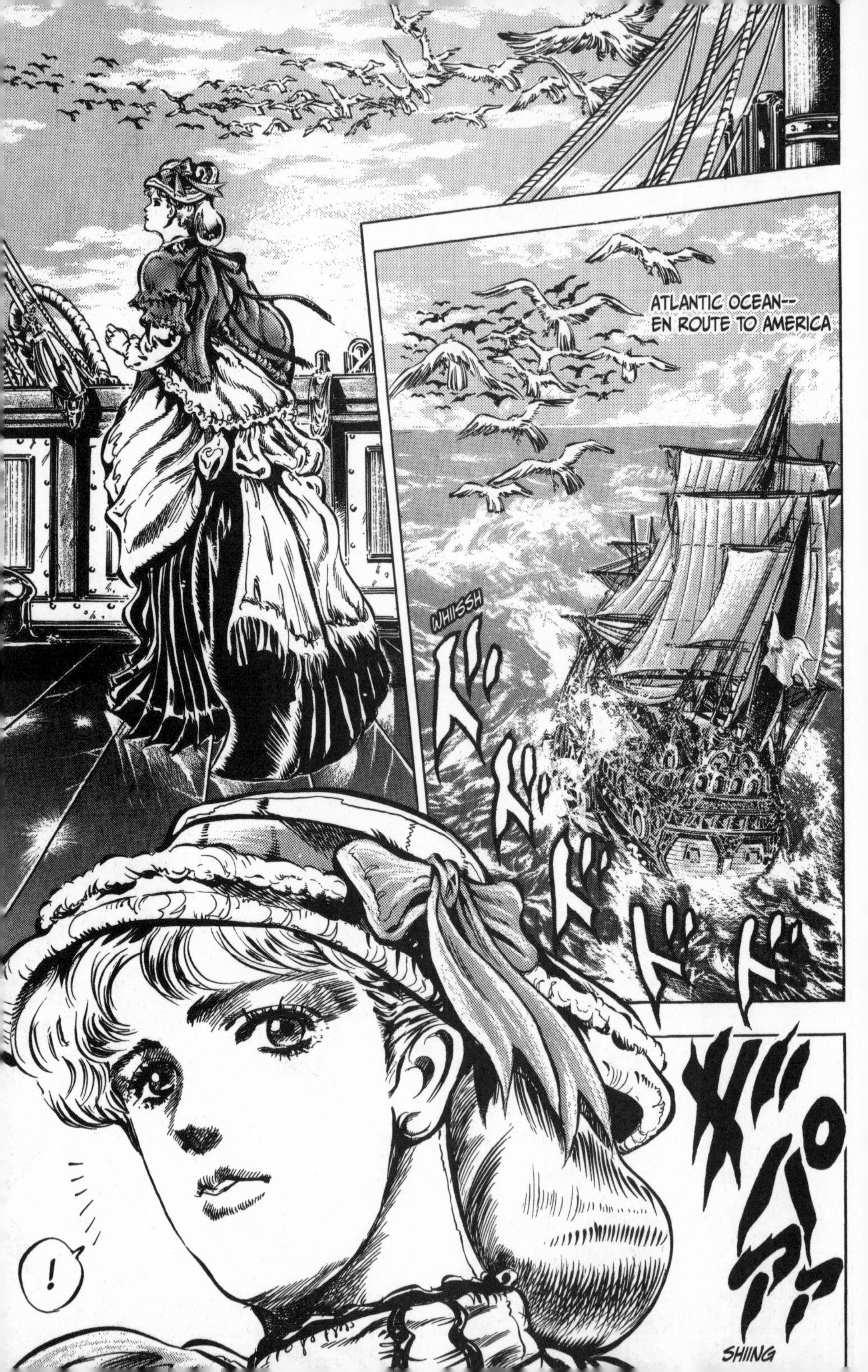
ATLANTIC OCEAN--
EN ROUTE TO AMERICA
WHIISSH
SHIING
!

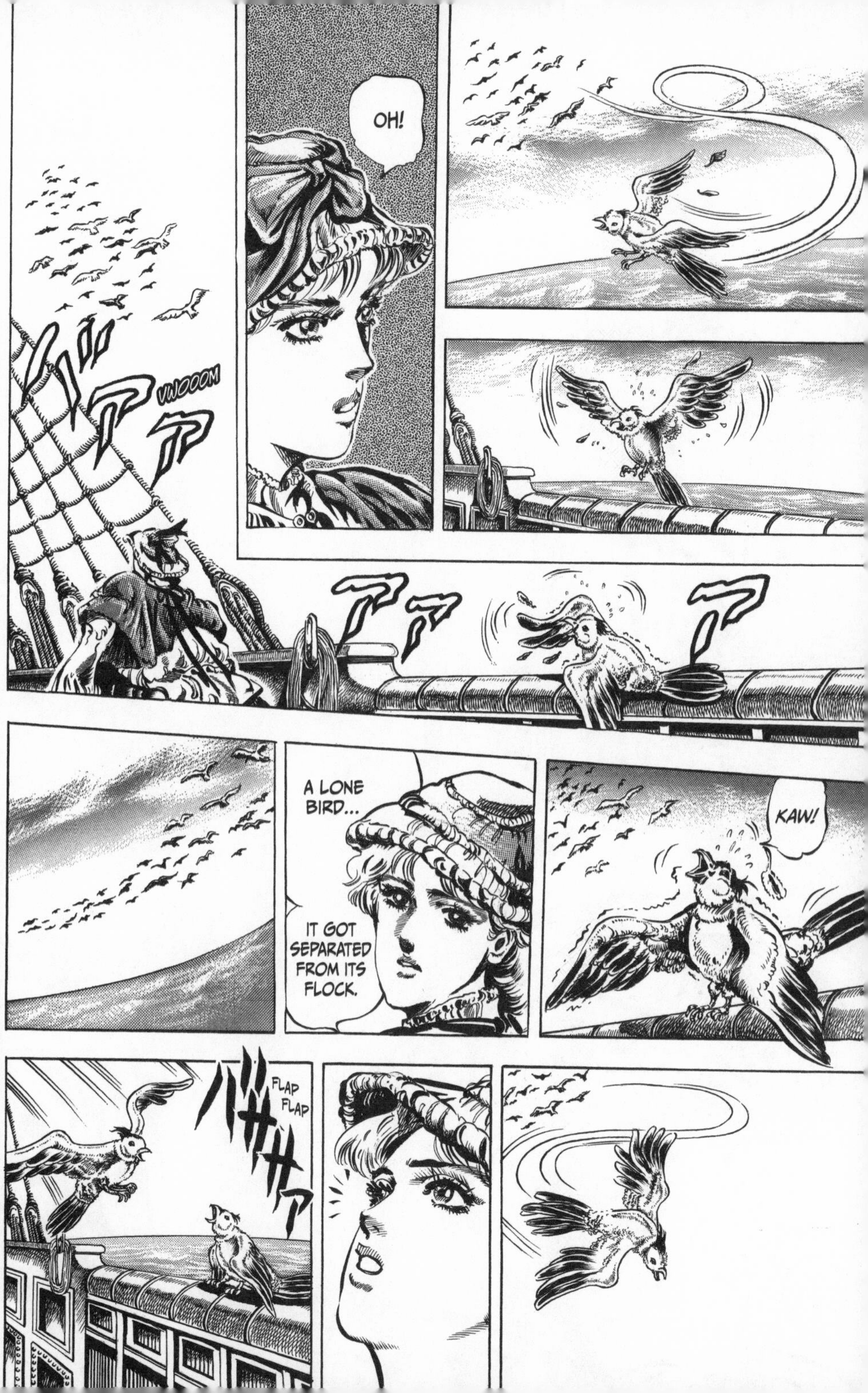
OH!
VWOOOM
KAW!
A LONE BIRD...
IT GOT SEPARATED FROM ITS FLOCK.
FLAP FLAP

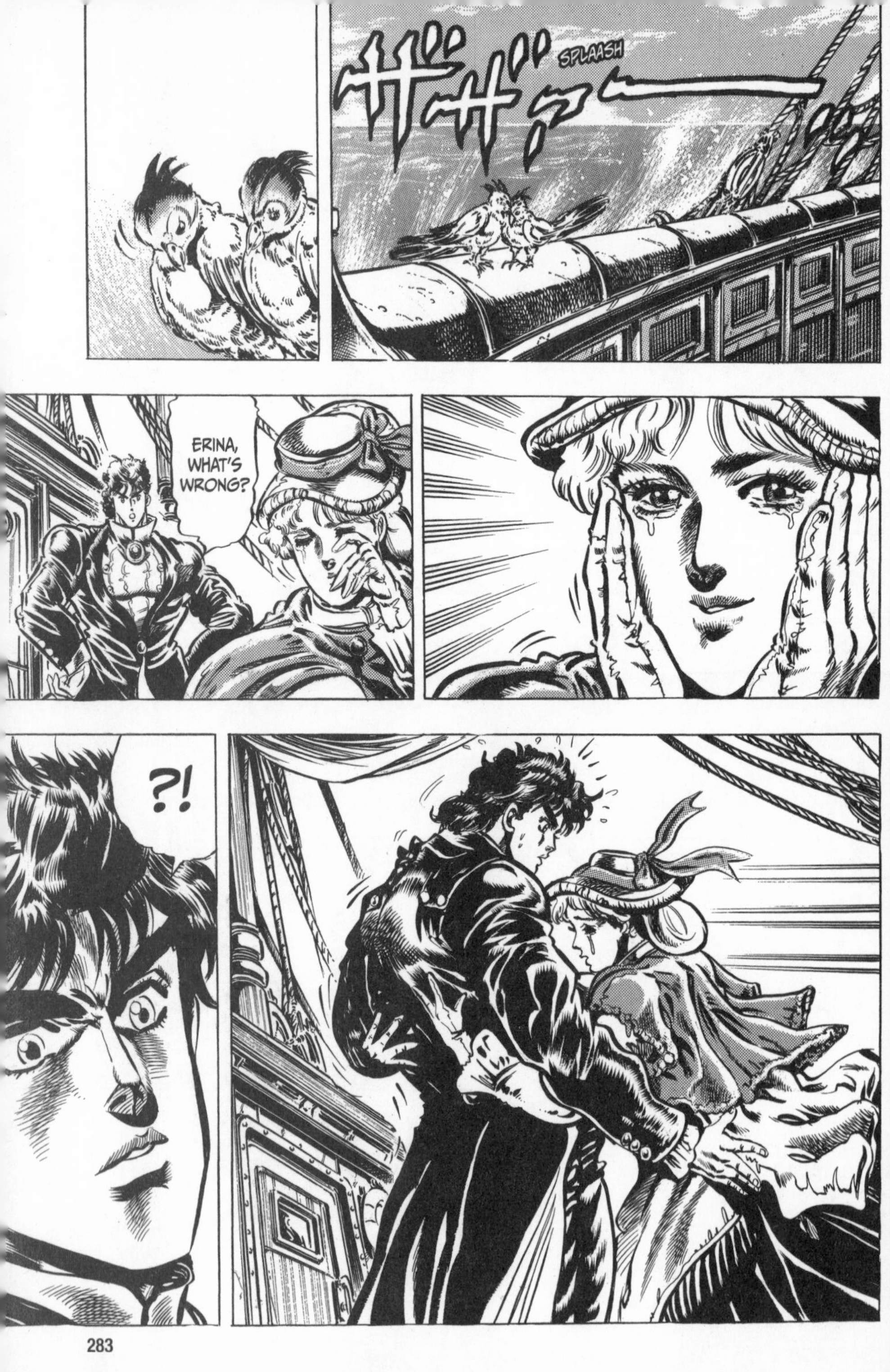
ザザァーー
SPLAASH
ERINA, WHAT'S WRONG?
?!

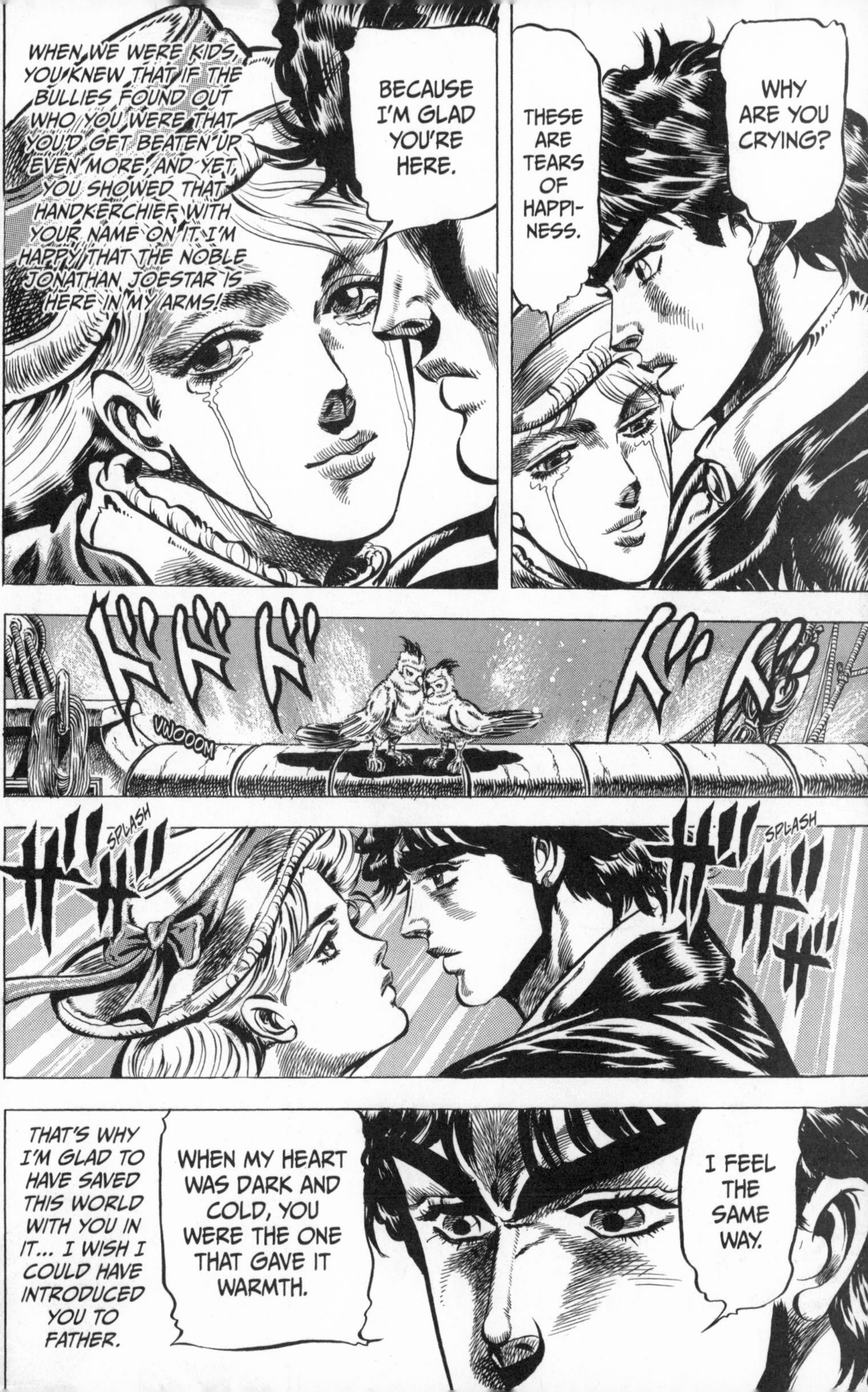
WHY ARE YOU CRYING?
THESE ARE TEARS OF HAPPINESS.
BECAUSE I'M GLAD YOU'RE HERE.
WHEN WE WERE KIDS, YOU KNEW THAT IF THE BULLIES FOUND OUT WHO YOU WERE THAT YOU'D GET BEATEN UP EVEN MORE, AND YET, YOU SHOWED THAT HANDKERCHIEF WITH YOUR NAME ON IT. I'M HAPPY THAT THE NOBLE JONATHAN JOESTAR IS HERE IN MY ARMS!
VNOOOM
SPLASH
SPLASH
I FEEL THE SAME WAY.
WHEN MY HEART WAS DARK AND COLD, YOU WERE THE ONE THAT GAVE IT WARMTH.
THAT'S WHY I'M GLAD TO HAVE SAVED THIS WORLD WITH YOU IN IT... I WISH I COULD HAVE INTRODUCED YOU TO FATHER.

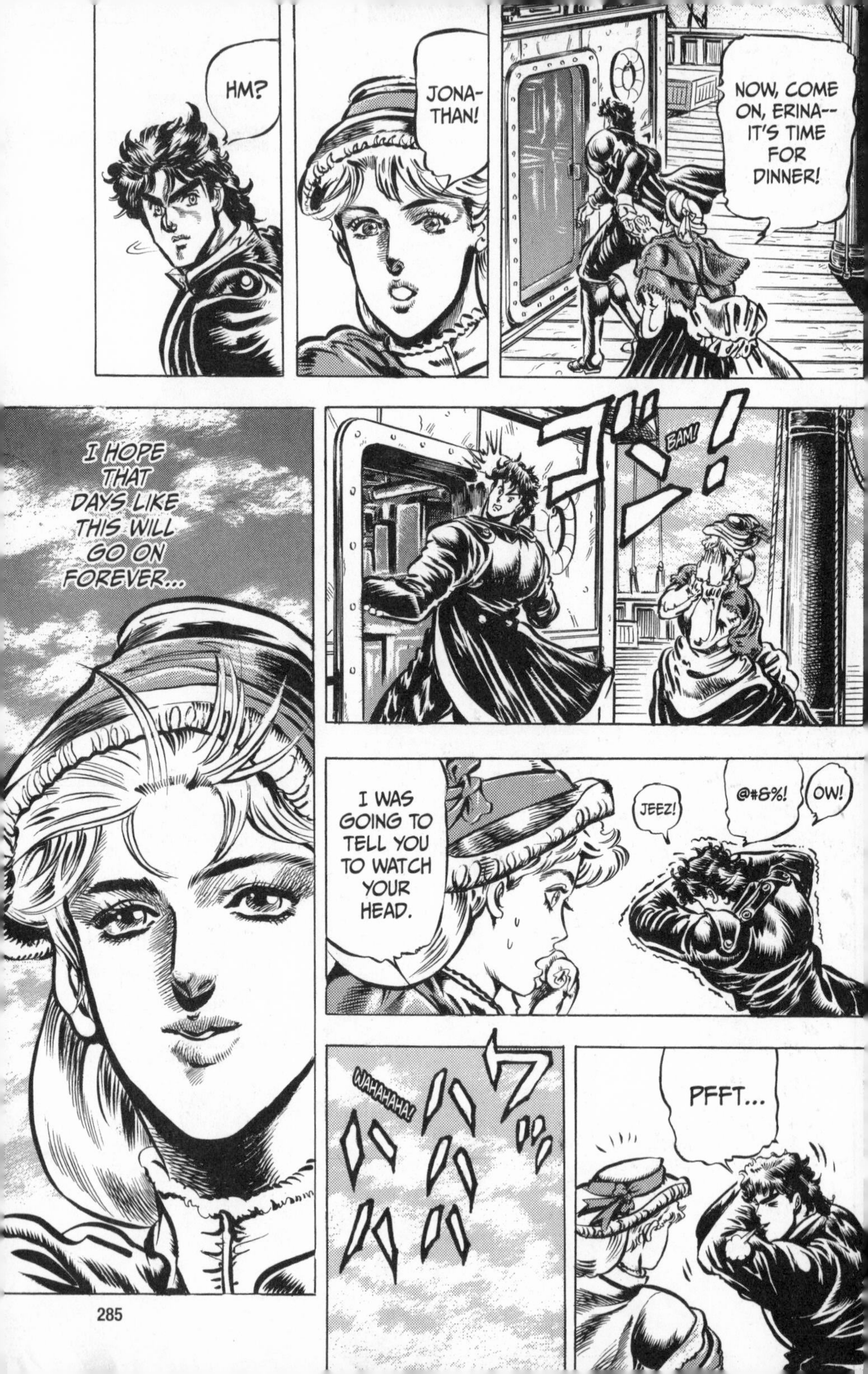
NOW, COME ON, ERINA-- IT'S TIME FOR DINNER!
JONA-THAN!
HM?
BAM!
OW!
@#8%!
JEEZ!
I WAS GOING TO TELL YOU TO WATCH YOUR HEAD.
PFFT...
WAHAHAHA!
I HOPE THAT DAYS LIKE THIS WILL GO ON FOREVER...

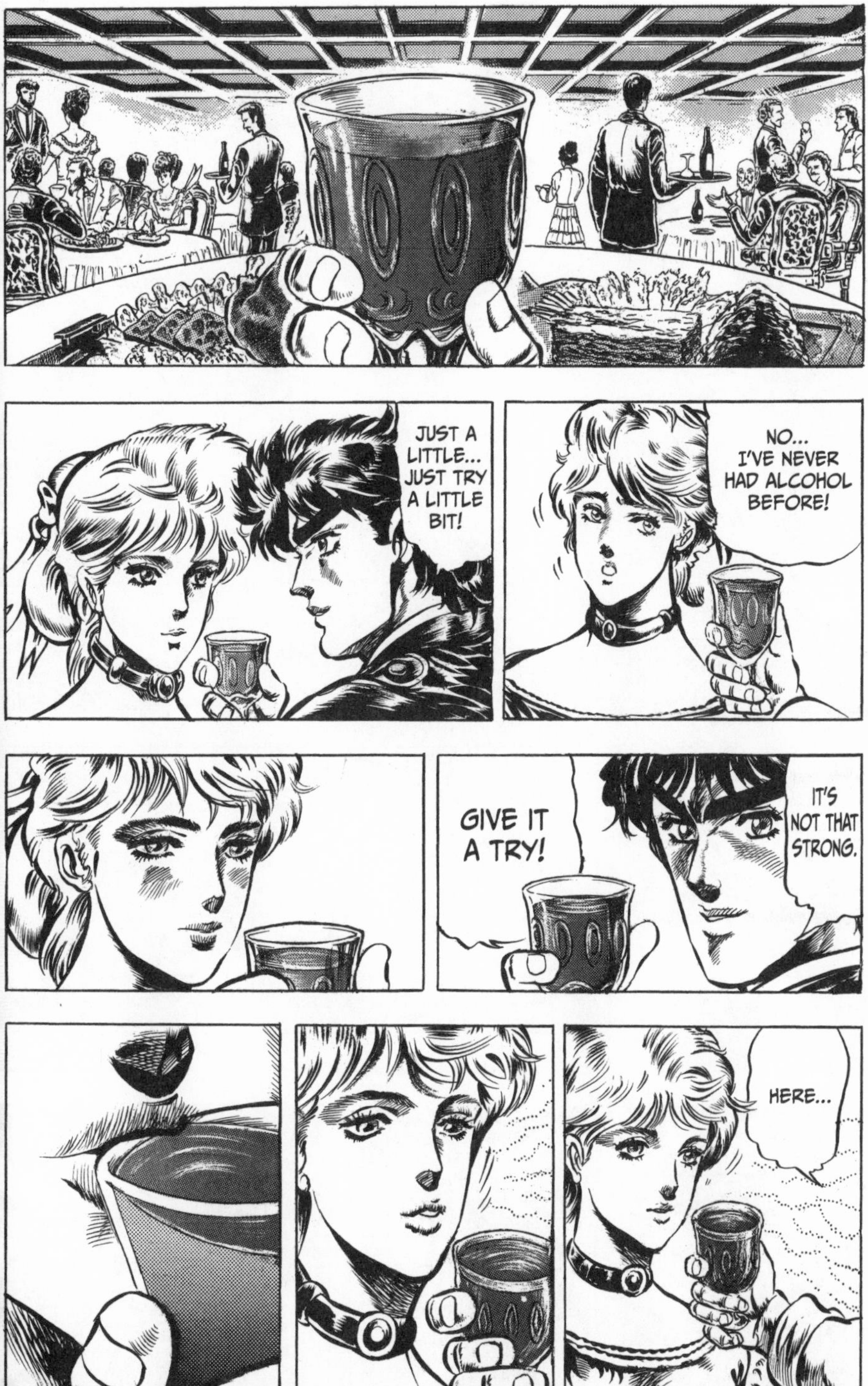
NO... I'VE NEVER HAD ALCOHOL BEFORE!
JUST A LITTLE... JUST TRY A LITTLE BIT!
IT'S NOT THAT STRONG.
GIVE IT A TRY!
HERE...

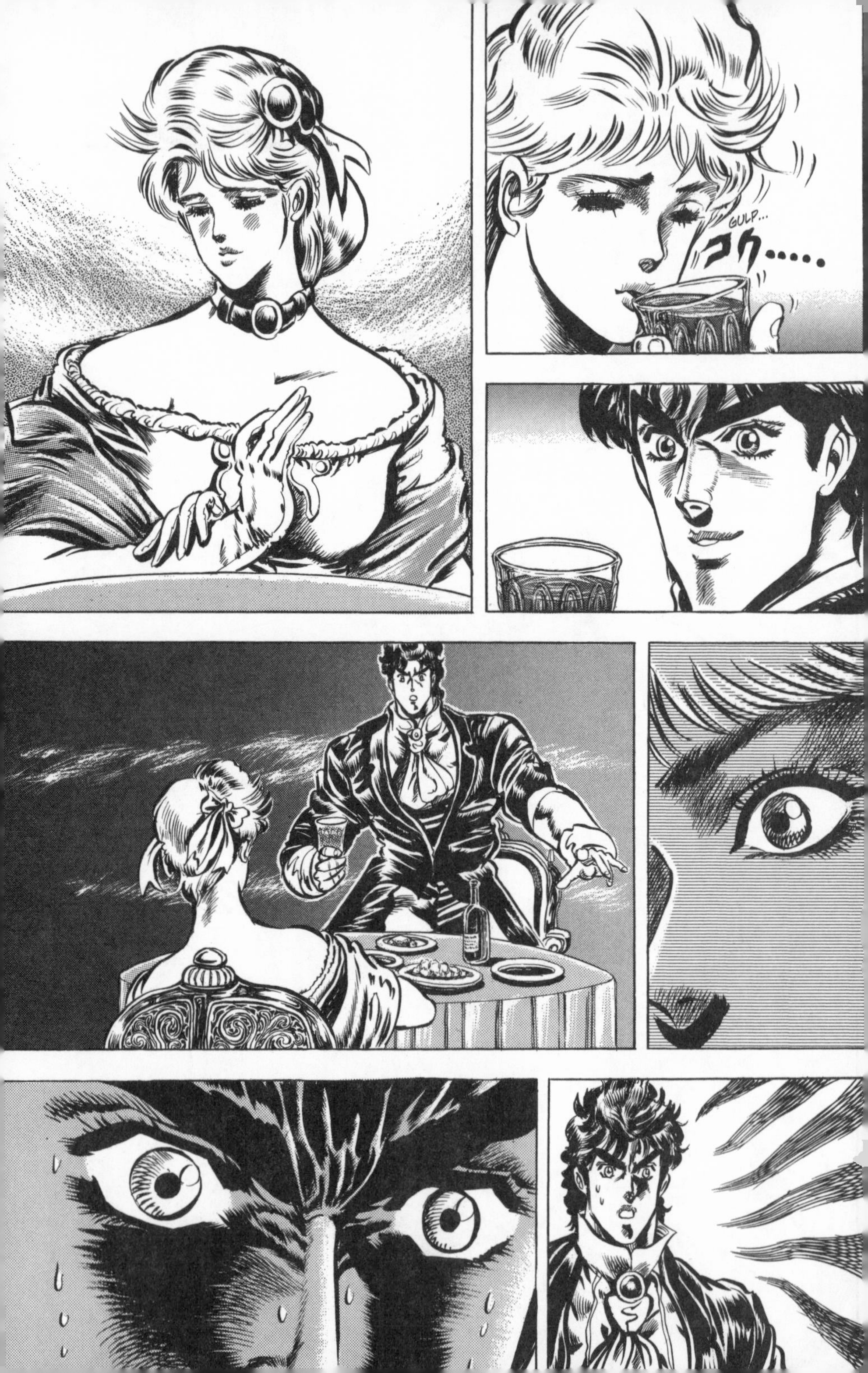
GULP...
ゴク……

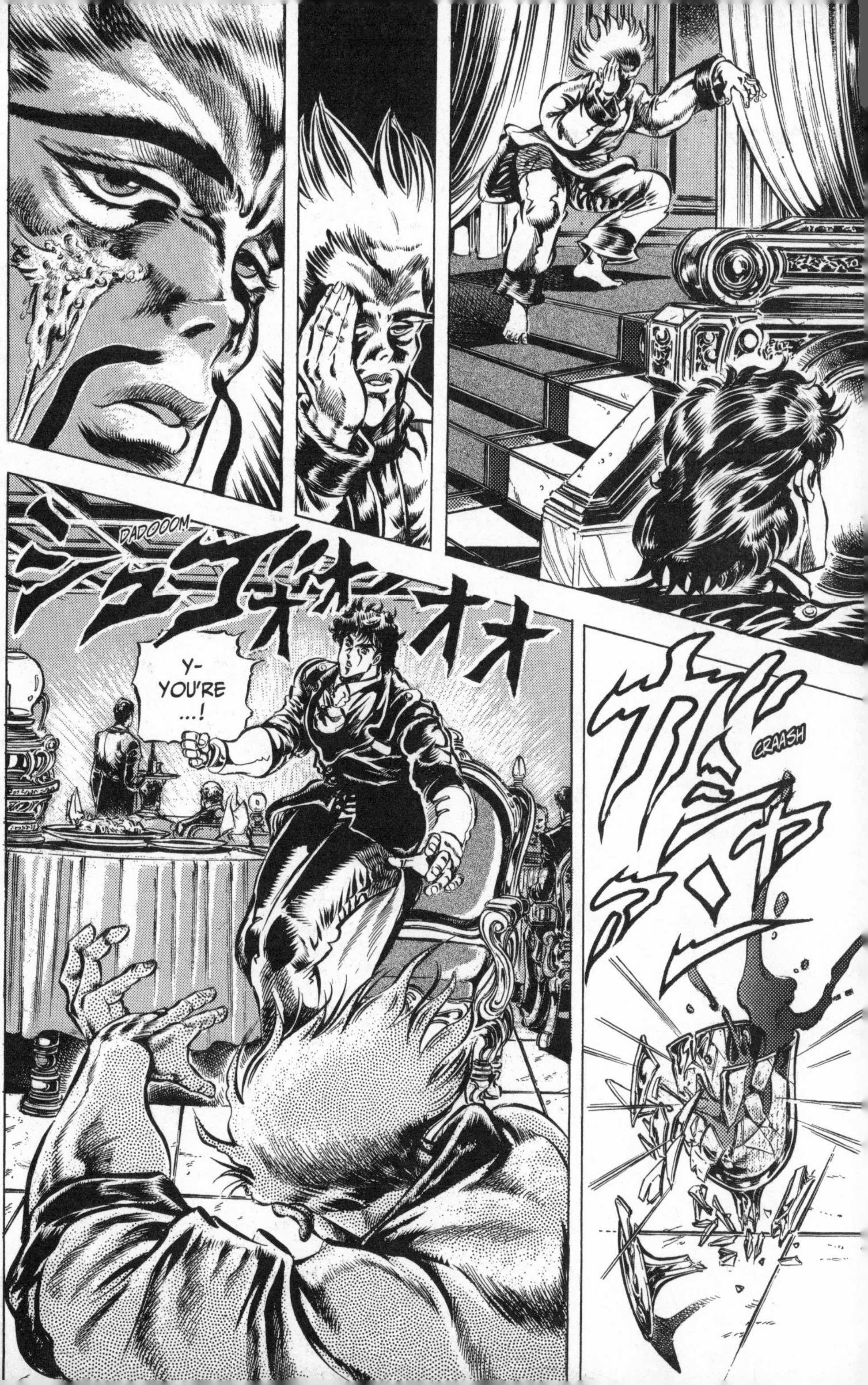
CRAASH
DADOOOM
Y-YOU'RE ...!

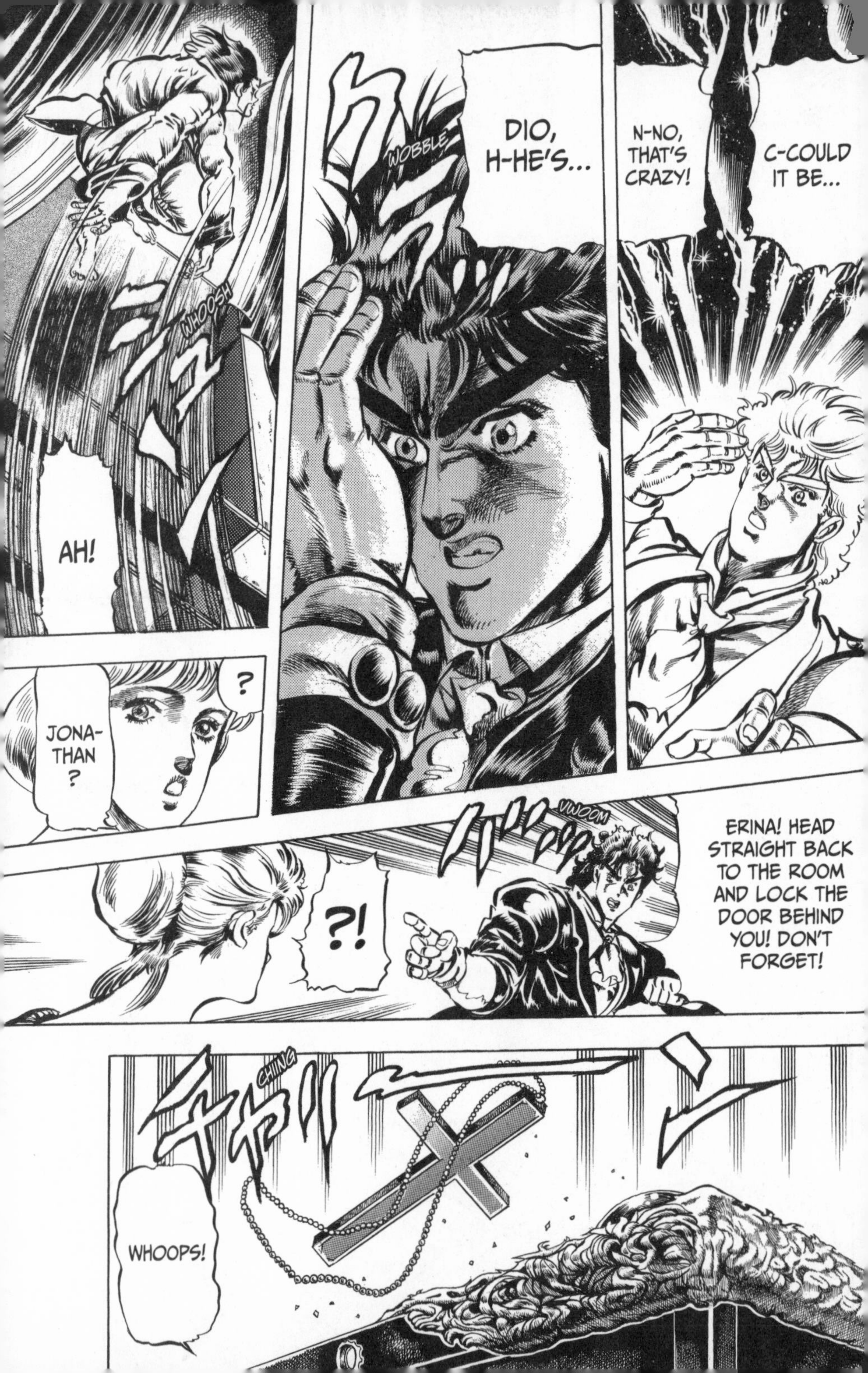
C-COULD IT BE...
N-NO, THAT'S CRAZY!
WOBBLE
DIO, H-HE'S...
WHOOSH
AH!
?
JONA-THAN ?
ERINA! HEAD STRAIGHT BACK TO THE ROOM AND LOCK THE DOOR BEHIND YOU! DON'T FORGET!
VWOOM
?!
CHING
WHOOPS!

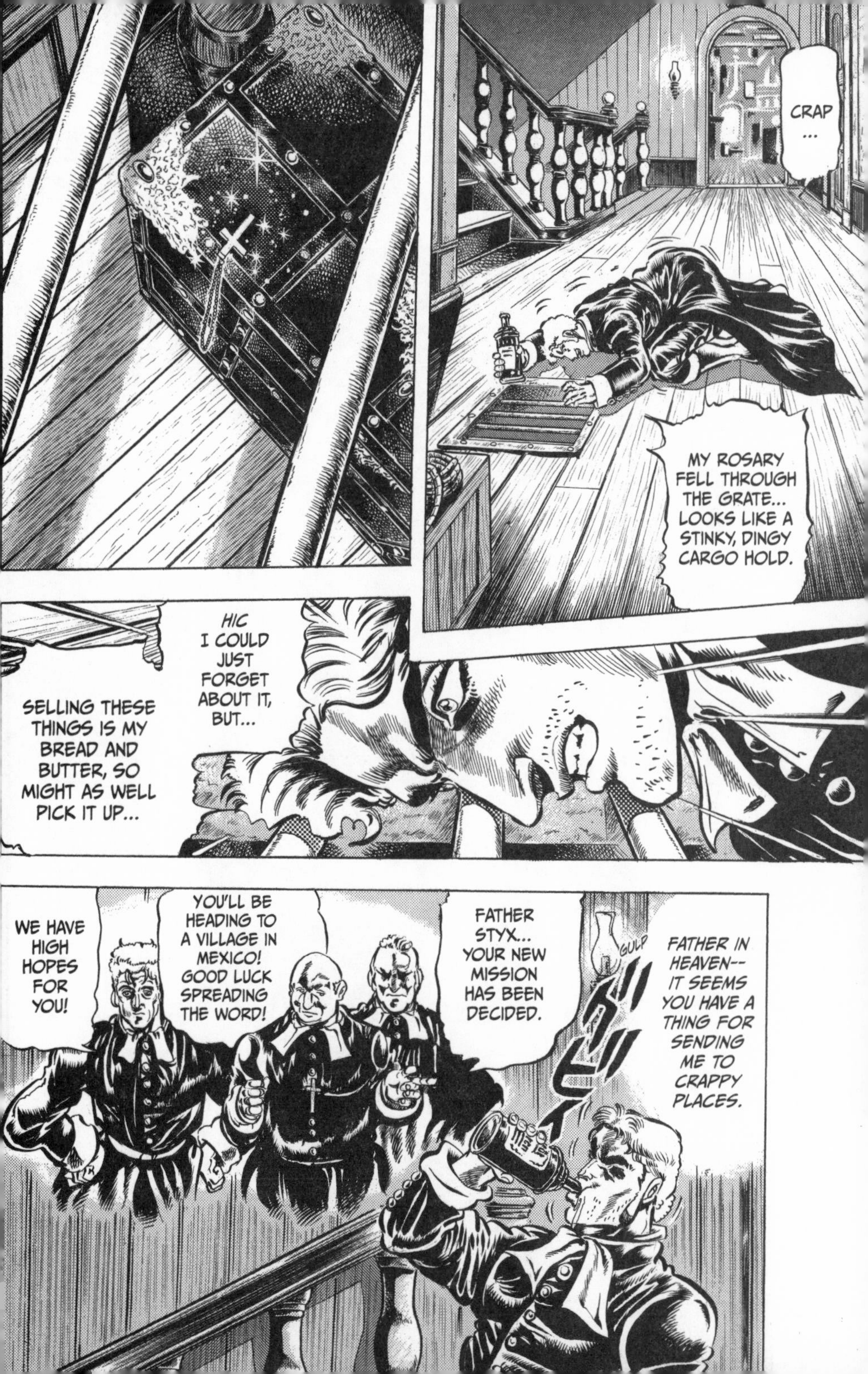
CRAP ...
MY ROSARY FELL THROUGH THE GRATE... LOOKS LIKE A STINKY, DINGY CARGO HOLD.
HIC I COULD JUST FORGET ABOUT IT, BUT...
SELLING THESE THINGS IS MY BREAD AND BUTTER, SO MIGHT AS WELL PICK IT UP...
FATHER IN HEAVEN-- IT SEEMS YOU HAVE A THING FOR SENDING ME TO CRAPPY PLACES.
GULP
FATHER STYX... YOUR NEW MISSION HAS BEEN DECIDED.
YOU'LL BE HEADING TO A VILLAGE IN MEXICO! GOOD LUCK SPREADING THE WORD!
WE HAVE HIGH HOPES FOR YOU!

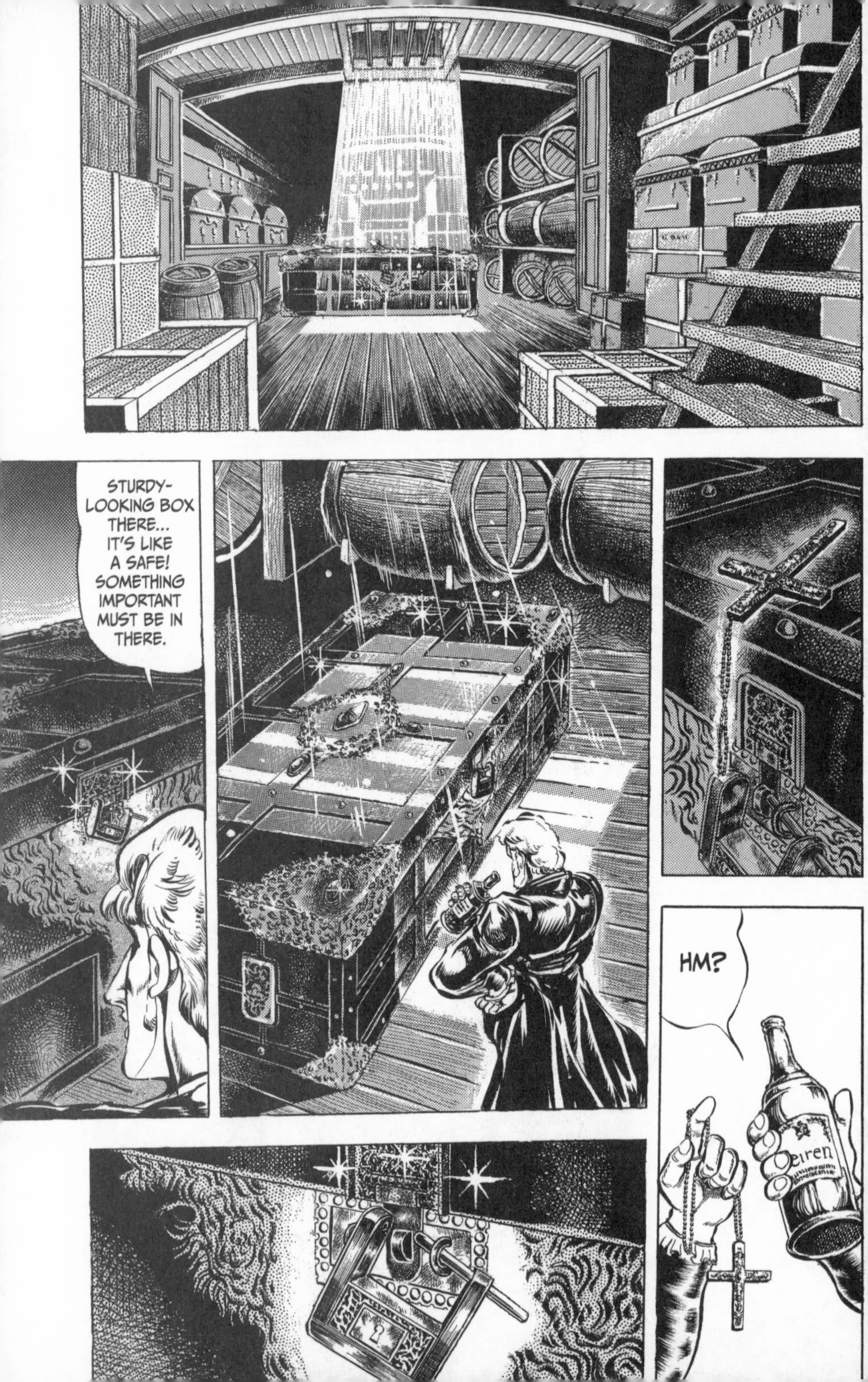
STURDY-LOOKING BOX THERE... IT'S LIKE A SAFE! SOMETHING IMPORTANT MUST BE IN THERE.
HM?

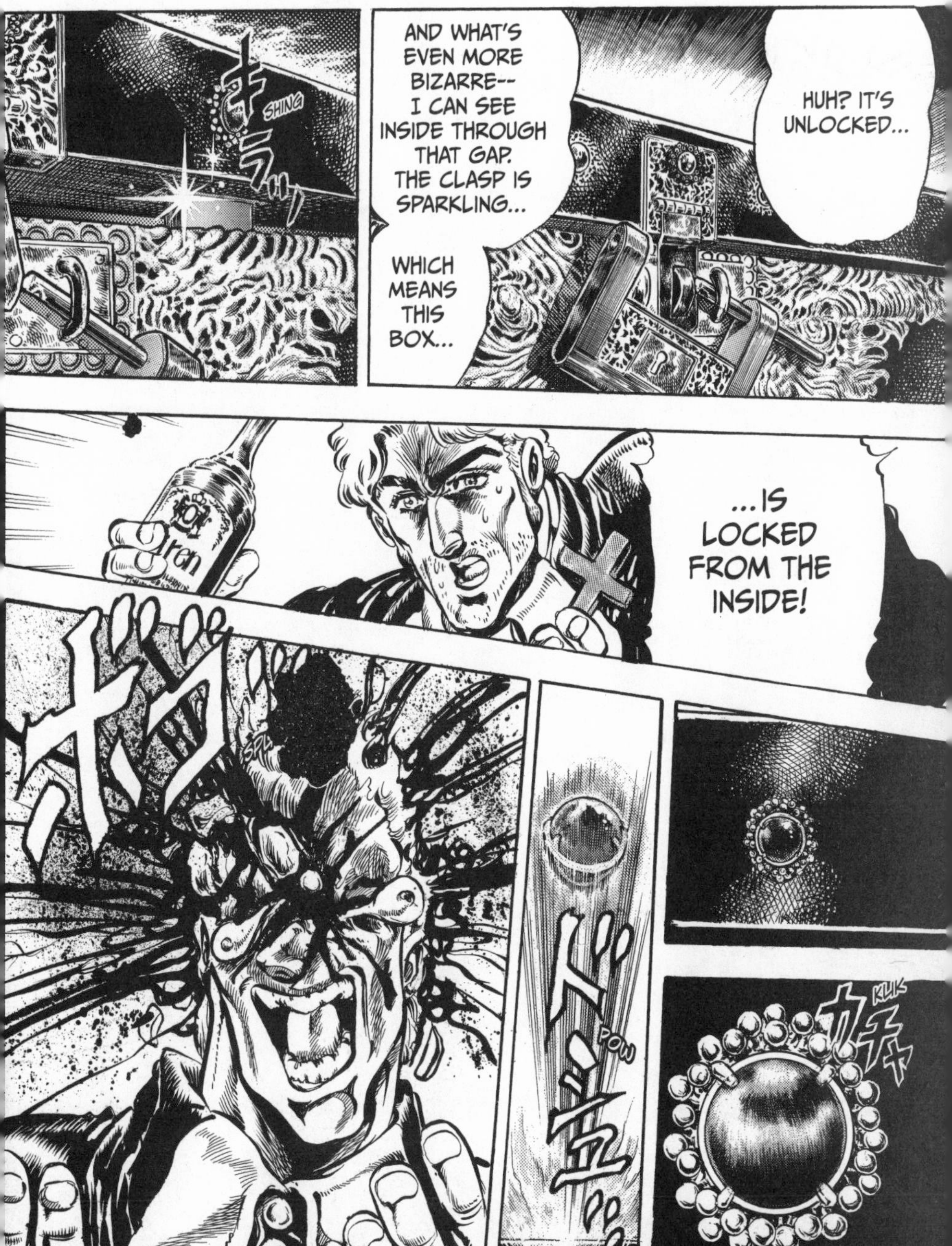
HUH? IT'S UNLOCKED...
AND WHAT'S EVEN MORE BIZARRE-- I CAN SEE INSIDE THROUGH THAT GAP. THE CLASP IS SPARKLING...
WHICH MEANS THIS BOX...
SHING
...IS LOCKED FROM THE INSIDE!
KLIK
POW

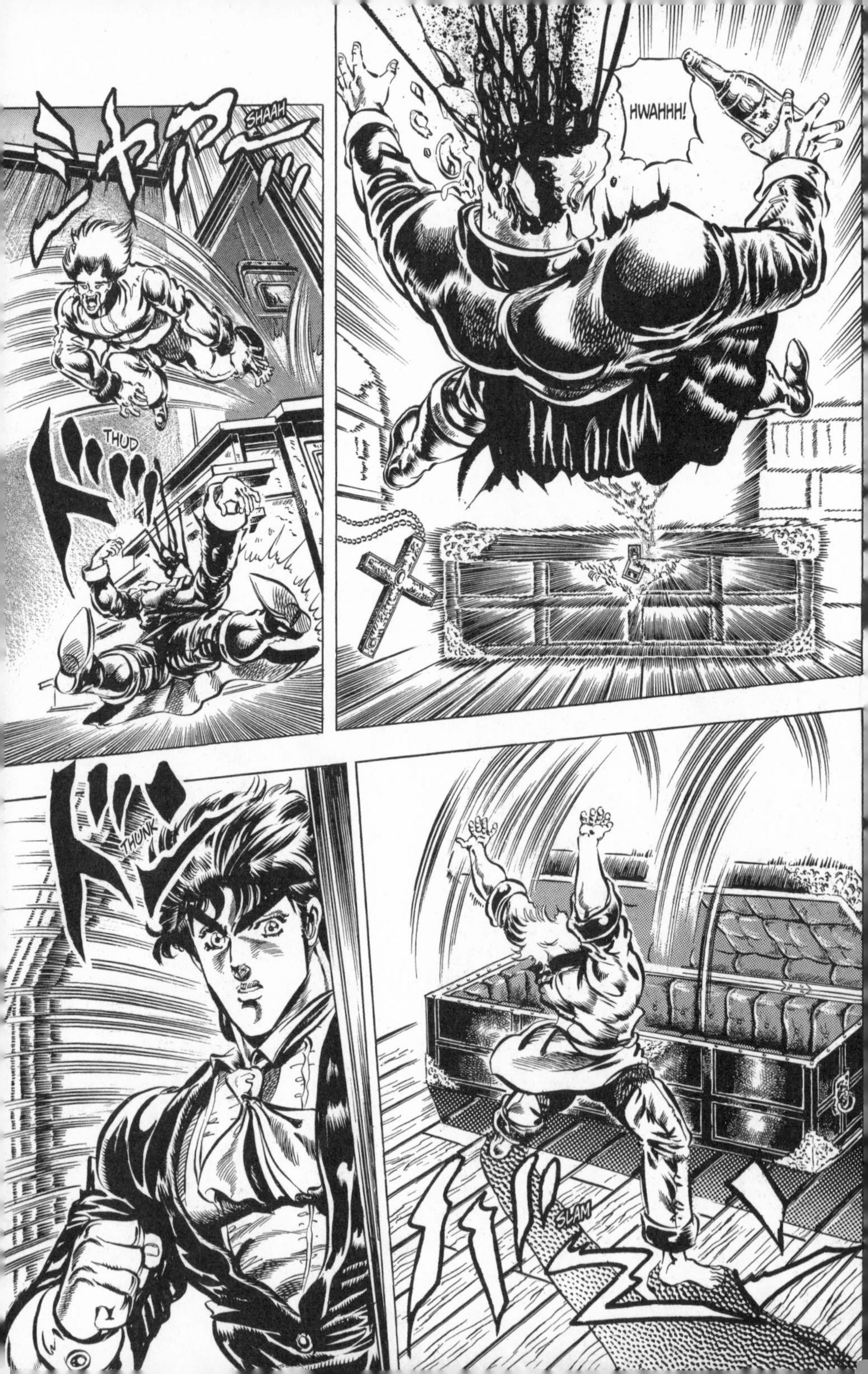
HWAHHH!
SHAAH
THUD
SLAM
THUNK

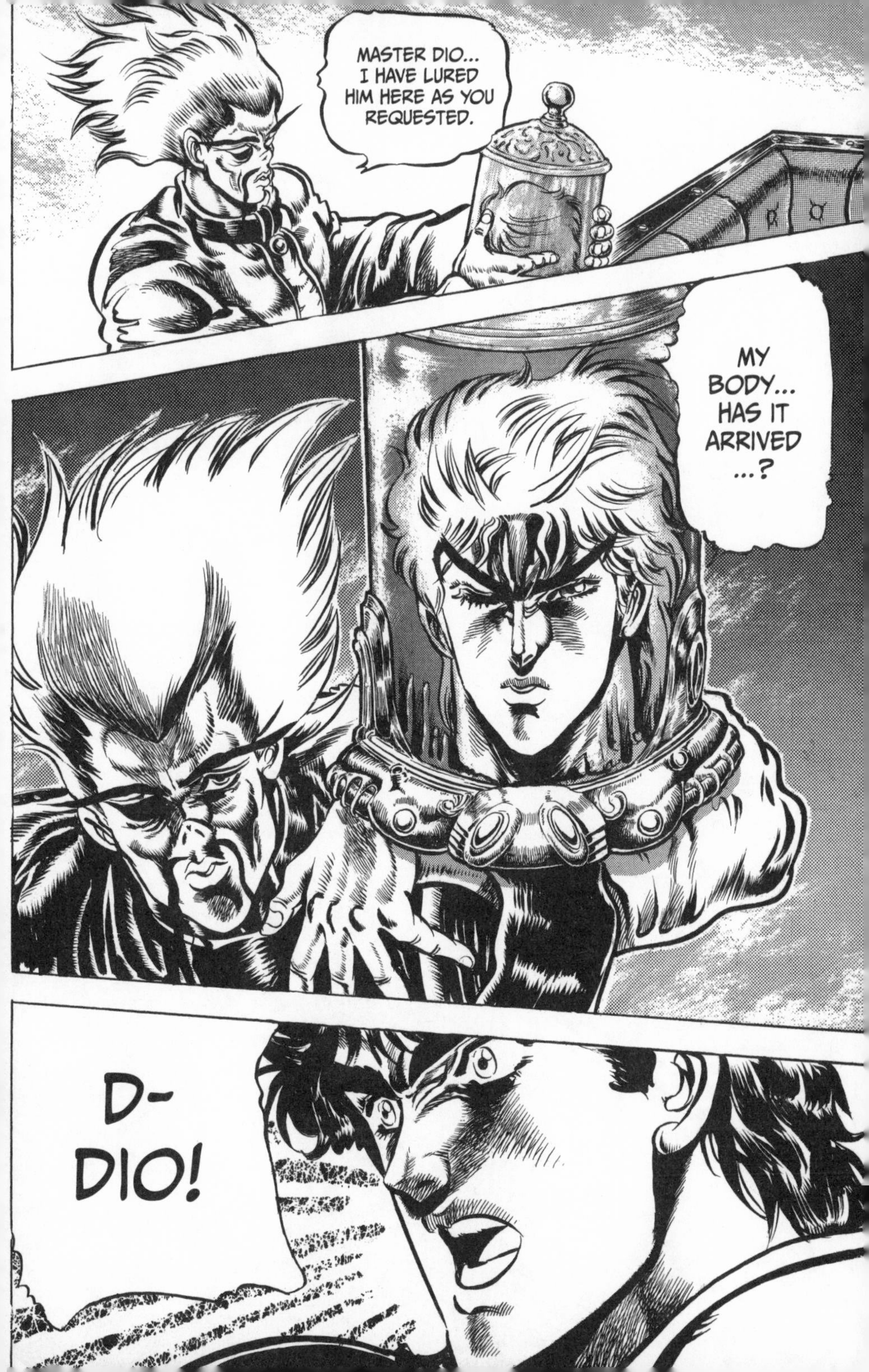
MASTER DIO... I HAVE LURED HIM HERE AS YOU REQUESTED.
MY BODY... HAS IT ARRIVED ...?
D-DIO!

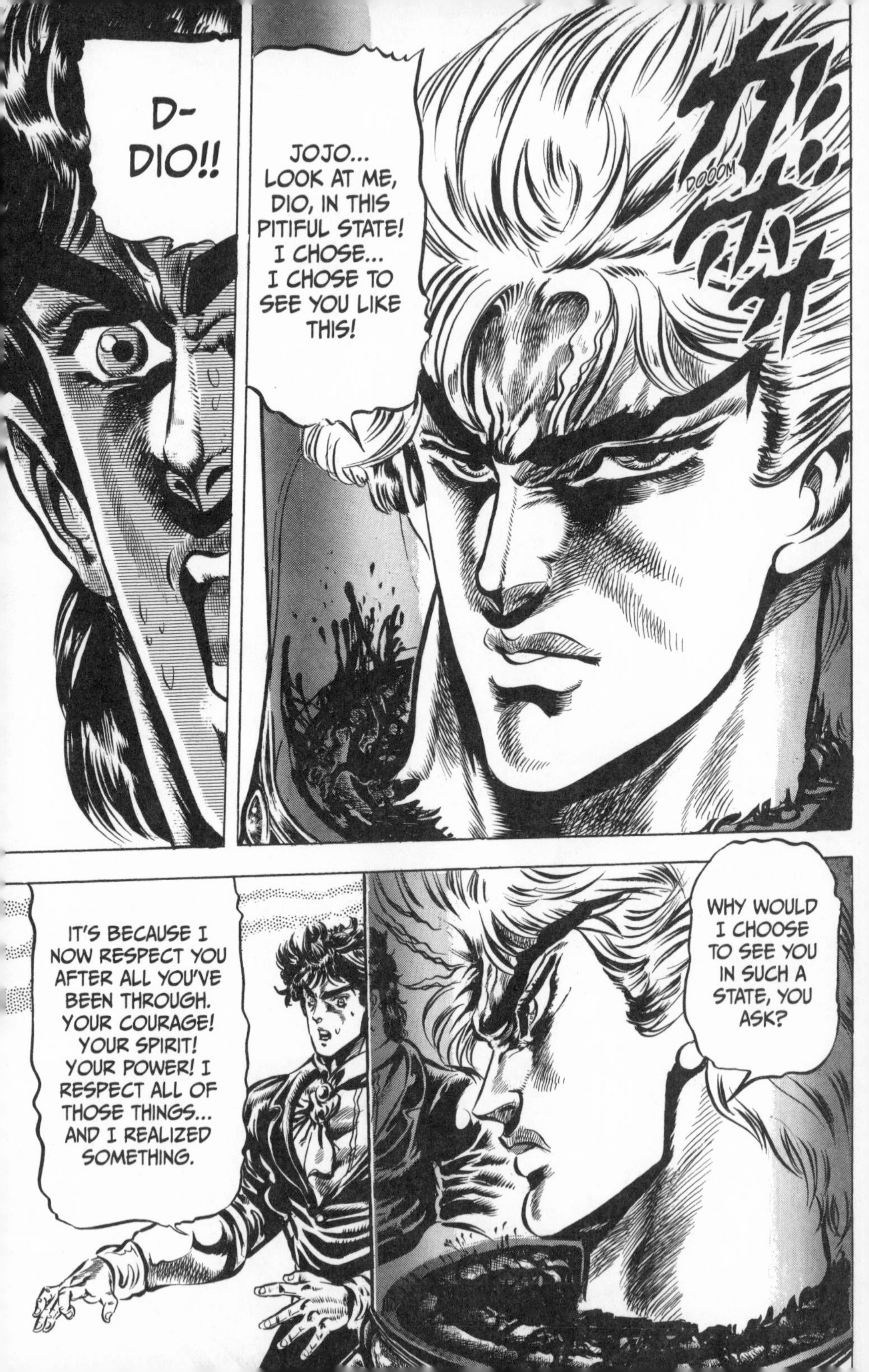
JOJO... LOOK AT ME, DIO, IN THIS PITIFUL STATE! I CHOSE... I CHOSE TO SEE YOU LIKE THIS!
DOOOM
D- DIO!!
WHY WOULD I CHOOSE TO SEE YOU IN SUCH A STATE, YOU ASK?
IT'S BECAUSE I NOW RESPECT YOU AFTER ALL YOU'VE BEEN THROUGH. YOUR COURAGE! YOUR SPIRIT! YOUR POWER! I RESPECT ALL OF THOSE THINGS... AND I REALIZED SOMETHING.

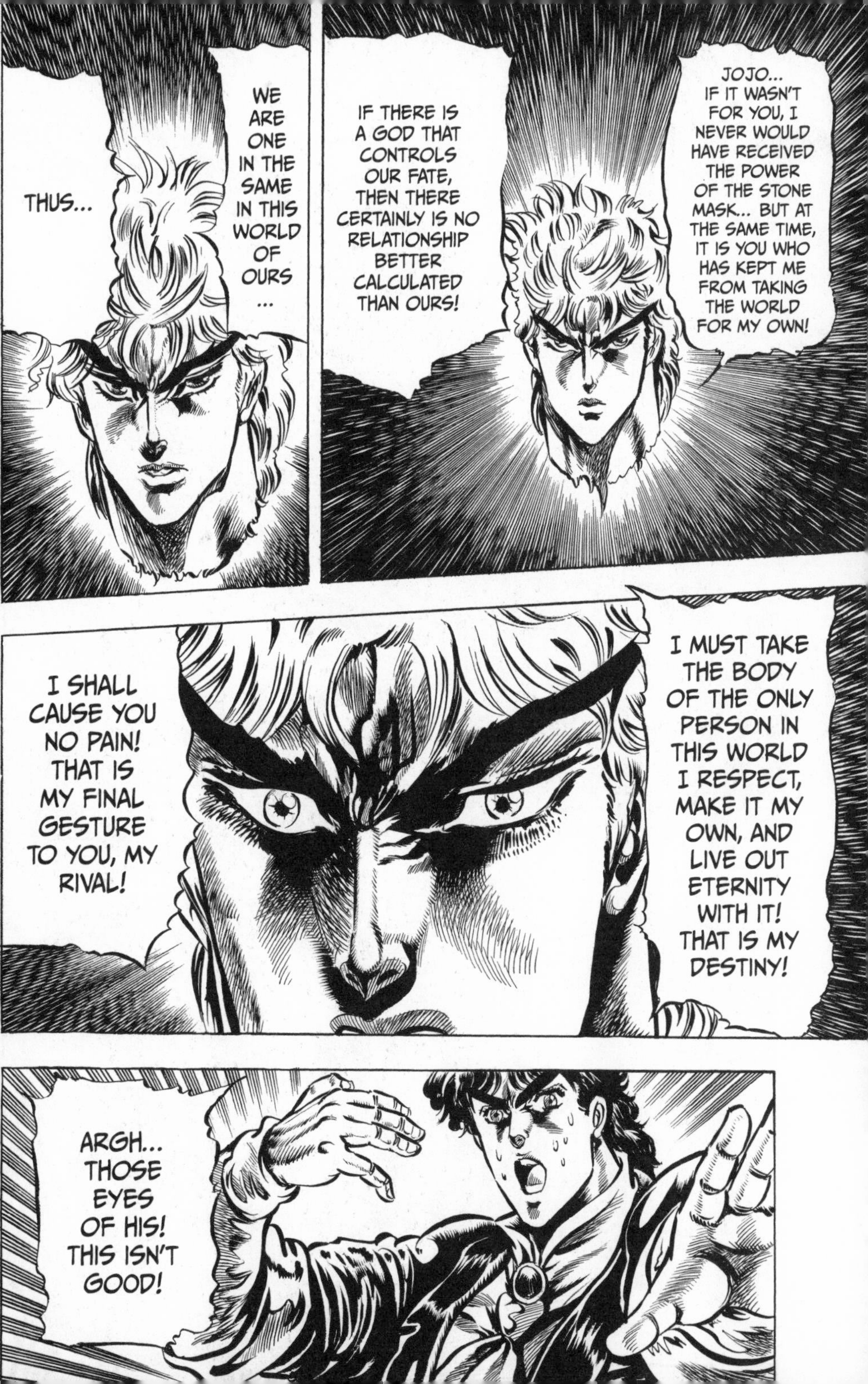
JOJO... IF IT WASN'T FOR YOU, I NEVER WOULD HAVE RECEIVED THE POWER OF THE STONE MASK... BUT AT THE SAME TIME, IT IS YOU WHO HAS KEPT ME FROM TAKING THE WORLD FOR MY OWN!
IF THERE IS A GOD THAT CONTROLS OUR FATE, THEN THERE CERTAINLY IS NO RELATIONSHIP BETTER CALCULATED THAN OURS!
WE ARE ONE IN THE SAME IN THIS WORLD OF OURS ...
THUS...
I MUST TAKE THE BODY OF THE ONLY PERSON IN THIS WORLD I RESPECT, MAKE IT MY OWN, AND LIVE OUT ETERNITY WITH IT! THAT IS MY DESTINY!
I SHALL CAUSE YOU NO PAIN! THAT IS MY FINAL GESTURE TO YOU, MY RIVAL!
ARGH... THOSE EYES OF HIS! THIS ISN'T GOOD!

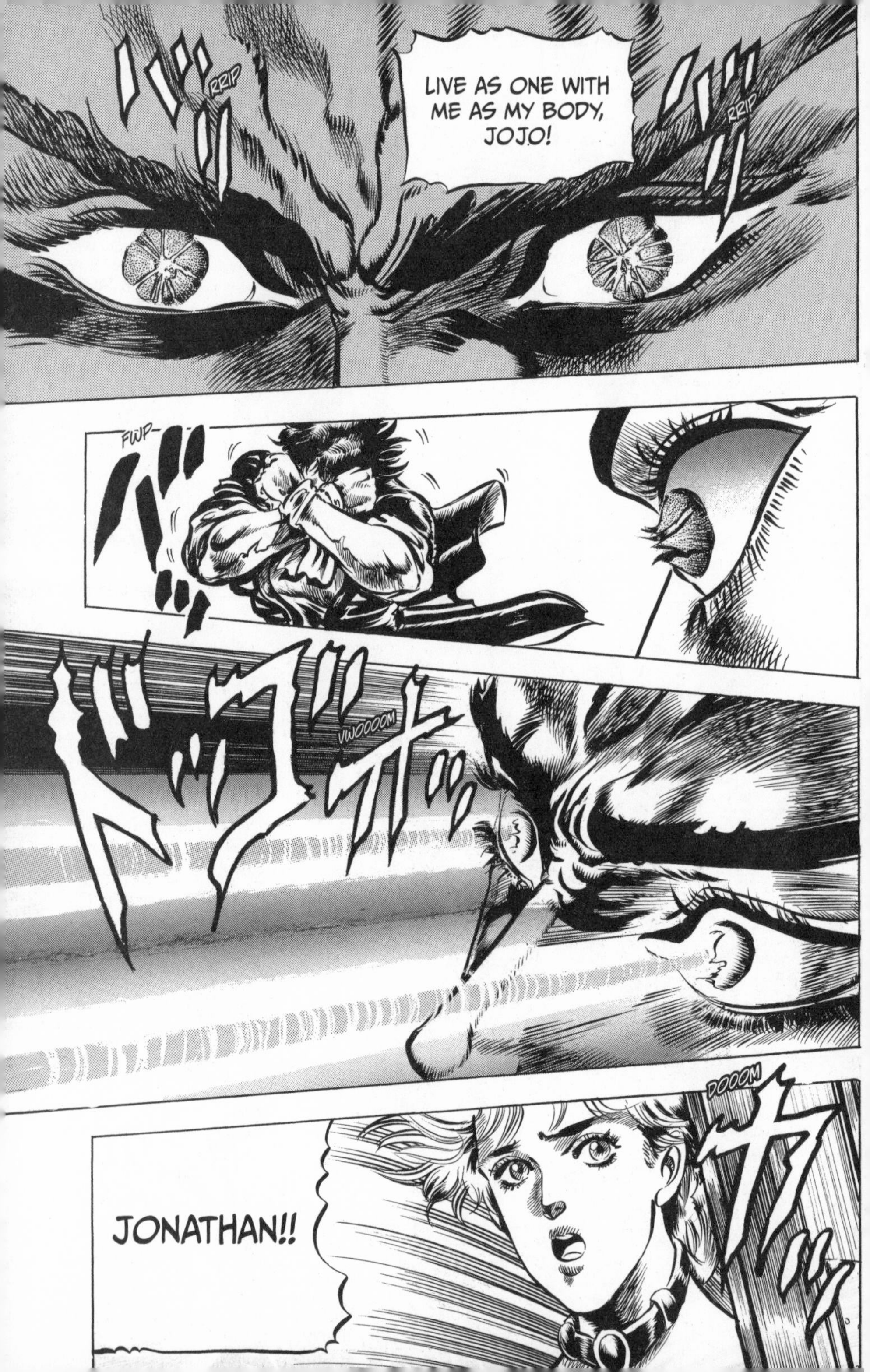
LIVE AS ONE WITH ME AS MY BODY, JOJO!
RRIP
RRIP
FWP
VWOOOOM
DOOOM
JONATHAN!!

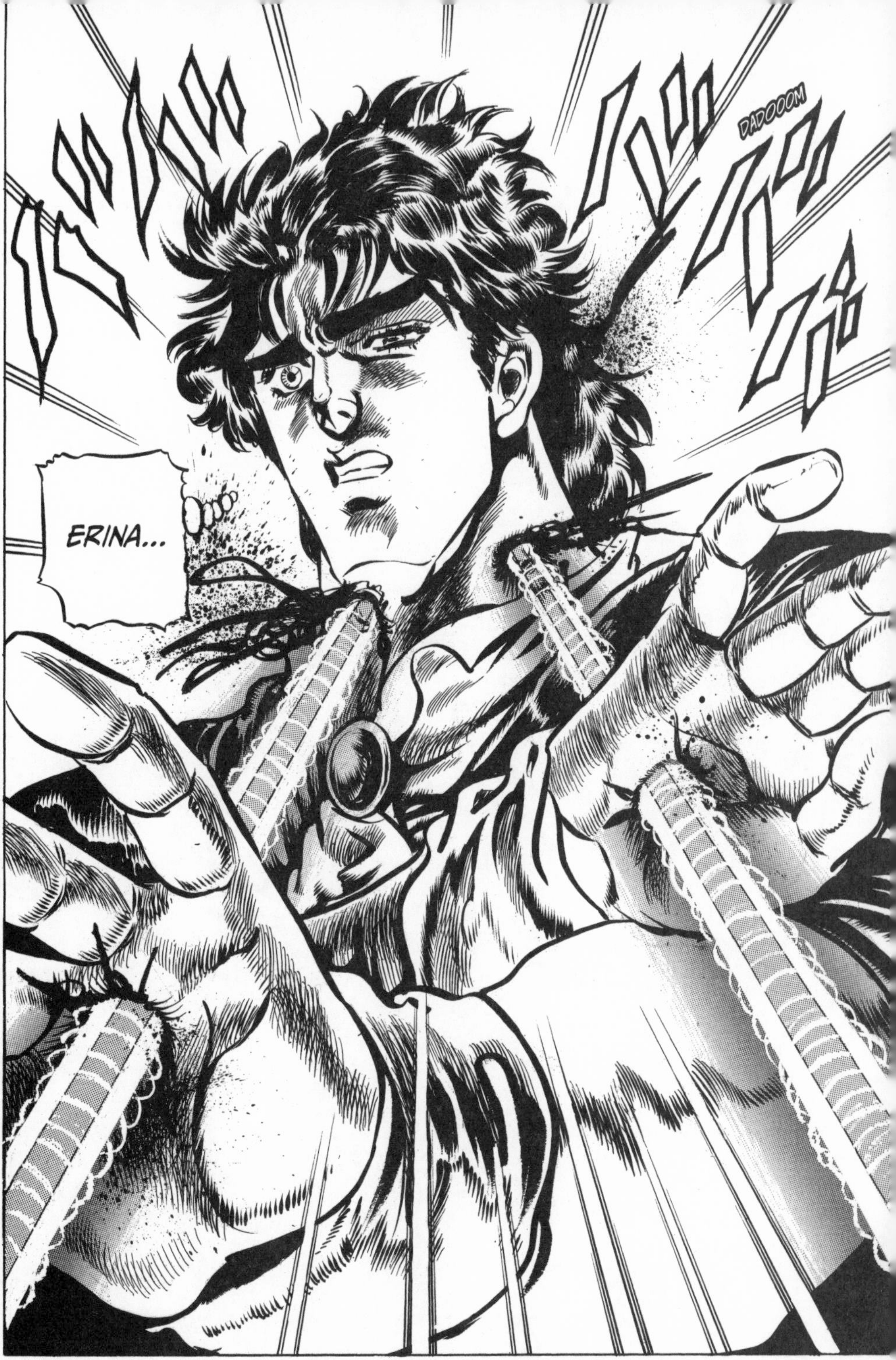
DADOOOM
ERINA...

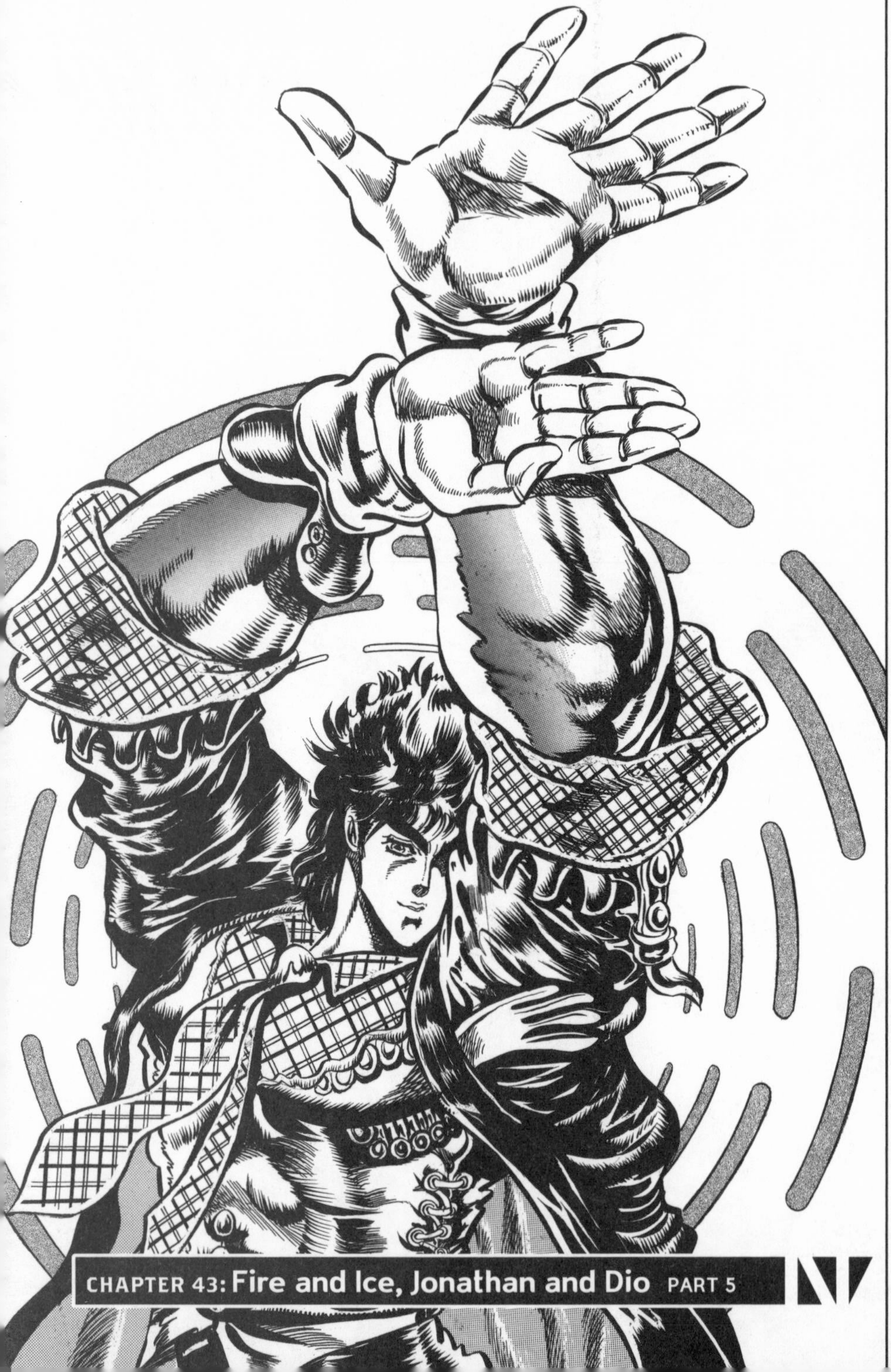

CHAPTER 43: Fire and Ice, Jonathan and Dio PART 5

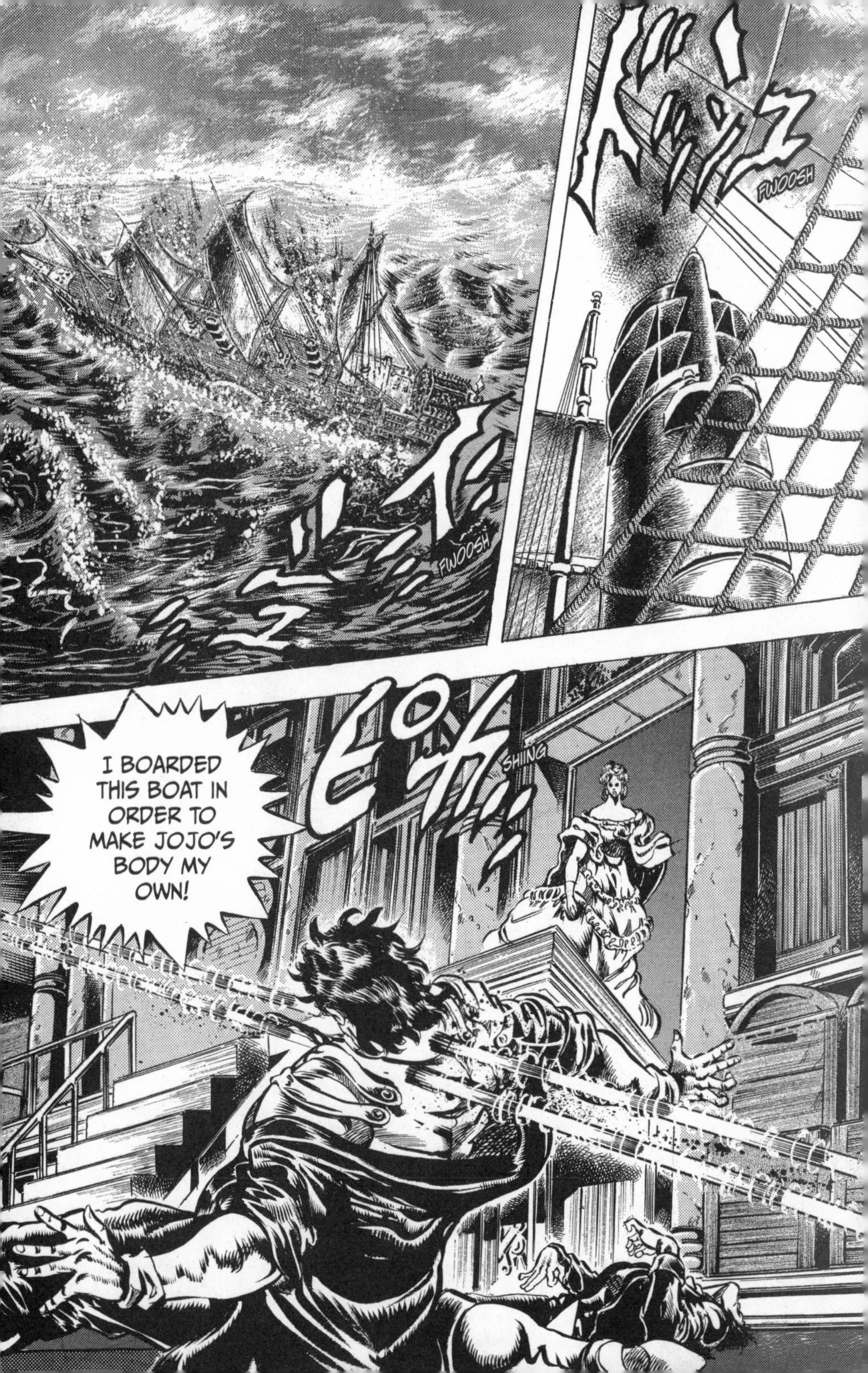
FWOOSH
FWOOSH
SHING
I BOARDED THIS BOAT IN ORDER TO MAKE JOJO'S BODY MY OWN!

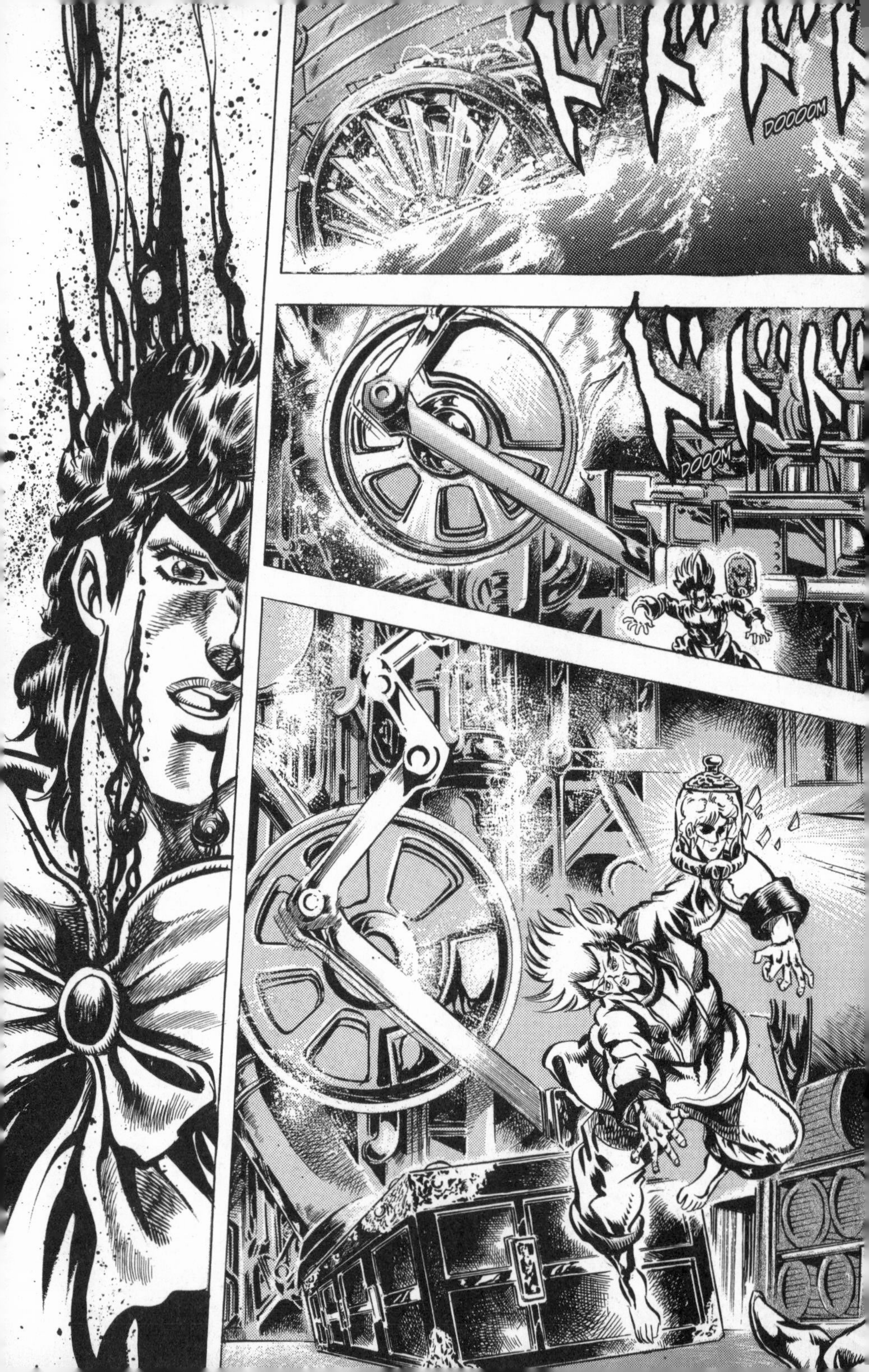
DOOOOM
DOOOM

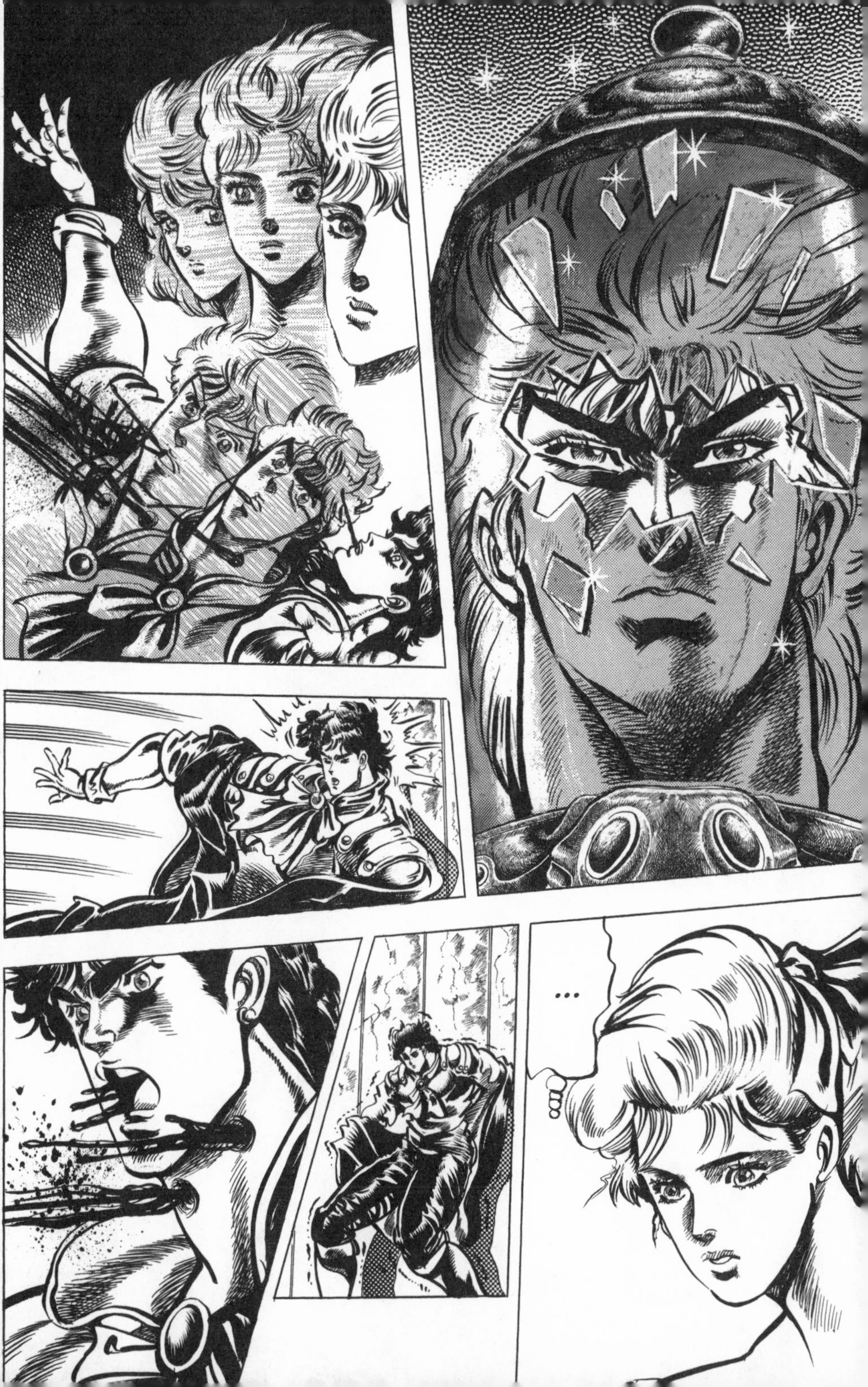
...

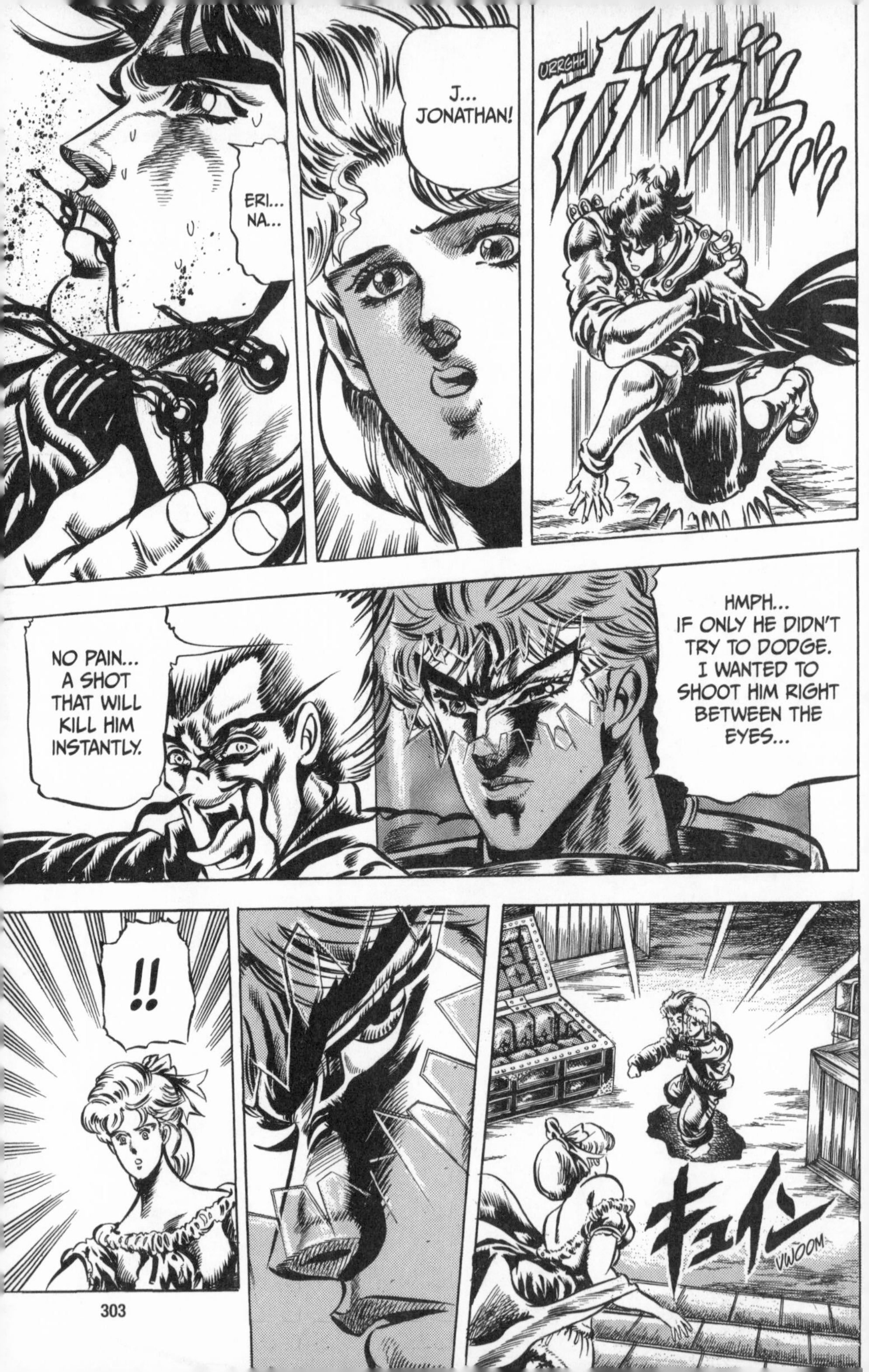
URRGHH
J... JONATHAN!
ERI... NA...
HMPH... IF ONLY HE DIDN'T TRY TO DODGE. I WANTED TO SHOOT HIM RIGHT BETWEEN THE EYES...
NO PAIN... A SHOT THAT WILL KILL HIM INSTANTLY.
VWOOM
!!

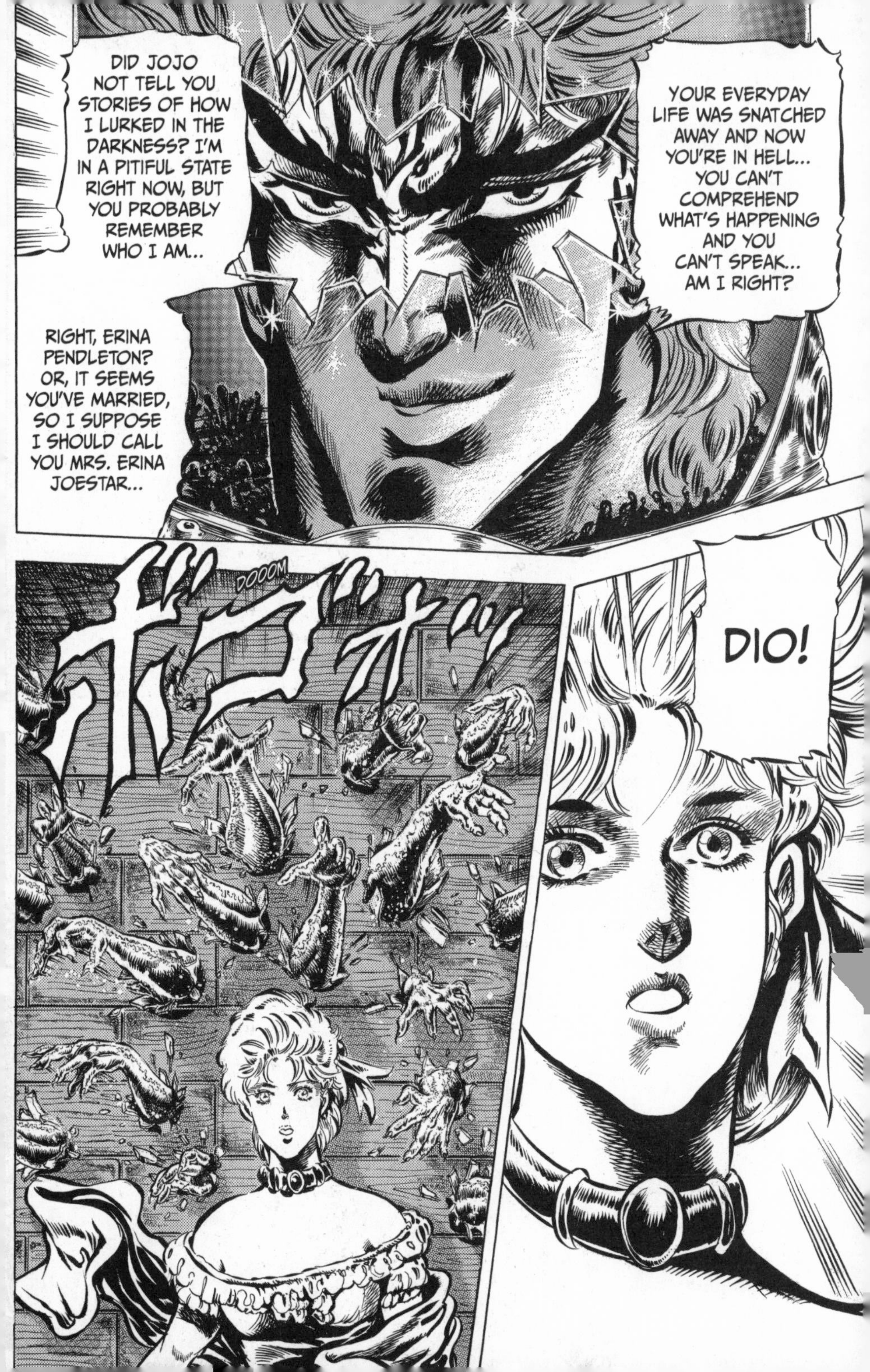
YOUR EVERYDAY LIFE WAS SNATCHED AWAY AND NOW YOU'RE IN HELL... YOU CAN'T COMPREHEND WHAT'S HAPPENING AND YOU CAN'T SPEAK... AM I RIGHT?
DID JOJO NOT TELL YOU STORIES OF HOW I LURKED IN THE DARKNESS? I'M IN A PITIFUL STATE RIGHT NOW, BUT YOU PROBABLY REMEMBER WHO I AM...
RIGHT, ERINA PENDLETON? OR, IT SEEMS YOU'VE MARRIED, SO I SUPPOSE I SHOULD CALL YOU MRS. ERINA JOESTAR...
DIO!
DOOOM

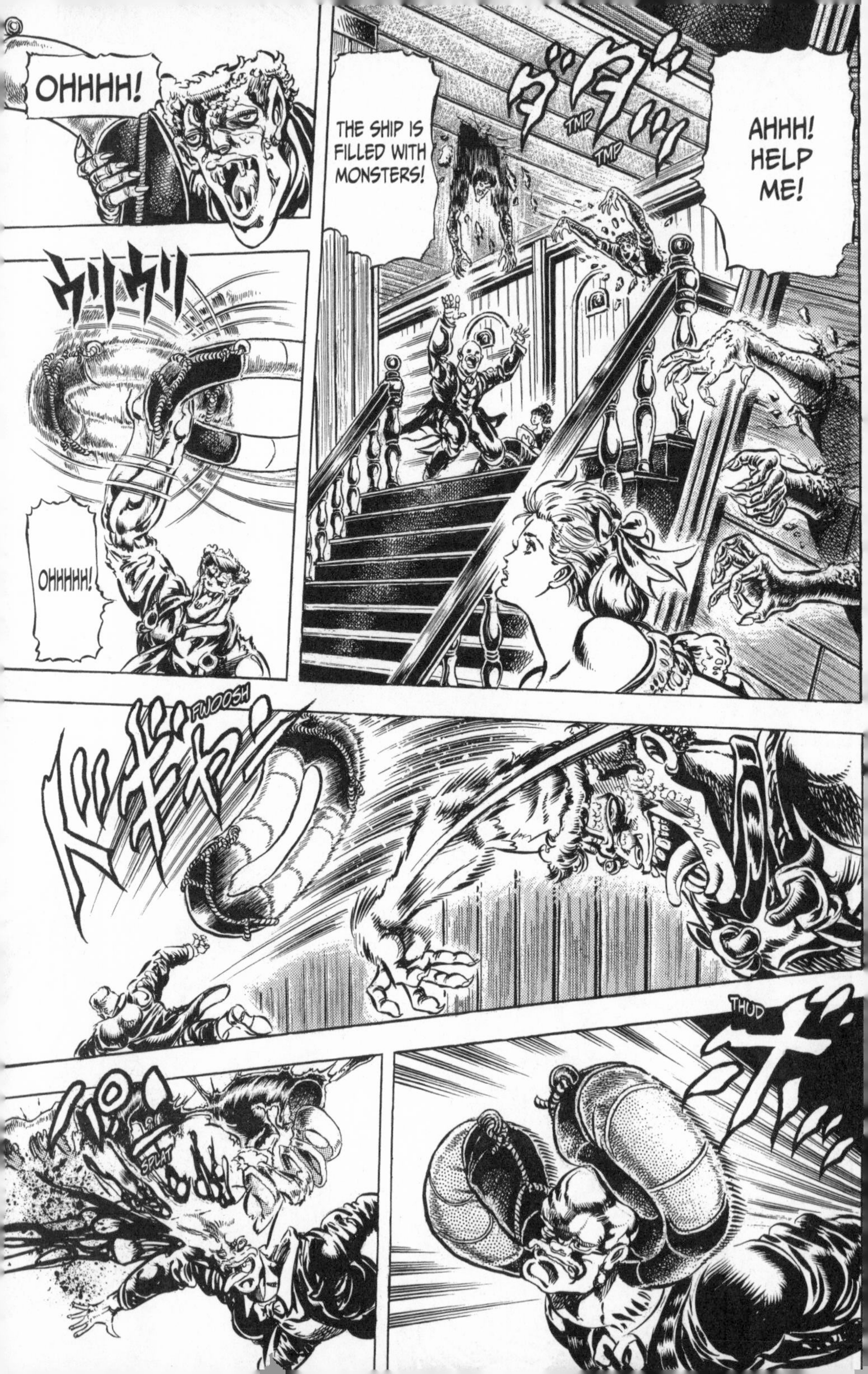
AHHH! HELP ME!
TMP
TMP
THE SHIP IS FILLED WITH MONSTERS!
OHHHH!
OHHHHH!
FWOOSH
THUD
SPLAT

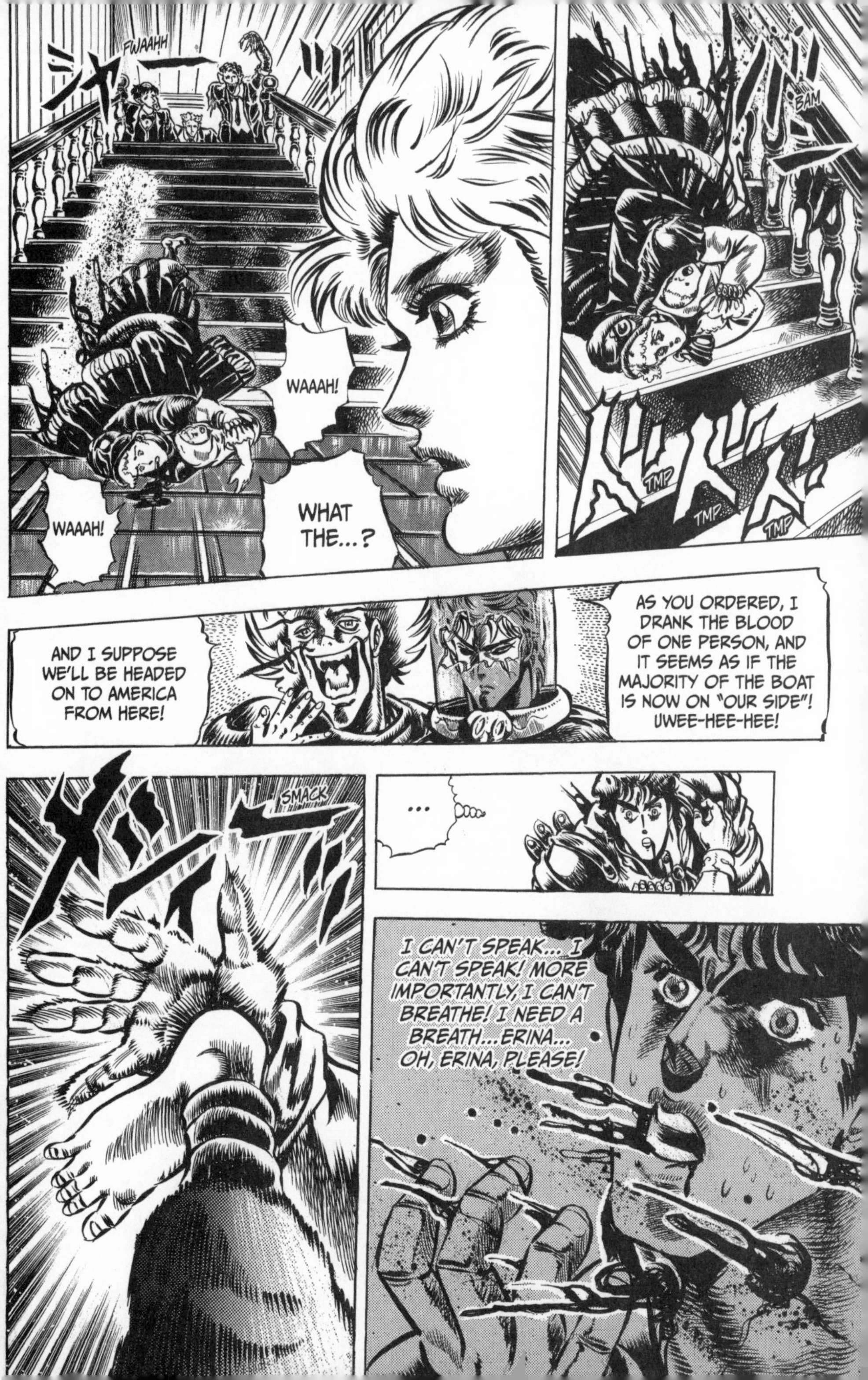
BAM
TMP
TMP
TMP
FWAAHH
WAAAH!
WAAAH!
WHAT THE...?
AS YOU ORDERED, I DRANK THE BLOOD OF ONE PERSON, AND IT SEEMS AS IF THE MAJORITY OF THE BOAT IS NOW ON "OUR SIDE"! UWEE-HEE-HEE!
AND I SUPPOSE WE'LL BE HEADED ON TO AMERICA FROM HERE!
...
I CAN'T SPEAK... I CAN'T SPEAK! MORE IMPORTANTLY, I CAN'T BREATHE! I NEED A BREATH...ERINA... OH, ERINA, PLEASE!
SMACK

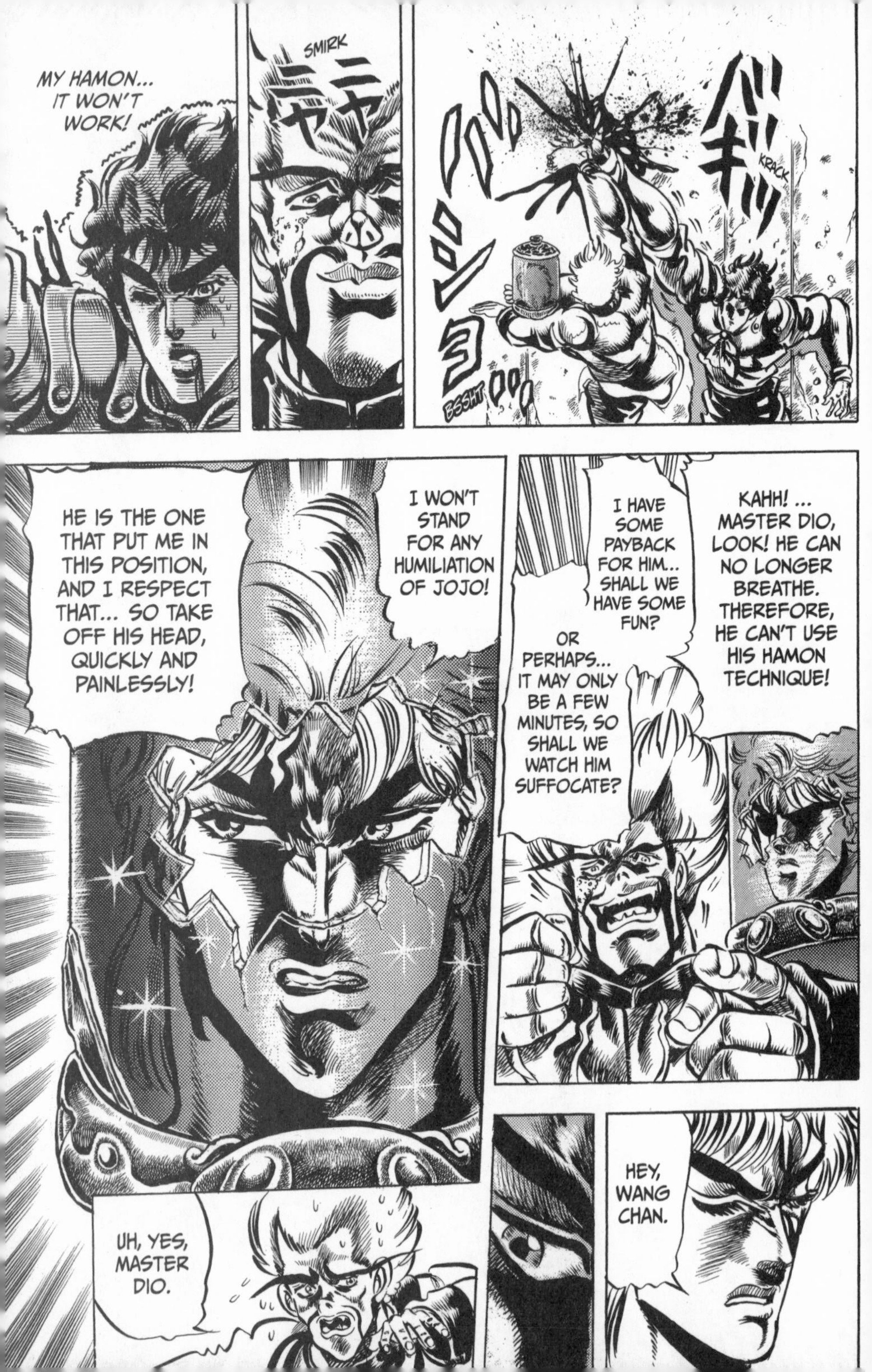
KRACK
BSSHT
SMIRK
MY HAMON... IT WON'T WORK!
KAHH! ... MASTER DIO, LOOK! HE CAN NO LONGER BREATHE. THEREFORE, HE CAN'T USE HIS HAMON TECHNIQUE!
I HAVE SOME PAYBACK FOR HIM... SHALL WE HAVE SOME FUN?
OR PERHAPS... IT MAY ONLY BE A FEW MINUTES, SO SHALL WE WATCH HIM SUFFOCATE?
I WON'T STAND FOR ANY HUMILIATION OF JOJO!
HE IS THE ONE THAT PUT ME IN THIS POSITION, AND I RESPECT THAT... SO TAKE OFF HIS HEAD, QUICKLY AND PAINLESSLY!
HEY, WANG CHAN.
UH, YES, MASTER DIO.

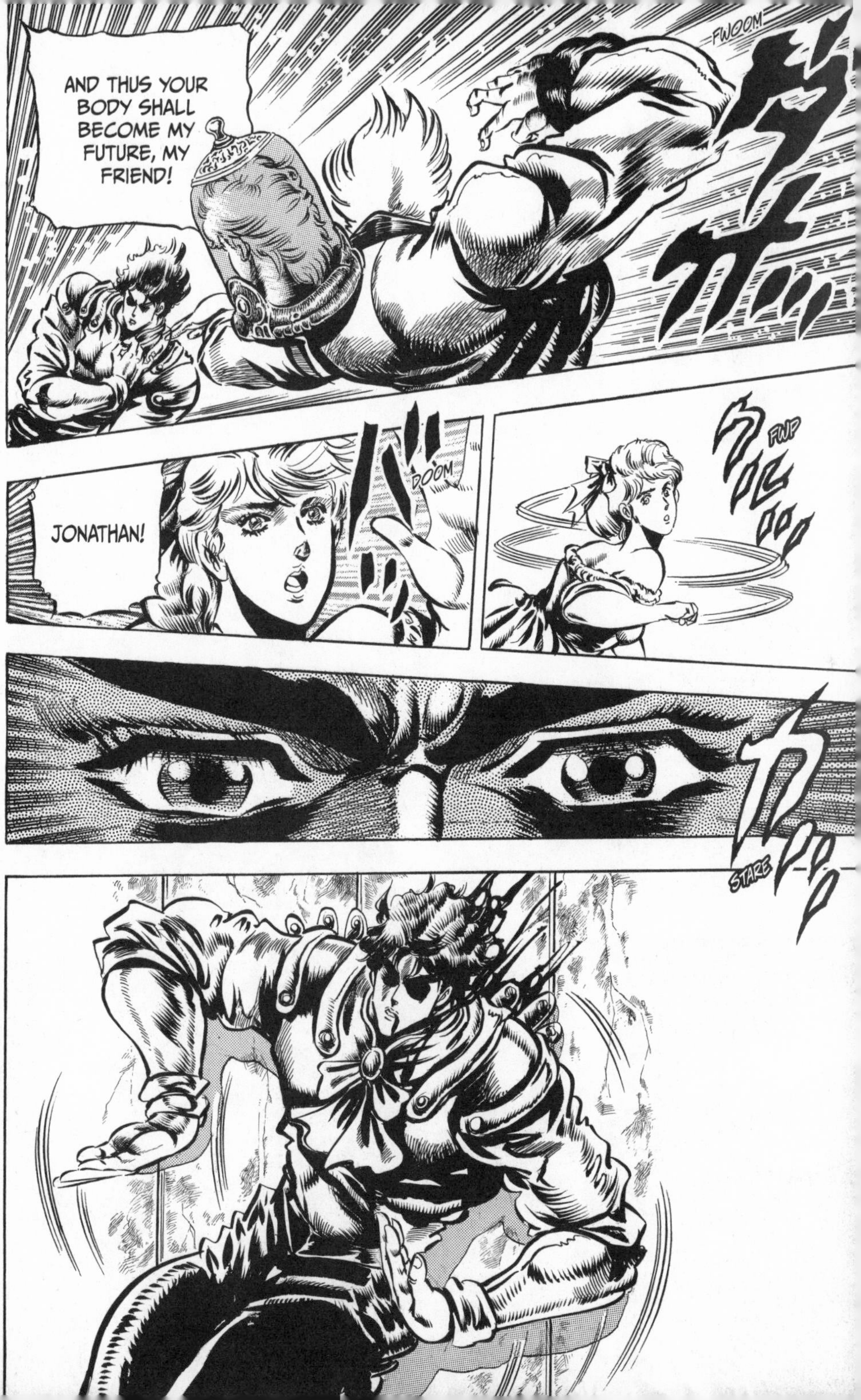
FWOOM
AND THUS YOUR BODY SHALL BECOME MY FUTURE, MY FRIEND!
FWP
DOOM
JONATHAN!
STARE

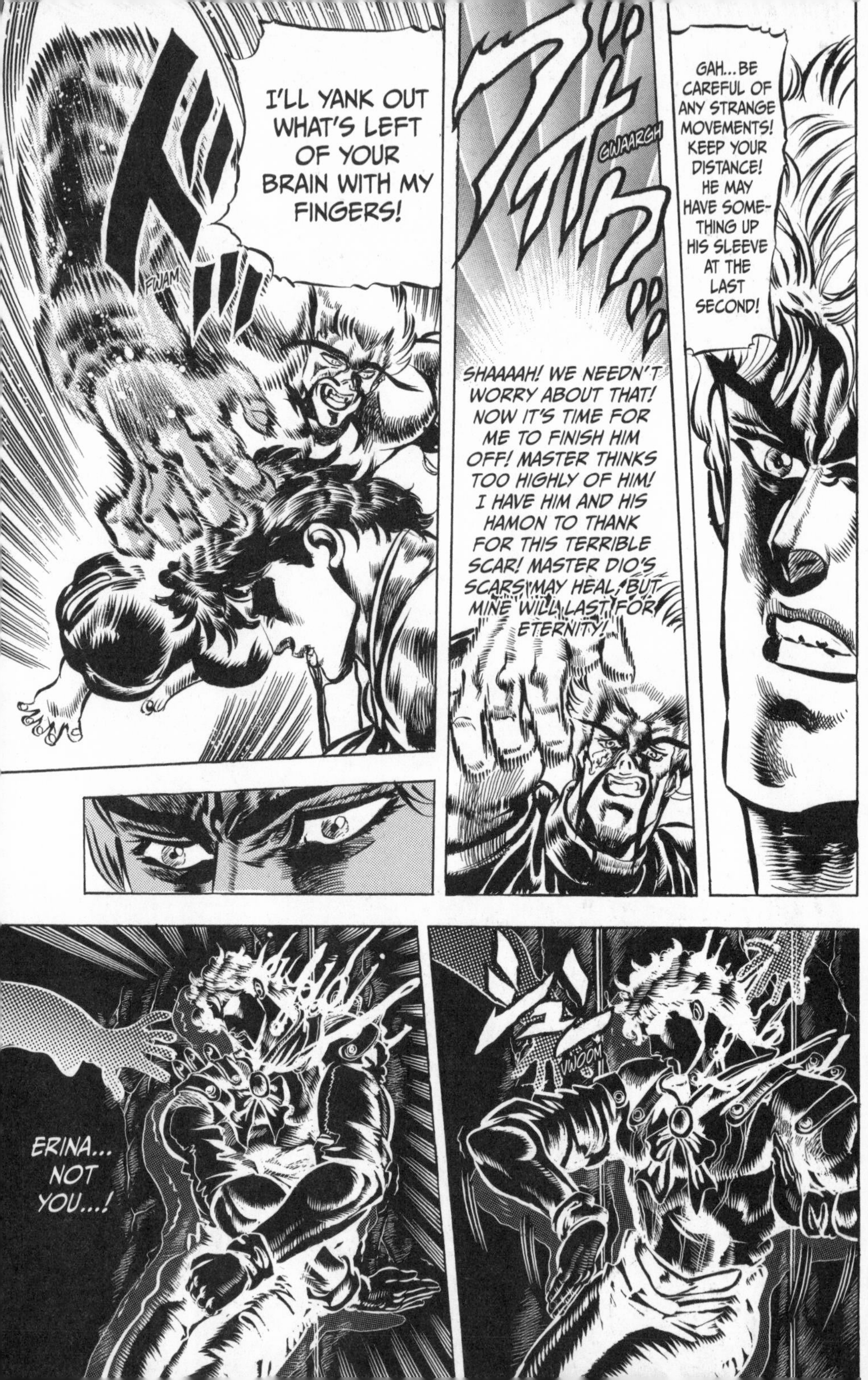
GAH...BE CAREFUL OF ANY STRANGE MOVEMENTS! KEEP YOUR DISTANCE! HE MAY HAVE SOME-THING UP HIS SLEEVE AT THE LAST SECOND!
CWAARCH
SHAAAAH! WE NEEDN'T WORRY ABOUT THAT! NOW IT'S TIME FOR ME TO FINISH HIM OFF! MASTER THINKS TOO HIGHLY OF HIM! I HAVE HIM AND HIS HAMON TO THANK FOR THIS TERRIBLE SCAR! MASTER DIO'S SCARS MAY HEAL, BUT MINE WILL LAST FOR ETERNITY!
I'LL YANK OUT WHAT'S LEFT OF YOUR BRAIN WITH MY FINGERS!
FWAM
VWOOM
ERINA... NOT YOU...!

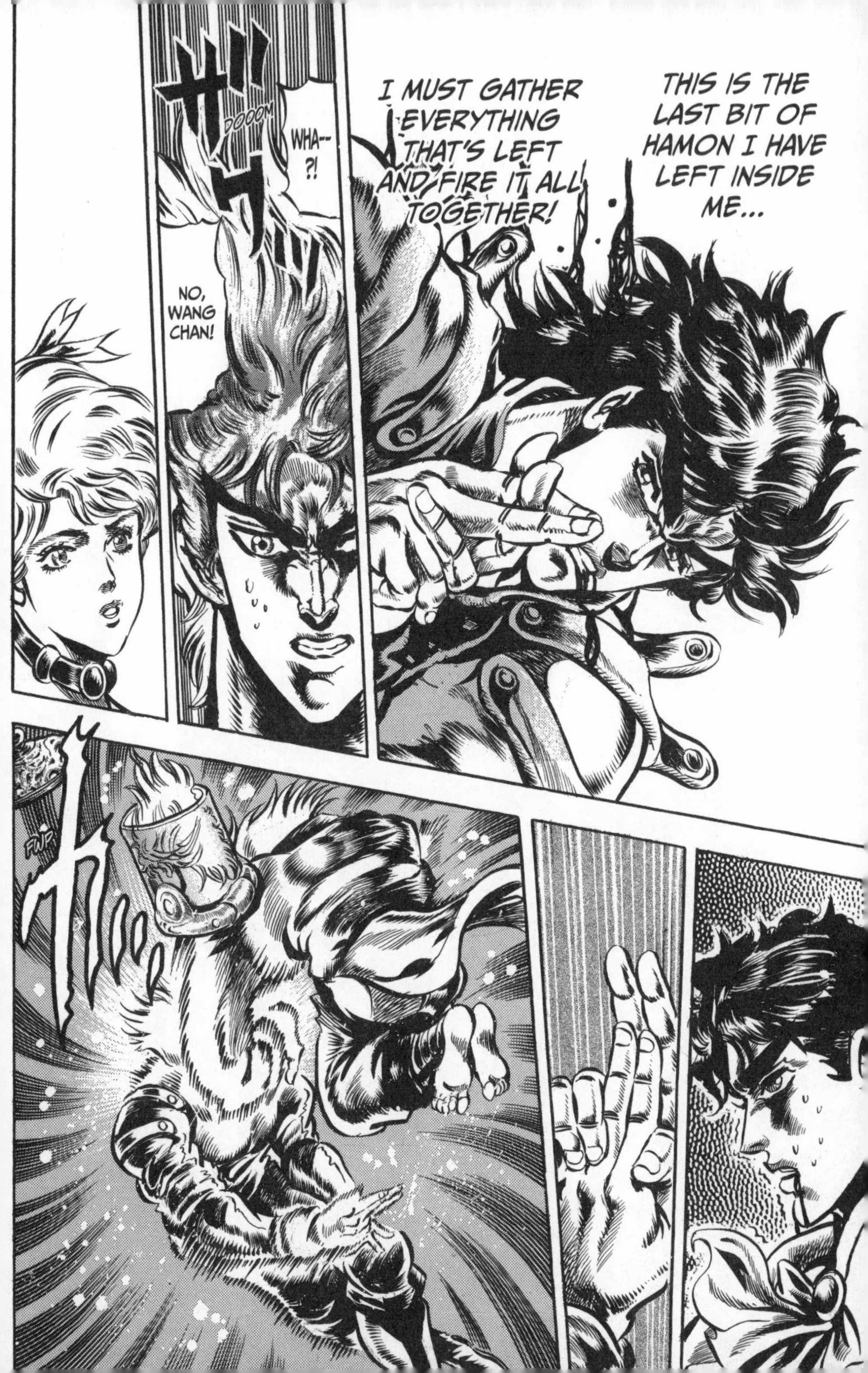

THIS IS THE LAST BIT OF HAMON I HAVE LEFT INSIDE ME...
I MUST GATHER EVERYTHING THAT'S LEFT AND FIRE IT ALL TOGETHER!
DOOOM
WHA-- ?!
NO, WANG CHAN!
FWP

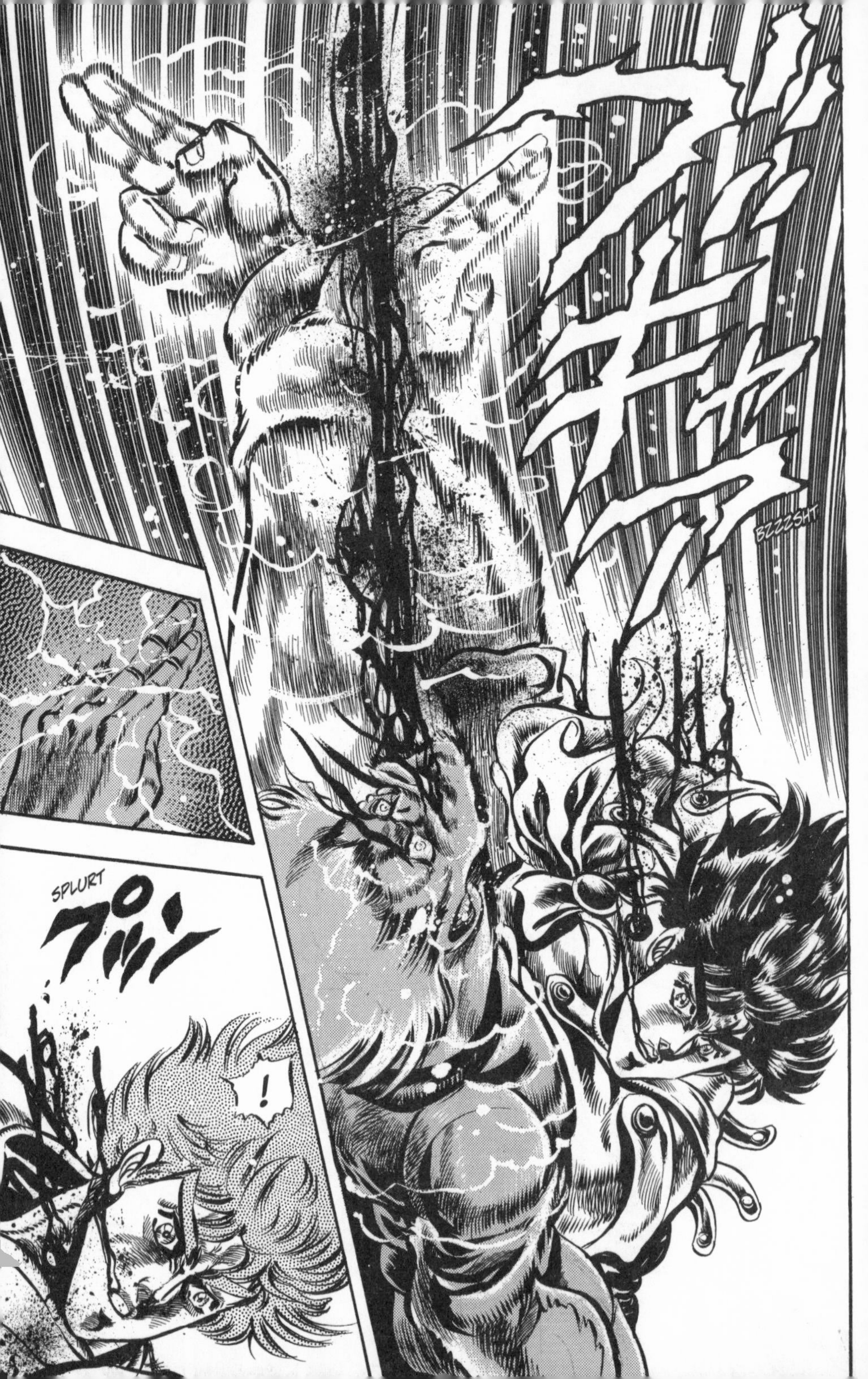
BZZZSHT
SPLURT
!

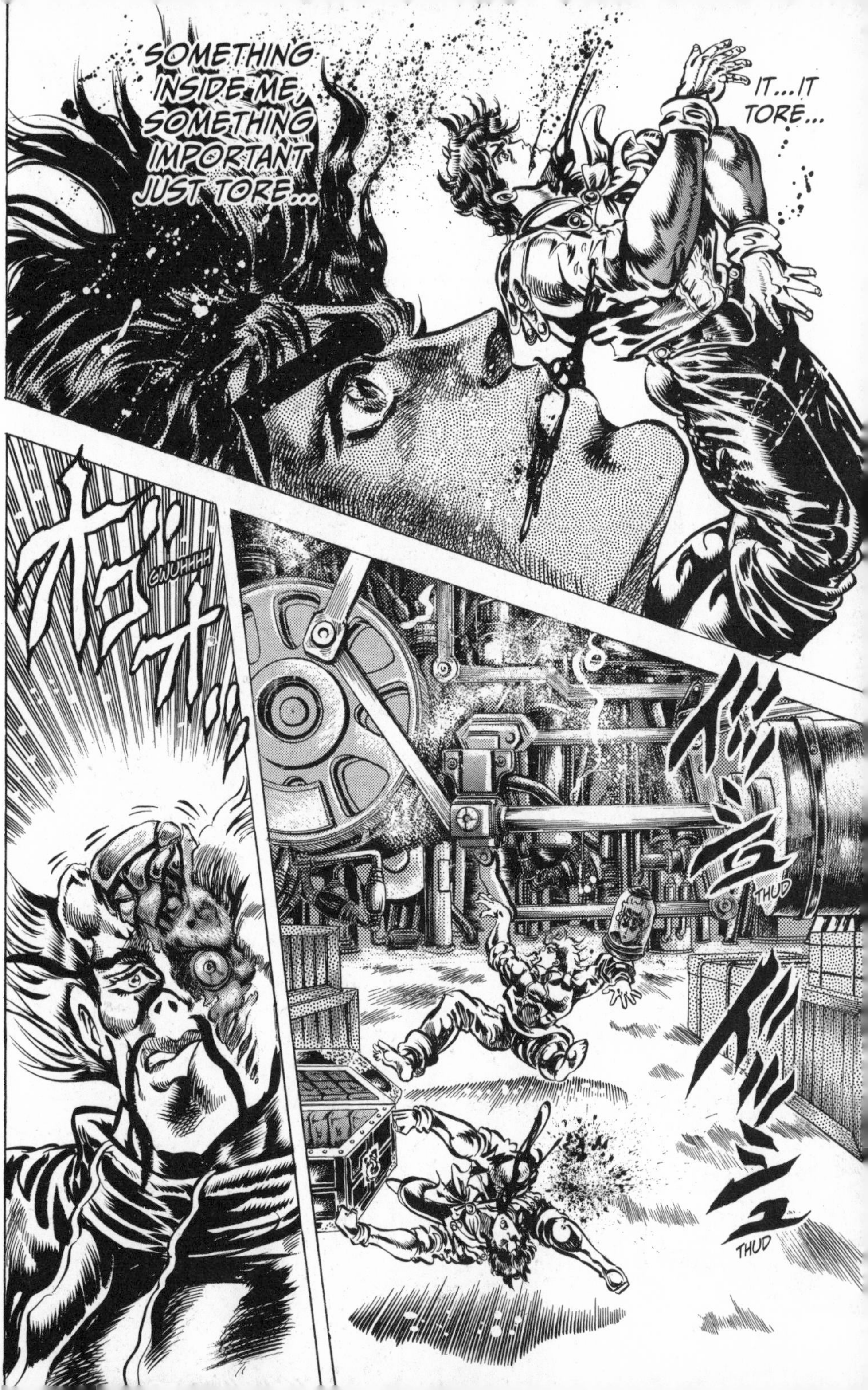
IT...IT TORE...
SOMETHING INSIDE ME, SOMETHING IMPORTANT JUST TORE...
THUD
THUD
GWUHHHH

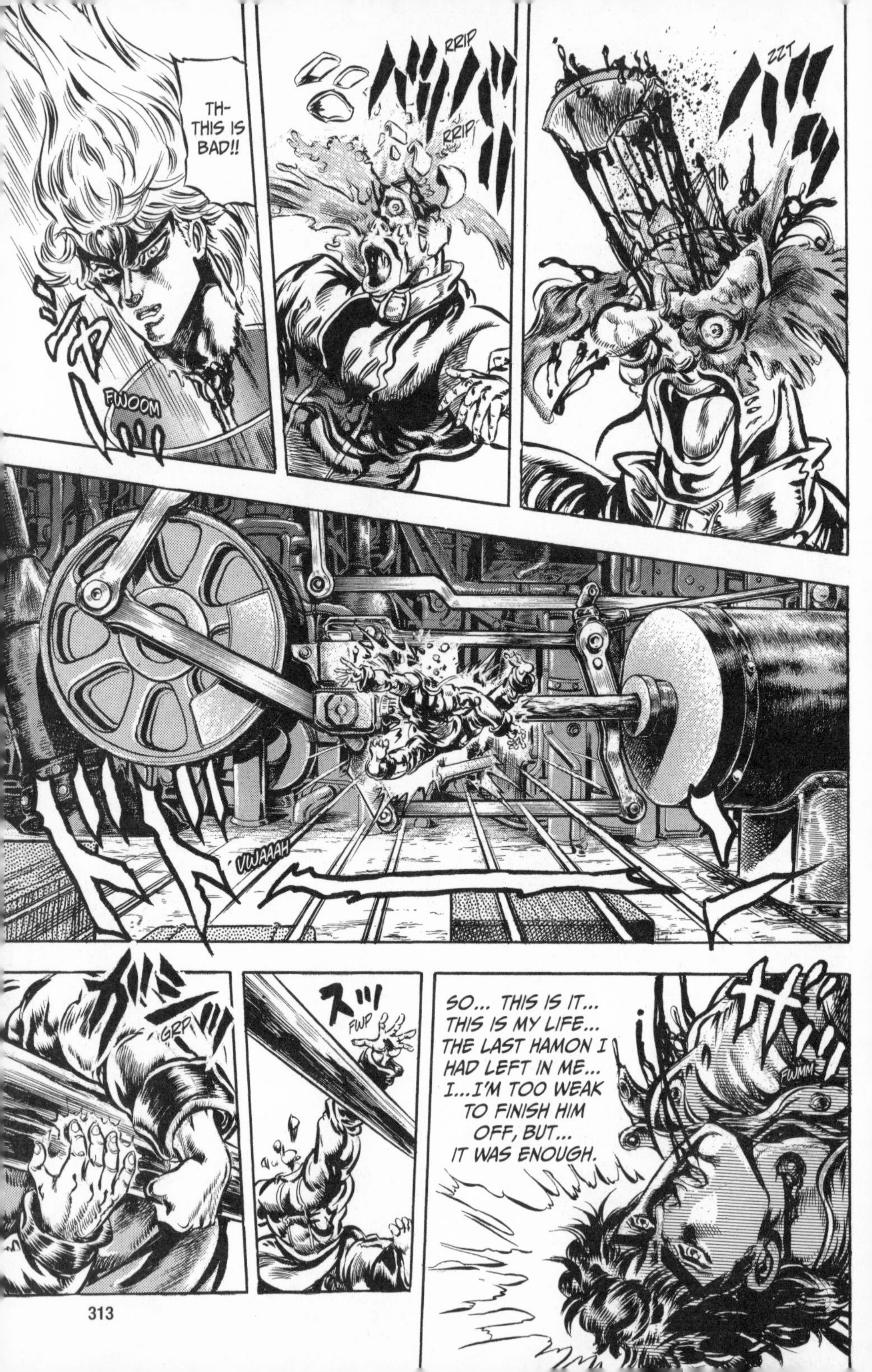
ZZT
RRIP
RRIP
TH-
THIS IS
BAD!!
FWOOM
VWAAAH
SO... THIS IS IT...
THIS IS MY LIFE...
THE LAST HAMON I
HAD LEFT IN ME...
I...I'M TOO WEAK
TO FINISH HIM
OFF, BUT...
IT WAS ENOUGH.
FWMM
FWP
GRP

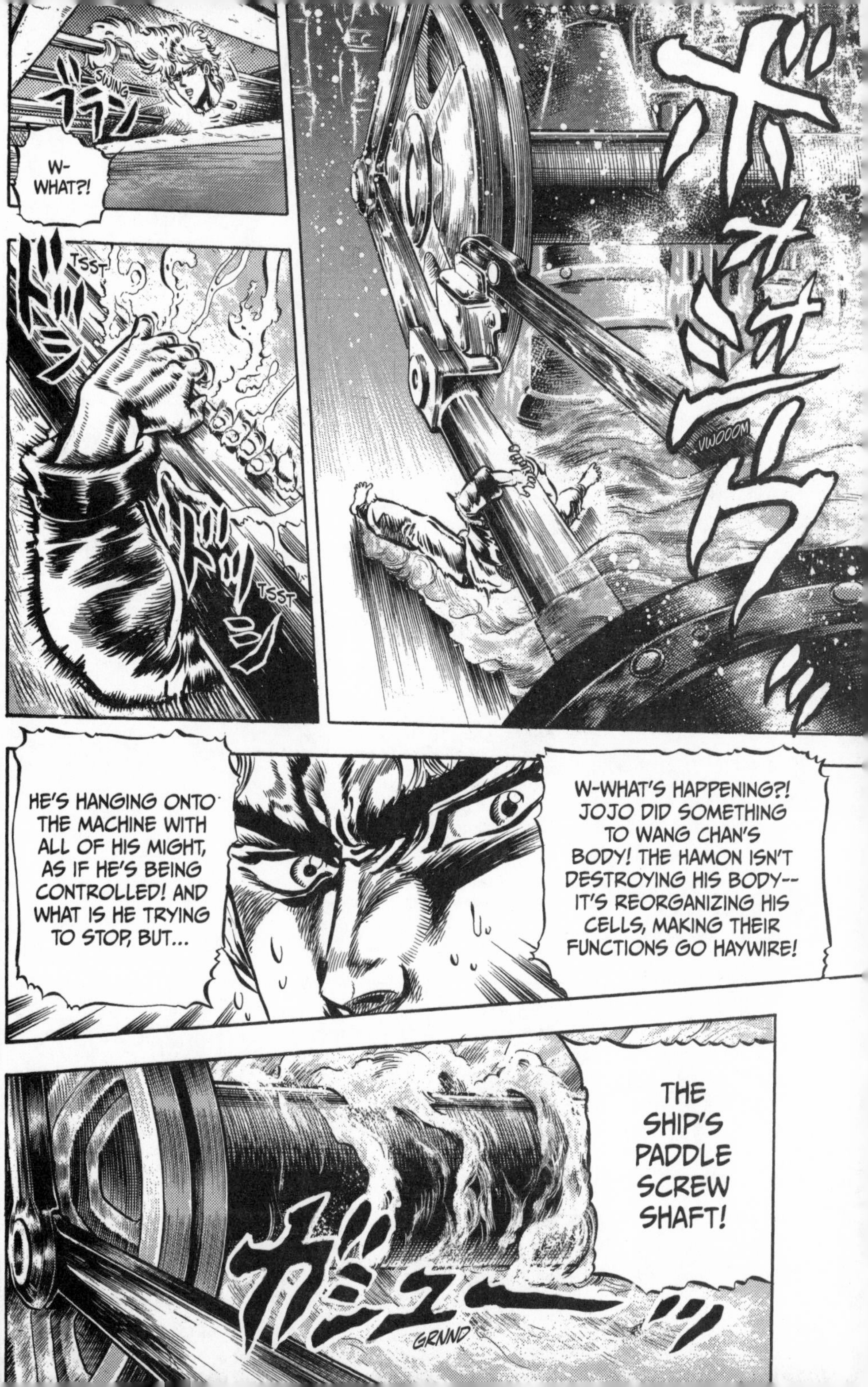

VWOOOM
SWING
W-WHAT?!
TSST
TSST
W-WHAT'S HAPPENING?! JOJO DID SOMETHING TO WANG CHAN'S BODY! THE HAMON ISN'T DESTROYING HIS BODY-- IT'S REORGANIZING HIS CELLS, MAKING THEIR FUNCTIONS GO HAYWIRE!
HE'S HANGING ONTO THE MACHINE WITH ALL OF HIS MIGHT, AS IF HE'S BEING CONTROLLED! AND WHAT IS HE TRYING TO STOP, BUT...
THE SHIP'S PADDLE SCREW SHAFT!
GRNND

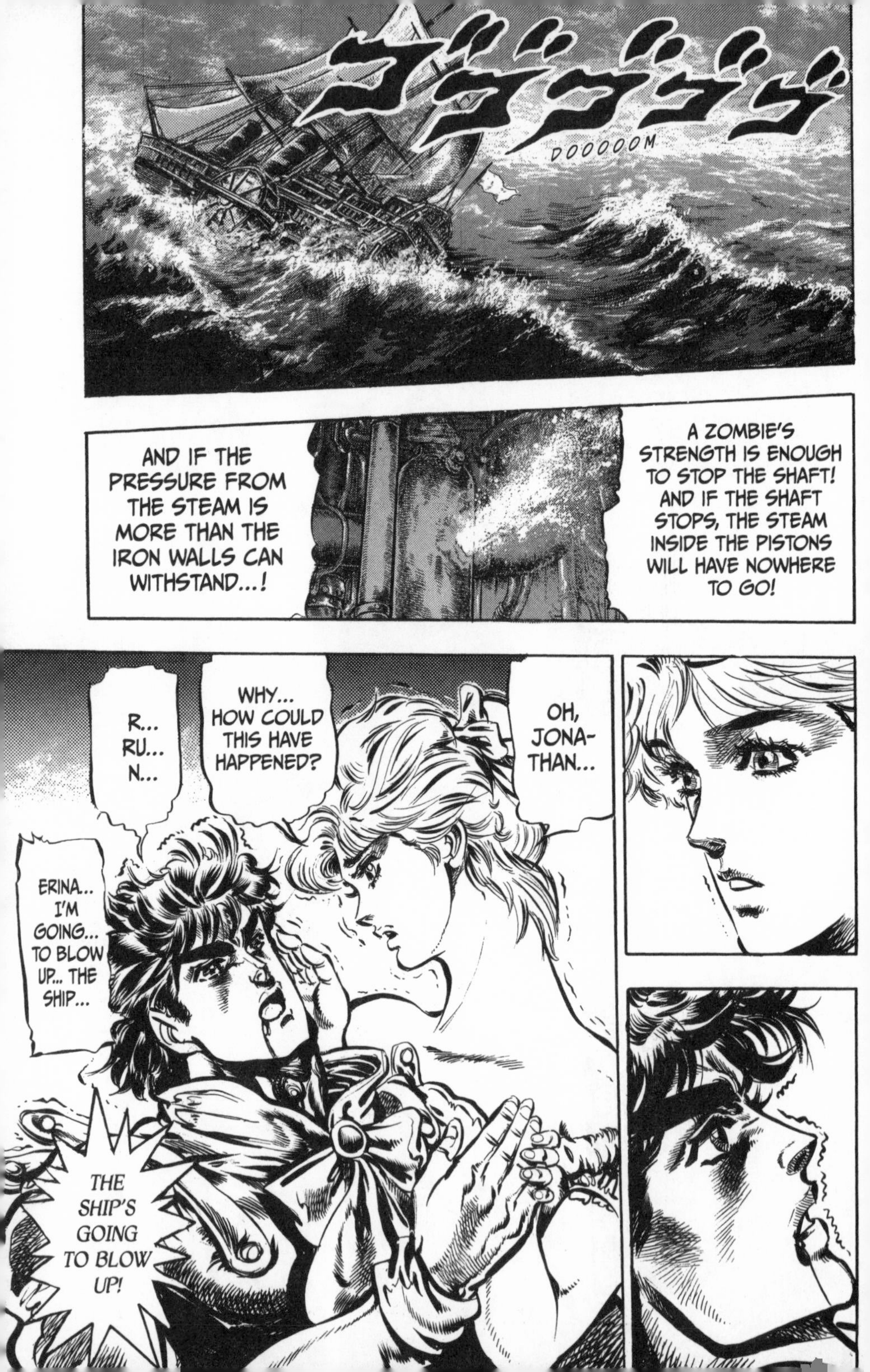
ゴゴゴゴゴ
DOOOOOOM
A ZOMBIE'S STRENGTH IS ENOUGH TO STOP THE SHAFT! AND IF THE SHAFT STOPS, THE STEAM INSIDE THE PISTONS WILL HAVE NOWHERE TO GO!
AND IF THE PRESSURE FROM THE STEAM IS MORE THAN THE IRON WALLS CAN WITHSTAND...!
OH, JONA-THAN...
WHY... HOW COULD THIS HAVE HAPPENED?
R... RU... N...
ERINA... I'M GOING... TO BLOW UP... THE SHIP...
THE SHIP'S GOING TO BLOW UP!

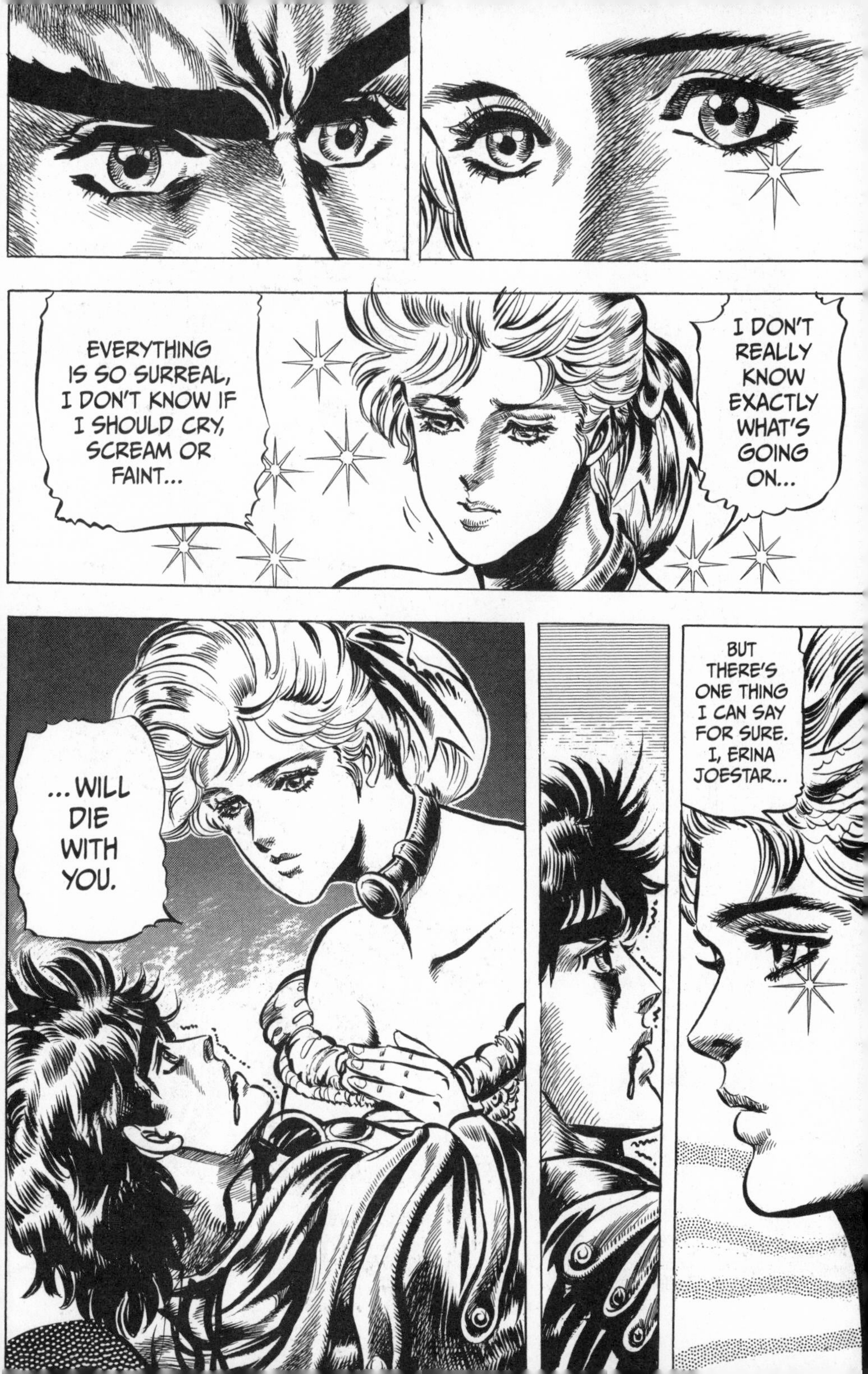
I DON'T REALLY KNOW EXACTLY WHAT'S GOING ON...
EVERYTHING IS SO SURREAL, I DON'T KNOW IF I SHOULD CRY, SCREAM OR FAINT...
BUT THERE'S ONE THING I CAN SAY FOR SURE. I, ERINA JOESTAR...
...WILL DIE WITH YOU.

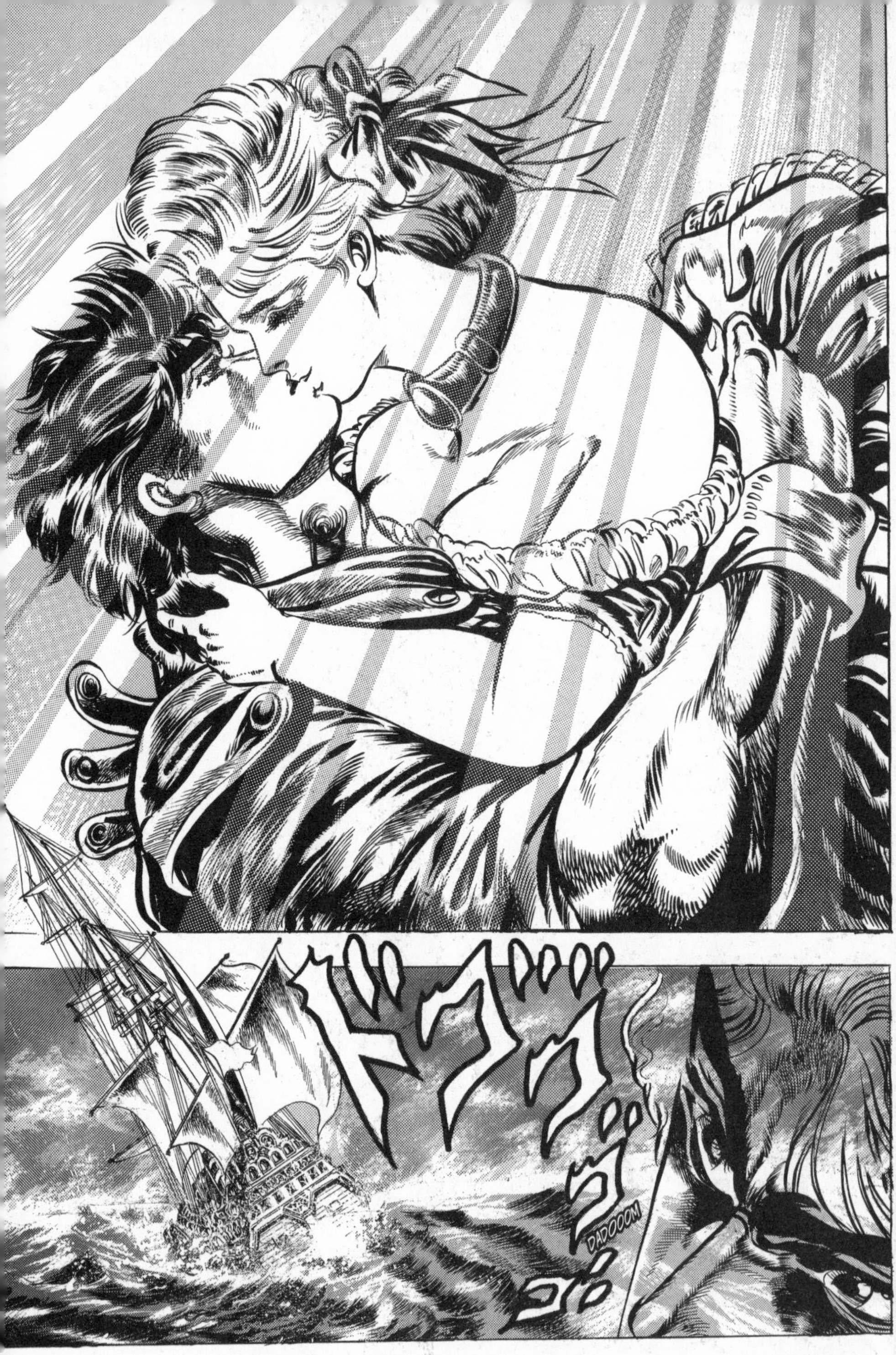
DADOOOM

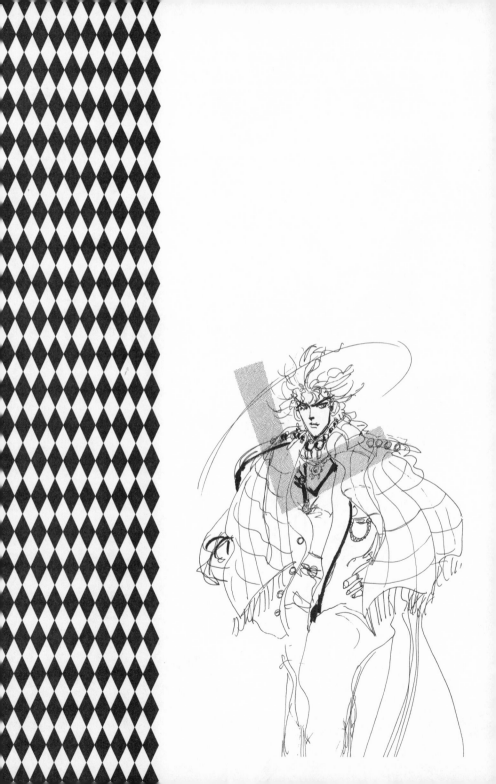

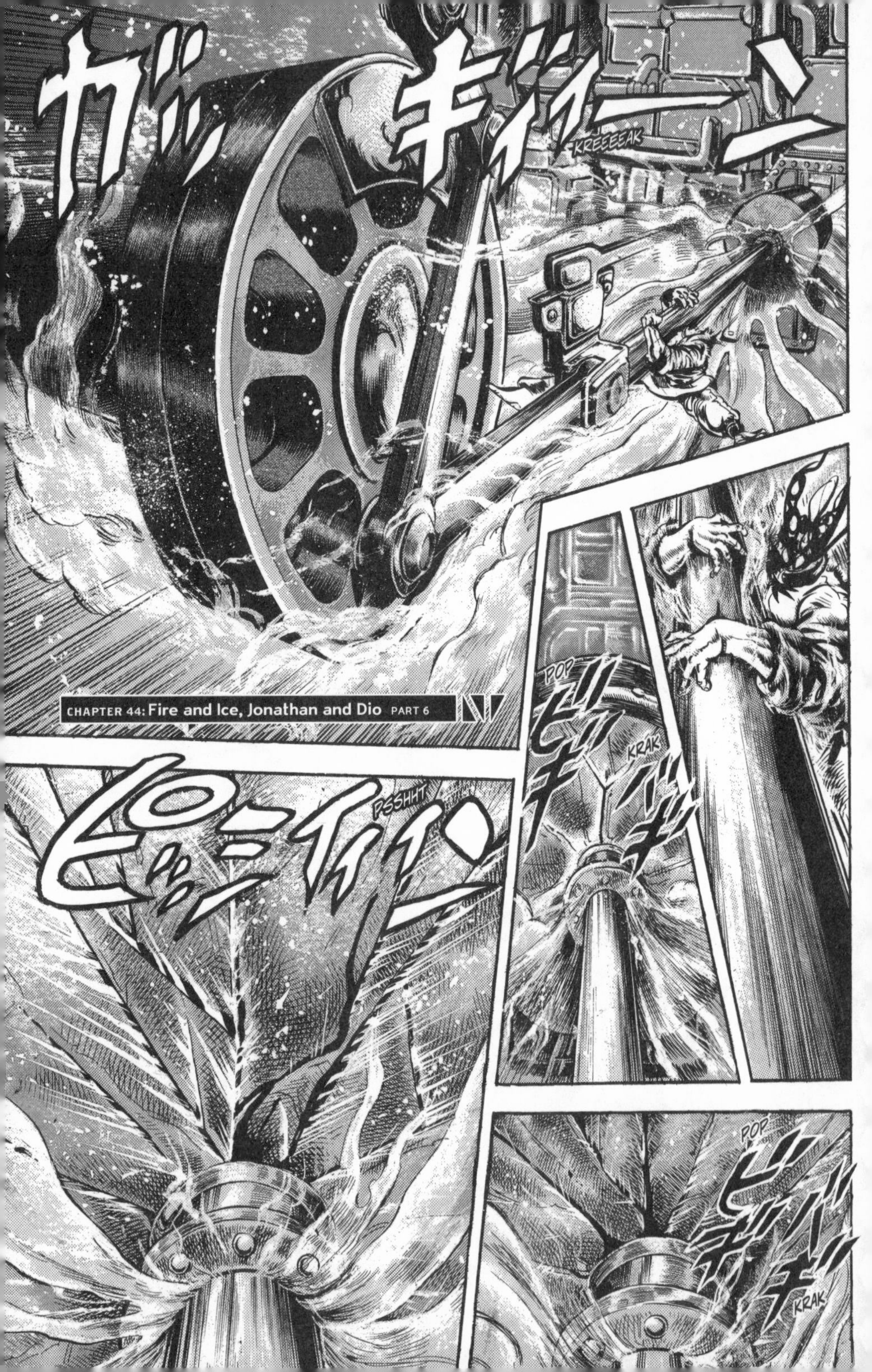
KREEEEAK
CHAPTER 44: Fire and Ice, Jonathan and Dio PART 6
POP
KRAK
PSSHHT
POP
KRAK

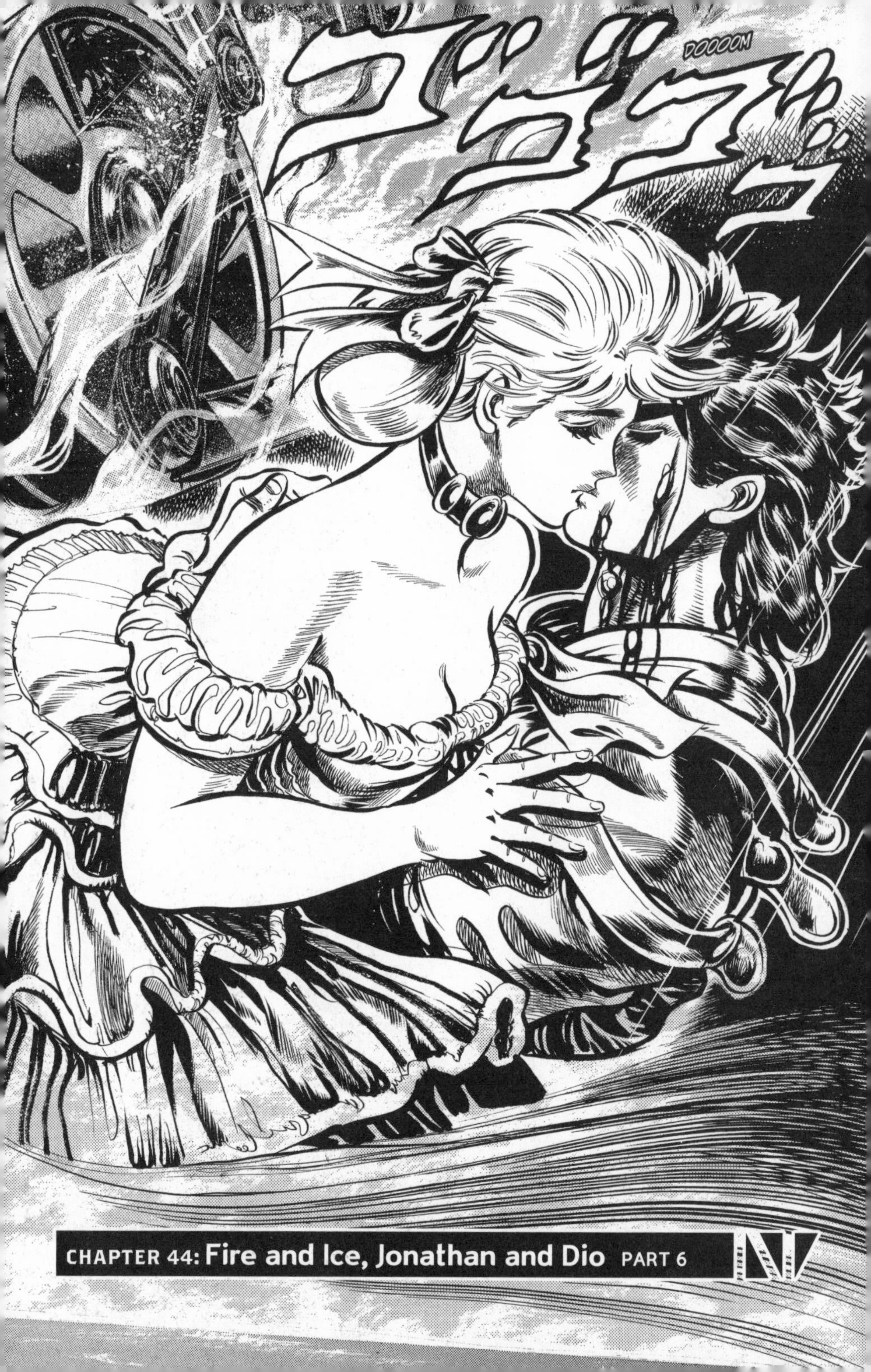
DOOOOM

CHAPTER 44: Fire and Ice, Jonathan and Dio PART 6

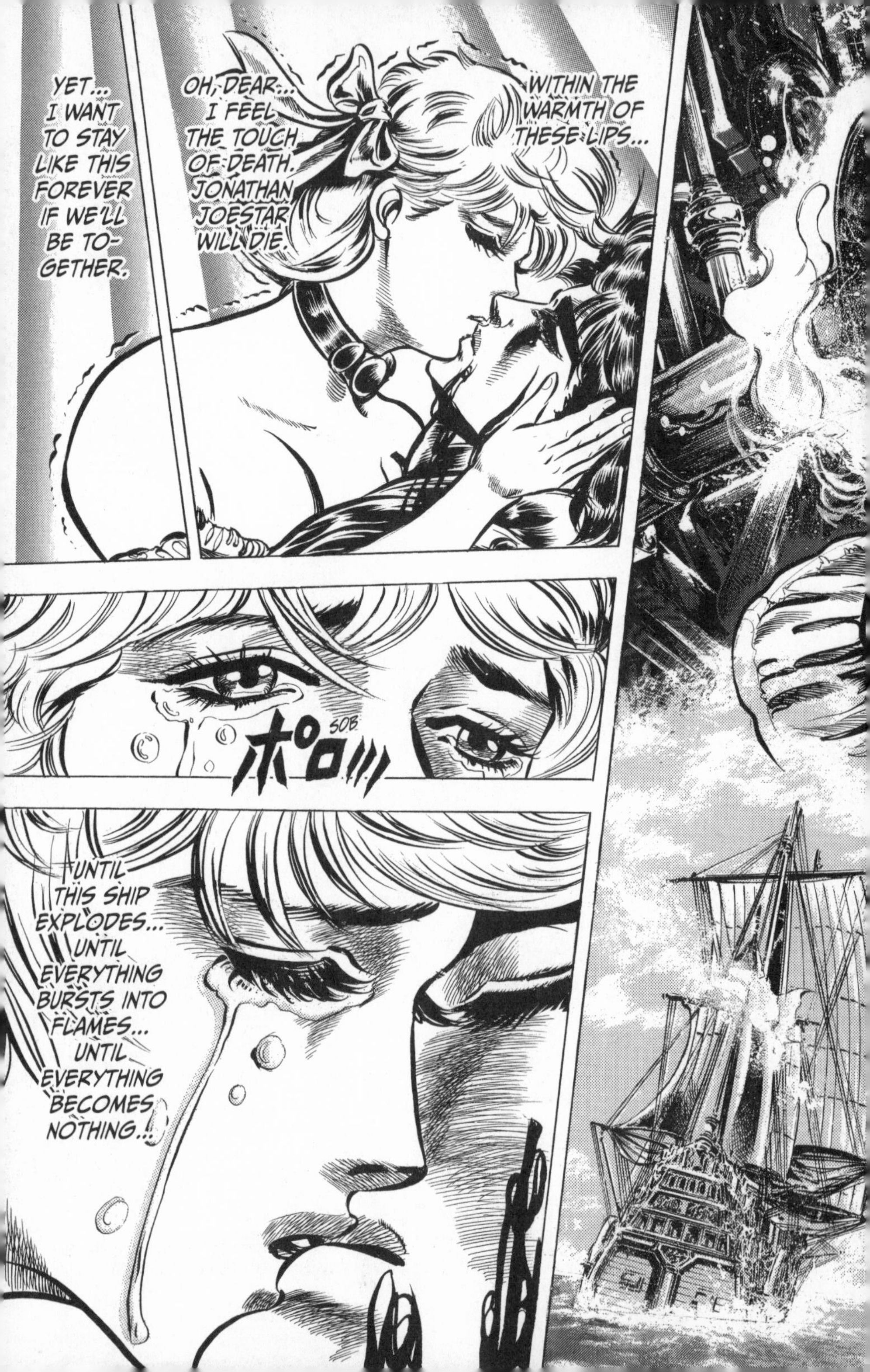
WITHIN THE WARMTH OF THESE LIPS...
OH, DEAR... I FEEL THE TOUCH OF DEATH. JONATHAN JOESTAR WILL DIE.
YET... I WANT TO STAY LIKE THIS FOREVER IF WE'LL BE TO-GETHER.
SOB
ポロ
UNTIL THIS SHIP EXPLODES... UNTIL EVERYTHING BURSTS INTO FLAMES... UNTIL EVERYTHING BECOMES NOTHING...!

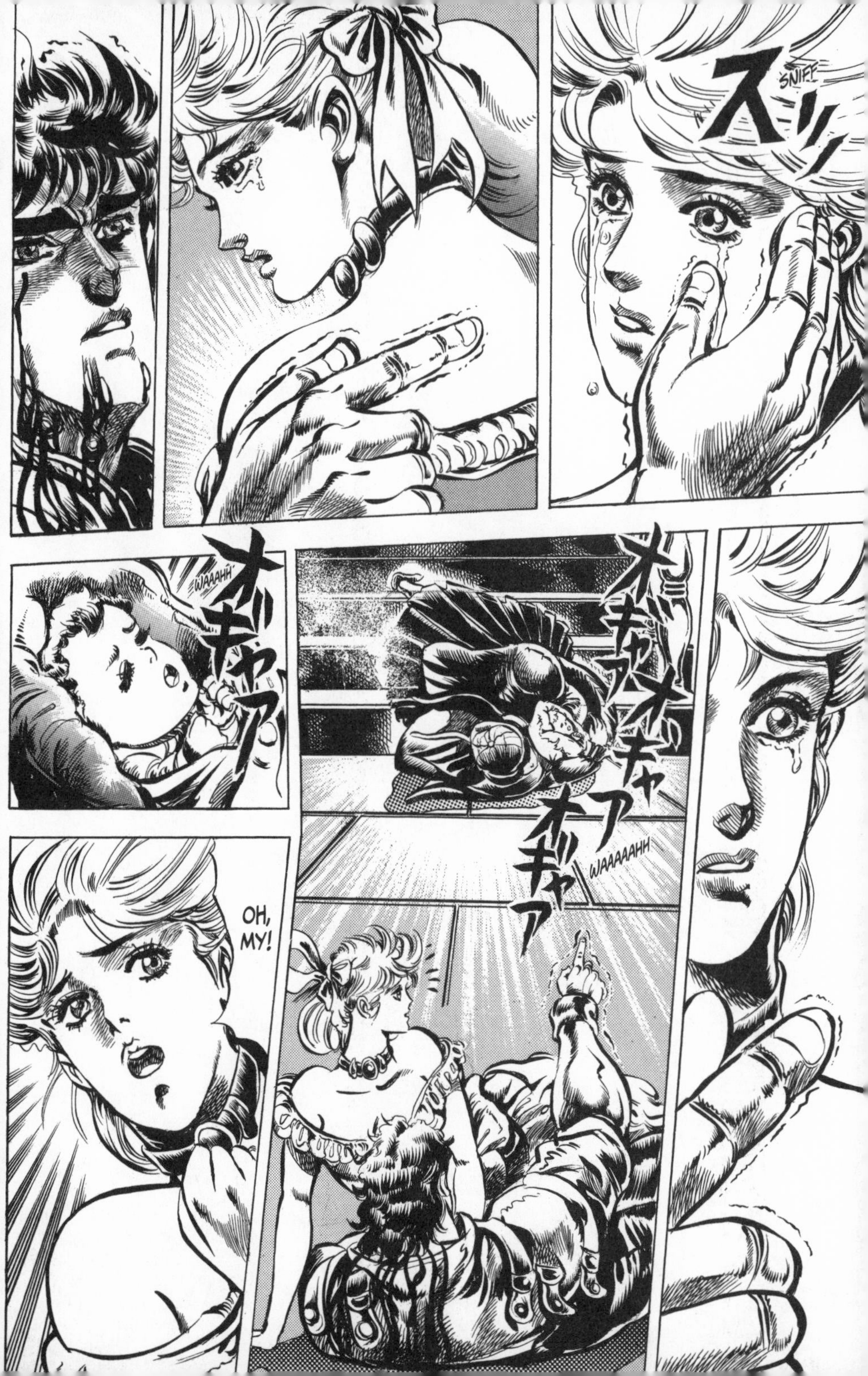
スリ
SNIFF
オギャアオギャア
オギャア
WAAAAAHH
オギャア
WAAAHH
OH, MY!

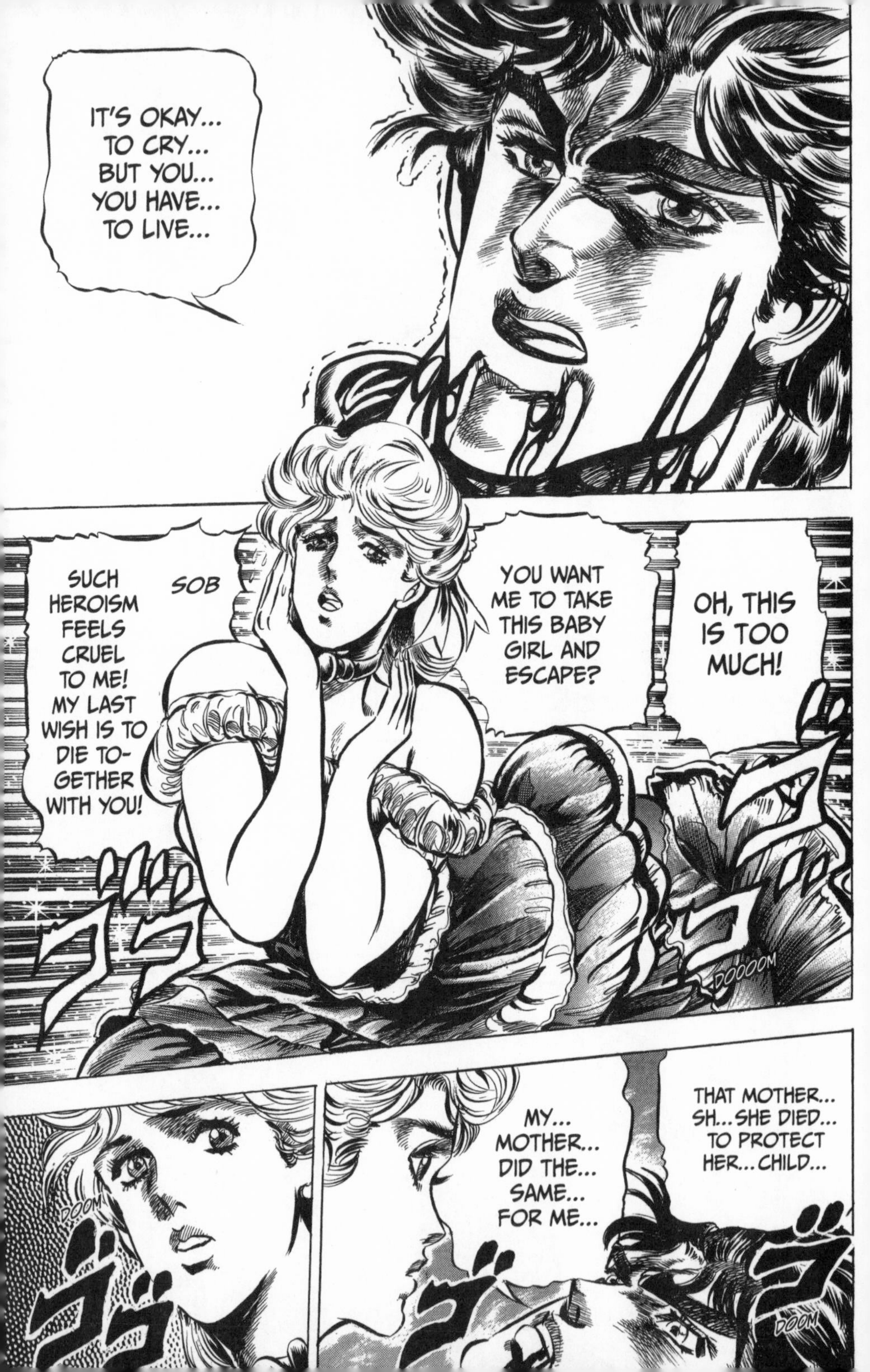
IT'S OKAY... TO CRY... BUT YOU... YOU HAVE... TO LIVE...
OH, THIS IS TOO MUCH!
YOU WANT ME TO TAKE THIS BABY GIRL AND ESCAPE?
SOB
SUCH HEROISM FEELS CRUEL TO ME! MY LAST WISH IS TO DIE TO-GETHER WITH YOU!
DOOOOM
THAT MOTHER... SH...SHE DIED... TO PROTECT HER...CHILD...
DOOM
MY... MOTHER... DID THE... SAME... FOR ME...
DOOM

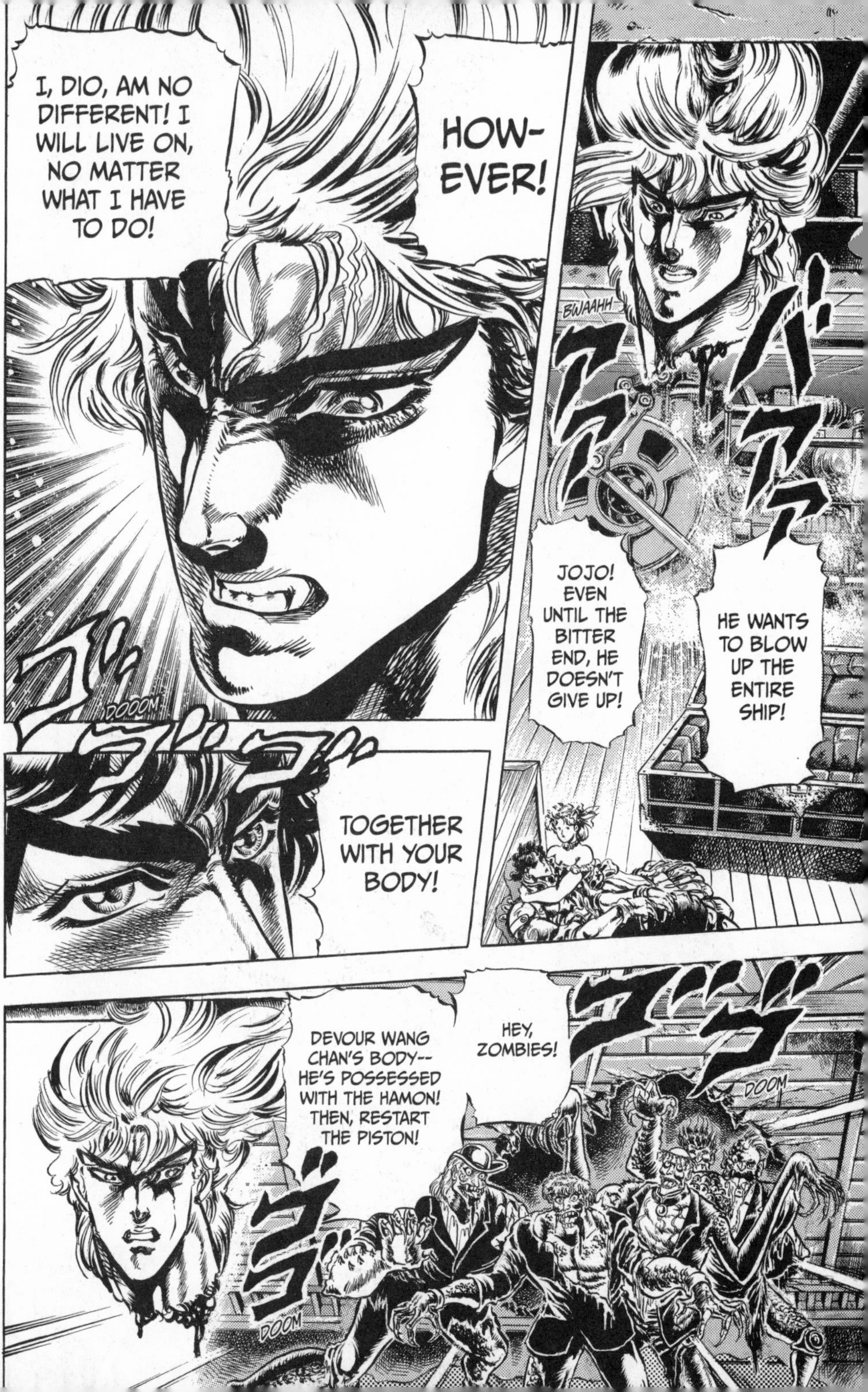
BWAAHH
JOJO! EVEN UNTIL THE BITTER END, HE DOESN'T GIVE UP!
HE WANTS TO BLOW UP THE ENTIRE SHIP!
I, DIO, AM NO DIFFERENT! I WILL LIVE ON, NO MATTER WHAT I HAVE TO DO!
HOW-EVER!
DOOOM
TOGETHER WITH YOUR BODY!
HEY, ZOMBIES!
DEVOUR WANG CHAN'S BODY-- HE'S POSSESSED WITH THE HAMON! THEN, RESTART THE PISTON!
DOOM
DOOM

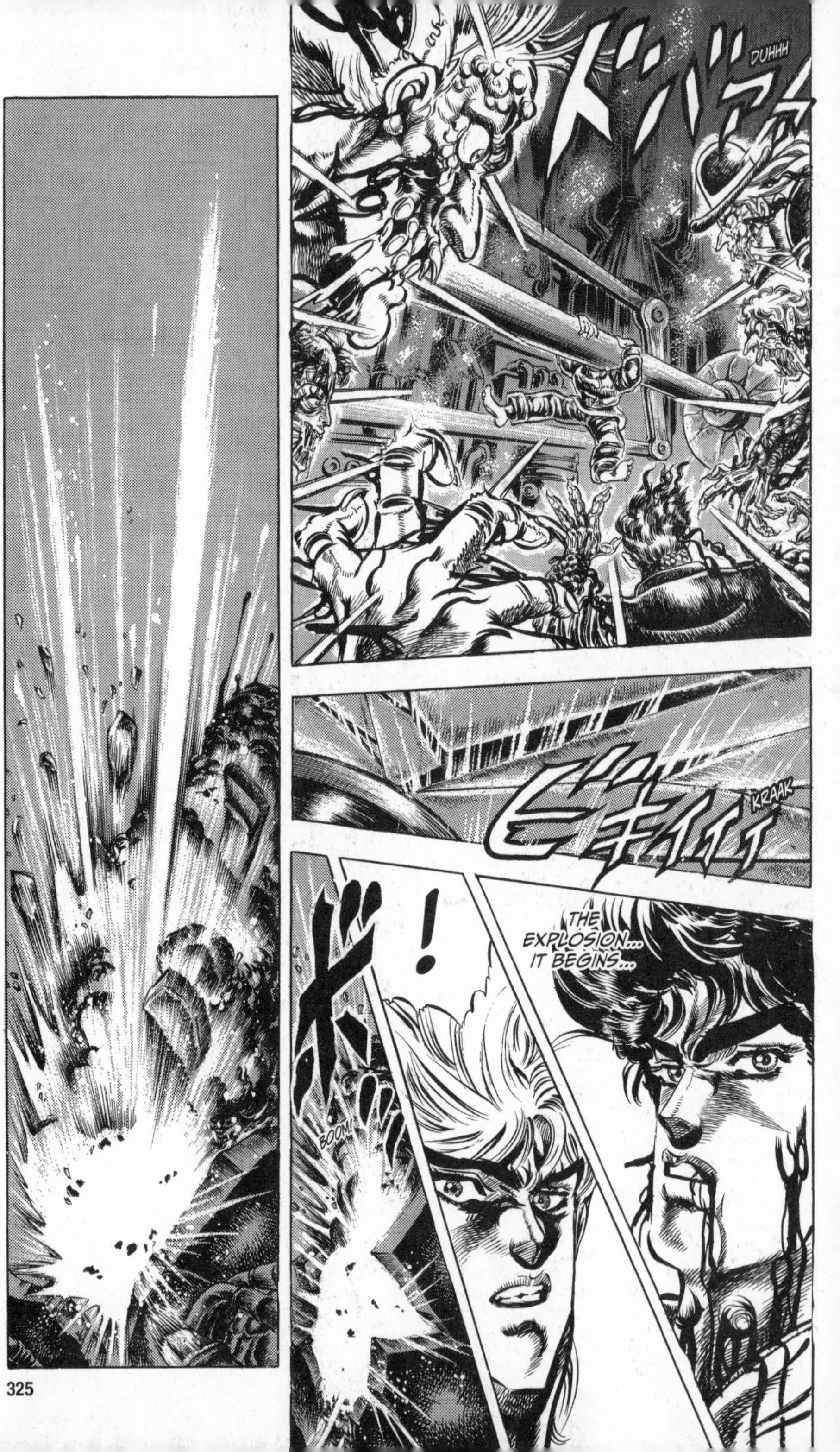
DUHHH
KRAAK
THE EXPLOSION... IT BEGINS...
!
BOOM!

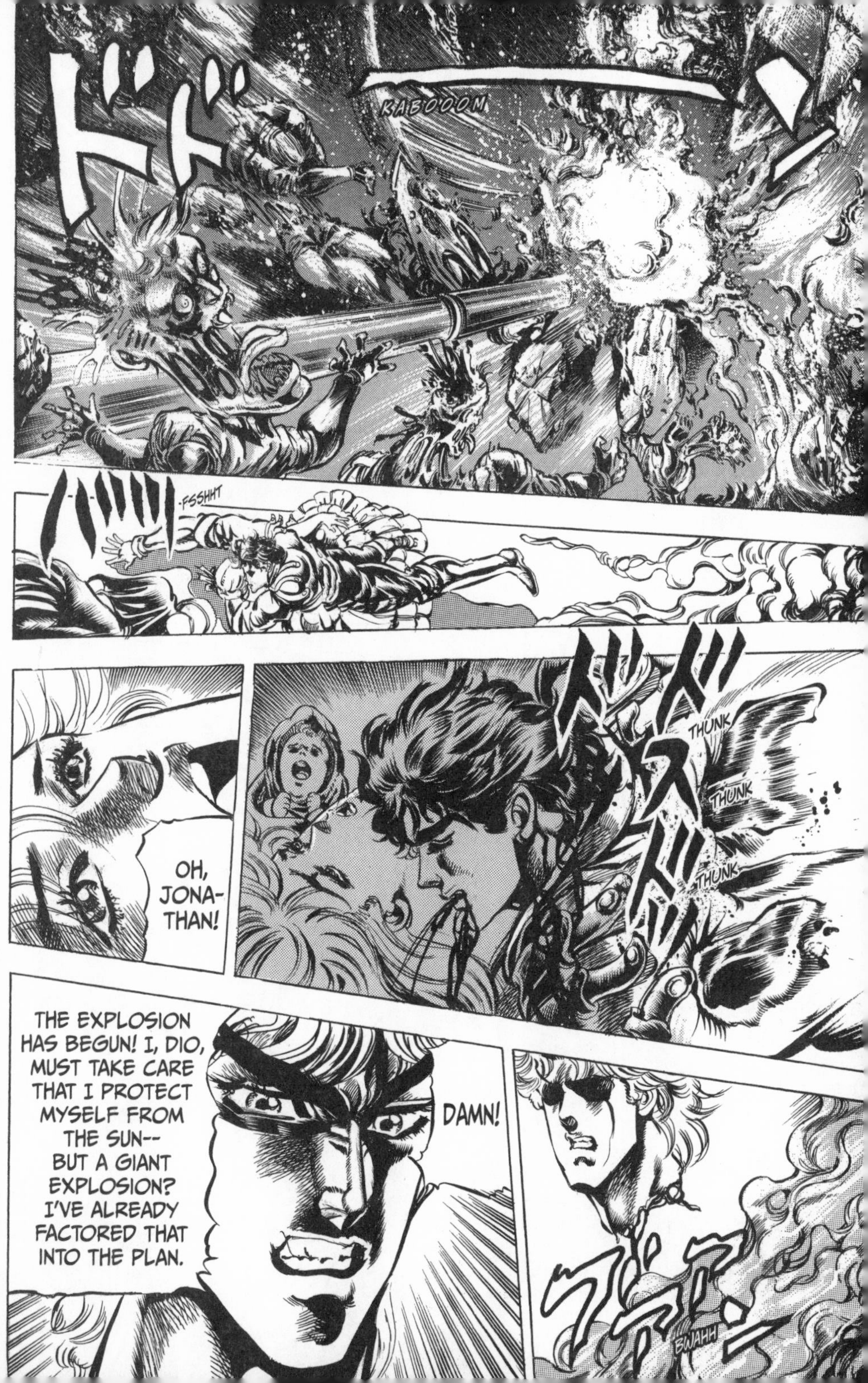
KABOOOM
FSSHHT
THUNK
THUNK
THUNK
OH, JONATHAN!
BWAHH
THE EXPLOSION HAS BEGUN! I, DIO, MUST TAKE CARE THAT I PROTECT MYSELF FROM THE SUN-- BUT A GIANT EXPLOSION? I'VE ALREADY FACTORED THAT INTO THE PLAN.
DAMN!

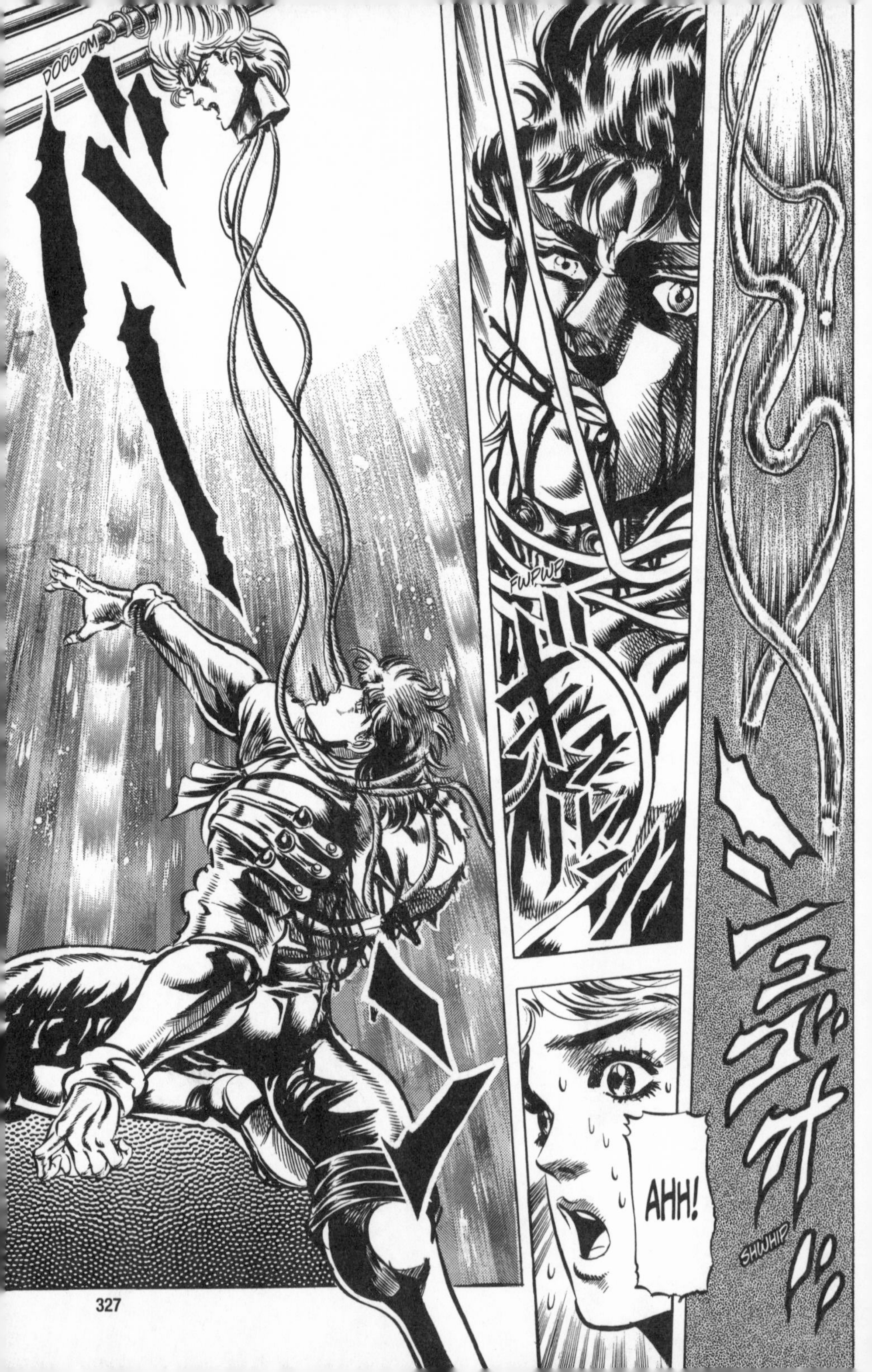
SHWHIP
FWPWP
AHH!
DOOOOM

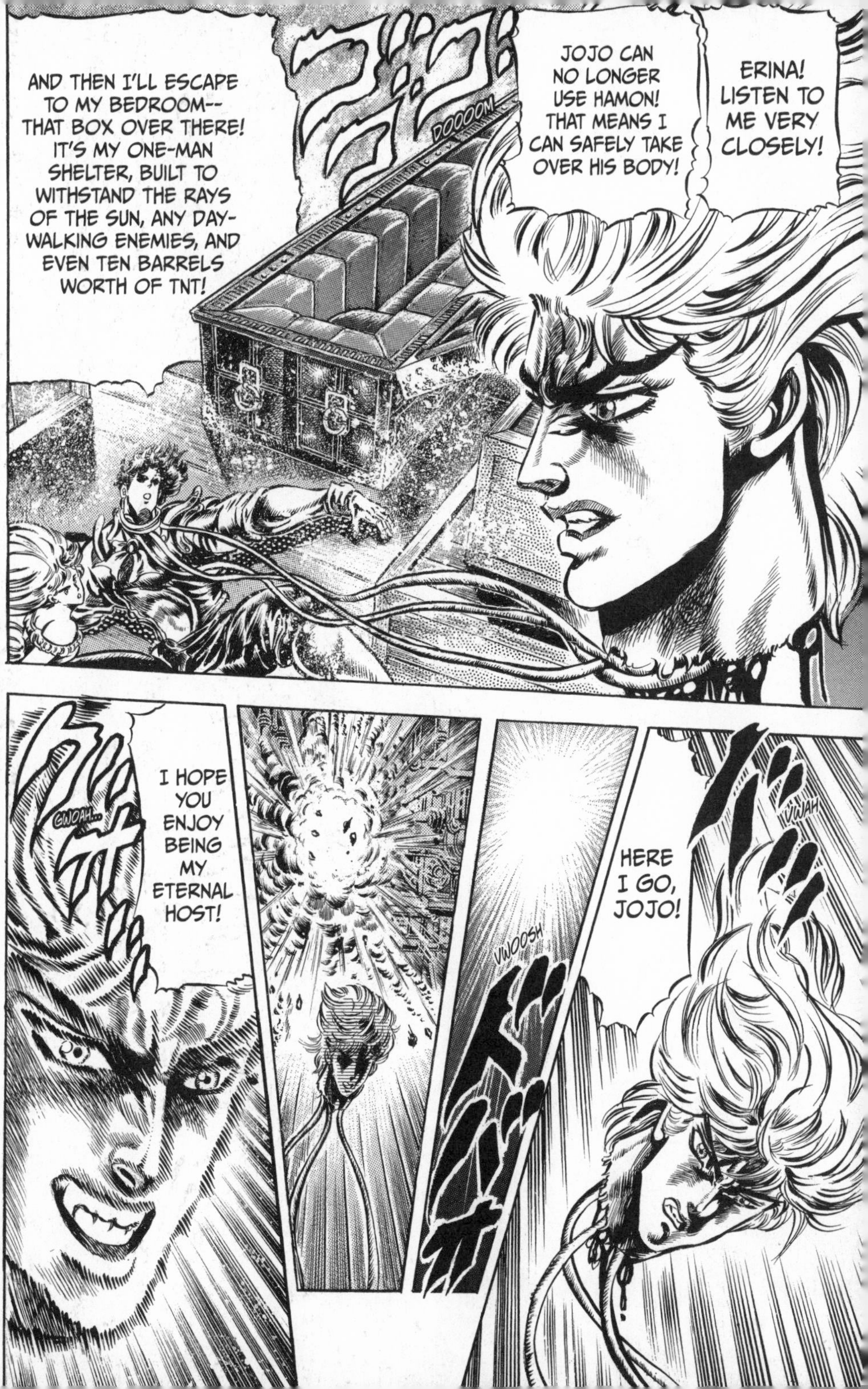
ERINA! LISTEN TO ME VERY CLOSELY!
JOJO CAN NO LONGER USE HAMON! THAT MEANS I CAN SAFELY TAKE OVER HIS BODY!
DOOOOM
AND THEN I'LL ESCAPE TO MY BEDROOM-- THAT BOX OVER THERE! IT'S MY ONE-MAN SHELTER, BUILT TO WITHSTAND THE RAYS OF THE SUN, ANY DAY-WALKING ENEMIES, AND EVEN TEN BARRELS WORTH OF TNT!
VWAH
HERE I GO, JOJO!
VWOOSH
GWOAH...
I HOPE YOU ENJOY BEING MY ETERNAL HOST!

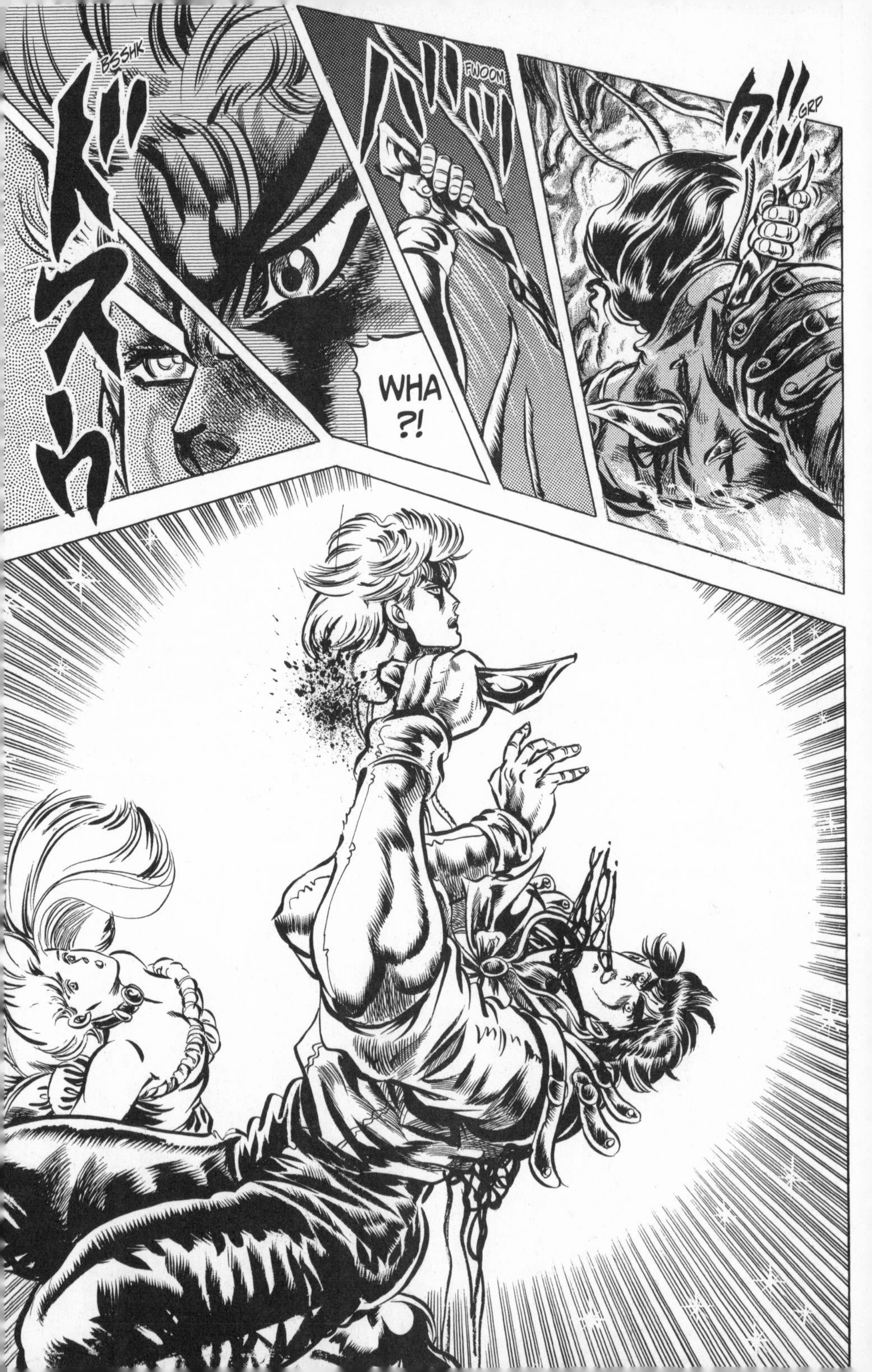
GRP
FWOOM
WHA ?!
BSSHK

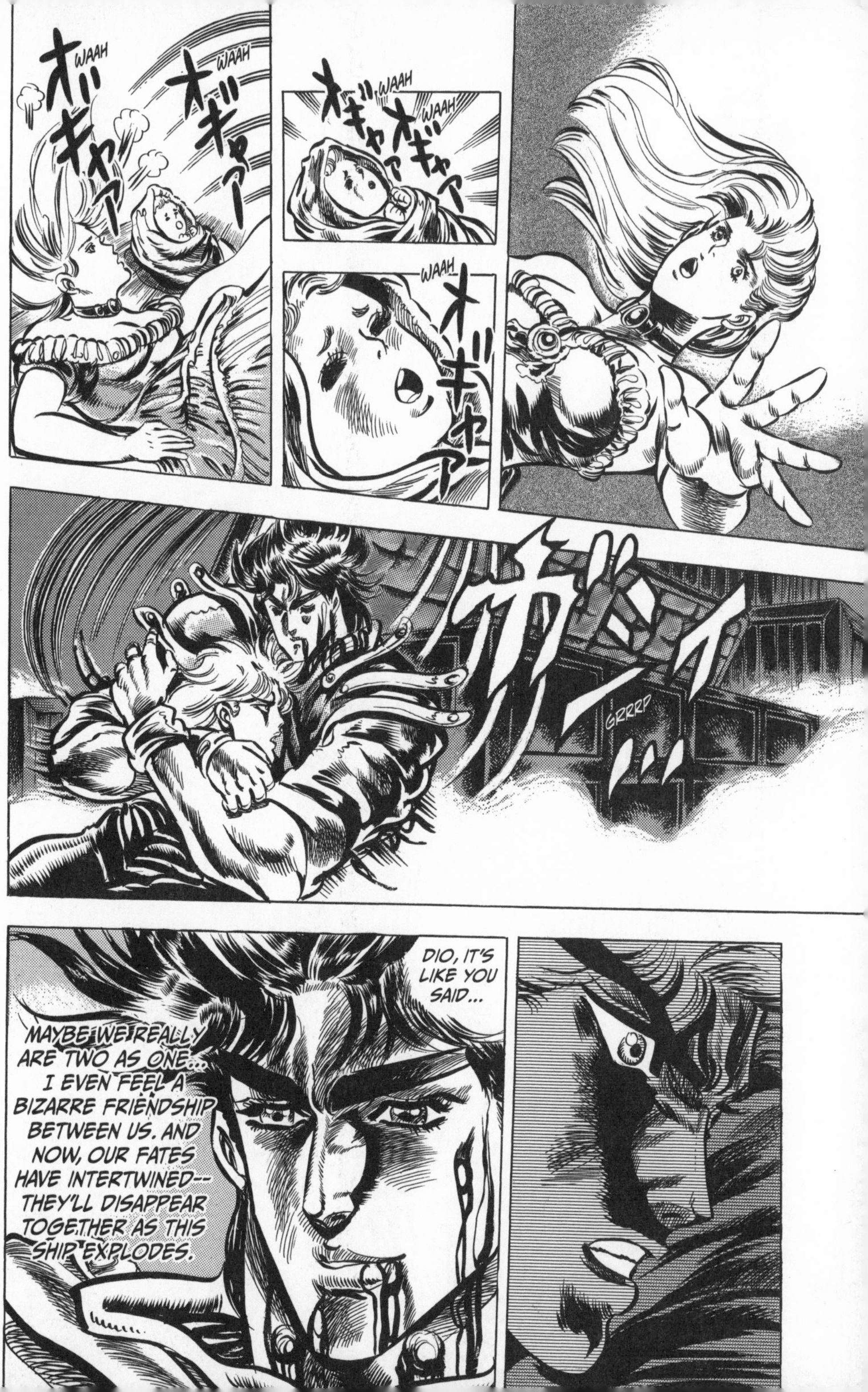
WAAH
WAAH
WAAH
WAAH
WAAH
GRRRP
DIO, IT'S LIKE YOU SAID...
MAYBE WE REALLY ARE TWO AS ONE... I EVEN FEEL A BIZARRE FRIENDSHIP BETWEEN US. AND NOW, OUR FATES HAVE INTERTWINED-- THEY'LL DISAPPEAR TOGETHER AS THIS SHIP EXPLODES.

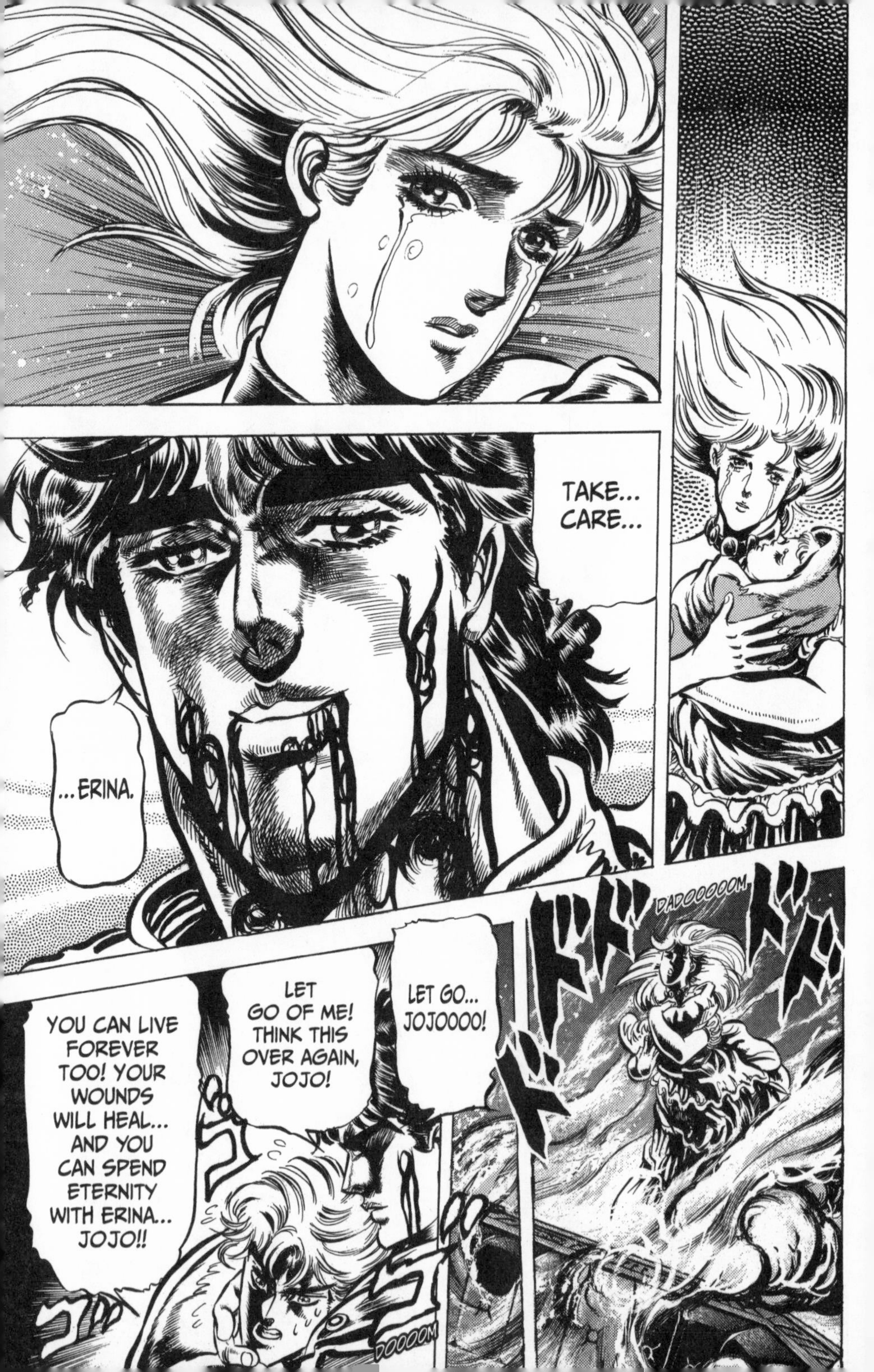
TAKE... CARE...
...ERINA.
DADOOOOOM
LET GO... JOJOOOO!
LET GO OF ME! THINK THIS OVER AGAIN, JOJO!
YOU CAN LIVE FOREVER TOO! YOUR WOUNDS WILL HEAL... AND YOU CAN SPEND ETERNITY WITH ERINA... JOJO!!
DOOOOM

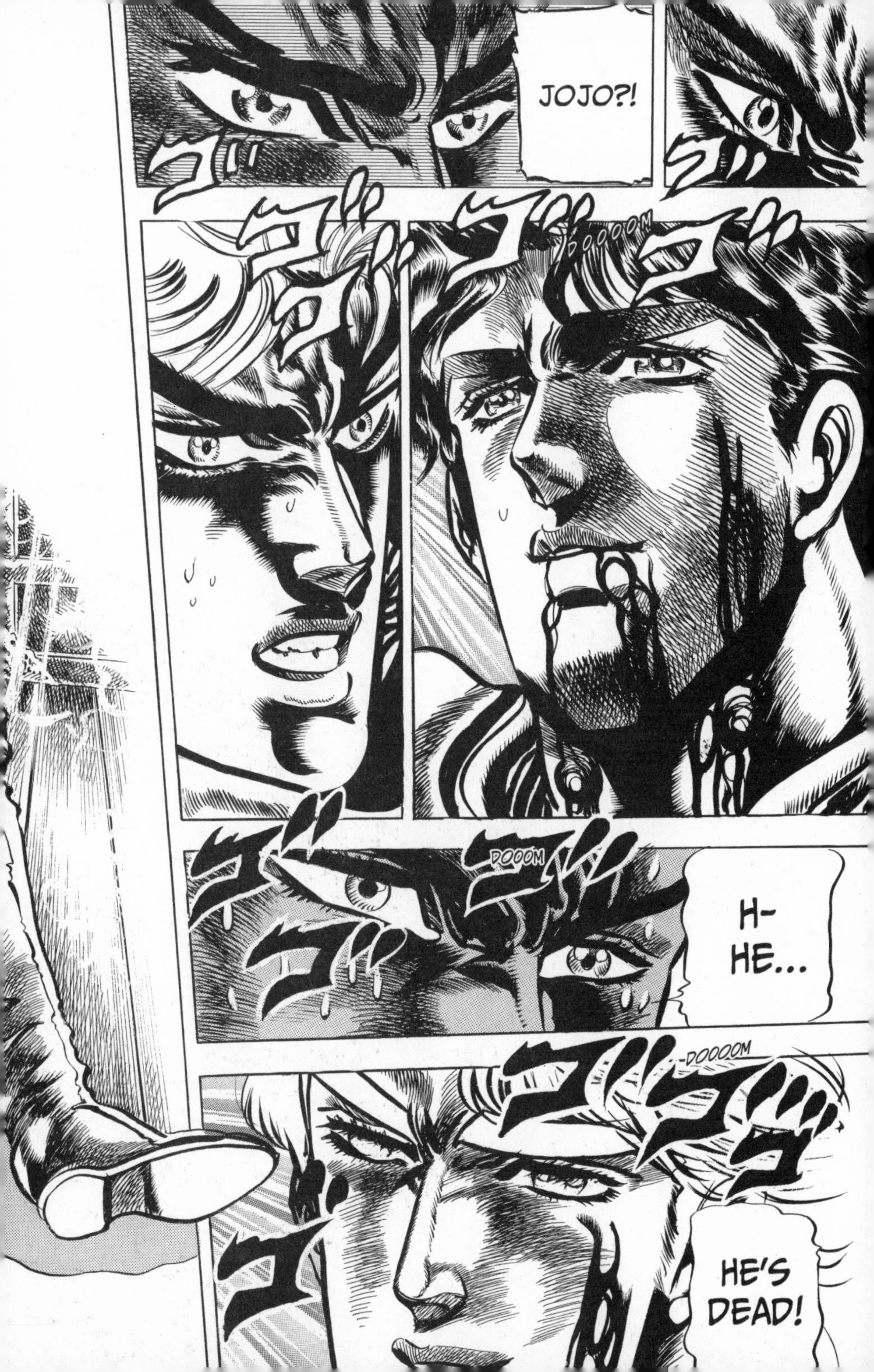
JOJO?!
DOOOOM
H-
HE...
DOOOM
DOOOOM
HE'S
DEAD!

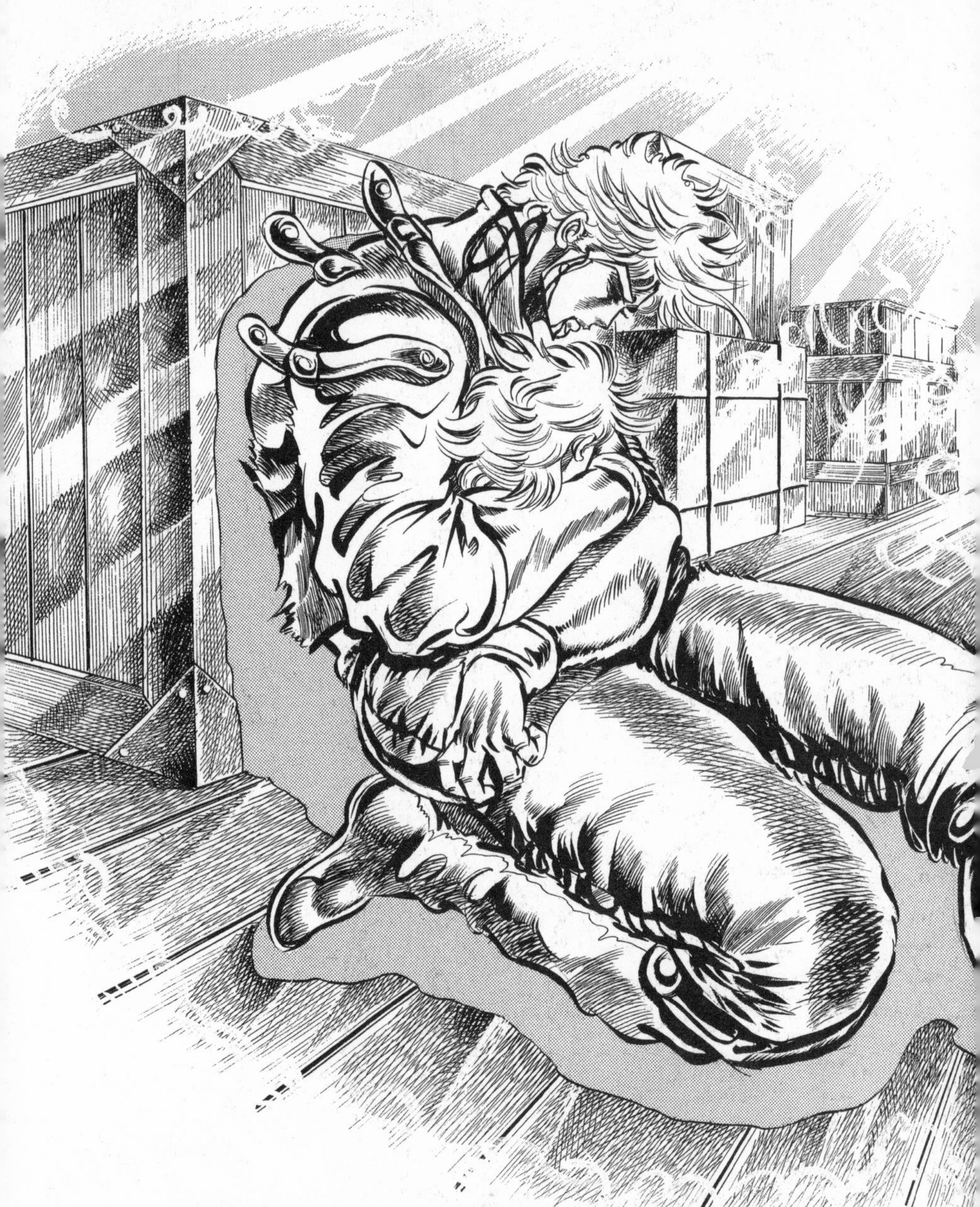

JONATHAN JOESTAR,
DIED FEBRUARY 7, 1889

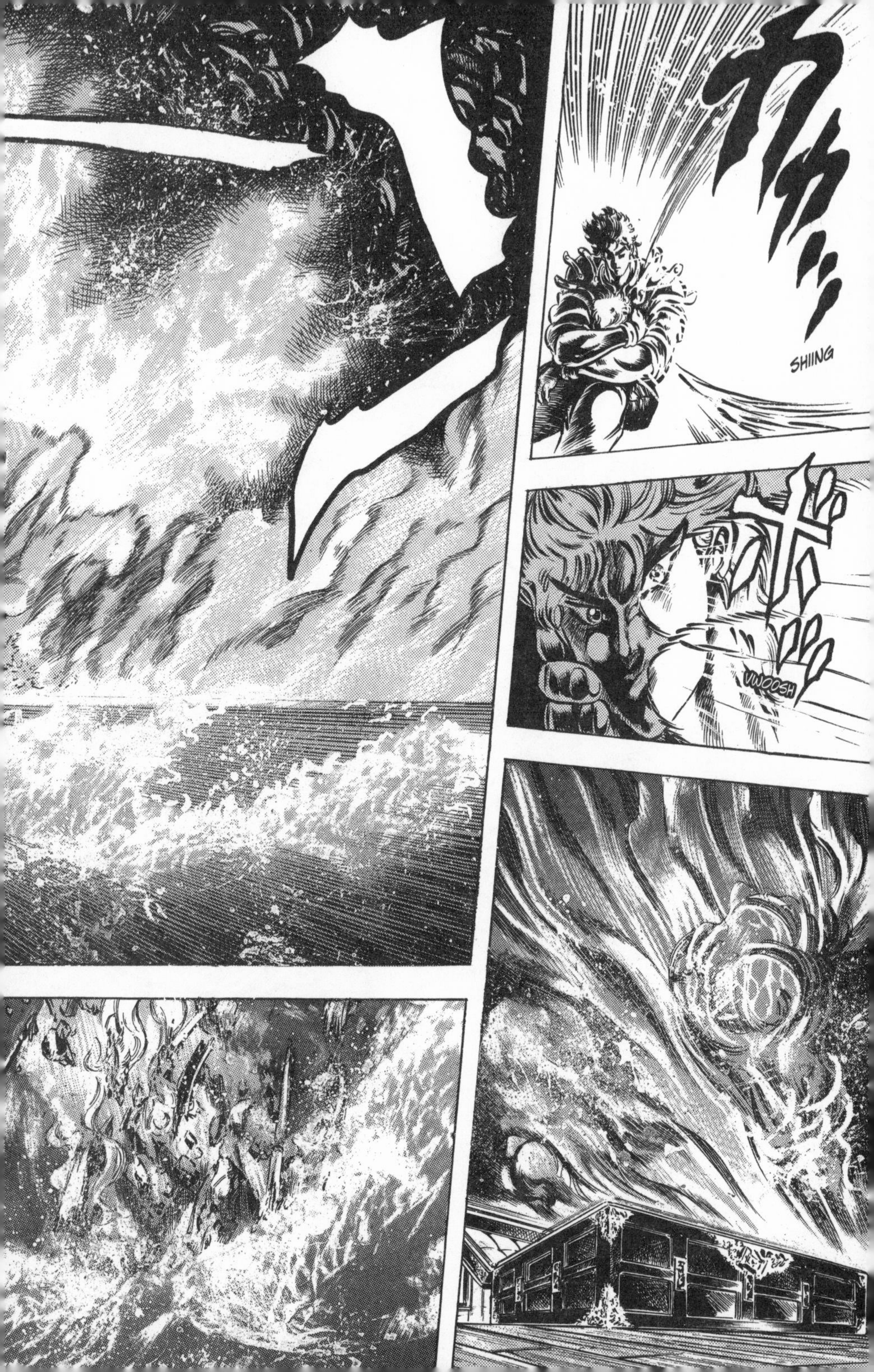
SHIING
VWOOSH

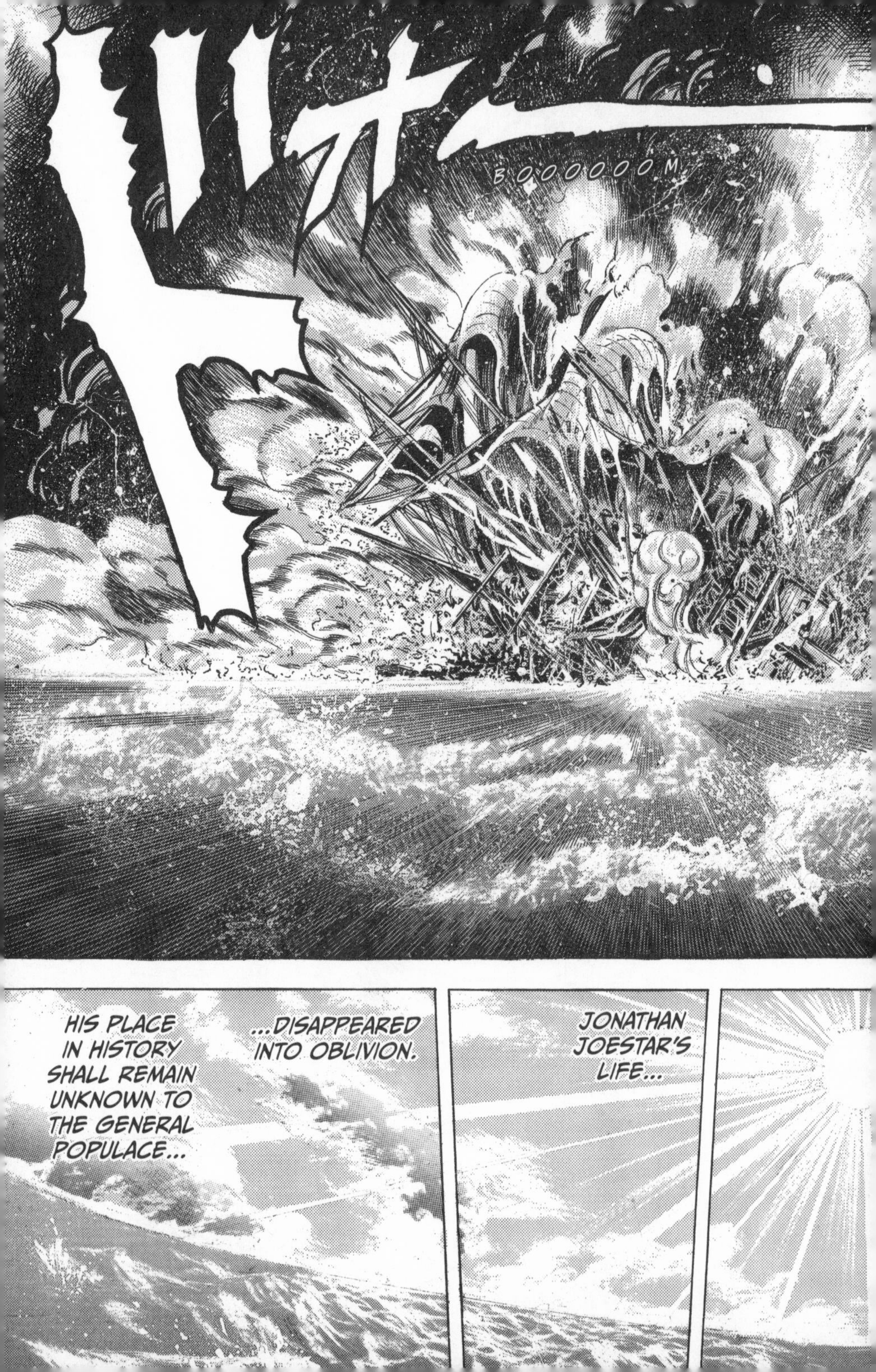
BOOOOOOOM
JONATHAN JOESTAR'S LIFE...
...DISAPPEARED INTO OBLIVION.
HIS PLACE IN HISTORY SHALL REMAIN UNKNOWN TO THE GENERAL POPULACE...

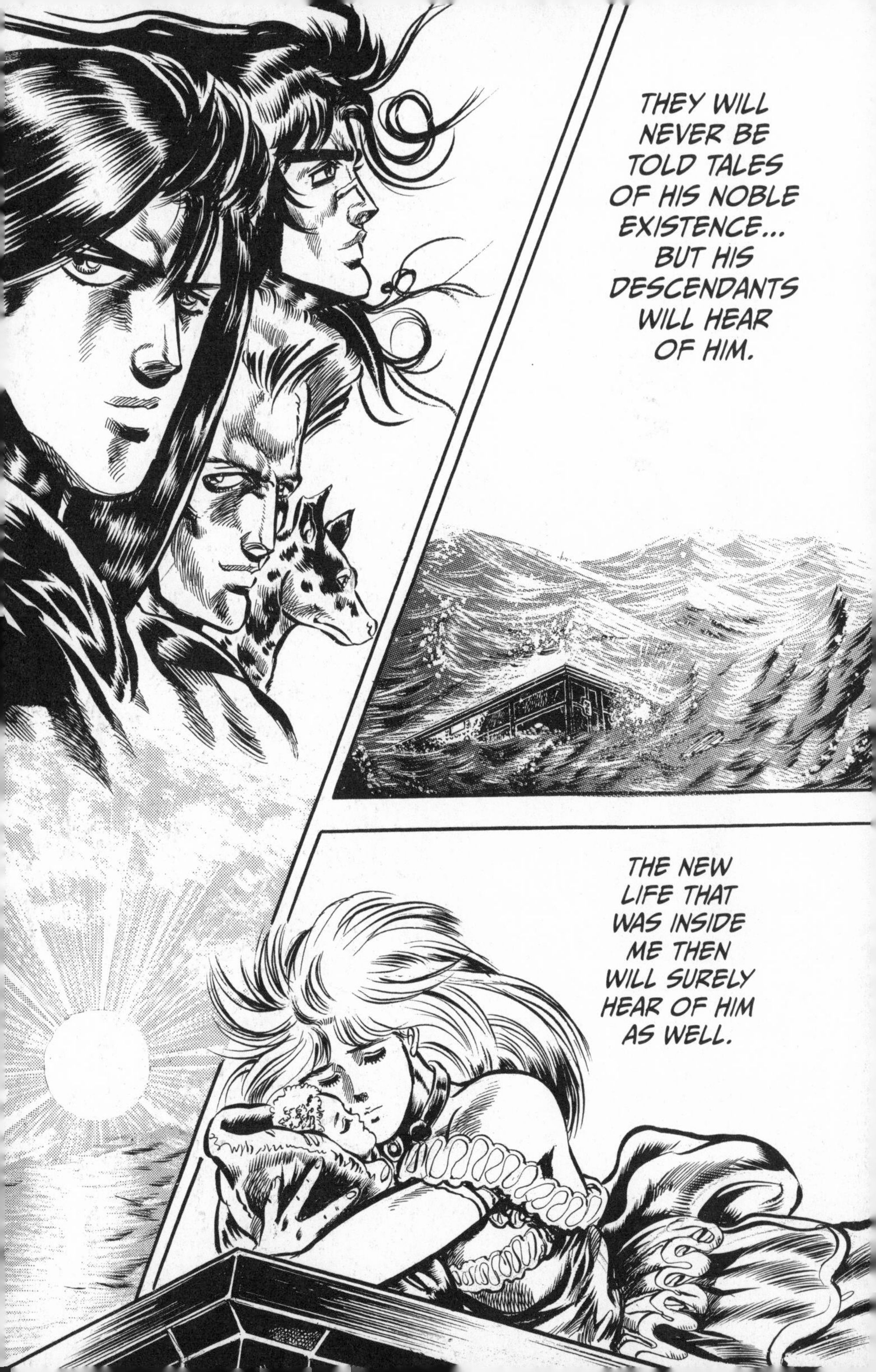
THEY WILL NEVER BE TOLD TALES OF HIS NOBLE EXISTENCE... BUT HIS DESCENDANTS WILL HEAR OF HIM.
THE NEW LIFE THAT WAS INSIDE ME THEN WILL SURELY HEAR OF HIM AS WELL.

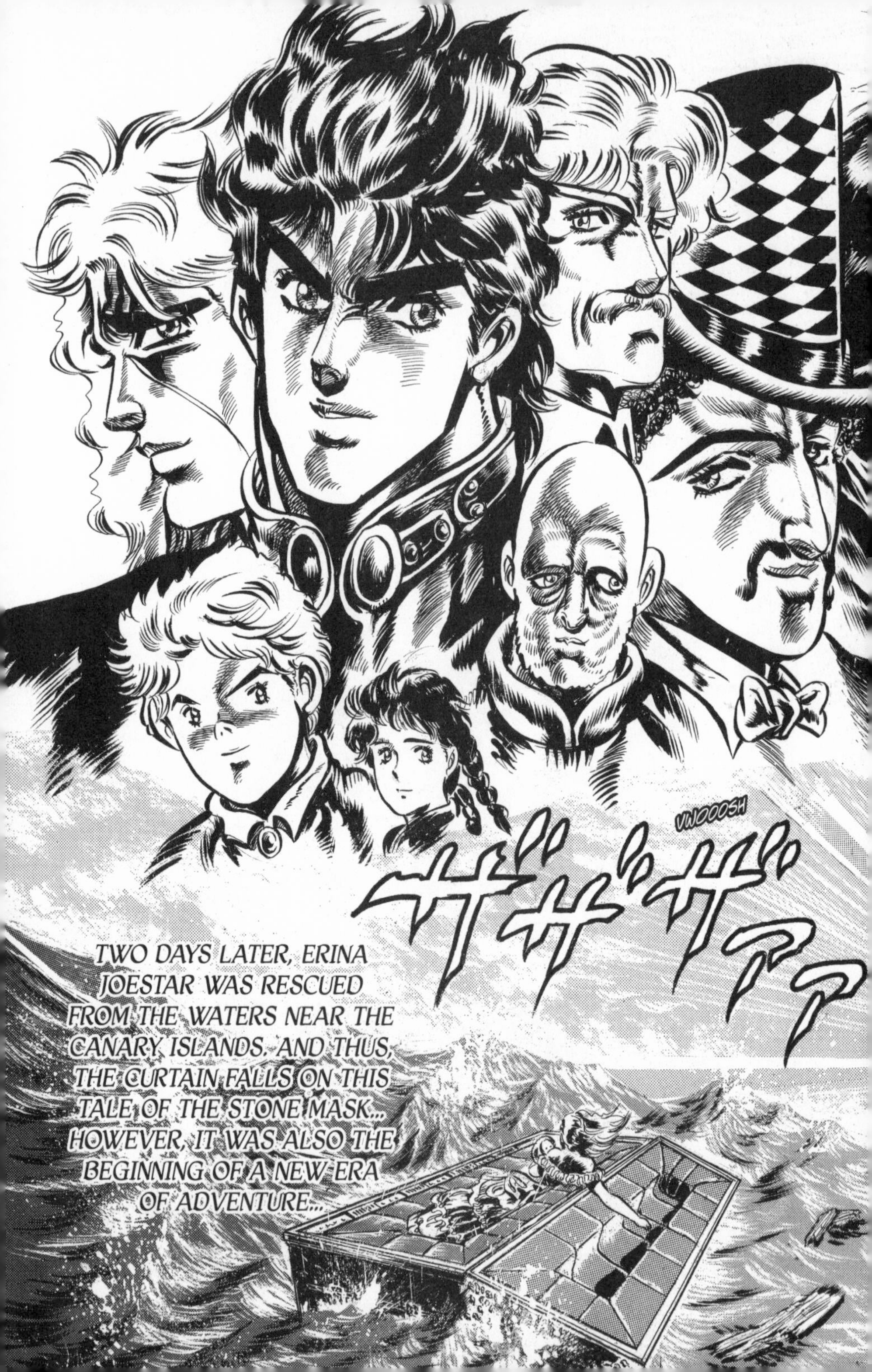
VWOOOSH
ザザザア
TWO DAYS LATER, ERINA JOESTAR WAS RESCUED FROM THE WATERS NEAR THE CANARY ISLANDS. AND THUS, THE CURTAIN FALLS ON THIS TALE OF THE STONE MASK... HOWEVER, IT WAS ALSO THE BEGINNING OF A NEW ERA OF ADVENTURE...

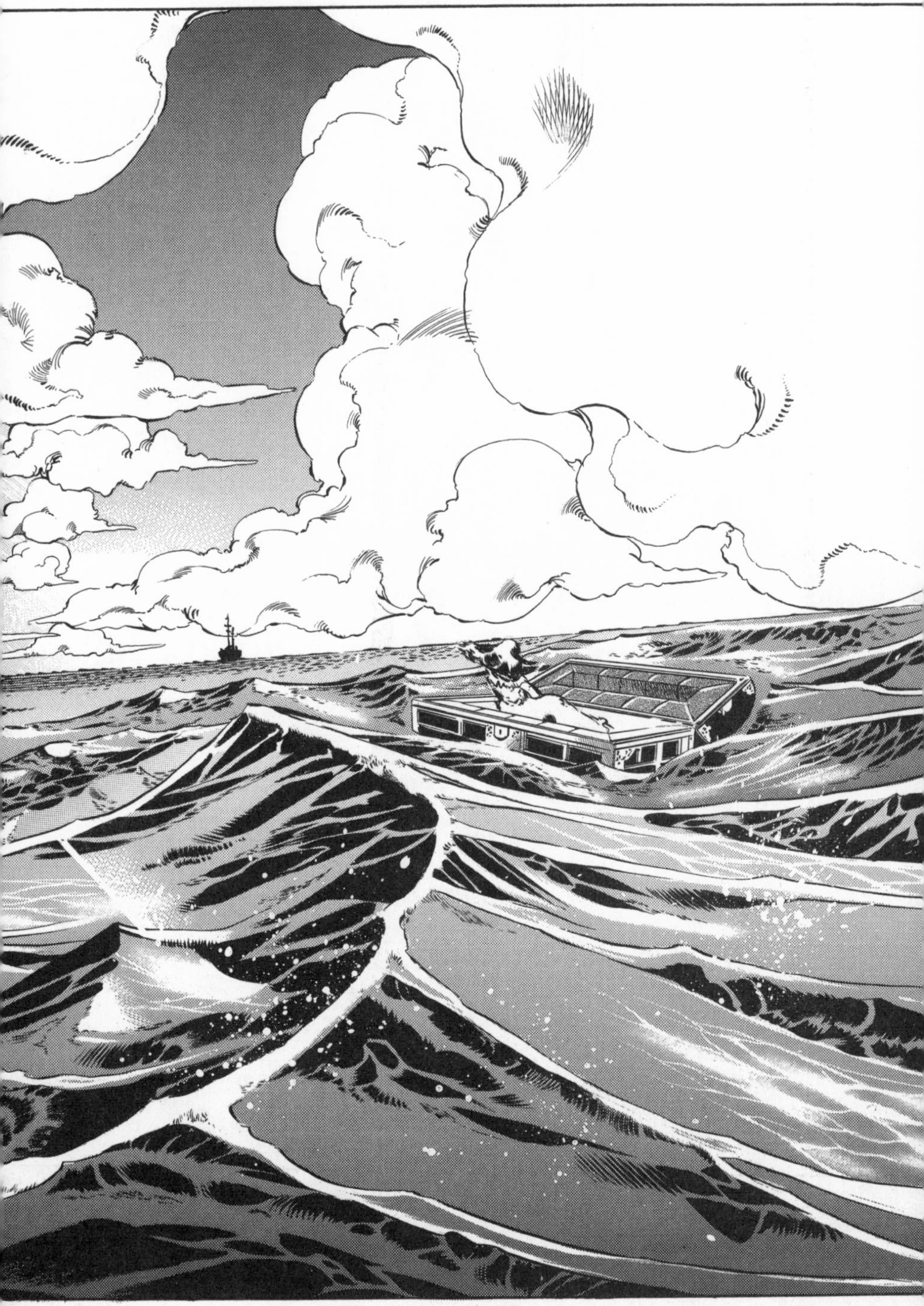

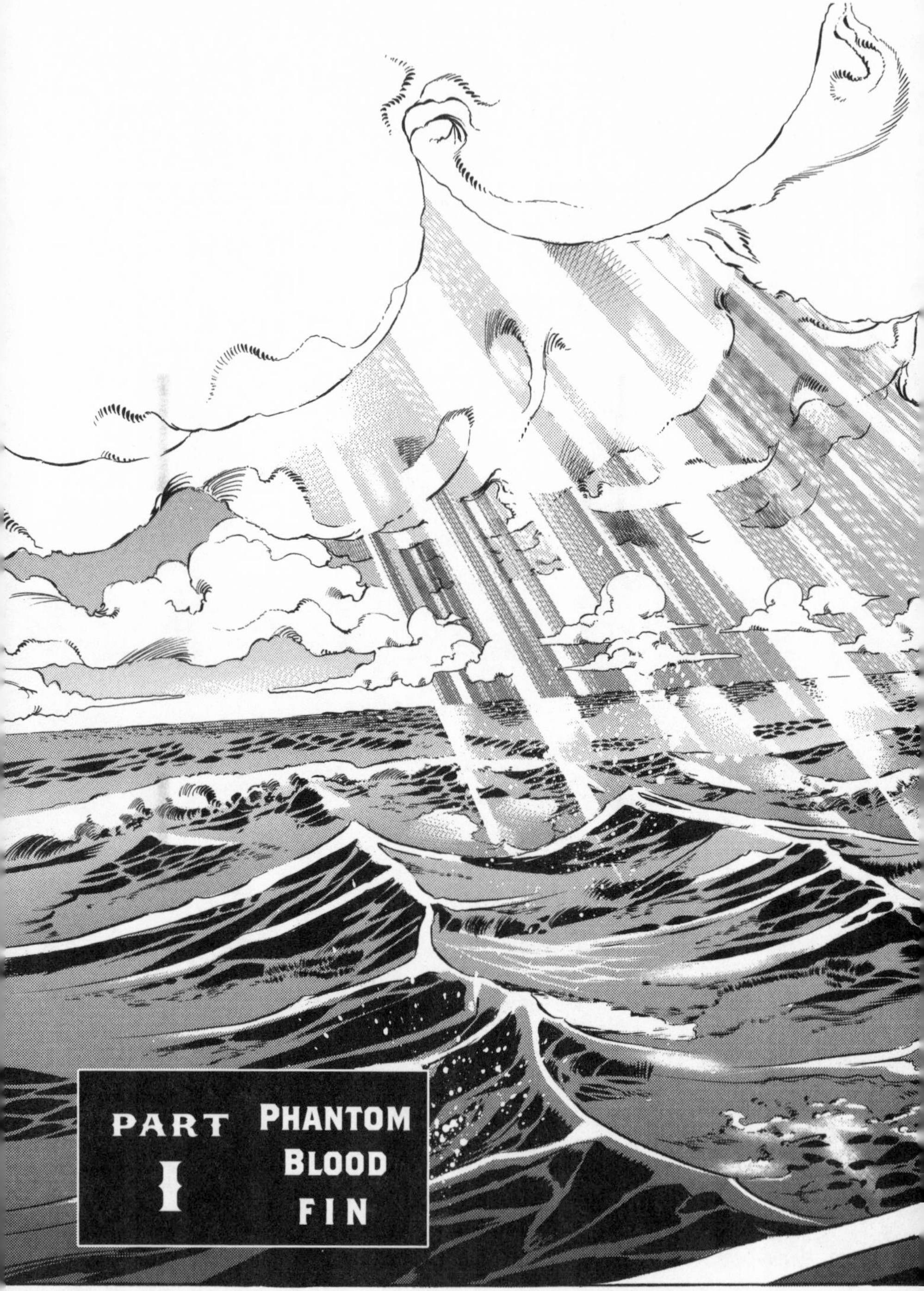
PART I
PHANTOM BLOOD
FIN

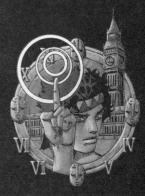

JoJo's
BIZARRE ADVENTURE

03

END

To Be Continued

JoJo's BIZARRE ADVENTURE

03

Di

荒木飛呂彦が
語る
キャラクター
誕生秘話

Hirohiko Araki talks about character creation!

JoJo's BIZARRE ADVENTURE
PART I
PHANTOM BLOOD

03

"THE 'ULTIMATE EVIL' ISN'T SOLELY ABOUT STRENGTH—IT MUST BE COMBINED WITH THE POWER TO CONTROL OTHERS."

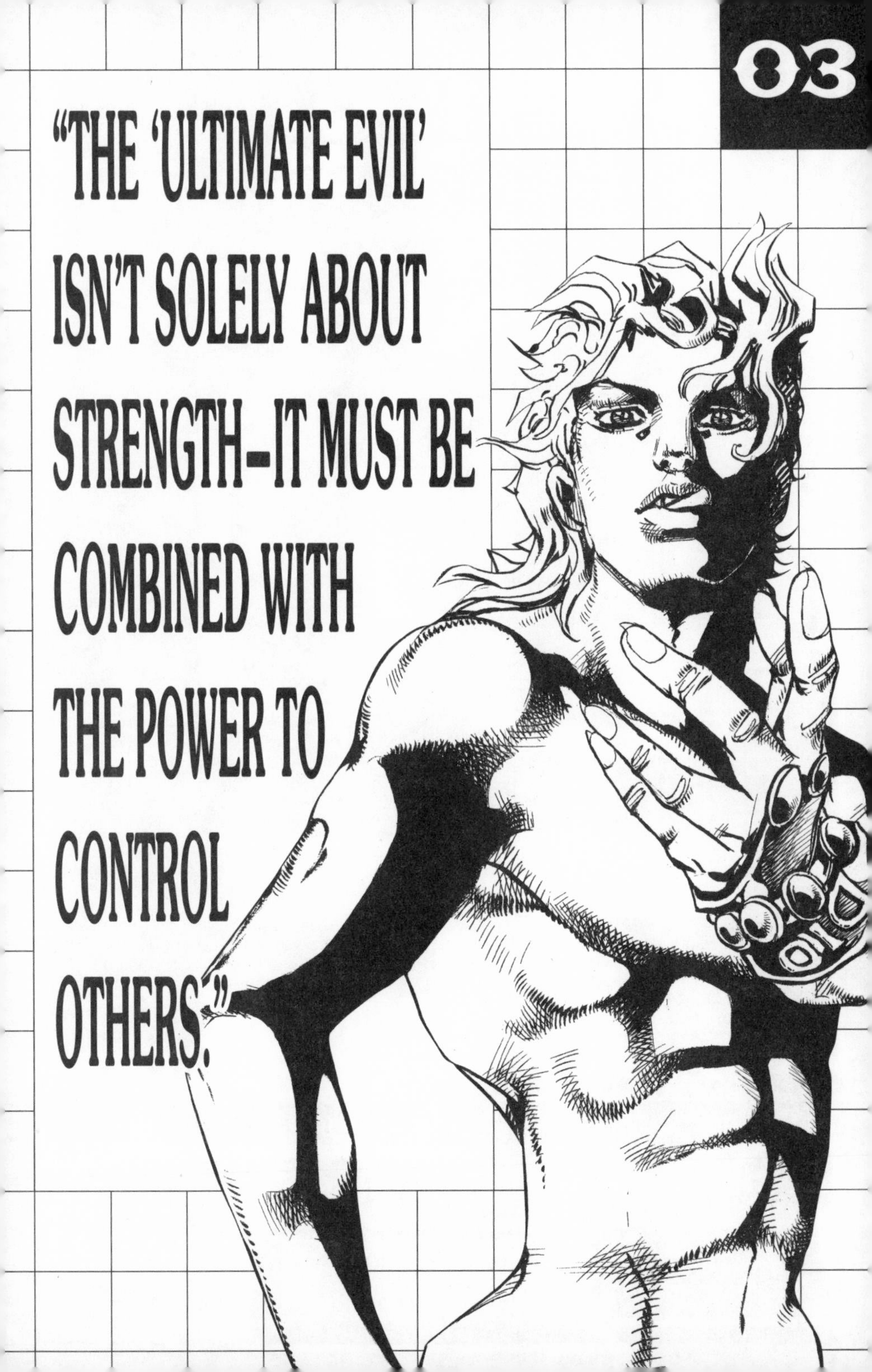

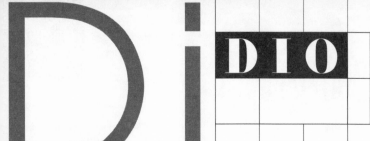

Di

DIO

DATA

Birthday: **Self-Reported,
So Unknown**
(Approx. 1867-1868)

Height: **Unknown**
Weight: **Unknown**
Sign: **Unknown**
Blood Type: **Unknown**

I mentioned this back when I was talking about Jonathan, but Dio was actually the one I wanted to draw most for Part 1. How far can a man's ambition drive him when he takes it to the ultimate extreme? That's what I wanted to depict. I wanted his name to sound cool when paired with JoJo's, so I ended up going with Dio, which means "god" in Italian. I always hear theories about how I got his name from the Dio scooter, but that's not true! I'll just put that out there, along with the *Kimyou na Bouken* thing from last volume.

In regards to how he contrasts with Jonathan, I wanted to tackle how you'd represent the ultimate villain as depicted against a symbol of justice. How exactly would he fall into that role of "villain"? People always love to compare who's stronger or who's cooler. You've got Godzilla versus Mechagodzilla, Schwarzenegger vs. Stallone… I wanted there to be that sort of contest or struggle between Dio and Jonathan.

Additonally, FBI psychological profiling was a hot topic around the time that I wrote this. Why do serial killers do what they do, scientifically speaking? I was inspired by that when I was working on Dio. Guys like that are true scumbags, rotten down to the core. Yet, I've always sort of thought that they're actually incredibly strong for being able to commit such crimes. Why do they go so far? Do they do it just to see if they can? The "control" aspect of it interests me as well. There was a famous case in America where a man trapped several women in a room and brought them out, one at a time, into another room to kill them. All of these women were waiting, together, for their turn to get killed. I can't imagine what their mental state was like at that point… Thinking rationally, you wonder why they wouldn't try to make a break for it, or why they wouldn't try to band together and overpower the killer? There has to be some way to resist. However, if you look into the process by which people control others, you start to see what's effective. There are many ways, including instilling fear, but I always found the act of controlling others strangely fascinating.

That's why Dio wasn't simply a strong villain, but a character that controls others and had admirers that served him. As an antagonist, it makes it suspenseful for the reader, as they wonder how he can be beaten. During serialization, I actually hadn't prepared a weakness for Dio. It's the best kind of suspense when you are on edge. How will they overcome him if Hamon doesn't work? The stronger the enemy, the better. It was hard coming up with a way for him to be defeated, though.

The story behind the new illustration for **JoJo 03!**

Q. Why is Dio naked?

A. He wanted to show off his beautiful body.

If I try, I can draw these characters to look the way they did, but they're living, breathing things. They *do* end up looking like completely different people when drawn in a modern style.

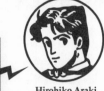

Hirohiko Araki

JoJo's Bizarre Adventure

PART I PHANTOM BLOOD

BY

HIROHIKO ARAKI

Translation ☆ Evan Galloway
Touch-Up Art & Lettering ☆ Mark McMurray
Design ☆ Fawn Lau
Editor ☆ Urian Brown

JOJO'S BIZARRE ADVENTURE © 1986 by Hirohiko Araki
All rights reserved.
First published in Japan in 1986 by SHUEISHA Inc., Tokyo.
English translation rights arranged by SHUEISHA Inc.

Original Japanese cover design by
MITSURU KOBAYASHI (GENI A LÒIDE)

Printed in the U.S.A.

Published by VIZ Media, LLC
P.O. Box 77010
San Francisco, CA 94107

10
First printing, August 2015
Tenth printing, February 2022

PARENTAL ADVISORY
JOJO'S BIZARRE ADVENTURE PART ONE PHANTOM BLOOD
is rated T+ for Older Teen and is recommended for ages 16 and up.
This volume contains graphic violence and some mature themes.

www.viz.com

www.shonenjump.com

JO

THIS IS THE LAST PAGE

ドドド

JoJo's Bizarre Adventure
has been printed in the original Japanese format in order to preserve the orientation of the original artwork.

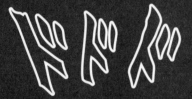

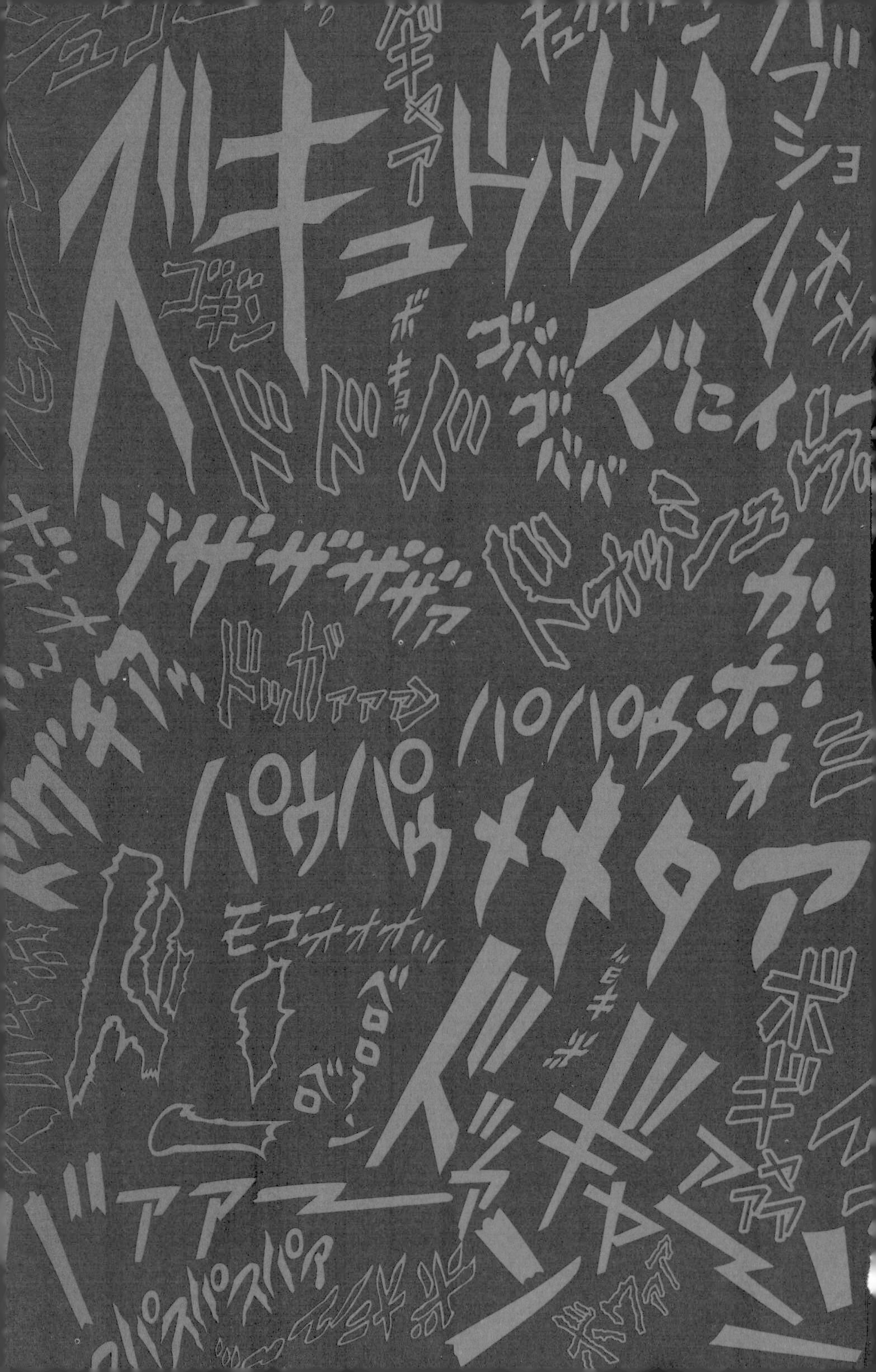

メメタァ
パウパウ
ゴバッゴババ